CALIFORNIA

Made in the United States
Text printed on 90%
recycled paper

Houghton Mifflin Harcourt

CALIFORNIA

GO MATH!

Printed in the U.S.A.

ISBN 978-0-544-20383-9

14 15 16 17 18 19 20 0029 27 26 25 24 23 22 21

4500821344 B C D E F G

Dear Students and Families,

Welcome to **California Go Math!**, Grade 1! In this exciting mathematics program, there are hands-on activities to do and real-world problems to solve. Best of all, you will write your ideas and answers right in your book. In **California Go Math!**, writing and drawing on the pages helps you think deeply about what you are learning, and you will really understand math!

By the way, all of the pages in your **California Go Math!** book are made using recycled paper. We wanted you to know that you can Go Green with **California Go Math!**

Sincerely,

The Authors

Made in the United States
Text printed on 90% recycled paper

CALIFORNIA

GO MATH!

Authors

Juli K. Dixon, Ph.D.
Professor, Mathematics Education
University of Central Florida
Orlando, Florida

Edward B. Burger, Ph.D.
President, Southwestern University
Georgetown, Texas

Steven J. Leinwand
Principal Research Analyst
American Institutes for Research (AIR)
Washington, D.C.

Matthew R. Larson, Ph.D.
K-12 Curriculum Specialist for Mathematics
Lincoln Public Schools
Lincoln, Nebraska

Martha E. Sandoval-Martinez
Math Instructor
El Camino College
Torrance, California

Contributor

Rena Petrello
Professor, Mathematics
Moorpark College
Moorpark, CA

English Language Learners Consultant

Elizabeth Jiménez
CEO, GEMAS Consulting
Professional Expert on English Learner Education
Bilingual Education and Dual Language
Pomona, California

Operations and Algebraic Thinking

Critical Area Developing understanding of addition, subtraction, and strategies for addition and subtraction within 20

Critical Area

GO DIGITAL

Go online! Your math lessons are interactive. Use *i*Tools, Animated Math Models, the Multimedia *e*Glossary, and more.

Chapter 1 Overview

In this chapter, you will explore and discover answers to the following **Essential Questions**:

- How can you model adding within 10?
- How do you show adding to a group?
- How do you model putting together?
- How do you show adding in any order?

Chapter 2 Overview

In this chapter, you will explore and discover answers to the following **Essential Questions**:

- How can you subtract numbers from 10 or less?
- How do you model taking apart?
- How do you show taking from a group?
- How do you subtract to compare?

Chapter 3 Overview

In this chapter, you will explore and discover answers to the following **Essential Questions**:

- How do you solve addition problems?
- What strategies can you use to add facts?
- Why can you add in any order?
- How can you add three numbers?

3 Addition Strategies 93

Domain Operations and Algebraic Thinking

COMMON CORE CALIFORNIA STANDARDS
1.OA.2, 1.OA.3, 1.OA.5, 1.OA.6

Chapter 4 Overview

In this chapter, you will explore and discover answers to the following **Essential Questions**:

- How do you solve subtraction problems?
- What strategies can you use to subtract facts?
- How can an addition fact help you solve a related subtraction fact?
- How can you make a ten to help you subtract?

4 Subtraction Strategies 149

Domain Operations and Algebraic Thinking

COMMON CORE CALIFORNIA STANDARDS
1.OA.1, 1.OA.4, 1.OA.5, 1.OA.6

5 Addition and Subtraction Relationships 181

Domain Operations and Algebraic Thinking

COMMON CORE CALIFORNIA STANDARDS

1.OA.1, 1.OA.6, 1.OA.7, 1.OA.8

Chapter 5 Overview

In this chapter, you will explore and discover answers to the following **Essential Questions**:

- How can relating addition and subtraction help you to learn and understand facts within 20?
- How do addition and subtraction undo each other?
- What is the relationship between related facts?
- How can you find unknown numbers in related facts?

Critical Area

Go online! Your math lessons are interactive. Use *i*Tools, Animated Math Models, the Multimedia *e*Glossary, and more.

Chapter 6 Overview

In this chapter, you will explore and discover answers to the following **Essential Questions**:

- How do you use place value to model, read, and write numbers to 120?
- What ways can you use tens and ones to model numbers to 120?
- How do numbers change as you count by tens to 120?

Number and Operations in Base Ten

COMMON CORE **Critical Area** Developing understanding of whole number relationships and place value, including grouping in tens and ones

7 Compare Numbers 285

Domain Number and Operations in Base Ten

COMMON CORE CALIFORNIA STANDARDS
1.NBT.3, 1.NBT.5

Chapter 7 Overview

In this chapter, you will explore and discover answers to the following **Essential Questions**:

- How do you use place value to compare numbers?
- What ways can you use tens and ones to compare two-digit numbers?
- How can you find 10 more and 10 less than a number?

8 Two-Digit Addition and Subtraction 313

Domains Operations and Algebraic Thinking
Number and Operations in Base Ten

COMMON CORE CALIFORNIA STANDARDS
1.OA.6, 1.NBT.4, 1.NBT.6

Chapter 8 Overview

In this chapter, you will explore and discover answers to the following **Essential Questions**:

- How can you add and subtract two-digit numbers?
- What ways can you use tens and ones to add and subtract two-digit numbers?
- How can making a ten help you add a two-digit number and a one-digit number?

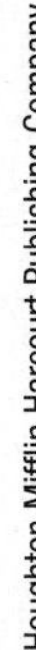

Critical Area

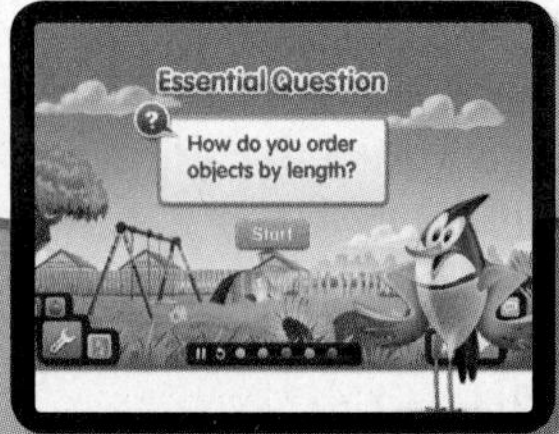

Go online! Your math lessons are interactive. Use *i*Tools, Animated Math Models, the Multimedia *e*Glossary, and more.

Chapter 9 Overview

In this chapter, you will explore and discover answers to the following **Essential Questions**:

- How can you measure a length and tell time?
- How can you describe using paper clips to measure the length of an object?
- How can you use the hour and minute hands of a clock to tell time to the hour and to the half hour?

Measurement and Data

Critical Area Developing understanding of linear measurement and measuring lengths as iterating length units

10 Represent Data 413

Domain Measurement and Data

COMMON CORE CALIFORNIA STANDARDS

1.MD.4

Chapter 10 Overview

In this chapter, you will explore and discover answers to the following **Essential Questions**:

- How can graphs and charts help you organize, represent, and interpret data?
- How can you look at a graph or chart to tell the most or least popular item without counting?
- How are tally charts, picture graphs, and bar graphs alike? How are they different?
- How can you compare information recorded in a graph?

Critical Area

GO DIGITAL

Go online! Your math lessons are interactive. Use *i*Tools, Animated Math Models, the Multimedia *e*Glossary, and more.

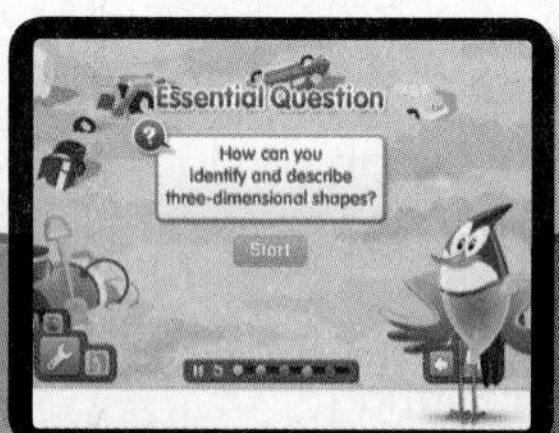

Chapter 11 Overview

In this chapter, you will explore and discover answers to the following **Essential Questions**:

- How can you identify and describe three-dimensional shapes?
- How can you combine three-dimensional shapes to make new shapes?
- How can you use a combined shape to make a new shape?
- What two-dimensional shapes are on three-dimensional shapes?

Chapter 12 Overview

In this chapter, you will explore and discover answers to the following **Essential Questions**:

- How do you sort and describe two-dimensional shapes?
- How can you describe two-dimensional shapes?
- How can you identify equal and unequal parts in two-dimensional shapes?

Geometry

Critical Area Reasoning about attributes of, and composing and decomposing geometric shapes

Animals in Our World

written by Martha Sibert

CRITICAL AREA Developing understanding of addition, subtraction, and strategies for addition and subtraction within 20

Two parrots sit on the branch of a tree.

How many beaks do you see? ___

Science

Where do parrots live?

Four elephants walk. They are all the same kind.

How many trunks can you find? ____

Science

Where do elephants live?

Three penguins stand. One is very small.

Each has two feet. How many feet in all? ____

Science

Where do penguins live?

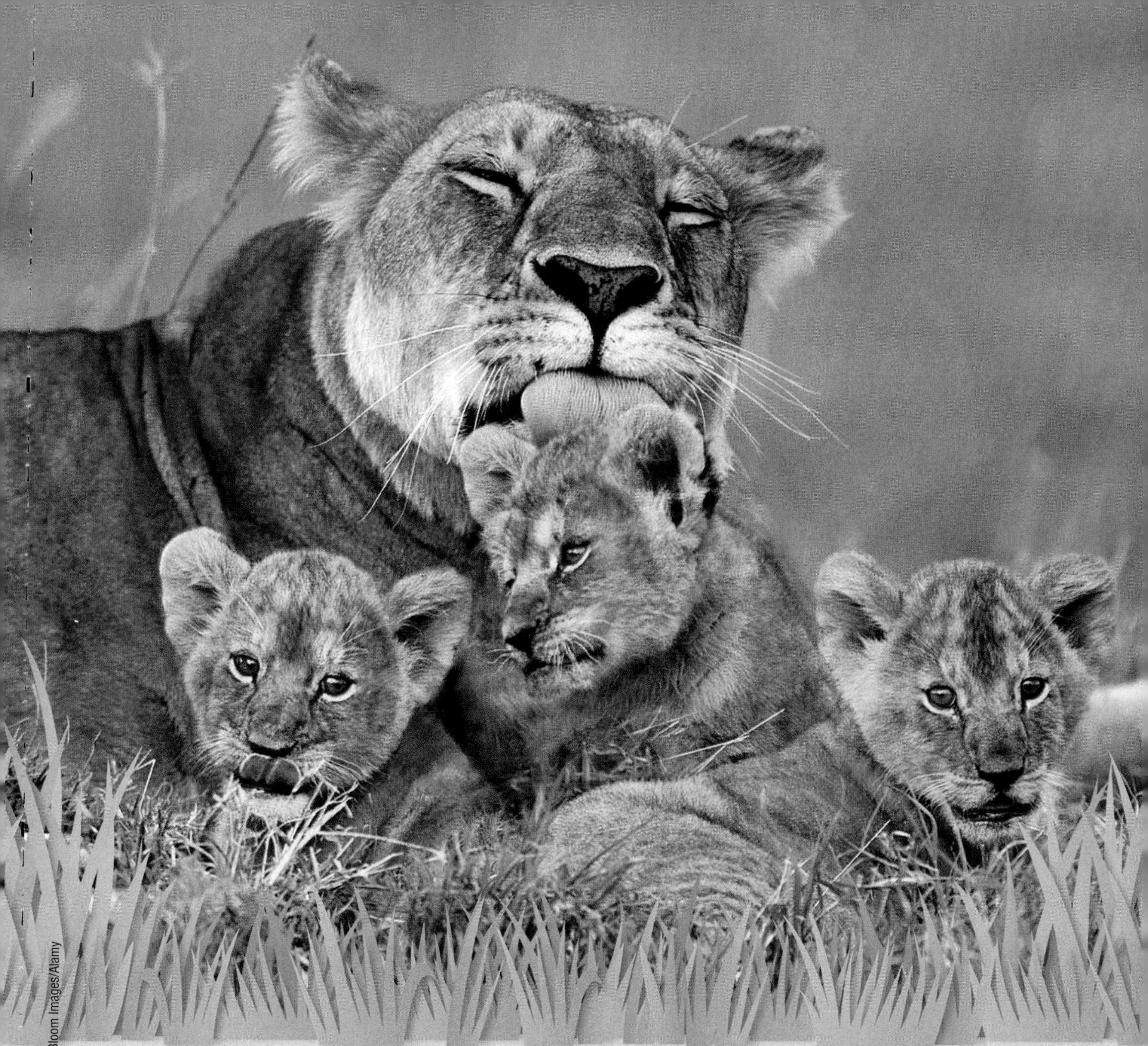

Four lions rest happy as can be.

Look at their ears. How many do you see? ____

Science

Where do lions live?

Five giraffes stand straight and tall.

How many small horns do they have in all? ____

Science

Where do giraffes live?

Name ______________________________

Write About the Story

WRITE Math Draw more bears. Then write an addition story problem or a subtraction story problem.

Vocabulary Review

plus + minus –

Write the addition or subtraction sentence. ___ ◯ ___ ◯ ___

How Many Ears?

Look at the picture of the pandas.
What if there were five pandas?
How many ears would there be?

Draw to explain.

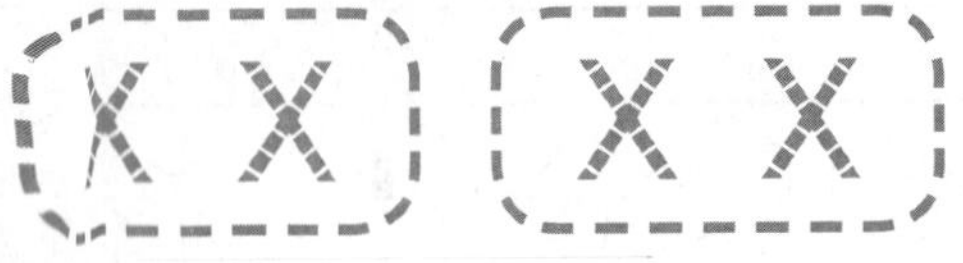

Five pandas would have ____ ears.

Make up a question about another animal in the story. Have a classmate draw to answer your question.

Chapter 1

Addition Concepts

Curious About Math with Curious George

How many kittens can you add to the group to have 10 kittens? Explain.

Name ________________________________

Show What You Know

Explore Numbers 1 to 4

Use  to show the number.
Draw the ●.

1. 1 

2. 3 

Numbers 1 to 10

How many objects are in each group?

3. 

____ chicks

4. 

____ eggs

5. 

____ flowers

Numbers 0 to 10

How many spots are on the ladybug?

6. 

____

7. 

____

8. 

____

9. 

____

This page checks understanding of important skills needed for success in Chapter 1.

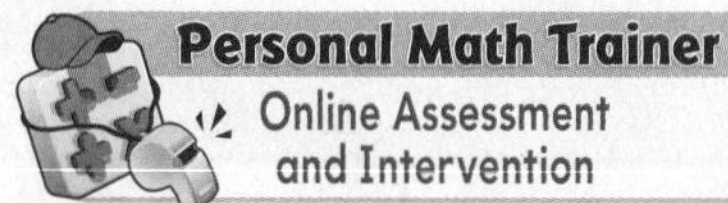

Name ______________________________

Review Words
add to
add
1 more

Vocabulary Builder

Visualize It

Draw to show 1 more.
Draw to show adding to.

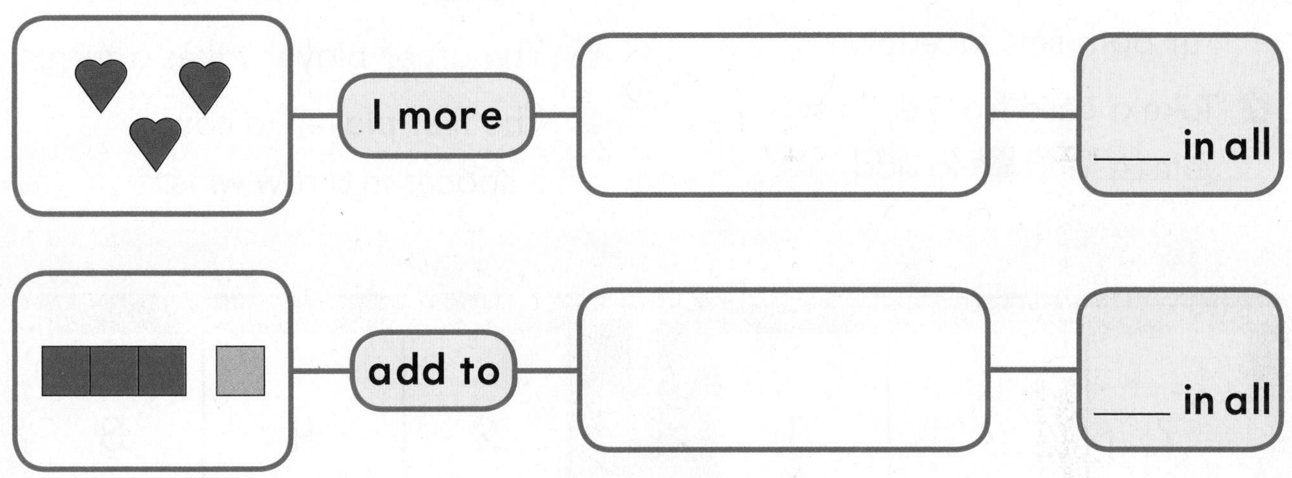

Understand Vocabulary

Complete the sentences with review words.

1. Sue wants to know how many counters are in two groups. She can ______________ to find out.

2. Pete has 2 apples. May has 3 apples. May has ______________ apple than Pete.

GO DIGITAL
- Interactive Student Edition
- Multimedia eGlossary

Game Addition Bingo

Materials

- 2 sets of Numeral Cards 0–4
- 18 ● • 4 ■ • 4 ■

Play with a partner.

1. Mix the cards in each set. Put both sets facedown.
2. Take a card from each set. Join ■ and ■ to add.
3. The other player checks your answer.
4. If you are correct, cover the answer with a ●.
5. The other player takes a turn.
6. The first player to cover 3 spaces in a row wins.

Player 1

7	1	8
3	6	5
0	2	4

Player 2

2	4	3
7	5	0
1	8	6

Name ______________________________

Algebra • Use Pictures to Add To

Essential Question How do pictures show adding to?

Operations and Algebraic Thinking—1.OA.1

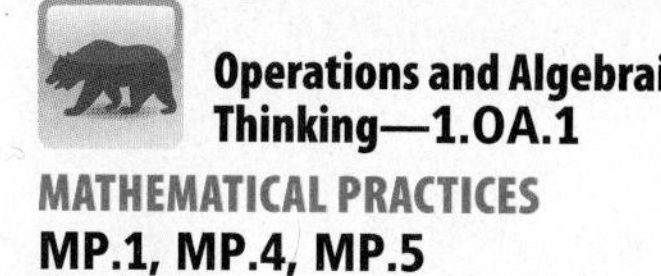

MATHEMATICAL PRACTICES
MP.1, MP.4, MP.5

Listen and Draw (Real World)

Draw to show adding to.
Write how many there are.

______ ladybugs

Math Talk — Mathematical Practices

How does your drawing show the problem? **Explain.**

FOR THE TEACHER • Read the following problem. Have children draw a picture to show the problem. There are 3 ladybugs on a leaf. 2 more ladybugs join them. How many ladybugs are there?

Model and Draw

2 cats  and I more cat 3 cats in all

Share and Show

Write how many.

1.

3 fish and I more fish ____ fish

2.

4 bees 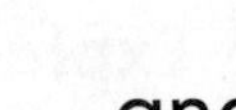 and 4 more bees ____ bees

Name ______________________________

On Your Own

MATHEMATICAL PRACTICE 4 **Model Mathematics** Write how many.

3.

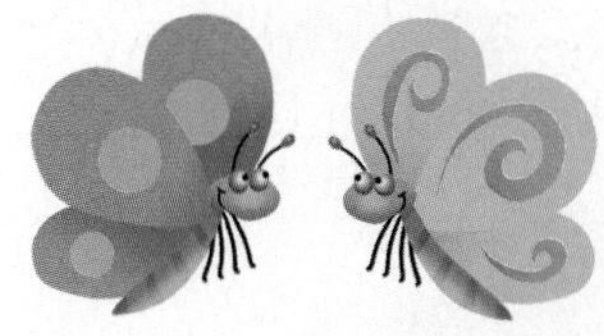

2 butterflies and 4 more butterflies _____ butterflies

4.

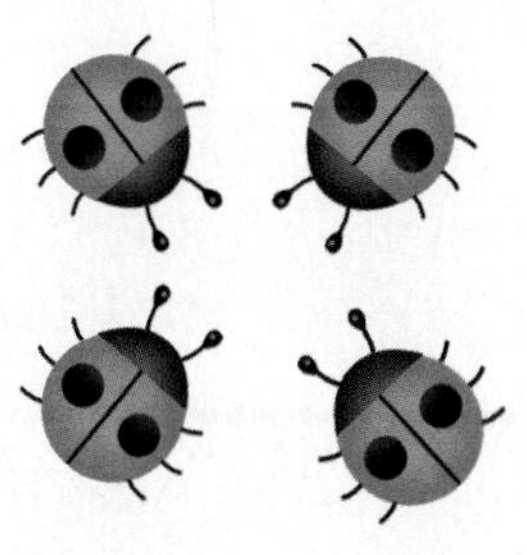

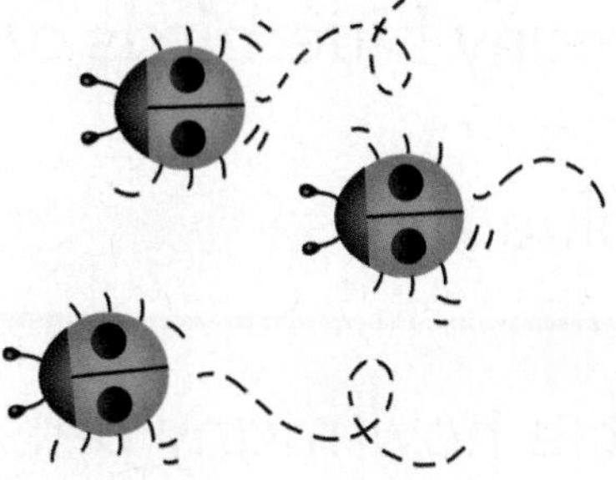

4 ladybugs and 3 more ladybugs _____ ladybugs

5. THINK SMARTER Evan and Luke see 8 worms on the path. Luke sees 2 more worms than Evan. Evan sees 3 worms. How many worms does Luke see?

_____ worms

Problem Solving • Applications

6. THINK SMARTER Color the birds to show how to solve.

There are 3 red birds. Some blue birds join them. How many blue birds are there?

There are ____ blue birds.

7. THINK SMARTER Circle how many ants in all.

3 ants and 2 more ants

3
4
5

ants

TAKE HOME ACTIVITY • Have your child use stuffed animals or other toys to show 3 animals. Then add to the group showing 2 more animals. Ask how many animals there are. Repeat for other combinations of animals with totals up to 10.

FOR MORE PRACTICE: Standards Practice Book

Name ______________________________

Model Adding To

Essential Question How do you model adding to a group?

Operations and Algebraic Thinking—1.OA.1 *Also 1.OA.7*

MATHEMATICAL PRACTICES
MP.1, MP.4, MP.5

Listen and Draw

Use ▪ to show adding to.
Draw to show your work.

FOR THE TEACHER • Read the following problem. Have children use connecting cubes to model the problem and draw to show their work. There are 6 children on the playground. 2 more children join them. How many children are on the playground?

Mathematical Practices

Explain how you use cubes to find your answer.

Model and Draw

5 turtles and 2 more turtles

5 + 2 = 7

plus is equal to sum

5 + 2 = 7 is an **addition sentence.**

Share and Show

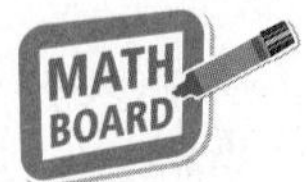

Use ▪ to show adding to.
Draw the ▪. Write the sum.

1. 3 cats and 1 more cat

3 + 1 = ____

2. 2 birds and 3 more birds

2 + 3 = ____

✓3. 4 bugs and 4 more bugs

4 + 4 = ____

✓4. 4 fish and 2 more fish

4 + 2 = ____

Name ______________________________

On Your Own

MATHEMATICAL PRACTICE 5 **Use Appropriate Tools** Use ▪ to show adding to. Draw the ▪. Write the sum.

5. 5 dogs and 4 more dogs

$5 + 4 =$ ____

6. 4 bees and 3 more bees

$4 + 3 =$ ____

7. THINK SMARTER Julia has 4 books on the table. She puts 1 more book on the table. Then she puts 2 more books on the table. How many books are on the table?

____ books

8. GO DEEPER Diego drew cubes to show adding to. Draw to show how Diego should fix his picture. Write the sum.

$2 + 8 =$ ____

Problem Solving • Applications

THINK SMARTER Use the picture to help you complete the addition sentences. Write the sum.

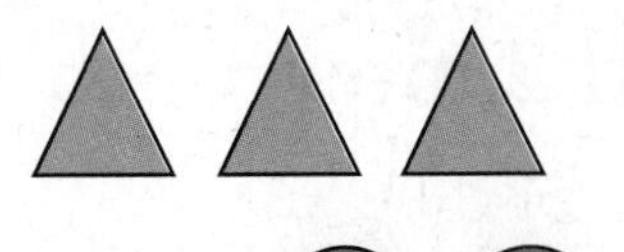
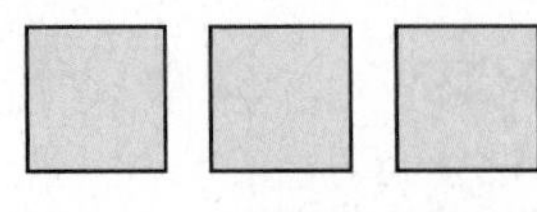
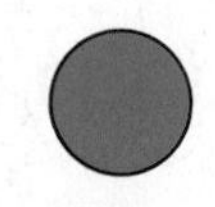
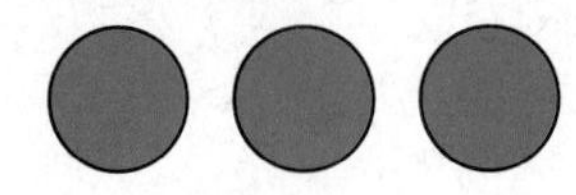
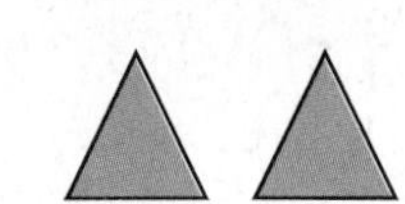
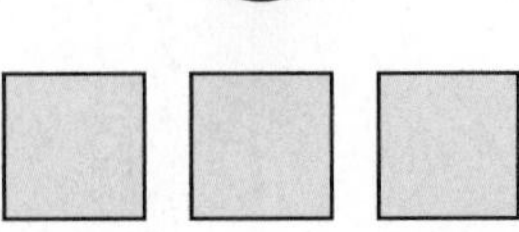

9. ____ ▲ + ____ ▲ = ____ ▲ in all

10. ____ ● + ____ ● = ____ ● in all

11. ____ ■ + ____ ■ = ____ ■ in all

Personal Math Trainer

12. THINK SMARTER + Use ▪ to show adding to. Draw the ▪. Write the sum.

3 bunnies and 5 more bunnies

$3 + 5 = \square$

TAKE HOME ACTIVITY • Put 3 pennies in one group and 2 pennies in another group. Have your child write an addition sentence to tell about the pennies. Repeat for other combinations of pennies with sums of up to 10.

FOR MORE PRACTICE: Standards Practice Book

Name ______________________________

HANDS ON
Lesson 1.3

Model Putting Together

Essential Question How do you model putting together?

Operations and Algebraic Thinking—1.OA.1

MATHEMATICAL PRACTICES
MP.1, MP.4, MP.5

Use ● to model the problem. Draw the ● .
Write the numbers and addition sentence.

____ red crayons ____ yellow crayons

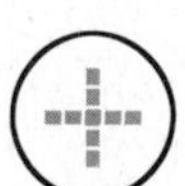  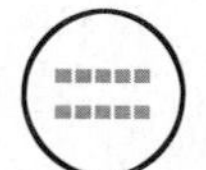

2 + 3 = ____

There are ____ crayons.

Mathematical Practices

Describe how the drawing helps you write the addition sentence.

FOR THE TEACHER • Read the following problem. There are 2 red crayons and 3 yellow crayons. How many crayons are there?

Model and Draw

Add to find how many books there are.

There are 2 small books and 1 big book. How many books are there?

____ books

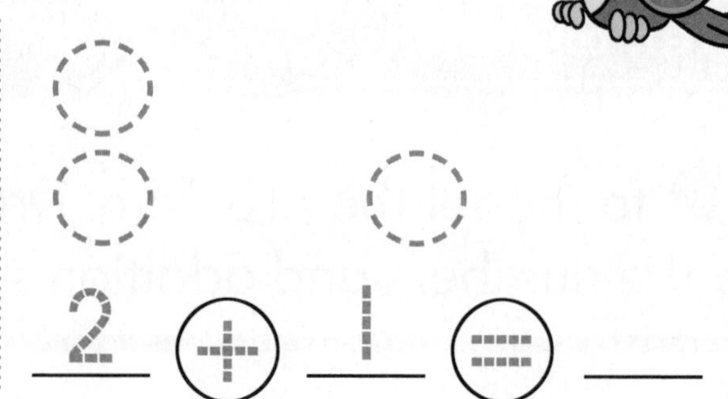

Share and Show

Use ● to solve. Draw to show your work. Write the number sentence and how many.

1. There are 4 red pencils and 2 green pencils. How many pencils are there?

____ pencils

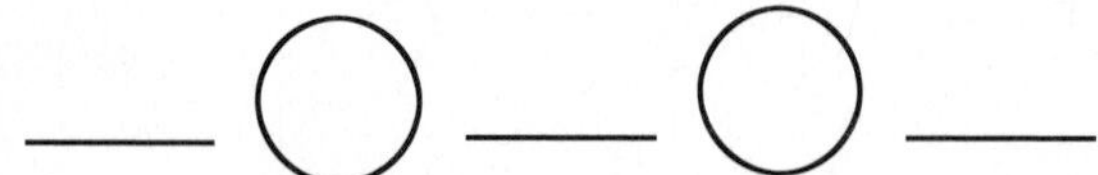

2. There are 5 blue cups and 3 yellow cups. How many cups are there?

____ cups

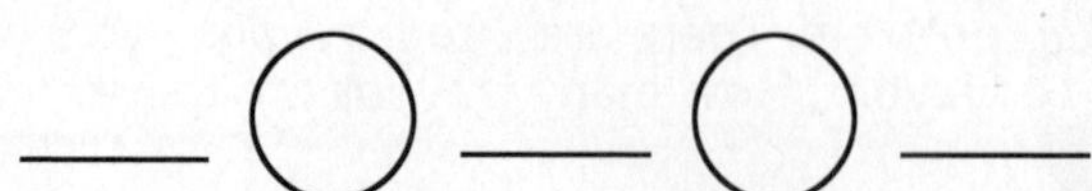

Name ______________________________

On Your Own

MATHEMATICAL PRACTICE 4 **Write an Equation** Use ● to solve. Draw to show your work. Write the number sentence and how many.

3. There are 3 small cats and 4 big cats. How many cats are there?

____ cats

4. There are 6 red cubes and 3 blue cubes. How many cubes are there?

____ cubes

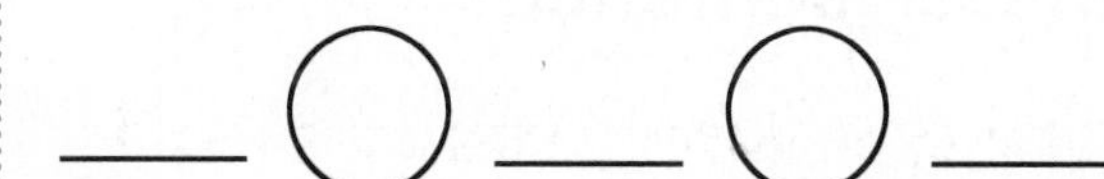

5. There are 2 red flowers and 8 yellow flowers. How many flowers are there?

____ flowers

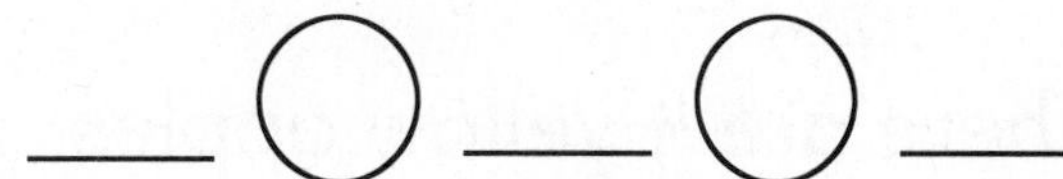

6. THINKSMARTER 4 girls and 4 boys run. Then 2 more children run. The same number of girls and boys run. How many of each run?

____ girls ____ boys

Problem Solving • Applications  

7. THINK SMARTER Write your own addition story problem.

8. Use ● to solve your story problem. Draw to show your work. Write the number sentence.

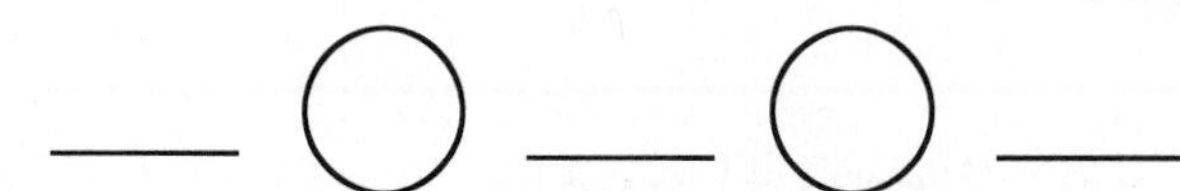

9. THINK SMARTER Draw ● to solve. Write the number sentence and how many.

There are 4 yellow apples and 4 red apples. How many apples are there?

____ apples

TAKE HOME ACTIVITY • Have your child collect a group of up to 10 small objects and use them to make up addition stories.

FOR MORE PRACTICE: Standards Practice Book

Name ____________________

Problem Solving • Model Addition

Essential Question How do you solve addition problems by making a model?

Operations and Algebraic Thinking—1.OA.1

MATHEMATICAL PRACTICES
MP.1, MP.4, MP.5

Hanna has 4 red flowers in a vase.
She puts 2 more flowers in the vase.
How many flowers are in the vase?
How can you use a model to find out?

Unlock the Problem

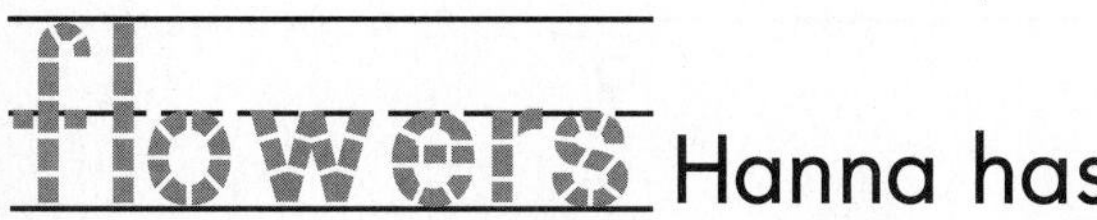

What do I need to find?

______ flowers Hanna has

What information do I need to use?

4 red flowers
2 more flowers

Show how to solve the problem.

4	2

6

4 + 2 = ______

HOME CONNECTION • Your child can model the concepts of adding to and putting together. He or she used a bar model to show the problems and solve.

Try Another Problem

- What do I need to find?
- What information do I need to use?

Read the problem. Use the bar model to solve. Complete the model and the number sentence.

1. There are 7 dogs in the park. Then 1 more dog joins them. How many dogs are in the park now?

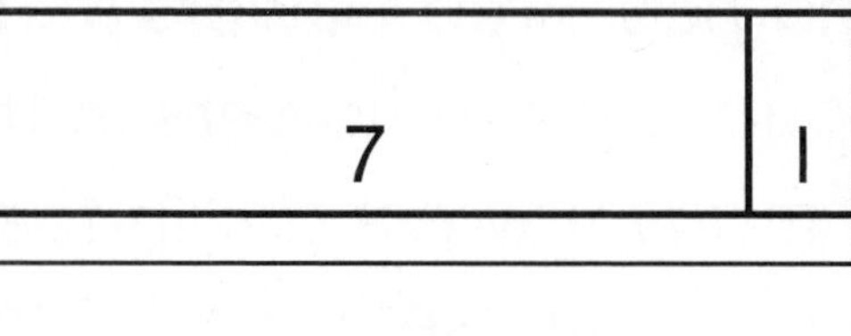

$7 + 1 =$ ____

2. Some birds are sitting in the tree. Four more birds sit in the tree. Then there are 9 birds. How many birds were in the tree before?

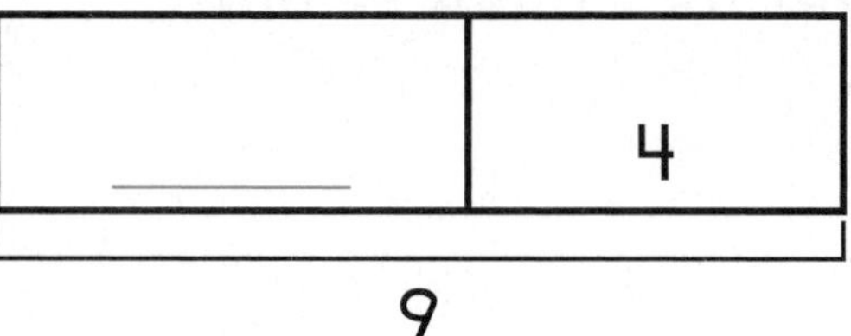

____ $+ 4 = 9$

3. There are 4 horses in the field. Some more horses run to the field. Now there are 10 horses in the field. How many horses run to the field?

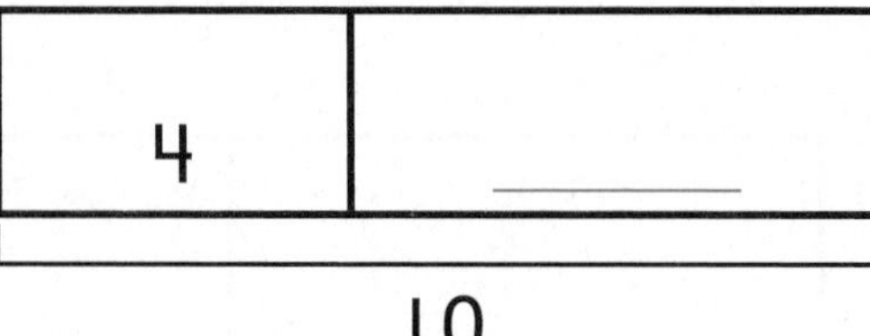

$4 +$ ____ $= 10$

Math Talk **Mathematical Practices**

How does a model help you solve Exercise 1? **Explain.**

Name ______________________________

Share and Show

MATHEMATICAL PRACTICE 4 **Use Diagrams** Read the problem. Use the bar model to solve. Complete the model and the number sentence.

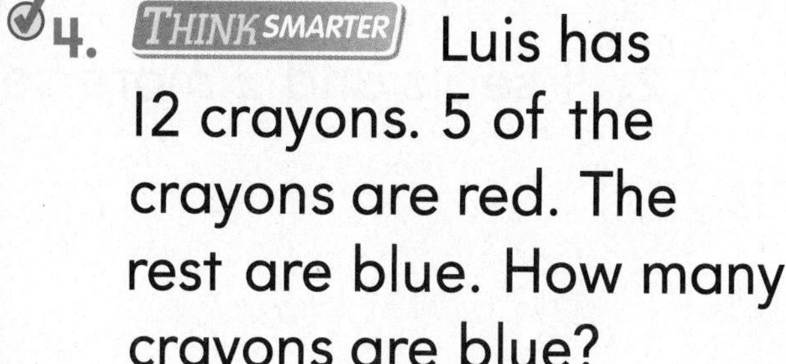

4. THINK SMARTER Luis has 12 crayons. 5 of the crayons are red. The rest are blue. How many crayons are blue?

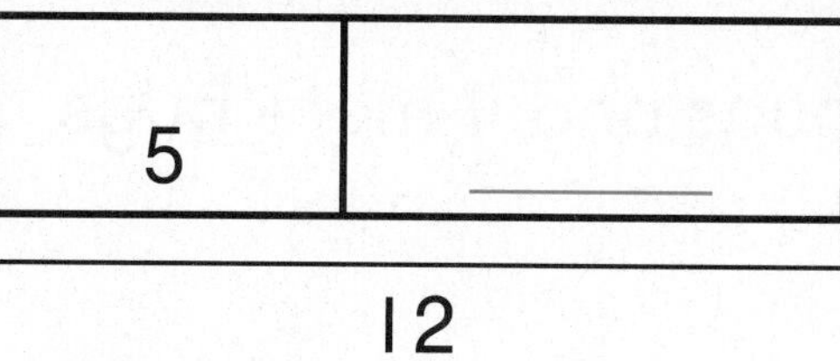

5 + ____ = 12

5. 8 bugs are flying. 2 more bugs fly with them. How many bugs are flying now?

8 | 2

____

8 + 2 = ____

6. THINK SMARTER Some ducks are swimming in a pond. 3 more ducks swim in the pond. Then there are 6 ducks in the pond. How many ducks were in the pond before?

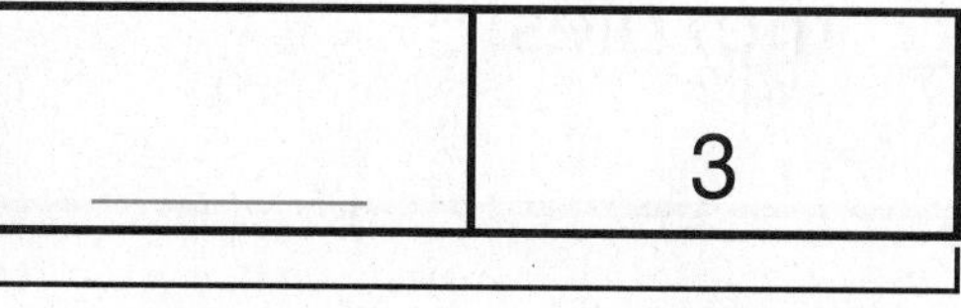

____ + 3 = 6

Math on the Spot

TAKE HOME ACTIVITY • Have your child describe each of the parts of a bar model using the number sentence 7 + 3 = 10.

FOR MORE PRACTICE: Standards Practice Book

Name ______________________________

Mid-Chapter Checkpoint

Concepts and Skills

Use ▪ to show adding to.
Draw the ▪. Write the sum. (1.OA.1)

I. 3 bugs and 4 more bugs

$3 + 4 =$ ____

2. 4 seals and 2 more seals

$4 + 2 =$ ____

Use ● to solve. Draw to show your work.
Write the number sentence and how many. (1.OA.1)

3. There are 5 red marbles and 4 blue marbles. How many marbles are there?

____ marbles

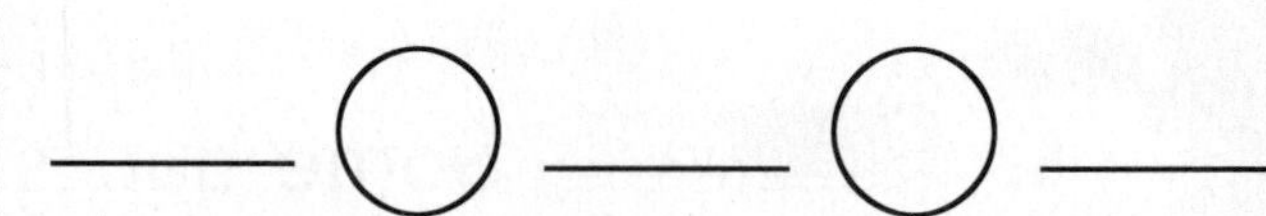

Personal Math Trainer

4. THINK SMARTER + There are 6 bunnies in the garden. More bunnies join them. Then there are 8 bunnies in the garden. How many bunnies join them? (1.OA.1)

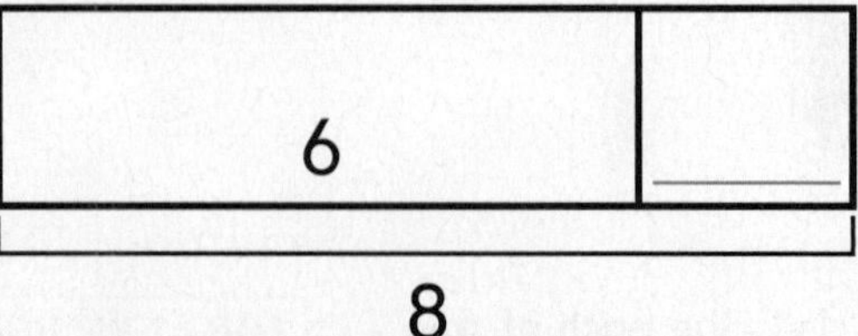

$6 +$ ____ $= 8$

Name

Algebra • Add Zero

Essential Question What happens when you add 0 to a number?

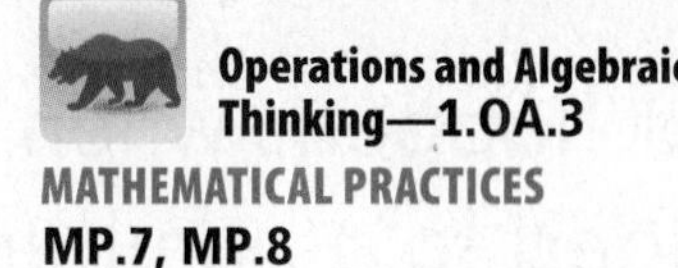

MATHEMATICAL PRACTICES
MP.7, MP.8

Listen and Draw

Use ● to model the problem.
Draw the ● you use.

FOR THE TEACHER • Read the following problem. Scott has 4 marbles. Jennifer has no marbles. How many marbles do they have?

Mathematical Practices

Explain your drawing.

Model and Draw

What happens when **zero** is added to a number?

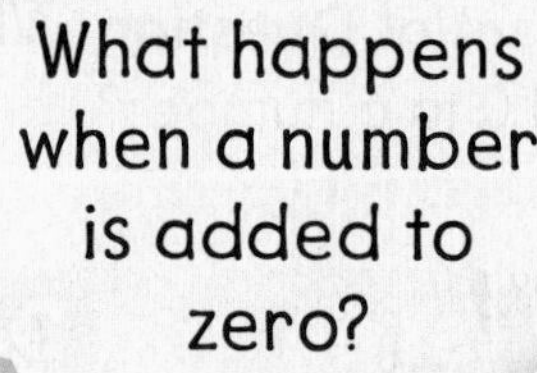

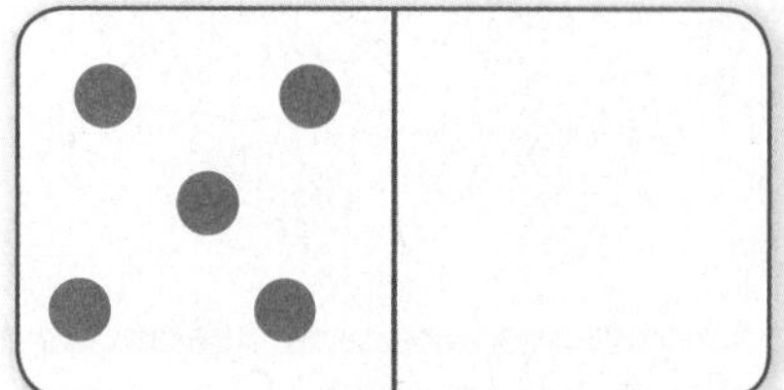

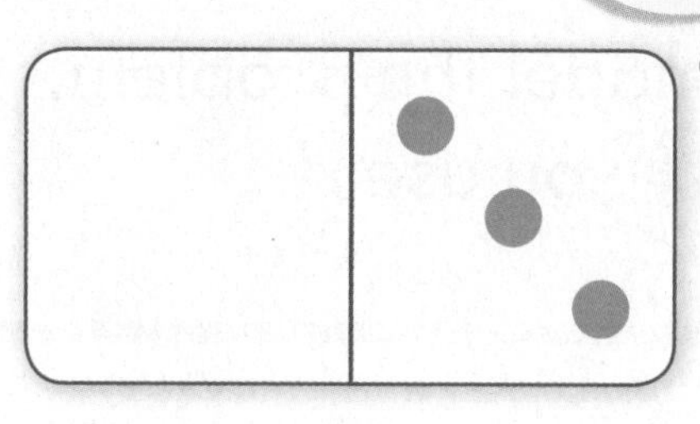

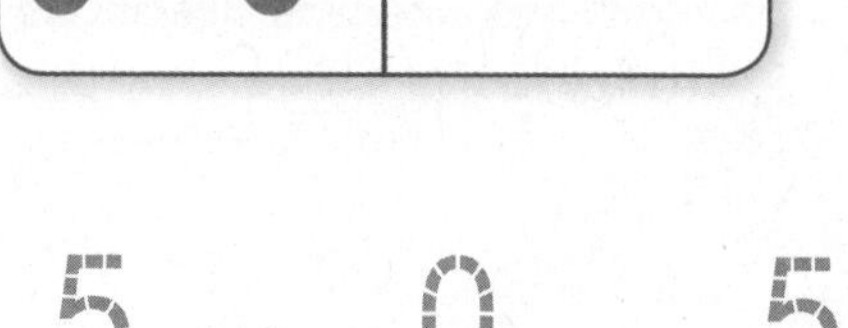

5 + 0 = 5
sum

0 + 3 = 3
sum

Share and Show

Use the picture to write each part. Write the sum.

1. 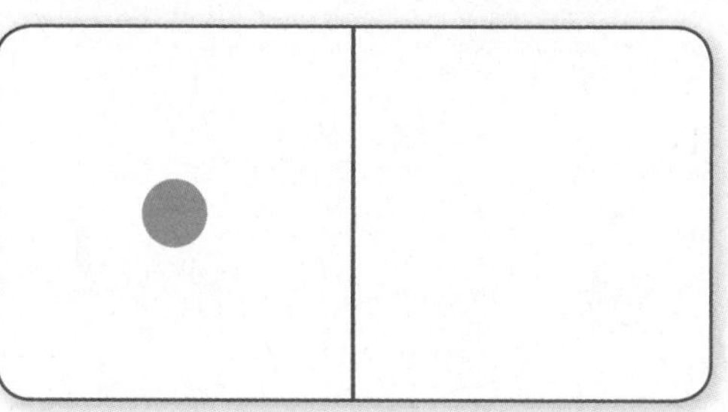

____ + ____ = ____

2. 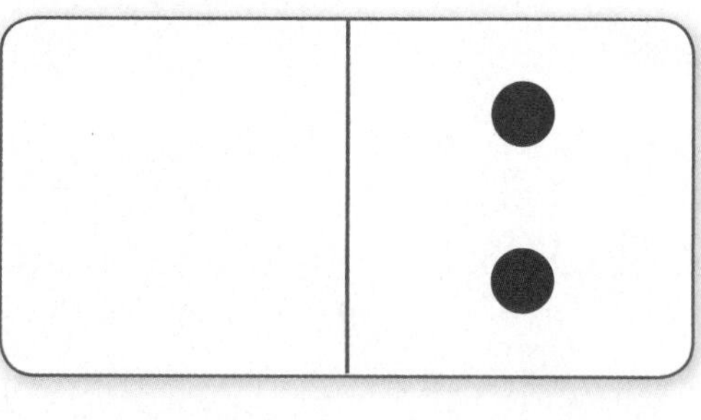

____ + ____ = ____

3. 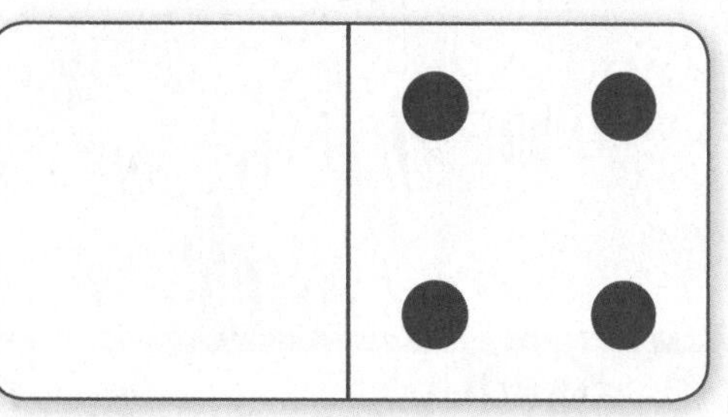

____ + ____ = ____

4. 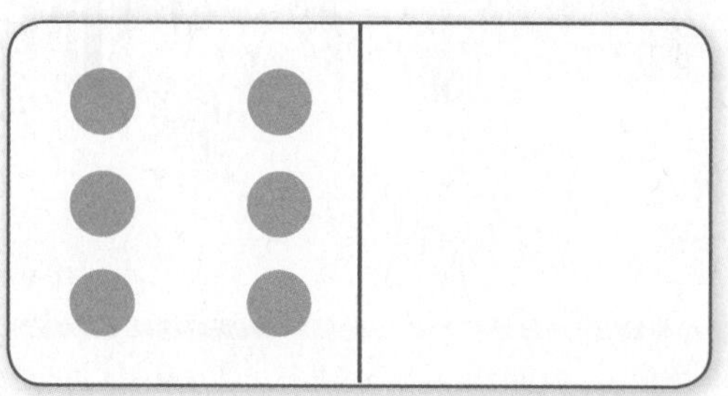

____ + ____ = ____

Name ______________________________

On Your Own

Draw circles to show the number.
Write the sum.

5. $2 + 0 =$ ____

6. $0 + 1 =$ ____

7. $4 + 6 =$ ____

8. $0 + 5 =$ ____

9. $3 + 4 =$ ____

10. $0 + 6 =$ ____

11. $3 + 0 =$ ____

12. $1 + 4 =$ ____

13. $4 + 0 =$ ____

14. THINK SMARTER Maya has 7 books. Eli has no books. Then Maya gives 7 books to Eli. How many books does Maya have?

____ books

15. THINK SMARTER Complete the addition sentence.

____ $+$ ____ $= 0$

Problem Solving • Applications

MATHEMATICAL PRACTICE 8 **Generalize** Write the addition sentence to solve.

16. Mike has 7 books. Cheryl does not have any books. How many books do they both have?

____ + ____ = ____

____ books

17. THINK SMARTER There are 5 birds in all. How many birds are in the house?

____ birds

18. THINK SMARTER There are no dogs in the park. Then 5 dogs come to the park. How many dogs are in the park now?

____ dogs

TAKE HOME ACTIVITY • Write the numbers 0 to 9 on small squares of paper. Shuffle and place the cards facedown. Have your child turn the top card and add zero to that number. Say the sum. Repeat the activity for each card.

FOR MORE PRACTICE: Standards Practice Book

Name ______________________________

Algebra • Add in Any Order

Essential Question Why can you add addends in any order?

HANDS ON
Lesson 1.6

Operations and Algebraic Thinking—1.OA.3

MATHEMATICAL PRACTICES
MP.7, MP.8

Listen and Draw

Use cubes to model the addition sentence.
Draw to show your work.

Math Talk **Mathematical Practices**

How is 2 + 3 = 5 the same as 3 + 2 = 5? **Explain** how it is different.

FOR THE TEACHER • Direct children to do the following. Use connecting cubes to show 2 + 3 and then 3 + 2.

Model and Draw

The **order** of the **addends** changes.
What do you notice about the sum?

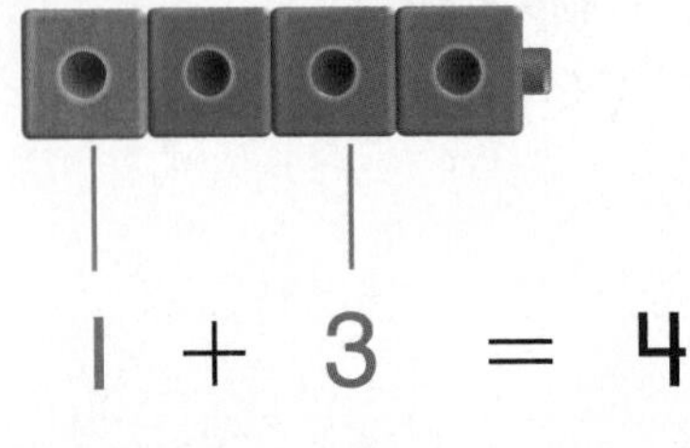

1 + 3 = 4

addends sum

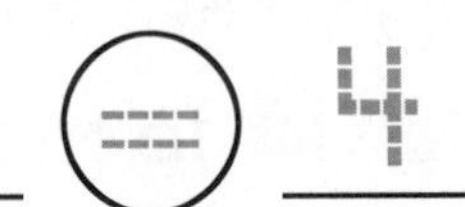

3 + 1 = 4

Share and Show

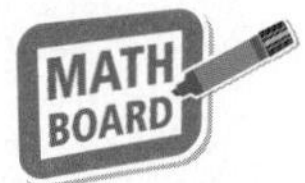

Use cubes to add.
Color to match.
Write the sum.

Change the order of the addends. Color to match.
Write the addition sentence.

1.

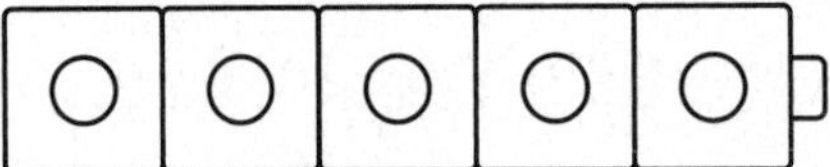

2 + 3 = ____

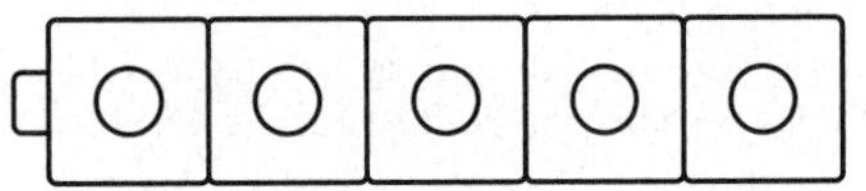

____ ◯ ____ ◯ ____

2.

2 + 4 = ____

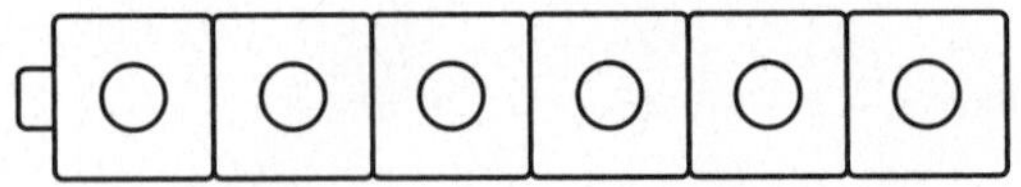

____ ◯ ____ ◯ ____

3.

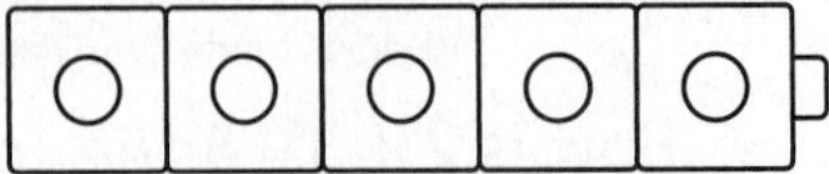

4 + 1 = ____

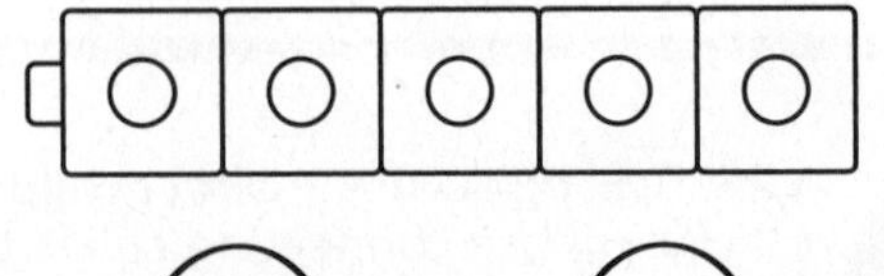

____ ◯ ____ ◯ ____

Name ______________________

On Your Own

MATHEMATICAL PRACTICE 7 **Look for Structure** Use cubes. Write the sum. Circle the addition sentences in each row that have the same addends in a different order.

4. $1 + 2 =$ ____ $1 + 3 =$ ____ $2 + 1 =$ ____

5. $1 + 5 =$ ____ $4 + 2 =$ ____ $2 + 4 =$ ____

6. THINK SMARTER Choose addends to complete the addition sentence. Change the order. Write the numbers.

____ + ____ = 10 ____ + ____ = ____

7. GO DEEPER Write two addition sentences that tell about the picture.

Problem Solving • Applications

WRITE Math

Draw pictures to match the addition sentences.
Write the sum.

8. $2 + 6 =$ ____

$6 + 2 =$ ____

9. $1 + 5 =$ ____

$5 + 1 =$ ____

10. THINK SMARTER Draw lines to match the same addends in a different order.

$7 + 3 = 10$	$3 + 6 = 9$	$4 + 6 = 10$
•	•	•
•	•	•
$6 + 4 = 10$	$3 + 7 = 10$	$6 + 3 = 9$

TAKE HOME ACTIVITY • Ask your child to use small objects of the same kind to show 2 + 4 and 4 + 2 and then explain to you why the sums are the same. Repeat with other addition sentences.

FOR MORE PRACTICE: Standards Practice Book

Name ______________________________

Algebra • Put Together Numbers to 10

Essential Question How can you show all the ways to make a number?

HANDS ON
Lesson 1.7

Operations and Algebraic Thinking— 1.OA.1 *Also 1.OA.6*

MATHEMATICAL PRACTICES
MP.4, MP.7, MP.8

Listen and Draw

Use cubes to show all the ways to make 5.
Color to show your work.

Ways to Make 5

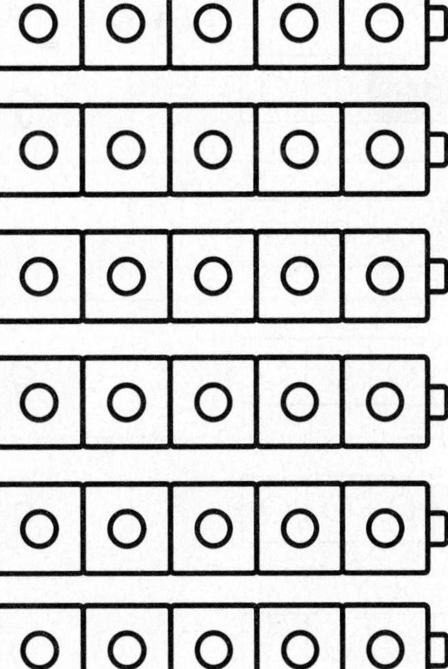

Math Talk Mathematical Practices

How do you know you showed all the ways? **Explain.**

FOR THE TEACHER • Read the following problem and have children show all the ways to solve the problem. Grandma has 5 flowers. How many can she put in her red vase and how many in her blue vase?

Model and Draw

Now Grandma has 9 flowers. How many can she put in her red vase and how many in her blue vase?

Complete the addition sentences.

1. $9 = 9 + 0$

2. $9 = 8 + 1$

Share and Show

Use cubes. Color to show how to make 9. Complete the addition sentences.

Show all the ways to make 9.

3. $9 = 7 + \_\_\_$

4. $9 = \_\_\_ + \_\_\_$

5. $9 = \_\_\_ + \_\_\_$

6. $9 = \_\_\_ + \_\_\_$

7. $9 = \_\_\_ + \_\_\_$

8. $9 = \_\_\_ + \_\_\_$

9. $9 = \_\_\_ + \_\_\_$

10. $9 = \_\_\_ + \_\_\_$

Name ______________________________

On Your Own

MATHEMATICAL PRACTICE 8 **Generalize** Use ▪▪. Color to show ways to make 10. Complete the addition sentences.

11. ○○○○○○○○○○ $10 = \underline{10} + \underline{0}$

12. ○○○○○○○○○○ $10 = \_\_\_ + \_\_\_$

13. ○○○○○○○○○○ $10 = \_\_\_ + \_\_\_$

14. ○○○○○○○○○○ $10 = \_\_\_ + \_\_\_$

15. ○○○○○○○○○○ $10 = \_\_\_ + \_\_\_$

16. ○○○○○○○○○○ $10 = \_\_\_ + \_\_\_$

17. THINK SMARTER Zach has 6 rocks. He places some in a box and some in a bag. Draw two ways he can place the rocks.

Problem Solving • Applications

WRITE Math

18. THINK SMARTER I have 8 marbles.
Some are red. Some are blue.
How many of each could I have?
Find and write as many ways as you can.

Red	Blue	Sum

19. THINK SMARTER Color two ways to make 7.

TAKE HOME ACTIVITY • Write 6 = 6 + 0. Model the problem with pennies. Ask your child to make 6 another way. Take turns until you and your child model all of the ways to make 6.

FOR MORE PRACTICE:
Standards Practice Book

Name ______________________

Addition to 10

Essential Question Why are some addition facts easy to add?

Operations and Algebraic Thinking—1.OA.6

MATHEMATICAL PRACTICES
MP.6, MP.7

Listen and Draw Real World

Draw a picture to show the problem.
Then write the addends and the sum in two ways.

___ + ___ = ___

$\begin{array}{r} \square \\ + \square \\ \hline \square \end{array}$

___ + ___ = ___

$\begin{array}{r} \square \\ + \square \\ \hline \square \end{array}$

FOR THE TEACHER • Read the following for the top of the page. There are 2 children in line for the slide. 4 more children get in line. How many children are in line for the slide? Read the following for the bottom of the page. Christy has 3 stickers. Bruce gives her 2 more stickers. How many stickers does Christy have now?

Mathematical Practices

Why is the sum the same when you add across or down? **Explain.**

Model and Draw

Write the addition problem.

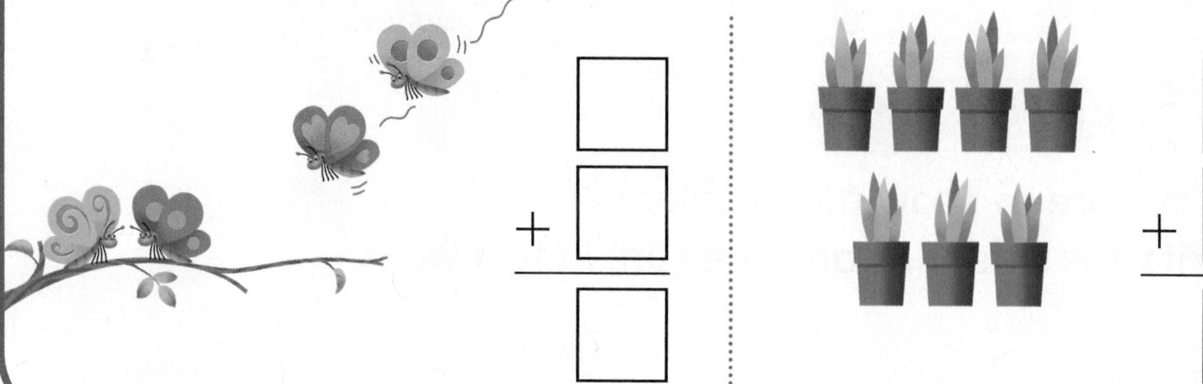

+

Share and Show

Write the addition problem.

1.

+

2.

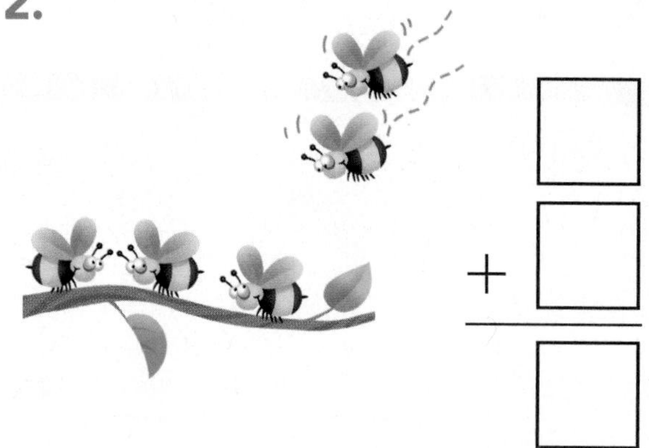

+

3.

+

4.

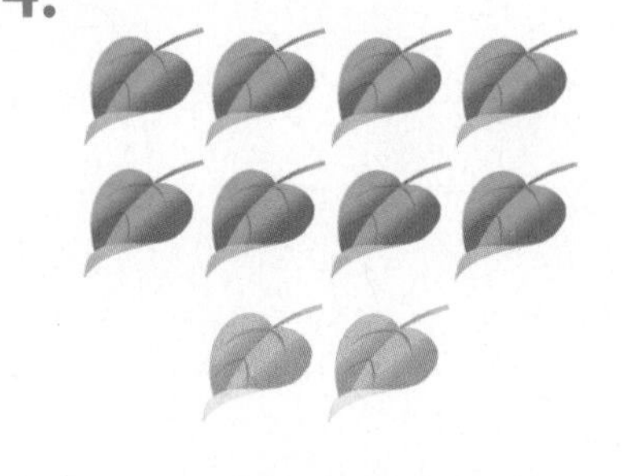

+

Name ______________________________

On Your Own

MATHEMATICAL PRACTICE 6 **Attend to Precision** **Write the sum.**

5. $\begin{array}{r} 1 \\ +\ 2 \\ \hline \end{array}$

6. $\begin{array}{r} 2 \\ +\ 2 \\ \hline \end{array}$

7. $\begin{array}{r} 0 \\ +\ 3 \\ \hline \end{array}$

8. $\begin{array}{r} 1 \\ +\ 1 \\ \hline \end{array}$

9. $\begin{array}{r} 4 \\ +\ 2 \\ \hline \end{array}$

10. $\begin{array}{r} 8 \\ +\ 1 \\ \hline \end{array}$

11. $\begin{array}{r} 0 \\ +\ 4 \\ \hline \end{array}$

12. $\begin{array}{r} 2 \\ +\ 5 \\ \hline \end{array}$

13. $\begin{array}{r} 4 \\ +\ 4 \\ \hline \end{array}$

14. $\begin{array}{r} 9 \\ +\ 1 \\ \hline \end{array}$

15. $\begin{array}{r} 6 \\ +\ 3 \\ \hline \end{array}$

16. $\begin{array}{r} 4 \\ +\ 3 \\ \hline \end{array}$

17. $\begin{array}{r} 1 \\ +\ 6 \\ \hline \end{array}$

18. $\begin{array}{r} 4 \\ +\ 6 \\ \hline \end{array}$

19. $\begin{array}{r} 7 \\ +\ 3 \\ \hline \end{array}$

20. $\begin{array}{r} 6 \\ +\ 2 \\ \hline \end{array}$

21. $\begin{array}{r} 3 \\ +\ 3 \\ \hline \end{array}$

22. $\begin{array}{r} 3 \\ +\ 5 \\ \hline \end{array}$

23. THINK SMARTER **Explain.** Sam showed how he added 4 + 2. Tell how Sam could find the correct sum.

$\begin{array}{r} 4 \\ +\ 2 \\ \hline 7 \end{array}$

____

____

____

____

Problem Solving • Applications

WRITE Math

24. Add. Write the sum. Use the sum and the key to color the flower.

KEY

7	YELLOW
8	RED
9	PURPLE
10	PINK

$3 + 7 =$ ____

$2 + 7$

$5 + 2 =$ ____

$0 + 9 =$ ____

$5 + 5$

$7 + 1 =$ ____

$6 + 4 =$ ____

$7 + 0$

$4 + 5$

$2 + 6$

$3 + 5 =$ ____

$3 + 4 =$ ____

25. GO DEEPER How many flowers are yellow or purple?

____ ◯ ____ ◯ ____

26. THINK SMARTER Write the sum. **Explain** how you solved the problem.

$$\begin{array}{r} 5 \\ +\,4 \\ \hline \square \end{array}$$

____

____

TAKE HOME ACTIVITY • Write addition sentences to add across. Then write addition sentences to add down. Have your child find the sum for each.

FOR MORE PRACTICE: Standards Practice Book

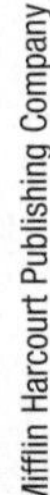

Name ____________________

Chapter 1 Review/Test

1.

2 bears and 1 more bear

How many bears?

1
2
3

bears

2. Write the addition problem.

$\square$
$+ \square$
$\square$

3. Color two ways to make 6.

○ ○ ○ ○ ○ ○

○ ○ ○ ○ ○ ○

GO DIGITAL Assessment Options Chapter Test

4. Choose all the pictures that show adding zero.

○ 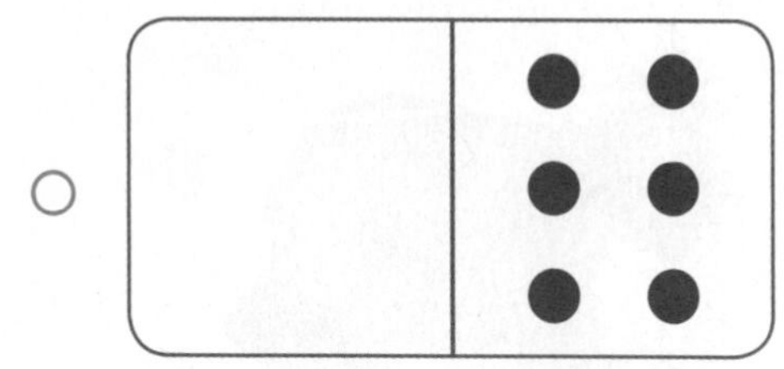

○ 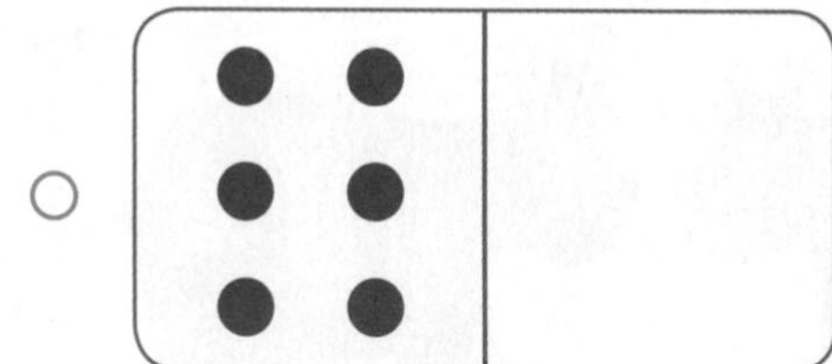

○ 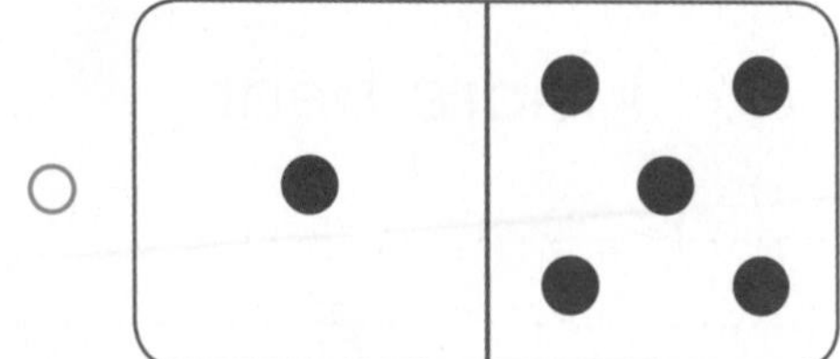

○ 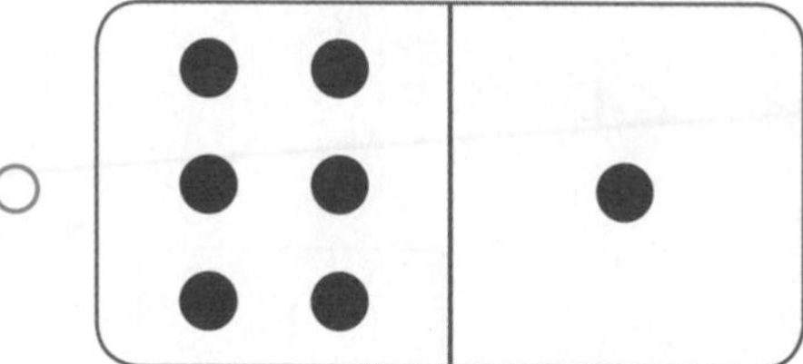

5. Draw lines to match addition sentences with the same addends in a different order.

8 + 2 = 10 2 + 7 = 9 4 + 5 = 9

5 + 4 = 9 2 + 8 = 10 7 + 2 = 9

Use ▪ to show adding to.
Draw the ▪. Write the sum.

6. 2 ducks and 3 more ducks

2 + 3 = ____

7. 5 lions and 2 more lions

5 + 2 = ____

Name ___________________________

8. Write each addition sentence in the box that shows the sum.

$4 + 3$ $3 + 4$ $3 + 3$ $3 + 5$ $5 + 3$

6	7	8

---

9. There are 5 red marbles and 4 blue marbles. How many marbles are there?

Draw to show your work.

Write the number sentence and how many.

_____ ◯ _____ ◯ _____

---

10. There are 2 people in the house. More people go in the house. Then there are 6 people in the house. How many people go in the house?

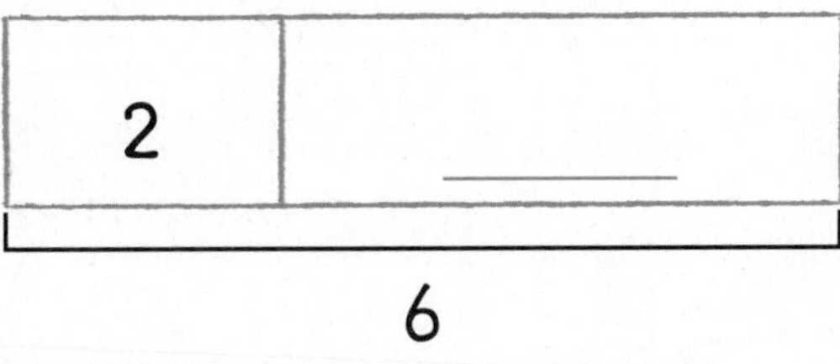

$2 +$ _____ $= 6$

11. Katie is drawing dots on cards to show ways to make 7. Draw dots for Katie.

Write addition sentences for two of the cards.

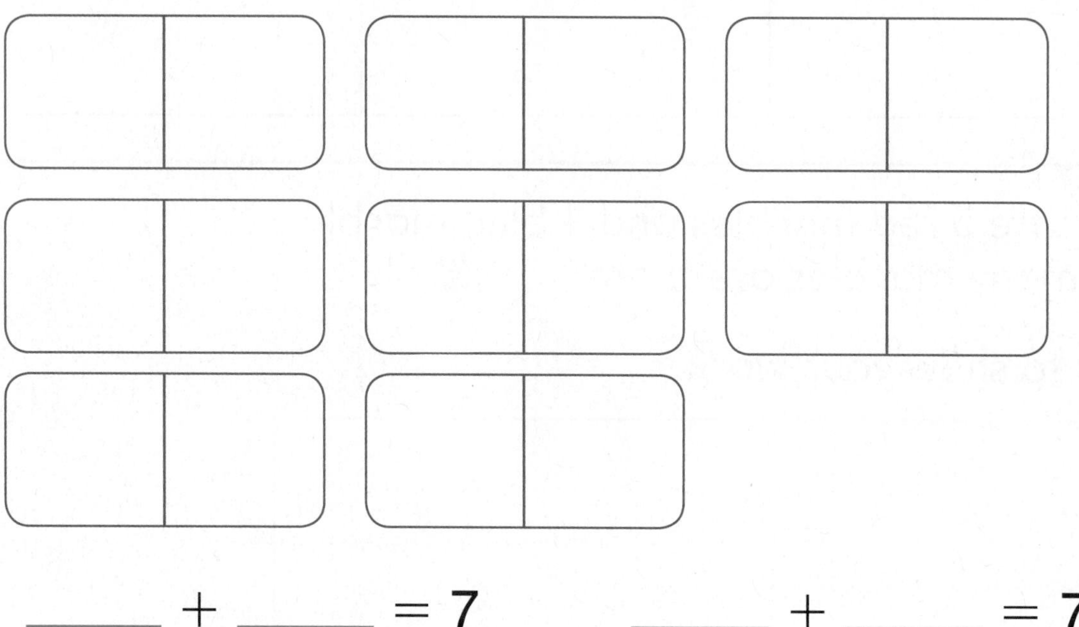

____ + ____ = 7 ____ + ____ = 7

12. Draw a model to show that 1 + 4 is the same as 4 + 1. Show how you know.

Chapter 2

Subtraction Concepts

Look at the picture.
Make up a subtraction
story problem.

Name ______________________

Show What You Know

Explore Numbers 1 to 4

Show the number with ●.
Draw the ●.

1. 4 

2. 2

Numbers 1 to 10

How many objects are in each set?

3. 

____ butterflies

4. 

____ cat

5. 

____ leaves

Use Pictures to Subtract

How many are left?

6. 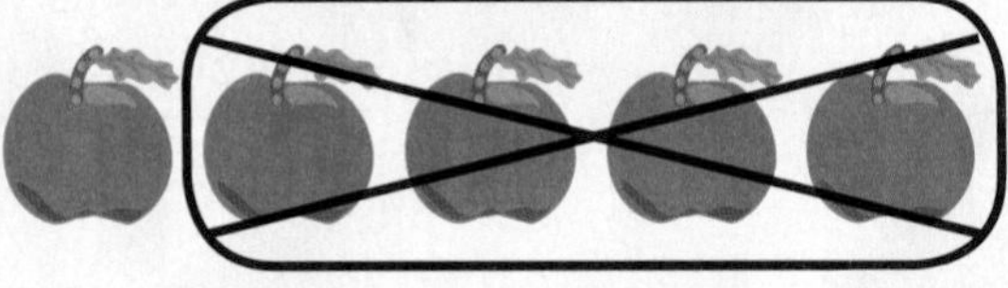

$5 - 4 =$ ____

7.   

$4 - 2 =$ ____

This page checks understanding of important skills needed for success in Chapter 2.

Personal Math Trainer
Online Assessment and Intervention

Name ______________________________

Vocabulary Builder

Review Words
add to
take apart
put together
take from

Visualize It

Sort the review words from the box.

Subtraction **Addition**

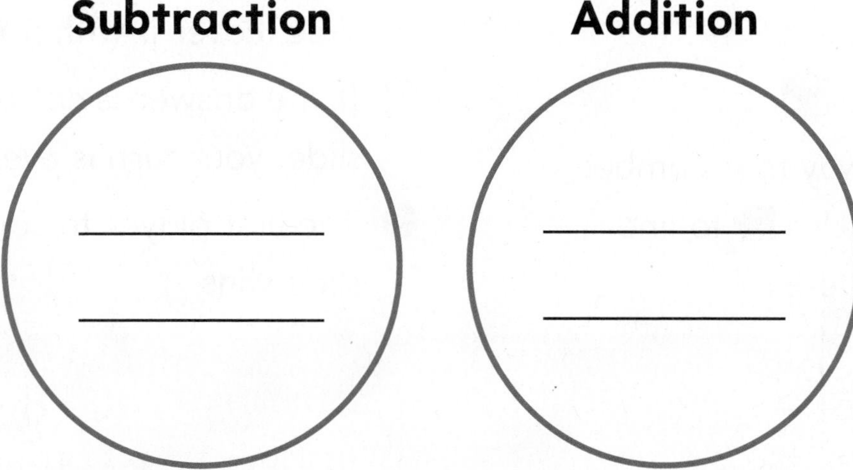

Understand Vocabulary

Circle the part you take from the group. Then cross it out.

1.  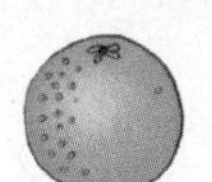 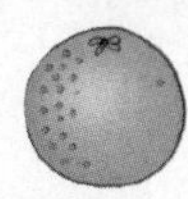 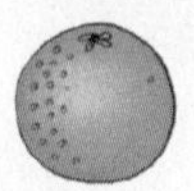

5 oranges 2 are eaten.

2.    

4 balloons 3 fly away.

3.  

3 toy cars 1 rolls away.

• Interactive Student Edition
• Multimedia eGlossary

Chapter 2

Subtraction Slide

Materials •  • 5 ●
 • 8 ■

Play with a partner.
Take turns.

1. Toss the 🎲.
2. Take away that number from 8. Use ■ to find what is left.
3. If you see the answer on your slide, cover it with a ●.
4. If the answer is not on your slide, your turn is over.
5. The first player to cover a whole slide wins.

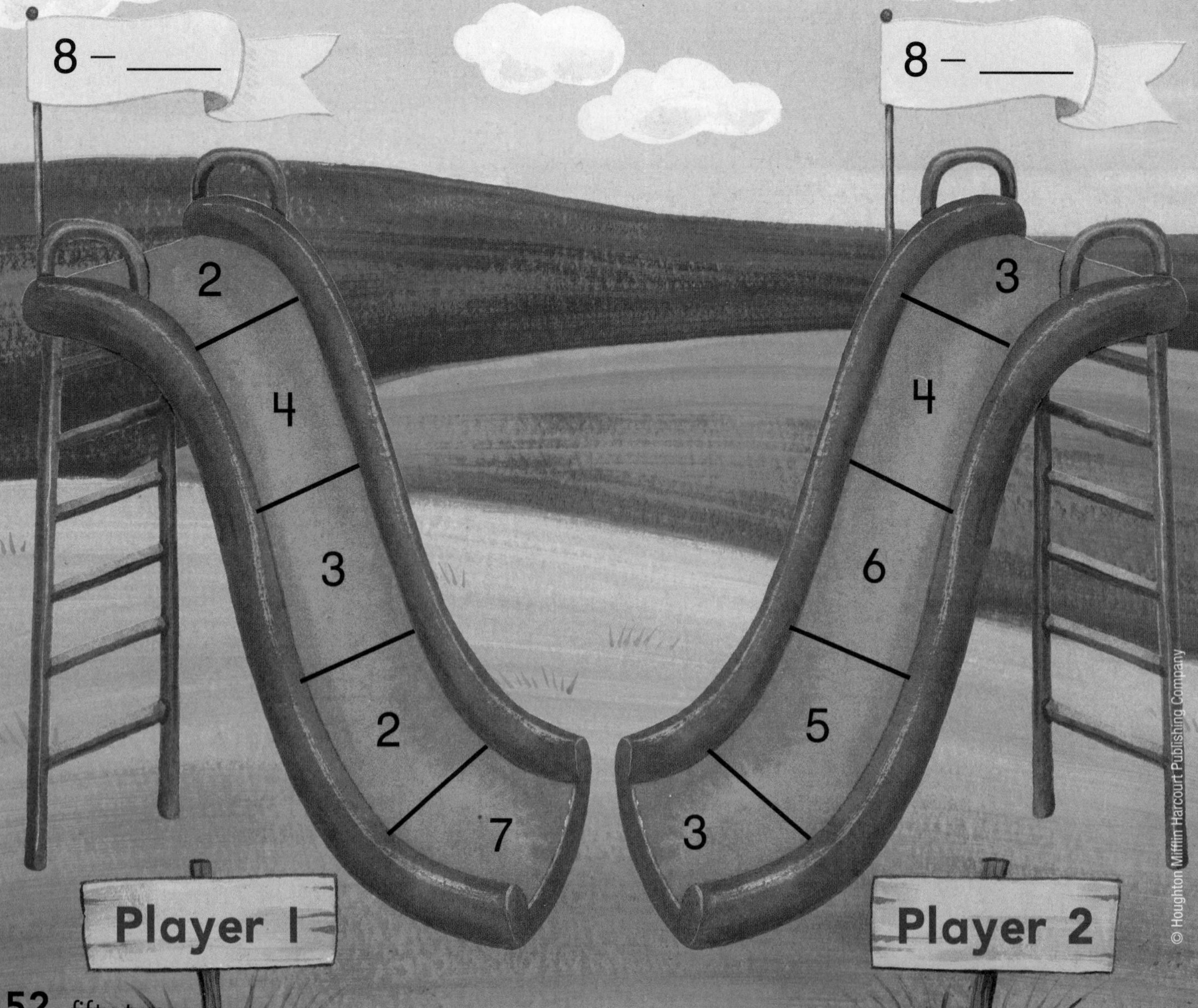

8 − ____

2
4
3
2
7

Player 1

8 − ____

3
4
6
5
3

Player 2

Name ______________________________

Use Pictures to Show Taking From

Essential Question How can you show taking from with pictures?

Operations and Algebraic Thinking—1.OA.1

MATHEMATICAL PRACTICES
MP.1, MP.2, MP.4

Listen and Draw Real World

Draw to show taking from.
Write how many there are now.

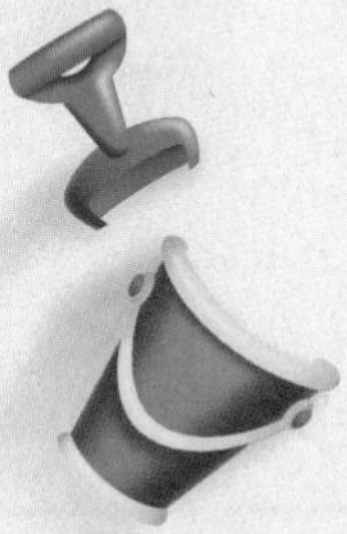

____ children now

Math Talk **Mathematical Practices**

How did you find how many are in the sandbox now? **Explain.**

FOR THE TEACHER • Read the following problem. Have children draw a picture to show the problem. There are 5 children in the sandbox. 2 walk away. How many children are in the sandbox now?

Model and Draw

There are 4 cats in the whole group.

4 cats   1 cat walks away.   __3__ cats now

Share and Show

Circle the part you are taking from the group.
Then cross it out. Write how many there are now.

1.

6 bugs   2 bugs fly away.   ____ bugs now

2.

3 dogs   1 dog walks away.   ____ dogs now

Name ______________________________

On Your Own

Circle the part you are taking from the group.
Then cross it out. Write how many there are now.

3. 

7 chicks 2 chicks walk away. ____ chicks now

4.  

6 ducks 3 ducks walk away. ____ ducks now

5. THINK SMARTER Ellie and Sara see 8 birds in the tree. Ellie sees 2 fewer birds than Sara. Sara sees 5 birds. How many birds does Ellie see? ____ birds

6. GO DEEPER Choose numbers to complete the story. Write the numbers. Draw to show the problem.

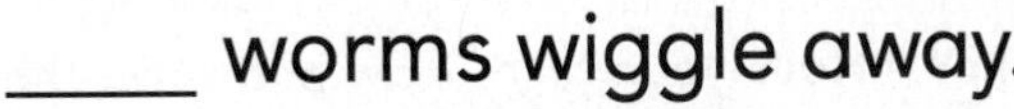

____ worms ____ worms wiggle away. 3 worms now

Problem Solving • Applications

Use Diagrams Solve.

7. There are 6 cats. I cat runs away. How many cats are there now? Draw to show your work.

____ cats

8. There are 5 rabbits. 3 rabbits hop away. How many rabbits are there now?

____ rabbits

9. THINK SMARTER Use the picture. Write the numbers.

8 birds ____ birds fly away. ____ birds now

10. THINK SMARTER Circle and cross out the part that goes away. Write how many there are now.

10 fish 6 fish swim away. ____ fish now

TAKE HOME ACTIVITY • Have your child draw and solve the subtraction problem: There are 6 cows. 3 cows walk away. How many cows are there now?

FOR MORE PRACTICE: Standards Practice Book

Name ______________________________

Model Taking From

Essential Question How do you model taking from a group?

Operations and Algebraic Thinking—1.OA.1

MATHEMATICAL PRACTICES
MP.1, MP.2, MP.4

Listen and Draw

Use [cube] to show taking from.
Draw to show your work.

Math Talk — **Mathematical Practices**

Are there more than or fewer than 9 butterflies now? **Explain.**

FOR THE TEACHER • Read the following problem. Have children use connecting cubes to model the problem and draw to show their work. There are 9 butterflies. 2 butterflies fly away. How many butterflies are there now?

Model and Draw

4 bunnies   3 bunnies hop away.

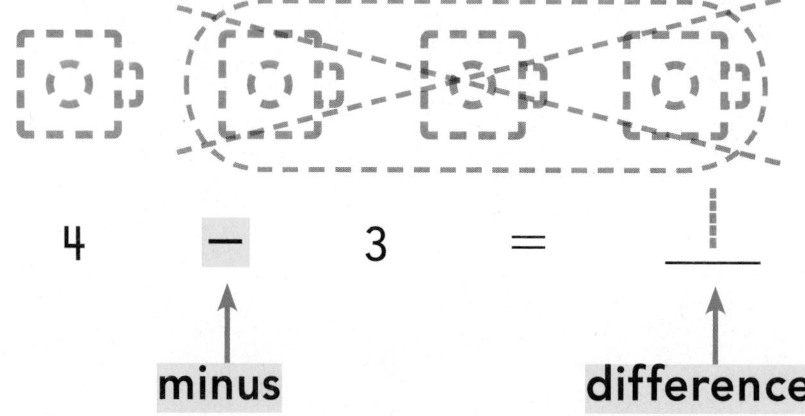

4 − 3 = 1

minus   difference

4 − 3 = 1 is a **subtraction sentence**.

Share and Show

Use ▪ to show taking from. Draw the ▪.
Circle the part you take away from the group.
Then cross it out. Write the difference.

1. 8 dogs   3 dogs run away.

8 − 3 = ____

2. 6 frogs   4 frogs hop away.

6 − 4 = ____

Name ______________________

On Your Own

Use ▪ to show taking from. Draw the ▪.
Circle the part you take away from the group.
Then cross it out. Write the difference.

3. 5 seals 4 seals swim away.

$5 - 4 =$ ____

4. 9 bears 6 bears run away.

$9 - 6 =$ ____

5. THINK SMARTER Kelly sees some fish at the pet shop. A man buys 2 fish. A boy buys 4 fish. Now there are 3 fish. How many fish did Kelly see at first?

____ fish

6. GO DEEPER Use the picture. Circle a part to take from the group. Then cross it out. Write the subtraction sentence.

____ ◯ ____ ◯ ____

Problem Solving • Applications

MATHEMATICAL PRACTICE 1 **Make Sense of Problems**

Draw ■ to solve. Complete the subtraction sentence.

7. There are 5 boys.
3 boys go home.
How many are there now?

___ − ___ = ___

___ boys

8. There are 8 bunnies.
2 bunnies hop away.
How many bunnies are there now?

___ − ___ = ___

___ bunnies

9. THINK SMARTER Draw a picture to show a subtraction sentence. Write the subtraction sentence.

___ − ___ = ___

Personal Math Trainer

10. THINK SMARTER + Take away ■ to show the problem. Write the difference.

There are 7 mice. 5 run away.

$7 - 5 =$ ___

TAKE HOME ACTIVITY • Use pennies or other small objects of the same kind to model a subtraction situation for numbers within 10. Ask your child to write the subtraction sentence for it. Then switch roles and repeat the activity.

FOR MORE PRACTICE: Standards Practice Book

Name ____________________

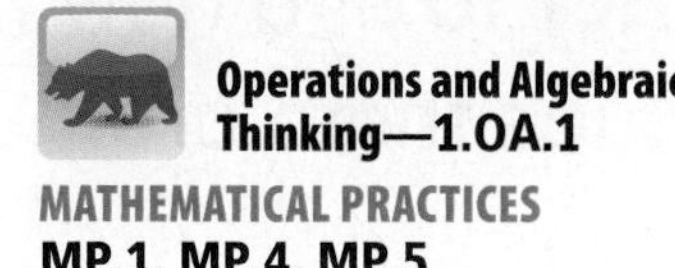

Model Taking Apart

Essential Question How do you model taking apart?

Operations and Algebraic Thinking—1.OA.1

MATHEMATICAL PRACTICES
MP.1, MP.4, MP.5

Use ● to model the problem. Draw and color to show your model. Write the numbers and a subtraction sentence.

____ red apples ____ yellow apples

5 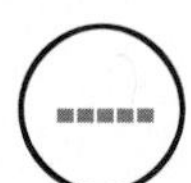 3 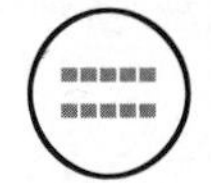 ____

Jeff has ____ yellow apples.

Math Talk Mathematical Practices

How did you solve this problem? **Explain.**

FOR THE TEACHER • Have children model the problem using counters. Jeff has 5 apples. 3 apples are red. The rest are yellow. How many apples are yellow?

Model and Draw

Subtract to find how many small cups there are.

Maria has 6 cups. 2 cups are big. The rest are small. How many cups are small?

2 cups are big.

The rest are small.

_____ small cups

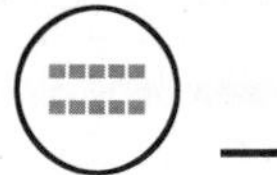

Share and Show

Use ● to solve. Draw to show your work. Write the number sentence and how many.

1. There are 7 folders. 6 folders are red. The rest are yellow. How many folders are yellow?

_____ yellow folder

_____ 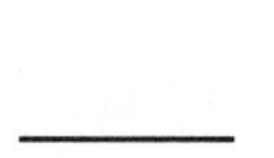 _____  _____

2. There are 8 pencils. 3 pencils are short. The rest are long. How many pencils are long?

_____ long pencils

_____ 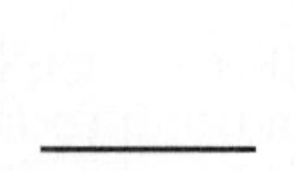 _____ 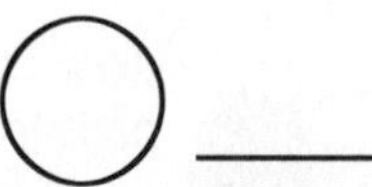 _____

Name ______________________________

On Your Own

MATHEMATICAL PRACTICE 4 **Write an Equation**

Use ● to solve. Draw to show your work.
Write the number sentence and how many.

3. There are 9 fish. 5 fish are red. The rest are yellow. How many fish are yellow?

____ yellow fish ____ ◯ ____ ◯ ____

4. There are 7 ants. 4 ants are big. The rest are small. How many ants are small?

____ small ants  ____ ◯ ____ ◯ ____

5. There are 8 hats. 2 hats are small. The rest are big. How many hats are big?

____ big hats ____ ◯ ____ ◯ ____

6. There are 5 trees. 1 tree is short. The rest are tall. How many trees are tall?

____ tall trees ____ ◯ ____ ◯ ____

Problem Solving • Applications

Solve. Draw a model to explain.

7. There are 6 bears. 4 are big. The rest are small. How many bears are small?

____ small bears

8. THINK SMARTER There are 7 bears. 1 bear walks away. Then 4 more bears walk away. How many bears are there now?

____ bears

9. GO DEEPER There are 4 bears. Some are black and some are brown. There are fewer than 2 black bears. How many bears are brown?

____ brown bears

10. THINK SMARTER Draw ● to solve. Write the number sentence. There are 8 flowers. 4 flowers are red. The rest are yellow. How many flowers are yellow?

TAKE HOME ACTIVITY • Have your child collect a group of up to 10 small objects of the same kind and use them to make up subtraction stories.

FOR MORE PRACTICE: Standards Practice Book

Name ______________________

Problem Solving • Model Subtraction

Essential Question How do you solve subtraction problems by making a model?

Operations and Algebraic Thinking—1.OA.1
MATHEMATICAL PRACTICES
MP.1, MP.4, MP.5

Tom has 6 crayons in a box.
He takes 2 crayons out of the box.
How many crayons are in the box now?
How can you use a model to find out?

Unlock the Problem Real World

What do I need to find?

how many  crayons
are in the box now

What information do I need to use?

6 crayons in a box
2 crayons taken out

Show how to solve the problem.

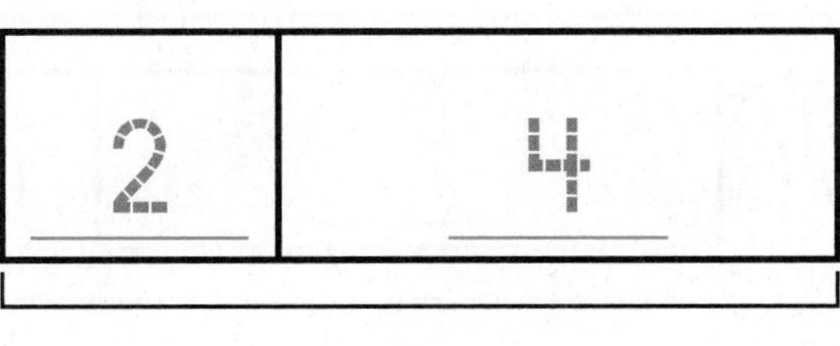

6 − 2 = ____

HOME CONNECTION • Your child used a bar model to help him or her understand and solve the subtraction problem.

Try Another Problem

Read the problem. Use the bar model to solve. Complete the model and the number sentence.

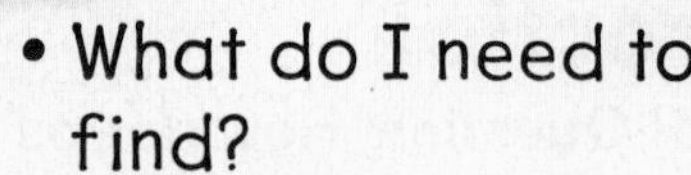

1. There are 10 stickers. 7 stickers are orange. The rest are brown. How many stickers are brown?

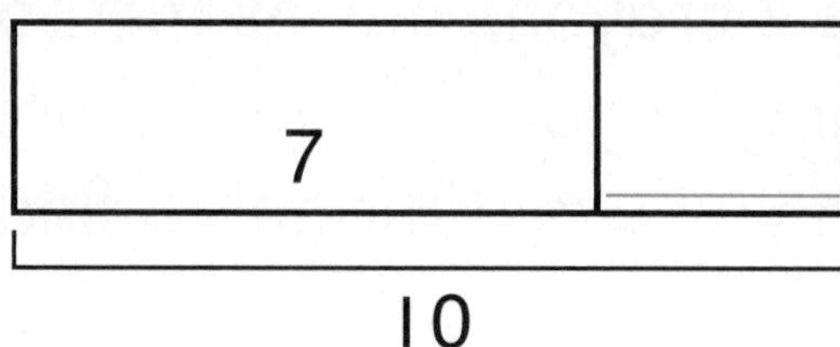

10 − 7 = ____

2. Some birds were in the tree. 2 birds flew away. Then there were 6 birds. How many birds were in the tree before?

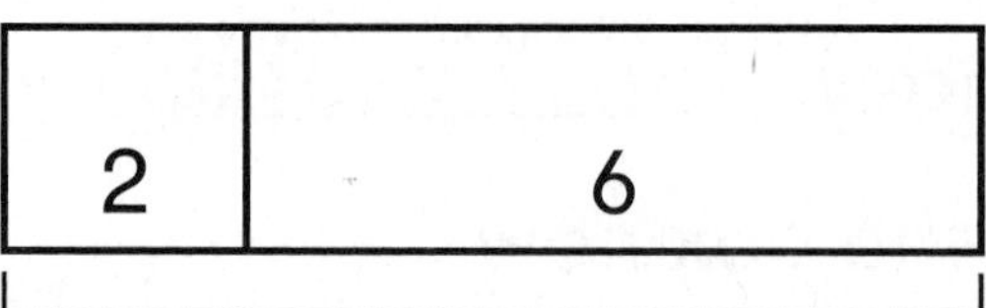

____ − 2 = 6

3. There were 5 cars. Some cars drove away. Then there was 1 car. How many cars drove away?

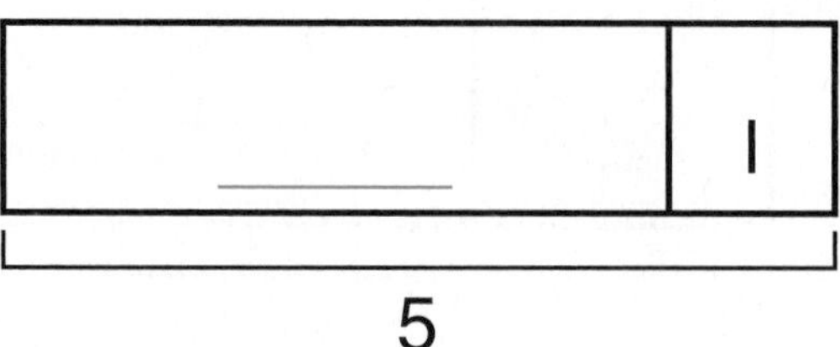

5 − ____ = 1

Math Talk **Mathematical Practices**

What does each part of the model show? **Explain.**

Name ______________________

Share and Show 

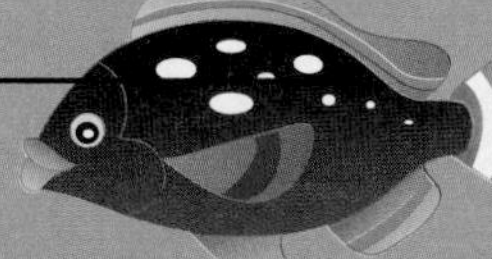

MATHEMATICAL PRACTICE 4 **Use Models** Read the problem. Use the bar model to solve. Complete the model and the number sentence.

4. Some goats were in the field. 3 goats ran away. Then there were 4 goats. How many goats were in the field before?

3	4

_____

_____ − 3 = 4

---

5. There are 8 sleds. Some sleds slide down the hill. Then there are 4 sleds. How many sleds slide down the hill?

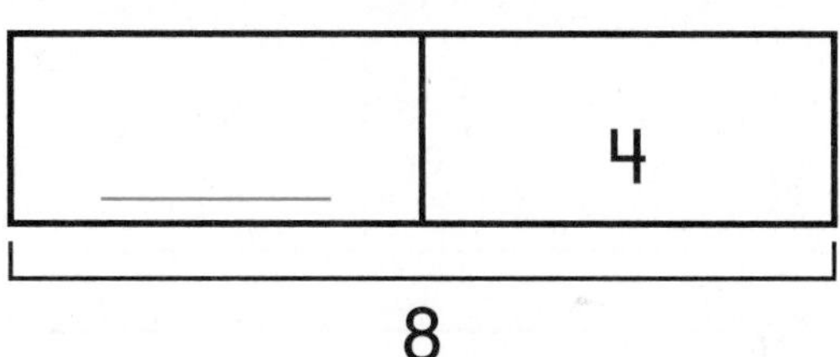

8 − _____ = 4

---

6. There are 10 buttons. 3 buttons are small. The rest are big. How many buttons are big?

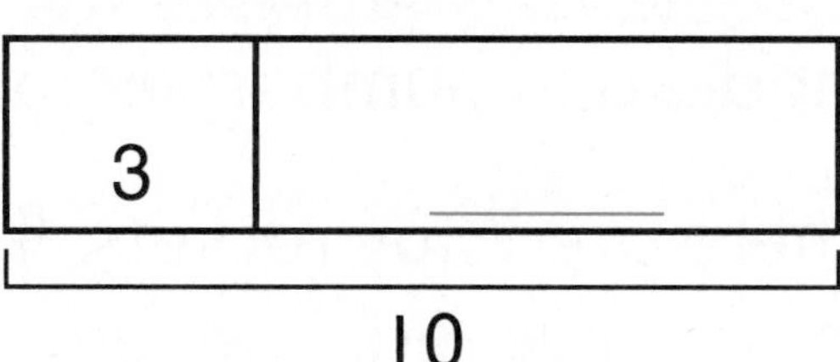

10 − 3 = _____

On Your Own

WRITE Math

Solve.

7. GO DEEPER There were 8 spiders in the grass. Some spiders crawled away. Then there were 3 spiders. How many spiders crawled away? Complete the number sentence.

____ spiders

8. THINK SMARTER Write your own story problem using the model.

7	2

9

____

____

9. THINK SMARTER Complete the model and number sentence.

4	____

7

There are 7 toy rockets. 4 toy rockets are red. The rest are black. How many toy rockets are black?

$7 - 4 =$ ____

TAKE HOME ACTIVITY • Ask your child to describe what the bottom part of a bar model means when subtracting.

FOR MORE PRACTICE: Standards Practice Book

Name ______________________________

Use Pictures and Subtraction to Compare

Essential Question How can you use pictures to compare and subtract?

Operations and Algebraic Thinking—1.OA.8

MATHEMATICAL PRACTICES
MP.1, MP.2, MP.4

Listen and Draw (Real World)

Draw bowls to show the problems.
Draw lines to match.

Math Talk Mathematical Practices

Explain how many more dogs or bowls there are.

FOR THE TEACHER • Read the problem. There are 9 brown dogs. There are 5 bowls. How many more dogs need a bowl? There are 7 white dogs. There are 8 bowls. How many bowls are not needed?

Model and Draw

Compare the groups.
Subtract to find how many **fewer** or how many **more**.

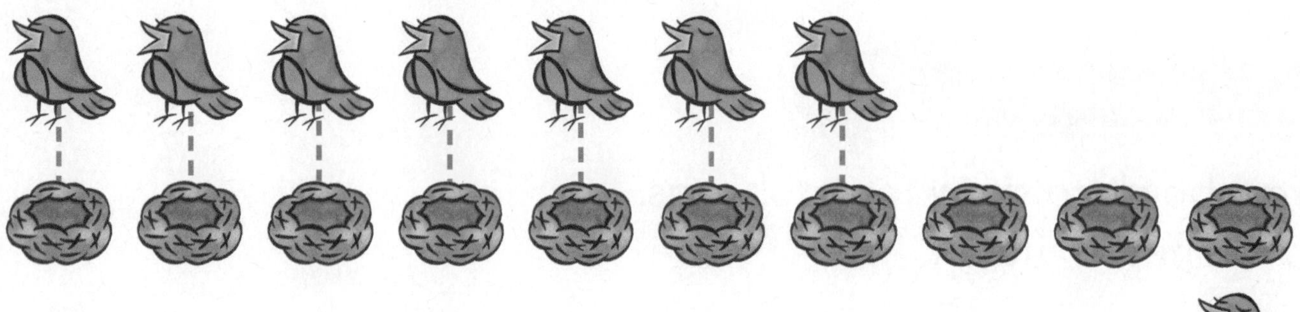

10 − 7 = 3   3 fewer 

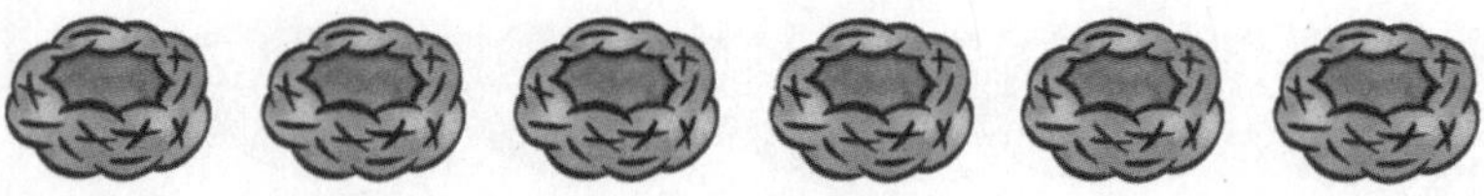

6 − 4 = ______   ______ more 

Share and Show

Draw lines to match.
Subtract to compare.

1.     

8 − 5 = ______   ______ fewer 

Name ___________________________

On Your Own

MATHEMATICAL PRACTICE 2 **Reason Quantitatively**

Draw lines to match. Subtract to compare.

2.         

9 − 3 = ______ ______ more 

3.        

10 − 6 = ______ ______ fewer 

4.    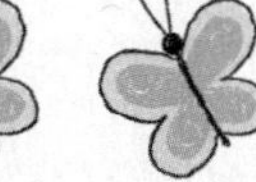   

9 − 7 = ______ ______ fewer 

5. GO DEEPER       

______ more 

7 − 2 = ______ ______ fewer 

Problem Solving • Applications

Draw a picture to show the problem. Write a subtraction sentence that your picture shows.

6. Aki has 5 baseball bats and 3 baseballs. How many fewer baseballs does Aki have?

____ − ____ = ____ ____ fewer baseballs

7. THINK SMARTER Jill has 2 more cats than she has dogs. How many fewer dogs does Jill have?

____ fewer dogs

8. THINK SMARTER Look at the picture. How many fewer leaves are there than ladybugs? Choose the answer.

2
3
5
8

fewer leaves

Name ______________________

Subtract to Compare

Essential Question How can you use models to compare and subtract?

Operations and Algebraic Thinking—1.OA.1 *Also 1.OA.8*

MATHEMATICAL PRACTICES
MP.1, MP.4, MP.6

Listen and Draw

Use ● to show the problem. Draw the ●.
Model the problem using the bar model.

Math Talk Mathematical Practices

Explain how you find how many more puzzle pieces Mindy has than David.

FOR THE TEACHER • Read the problem. Mindy has 8 puzzle pieces. David has 5 puzzle pieces. How many more puzzle pieces does Mindy have than David?

Model and Draw

James has 4 stones. Heather has 7 stones. How many fewer stones does James have than Heather?

____ fewer stones

____ ◯ ____ ◯ ____

Share and Show

MATH BOARD

Read the problem. Use the bar model to solve. Write the number sentence. Then write how many.

1. Abby has 8 stamps. Ben has 6 stamps. How many more stamps does Abby have than Ben?

____ more stamps

____ ◯ ____ ◯ ____

2. Daniel has 3 books. Vicky has 6 books. How many fewer books does Daniel have than Vicky?

____ fewer books

____ ◯ ____ ◯ ____

Name ______________________________

On Your Own

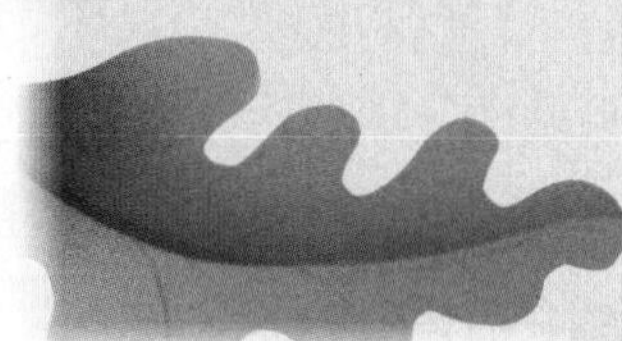

MATHEMATICAL PRACTICE 4 **Use Models** Read the problem. Use the bar model to solve. Write the number sentence. Then write how many.

3. THINK SMARTER Pam has 4 marbles. Rick has 10 marbles. How many fewer marbles does Pam have than Rick?

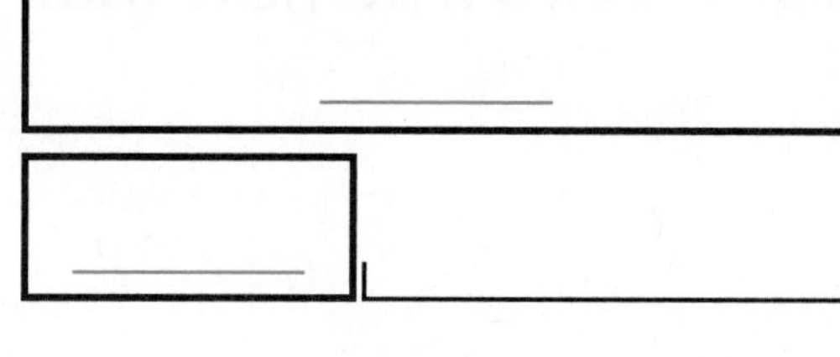

____ fewer marbles

____ ◯ ____ ◯ ____

4. Sally has 5 feathers. James has 2 feathers. How many more feathers does Sally have than James?

____ more feathers

____ ◯ ____ ◯ ____

5. GO DEEPER Kyle has 6 keys. Kyle has 4 more keys than Lee. How many keys does Lee have?

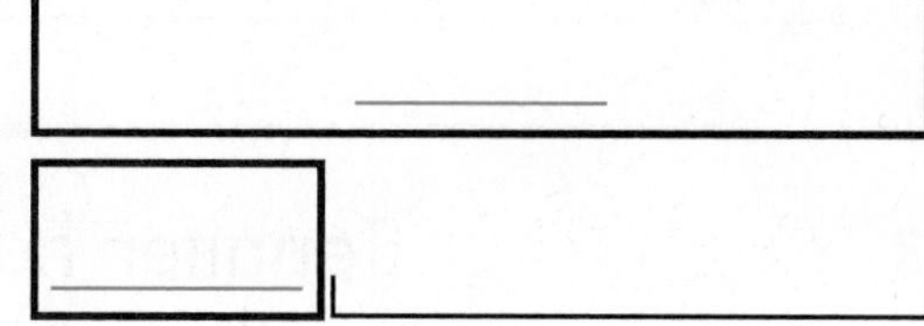

____ keys

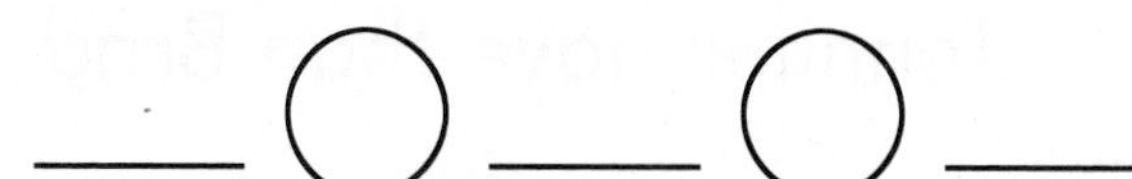

____ ◯ ____ ◯ ____

TAKE HOME ACTIVITY • Have your child explain how he or she solved exercise 3 using the bar model.

FOR MORE PRACTICE: Standards Practice Book

Name ______________________________

Mid-Chapter Checkpoint

Concepts and Skills

Circle the part you are taking from the group. Then cross it out. Write how many there are now. (1.OA.1)

1\.

7 birds 3 birds fly away. ____ birds now

Use ● to solve. Draw to show your work. Write the number sentence and how many. (1.OA.1)

2\. There are 4 cans. 1 can is red. The rest are yellow. How many cans are yellow?

____ yellow cans

3\. THINK SMARTER Jennifer has 3 pennies. Brad has 9 pennies. How many fewer pennies does Jennifer have than Brad? (1.OA.1)

9	
3	

9 − 3 = ____

____

Name ______________________________

Subtract All or Zero

Essential Question What happens when you subtract 0 from a number?

Operations and Algebraic Thinking—1.OA.8

MATHEMATICAL PRACTICES
MP.3, MP.4, MP.8

Listen and Draw Real World

Use ● to show the problem. Draw the ●.
Write the numbers.

___ – ___ – ___

___ – ___ = ___

Math Talk **Mathematical Practices**

Does your first answer make sense? **Explain.**

FOR THE TEACHER • Read the following problem. 4 toys are on the shelf. 0 toys are taken off. How many toys are on the shelf? Then read the following problem. 4 toys are on the shelf. 4 toys are taken off. How many toys are there now?

Model and Draw

When you subtract zero, how many are left?

$\underline{5} - 0 = \underline{5}$

When you subtract all, how many are left?

$\underline{5} - \underline{5} = 0$

Share and Show

Use the picture to complete the subtraction sentence.

1.

$\_\_\_\_ - 0 = \_\_\_\_$

2.

$\_\_\_\_ - \_\_\_\_ = 0$

3.

$\_\_\_\_ - \_\_\_\_ = 0$

4.

$\_\_\_\_ - 0 = \_\_\_\_$

✓5.

$\_\_\_\_ - 0 = \_\_\_\_$

✓6.

$\_\_\_\_ - \_\_\_\_ = 0$

Name ________________________________

On Your Own

MATHEMATICAL PRACTICE 8 **Use Repeated Reasoning**

Complete the subtraction sentence.

7. 

1 − 0 = ____

8. 

____ = 6 − 6

9. 

0 = ____ − 3

10. 

1 − 1 = ____

11. 3 − 0 = ____

12. ____ = 8 − 0

13. 7 − ____ = 7

14. 8 − 8 = ____

15. 5 − 5 = ____

16. ____ = 0 − 0

GO DEEPER Choose numbers to complete the subtraction sentence.

17. ____ − ____ = 0

18. ____ − ____ = 0

Problem Solving • Applications

WRITE Math

Write the number sentence and tell how many.

19. There are 6 bookmarks on the table. 0 are blue and the rest are yellow. How many bookmarks are yellow?

____ ◯ ____ ◯ ____

____ yellow bookmarks

20. Jared has 8 pictures. He gave some to Wendy. Jared has 0 pictures now. How many pictures did Jared give to Wendy?

____ ◯ ____ ◯ ____

____ pictures

21. THINK SMARTER Kevin has 3 fewer leaves than Sandy. Sandy has 3 leaves. How many leaves does Kevin have?

____ leaves

22. THINK SMARTER Is the answer correct? Choose Yes or No.

$5 - 0 = 0$	○ Yes	○ No
$5 - 0 = 5$	○ Yes	○ No
$5 - 5 = 0$	○ Yes	○ No

TAKE HOME ACTIVITY • Have your child explain how 4 − 4 and 4 − 0 are different.

FOR MORE PRACTICE: Standards Practice Book

Name ________________________________

Algebra • Take Apart Numbers

Essential Question How can you show all the ways to take apart a number?

Operations and Algebraic Thinking—1.OA.1 *Also 1.OA.6*

MATHEMATICAL PRACTICES
MP.3, MP.4, MP.7

Listen and Draw (Real World) (Hands On)

Use [cube] to show all the ways to take apart 5.
Color and draw to show your work.

Take Apart 5

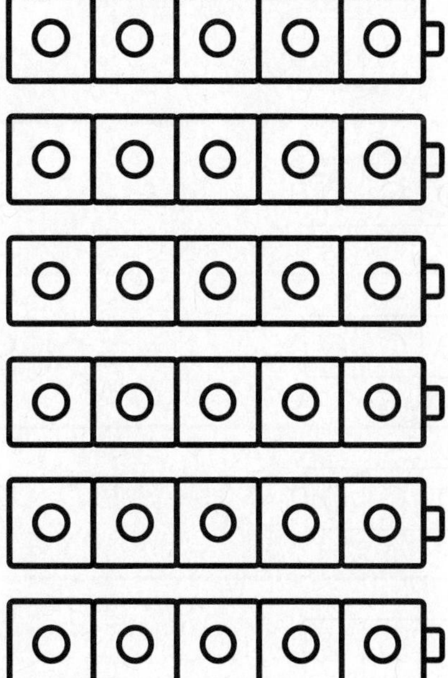

Math Talk **Mathematical Practices**

How do you know you showed all the ways? **Explain.**

FOR THE TEACHER • Read the following problem and have children show all the ways to solve the problem. Jada has 5 grapes. What are all the ways she can share the grapes with her sister?

Model and Draw

Now Jada has 9 grapes. What are all the ways she can share the grapes with her sister?

Complete the number sentence.

1. 9 − 0 = 9

2. 9 − 1 = 8

Share and Show

MATH BOARD

Use . Color and draw to show how to take apart 9. Complete the subtraction sentence.

Show all the ways to take apart 9.

3. 9 − ___ = ___

4. 9 − ___ = ___

5. 9 − ___ = ___

6. 9 − ___ = ___

7. 9 − ___ = ___

8. 9 − ___ = ___

9. 9 − ___ = ___

10. 9 − ___ = ___

Name ____________________

On Your Own

MATHEMATICAL PRACTICE 7 **Look for a Pattern** Use ▪. Color and draw to show how to take apart 10. Complete the subtraction sentence.

Show all the ways to take apart 10.

11. ○○○○○○○○○○ 10 − ___ = ___

12. ○○○○○○○○○○ 10 − ___ = ___

13. ○○○○○○○○○○ 10 − ___ = ___

14. ○○○○○○○○○○ 10 − ___ = ___

15. ○○○○○○○○○○ 10 − ___ = ___

16. ○○○○○○○○○○ 10 − ___ = ___

17. ○○○○○○○○○○ 10 − ___ = ___

18. ○○○○○○○○○○ 10 − ___ = ___

19. ○○○○○○○○○○ 10 − ___ = ___

20. ○○○○○○○○○○ 10 − ___ = ___

21. ○○○○○○○○○○ 10 − ___ = ___

Problem Solving • Applications  

22. James has 10 books. He shares them with his sister. Draw one way he can share the books.

23. THINK SMARTER Hannah has 7 shells. She shares them with Emily. Draw two ways she can share the shells.

Math on the Spot

24. GO DEEPER I use 6 marbles to play a game. I lose 1 marble. Then I lose 1 more marble. How many marbles do I have left?

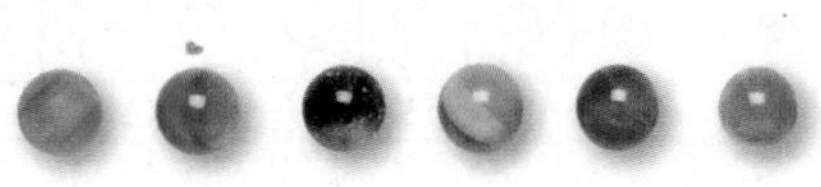

____ marbles

25. THINK SMARTER Circle all the models that show a way to take apart 8.

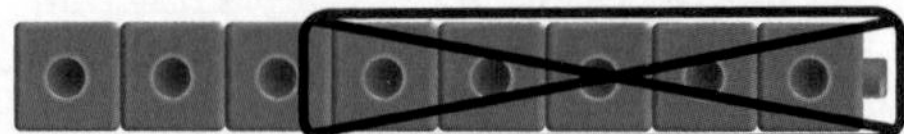

TAKE HOME ACTIVITY • Write 5 − 0 = 5 and 5 − 1 = 4. Ask your child to subtract from 5 another way. Take turns to show all the ways to subtract from 5.

FOR MORE PRACTICE: Standards Practice Book

Name ______________________________

Subtraction from 10 or Less

Essential Question Why are some subtraction facts easy to subtract?

Operations and Algebraic Thinking—1.OA.6

MATHEMATICAL PRACTICES
MP.4, MP.6, MP.8

Listen and Draw (Real World)

Draw a picture to show the problem. Then write the subtraction problem two different ways.

___ − ___ = ___

$\square$
$- \square$
$\square$

___ − ___ = ___

$\square$
$- \square$
$\square$

FOR THE TEACHER • Read the following problem for the top section. There are 5 birds in a tree. 2 birds fly away. How many birds are still in the tree? Read the following problem for the bottom section. Steve has 6 crayons. He gives 4 to Matt. How many crayons does Steve have now?

Math Talk **Mathematical Practices**

Look at the top problem. **Explain** why the difference is the same.

Model and Draw

Write the subtraction problem.

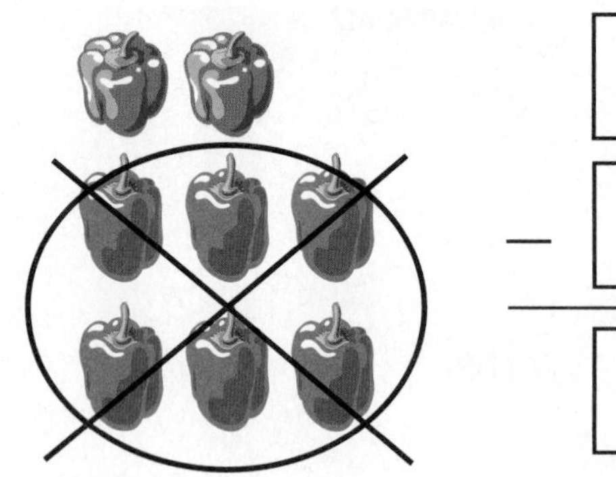

$-$

$-$

Share and Show

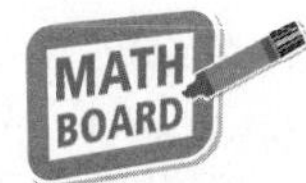

Write the subtraction problem.

1.

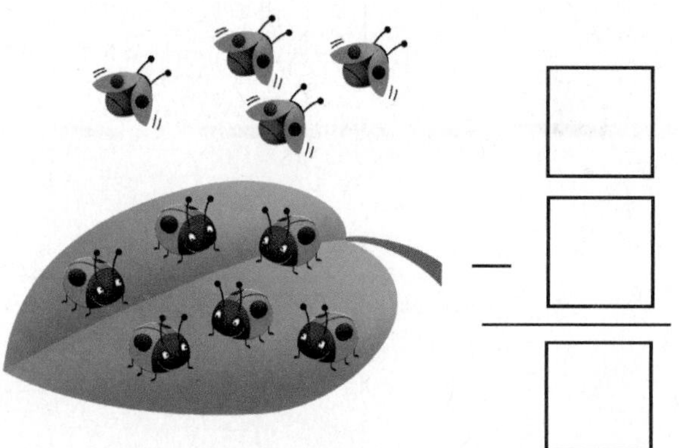

$-$

2.

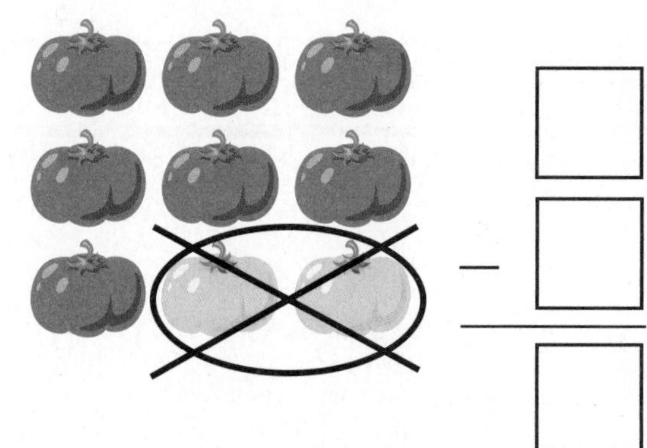

$-$

3.

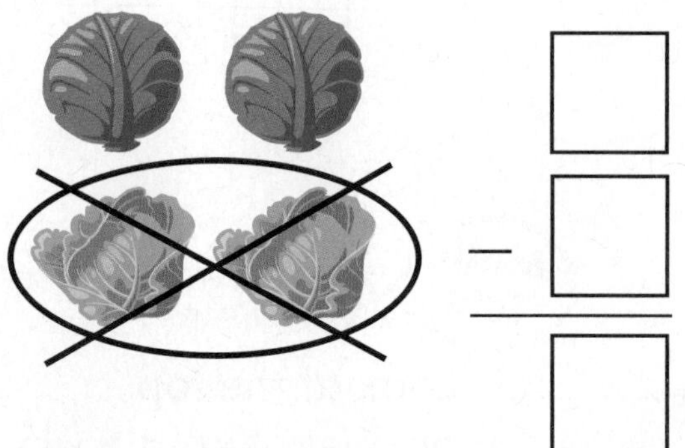

$-$

4.

$-$

Name ______________________________

On Your Own

MATHEMATICAL PRACTICE 6 **Attend to Precision**

Write the difference.

5. $2 - 1 =$ ____
6. $3 - 3 =$ ____
7. $5 - 4 =$ ____
8. $7 - 3 =$ ____
9. $6 - 2 =$ ____
10. $10 - 7 =$ ____
11. $9 - 9 =$ ____
12. $8 - 2 =$ ____
13. $7 - 4 =$ ____
14. $6 - 3 =$ ____
15. $8 - 0 =$ ____
16. $9 - 4 =$ ____
17. $8 - 7 =$ ____
18. $7 - 5 =$ ____
19. $8 - 6 =$ ____
20. $10 - 1 =$ ____
21. $6 - 5 =$ ____
22. $9 - 7 =$ ____

23. THINK SMARTER Explain how the picture shows subtraction.

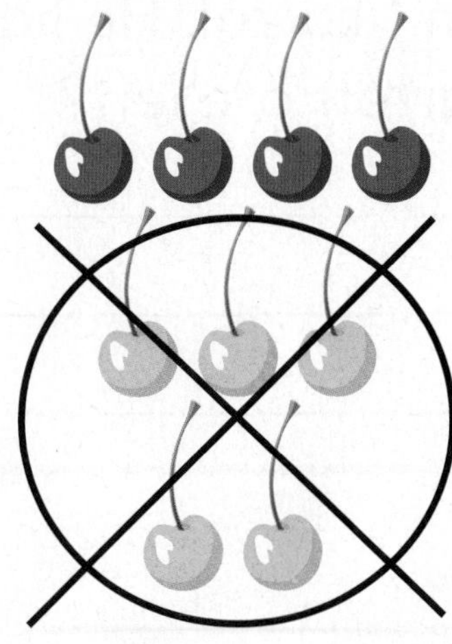

____

____

____

Problem Solving • Applications

24. GO DEEPER Draw a picture to show subtraction. Write the subtraction problem to match the picture.

25. Write the number sentence.

10 ducks are at the pond. All the ducks fly away. How many ducks are still at the pond?

___ − ___ = ___

Personal Math Trainer

26. THINK SMARTER + Write all of the subtraction sentences that can tell the story. Tell how you know.

Max has 6 carrots. He eats more than 1 carrot. He has more than 1 carrot left. How many carrots are left?

____

____

____

TAKE HOME ACTIVITY • Tell your child a subtraction problem. Have your child write the problem to subtract two different ways. Then have your child find the difference.

FOR MORE PRACTICE: Standards Practice Book

Name ______________________________

Chapter 2 Review/Test

1. Circle the part you are taking from the group. Then cross it out. Write how many there are now.

5 zebras 3 zebras walk away. ______ zebras now

Circle the part you take away from the group. Then cross it out. Write the difference.

2. There are 6 cats. 5 cats run away.

$6 - 5 =$ ______

3. There are 4 dogs. 1 dog runs away.

$4 - 1 =$ ______

---

4. Is the subtraction sentence true? Choose Yes or No.

$5 - 5 = 0$	○ Yes	○ No
$2 - 2 = 2$	○ Yes	○ No
$4 - 0 = 4$	○ Yes	○ No

GO DIGITAL Assessment Options Chapter Test

5. Color ● to solve. Write the number sentence and how many.

There are 9 pencils. 5 pencils are red. The rest are yellow. How many pencils are yellow?

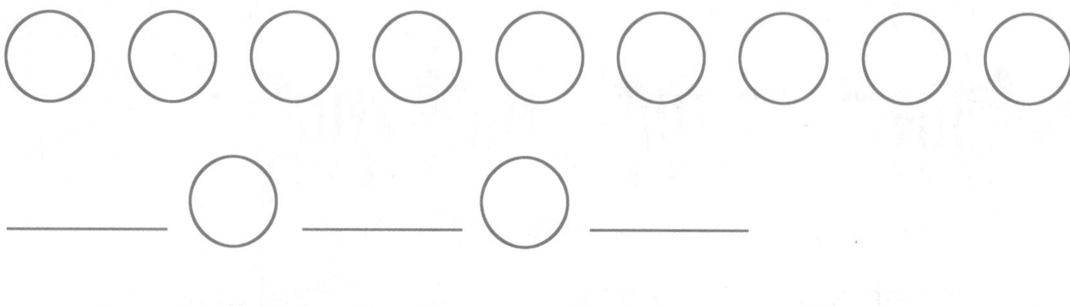

_____ yellow pencils

6. Read the problem. Use the model to solve. Complete the model and the number sentence.

There are 6 frogs on a log. 1 frog is big. The others are small. How many frogs are small?

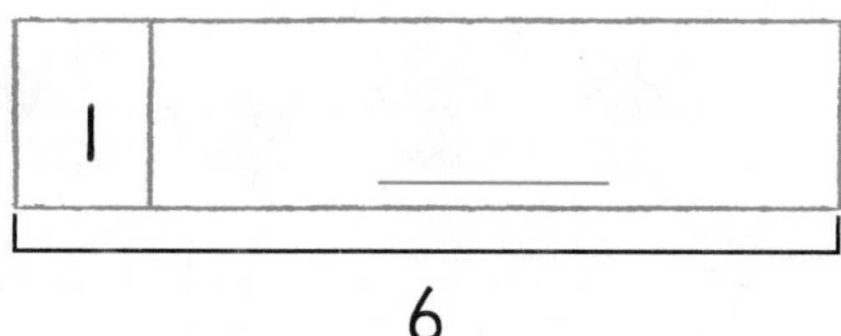

6 − 1 = _____

7. Look at the picture. How many fewer bats are there than balls? Choose the number.

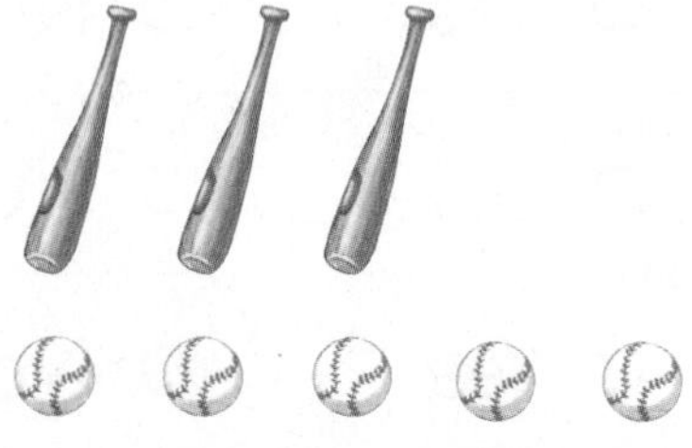

5
3
2

fewer bats

Name ______________________________

8. Read the problem. Use the bar model to solve.

Maria has 2 rocks. Peter has 8 rocks. How many more rocks does Peter have than Maria?

8	
2	______

______ rocks

9. The models show two ways to take apart 6. Complete the subtraction sentences. Use these numbers.

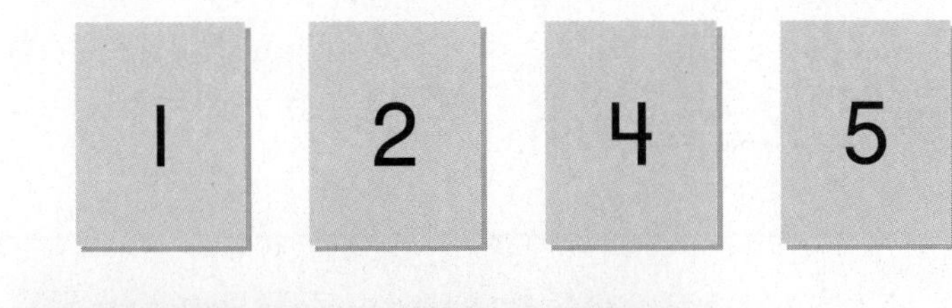

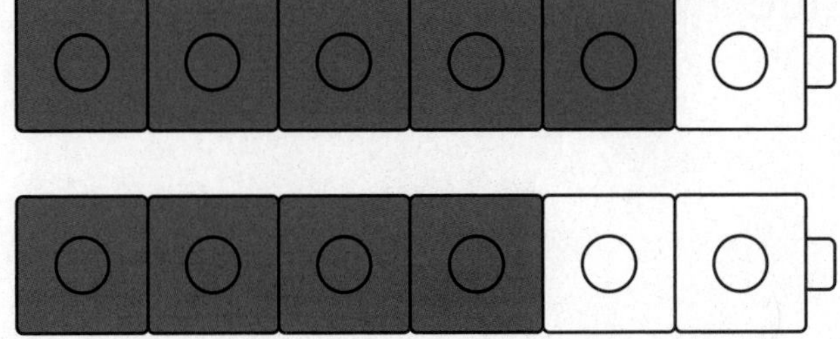

6 − ______ = ______

6 − ______ = ______

10. Write the subtraction sentence in the box that shows the difference.

$$\begin{array}{r} 10 \\ -\ 5 \\ \hline \end{array} \qquad \begin{array}{r} 5 \\ -\ 1 \\ \hline \end{array} \qquad \begin{array}{r} 7 \\ -\ 4 \\ \hline \end{array}$$

3	4	5
☐	☐	☐

11. Read the problem. Draw a model to solve. Complete the number sentence.

Mr. Bear catches 8 fish. He takes 3 fish home. He throws the other fish back in the water. How many fish does he throw back in the water?

______ − ______ = ______ fish

---

12. Write the subtraction sentence the picture shows.

______ − ______ = ______

Explain.

____

____

____

Chapter 3 Addition Strategies

Curious About Math with Curious George

There are 4 fish in the tank. If you doubled the number of fish, how many would there be?

Name ______________________________

Show What You Know

Model Addition

Use ▪ to show each number. Draw the cubes.
Write how many in all.

1.

2 + 3 ______

Use Symbols to Add

Use the picture. Write the addition sentence.

2.

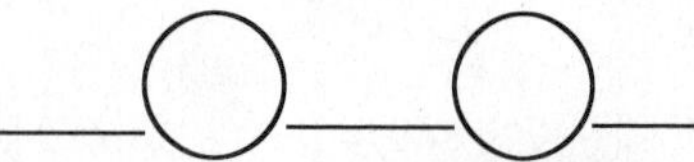

3.

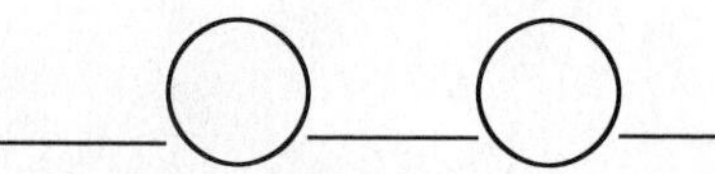

Add in Any Order

Use ▪ and ▪ to add. Color to match.
Write each sum.

4.

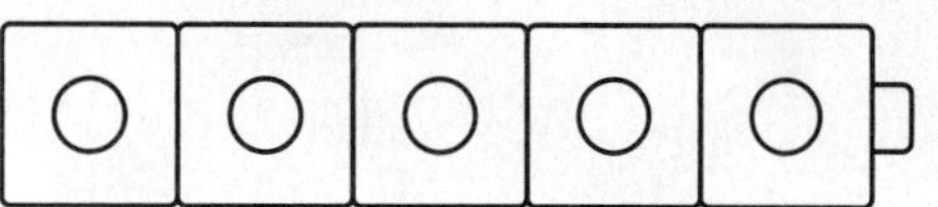

1 + 4 = ___

5.

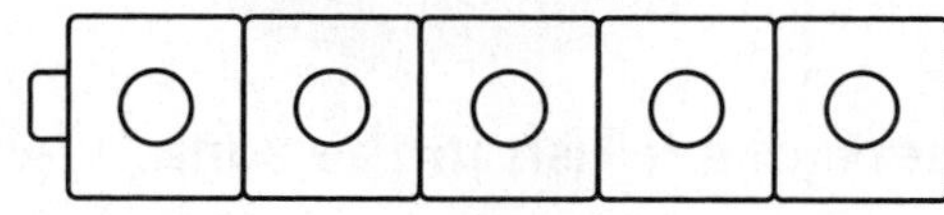

4 + 1 = ___

This page checks understanding of important skills needed for success in Chapter 3.

Personal Math Trainer
Online Assessment and Intervention

Name ______________________________

Vocabulary Builder

Review Words
add
addends
addition sentence
sum

Visualize It

Write the addends and the sum for the addition sentence.

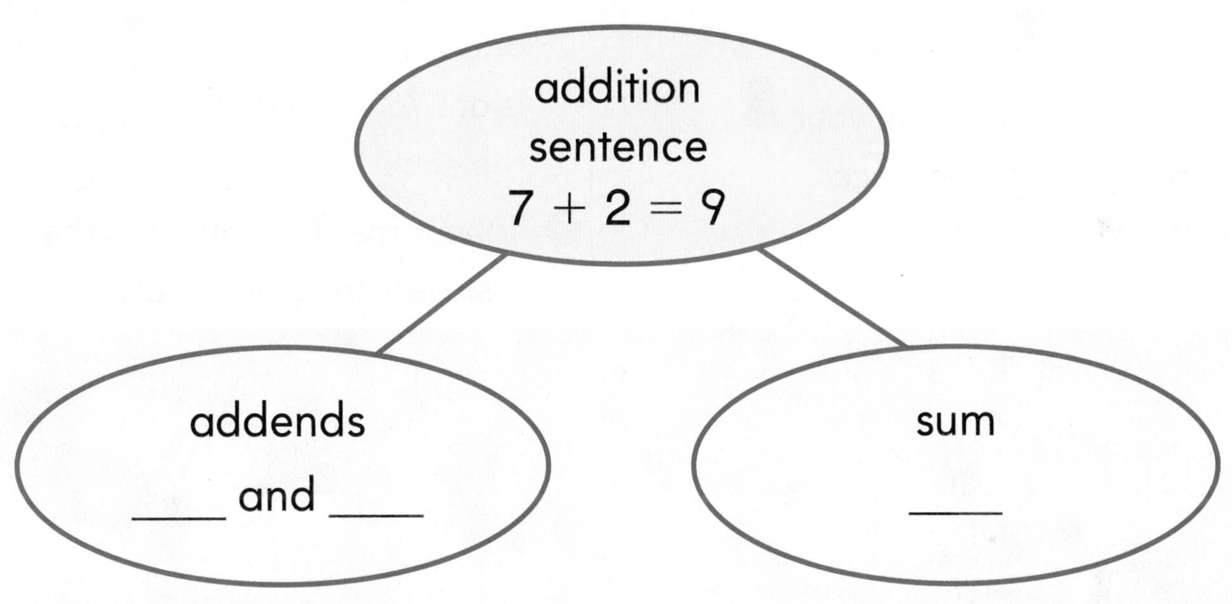

Understand Vocabulary

Use a review word to complete the sentence.

1. 4 and 3 in 4 + 3 = 7 are ______________________.

2. 4 + 3 = 7 is an ______________________.

3. 4 cubes and 3 cubes are put together to ______________________ the groups.

GO DIGITAL • Interactive Student Edition • Multimedia eGlossary

Chapter 3

Game Ducky Sums

Materials •  • •
•  •

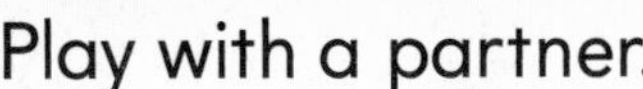

Play with a partner.

1. Put your pawn on START.
2. Toss the number cube. Move your pawn that number of spaces.
3. Use a spinner, a paper clip, and a pencil to make the spinner. Spin.
4. Add the number you spin and the number your pawn is on. Your partner checks the sum.
5. Take turns. The winner is the first person to get to END.

START

8 9 4 6 5 7 3 8 5 9 6 7 4 8 3 6 5 7 9

END

Name ______________________________

Algebra • Add in Any Order

Essential Question What happens if you change the order of the addends when you add?

Operations and Algebraic Thinking—1.OA.3
MATHEMATICAL PRACTICES
MP.1, MP.4, MP.6

Listen and Draw Real World

Use [crayon] and [crayon]. Color to model the problem.
Write the addition sentence.

___ + ___ = ___

Use [crayon] and [crayon]. Color to change the order.
Write the addition sentence.

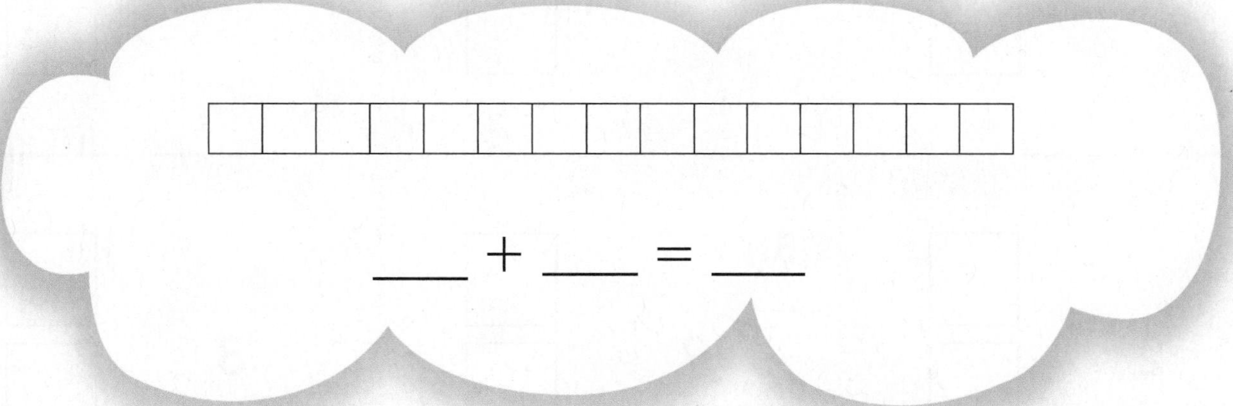

___ + ___ = ___

FOR THE TEACHER • Read the problem. George sees 7 blue birds and 8 red birds. How many birds does he see? Help children work through changing the order of the addends.

Math Talk Mathematical Practices

Explain how knowing the fact 7 + 8 helps you find 8 + 7.

Model and Draw

If you use the same addends, what other fact can you write?

$$\begin{array}{r} 5 \\ +6 \\ \hline \end{array}$$

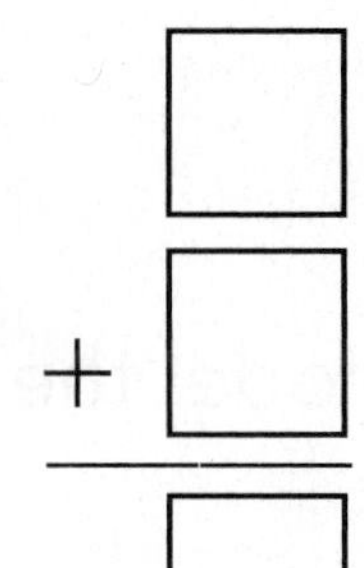

Share and Show

Add. Change the order of the addends. Add again.

1. $\begin{array}{r} 8 \\ +9 \\ \hline \end{array}$ $\quad + \square$

2. $\begin{array}{r} 6 \\ +7 \\ \hline \end{array}$ $\quad + \square$

3. $\begin{array}{r} 7 \\ +5 \\ \hline \end{array}$ $\quad + \square$

4. $\begin{array}{r} 2 \\ +8 \\ \hline \end{array}$ $\quad + \square$

✓5. $\begin{array}{r} 9 \\ +2 \\ \hline \end{array}$ $\quad + \square$

✓6. $\begin{array}{r} 8 \\ +4 \\ \hline \end{array}$ $\quad + \square$

Name ______________________

On Your Own

MATHEMATICAL PRACTICE 6 **Attend to Precision** Add. Change the order of the addends. Add again.

7. $\begin{array}{r} 9 \\ +6 \\ \hline \end{array}$ $\begin{array}{r} \square \\ +\square \\ \hline \square \end{array}$

8. $\begin{array}{r} 0 \\ +6 \\ \hline \end{array}$ $\begin{array}{r} \square \\ +\square \\ \hline \square \end{array}$

9. $\begin{array}{r} 8 \\ +3 \\ \hline \end{array}$ $\begin{array}{r} \square \\ +\square \\ \hline \square \end{array}$

10. $\begin{array}{r} 5 \\ +9 \\ \hline \end{array}$ $\begin{array}{r} \square \\ +\square \\ \hline \square \end{array}$

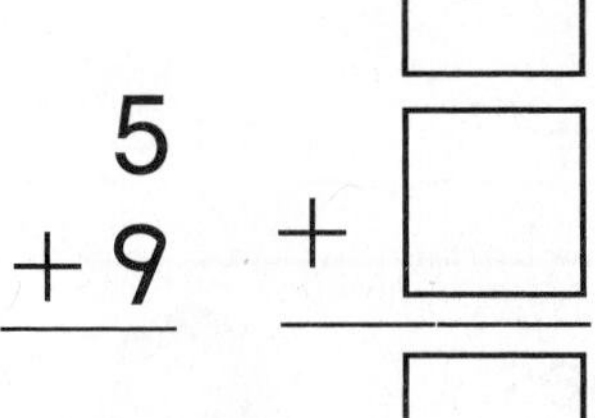

11. $\begin{array}{r} 4 \\ +5 \\ \hline \end{array}$ $\begin{array}{r} \square \\ +\square \\ \hline \square \end{array}$

12. $\begin{array}{r} 8 \\ +5 \\ \hline \end{array}$ $\begin{array}{r} \square \\ +\square \\ \hline \square \end{array}$

13. $\begin{array}{r} 9 \\ +1 \\ \hline \end{array}$ $\begin{array}{r} \square \\ +\square \\ \hline \square \end{array}$

14. $\begin{array}{r} 7 \\ +9 \\ \hline \end{array}$ $\begin{array}{r} \square \\ +\square \\ \hline \square \end{array}$

15. $\begin{array}{r} 4 \\ +6 \\ \hline \end{array}$ $\begin{array}{r} \square \\ +\square \\ \hline \square \end{array}$

16. GO DEEPER **Explain** If Adam knows $4 + 7 = 11$, what other addition fact does he know? Write the new fact in the box. Tell how Adam knows the new fact.

____

____

____

Problem Solving • Applications

WRITE Math

Write two addition sentences you can use to solve the problem. Write the answer.

17. Roy sees 4 big fish and 9 small fish. How many fish does Roy see?

____ fish

____ + ____ = ____

____ + ____ = ____

18. THINK SMARTER Justin has 6 toys. He gets 8 more toys. How many toys does he have now?

____ toys

____ + ____ = ____

____ + ____ = ____

19. THINK SMARTER Anna has two groups of pennies. She has 10 pennies in all. When she changes the order of the addends, the addition sentence is the same. What sentence can Anna write?

____ = ____ + ____

20. THINK SMARTER Write the addends in a different order.

$3 + 4 = 7$

____ + ____ = 7

TAKE HOME ACTIVITY • Ask your child to explain what happens to the sum when you change the order of the addends.

FOR MORE PRACTICE: Standards Practice Book

Name ______________________

Count On

Essential Question How do you count on 1, 2, or 3?

Operations and Algebraic Thinking—1.OA.5
Also 1.OA.6, 1.OA.8

MATHEMATICAL PRACTICES
MP.1, MP.6, MP.8

Start at 9. How can you count on to add?

Add 1.

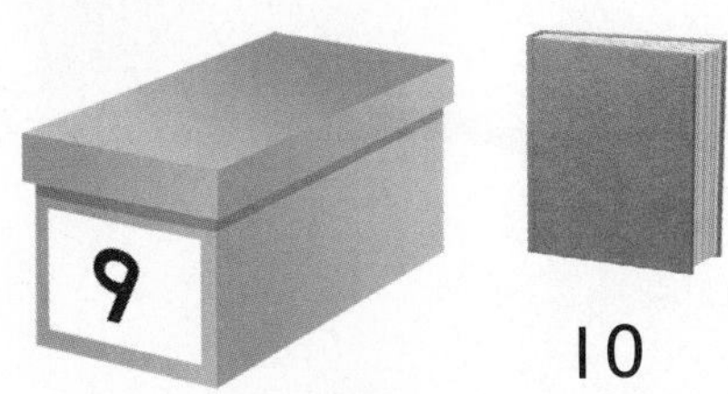

10

9 + 1 = ____

Add 2.

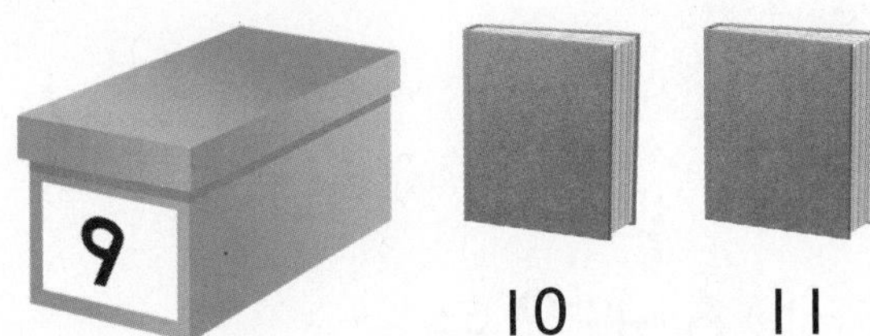

10 11

9 + 2 = ____

Add 3.

10 11 12

9 + 3 = ____

Mathematical Practices

How is counting on 2 like adding 2? **Explain.**

FOR THE TEACHER • Read the problem and use the top workspace to solve. Sam has 9 books in a box. He gets 1 more. How many books does he have? Repeat for the other two workspaces, saying, *He gets 2 more.* and *He gets 3 more.*

Model and Draw

You can **count on** to add 1, 2, or 3.
Start with the greater addend.

Start with 5.
Count on 3.

3 + (5) = 8

Circle the greater addend. Draw ▮ to count on 1, 2, or 3. Write the sum.

1. 

2 + (6) = 8

2. 

6 + 3 = ____

3. 

____ = 1 + 6

4. 

____ = 7 + 1

✓5. 

2 + 7 = ____

✓6. 

____ = 7 + 3

Name ____________________

On Your Own

GO DEEPER Circle the greater addend.
Count on to find the sum.

7. $1 + 9$	8. $8 + 3$	9. $1 + 8$	10. $1 + 6$	11. $9 + 3$	12. $7 + 2$
13. $2 + 6$	14. $5 + 3$	15. $7 + 1$	16. $3 + 7$	17. $9 + 2$	18. $3 + 4$
19. $4 + 1$	20. $2 + 8$	21. $2 + 4$	22. $5 + 2$	23. $3 + 6$	24. $5 + 1$
25. $9 + 3$	26. $2 + 7$	27. $6 + 2$	28. $3 + 4$	29. $8 + 1$	30. $3 + 5$

31. MATHEMATICAL PRACTICE 6 **Explain** Terry added 3 and 7. He got a sum of 9. His answer is **not** correct. Describe how Terry can find the correct sum.

____

____

Problem Solving • Applications

Draw to solve. Write the addition sentence.

32. THINK SMARTER Cindy and Joe pick 8 oranges. Then they pick 3 more oranges. How many oranges do they pick?

____ + ____ = ____ oranges

Which three numbers can you use to complete the problem?

33. THINK SMARTER Jennifer has ____ stamps. She gets ____ more stamps. How many stamps does she have now?

____ + ____ = ____ stamps

34. THINK SMARTER Count on from 3. Write the number that shows 2 more in the box below.

☐

TAKE HOME ACTIVITY • Have your child tell you how to count on to find the sum for 6 + 3.

FOR MORE PRACTICE: Standards Practice Book

Name ________________________

Add Doubles

Essential Question What are doubles facts?

HANDS ON
Lesson 3.3

Operations and Algebraic Thinking—1.OA.6 *Also 1.OA.8*

MATHEMATICAL PRACTICES
MP.5, MP.7

Listen and Draw Real World

Use ▣. Draw ▣ to solve.
Write the addition sentence.

___ + ___ = ___

Math Talk Mathematical Practices

Describe how your model shows a doubles fact.

FOR THE TEACHER • Read the following problem. Sal built two towers. Each tower has 4 cubes. How many cubes does Sal use to build both towers?

Model and Draw

Why are these **doubles** facts?

$$\begin{array}{r} 1 \\ +\ 1 \\ \hline 2 \end{array}$$

$$\begin{array}{r} 2 \\ +\ 2 \\ \hline \end{array}$$

Share and Show

Use . Draw to show your work.
Write the sum.

1.
$$\begin{array}{r} 3 \\ +\ 3 \\ \hline \end{array}$$

2.
$$\begin{array}{r} 4 \\ +\ 4 \\ \hline \end{array}$$

✓3.
$$\begin{array}{r} 5 \\ +\ 5 \\ \hline \end{array}$$

✓4.
$$\begin{array}{r} 6 \\ +\ 6 \\ \hline \end{array}$$

Name ______________________

On Your Own

GO DEEPER Use ■. Draw ■ to show your work. Write the sum.

5. $\begin{array}{r} 7 \\ +\ 7 \\ \hline \end{array}$

6. $\begin{array}{r} 8 \\ +\ 8 \\ \hline \end{array}$

7. MATHEMATICAL PRACTICE 7 **Look for a Pattern** Look back at Exercises 1–6. Write the fact that would be next in the pattern. Draw ■ to show your work.

$\begin{array}{r} \square \\ +\ \square \\ \hline \square \end{array}$

Add.

8. $\begin{array}{r} 5 \\ +\ 5 \\ \hline \end{array}$

9. $\begin{array}{r} 7 \\ +\ 7 \\ \hline \end{array}$

10. $\begin{array}{r} 6 \\ +\ 6 \\ \hline \end{array}$

11. $\begin{array}{r} 10 \\ +\ 10 \\ \hline \end{array}$

12. $\begin{array}{r} 4 \\ +\ 4 \\ \hline \end{array}$

13. $\begin{array}{r} 8 \\ +\ 8 \\ \hline \end{array}$

Problem Solving • Applications 

Write a doubles fact to solve.

14. THINK SMARTER Meg and Paul each put 8 apples into a basket. How many apples are in the basket?

____ + ____ = ____ apples

15. THINK SMARTER There are 18 people at the party. Some are boys and some are girls.The number of boys is the same as the number of girls.

____ = ____ + ____

16. THINK SMARTER The cubes show a doubles fact. Choose the doubles fact and the sum.

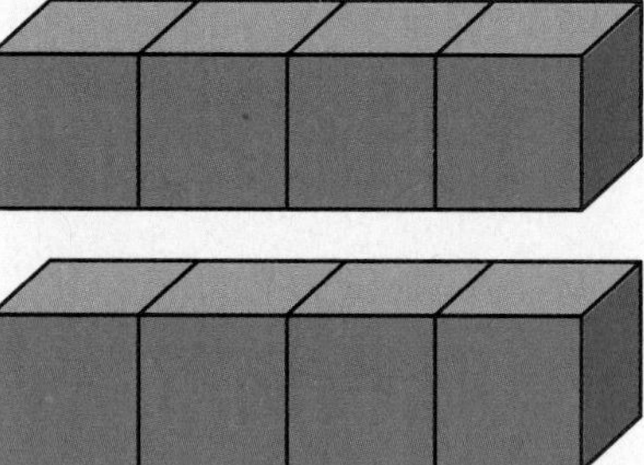

4 + [3 / 4] = [7 / 8]

TAKE HOME ACTIVITY • Have your child choose a number from 1 to 10 and use that number in a doubles fact. Repeat with other numbers.

FOR MORE PRACTICE: Standards Practice Book

Name ______________________________

Use Doubles to Add

HANDS ON
Lesson 3.4

Essential Question How can you use doubles to help you add?

Operations and Algebraic Thinking—1.OA.6 *Also 1.OA.8*

MATHEMATICAL PRACTICES
MP.1, MP.5, MP.7

Listen and Draw (Real World)

Draw to show the problem.
Write the number of fish.

There are ____ fish.

Math Talk **Mathematical Practices**

How does knowing 3 + 3 help you solve the problem? **Explain.**

FOR THE TEACHER • Read the following problem. There are 3 orange fish, 3 red fish, and 1 white fish in the fish tank. How many fish are in the fish tank?

Model and Draw

How can a doubles fact help you solve 6 + 7?

Break apart the 7. 7 is the same as 6 + 1. ⇨ Solve the doubles fact, 6 + 6. ⇨ **THINK** What is one more than 12?

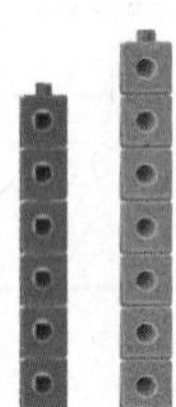

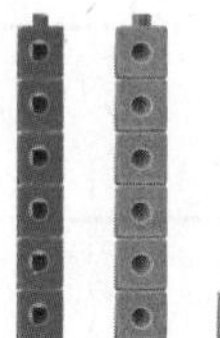

6 + 7 = 6 + 6 + 1 = 12 + 1 = 13

So, 6 + 7 = ____.

Share and Show

Use cubes to model. Make doubles. Add.

✓ 1.

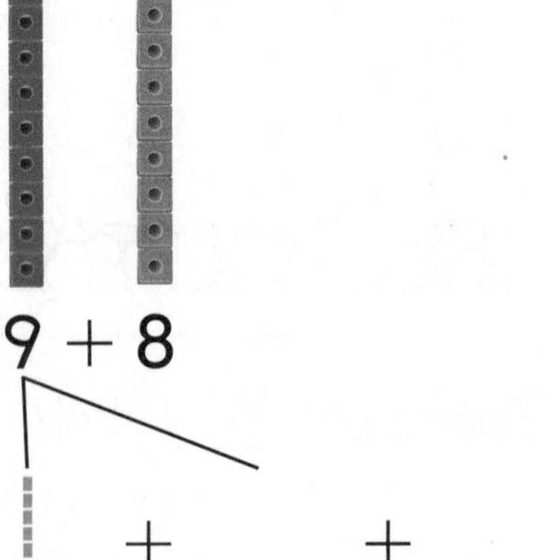

9 + 8

1 + ____ + ____

____ + ____ = ____

So, 9 + 8 = ____.

✓ 2.

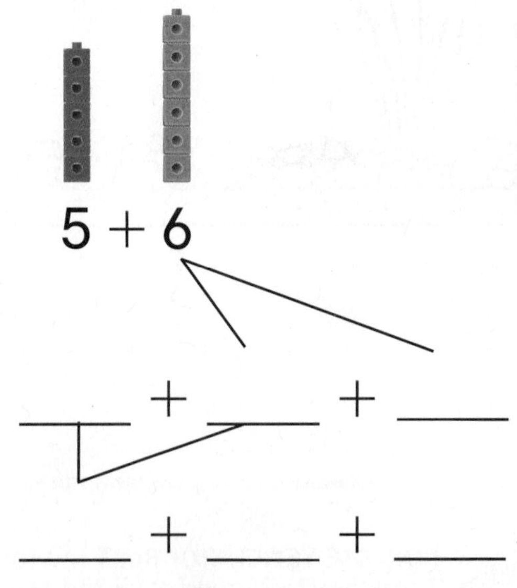

5 + 6

____ + ____ + ____

____ + ____ + ____

So, 5 + 6 = ____.

Name ______________________________

On Your Own

MATHEMATICAL PRACTICE 5 **Use a Concrete Model**

Use ▪ ▪. Make doubles. Add.

3. 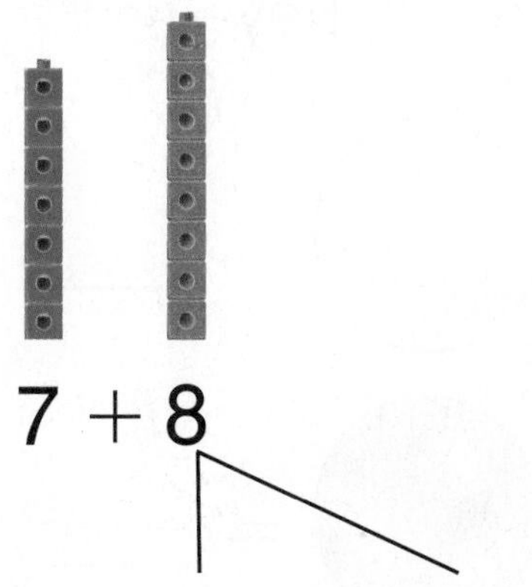

7 + 8

____ + ____ + ____

So, 7 + 8 = ____.

4. 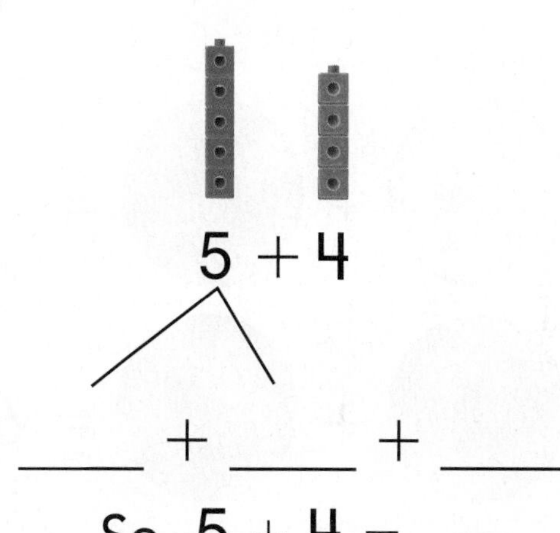

5 + 4

____ + ____ + ____

So, 5 + 4 = ____.

5. THINK SMARTER Mandy has the same number of red and yellow leaves. Then she finds one more yellow leaf. There are 17 leaves in all. How many leaves are red? How many leaves are yellow?

____ red leaves ____ yellow leaves

GO DEEPER **Explain** Would you use count on or doubles to solve? Why?

6. 3 + 4

____

7. 3 + 9

____

Problem Solving • Applications

WRITE Math

8. THINK SMARTER Use what you know about doubles to complete the Key. Write the missing sums.

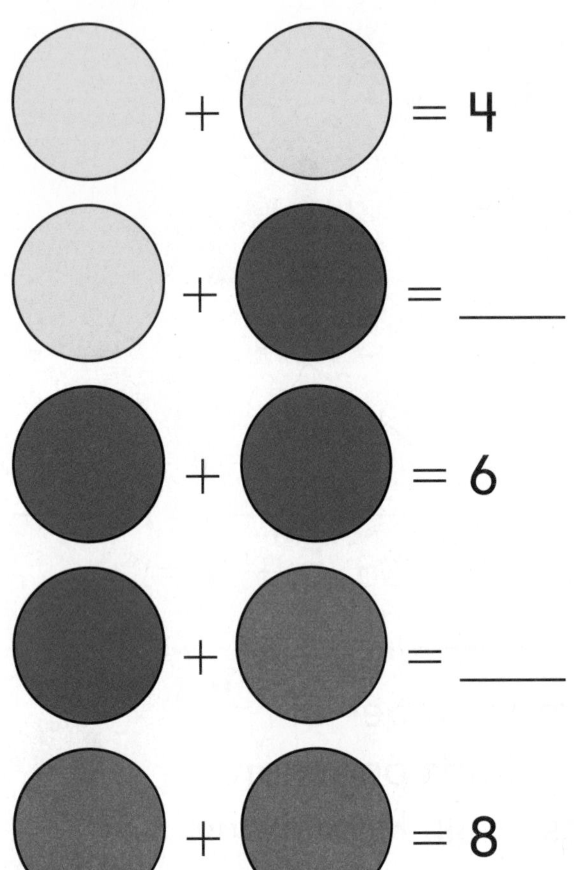

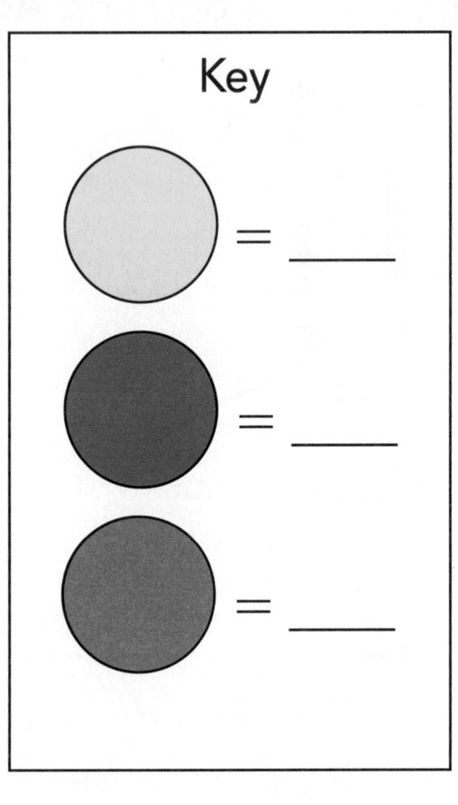

Personal Math Trainer

9. THINK SMARTER + There are 7 red cubes. There are 8 yellow cubes. How many cubes are there in all? Use a double to add. Write the missing numbers.

$7 + 8 = \square + \square + 1$

So, $7 + 8 = \square$

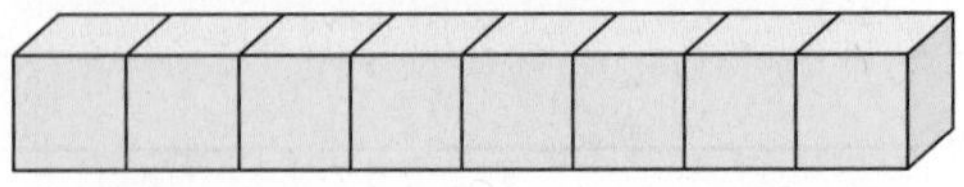

TAKE HOME ACTIVITY • Ask your child to show you how to use what he or she knows about doubles to help solve 6 + 5.

FOR MORE PRACTICE: Standards Practice Book

Name ____________________

Doubles Plus 1 and Doubles Minus 1

HANDS ON
Lesson 3.5

Essential Question How can you use what you know about doubles to find other sums?

Operations and Algebraic Thinking—1.OA.6 *Also 1.OA.8*

MATHEMATICAL PRACTICES
MP.6, MP.7

Listen and Draw

How can you use the doubles fact, 4 + 4, to solve each problem? Draw to show how. Complete the addition sentence.

4 + ___ = 9

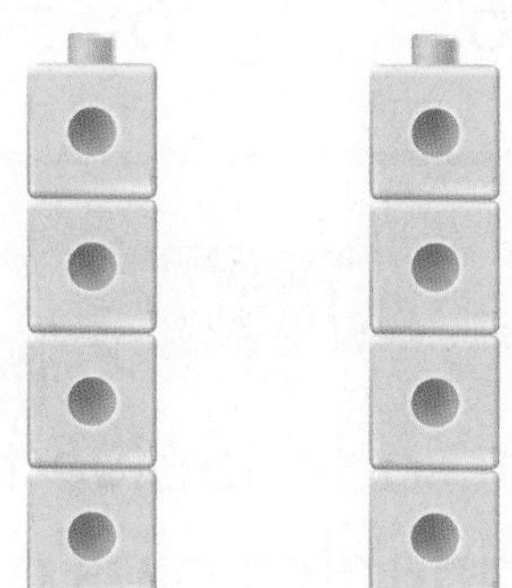

4 + ___ = 7

Math Talk **Mathematical Practices**

Explain what happens to the doubles fact when you increase one addend by one or decrease one addend by one.

FOR THE TEACHER • Read the problems. Look at the doubles fact, 4 + 4. Draw to show 1 more in the first workspace. Draw to show 1 less in the second workspace.

Model and Draw

Use the doubles fact 5 + 5 to add.

Use **doubles plus one**.
Add 1 to the doubles fact 5 + 5.

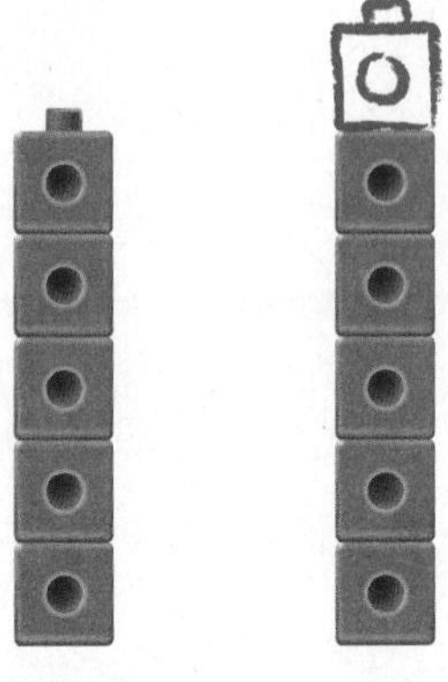

5 + 6 = 11

Use **doubles minus one**.
Subtract 1 from the doubles fact 5 + 5.

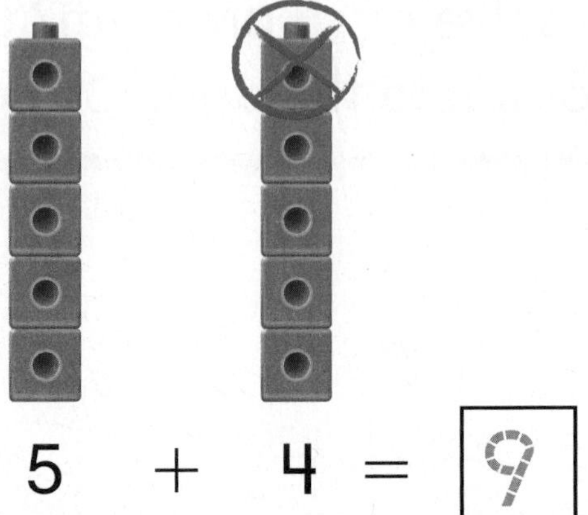

5 + 4 = 9

Share and Show

Use [cubes] to add. Solve the doubles fact.
Then use doubles plus one or doubles minus one.
Circle + or − to show how you solved each one.

1. 2 + 2 = ☐ 2 + 3 = ☐ doubles ± one 2 + 1 = ☐ doubles ± one

2. 3 + 3 = ☐ 3 + 4 = ☐ doubles ± one 3 + 2 = ☐ doubles ± one

3. 4 + 4 = ☐ 4 + 5 = ☐ doubles ± one 4 + 3 = ☐ doubles ± one

Name ______________________________

On Your Own

MATHEMATICAL PRACTICE 6 **Make Connections** Add. Write the doubles fact you used to solve the problem.

4. $8 + 9 =$ ____

____ ◯ ____ ◯ ____

5. $2 + 3 =$ ____

____ ◯ ____ ◯ ____

6. $7 + 6 =$ ____

____ ◯ ____ ◯ ____

7. $6 + 5 =$ ____

____ ◯ ____ ◯ ____

8. $3 + 4 =$ ____

____ ◯ ____ ◯ ____

9. $4 + 5 =$ ____

____ ◯ ____ ◯ ____

10. THINK SMARTER Brianna has 6 toy ducks. Ian has the same number of toy ducks and a toy fish. How many toys do Brianna and Ian have?

____ ◯ ____ ◯ ____ toys

THINK SMARTER Add. Write the doubles plus one fact. Write the doubles minus one fact.

11. $\begin{array}{r} 6 \\ + \ 6 \\ \hline \end{array}$

doubles plus one	doubles minus one

Problem Solving • Applications  WRITE ▸ Math

12. GO DEEPER Grace wants to write the sums for the doubles plus one and doubles minus one facts. She has started writing sums. Help her find the rest of the sums.

+	0	1	2	3	4	5	6	7	8	9
0	0	1								
1	1	2	3							
2		3	4	5						
3			5	6	7					
4				7	8					
5						10	11			
6						11	12			
7								14	15	
8								15	16	
9										18

13. THINK SMARTER Choose all the doubles facts that can help you solve 4 + 5.

○ 9 + 9 = 18

○ 5 + 5 = 10

○ 4 + 4 = 8

TAKE HOME ACTIVITY • Have your child explain how to use a doubles fact to solve the doubles plus one fact 4 + 5 and the doubles minus one fact 4 + 3.

FOR MORE PRACTICE: Standards Practice Book

Name ______________________________

Practice the Strategies

Essential Question What strategies can you use to solve addition fact problems?

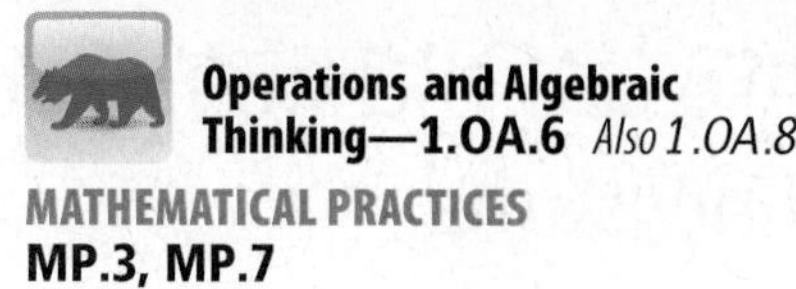

Listen and Draw

Think of different addition strategies. Write or draw two ways you can solve 4 + 3.

4 + 3 = ____	
Way 1	**Way 2**

Math Talk Mathematical Practices

Explain why the sum is the same when you use different strategies.

FOR THE TEACHER • Encourage children to use different strategies to show two ways they can solve 4 + 3. Have children share answers and discuss all strategies.

Model and Draw

These are the ways you have learned to find sums.

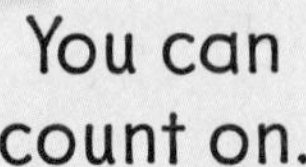

$9 + 1 =$ 10

$9 + 2 =$ ____

$9 + 3 =$ ____

$5 + 5 =$ 10

$5 + 6 =$ ____

$5 + 4 =$ ____

Share and Show

1.

Count On 1
$4 + 1 =$ ____
$5 + 1 =$ ____
$6 + 1 =$ ____
$7 + 1 =$ ____

2.

Count On 2
$5 + 2 =$ ____
$6 + 2 =$ ____
$7 + 2 =$ ____
$8 + 2 =$ ____

✓ 3.

Count On 3
$6 + 3 =$ ____
$7 + 3 =$ ____
$8 + 3 =$ ____
$9 + 3 =$ ____

4.

Doubles
$7 + 7 =$ ____
$8 + 8 =$ ____
$9 + 9 =$ ____
$10 + 10 =$ ____

✓ 5.

Doubles Plus One
$5 + 6 =$ ____
$6 + 7 =$ ____

Doubles Minus One
$8 + 7 =$ ____
$9 + 8 =$ ____

Name ______________________

On Your Own

MATHEMATICAL PRACTICE 3 Apply Add. Color doubles facts (crayon). Color count on facts (crayon). Color doubles plus one or doubles minus one facts (crayon).

6. $9 + 9 =$ ____	7. $7 + 1 =$ ____	8. $5 + 3 =$ ____
9. $2 + 9 =$ ____	10. $7 + 3 =$ ____	11. $7 + 7 =$ ____
12. $6 + 5 =$ ____	13. $2 + 8 =$ ____	14. $8 + 8 =$ ____
15. $8 + 9 =$ ____	16. $9 + 3 =$ ____	17. $7 + 8 =$ ____

THINK SMARTER Make a counting on problem. Write the missing numbers.

18. ____ birds were in a tree.
____ more birds flew there.
How many birds are in the tree now?

____ birds

TAKE HOME ACTIVITY • Have your child point out a doubles fact, a doubles plus one fact, a doubles minus one fact, and a fact he or she solved by counting on. Have him or her describe how each strategy works.

FOR MORE PRACTICE: Standards Practice Book

Name ______________________________

Mid-Chapter Checkpoint

Concepts and Skills

Add. Change the order of the addends. Add again. (1.OA.3)

1.

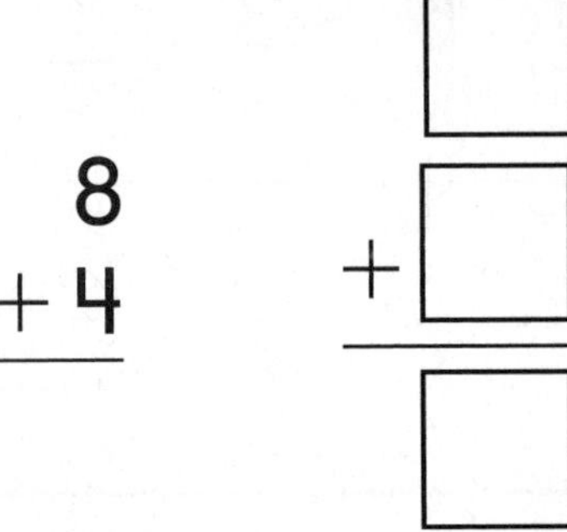

$\begin{array}{r} 8 \\ +4 \\ \hline \end{array}$ $\qquad \begin{array}{r} \square \\ +\square \\ \hline \square \end{array}$

2.

$\begin{array}{r} 7 \\ +9 \\ \hline \end{array}$ $\qquad \begin{array}{r} \square \\ +\square \\ \hline \square \end{array}$

Circle the greater addend. Count on to find the sum. (1.OA.5)

3. $\begin{array}{r} 1 \\ +8 \\ \hline \end{array}$ **4.** $\begin{array}{r} 3 \\ +7 \\ \hline \end{array}$ **5.** $\begin{array}{r} 9 \\ +2 \\ \hline \end{array}$ **6.** $\begin{array}{r} 6 \\ +3 \\ \hline \end{array}$ **7.** $\begin{array}{r} 7 \\ +1 \\ \hline \end{array}$ **8.** $\begin{array}{r} 2 \\ +8 \\ \hline \end{array}$

Use doubles to help you add. (1.OA.6)

9. $7 + 8 =$ ____ **10.** $6 + 7 =$ ____ **11.** $9 + 8 =$ ____

Personal Math Trainer

12. THINK SMARTER + Write a count on 1 fact to show a sum of 8. Then write a doubles fact to show a sum of 8.

Name ______________________

Add 10 and More

Essential Question How can you use a ten frame to add 10 and some more?

HANDS ON
Lesson 3.7

Operations and Algebraic Thinking—1.OA.6 *Also 1.OA.8*

MATHEMATICAL PRACTICES
MP.2, MP.5

Listen and Draw

What is 10 + 5? Use ● ● and the ten frame. Model and draw to solve.

FOR THE TEACHER • Read the following problem. Ali has 10 red apples in a bag. She has 5 yellow apples next to the bag. How many apples does Ali have?

Math Talk **Mathematical Practices**

Explain how your model shows 10 + 5.

Model and Draw

You can use a ten frame to add 10 + 6.

$$\begin{array}{r} 10 \\ +\ 6 \\ \hline 16 \end{array}$$

Color the counters to show 10 red. Color the counters to show 6 yellow.

Share and Show

Draw ● to show 10. Draw ● to show the other addend. Write the sum.

1. $\begin{array}{r} 10 \\ +\ 3 \\ \hline \end{array}$

2. $\begin{array}{r} 10 \\ +\ 5 \\ \hline \end{array}$

3. $\begin{array}{r} 10 \\ +\ 1 \\ \hline \end{array}$

4. $\begin{array}{r} 10 \\ +\ 2 \\ \hline \end{array}$

✓ 5. $\begin{array}{r} 10 \\ +\ 4 \\ \hline \end{array}$

✓ 6. $\begin{array}{r} 10 \\ +\ 7 \\ \hline \end{array}$

Name ______________________________

On Your Own

MATHEMATICAL PRACTICE 2 **Represent a Problem**

Draw ● to show 10. Draw ○ to show the other addend. Write the sum.

7. $\begin{array}{r} 10 \\ +\ 8 \\ \hline \end{array}$

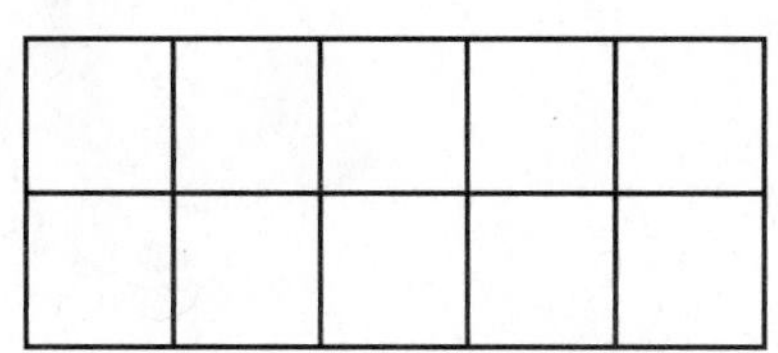

8. $\begin{array}{r} 10 \\ +\ 2 \\ \hline \end{array}$

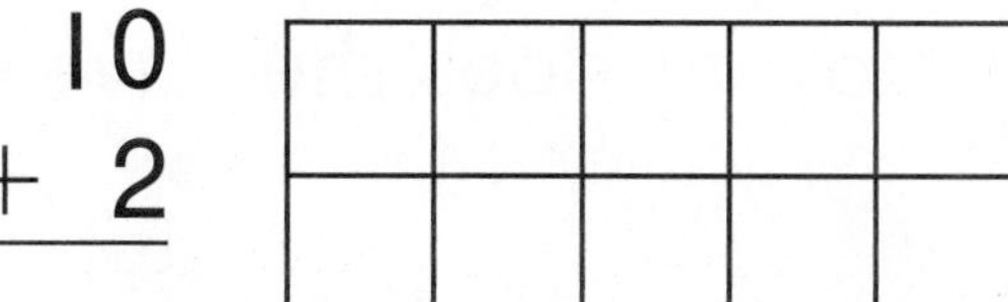

9. $\begin{array}{r} 10 \\ +\ 6 \\ \hline \end{array}$

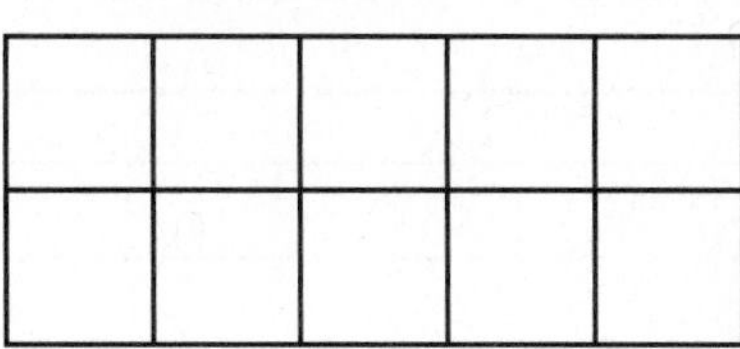

10. $\begin{array}{r} 10 \\ +\ 9 \\ \hline \end{array}$

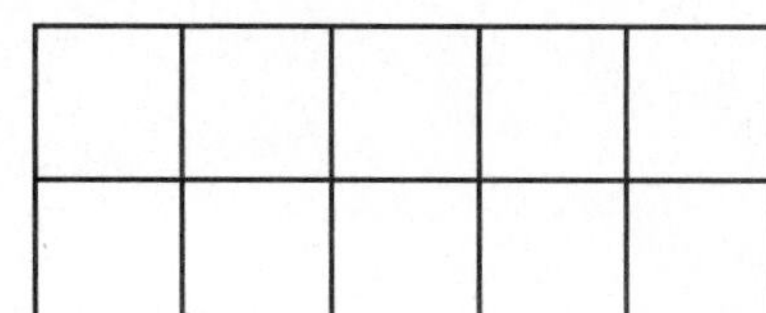

Add.

11. $\begin{array}{r} 10 \\ +\ 1 \\ \hline \end{array}$

12. $\begin{array}{r} 4 \\ +10 \\ \hline \end{array}$

13. $\begin{array}{r} 5 \\ +10 \\ \hline \end{array}$

14. $\begin{array}{r} 10 \\ +\ 3 \\ \hline \end{array}$

15. $\begin{array}{r} 0 \\ +10 \\ \hline \end{array}$

16. THINK SMARTER Draw ● to show 10. Draw ○ to show the missing addend. Write the missing addend.

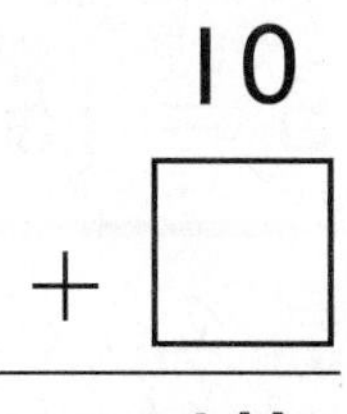

$\begin{array}{r} 10 \\ +\ \square \\ \hline 14 \end{array}$

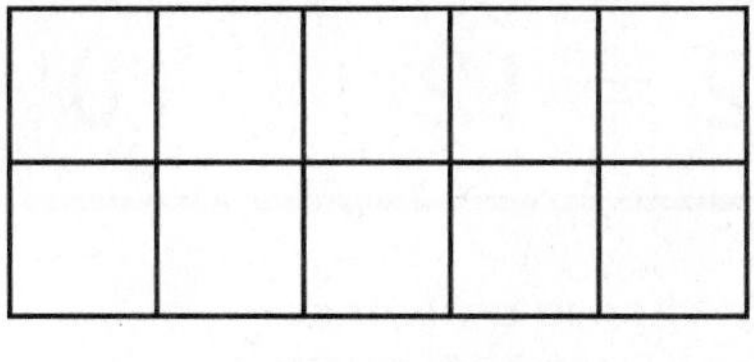

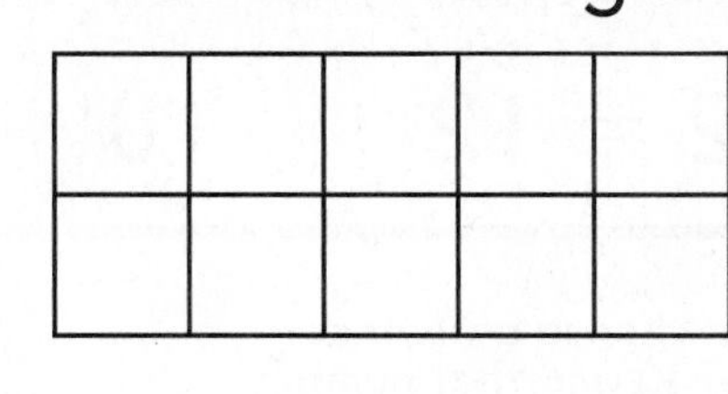

Problem Solving • Applications Real World

WRITE Math

GO DEEPER Draw ● ●. Write the addition sentence. Explain your model.

17. Marina has 10 crayons. She gets 7 more crayons. How many crayons does she have now?

____ + ____ = ____ crayons

18. THINK SMARTER Match the models to the number sentences.

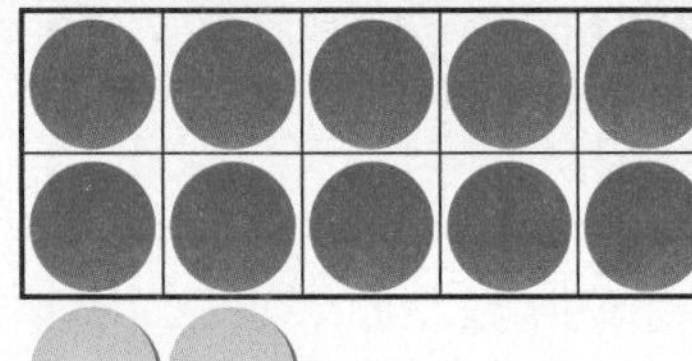

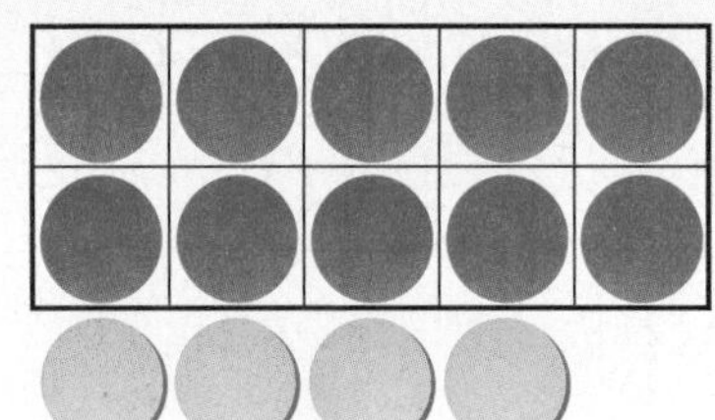

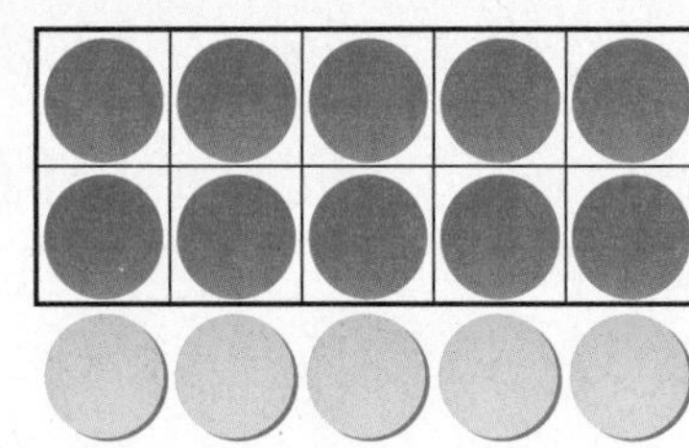

10 + 4 = 14 10 + 2 = 12 10 + 5 = 15

TAKE HOME ACTIVITY • Have your child choose a number between 1 and 10 and then find the sum of 10 and that number. Repeat using other numbers.

FOR MORE PRACTICE: Standards Practice Book

Name ____________________

Make a 10 to Add

Essential Question How do you use the make a ten strategy to add?

Operations and Algebraic Thinking—1.OA.6 *Also 1.OA.8*

MATHEMATICAL PRACTICES
MP.2, MP.5

Listen and Draw

Real World

Hands On

What is 9 + 6? Use ●● and the ten frame. Model and draw to solve.

FOR THE TEACHER • Ask children: What is 9 + 6? Have children use red and yellow counters to model. Then move one counter from the 6 to make a ten.

Math Talk — Mathematical Practices

Explain why you start by putting 9 counters in the ten frame.

Model and Draw

Why do you show 8 in the ten frame to find 4 + 8?

Put 8 ● in the ten frame.
Then show 4 ●.

$$\begin{array}{r} 4 \\ +\ 8 \\ \hline \end{array}$$

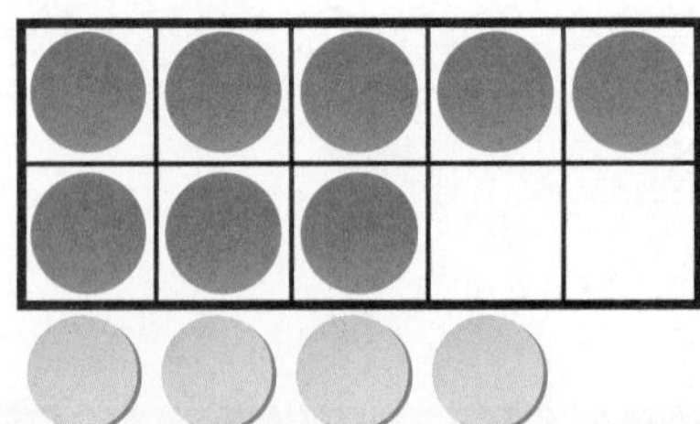

Draw to **make a ten**.
Then write the new fact.

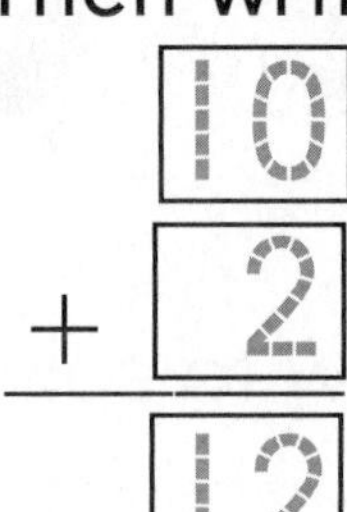

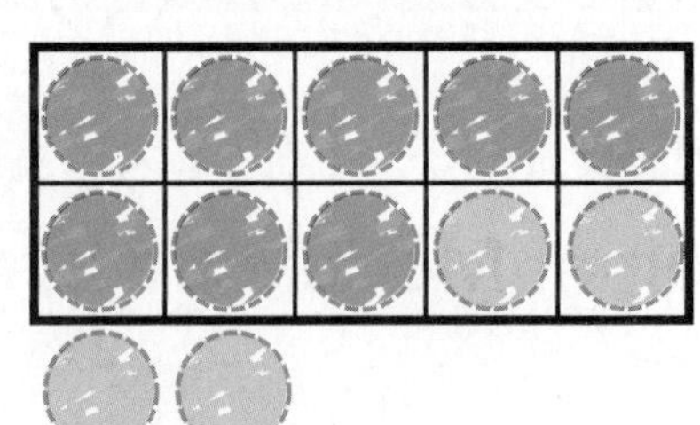

Share and Show

Use ● ● and a ten frame. Show both addends.
Draw to make a ten. Then write the new fact. Add.

1. $$\begin{array}{r} 9 \\ +\ 5 \\ \hline \end{array}$$

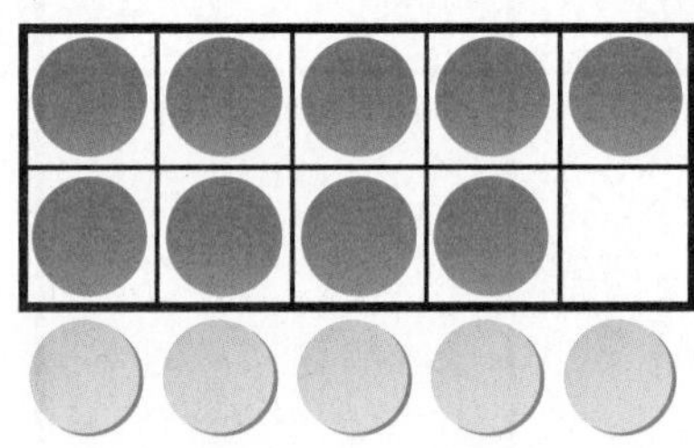

+

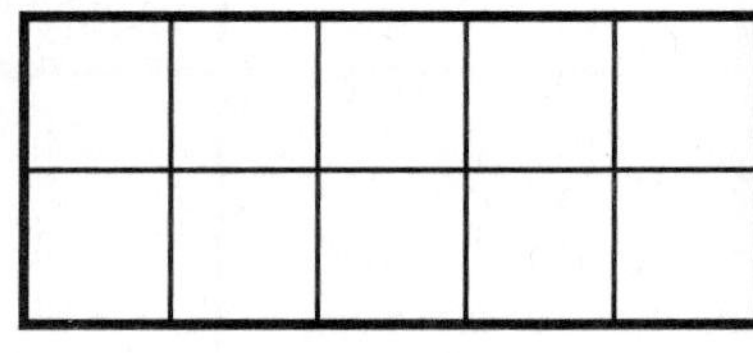

2. $$\begin{array}{r} 4 \\ +\ 7 \\ \hline \end{array}$$

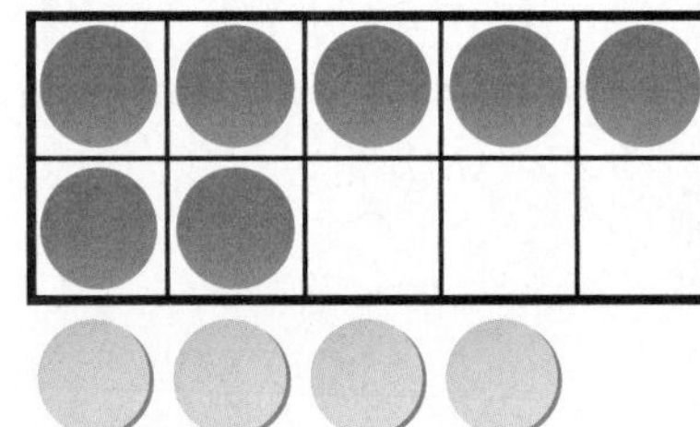

+

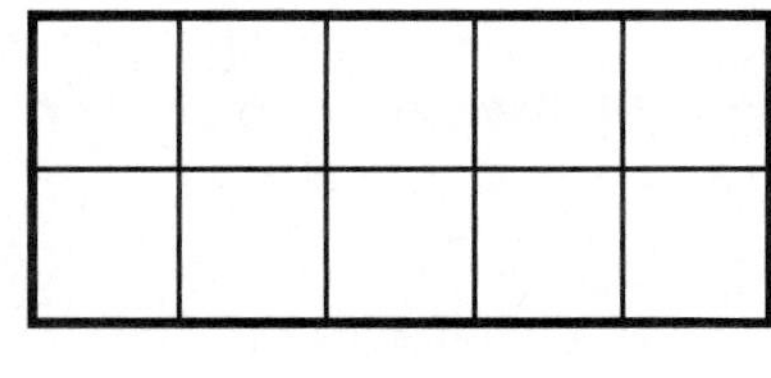

3. $$\begin{array}{r} 9 \\ +\ 8 \\ \hline \end{array}$$

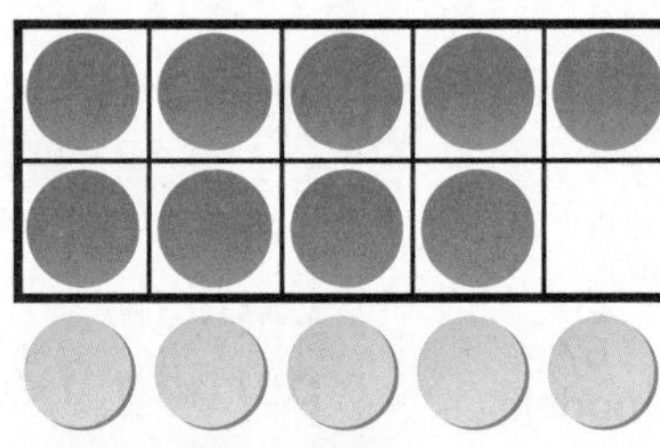

+

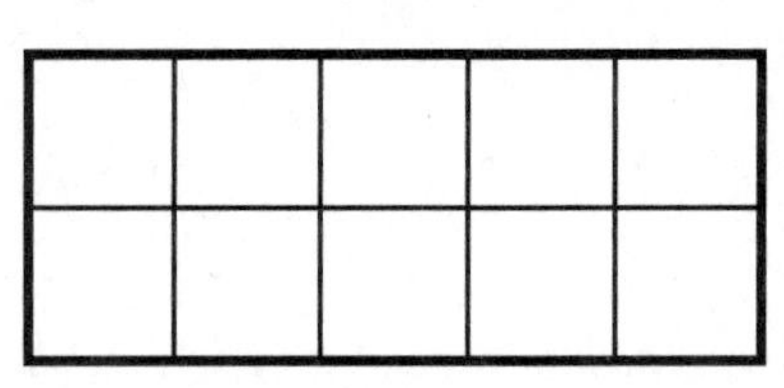

Name ______________________________

REMEMBER
Start with the greater addend.

On Your Own

MATHEMATICAL PRACTICE 5 **Use a Concrete Model**

Use and a ten frame. Show both addends. Draw to make a ten. Then write the new fact. Add.

4. $5 + 8$

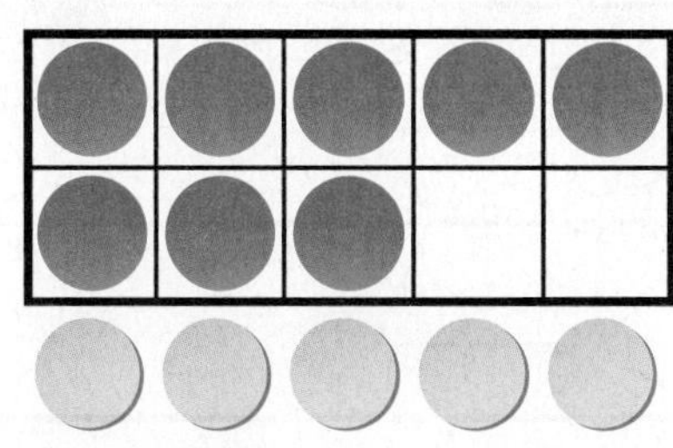

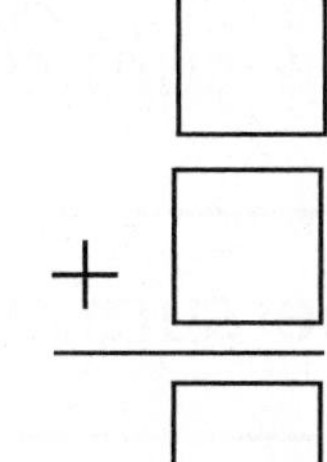

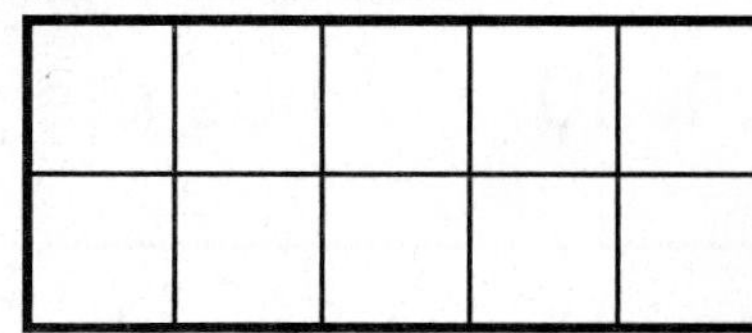

5. $9 + 6$

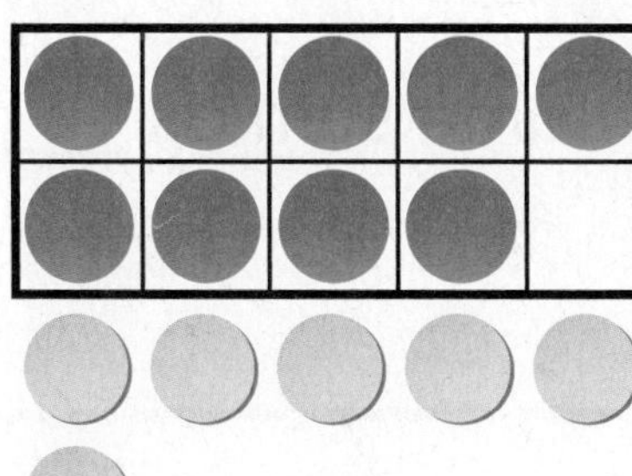

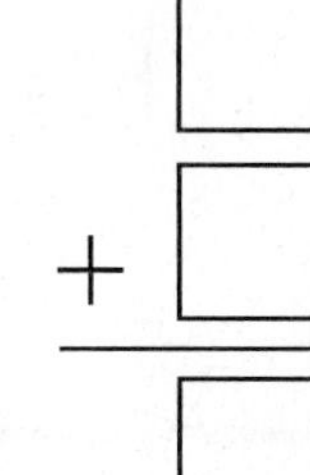

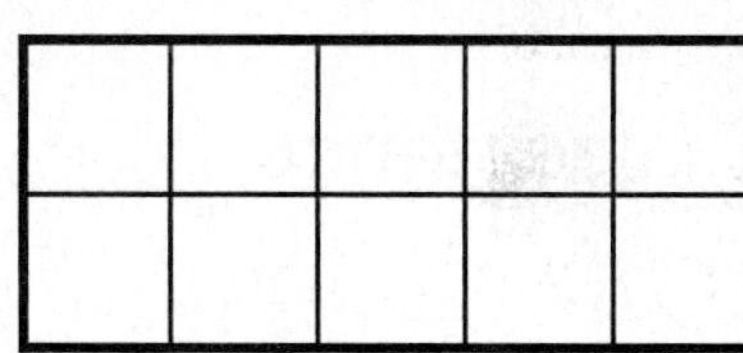

6. $7 + 9$

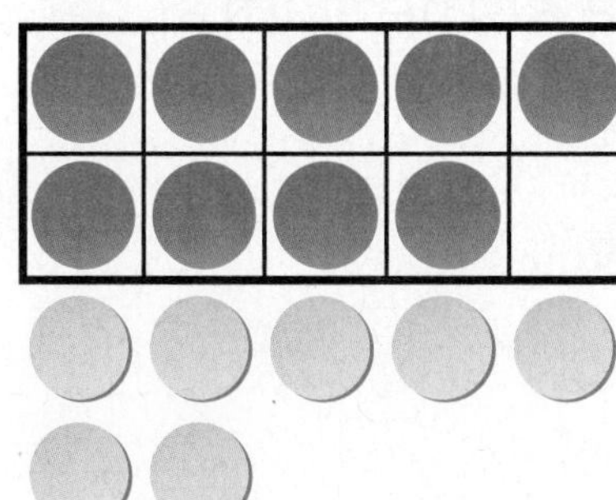

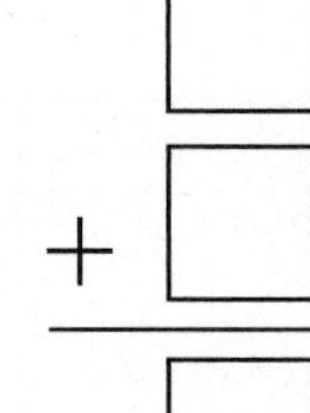

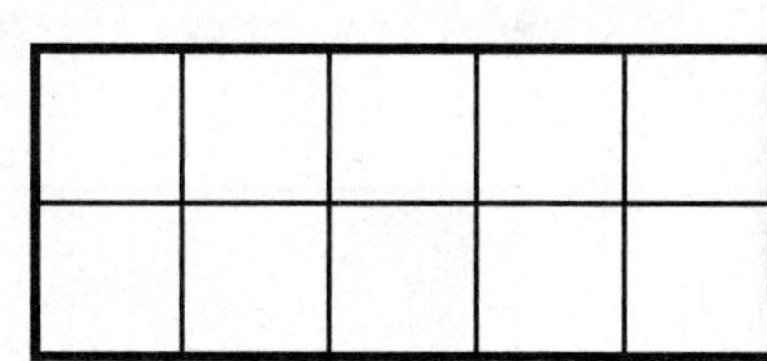

7. THINK SMARTER What strategy would you choose to solve 7 + 8? Why?

____

____

Problem Solving • Applications Real World

WRITE Math

Solve.

8. 10 + 8 has the same sum as 9 + ____.

9. 10 + 7 has the same sum as 8 + ____.

10. 10 + 5 has the same sum as 6 + ____.

11. GO DEEPER Write the numbers **6, 8,** or **10** to complete the sentence. ____ + ____ has the same sum as ____ + 8.

12. THINK SMARTER The model shows 7 + 4 = 11. Write the 10 fact that has the same sum.

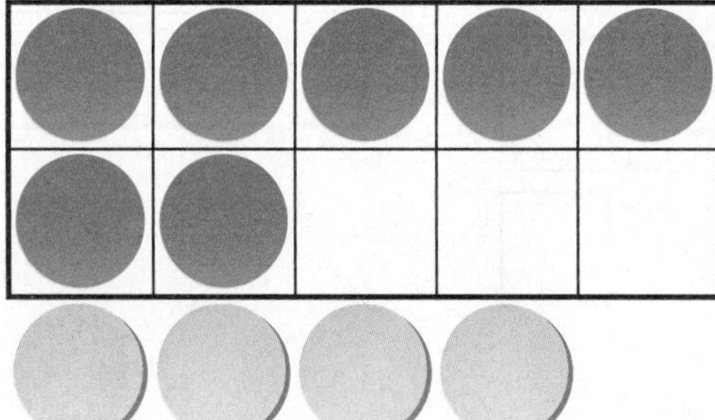

TAKE HOME ACTIVITY • Cut off 2 cups from an egg carton or draw a 5-by-2 grid on a sheet of paper to create a ten frame. Have your child use small objects to show how to make a ten to solve 8 + 3, 7 + 6, and 9 + 9.

FOR MORE PRACTICE: Standards Practice Book

Name ______________________________

Use Make a 10 to Add

Essential Question How can you make a ten to help you add?

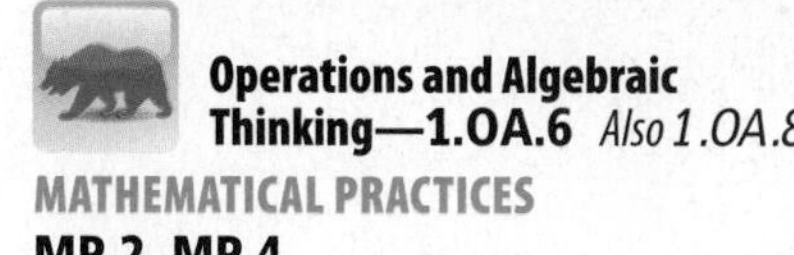

MATHEMATICAL PRACTICES
MP.2, MP.4

Listen and Draw (Real World)

Draw to show the addends. Then draw to show how to make a ten. Write the sum.

$$\begin{array}{r} 6 \\ +\ 7 \\ \hline \end{array}$$

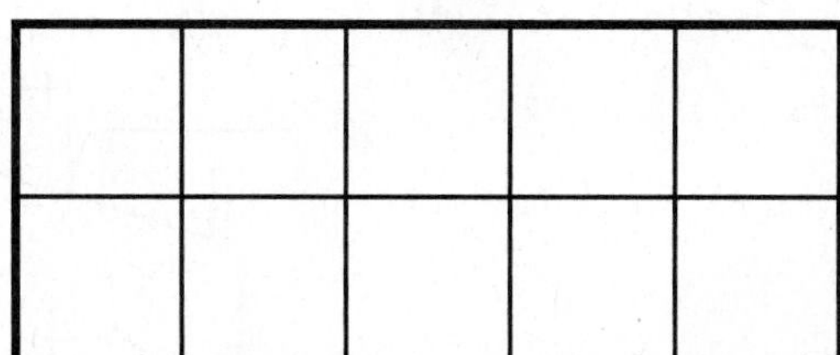

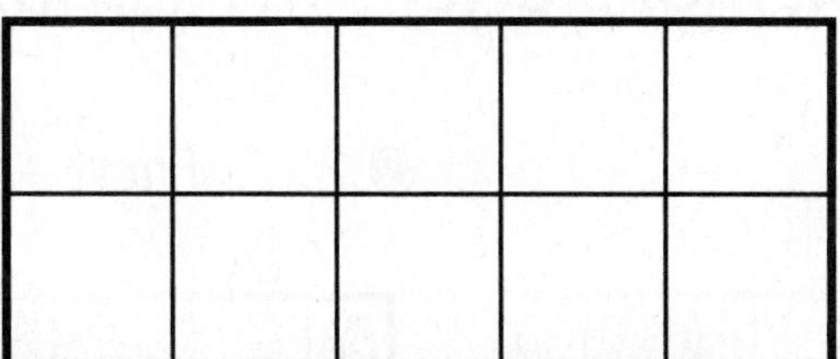

Math Talk Mathematical Practices

Describe how the drawings show how to make a ten to solve 6 + 7.

FOR THE TEACHER • Read the following problem. Sean has 6 red blocks and 7 blue blocks. How many blocks does he have? Ask children to draw counters in the ten frames to show how to solve by making a ten.

Model and Draw

What is 9 + 6?

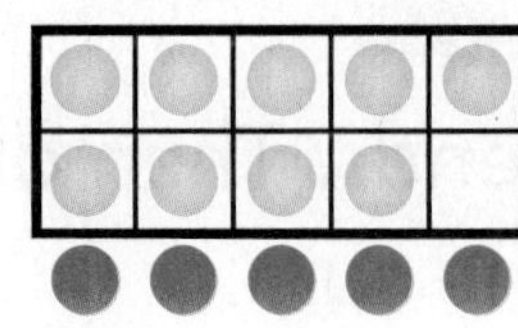

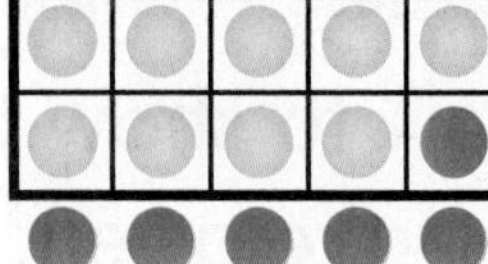

Find the sum.

9 + 1 + 5

10 + 5 = ____

So, 6 + 9 = ____.

Share and Show

Write to show how you make a ten. Then add.

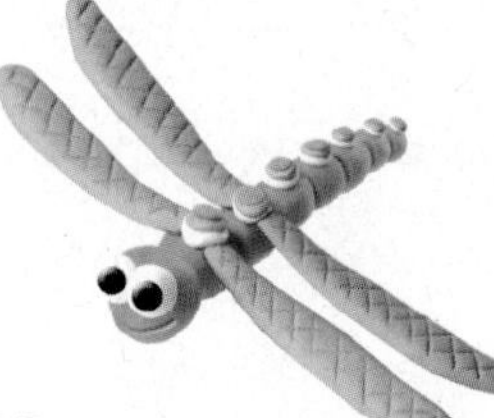

1. What is 8 + 4?

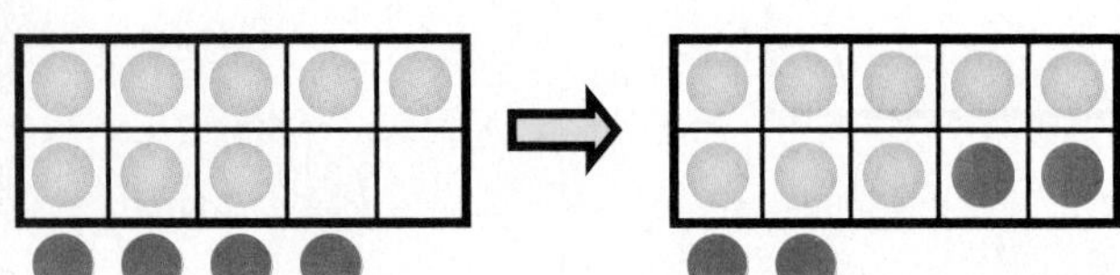

____ + ____ + 2

____ + ____ = ____

So, 8 + 4 = ____.

2. What is 5 + 7?

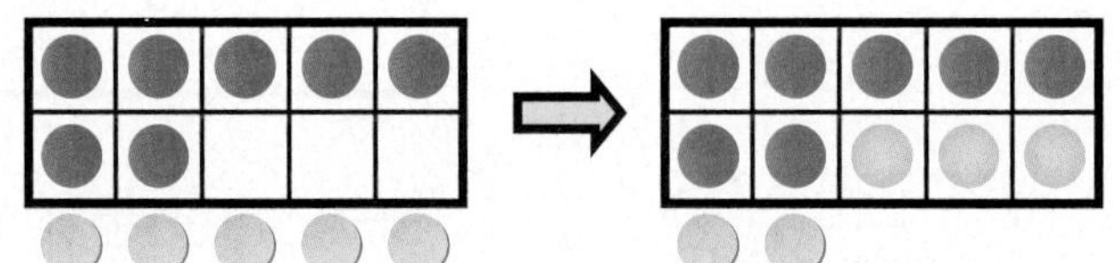

____ + ____ + 2

____ + ____ = ____

So, 5 + 7 = ____.

Name ___________________________

On Your Own

THINK SMARTER Write to show how you make a ten. Then add.

3. What is 7 + 8?

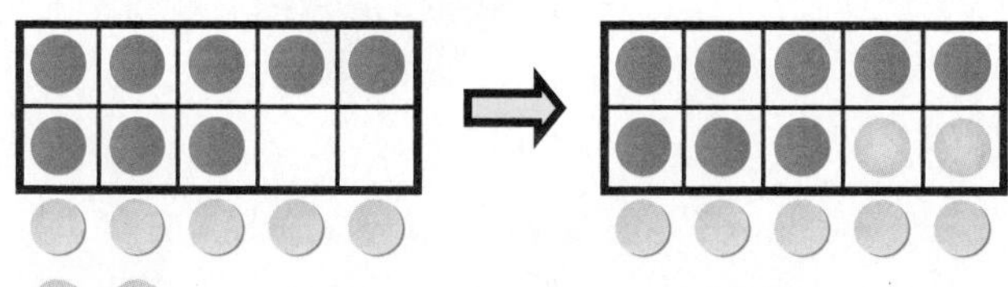

____ + ____ + ____

____ + ____ = ____

So, 7 + 8 = ____.

4. What is 9 + 8?

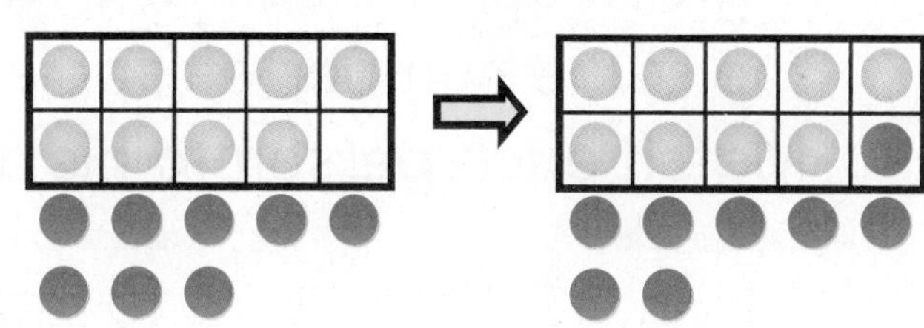

____ + ____ + ____

____ + ____ = ____

So, 9 + 8 = ____.

MATHEMATICAL PRACTICE 4 **Use Models**

Use the model. Write to show how you make a ten. Then add.

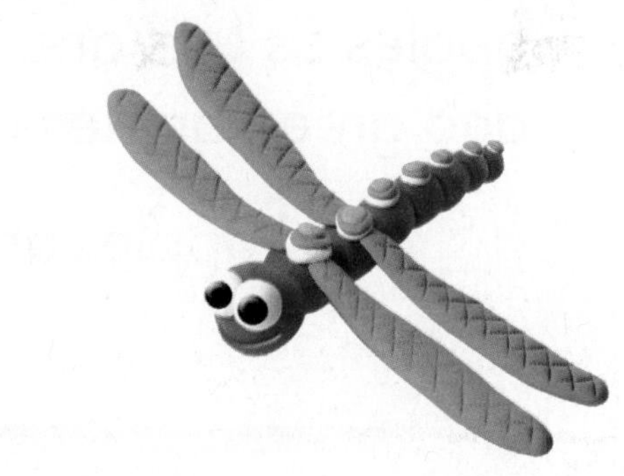

5. 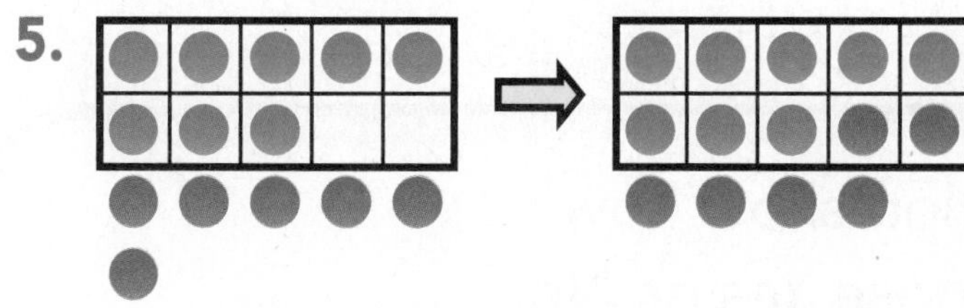

____ + ____ + ____

____ + ____ = ____

So, ____ + ____ = ____.

Problem Solving • Applications

Use the clues to solve. Draw lines to match.

6. Han, Luis, and Mike buy apples. Mike buys 10 red apples and 4 green apples. Luis and Mike buy the same number of apples. Match each person to his apples.

Han	10 red apples and 4 green apples
Luis	6 red apples and 8 green apples
Mike	8 red apples and 7 green apples

---

7. GO DEEPER Look at Exercise 6. Han eats one apple. Now he has the same number of apples as Luis and Mike. How many red and green apples could he have?

_____ red apples and _____ green apples

8. THINK SMARTER Does the addition show how to make a ten to add? Choose Yes or No.

8 + 2 + 2	○ Yes	○ No
5 + 4 + 3	○ Yes	○ No
6 + 7 + 3	○ Yes	○ No

Name ____________________

Algebra • Add 3 Numbers

HANDS ON
Lesson 3.10

Essential Question How can you add three addends?

Operations and Algebraic Thinking—1.OA.3 *Also 1.OA.6*
MATHEMATICAL PRACTICES
MP.3

Listen and Draw

Use  to model the problem.
Draw to show your work.

____ birds

Mathematical Practices

Which two addends did you add first? **Explain.**

FOR THE TEACHER • Read the following problem. Kelly sees 7 birds. Bruno sees 2 birds. Joe sees 3 birds. How many birds do they see?

Model and Draw

$2 + 3 + 1 =$ ___

You can change which two addends you add first. The sum stays the same.

Add 2 and 3. Then add 1.

5 + 1 = 6

Add 3 and 1. Then add 2.

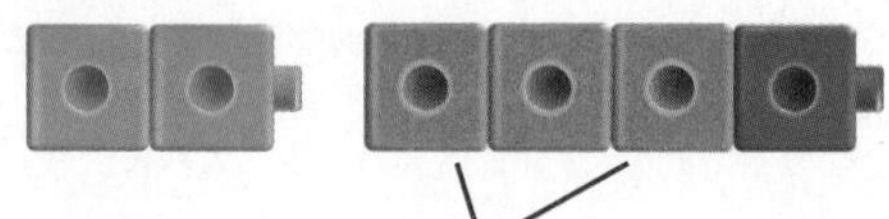

2 + 4 = 6

Share and Show

Use cubes to change which two addends you add first. Complete the addition sentences.

1. $5 + 2 + 3 =$ ___

___ + ___ = ___ ___ + ___ = ___

2. $3 + 4 + 6 =$ ___

___ + ___ = ___ ___ + ___ = ___

Name ________________________________

On Your Own

MATHEMATICAL PRACTICE 3 **Compare Models**

Look at the . Complete the addition sentences showing two ways to find the sum.

3. 7 + 3 + 1 = ____

____ + ____ = ____　　　____ + ____ = ____

4. 3 + 6 + 3 = ____

____ + ____ = ____　　　____ + ____ = ____

GO DEEPER Solve both ways.

5. 2 + 3 + 7 = ____　　　2 + 3 + 7 = ____

____ + ____ = ____　　　____ + ____ = ____

6. THINK SMARTER I used cubes to model 3 addends. Use my model. Write the 3 addends.

My Model

____ + ____ + ____ = 7

Problem Solving • Applications

WRITE ▶ Math

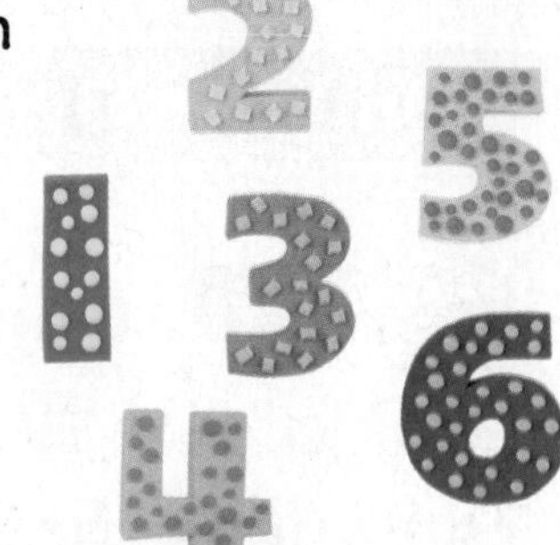

7. THINK SMARTER Choose three numbers from 1 to 6. Write the numbers in an addition sentence. Show two ways to find the sum.

8. THINK SMARTER Write each addition sentence in the box that shows the sum.

2 + 2 + 8	5 + 3 + 5	6 + 0 + 6	4 + 4 + 5

12	13

TAKE HOME ACTIVITY • Have your child draw to show two ways to add the numbers 2, 4, and 6.

FOR MORE PRACTICE: Standards Practice Book

Name ______________________________

Algebra • Add 3 Numbers

Essential Question How can you group numbers to add three addends?

Operations and Algebraic Thinking—1.OA.3 *Also 1.OA.6*

MATHEMATICAL PRACTICES
MP.3, MP.8

Listen to the problem. Show two ways to group and add the numbers.

3 6 3

FOR THE TEACHER • Read the following problem. There are 3 children at one table. There are 6 children at another table. There are 3 children in line. How many children are there?

Math Talk **Mathematical Practices**

Describe the two ways you grouped the numbers to add.

Model and Draw

You can group the addends in any order and in different ways to find the sum.

Add 8 and 2 to use the strategy make a ten. Then add 10 and 6.

Add 6 and 2 to use the strategy count on. Then add doubles 8 and 8.

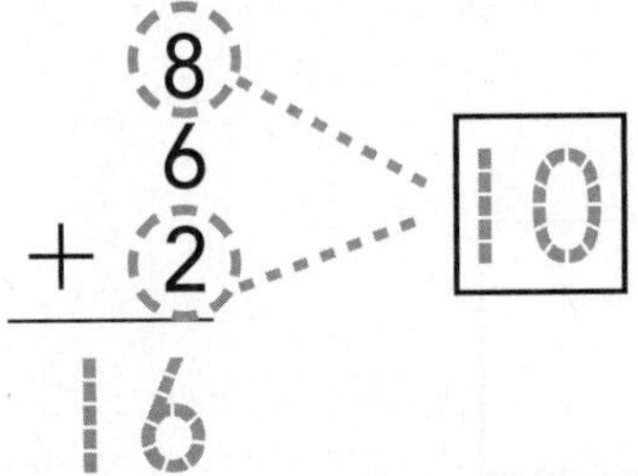

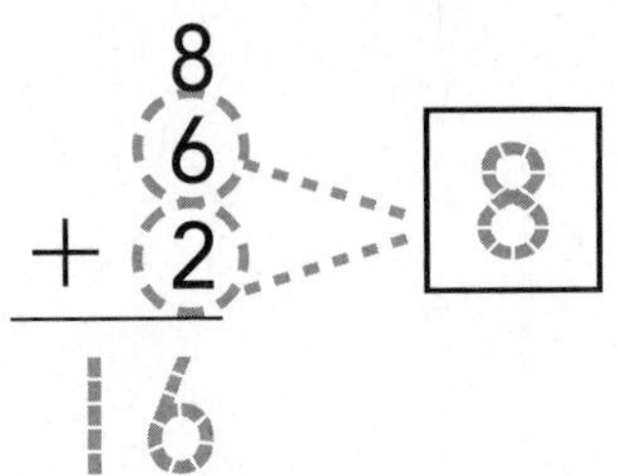

Share and Show

Choose a strategy. Circle two addends to add first. Write the sum. Then find the total sum. Then use a different strategy and add again.

THINK
Use count on, doubles, doubles plus one, doubles minus one, or make a ten to add.

1. $\begin{array}{r} 6 \\ 4 \\ +2 \\ \hline \end{array}$ ☐ $\begin{array}{r} 6 \\ 4 \\ +2 \\ \hline \end{array}$ ☐

2. $\begin{array}{r} 3 \\ 4 \\ +4 \\ \hline \end{array}$ ☐ $\begin{array}{r} 3 \\ 4 \\ +4 \\ \hline \end{array}$ ☐

✓ 3. $\begin{array}{r} 2 \\ 5 \\ +0 \\ \hline \end{array}$ ☐ $\begin{array}{r} 2 \\ 5 \\ +0 \\ \hline \end{array}$ ☐

✓ 4. $\begin{array}{r} 5 \\ 4 \\ +5 \\ \hline \end{array}$ ☐ $\begin{array}{r} 5 \\ 4 \\ +5 \\ \hline \end{array}$ ☐

Name ____________________

On Your Own

MATHEMATICAL PRACTICE 8 **Use Repeated Reasoning**

Choose a strategy. Circle two addends to add first. Write the sum.

5.
$$\begin{array}{r} 8 \\ 2 \\ +2 \\ \hline \end{array}$$

6.
$$\begin{array}{r} 6 \\ 0 \\ +8 \\ \hline \end{array}$$

7.
$$\begin{array}{r} 3 \\ 4 \\ +6 \\ \hline \end{array}$$

8.
$$\begin{array}{r} 2 \\ 3 \\ +7 \\ \hline \end{array}$$

9.
$$\begin{array}{r} 7 \\ 7 \\ +2 \\ \hline \end{array}$$

10.
$$\begin{array}{r} 1 \\ 9 \\ +1 \\ \hline \end{array}$$

11.
$$\begin{array}{r} 5 \\ 4 \\ +4 \\ \hline \end{array}$$

12.
$$\begin{array}{r} 5 \\ 5 \\ +5 \\ \hline \end{array}$$

13.
$$\begin{array}{r} 3 \\ 5 \\ +2 \\ \hline \end{array}$$

14.
$$\begin{array}{r} 2 \\ 6 \\ +4 \\ \hline \end{array}$$

15.
$$\begin{array}{r} 9 \\ 9 \\ +1 \\ \hline \end{array}$$

16.
$$\begin{array}{r} 1 \\ 2 \\ +8 \\ \hline \end{array}$$

THINK SMARTER Write the missing addends. Add.

17.
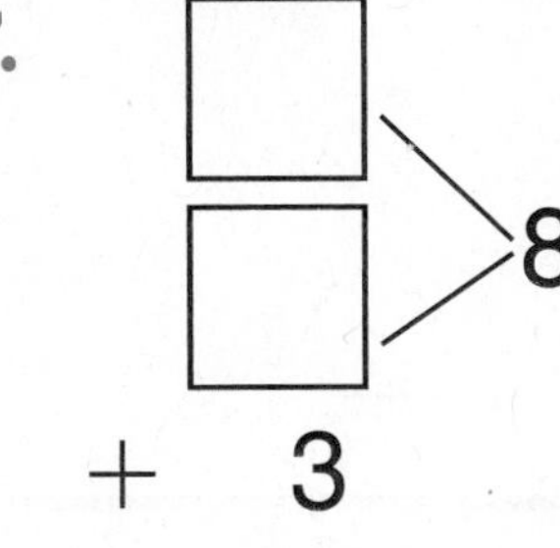

18.
$$\begin{array}{r} \square \\ 3 \\ +\square \\ \hline \end{array}$$
(first two addends → 7)

Problem Solving • Applications

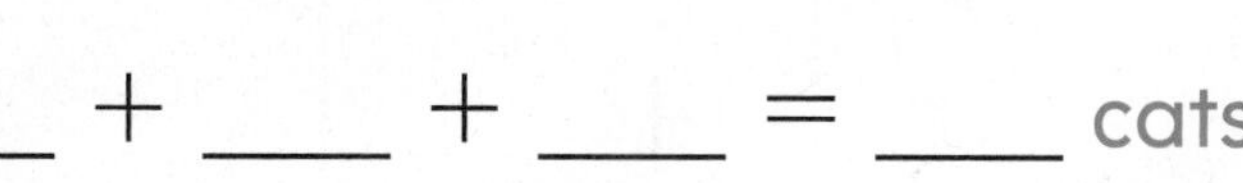

Draw a picture. Write the number sentence.

19. Maria has 3 cats. Jim has 2 cats. Cheryl has 5 cats. How many cats do they have?

____ + ____ + ____ = ____ cats

20. Tony sees 5 small turtles. He sees 0 medium turtles. He sees 4 big turtles. How many turtles does he see?

____ + ____ + ____ = ____ turtles

21. GO DEEPER Kathy sees 13 fish in the tank. 6 fish are gold. The rest are blue or red. How many of each could she see?

____ + ____ + 6 = 13 fish

22. THINK SMARTER Write two ways to group and add 2 + 3 + 4.

____ + ____ = ____ ____ + ____ = ____

TAKE HOME ACTIVITY • Have your child look at Exercise 21. Have your child tell you how he or she decided which numbers to use. Have him or her tell you two new numbers that would work.

FOR MORE PRACTICE: Standards Practice Book

Name ______________________________

Problem Solving • Use Addition Strategies

Essential Question How do you solve addition word problems by drawing a picture?

Operations and Algebraic Thinking—1.OA.2 *Also 1.OA.6*

MATHEMATICAL PRACTICES
MP.1, MP.2, MP.4

Megan put 8 fish in the tank. Tess put in 2 more fish. Then Bob put in 3 more fish. How many fish are in the tank now?

Unlock the Problem — Real World

What do I need to find?

how many  fish

are in the tank

What information do I need to use?

Megan put in 8 fish.

Tess put in 2 fish.

Bob put in 3 fish.

Show how to solve the problem.

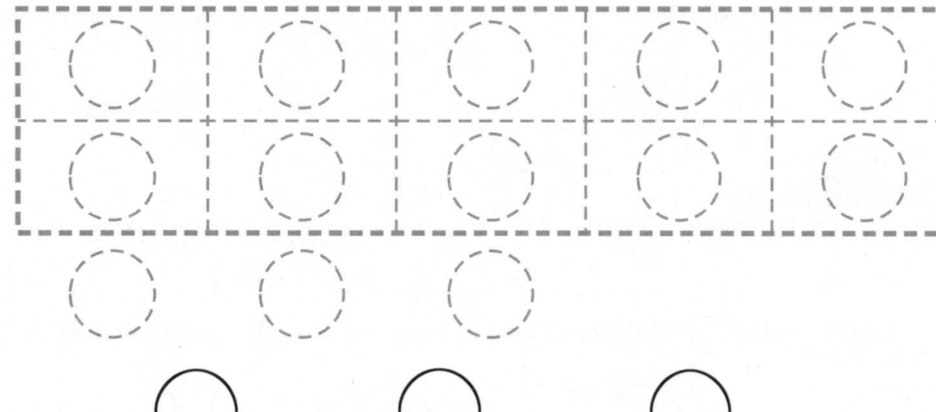

___ ◯ ___ ◯ ___ ◯ ___

___ fish

HOME CONNECTION • Your child will continue to use this chart throughout the year to help him or her unlock the problem. In this lesson, your child used the strategy draw a picture to solve problems.

Try Another Problem

Draw a picture to solve.

- What do I need to find?
- What information do I need to use?

1. Mark has 9 green toy cars.
He has 1 yellow toy car.
He also has 5 blue toy cars.
How many toy cars does he have?

_____ ◯ _____ ◯ _____ ◯ _____

_____ toy cars

Math Talk **Mathematical Practices**

Explain how make a ten helps you solve the problem.

Name ___________________________

Share and Show

MATHEMATICAL PRACTICE 4 **Write an Equation**

Draw a picture to solve.

2. Ken put 5 pennies in a jar. Lou put in 0 pennies. Mae put in 5 pennies. How many pennies did they put in the jar?

___ ◯ ___ ◯ ___ ◯ ___   ___ pennies

3. Ava has 3 kites. Lexi has 3 kites. Fred has 5 kites. How many kites do they have?

___ ◯ ___ ◯ ___ ◯ ___   ___ kites

4. Al got 8 books at the library. Ryan got 7 books. Dee got 1 book. How many books do they have?

___ ◯ ___ ◯ ___ ◯ ___   ___ books

5. Pete sends 4 letters. Then he sends 3 more letters. Then he sends 2 more letters. How many letters did Pete send?

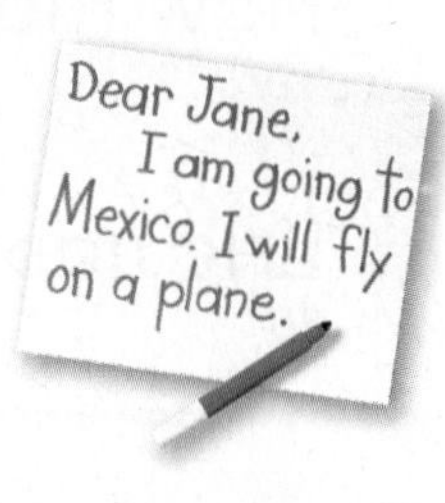

___ letters

On Your Own

Solve. Draw or write to show your work.

6. Kevin has 15 baseball cards. He gives away 8 baseball cards. How many baseball cards does he have?

____ baseball cards

---

7. There are 14 pencils. Haley has 6 pencils. Mac has 4 pencils. Sid has some pencils. How many pencils does Sid have?

____ pencils

---

8. GO DEEPER 12 marbles are in a bag. Shelly takes 3 marbles. Dan puts in 4. How many marbles are in the bag now?

____ marbles

9. 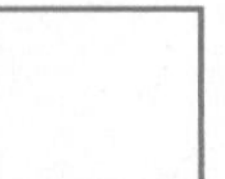

Eric has 4 pencils. Sandy gives Eric 3 pencils. Tracy gives Eric 5 more pencils. How many pencils does Eric have in all?

Eric has ☐ pencils in all.

TAKE HOME ACTIVITY • Ask your child to look at Exercise 8 and tell how he or she found the answer.

FOR MORE PRACTICE: Standards Practice Book

Name ____________________

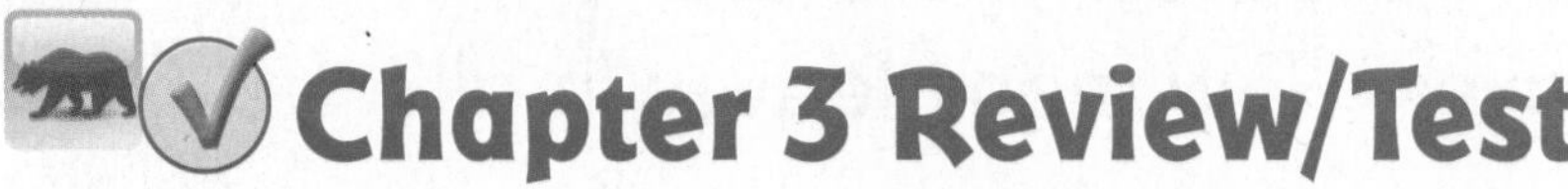

Chapter 3 Review/Test

1. Write the addends in a different order.

$$5 + 4 = 9$$

_____ + _____ = _____

2. Count on from 4. Write the number that shows 1 more.

_____

3. The cubes show a doubles fact. Choose the doubles fact and the sum.

_____ + [5 / 6] = [9 / 10]

GO DIGITAL Assessment Options Chapter Test

4. There are 3 red leaves. There are 4 yellow leaves. How many leaves in all?

Use a double to add.
Write the missing numbers.

3 + 4 = ☐ + ☐ + ☐

So, 3 + 4 = ☐

---

5. Choose all the doubles facts that can help you solve 8 + 7.

○ 4 + 4 = 8
○ 7 + 7 = 14
○ 8 + 8 = 16

---

6. Write a count on 2 fact to show a sum of 10.

Then write a doubles fact to show a sum of 10.

☐ + ☐ = ☐

☐ + ☐ = ☐

Name ______________________________

7. Match the models to the number sentences.

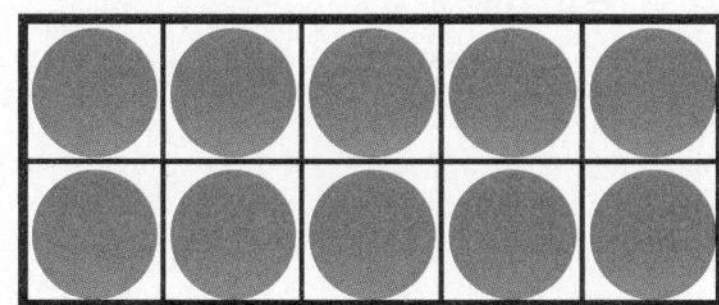

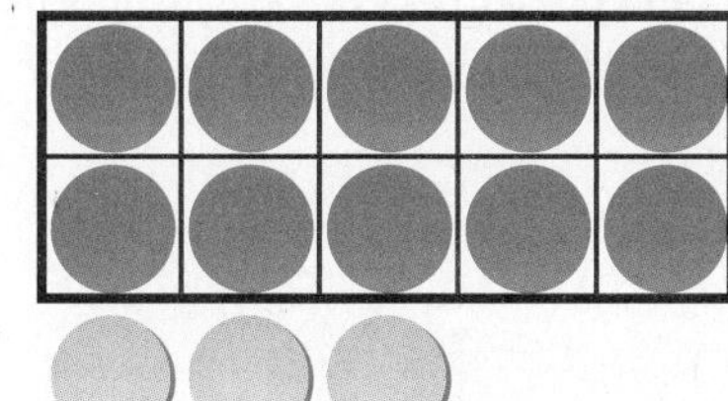

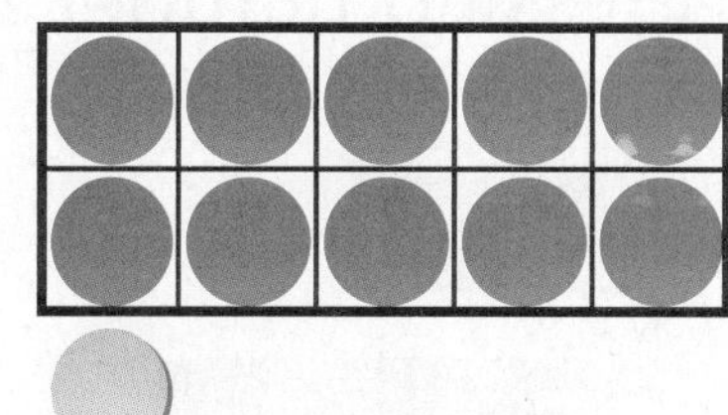

10 + 3 = 13   10 + 1 = 11   10 + 0 = 10

---

8. The model shows 8 + 5 = 13.

Write the 10 fact that has the same sum.

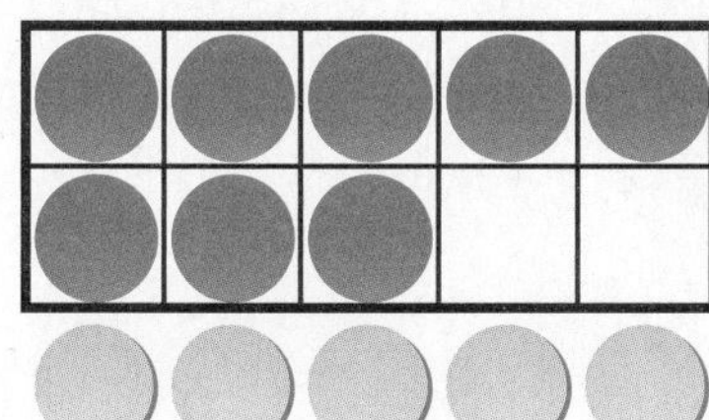

☐ + ☐ = ☐

---

9. Does the addition show how to make a ten to add? Choose Yes or No.

7 + 3 + 2	○ Yes	○ No
7 + 5 + 5	○ Yes	○ No
5 + 4 + 7	○ Yes	○ No

10. Look at the ▪ ▪ ▪ . Complete the addition sentence to show the sum. Choose the missing number and the sum.

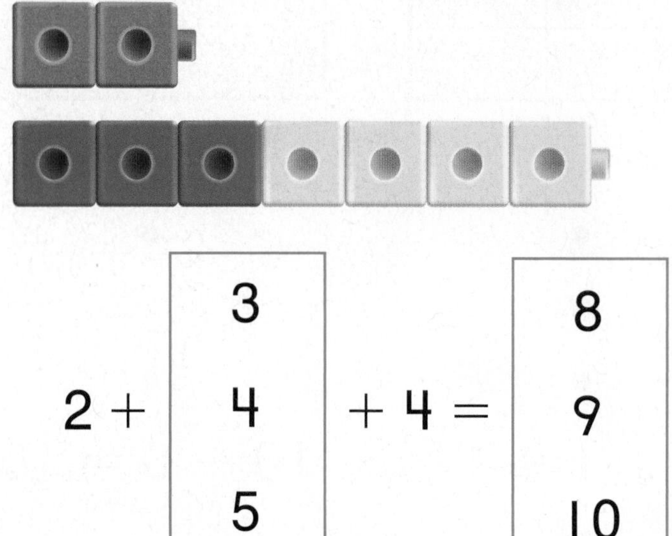

	Choose one		Choose one
2 +	3 4 5	+ 4 =	8 9 10

---

11. Write two ways to group and add 4 + 2 + 5.

_____ + _____ = _____

_____ + _____ = _____

---

12. Beth sees 4 red birds. She sees 2 yellow birds. She sees 4 blue birds. Draw a picture of the birds.

Beth sees ☐ birds.

Chapter 4

Subtraction Strategies

Curious About Math with Curious George

Six little chicks are on the fence. Two chicks hop away. How many are there now?

Name ______________________________

Show What You Know 

Model Subtraction

Use [cube] to show each number.
Take away. Write how many are left.

1. 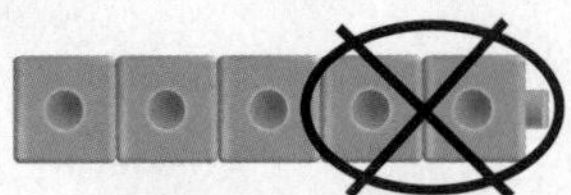

5 take away 2 ______

2. 

3 take away 1 ______

Use Symbols to Subtract

Use the picture. Write the subtraction sentence.

3. 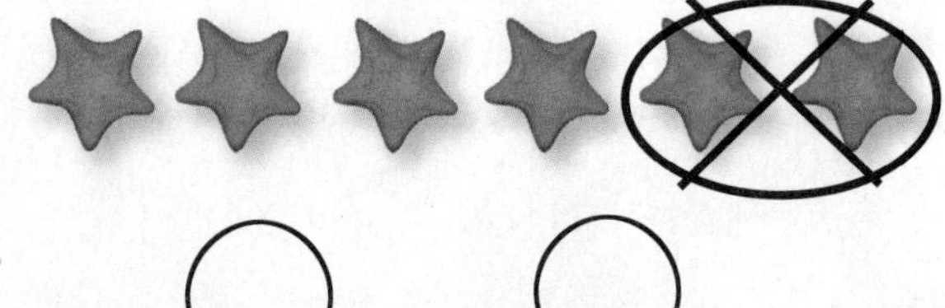

___ ○ ___ ○ ___

4. 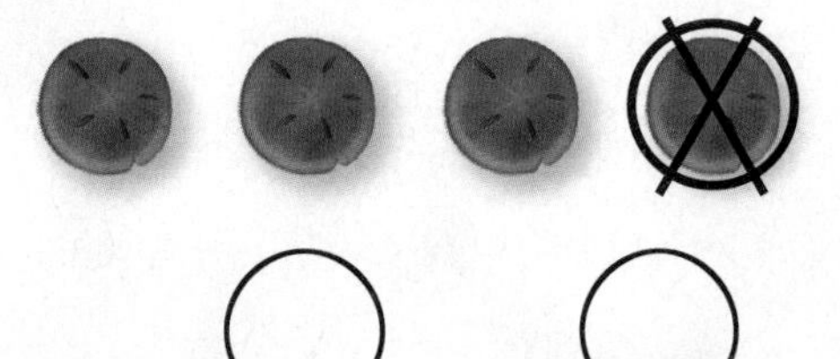

___ ○ ___ ○ ___

Subtract All or Zero

Write how many are left.

5. 

$3 - 0 =$ ____

6. 

$4 - 4 =$ ____

This page checks understanding of important skills needed for success in Chapter 4.

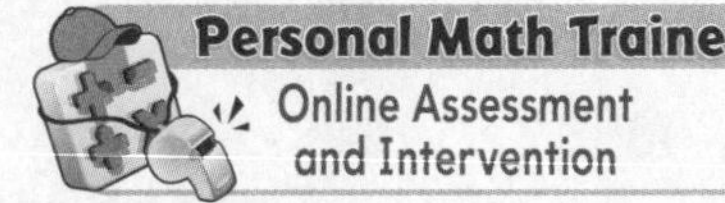

Name ______________________________

Review Words
difference
subtract
subtraction sentence
take away

Vocabulary Builder

Visualize It

Complete the chart.
Mark each row with a ✓.

Word	I Know	Sounds Familiar	I Do Not Know
difference			
subtract			
subtraction sentence			
take away			

Understand Vocabulary

Complete the sentences with review words.

1. 3 is the ______________________ for 5 − 2 = 3.

2. 7 − 4 = 3 is a ______________________.

3. You ______________________ to solve 5 − 1.

4. You can ______________________ 2 ● from 6 ●.

GO DIGITAL
• Interactive Student Edition
• Multimedia eGlossary

Chapter 4

Game Under the Sea

Materials • 2 playing pieces • spinner (1–2) • 12 cubes

Play with a partner. Take turns.

1. Put your playing piece on START.
2. Spin the spinner. Move that number of spaces.
3. Spin again. Subtract that number from the number on the game board space.
4. Use cubes to check your answer. If you are not correct, lose a turn.
5. The first player to get to END wins.

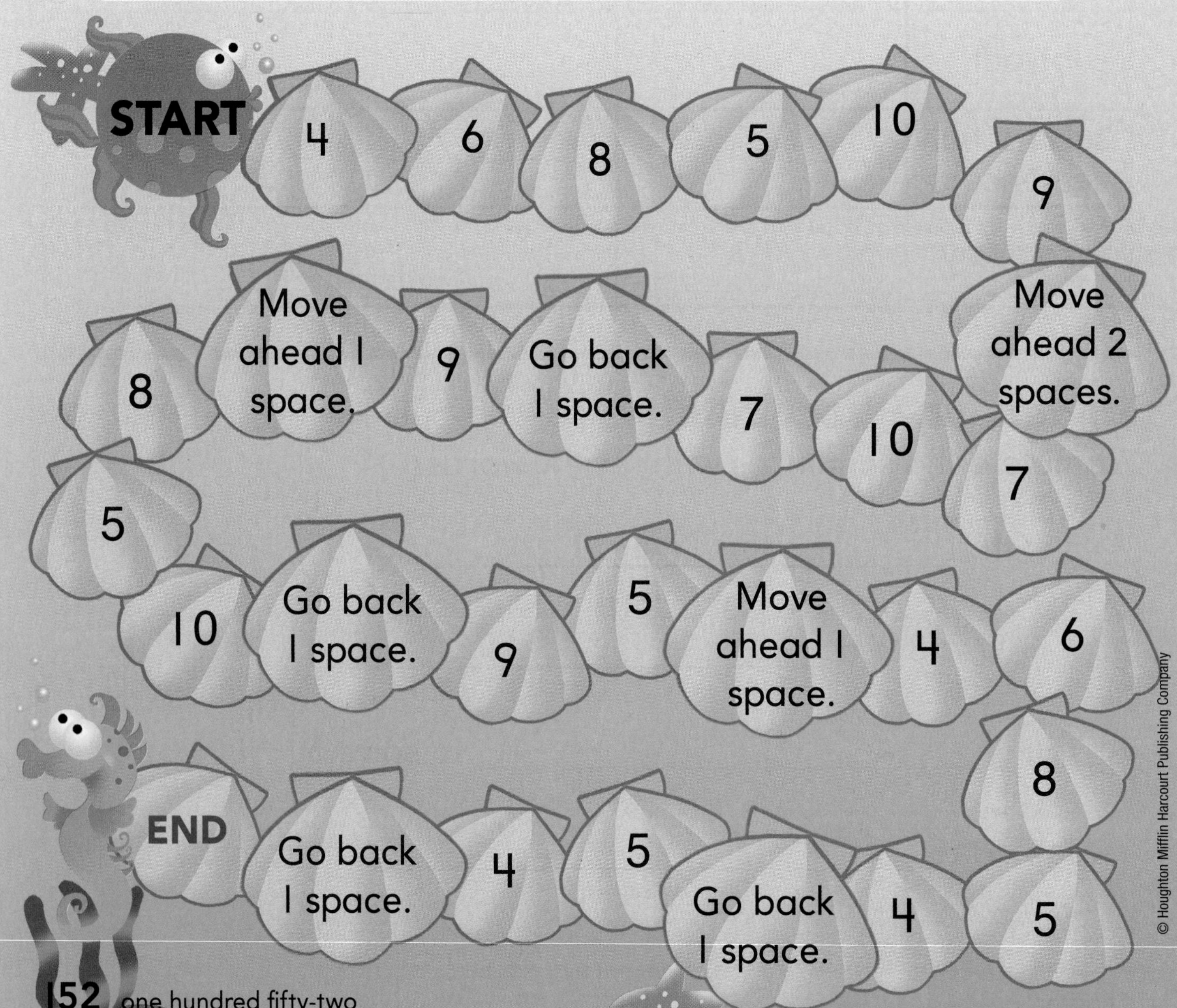

Name ______________________________

Count Back

Essential Question How can you count back 1, 2, or 3?

Operations and Algebraic Thinking—1.OA.5 *Also 1.OA.6, 1.OA.8*

MATHEMATICAL PRACTICES
MP.2, MP.4, MP.6

Listen and Draw

Start at 9. Count back to find the difference.

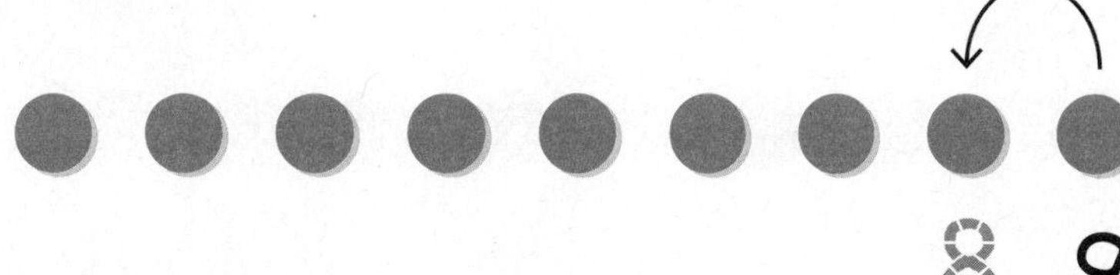

8 9

9 − 1 = ___

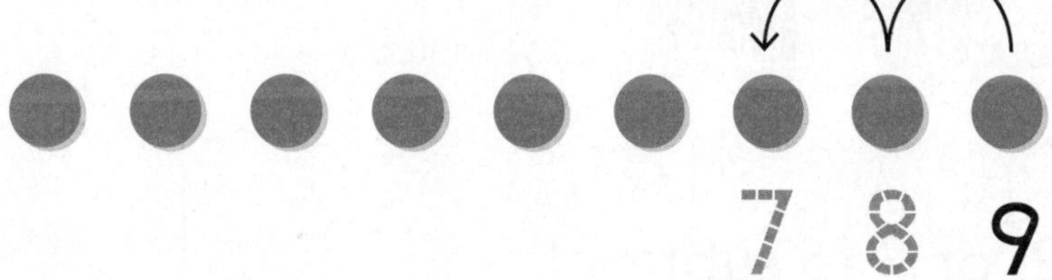

7 8 9

9 − 2 = ___

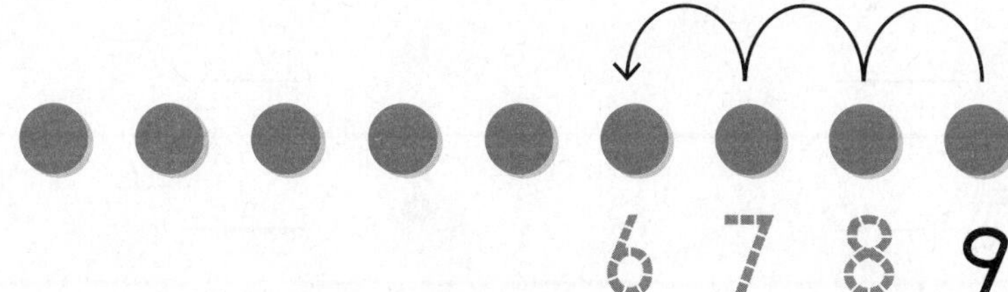

6 7 8 9

9 − 3 = ___

FOR THE TEACHER • Ask children: What is 9 – 1? Have children use the counters in the first workspace to count back 1 from 9. Repeat for the other two workspaces, having children count back 2 from 9 and then 3 from 9 to solve the subtraction sentences.

Math Talk — **Mathematical Practices**

Explain why you count backward to find the difference.

Model and Draw

You can **count back** to subtract.

Use 8 ●.
Count back 1 ●.
The difference is 7.

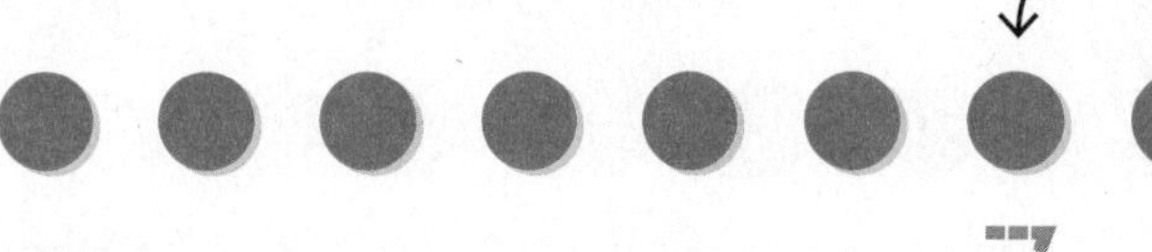

7 8

8 − 1 = 7

Share and Show

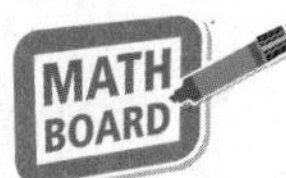

Use ●.
Count back 1, 2, or 3 to subtract.
Write the difference.

1. 5 − 1 = ____
2. ____ = 5 − 2
3. 6 − 1 = ____
4. ____ = 6 − 3
5. 7 − 2 = ____
6. ____ = 7 − 3
7. 10 − 1 = ____
8. ____ = 10 − 2
9. 12 − 3 = ____
10. ____ = 8 − 2
11. 4 − 3 = ____
12. ____ = 9 − 1

Name ____________________

On Your Own

MATHEMATICAL PRACTICE 6 **Attend to Precision**

Count back 1, 2, or 3.
Write the difference.

13. 9 − 3 = ___	14. ___ = 5 − 3	15. 6 − 3 = ___
16. 7 − 2 = ___	17. ___ = 10 − 1	18. 8 − 1 = ___
19. 5 − 2 = ___	20. ___ = 8 − 3	21. 11 − 3 = ___
22. 7 − 1 = ___	23. ___ = 9 − 1	24. 6 − 2 = ___
25. 4 − 1 = ___	26. ___ = 7 − 2	27. 3 − 1 = ___
28. 12 − 3 = ___	29. ___ = 11 − 2	30. 10 − 2 = ___
31. 3 − 2 = ___	32. ___ = 4 − 2	33. 9 − 2 = ___
34. 8 − 2 = ___	35. ___ = 10 − 3	36. 7 − 3 = ___

37. THINK SMARTER Alex subtracts 3 from 10. What is a subtraction sentence he could write?

___ ◯ ___ ◯ ___

Problem Solving • Applications

Write a subtraction sentence to solve.

38. GO DEEPER Carlos has 11 train cars. He puts 2 train cars on the track. How many train cars are off the track?

____ − ____ = ____ train cars

Then Carlos puts 1 more train car on the track. How many train cars are off the track now?

____ − ____ = ____ train cars

39. Sofia has 8 erasers. She gives 2 to Ben. How many erasers does Sofia have now?

____ − ____ = ____ erasers

40. THINK SMARTER Write the number that is 1 less.

9 − 1 = ☐

TAKE HOME ACTIVITY • Have your child show how to use the count back strategy to find the difference for 7 − 2. Repeat with other problems to count back 1, 2, or 3 from 12 or less.

FOR MORE PRACTICE: Standards Practice Book

Name ____________________

Think Addition to Subtract

Essential Question How can you use an addition fact to find the answer to a subtraction fact?

Operations and Algebraic Thinking—1.OA.4

MATHEMATICAL PRACTICES
MP.3, MP.4, MP.7

Listen and Draw

What is 12 - 5?

Use cubes to model the problem.
Draw cubes to show your work.

5 + ___ = 12

12 − 5 = ___

FOR THE TEACHER • Read the following problems. Joey had 5 cubes. Sarah gave him more cubes. Now Joey has 12 cubes. How many cubes did Sarah give him? Have children use the top workspace to solve. Then have children solve this problem: Joey had 12 cubes. He gave Sarah 5 cubes. How many cubes does Joey have now?

Mathematical Practices

Explain how 5 + 7 = 12 can help you find 12 - 5.

Model and Draw

What is $9 - 4$?

Think

$4 + \underline{\ ?\ } = 9$

Think $4 + \underline{5} = 9$ So $9 - 4 = \underline{5}$

Share and Show

Use [cubes] to add and to subtract.

1. What is $8 - 6$?

   Think $6 + \_\_\_\_ = 8$

   So $8 - 6 = \_\_\_\_$

2. What is $8 - 4$?

   Think $4 + \_\_\_\_ = 8$

   So $8 - 4 = \_\_\_\_$

3. What is $10 - 4$?

   Think $4 + \_\_\_\_ = 10$

   So $10 - 4 = \_\_\_\_$

4. What is $12 - 6$?

   Think $6 + \_\_\_\_ = 12$

   So $12 - 6 = \_\_\_\_$

Name ___________________________

On Your Own

MATHEMATICAL PRACTICE 4 Model Mathematics

Use cubes to add and to subtract.

5. $\begin{array}{r} 8 \\ -\ 3 \\ \hline ? \end{array}$ Think $\begin{array}{r} 3 \\ +\ \square \\ \hline 8 \end{array}$ So $\begin{array}{r} 8 \\ -\ 3 \\ \hline \end{array}$

6. $\begin{array}{r} 9 \\ -\ 5 \\ \hline ? \end{array}$ Think $\begin{array}{r} 5 \\ +\ \square \\ \hline 9 \end{array}$ So $\begin{array}{r} 9 \\ -\ 5 \\ \hline \end{array}$

7. $\begin{array}{r} 12 \\ -\ 7 \\ \hline ? \end{array}$ Think $\begin{array}{r} 7 \\ +\ \square \\ \hline 12 \end{array}$ So $\begin{array}{r} 12 \\ -\ 7 \\ \hline \end{array}$

8. THINK SMARTER Carol can use an addition sentence to write a subtraction sentence. Write a subtraction sentence she can solve using 6 + 8 = 14.

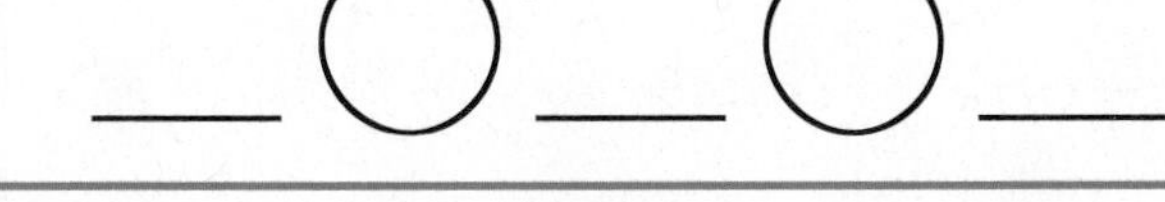

9. Write an addition sentence Carol can use to help her solve 13 − 9.

___ ◯ ___ ◯ ___

Problem Solving • Applications

Write a number sentence to solve.

10. There are 14 cats. 7 are black. The rest are yellow. How many yellow cats are there?

___ ◯ ___ ◯ ___

___ yellow cats

11. I had some pencils. I gave 4 pencils away. Now I have 2 pencils. How many pencils did I start with?

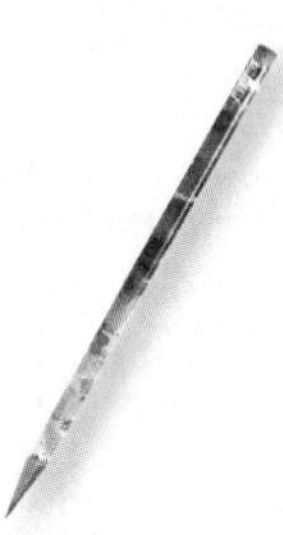

___ ◯ ___ ◯ ___

___ pencils

12. GO DEEPER Sarah has 8 fewer flowers than Ann. Ann has 16 flowers. How many flowers does Sarah have?

___ ◯ ___ ◯ ___

___ flowers

13. THINK SMARTER Look at the facts. Write the missing number in each fact.

$$\begin{array}{r} 5 \\ + \square \\ \hline 12 \end{array} \qquad \begin{array}{r} 12 \\ - 5 \\ \hline \square \end{array}$$

TAKE HOME ACTIVITY • Write 5 + 4 = ___ and ask your child to write the sum. Have him or her explain how to use 5 + 4 = 9 to solve ___ − 4 = 5 and then write the answer.

FOR MORE PRACTICE: Standards Practice Book

Name ______________________________

Use Think Addition to Subtract

Essential Question How can you use addition to help you find the answer to a subtraction fact?

Operations and Algebraic Thinking—1.OA.4 *Also 1.OA.8*
MATHEMATICAL PRACTICES
MP.1, MP.5, MP.6

Listen and Draw

What is 10 - 3?

Use [cubes]. Draw to show your work.
Write the number sentences.

___ ◯ ___ ◯ ___

___ ◯ ___ ◯ ___

FOR THE TEACHER • Read the problem. Maria has 7 crayons. She gets 3 more. How many crayons does she have? Have children use the top workspace to solve. Then have children solve this problem: Maria has 10 crayons. She gives 3 of them to her friends. How many crayons are there now?

Math Talk **Mathematical Practices**

Do your answers make sense? **Explain.**

Model and Draw

An addition fact can help you subtract.

What is 8 − 6?

Use 6 + ___ = 8

So 8 − 6 = ___

Share and Show

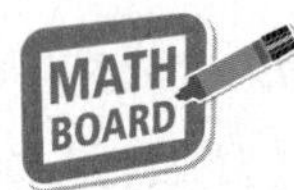

Think of an addition fact to help you subtract.

1. What is 9 − 6?

Use 6 + ___ = 9

So 9 − 6 = ___

2. What is 11 − 5?

Use ___ + ___ = 11

So 11 − 5 = ___

✓3. What is 10 − 8?

Use ___ + ___ = 10

So 10 − 8 = ___

✓4. What is 7 − 4?

Use ___ + ___ = 7

So 7 − 4 = ___

Name ____________________

On Your Own

MATHEMATICAL PRACTICE 1 **Analyze**

Think of an addition fact to help you subtract.

5. $\begin{array}{r} 16 \\ -\ 8 \\ \hline \end{array}$ $\begin{array}{r} 8 \\ +\ \blacksquare \\ \hline 16 \end{array}$

6. $\begin{array}{r} 10 \\ -\ 6 \\ \hline \end{array}$ $\begin{array}{r} 6 \\ +\ \blacksquare \\ \hline 10 \end{array}$

7. $\begin{array}{r} 7 \\ -\ 5 \\ \hline \end{array}$

8. $\begin{array}{r} 10 \\ -\ 5 \\ \hline \end{array}$

9. $\begin{array}{r} 8 \\ -\ 5 \\ \hline \end{array}$

10. $\begin{array}{r} 11 \\ -\ 6 \\ \hline \end{array}$

11. $\begin{array}{r} 13 \\ -\ 7 \\ \hline \end{array}$

12. $\begin{array}{r} 11 \\ -\ 4 \\ \hline \end{array}$

13. $\begin{array}{r} 14 \\ -\ 7 \\ \hline \end{array}$

14. $\begin{array}{r} 9 \\ -\ 3 \\ \hline \end{array}$

15. $\begin{array}{r} 11 \\ -\ 7 \\ \hline \end{array}$

16. $\begin{array}{r} 12 \\ -\ 7 \\ \hline \end{array}$

17. THINK SMARTER Emil has 13 pencils in a cup. He takes some pencils out. There are 6 pencils left in the cup. How many pencils does he take out?

What addition fact can you use to solve this problem?

____ + ____ = ____

So, Emil takes out ____ pencils.

TAKE HOME ACTIVITY • Ask your child to explain how the addition fact 8 + 6 = 14 can help him or her to find 14 − 6.

FOR MORE PRACTICE: Standards Practice Book

Name ______________________________

Mid-Chapter Checkpoint

Concepts and Skills

Count back 1, 2, or 3 to subtract.
Write the difference. (1.OA.5)

1. $7 - 1 =$ ____

2. ____ $= 7 - 2$

3. $12 - 3 =$ ____

4. $9 - 3 =$ ____

5. $6 - 2 =$ ____

6. $8 - 3 =$ ____

7. ____ $= 11 - 3$

8. $5 - 2 =$ ____

Use cubes to add and to subtract. (1.OA.4)

9. $11 - 5 = ?$

Think: $5 + \square = 11$

So: $11 - 5 =$ ____

10. $14 - 7 = ?$

Think: $7 + \square = 14$

So: $14 - 7 =$ ____

Personal Math Trainer

11. THINKSMARTER+ Write a subtraction sentence you can solve by using $3 + 9 = 12$. (1.OA.4)

____ − ____ = ____

Name ______________________________

Use 10 to Subtract

Essential Question How can you make a ten to help you subtract?

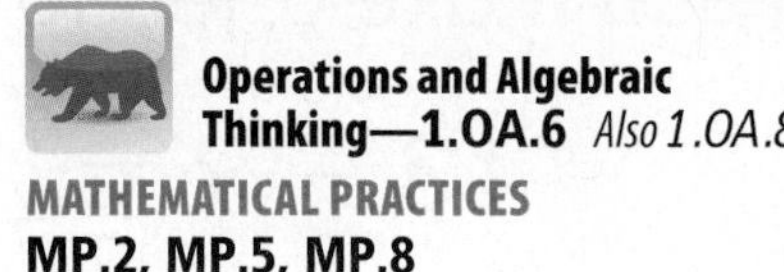

HANDS ON
Lesson 4.4

Operations and Algebraic Thinking—1.OA.6 *Also 1.OA.8*

MATHEMATICAL PRACTICES
MP.2, MP.5, MP.8

Listen and Draw

Real World · Hands On

Use ● to show the problem.
Draw to show your work.

Math Talk **Mathematical Practices**

Explain how your drawing can help you solve 15 − 9.

FOR THE TEACHER • Read the following problem. Austin puts 9 red counters in the first ten frame. Then he puts 1 yellow counter in the ten frame. How many more yellow counters does Austin need to make 15?

Model and Draw

You can make a ten to help you subtract.

$13 - 9 = \underline{\ ?\ }$

Start at 9.

Count up 1 to make 10.

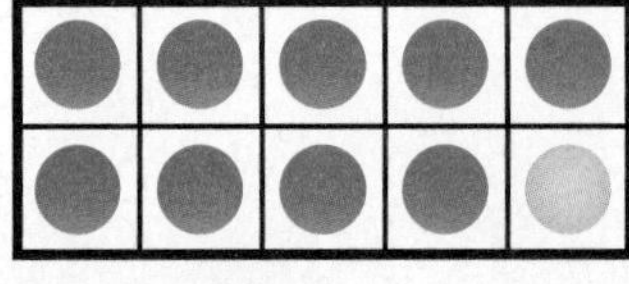

Count up 3 more to 13.

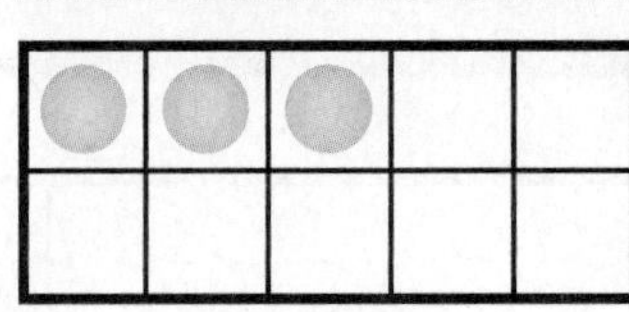

You counted up 4.

$13 - 9 = \_\_\_\_$

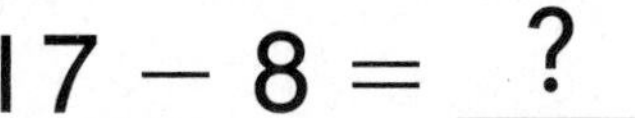

$17 - 8 = \underline{\ ?\ }$

Start at 8.

Count up 2 to make 10.

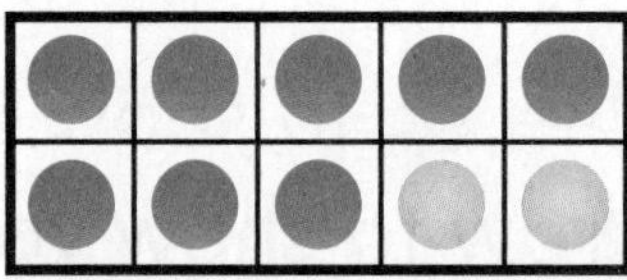

Count up 7 more to 17.

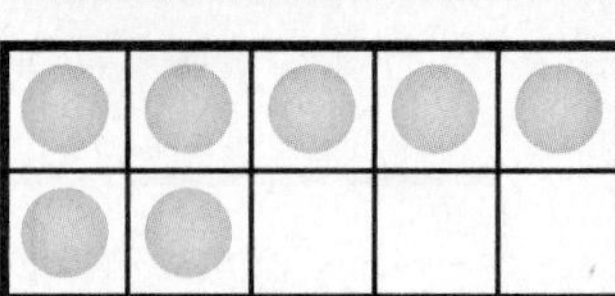

You counted up 9.

$17 - 8 = \_\_\_\_$

Share and Show

Use ● and ten frames. Make a ten to subtract. Draw to show your work.

1. $12 - 8 = \underline{\ ?\ }$

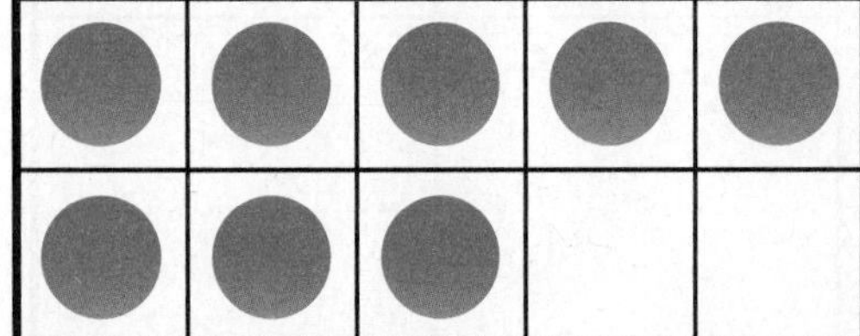

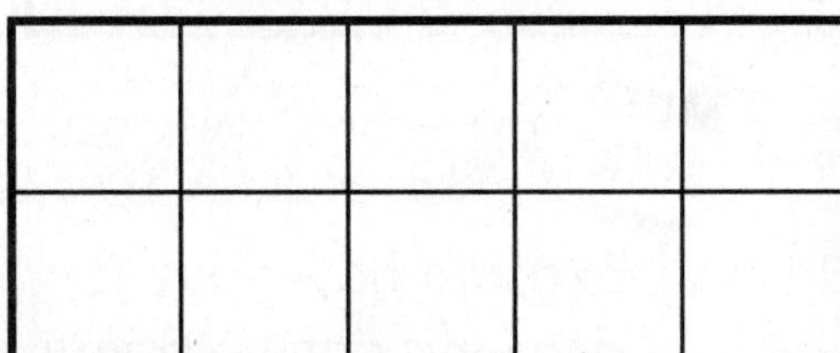

$12 - 8 = \_\_\_\_$

2. $11 - 9 = \underline{\ ?\ }$

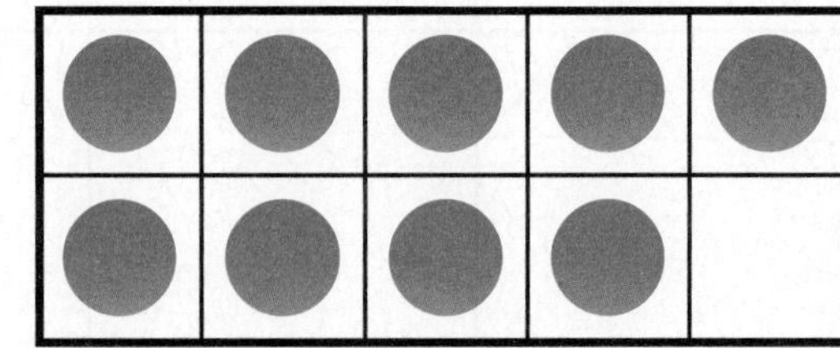

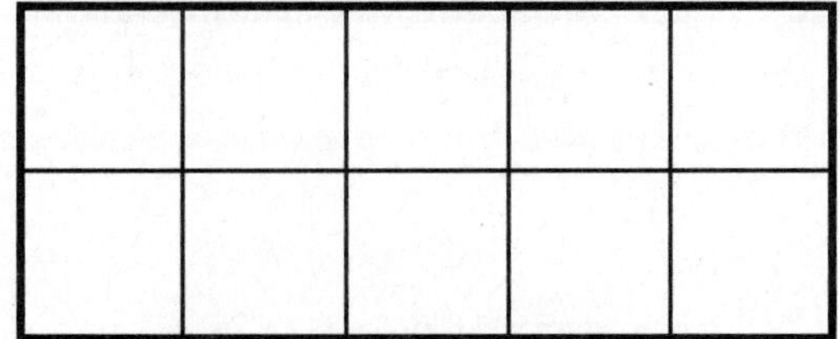

$11 - 9 = \_\_\_\_$

Name ____________________

On Your Own

MATHEMATICAL PRACTICE 5 **Use a Concrete Model**

Use ● and ten frames. Make a ten to subtract.
Draw to show your work.

3. 14 − 9 = ?

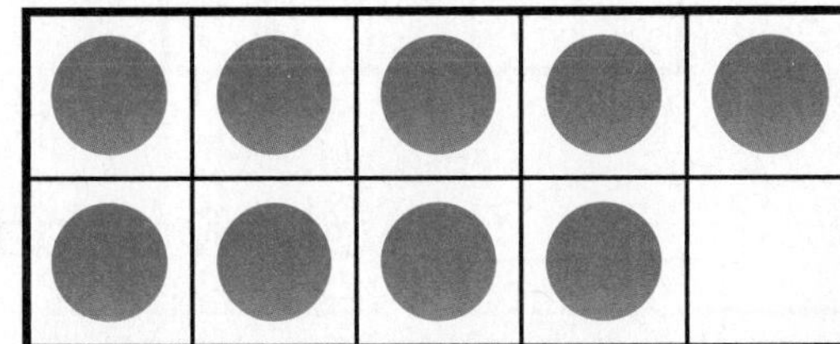

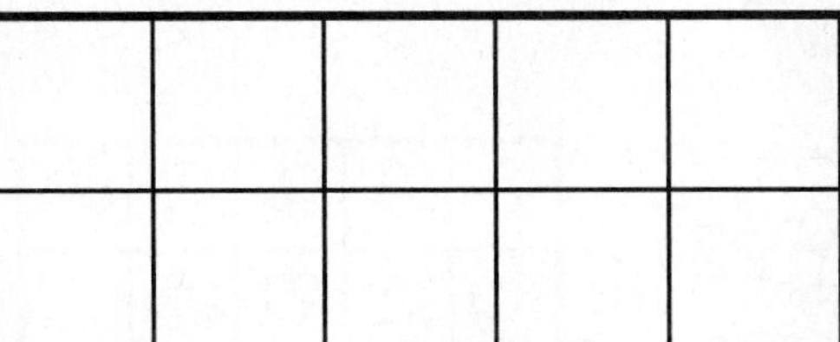

14 − 9 = ____

4. 11 − 8 = ?

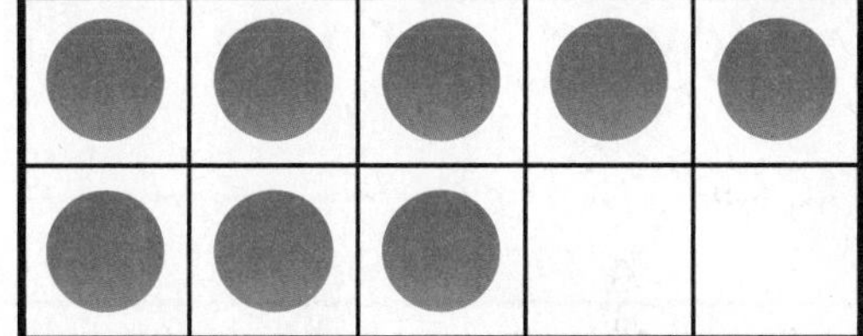

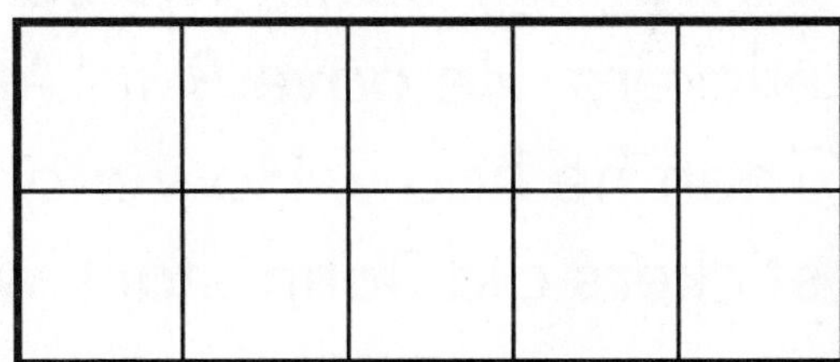

11 − 8 = ____

5. 15 − 8 = ?

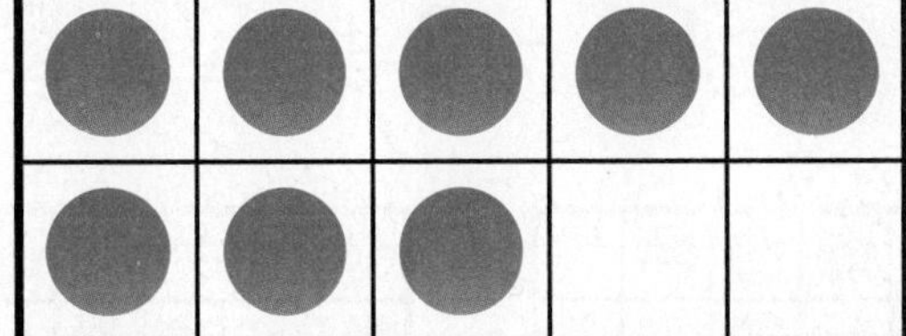

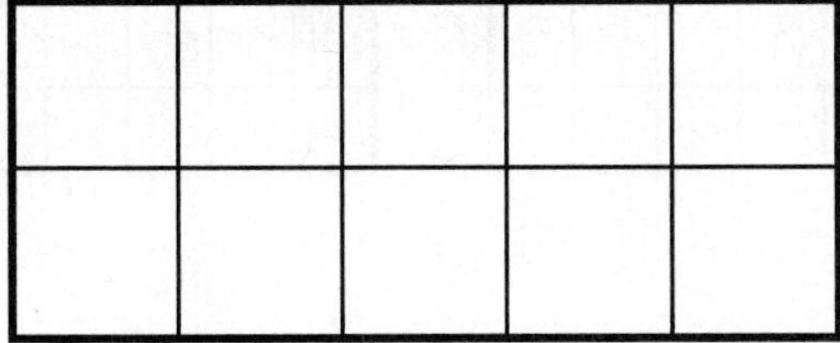

15 − 8 = ____

6. 17 − 9 = ?

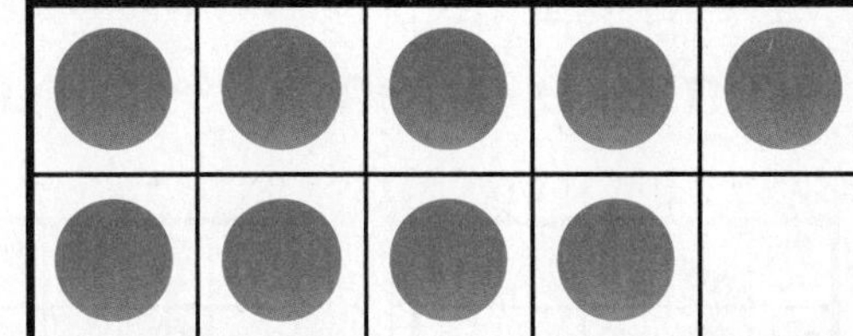

17 − 9 = ____

Problem Solving • Applications Real World

WRITE Math

Solve. Use the ten frames to make a ten to help you subtract.

7. GO DEEPER Mia has 18 beads. 9 are red and the rest are yellow. How many beads are yellow?

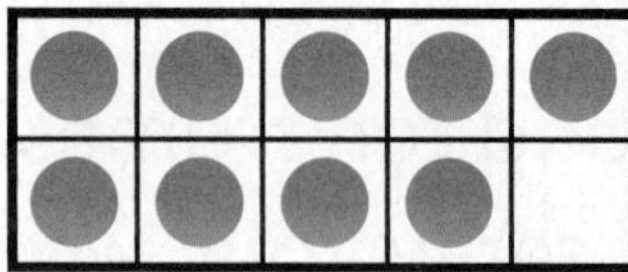

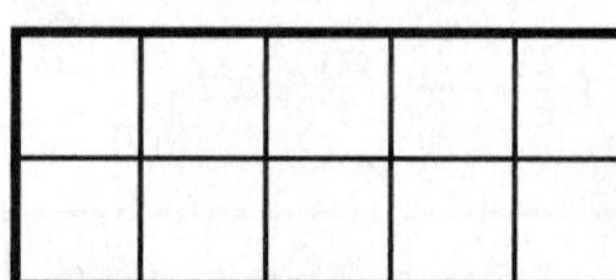

_______ yellow beads

8. THINK SMARTER John had some stickers. He gave 9 to April. Then he had 7. How many stickers did John start with?

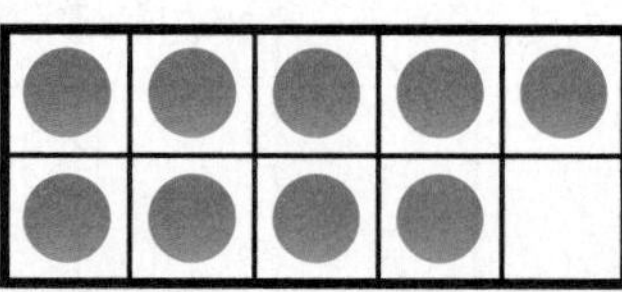

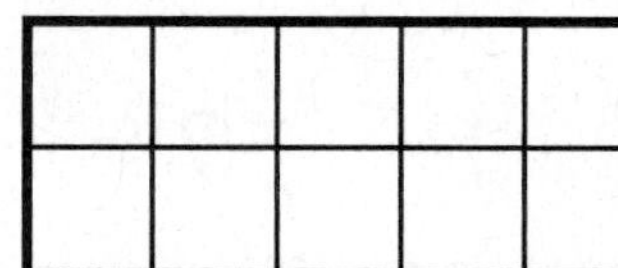

_______ stickers

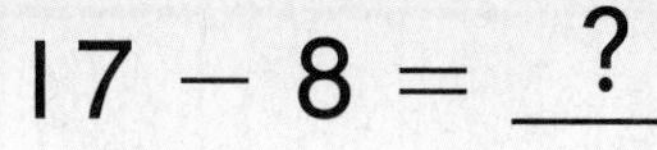

9. THINK SMARTER + Which shows a way to make a ten to subtract?

$17 - 8 = \underline{\ ?\ }$

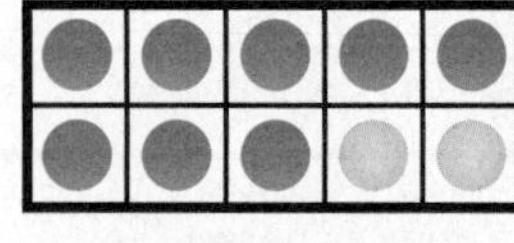
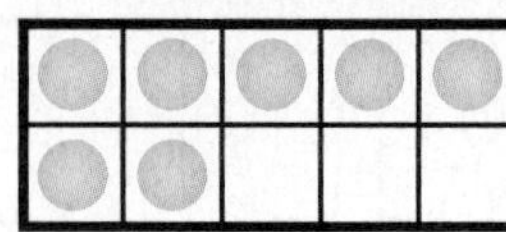
○

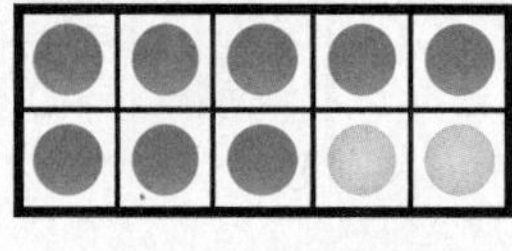
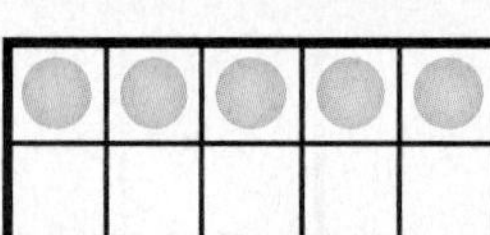
○

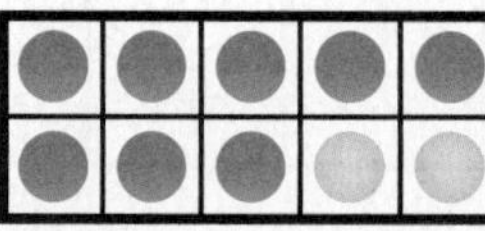
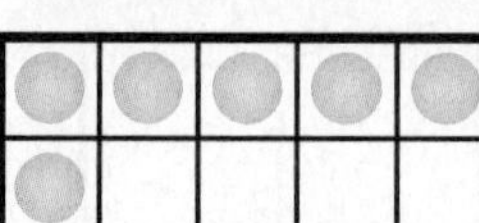
○

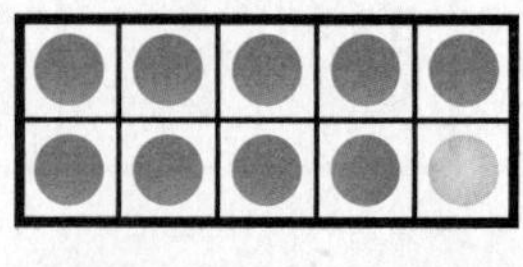
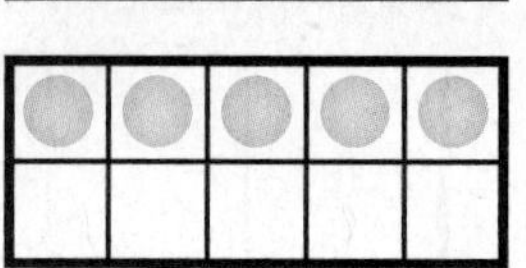
○

TAKE HOME ACTIVITY • Ask your child to explain how he or she solved Exercise 7.

FOR MORE PRACTICE: Standards Practice Book

Name ______________________

Break Apart to Subtract

Essential Question How do you break apart a number to subtract?

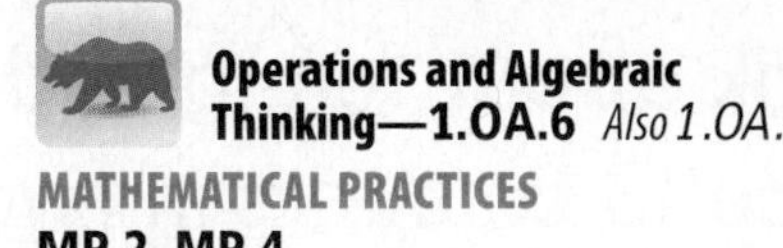

MATHEMATICAL PRACTICES
MP.2, MP.4

Listen and Draw — Real World — Hands On

Use ● to solve each problem.
Draw to show your work.

______ pennies

______ pennies

FOR THE TEACHER • Read the following problem. Tom had 14 pennies. He gave 4 pennies to his sister. How many pennies does Tom have now? Have children use the top workspace to solve. Then read this part of the problem: Then Tom gave 2 pennies to his brother. How many pennies does Tom have now?

Math Talk — Mathematical Practices

How many pennies did Tom give away? **Explain.**

Model and Draw

Think about ten to find 13 − 4.
Place 13 counters in two ten frames.

How many do you subtract to get to 10?

Subtract 3 to get to 10.

Step 1

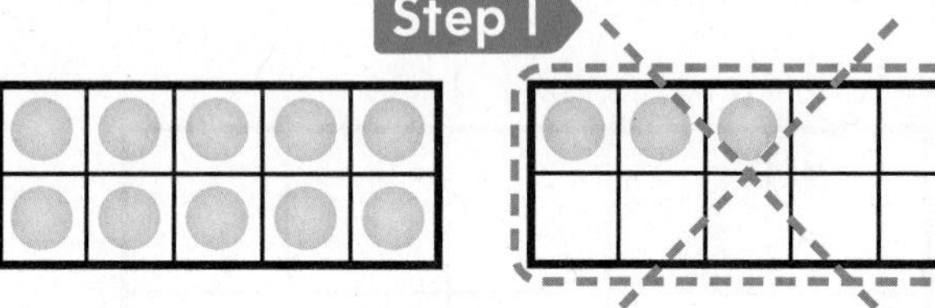

How many more to subtract 4?

Then subtract 1 more.

Step 2

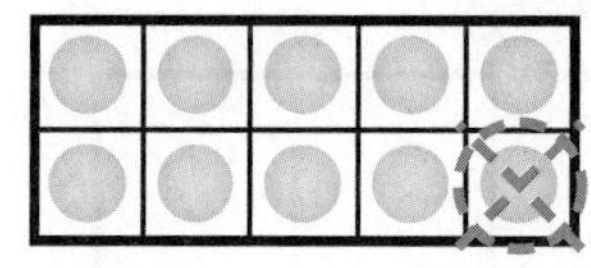

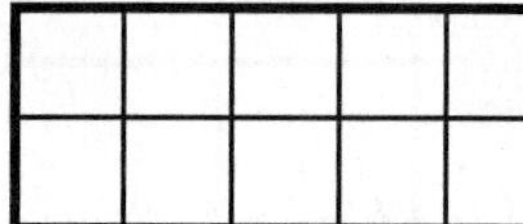

13 − 3 − 1

10 − 1 = ____

So, 13 − 4 = ____.

Share and Show

THINK
What is the best way to break apart the 7?

Subtract.

1. What is 15 − 7?

Step 1

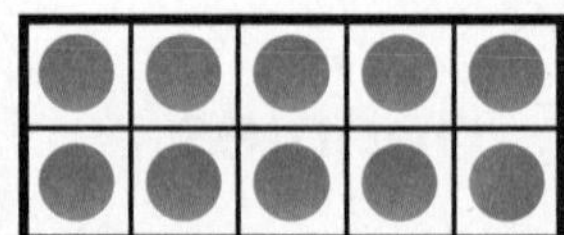

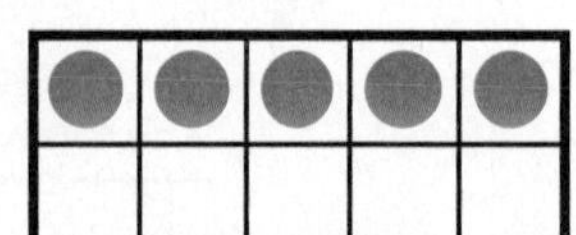

Step 2

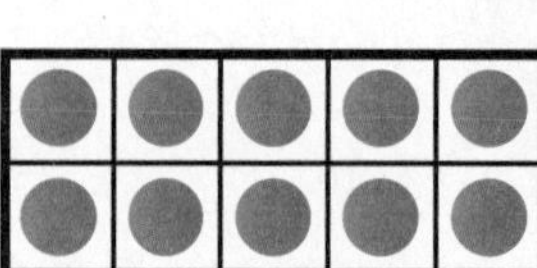

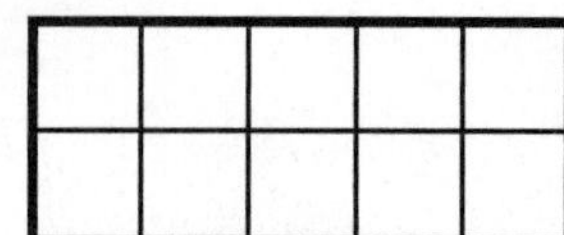

____ − ____ − ____

____ − ____ = ____

So, 15 − 7 = ____.

Name ____________________

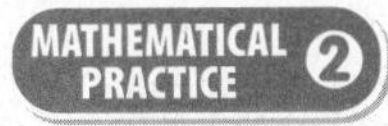

MATHEMATICAL PRACTICE 2 Reason Quantitatively

Subtract.

2. GO DEEPER What is 14 − 6?

Step 1

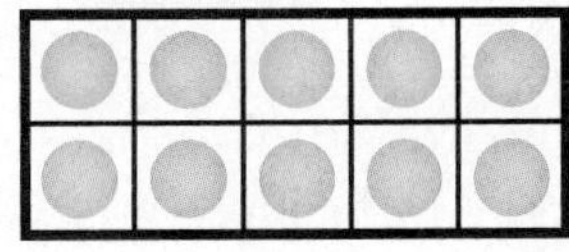

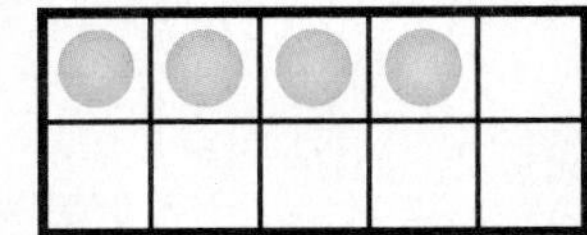

Step 2

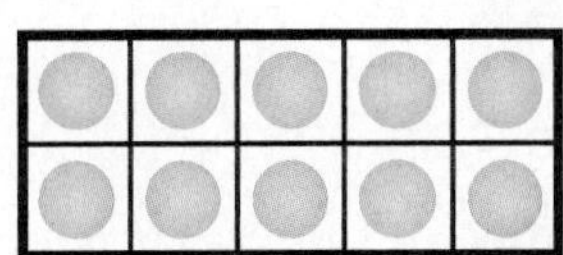

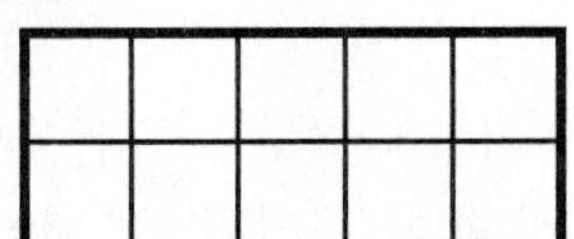

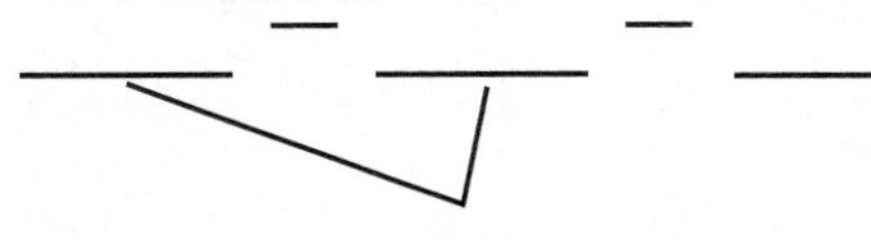

____ − ____ − ____

____ − ____ = ____

So, 14 − 6 = ____.

3. What is 16 − 7?

Step 1

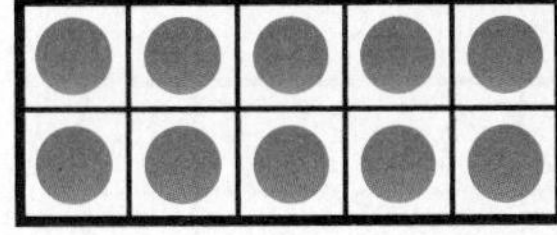

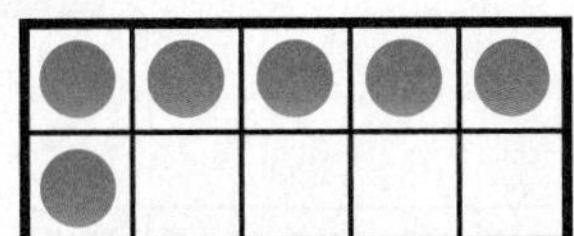

Step 2

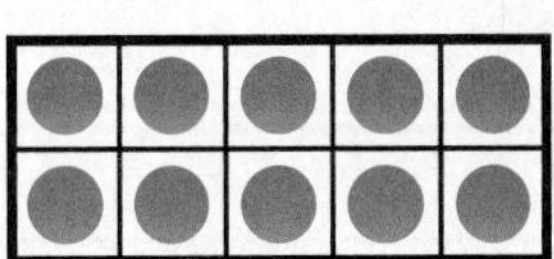

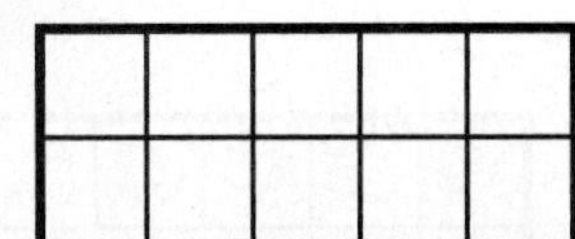

____ − ____ − ____

____ − ____ = ____

So, ____ − ____ = ____.

Problem Solving • Applications

Use the ten frames.
Write a number sentence to solve.

4. THINK SMARTER There are 14 sheep in the herd. 5 sheep run away. How many sheep are left in the herd?

Step 1

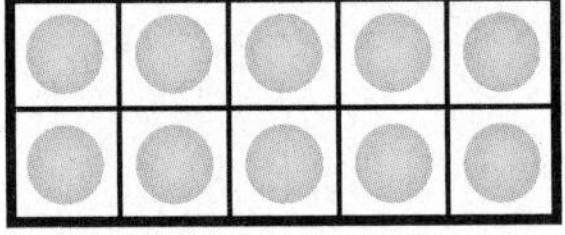

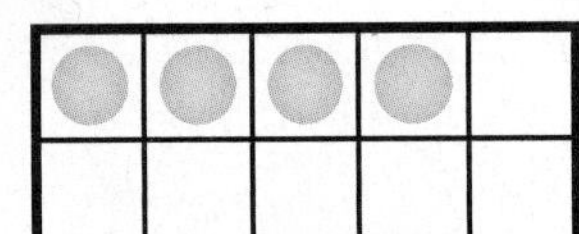

Step 2

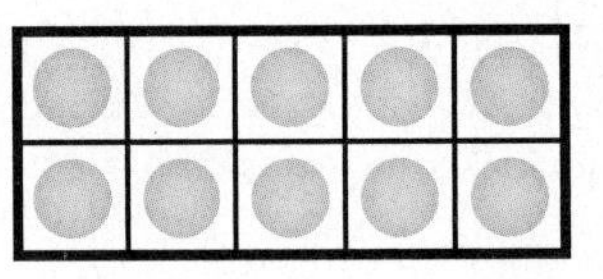

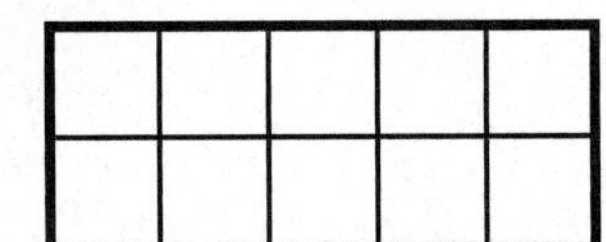

____ − ____ = ____

____ sheep

5. THINK SMARTER What subtraction sentence does the model show?

Step 1

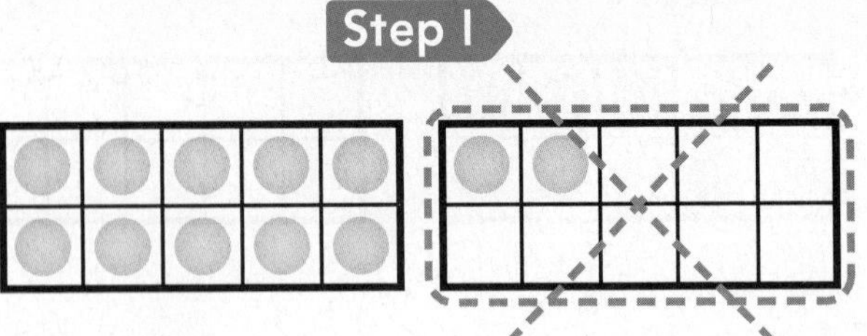

Step 2

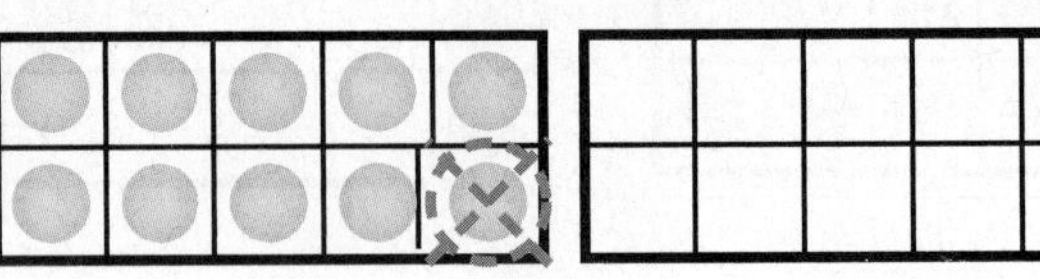

○ 10 − 1 = 9 ○ 12 − 3 = 9

○ 10 − 3 = 7 ○ 12 − 2 = 10

TAKE HOME ACTIVITY • Ask your child to explain how he or she solved Exercise 4.

FOR MORE PRACTICE: Standards Practice Book

Name ___

Problem Solving • Use Subtraction Strategies

Essential Question How can acting out a problem help you solve the problem?

Operations and Algebraic Thinking—1.OA.1

MATHEMATICAL PRACTICES
MP.1, MP.3, MP.4

Kyle had 13 hats. He gave 5 hats to Jake. How many hats does Kyle have now?

Unlock the Problem (Real World)

Hands On

What do I need to find?	What information do I need to use?
how many hats Kyle has now	Kyle had 13 hats. Kyle gave 5 to Jake.

Show how to solve the problem.

Step 1

Step 2

Kyle has 8 hats now.

HOME CONNECTION • Your child used counters to act out the subtraction story. The graphic organizer helps your child analyze the information given in the problem.

Try Another Problem

Act it out to solve. Draw to show your work.

- What do I need to find?
- What information do I need to use?

1. Heather has 14 crackers.
Some crackers are broken.
8 crackers are not broken. How many crackers are broken?

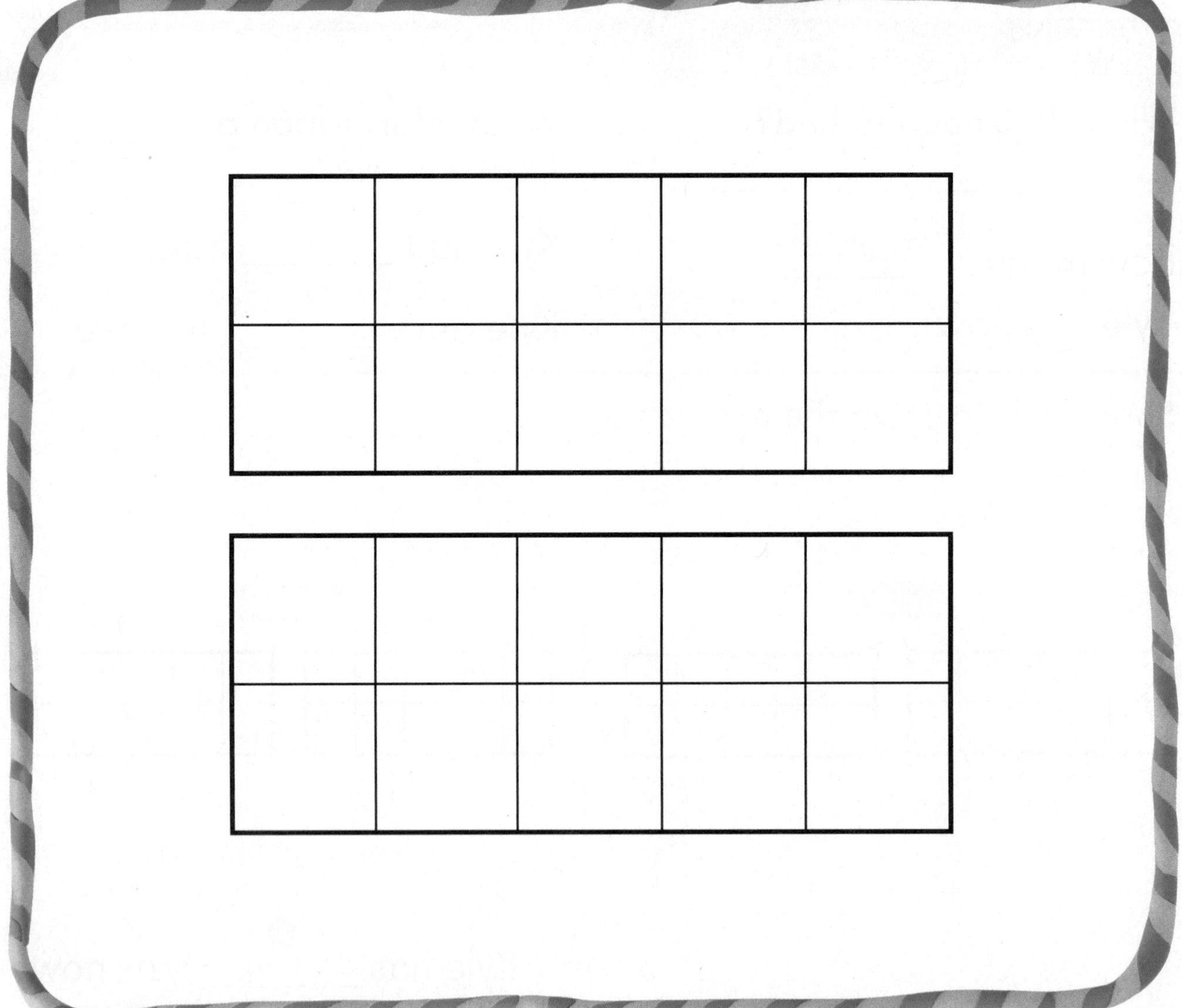

$14 - \square = 8$

_______ crackers are broken.

Math Talk **Mathematical Practices**

Explain how you can show how many crackers are broken.

Name ______________________________

Share and Show

MATHEMATICAL PRACTICE 1 **Analyze**

Act it out to solve. Draw to show your work.

2. Phil had some stickers. He lost 7 stickers. Now he has 9 stickers. How many stickers did Phil start with?

$\square - 7 = 9$

Phil started with ____ stickers.

3. Hillary has 9 dolls. Abby has 18 dolls. How many fewer dolls does Hillary have than Abby?

$18 - 9 = \square$

Hillary has ____ fewer dolls.

✓ 4. Josh had 12 pennies. He tossed some into a fountain. He has 5 left. How many pennies did he toss in the fountain?

$12 - \square = 5$

Josh tossed ____ pennies.

✓ 5. Cami has 13 apples. Some are green and some are red. She has 8 red apples. How many apples are green?

$13 - \square = 8$

____ apples are green.

On Your Own

WRITE Math

Choose a way to solve. Draw or write to explain.

6. THINK SMARTER 10 frogs are in the tree. 3 more frogs jump into the tree. Then 4 frogs jump out of the tree. How many frogs are in the tree now?

____ frogs

7. There are 9 more turtles in the water than on a log. 13 turtles are in the water. How many turtles are on a log?

____ turtles

8. GO DEEPER Choose a number to fill in the blank. Solve.
10 dogs are at the park.

____ dogs are brown. The rest have black spots. How many dogs have black spots?

____ dogs

9. THINK SMARTER Chris has 10 dollars. He spends some of his dollars. He has 6 dollars left. How many dollars did Chris spend?

Chris spent ☐ dollars.

TAKE HOME ACTIVITY • Tell your child a subtraction story. Ask your child to use small objects to act out the problem to solve it.

FOR MORE PRACTICE: Standards Practice Book

Name ______________________

Chapter 4 Review/Test

1. Count back. Write the number that is 2 less.

$8 - 2 = \square$

2. Look at the facts. A number is missing. Which number is missing?

$$\begin{array}{r} 8 \\ + \square \\ \hline 13 \end{array} \qquad \begin{array}{r} 13 \\ - 8 \\ \hline \square \end{array}$$

5 ○   6 ○   7 ○   8 ○

3. Write a subtraction sentence you can solve by using $5 + 4 = 9$.

$\square - \square = \square$

GO DIGITAL Assessment Options Chapter Test

4. Make a ten to subtract.
Draw to show your work.
Write the difference.

12 − 7 = ?

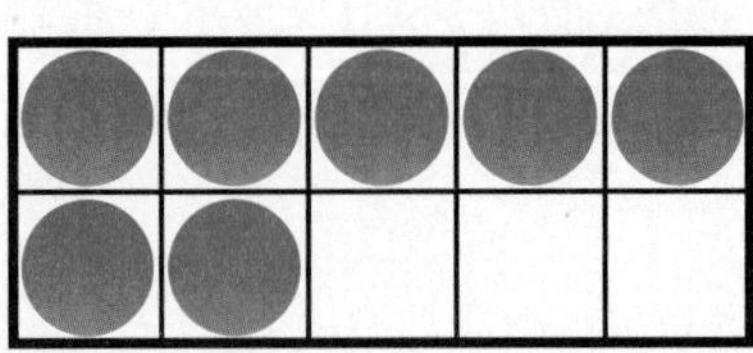

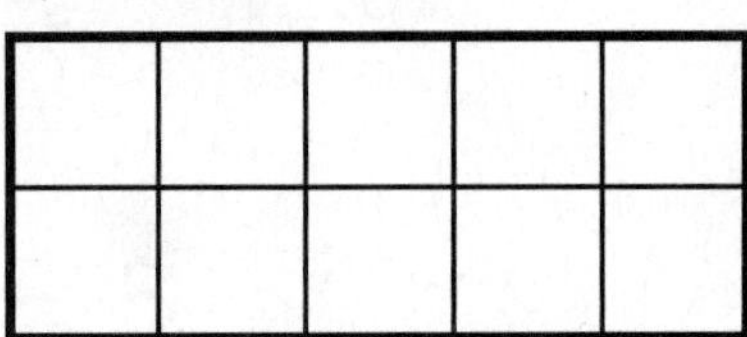

12 − 7 = ☐

5. What subtraction sentence does the model show?

Step 1

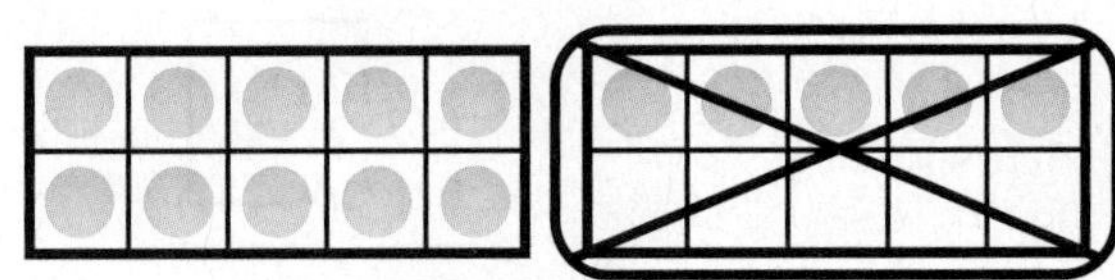

Step 2

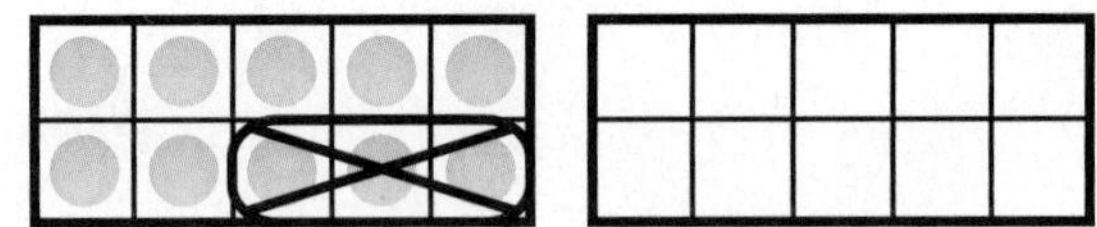

○ 10 − 5
○ 15 − 5
○ 10 − 5 − 1
○ 15 − 5 − 3

6. Lupe has 9 books. She gives some away. She has 7 left. How many books does she give away? Draw or write to explain.

Lupe gives away ☐ books.

Name ____________________

7. Look at the number sentences. What number is missing? Write the number in each box.

13 − ☐ = 9   9 + ☐ = 13

8. ★ means "count back 1."

■ means "count back 2."

● means "count back 3."

Match each picture to a number sentence.

 •   • 5 − ? = 2

 •   • 7 − ? = 6

 •   • 8 − ? = 6

9. Make a 10 to subtract.

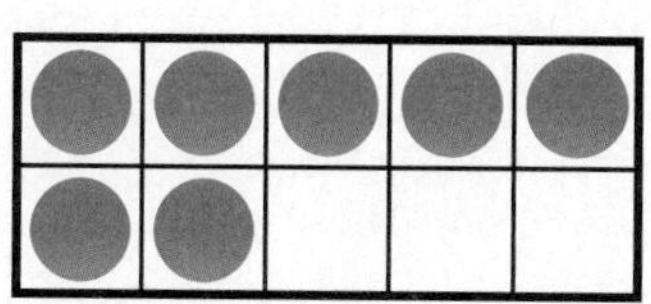

13 − 7 = ☐

13 − 7 = ?

10. How does the model show 15 − 6? Choose the numbers that make the number sentences true. Circle numbers in the boxes.

Step 1

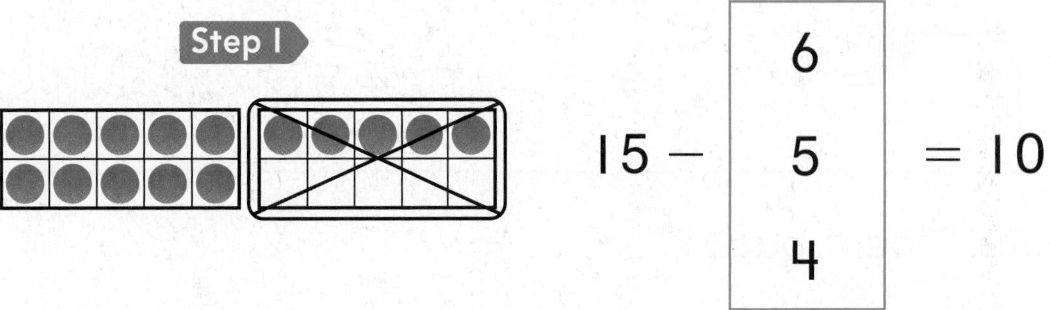

15 − [6 / 5 / 4] = 10

Step 2

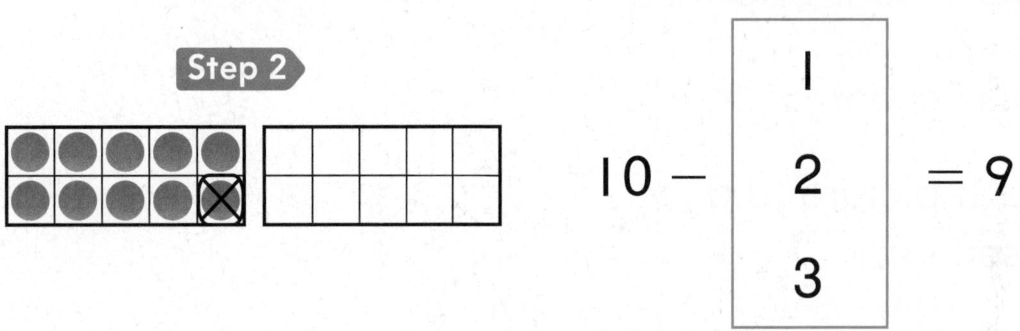

10 − [1 / 2 / 3] = 9

---

11. Mark has 11 crayons. He gives some away. He has 4 left. How many crayons does he give away? Draw a picture to help you subtract.

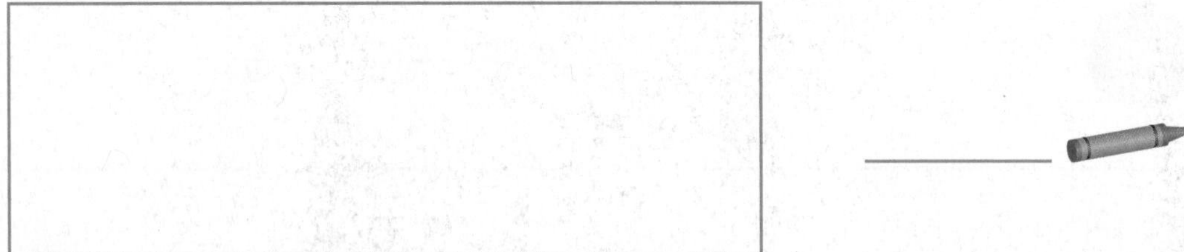

_____ crayons

How is drawing a picture like acting out a problem?

Chapter 5

Addition and Subtraction Relationships

Curious About Math with Curious George

Children tap the Liberty Bell 4 times. Then they tap it 9 more times. How many times do the children tap the bell?

Name ______________________

Show What You Know

Add in Any Order

Use cubes. Color to match.
Write each sum.

1\.
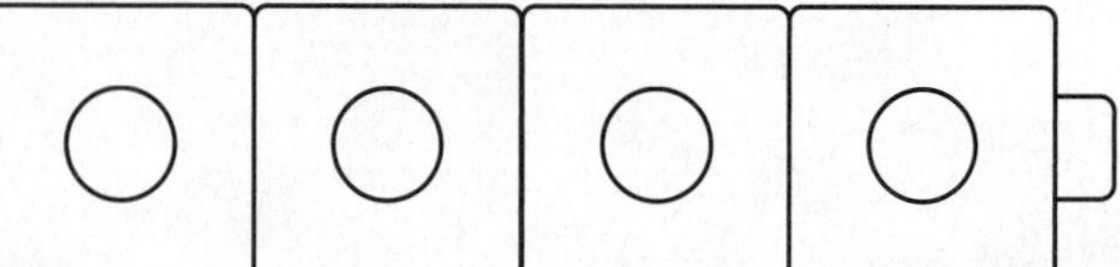
1 + 3 = ____

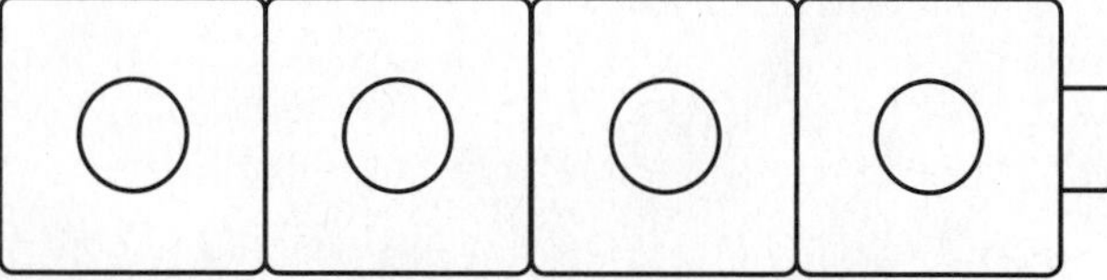
3 + 1 = ____

Count On

Use the number line to add. Write each sum.

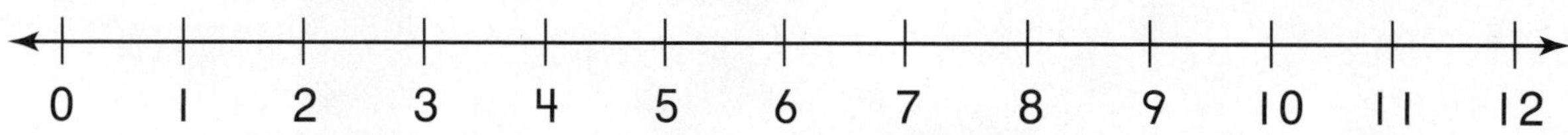

2\. 6 + 3 = ____ | 3. 7 + 1 = ____ | 4. 8 + 2 = ____

Count Back

Use the number line to subtract. Write each difference.

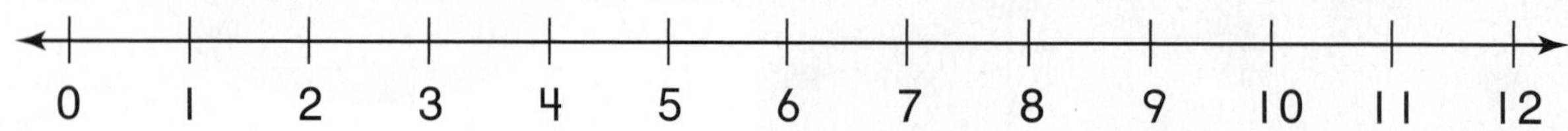

5\. 11 − 2 = ____ | 6. 8 − 3 = ____ | 7. 9 − 1 = ____

This page checks understanding of important skills needed for success in Chapter 5.

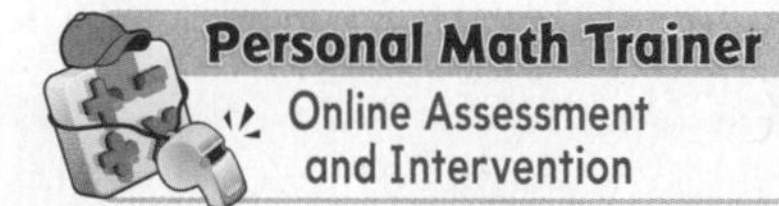

Name ______________________________

Vocabulary Builder

Review Words
add
addition fact
difference
subtract
subtraction fact
sum

Visualize It

Sort the review words from the box.

Addition Words

Subtraction Words

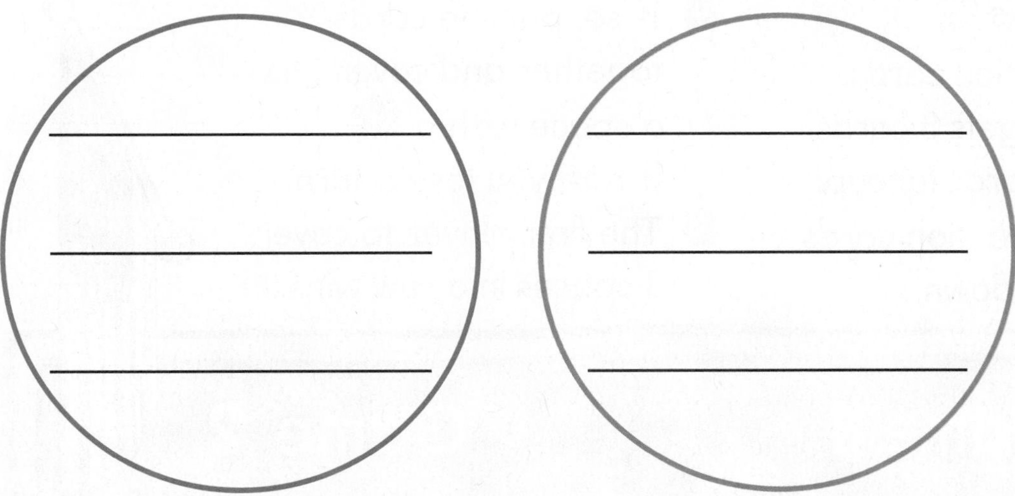

Understand Vocabulary

Follow the directions.

1. Write an addition fact.

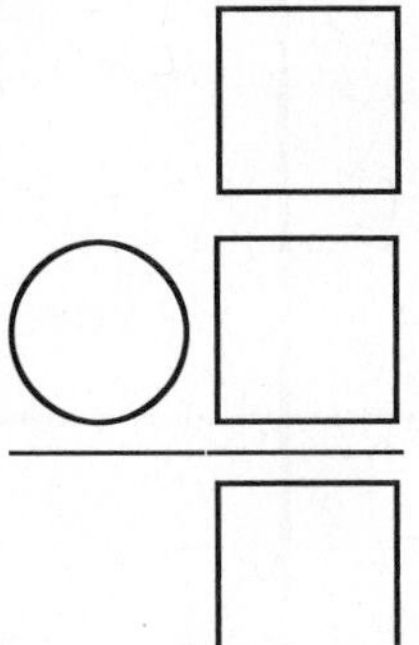

2. What is the sum?

____

3. Write a subtraction fact.

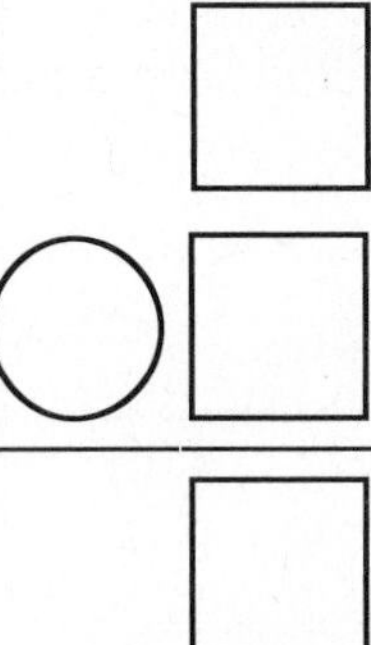

4. What is the difference?

____

GO DIGITAL • Interactive Student Edition • Multimedia eGlossary

Chapter 5

Game Add to Subtract Bingo

Materials • 16 $\boxed{5 + 3}$ • 16 $\boxed{8 - 3}$ • 18 ●

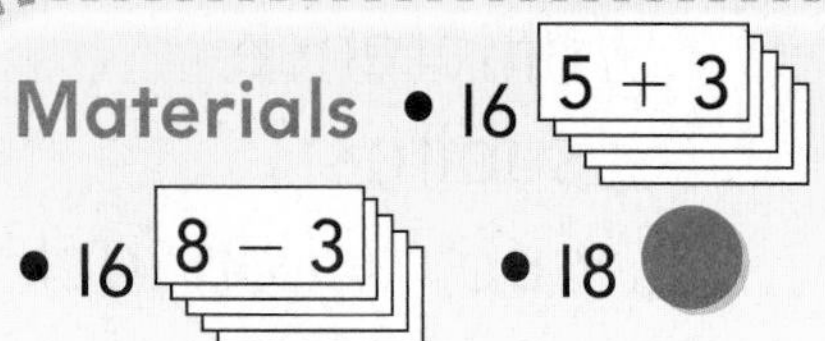

Play with a partner.

Each player picks ● or ●.

1. Mix the addition cards. Each player gets 8 cards. Show your cards faceup.
2. Put the subtraction cards in a pile facedown.
3. Take a subtraction card. Do you have the addition fact that helps you subtract?
4. If so, put the cards together and cover a space with a ●. If not, you lose a turn.
5. The first player to cover 3 spaces in a row wins.

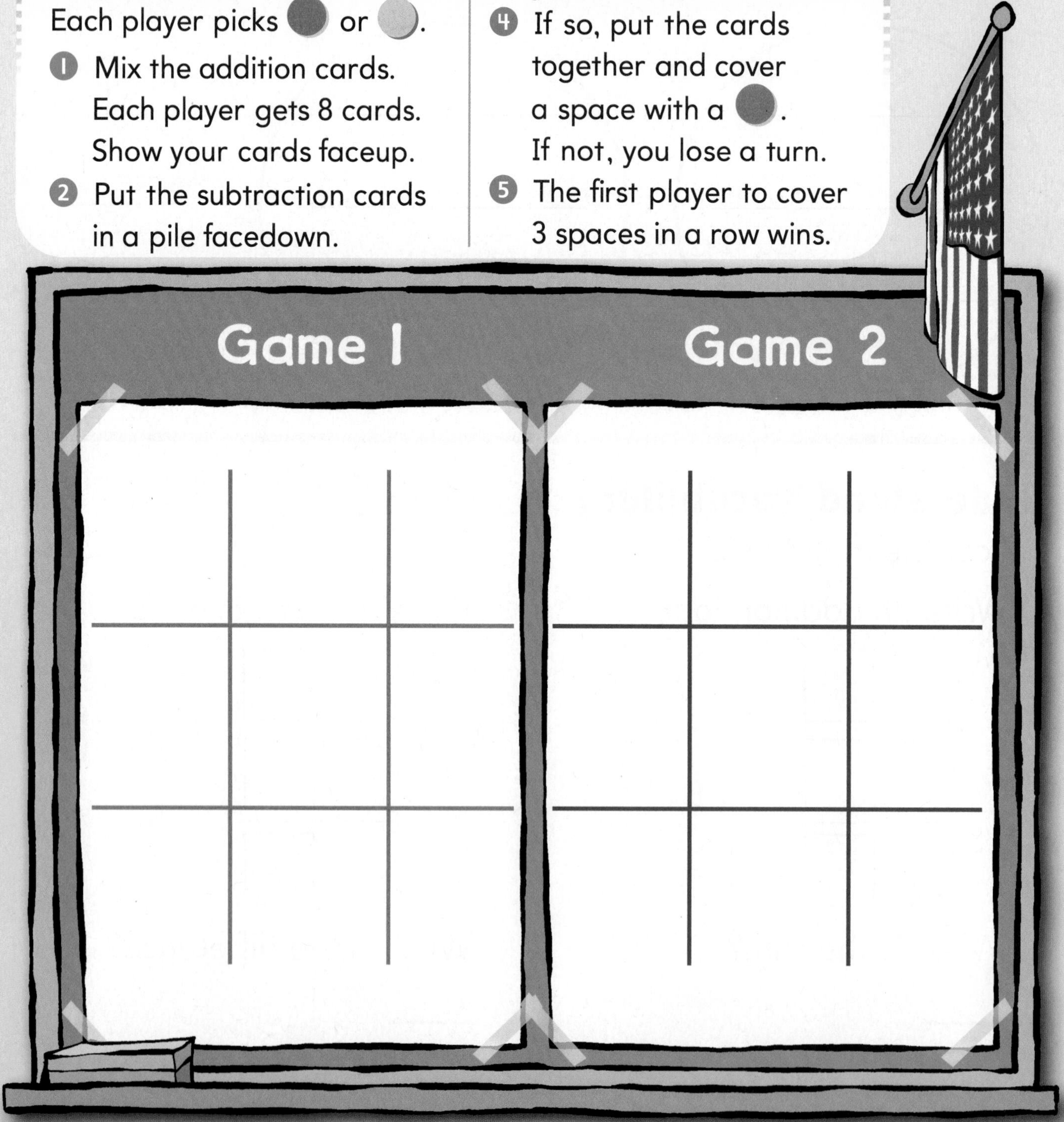

Game 1

Game 2

Name ______________________________

Problem Solving • Add or Subtract

Essential Question How can making a model help you solve a problem?

Operations and Algebraic Thinking—1.OA.1

MATHEMATICAL PRACTICES
MP.1, MP.2, MP.4

There are 16 turtles on the beach. Some swim away. Now there are 9 turtles on the beach. How many turtles swim away?

Unlock the Problem

What do I need to find?

how many turtles swim away

What information do I need to use?

16 turtles

? swim away

9 turtles now on the beach

Show how to solve the problem.

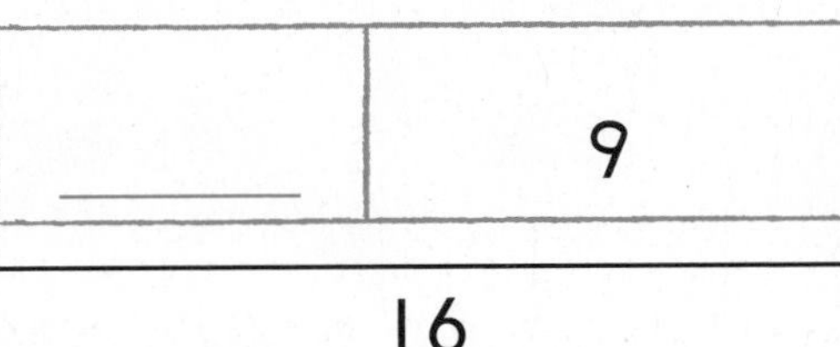

16 turtles ______ swim away 9 turtles now on the beach

HOME CONNECTION • Your child made a model to visualize the problem. The model helps your child see what part of the problem to find.

Try Another Problem

Make a model to solve.
Use ▪ to help you.

- What do I need to find?
- What information do I need to use?

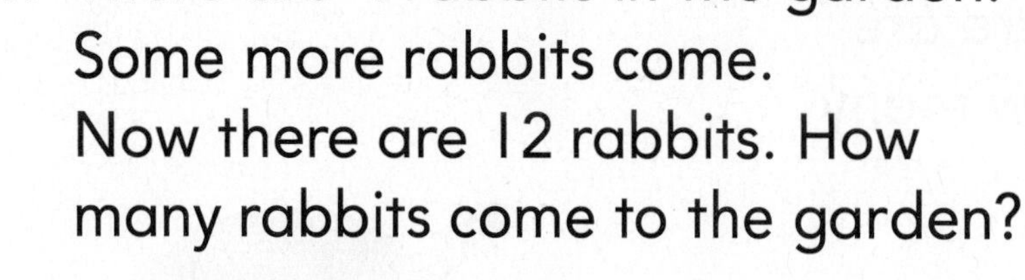

1. There are 4 rabbits in the garden. Some more rabbits come. Now there are 12 rabbits. How many rabbits come to the garden?

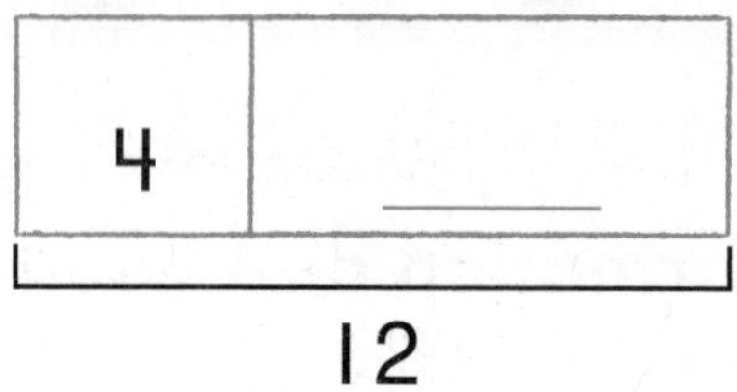

4 rabbits ______ rabbits come 12 rabbits in the garden

---

2. There are 14 birds in a tree. Some birds fly away. There are 9 birds still in the tree. How many birds fly away?

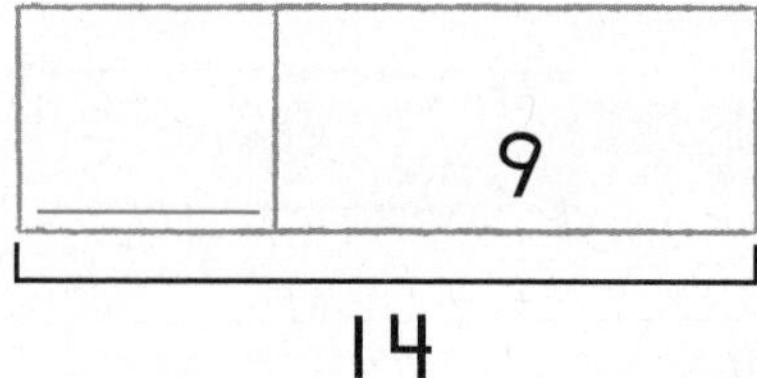

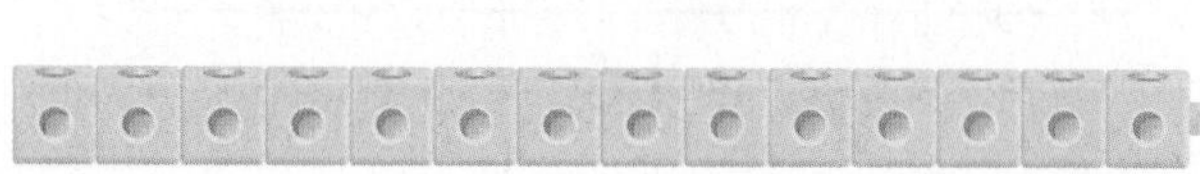

14 birds ______ birds fly away 9 birds still in the tree

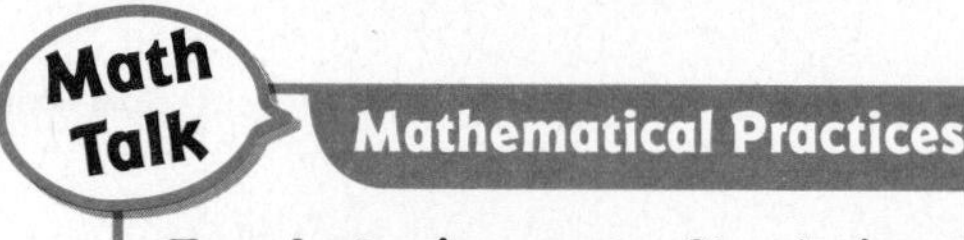

Math Talk **Mathematical Practices**

Explain how to find the missing number.

Name ______________________________

Share and Show

Make a model to solve.

✓3. There are 20 ducks in the pond. Then 10 ducks swim away. How many ducks are still in the pond?

10	____
20	

20 ducks 10 swim away ____ ducks still in the pond

---

4. THINK SMARTER 3 eagles land in the trees. Now 12 eagles are in the trees. How many eagles were in the trees to start?

____	3
12	

____ eagles 3 eagles land 12 eagles in the trees

✓5. 8 squirrels are in the park. Some more squirrels come. Now there are 16 squirrels. How many squirrels come to the park?

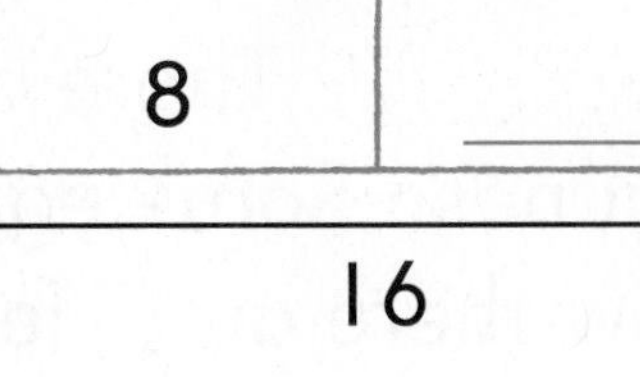

8	____
16	

8 squirrels ____ squirrels come 16 squirrels in the park

On Your Own

WRITE Math

MATHEMATICAL PRACTICE 2 Represent a Problem

Solve. Draw or write to show your work.

6. Liz picks 15 flowers. 7 are pink. The rest are yellow. How many are yellow?

____ yellow flowers

7. Cindy has 14 sand dollars. She has the same number of large and small sand dollars. Write a number sentence about the sand dollars.

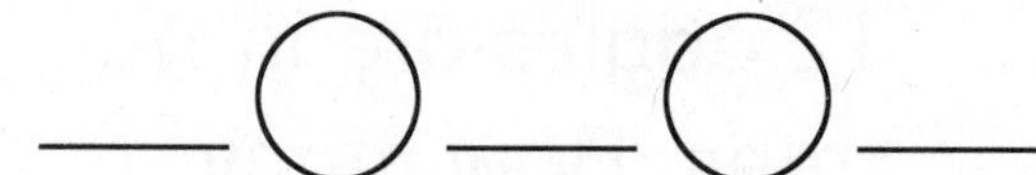

8. GO DEEPER Sam has 3 more books than Ed. Sam has 8 books. How many books does Ed have?

____ books

9. THINK SMARTER There are 7 eggs in a nest. Some eggs hatch. Now there are 5 left. How many eggs hatch?

____	5

7

7 eggs ____ hatch 5 eggs left

TAKE HOME ACTIVITY • Ask your child to look at Exercise 7 and use the number 18 as the total number of sand dollars. Then have your child write a number sentence.

FOR MORE PRACTICE: Standards Practice Book

Name ______________________________

Record Related Facts

Essential Question How do related facts help you find missing numbers?

Operations and Algebraic Thinking—1.OA.6 *Also 1.OA.8*

MATHEMATICAL PRACTICES
MP.5, MP.7, MP.8

Listen and Draw

Listen to the problem.
Model with cubes. Draw cubes.
Write the number sentence.

___ + ___ = ___

___ − ___ = ___

Math Talk **Mathematical Practices**

Explain how your model helps you write your number sentence.

FOR THE TEACHER • Read the following problem for the left box. Colin has 7 crackers. He gets 1 more cracker. How many crackers does Colin have now? Then read the following for the right box. Colin has 8 crackers. He gives one to Jacob. How many crackers does Colin have now?

Model and Draw

How can one model help you write four **related facts**?

4 + 5 = 9

9 − 5 = 4

5 + 4 = 9

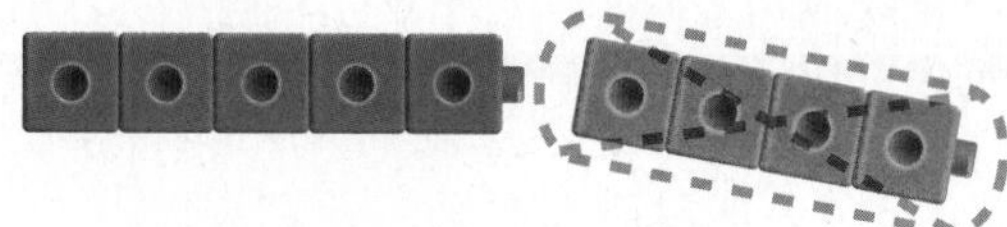

9 − 4 = 5

Share and Show

Use ▪ ▪. Add or subtract.
Complete the related facts.

1. 8 + ☐ = 15　　15 − 7 = ☐

7 + 8 = ☐　　☐ − ☐ = ☐

2. ☐ + 9 = 14　　14 − ☐ = 5

9 + 5 = ☐　　☐ − ☐ = ☐

3. 7 + ☐ = 13　　13 − 6 = ☐

6 + 7 = ☐　　☐ − ☐ = ☐

Name ______________________________

On Your Own

MATHEMATICAL PRACTICE 1 **Analyze Relationships**

Use cubes. Add or subtract. Complete the related facts.

4. $\square + 8 = 13$ $\quad$ $13 - \square = 5$

$8 + 5 = \square$ $\quad$ $\square - \square = \square$

5. $\square + 8 = 17$ $\quad$ $17 - \square = 9$

$8 + 9 = \square$ $\quad$ $\square - \square = \square$

6. $9 + \square = 15$ $\quad$ $\square - 6 = 9$

$6 + \square = 15$ $\quad$ $\square - \square = \square$

7. THINK SMARTER Circle the number sentence that has a mistake. Correct it to complete the related facts.

$7 + 9 = 16$

$16 + 9 = 7$

$9 + 7 = 16$

$16 - 7 = 9$

___ ◯ ___ ◯ ___

Problem Solving • Applications

WRITE Math

8. GO DEEPER Choose three numbers to make related facts. Choose numbers between 0 and 18. Write your numbers. Write the related facts.

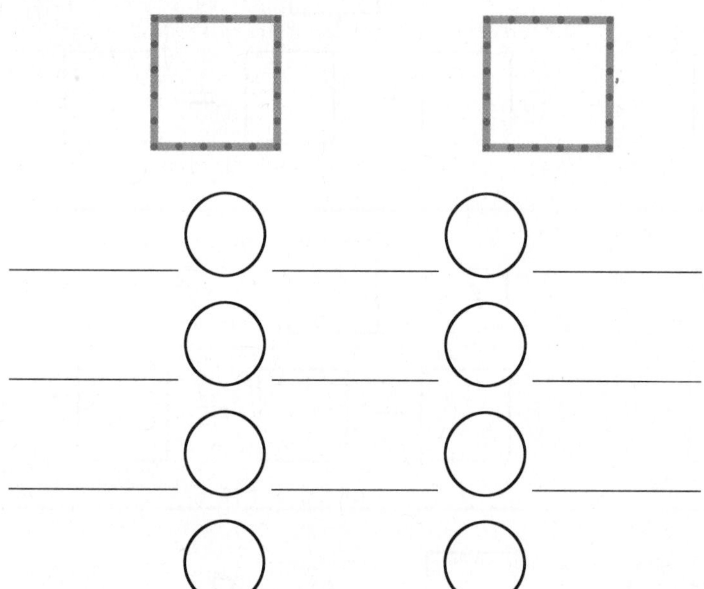

9. THINK SMARTER Which fact is a related fact?

$6 + 3 = 9$ $9 - 3 = 6$

$3 + 6 = 9$?

- ○ $6 + 9 = 15$
- ○ $9 + 3 = 12$
- ○ $9 - 6 = 3$
- ○ $6 - 3 = 3$

TAKE HOME ACTIVITY • Write an addition fact. Ask your child to write three other related facts.

FOR MORE PRACTICE: Standards Practice Book

Name ______________________________

Identify Related Facts

Essential Question How do you know if addition and subtraction facts are related?

Operations and Algebraic Thinking—1.OA.6 *Also 1.OA.8*

MATHEMATICAL PRACTICES
MP.4, MP.7, MP.8

Listen and Draw

Use cubes to show 4 + 9 = 13.
Draw cubes to show a related subtraction fact.
Write the subtraction sentence.

___ ◯ ___ ◯ ___

Math Talk Mathematical Practices

Explain why your subtraction sentence is related to 4 + 9 = 13.

FOR THE TEACHER • Have children use cubes to show 4 + 9 = 13. Then have them use cubes to show the related subtraction sentence, draw the cubes, and write the related sentence.

Model and Draw

Use the pictures. What two facts can you write?

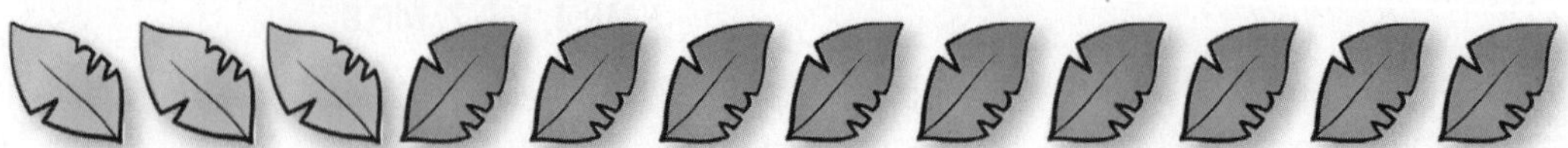

3 (+) 9 (=) 12

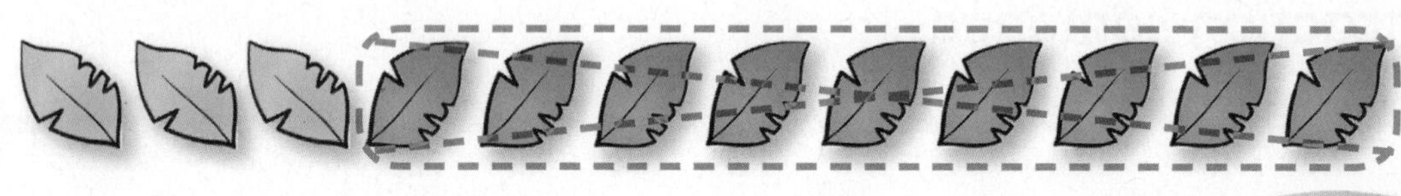

12 (−) 9 (=) 3

These are related facts. If you know one of these facts, you also know the other fact.

Share and Show

Add and subtract.
Circle the related facts.

1. $6 + 4 =$ ____
   $10 - 4 =$ ____

2. ____ $= 9 + 8$
   ____ $= 17 - 8$

3. $9 + 5 =$ ____
   $9 - 5 =$ ____

4. $8 + 7 =$ ____
   $15 - 7 =$ ____

5. ____ $= 9 + 2$
   ____ $= 9 - 2$

6. $6 + 3 =$ ____
   $12 - 3 =$ ____

7. $4 + 8 =$ ____
   $12 - 8 =$ ____

✓8. ____ $= 7 + 6$
   ____ $= 13 - 6$

✓9. $9 + 9 =$ ____
   $18 - 9 =$ ____

Name ___________________________

On Your Own

10. MATHEMATICAL PRACTICE 7 **Identify Relationships** Add and subtract. Color the leaves that have related facts.

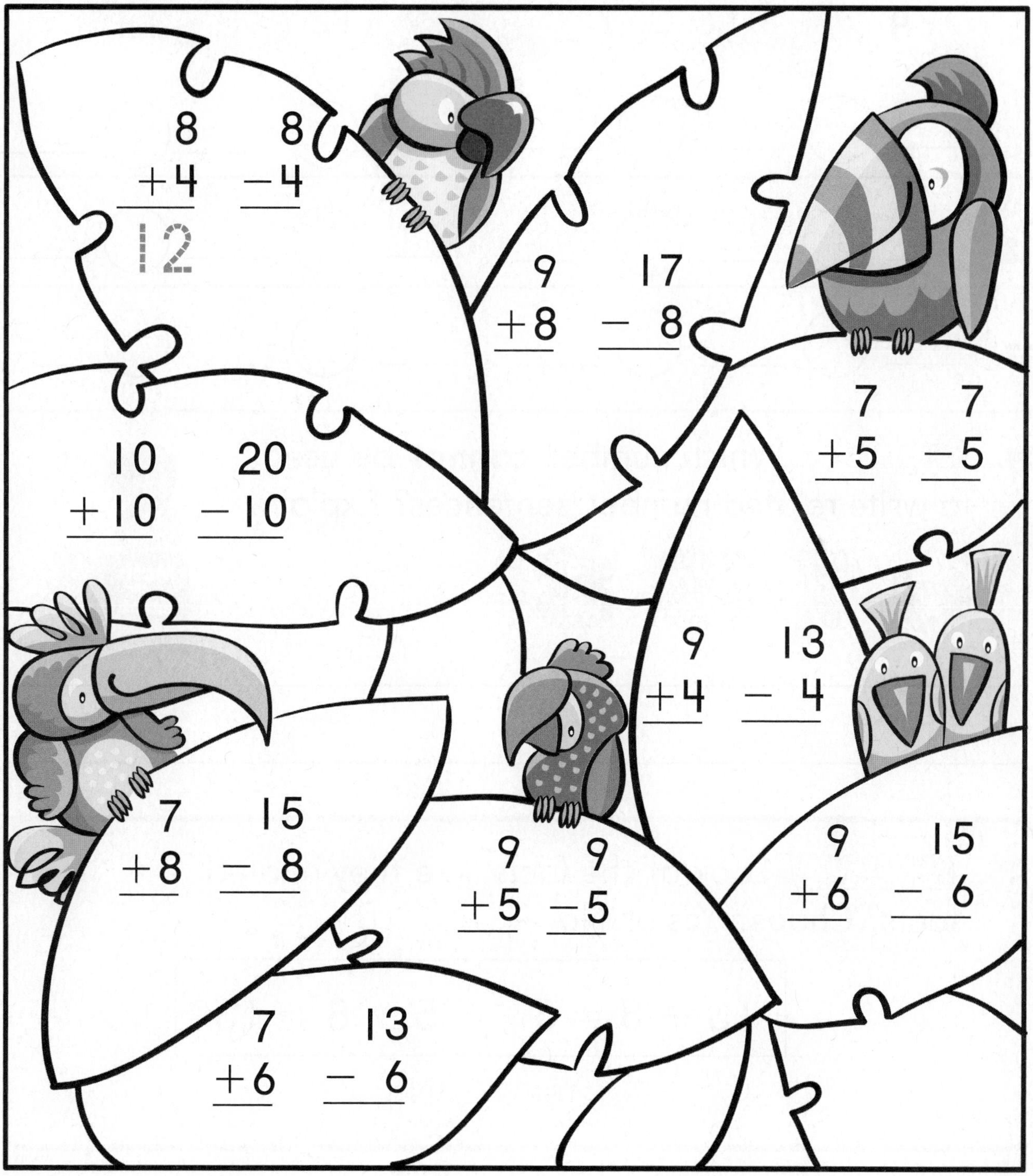

$$\begin{array}{r} 8 \\ +4 \\ \hline 12 \end{array} \quad \begin{array}{r} 8 \\ -4 \\ \hline \end{array}$$

$$\begin{array}{r} 9 \\ +8 \\ \hline \end{array} \quad \begin{array}{r} 17 \\ -8 \\ \hline \end{array}$$

$$\begin{array}{r} 10 \\ +10 \\ \hline \end{array} \quad \begin{array}{r} 20 \\ -10 \\ \hline \end{array}$$

$$\begin{array}{r} 7 \\ +5 \\ \hline \end{array} \quad \begin{array}{r} 7 \\ -5 \\ \hline \end{array}$$

$$\begin{array}{r} 9 \\ +4 \\ \hline \end{array} \quad \begin{array}{r} 13 \\ -4 \\ \hline \end{array}$$

$$\begin{array}{r} 7 \\ +8 \\ \hline \end{array} \quad \begin{array}{r} 15 \\ -8 \\ \hline \end{array}$$

$$\begin{array}{r} 9 \\ +5 \\ \hline \end{array} \quad \begin{array}{r} 9 \\ -5 \\ \hline \end{array}$$

$$\begin{array}{r} 9 \\ +6 \\ \hline \end{array} \quad \begin{array}{r} 15 \\ -6 \\ \hline \end{array}$$

$$\begin{array}{r} 7 \\ +6 \\ \hline \end{array} \quad \begin{array}{r} 13 \\ -6 \\ \hline \end{array}$$

Problem Solving • Applications

GO DEEPER Use the numbers to write related addition and subtraction sentences.

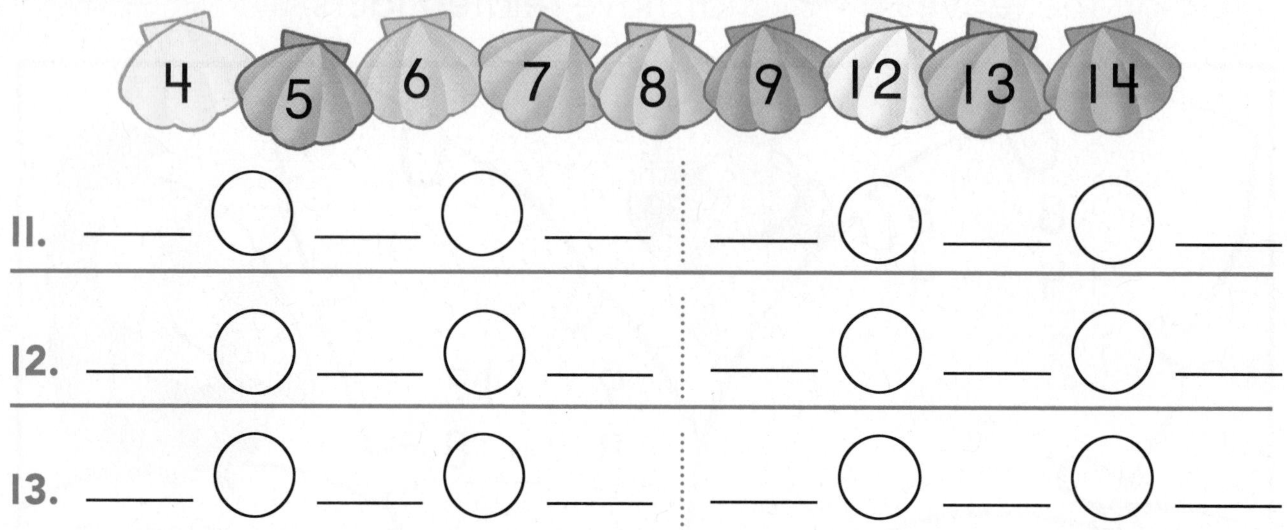

11. ___ ◯ ___ ◯ ___ | ___ ◯ ___ ◯ ___

12. ___ ◯ ___ ◯ ___ | ___ ◯ ___ ◯ ___

13. ___ ◯ ___ ◯ ___ | ___ ◯ ___ ◯ ___

14. THINK SMARTER Which number **cannot** be used to write related number sentences? Explain.

____

____

15. THINK SMARTER Look at the facts. Are they related facts? Choose Yes or No.

13 − 8 = 5	5 + 8 = 13

Yes　　No

TAKE HOME ACTIVITY • Write 7, 9, 16, +, −, and = on separate slips of paper. Have your child use the slips of paper to show related facts.

FOR MORE PRACTICE: Standards Practice Book

Name ______________________________

Use Addition to Check Subtraction

Essential Question How can you use addition to check subtraction?

Operations and Algebraic Thinking—1.OA.6 *Also 1.OA.8*

MATHEMATICAL PRACTICES
MP.4, MP.7, MP.8

Listen and Draw Real World

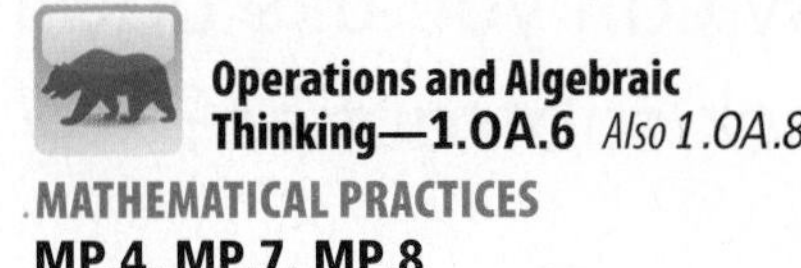

Draw and write to solve the problem.

____ ○ ____ ○ ____

____ ○ ____ ○ ____

FOR THE TEACHER • Read the problem. Erin has 11 books. I borrow 4 of them. How many books does Erin still have? Allow children time to solve, using the top workspace. Then read this part of the problem: I give 4 books back to Erin. How many books does Erin have now?

Math Talk **Mathematical Practices**

Does Erin get all her books back? Use the number sentences to **explain** how you know.

Model and Draw

Why can you use addition to check subtraction?

You subtract one part from the whole. The difference is the other part.

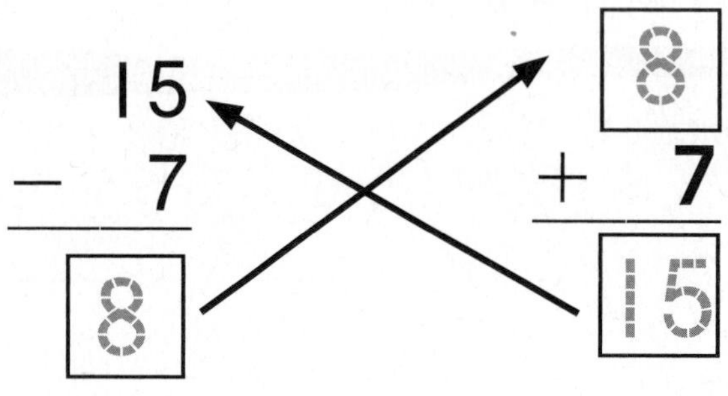

When you add the parts, you get the same whole.

Share and Show

Subtract. Then add to check your answer.

1.

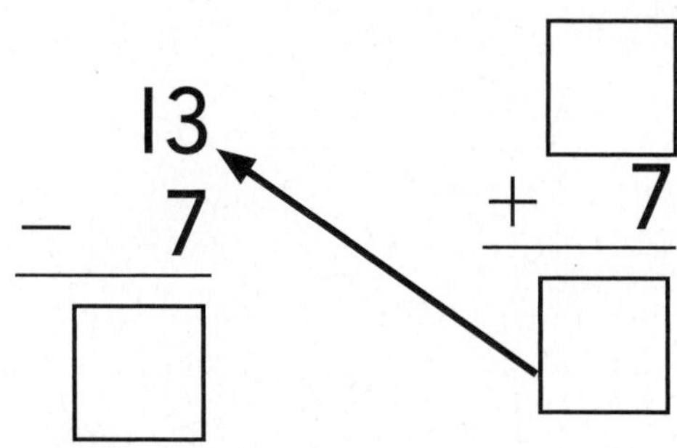

2.

14
− 5

+ 5

3.

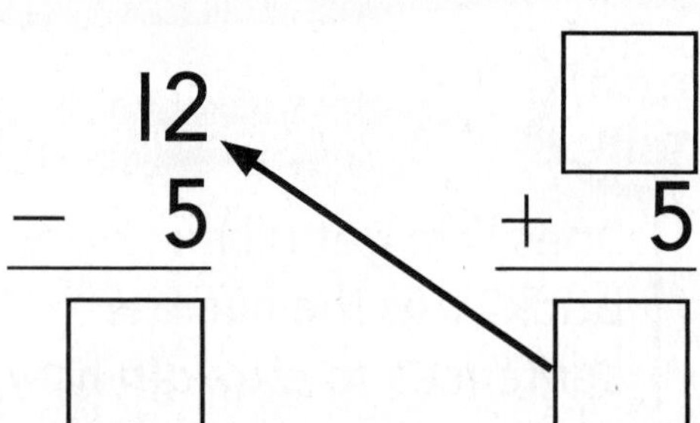

4.

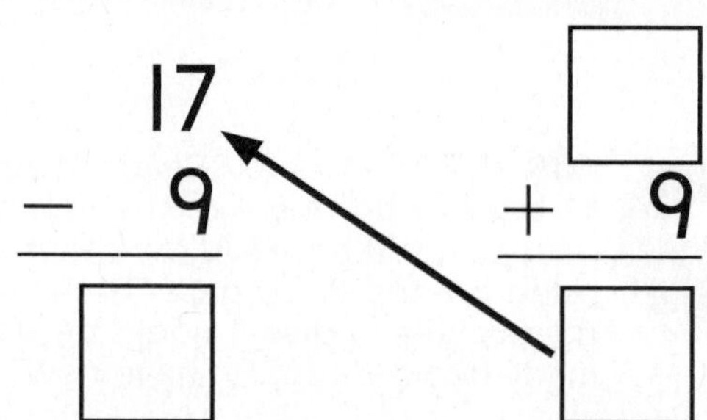

Name ________________________

On Your Own

MATHEMATICAL PRACTICE 7 **Look for Structure** Subtract. Then add to check your answer.

5. $11 - 3 = \square$

$\square + 3 = \square$

6. $13 - 9 = \square$

$\square + 9 = \square$

7. THINK SMARTER Brianna has 13 sand dollars. Some sand dollars are broken. 5 sand dollars are not broken. Write number sentences about the sand dollars.

___ ◯ ___ ◯ ___

___ ◯ ___ ◯ ___

8. GO DEEPER Subtract to solve. Then add to check your answer.

Liam took 15 balloons to the party. All but 6 of the balloons were red. How many balloons were red?

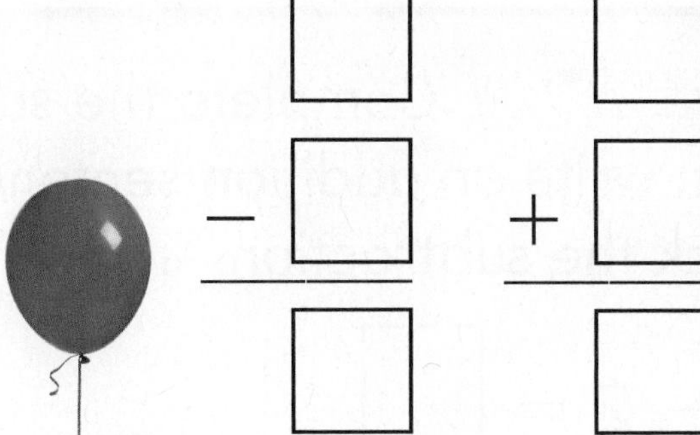

$\square - \square = \square$ $\square + \square = \square$

____ red balloons

TAKE HOME ACTIVITY • Write 11 − 7 = □ on a sheet of paper. Ask your child to find the difference and then write an addition sentence he or she can use to check the subtraction.

FOR MORE PRACTICE: Standards Practice Book

Name ______________________________

Concepts and Skills

Use [cubes]. Add or subtract.
Complete the related facts. (1.OA.6)

1. $\square + 8 = 14$ $\quad 14 - \square = 6$

$8 + 6 = \square$ $\quad \square - \square = \square$

2. $7 + \square = 13$ $\quad \square - 6 = 7$

$6 + \square = 13$ $\quad \square - \square = \square$

Add and subtract. Circle the related facts. (1.OA.6)

3. $9 + 3 =$ ___

$9 - 3 =$ ___

4. $7 + 8 =$ ___

$15 - 8 =$ ___

5. ___ $= 6 + 5$

___ $= 6 - 5$

Personal Math Trainer

6. THINK SMARTER + Complete the subtraction. Then write an addition sentence to check the subtraction. (1.OA.6)

$11 - 2 = \square$

___ ◯ ___ ◯ ___

Name ______________________________

Algebra • Unknown Numbers

Essential Question How can you use a related fact to find an unknown number?

Operations and Algebraic Thinking—1.OA.8 *Also 1.OA.6*

MATHEMATICAL PRACTICES
MP.1, MP.7, MP.8

Listen and Draw

Listen to the problem. Use cubes to show the story. Draw to show your work.

Math Talk **Mathematical Practices**

How many toy cars are blue? **Explain** how you got your answer.

FOR THE TEACHER • Read the problem. Calvin has 7 toy cars that are red. He has some blue toy cars. He has 10 toy cars. How many blue toy cars does Calvin have?

Model and Draw

What are the unknown numbers?

$8 + \boxed{3} = 11$

$11 - 8 = \boxed{3}$

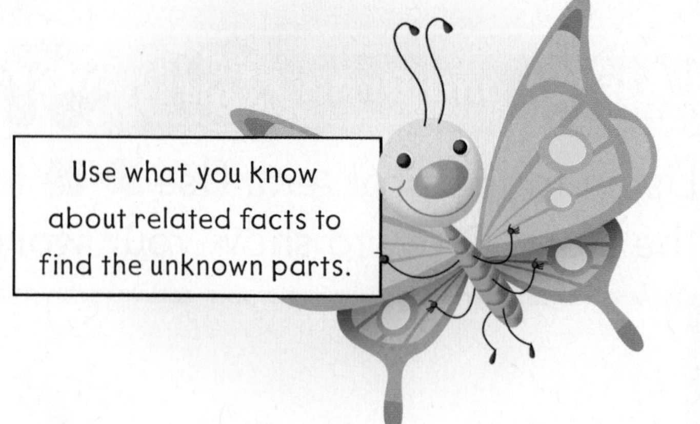

Share and Show

Use cubes to find the unknown numbers. Write the numbers.

1. $8 + \square = 15$

   $15 - 8 = \square$

2. $13 = 9 + \square$

   $\square = 13 - 9$

3. $5 + \square = 14$

   $14 - 5 = \square$

4. $14 = 6 + \square$

   $\square = 14 - 6$

5. $9 + \square = 16$

   $16 - 9 = \square$

6. $17 = 8 + \square$

   $\square = 17 - 8$

Name ____________________

On Your Own

HINT
Use a related fact to help you.

MATHEMATICAL PRACTICE 7 **Identify Relationships**

Write the unknown numbers.
Use cubes if you need to.

7. $7 + \square = 15$

$15 - 7 = \square$

8. $5 + \square = 11$

$11 - 5 = \square$

9. $\square + 10 = 20$

$20 - 10 = \square$

10. $\square + 9 = 16$

$16 - 9 = \square$

11. $\square = 9 + 9$

$9 = \square - 9$

12. $\square = 5 + 8$

$5 = \square - 8$

13. 

Solve.
Rick has 10 party hats.
He needs 19 hats for his party. How many more party hats does Rick need?

Math on the Spot

_____ party hats

Problem Solving • Applications

Use cubes or draw a picture to solve.

14. Todd has 12 bunnies. He gives 4 bunnies to his sister. How many bunnies does Todd have now?

____ bunnies

15. Brad has 11 trucks. Some are small trucks. 4 are big trucks. How many small trucks does he have?

____	4

11

____ small trucks

16. GO DEEPER There are 15 children at the park. 6 of the children go home. Then 4 more children come to the park. How many children are in the park now?

____ children

17. THINK SMARTER Use cubes to find the unknown numbers. Write the numbers.

$9 + \_\_\_\_ = 17$

$17 - 9 = \_\_\_\_$

TAKE HOME ACTIVITY • Have your child explain how using subtraction can help him or her find the unknown number in $7 + \square = 16$.

FOR MORE PRACTICE: Standards Practice Book

Name ________________________________

Algebra • Use Related Facts

Essential Question How can you use a related fact to find an unknown number?

Operations and Algebraic Thinking—1.OA.8 *Also 1.OA.6*

MATHEMATICAL PRACTICES
MP.2, MP.4

Listen and Draw Real World

What number can you add to 8 to get 10?
Draw a picture to solve. Write the unknown number.

8 + ☐ = 10

Math Talk **Mathematical Practices**

Describe how to solve this problem using cubes.

FOR THE TEACHER • Have children draw a picture and complete the number sentence to show the number that can be added to 8 to get 10.

Model and Draw

You can use an addition fact to find a related subtraction fact.

Find 10 − 3.

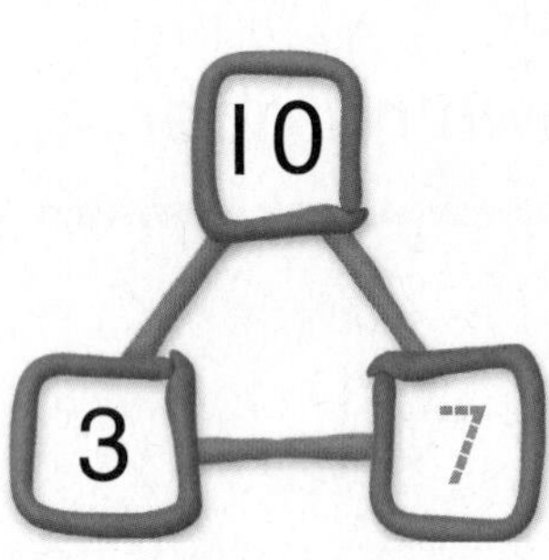

3 + 7 = 10

10 − 3 = 7

Share and Show

Write the unknown numbers.

1. Find 14 − 8.

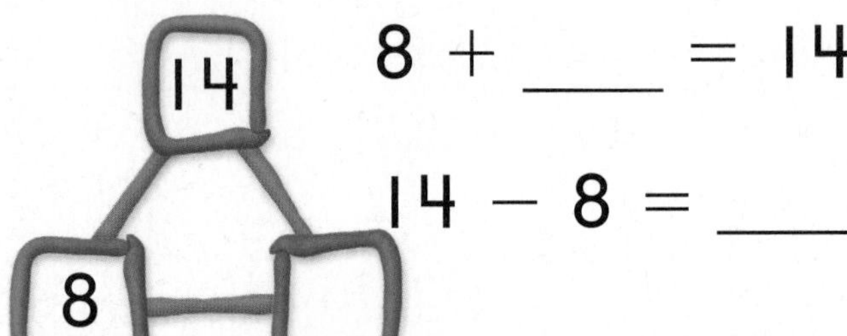

8 + ____ = 14

14 − 8 = ____

2. Find 17 − 8.

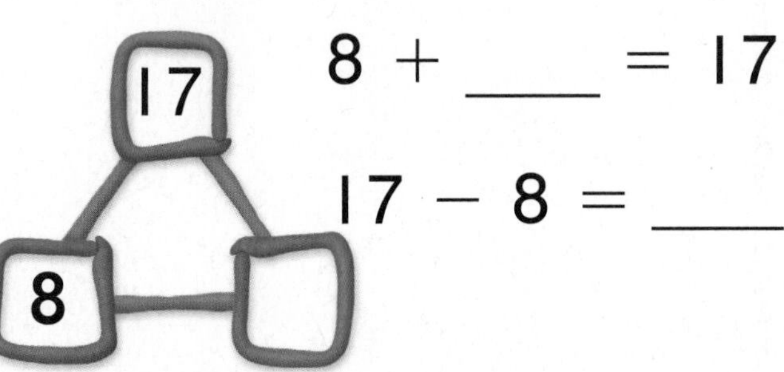

8 + ____ = 17

17 − 8 = ____

3. Find 11 − 6.

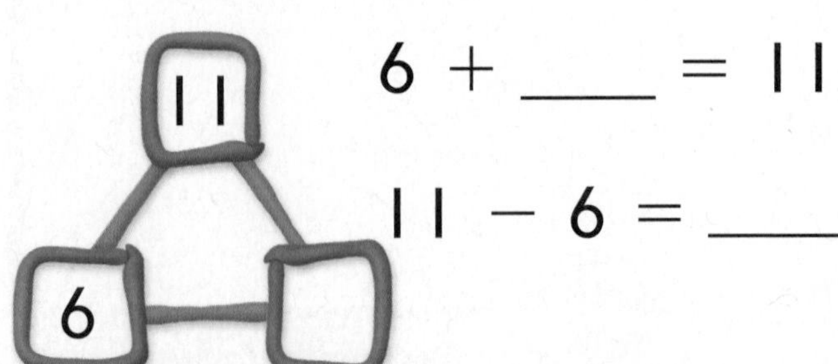

6 + ____ = 11

11 − 6 = ____

4. Find 15 − 9.

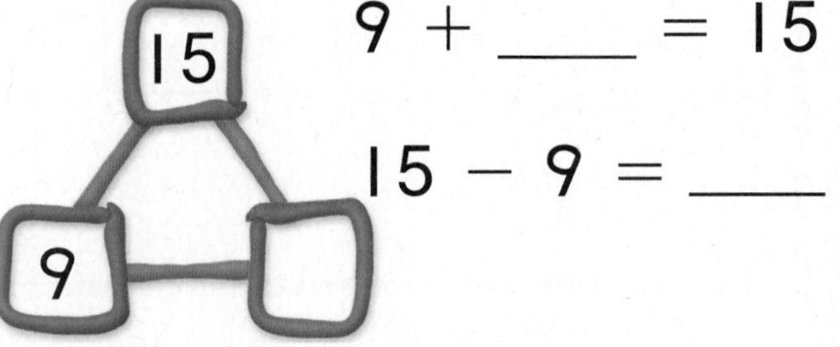

9 + ____ = 15

15 − 9 = ____

Name ________________

On Your Own

Write the unknown numbers.

5. Find 20 − 10.

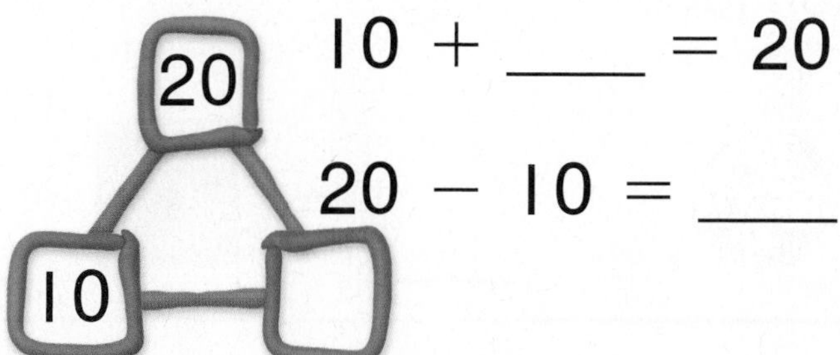

6. Find 13 − 4.

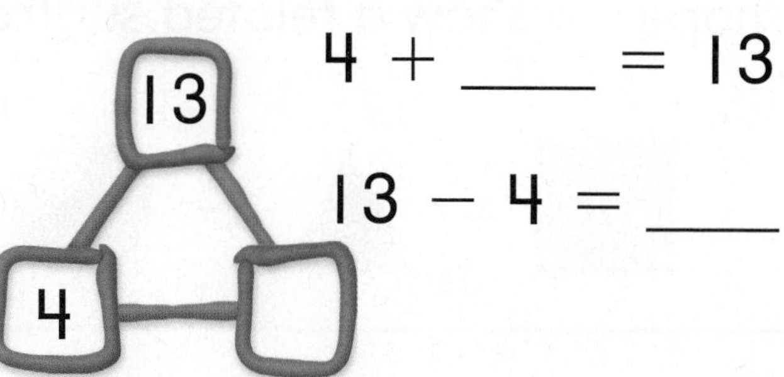

7. Find 12 − 7.

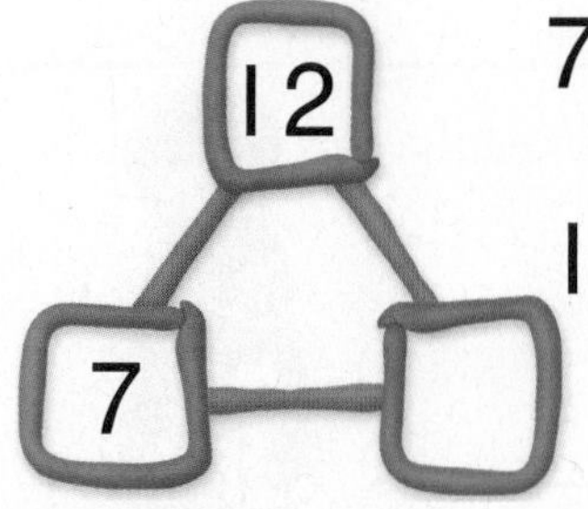

7 + ___ = 12

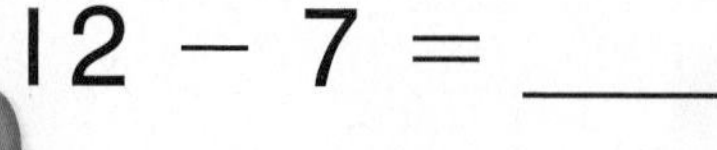

8. Find 15 − 8.

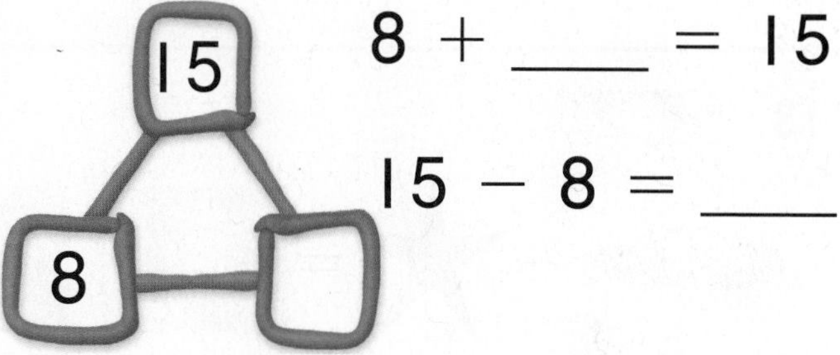

GO DEEPER Write an addition sentence to help you find the difference. Then write the related subtraction sentence to solve.

9. Find 11 − 5.

10. Find 13 − 6.

___ = ___ + ___

___ = ___ − ___

Problem Solving • Applications

WRITE Math

MATHEMATICAL PRACTICE 2 **Reason Abstractly** Look at the shapes in the addition sentence. Draw shapes to show a related subtraction fact.

11.

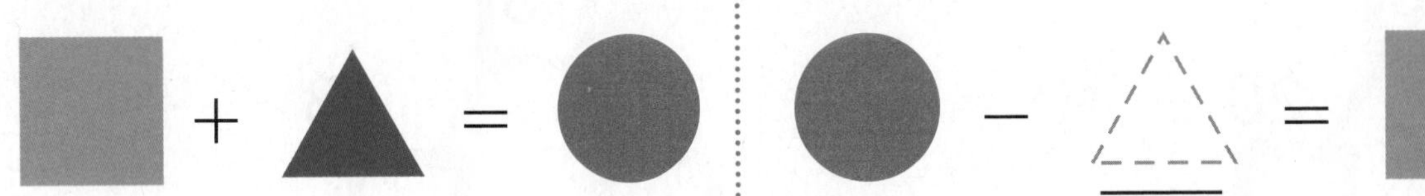

12.

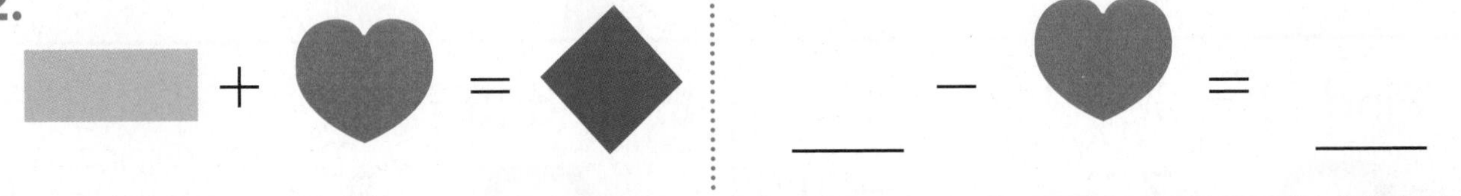

13. THINK SMARTER

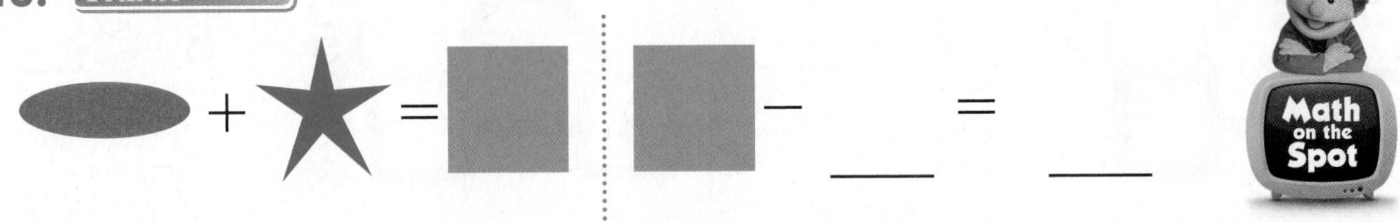

Math on the Spot

14. THINK SMARTER Which is the unknown number in these related facts?

$\square + 5 = 12$ $12 - 5 = \square$

$5 + \square = 12$ $12 - \square = 5$

○ 5 ○ 7 ○ 8 ○ 9

TAKE HOME ACTIVITY • Give your child 5 small objects, such as paper clips. Then ask your child how many more objects he or she would need to have 12.

FOR MORE PRACTICE: Standards Practice Book

Name ______________________

Choose an Operation

Essential Question How do you choose when to add and when to subtract to solve a problem?

Operations and Algebraic Thinking—1.OA.1 *Also 1.OA.6*

MATHEMATICAL PRACTICES
MP.3, MP.4, MP.6

Listen to the problem. Use ● to solve.
Draw a picture to show your work.

____ white balloons

Math Talk **Mathematical Practices**

How did you solve this problem? **Explain.**

FOR THE TEACHER • Read the following problem. Kira has 16 balloons. She has 8 pink balloons. The other balloons are white. How many white balloons does she have?

Model and Draw

Mary sees 8 squirrels. Jack sees 9 more squirrels than Mary. How many squirrels does Jack see?

Do you add or subtract to solve?

add   subtract    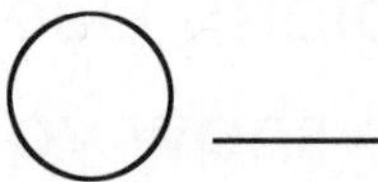

 ____ squirrels

Share and Show 

Circle **add** or **subtract**.
Write a number sentence to solve.

1. Hanna has 5 markers. Owen has 9 more markers than Hanna. How many markers does Owen have?

   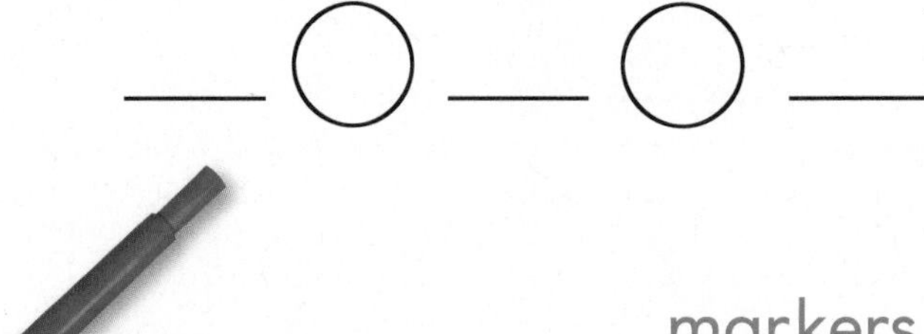

   ____ ◯ ____ ◯ ____

   add   **subtract**

   ____ markers

2. Angel has 13 apples. He gives some away. Then there were 5 apples. How many apples does he give away?

   ____ ◯ ____ ◯ ____

   add   **subtract**

   ____ apples

3. Deon has 18 blocks. He builds a house with 9 of the blocks. How many blocks does Deon have now?

   ____ ◯ ____ ◯ ____

   add   **subtract**

   ____ blocks

Name ______________________________

On Your Own

Circle **add** or **subtract.**
Write a number sentence to solve.

4. Rob sees 5 raccoons. Talia sees 4 more raccoons than Rob. How many raccoons do they see?

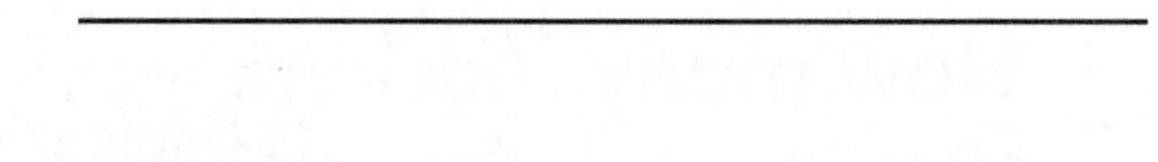

____ raccoons

add **subtract**

5. Eli has a box with 12 eggs. His other box has no eggs. How many eggs are in both boxes?

____ eggs

add **subtract**

6. Leah has a bowl with 16 fish. Some fish have long tails. 7 fish have short tails. How many fish have long tails?

____ fish

add **subtract**

7. GO DEEPER Sasha has 8 red apples. She has 3 fewer green apples than red apples. How many apples does she have?

____

____ apples

add **subtract**

Problem Solving • Applications

MATHEMATICAL PRACTICE 3 **Apply** Choose a way to solve. Write or draw to explain.

8. James has 4 big markers and 7 skinny markers. How many markers does he have?

____ markers

9. Sam has 9 baseball cards. She wants to have 17 cards. How many more cards does she need?

____ more cards

10. THINK SMARTER Annie gets 15 pennies on Monday. She gets 1 more penny each day. How many pennies does she have on Friday?

____ pennies

11. THINK SMARTER Beth has 5 grapes. A friend gives her 8 grapes. How many grapes does Beth have now? Draw a picture to show your work.

Beth has ____ grapes.

TAKE HOME ACTIVITY • Ask your child to write a number sentence that could be used to solve Exercise 9.

FOR MORE PRACTICE: Standards Practice Book

Name ______________________________

Algebra • Ways to Make Numbers to 20

Essential Question How can you add and subtract in different ways to make the same number?

Operations and Algebraic Thinking—1.OA.6

MATHEMATICAL PRACTICES
MP.5, MP.7

Listen and Draw

Use connecting cubes. Show two ways to make 10.
Draw to show your work.

Way One	Way Two

Math Talk — Mathematical Practices

Explain how your models show two ways to make 10.

FOR THE TEACHER • Have children use connecting cubes to show two ways to make 10. Then have them draw to show the two ways.

Model and Draw

How can you make the number 12 in different ways?

You can add or subtract to make 12.

12
6 + 6
5 + 4 + 3
12 − 0

Share and Show

Use cubes. Write ways to make the number at the top.

1.

13
___ + ___
___ − ___
___ + ___ + ___
___ + ___
___ ◯ ___

2.

10
___ − ___
___ + ___
___ − ___
___ + ___ + ___
___ ◯ ___

Name ___________________________________

On Your Own

MATHEMATICAL PRACTICE 5 **Use Appropriate Tools**

Use ▪ ▪ ▪. Write ways to make the number at the top.

3.

17
____ + ____ + ____
____ + ____
____ − ____
____ ◯ ____

4.

14
____ + ____
____ + ____ + ____
____ − ____
____ ◯ ____

5.

16
____ + ____
____ + ____ + ____
____ − ____
____ ◯ ____

6.

18
____ + ____
____ + ____
____ + ____ + ____
____ ◯ ____

THINK SMARTER Choose a number less than 20. Write the number. Write two ways to make your number. ☐

7.

8.

Problem Solving • Applications

WRITE Math

GO DEEPER Write numbers to make each line have the same sum.

9.

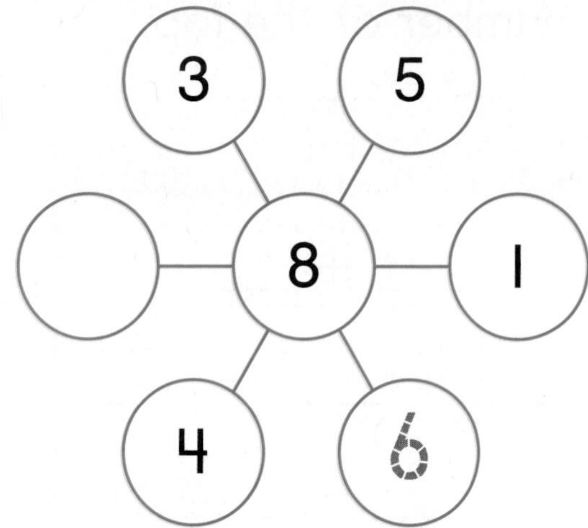

10.

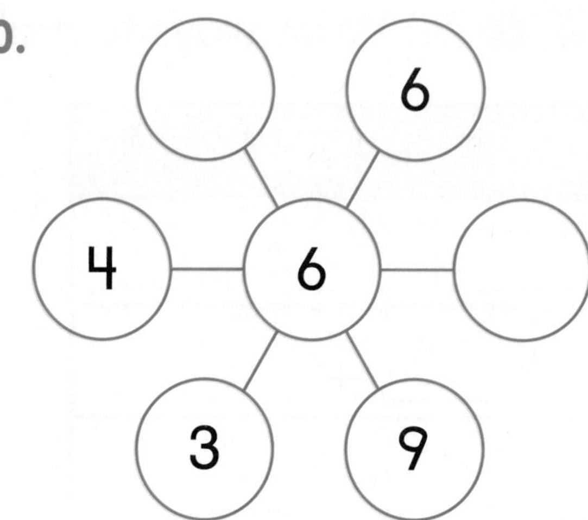

11. GO DEEPER Choose a number from 14 to 20 to be the sum. Write numbers to make each line have your sum.

sum for each line ☐

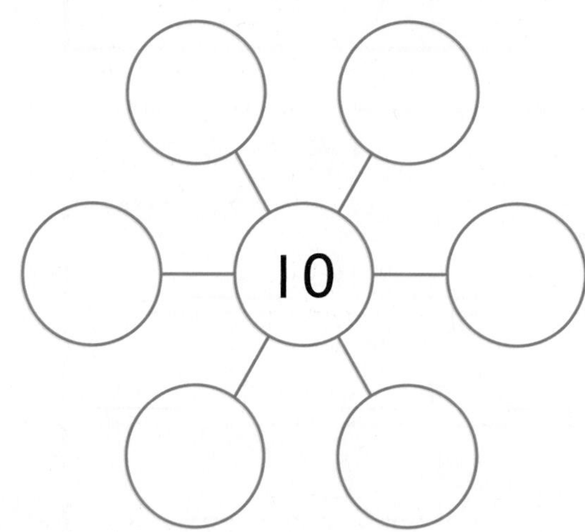

12. THINK SMARTER Choose all the ways that make 13.

- ○ 10 + 3
- ○ 9 + 3 + 1
- ○ 8 + 2 + 2

TAKE HOME ACTIVITY • Have your child explain three different ways to make 15. Encourage him or her to use addition and subtraction, including addition of three numbers.

FOR MORE PRACTICE: Standards Practice Book

Name ______________________________

Algebra • Equal and Not Equal

Essential Question How can you decide if a number sentence is true or false?

Operations and Algebraic Thinking—1.OA.7 *Also 1.OA.6*

MATHEMATICAL PRACTICES
MP.6, MP.7

Listen and Draw

Color the cards that make the same number.

2 + 6	12 − 6	6 + 1
13 − 6	3 + 3 + 1	10 + 6
3 + 4	4 + 3	5 + 2 + 5
3 + 2 + 2	11 − 2	16 − 9

Math Talk **Mathematical Practices**

Explain why you can use two of the cards you color and an equal sign to make a number sentence.

FOR THE TEACHER • Have children color the cards that make the same number.

Model and Draw

The equal sign means that both sides are the same.

Write a number to make each true.

$4 + 5 = 5 + 5$ is **not** true. It is false.

$9 = \underline{9}$ $4 + 5 = \_\_\_$ $4 + 5 = \_\_\_ + 4$

Share and Show

THINK
Are both sides equal?

Which is true? Circle your answer.
Which is false? Cross out your answer.

1. $7 = 8 - 1$

   $1 + 2 = 3 - 2$

2. $4 + 1 = 5 + 2$

   $6 - 6 = 7 - 7$

3. $7 + 2 = 6 + 3$

   $8 - 2 = 6 + 4$

4. $5 - 4 = 4 - 3$

   $10 = 1 + 0$

Name ______________________________

On Your Own

MATHEMATICAL PRACTICE 6 **Attend to Precision**

Which are true? Circle your answers.
Which are false? Cross out your answers.

5. $1 + 9 = 9 - 1$	$8 + 1 = 2 + 7$	$19 = 19$
6. $8 = 5 + 3$	$8 + 5 = 5 + 8$	$6 + 2 = 4 + 4$
7. $9 + 7 = 16$	$16 - 9 = 9 + 7$	$9 - 7 = 7 + 9$
8. $12 - 3 = 9 - 0$	$11 = 1 + 5 + 5$	$10 = 8 - 2$

Write numbers to make sentences that are true.

9. $2 + 10 = 7 +$ ____

10. ____ $= 2 + 3 + 4$

11. $0 + 9 =$ ____ $- 9$

12. ____ $+ 7 = 7 + 6$

13. THINK SMARTER Write numbers to show expressions of equal value.

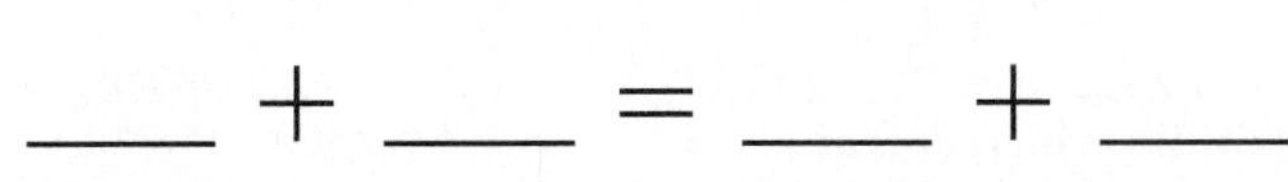

____ + ____ = ____ + ____

Problem Solving • Applications

WRITE Math

14. Which are true? Use [crayon] to color.

20 = 20	9 + 1 + 1 = 11	8 − 0 = 8
12 = 1 + 2	10 + 1 = 1 + 10	7 = 14 + 7
	6 = 2 + 2 + 2	
	11 − 5 = 1 + 5	
	1 + 2 + 3 = 4 + 5	

15. THINK SMARTER Use the same numbers. Write a different number sentence that is true.

7 + 8 = 15

___ = ___ ◯ ___

Personal Math Trainer

16. THINK SMARTER + Is the math sentence true? Circle Yes or No.

5 − 4 = 9 − 8	○ Yes	○ No
13 = 5 + 7	○ Yes	○ No
6 + 2 = 2 + 6	○ Yes	○ No

TAKE HOME ACTIVITY • Write 10 = 7 − 3 and 10 = 7 + 3 on a sheet of paper. Ask your child to explain which is true.

FOR MORE PRACTICE: Standards Practice Book

Name ______________________________

Facts Practice to 20

Essential Question How can addition and subtraction strategies help you find sums and differences?

Operations and Algebraic Thinking—1.OA.6
MATHEMATICAL PRACTICES
MP.2, MP.6

Listen and Draw

What is 2 + 8?
Use ●. Draw to show a strategy you can use to solve.

$2 + 8 = \_\_\_\_$

Math Talk — Mathematical Practices

What other strategy could you use to solve the addition fact?

FOR THE TEACHER • Have children use two-color counters to model a strategy to solve the addition fact. Then have them draw a picture to show the strategy they used.

Model and Draw

Sam is reading a story that has 10 pages. He has read 4 pages. How many pages does he have left to read?

THINK
I can use a related addition fact to solve 10 − 4.

What is 10 − 4?

4 + [6] = 10

So, 10 − 4 = 6.

Share and Show

Add or subtract.

1. 2 + 5 = ____	2. 9 − 6 = ____	3. ____ = 9 + 3
4. 15 − 7 = ____	5. 3 − 1 = ____	6. ____ = 2 + 6
7. 2 + ☐ = 11	8. 10 − ☐ = 2	9. 8 = 8 + ☐
10. 12 − 9 = ____	11. 12 − 4 = ____	12. ____ = 4 + 9
13. ☐ + 8 = 13	14. ☐ − 1 = 6	15. 9 = ☐ + 3
16. 16 − 7 = ____	✓17. 11 − 8 = ____	✓18. ____ = 8 + 7

Name ____________________

On Your Own

MATHEMATICAL PRACTICE 6 **Attend to Precision**

Add or subtract.

19. $6 + 0 = $ ___

20. $17 - 8 = $ ___

21. $7 + 4 = $ ___

22. $9 - 0 = $ ___

23. $17 - 9 = $ ___

24. $4 + 6 = $ ___

25. $7 + \square = 10$

26. $8 - \square = 3$

27. $8 + \square = 11$

28. $8 - \square = 2$

29. $10 - \square = 6$

30. $9 + \square = 17$

31. $6 + 7 = $ ___

32. $4 - \square = 0$

33. $5 + \square = 11$

34. $13 - 6 = $ ___

35. $17 - 9 = $ ___

36. $8 + \square = 16$

37. $10 + 5 = $ ___

38. $13 - 3 = $ ___

39. $10 + \square = 13$

40. $20 - 10 = $ ___

41. $10 - \square = 9$

42. $9 + \square = 19$

43. THINK SMARTER Use the clues to write the addition fact. The sum is 14. One addend is 2 more than the other.

$\square + \square = \square$

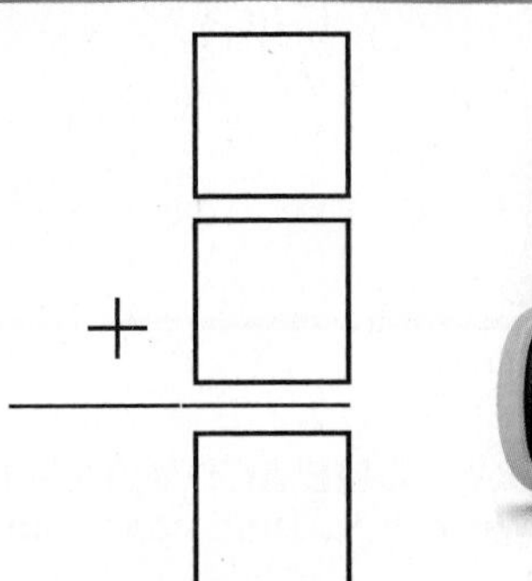

Problem Solving • Applications

Solve. Write or draw to explain.

44. There are 14 rabbits. Then 7 rabbits hop away. How many rabbits are there now?

_____ rabbits

---

45. There are 11 dogs at the park. 2 dogs are gray. The rest are brown. How many dogs are brown?

_____ brown dogs

---

46. GO DEEPER Fill in the blanks. Write the addition fact. Solve.

There are _____ ladybugs on a leaf. Then _____ more ladybugs come. How many ladybugs are there now?

_____ ladybugs

47. THINK SMARTER Marco has 13 marbles. Lucy has 8 marbles. How many more marbles does Marco have than Lucy? Write or draw to show your work.

_____ more marbles

TAKE HOME ACTIVITY • Have your child draw a picture to solve 7 + 4. Then have him or her tell a related subtraction fact.

FOR MORE PRACTICE: Standards Practice Book

Name ______________________

Chapter 5 Review/Test

1. There are 2 dogs in the park. Some more dogs come. Now there are 9 in all. How many dogs come?

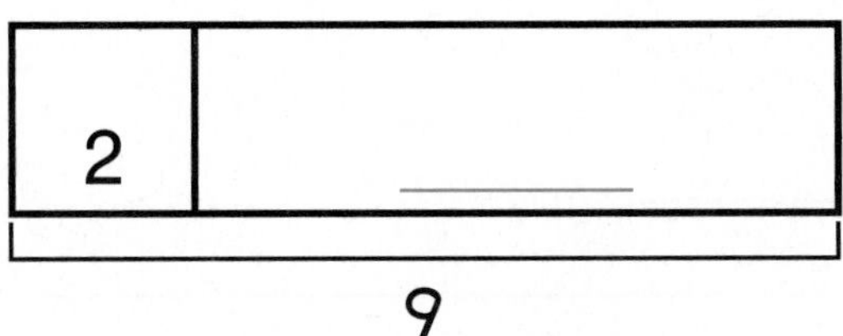

2 dogs ______ come 9 dogs in all

2. Which fact is a related fact?

$5 + 3 = 8$ $8 - 5 = 3$

$3 + 5 = 8$?

$8 - 3 = 5$	$8 + 5 = 13$	$8 + 3 = 11$	$5 - 3 = 2$
○	○	○	○

3. Look at the facts. Are they related facts? Choose Yes or No.

$14 - 6 = 8$	$8 + 6 = 14$

Yes No

4. Tom has 12 pennies. He spends 7 pennies. How many pennies does he have now?

Write a number sentence to solve. Then write an addition sentence to check.

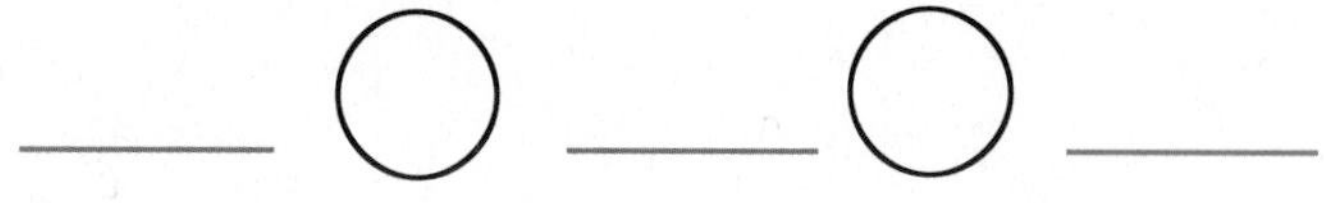

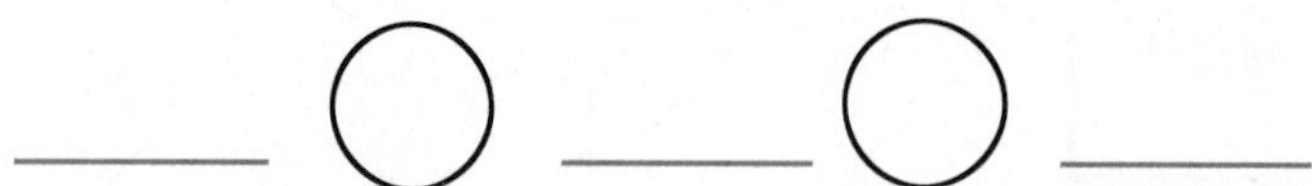

5. Use ■, ■ to find the unknown numbers. Write the numbers.

6 + ____ = 16

16 − 6 = ____

6. Which is the unknown number in these related facts?

□ + 4 = 13   13 − 4 = □

4 + □ = 13   13 − □ = 4

5	7	8	9
○	○	○	○

Name ___________________________

7. Joe has 7 blue marbles. A friend gives him 6 red marbles. How many marbles does Joe have now? Draw a picture to show your work.

Joe has _____ marbles.

---

8. Choose all the ways that make 12.

- ○ $4 + 8$
- ○ $6 + 5$
- ○ $5 + 5 + 2$

---

9. Is the math sentence true? Choose Yes or No.

$7 + 2 = 9 - 2$	○ Yes	○ No
$9 = 6 + 3$	○ Yes	○ No
$5 + 4 = 4 + 5$	○ Yes	○ No

10. Ann has 14 white socks. Bill has 6 white socks. How many more white socks does Ann have than Bill? Write or draw to show your work.

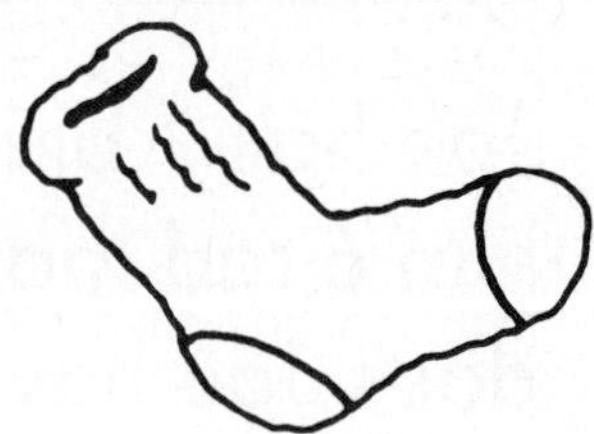

_____ more white socks

---

11. Alma has 5 crayons. Her dad gives her 7 more crayons. How many crayons does she have now? Use a related fact to check your answer.

Alma has _____ crayons.

Write a related fact to check.

_____ − _____ = 5

---

12. Julia buys 12 books. She gives 9 books away. How many books does she have left?

9	_____

12

_____ books left

Around the Neighborhood

written by John Hudson

UNITED STATES POST OFFICE

CRITICAL AREA Developing understanding of whole number relationships and place value, including grouping in tens and ones

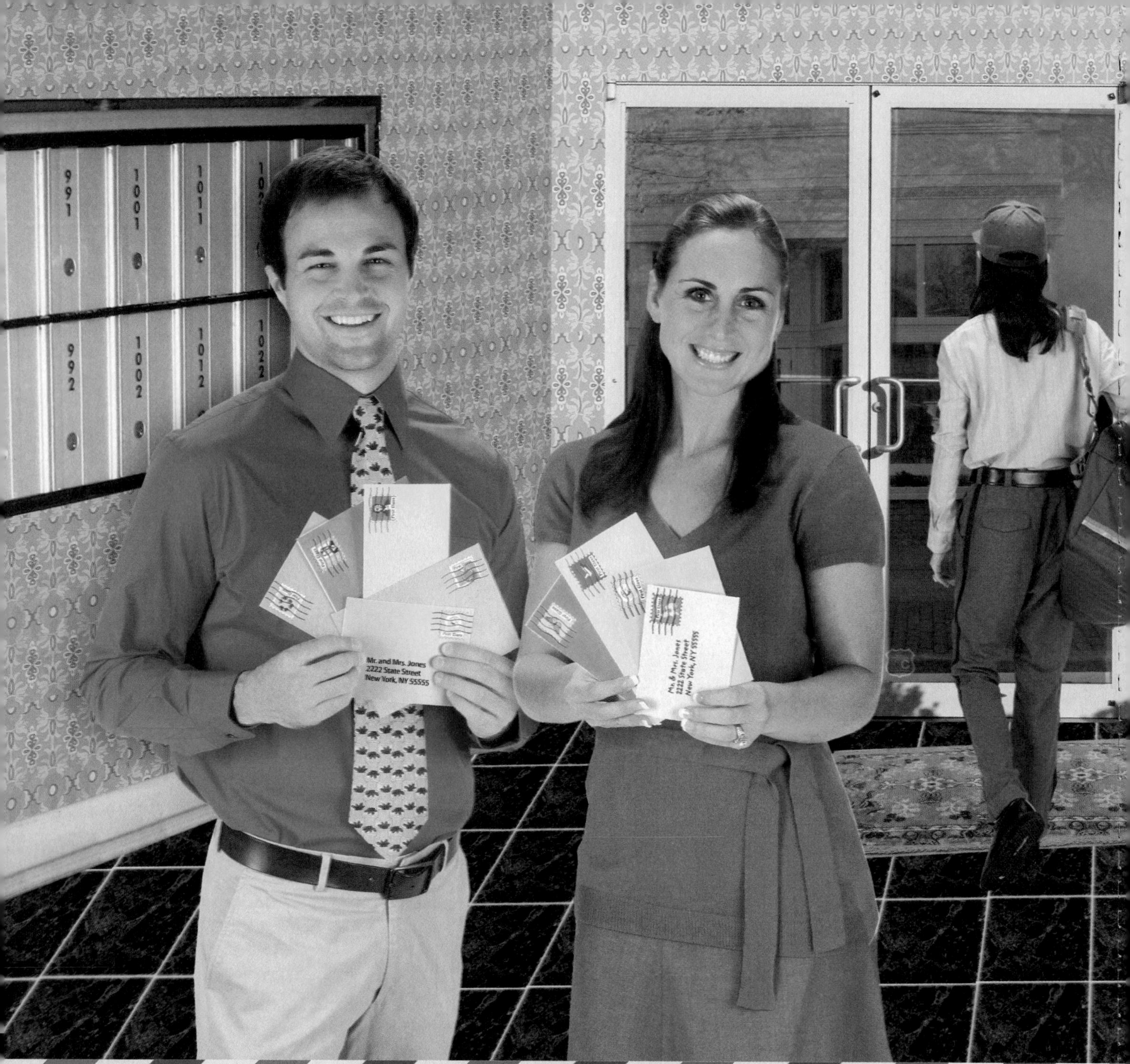

The mail carrier brings letters to Mr. and Mrs. Jones. How many letters does she bring?

_____ ◯ _____ ◯ _____

How do mail carriers help us?

The mail carrier brings packages to the fire station. Then she brings more packages. How many packages does she bring?

_____ ◯ _____ ◯ _____

Social Studies

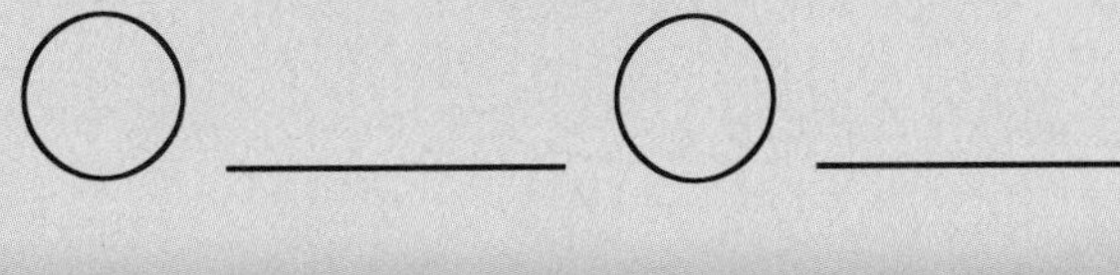

How do firefighters help us?

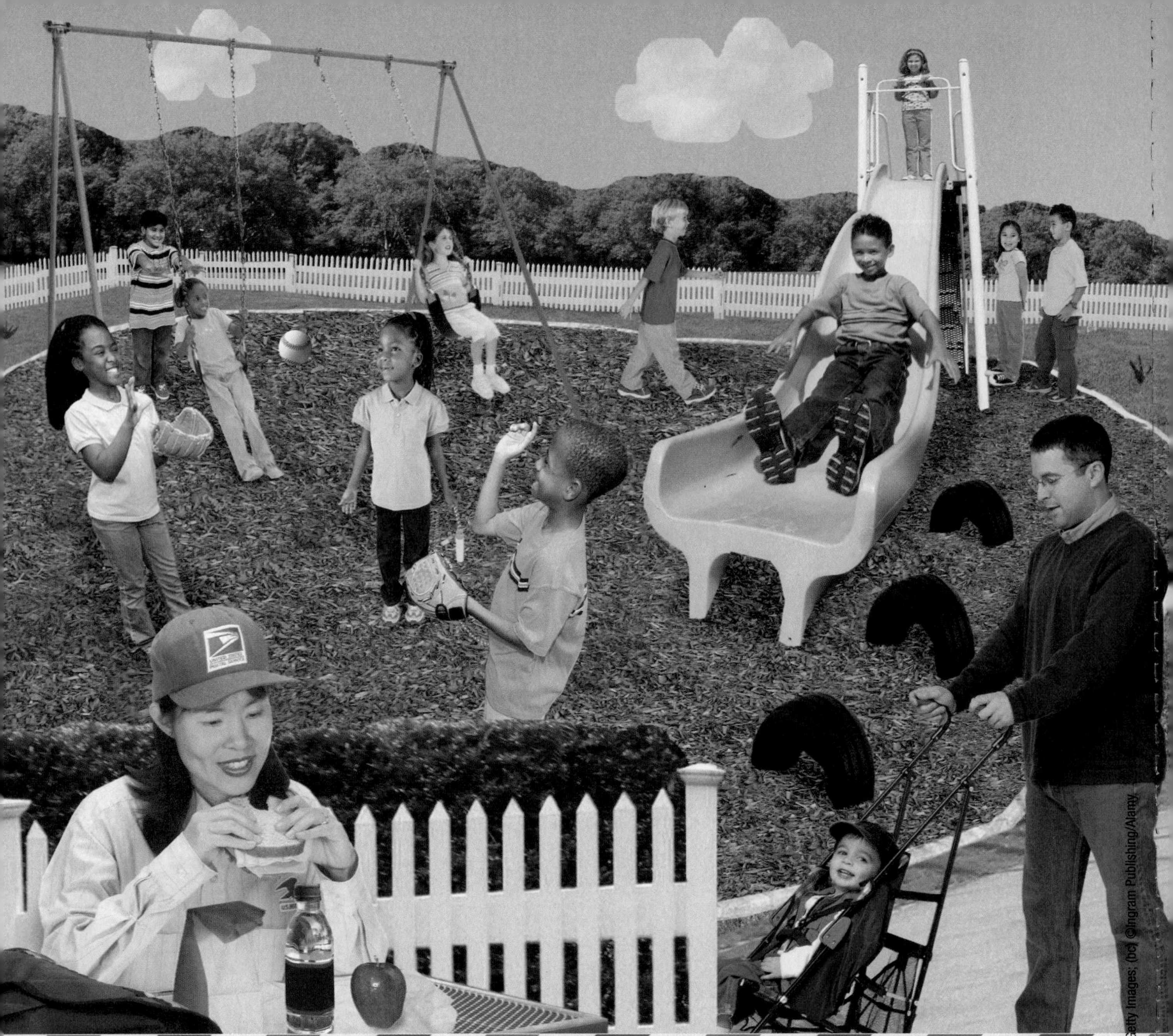

It is time for lunch. The mail carrier eats in the park. How many boys and girls are playing?

_____ ◯ _____ ◯ _____

How do parents help us?

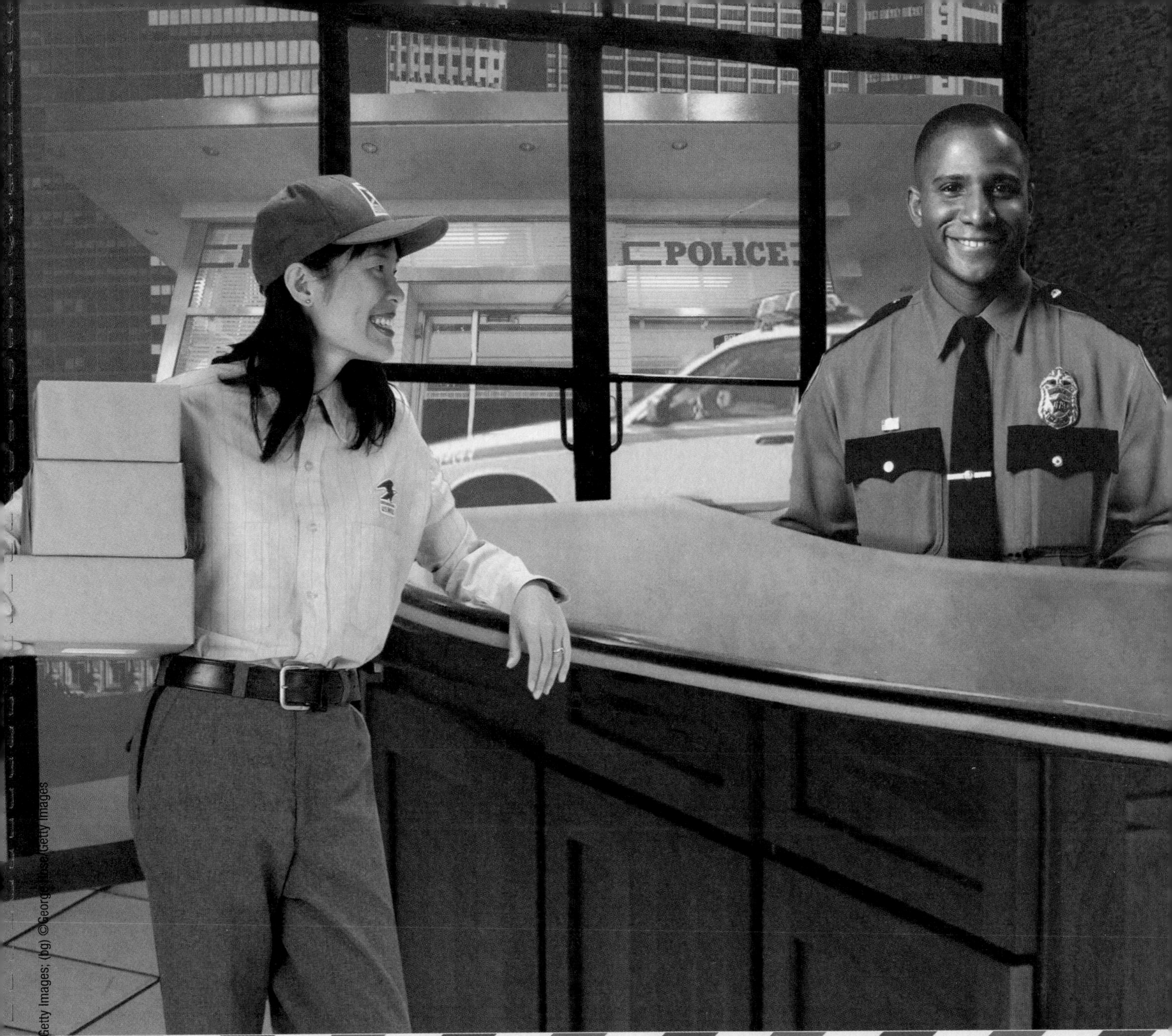

The mail carrier brings 12 packages to the police station. "This person has moved," says the police officer. "You need to take these back." How many packages does the officer keep?

____ ◯ ____ ◯ ____

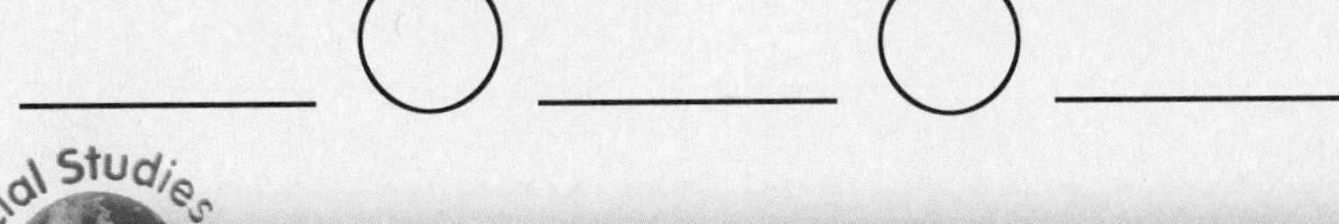

How do police officers help us?

The mail carrier stops at City Hall.
She brings 8 letters for the mayor.
She brings 4 letters for the city clerk.
How many letters does she bring?

_____ ◯ _____ ◯ _____

How do city workers help us?

Name ______________________________

Write About the Story

One day, Mr. and Mrs. Jones each got the same number of letters. They got 12 letters in all. Draw the two groups of letters.

Vocabulary Review

add
difference
doubles
subtract
sum

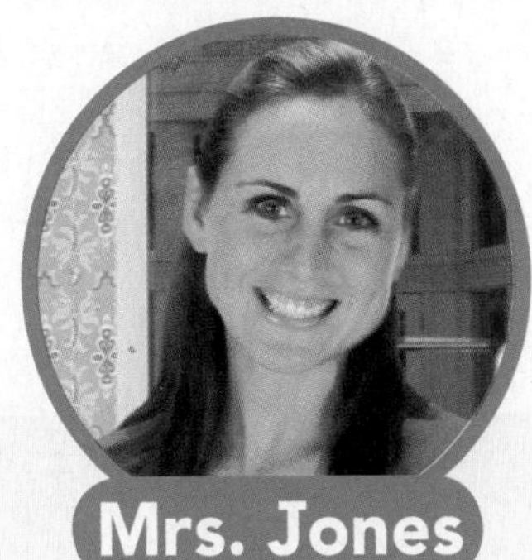

Letters for Mr. Jones

Letters for Mrs. Jones

Write the number sentence. ______ ◯ ______ ◯ ______

WRITE Math Describe your number sentence. Use a vocabulary word.

____

____

How Many Letters?

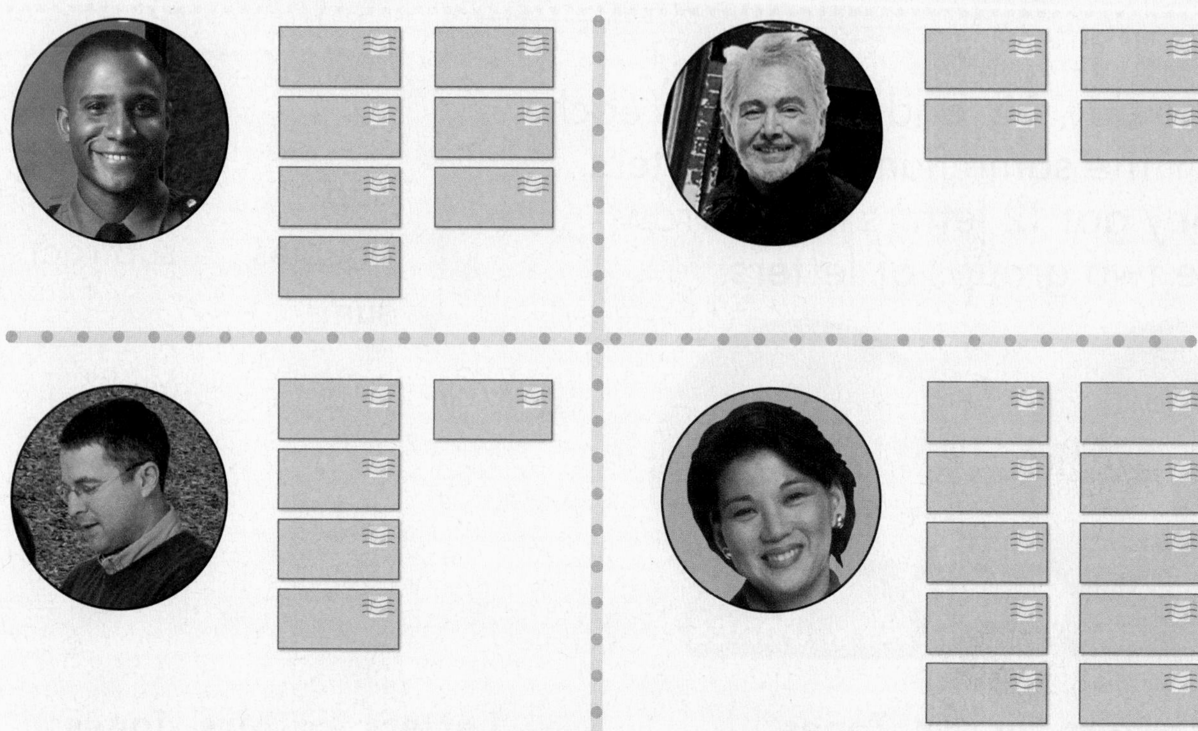

1. How many letters do  and  have in all?

_____ ◯ _____ ◯ _____

2. How many more letters does  have than ?

_____ ◯ _____ ◯ _____

3. Circle the two that have 11 letters in all.

Make up an addition story about the mail carrier bringing letters to you and a classmate. Write the number sentence.

Chapter 6

Count and Model Numbers

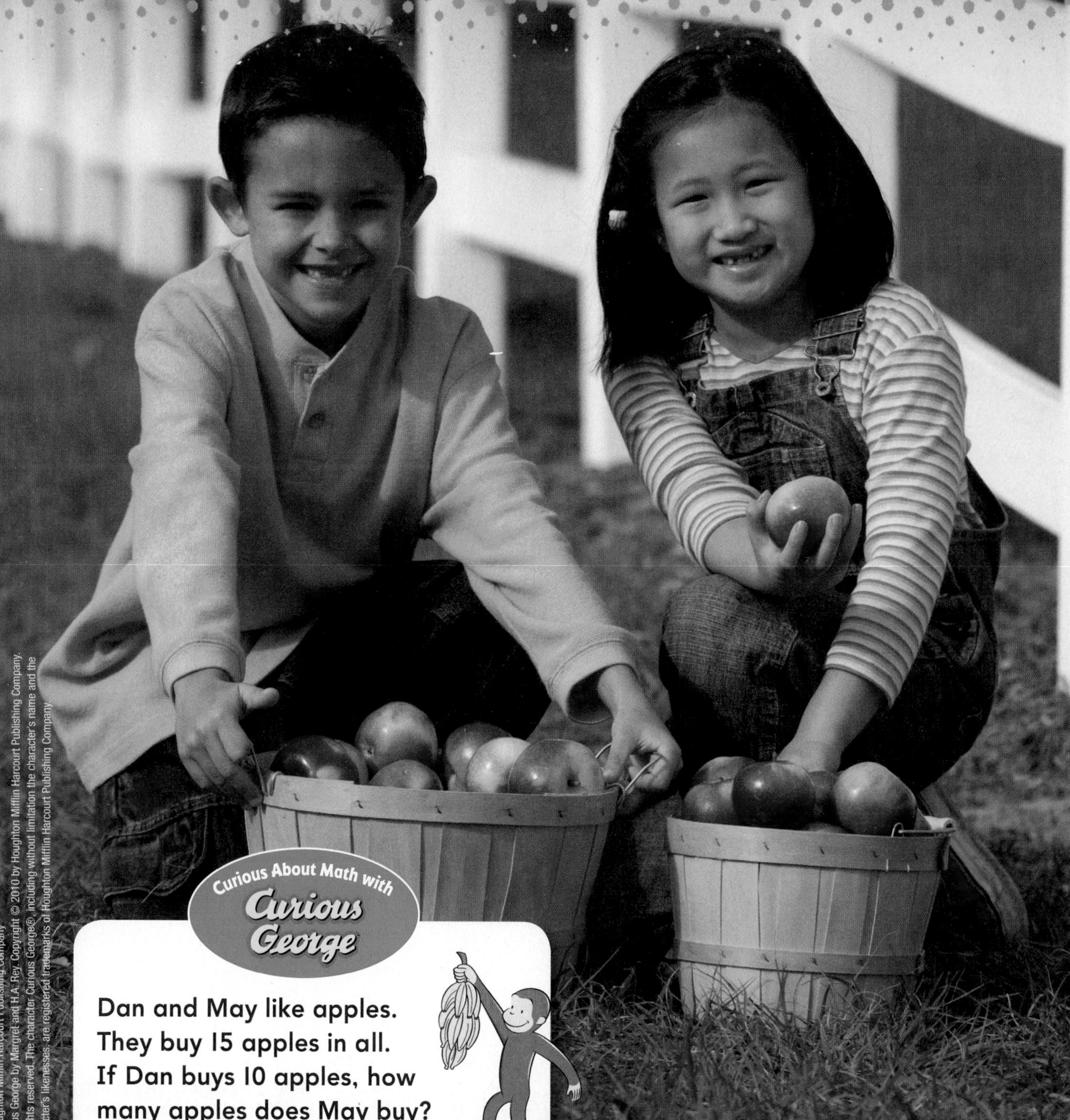

Dan and May like apples.
They buy 15 apples in all.
If Dan buys 10 apples, how
many apples does May buy?

Name ______________________________

Explore Numbers 6 to 9

Count how many. Circle the number.

1. 

6

7

2. 

8

9

Count Groups to 20

Circle groups of 10. Write how many.

3. 

____

4. 

____

Make Groups of 10

Use ●. Draw to show a group of 10 in two different ways.

5.

6.

This page checks understanding of important skills needed for success in Chapter 6.

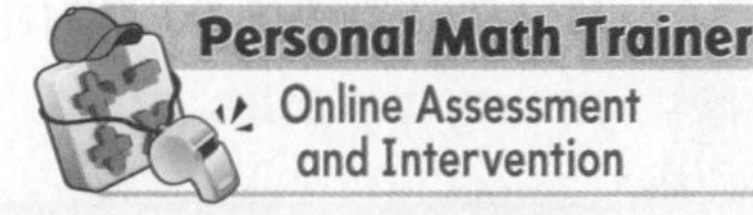

Name ______________________________

Vocabulary Builder

Review Words	
one	two
three	four
five	six
seven	eight
nine	ten

Visualize It

Draw pictures in the box to show the number.

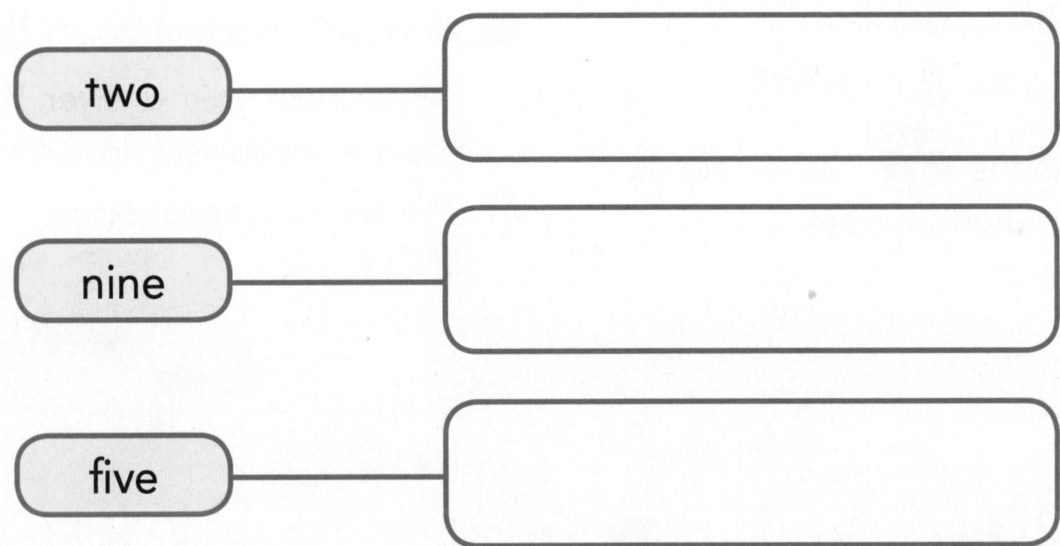

Understand Vocabulary

Write a review word to name the number.

1.  ______________

2. 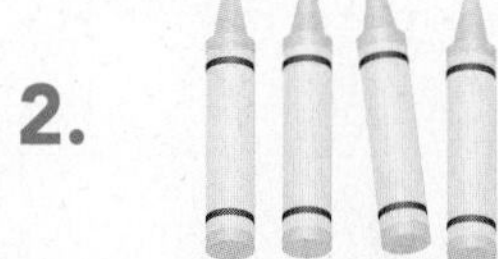 ______________

3.  ______________

GO DIGITAL • Interactive Student Edition • Multimedia eGlossary

Game Show the Numbers

Materials •  • 
• 20 ● • 

Play with a partner.

1. Put your ♟ on START.
2. Spin the ◉. Move your ♟ that many spaces.
3. Read the number. Use ● to show the number on a ten frame.
4. Have your partner count the ● to check your answer. If you are not correct, lose a turn.
5. The first player to get to END wins.

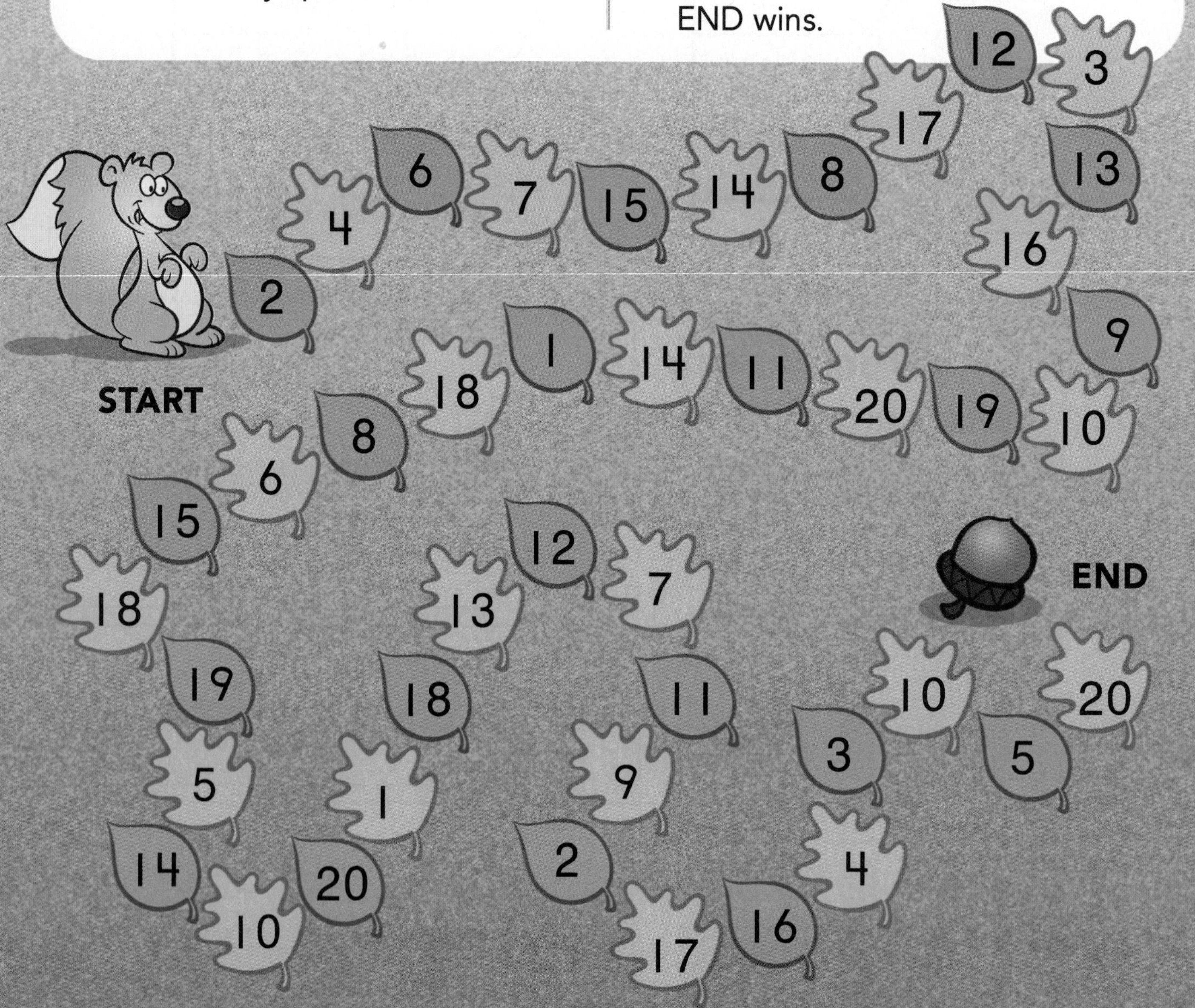

START

2 4 6 7 15 14 8 17 12 3 13 16 9 10 19 20 11 14 1 18 8 6 15 18 19 5 14 10 20 1 18 13 12 7 11 9 2 17 16 4 3 10 5 20

END

Name ____________________________________

Count by Ones to 120

Essential Question How can knowing a counting pattern help you count to 120?

Number and Operations in Base Ten—1.NBT.1

MATHEMATICAL PRACTICES
MP.5, MP.7, MP.8

Write the missing numbers.

21	22	23	24	25	26	27	28	29	30
31	32	33	34	35	36	37	38	39	40
41	42	43	44	45	46	47	48	49	50
51	52	53	54	55	56	57	58	59	60
61	62	63	64	65	66	67	68	69	70
71	72	73	74	75	76	77	78	79	80
81	82	83	84	85	86	87	88	89	90
91	92	93	94	95	96	97	98	99	100

FOR THE TEACHER • Read the following problem. Debbie saw this page in a puzzle book. Two rows of numbers are missing. Use what you know about counting to write the missing numbers.

Math Talk **Mathematical Practices**

Explain how you know which numbers are missing.

Model and Draw

Count forward.
Write the numbers.

10, 11, ___, ___, ___

100, 101, ___, ___, ___

110, 111, ___, ___, ___

1	2	3	4	5	6	7	8	9	10
11	12	13	14	15	16	17	18	19	20
21	22	23	24	25	26	27	28	29	30
31	32	33	34	35	36	37	38	39	40
41	42	43	44	45	46	47	48	49	50
51	52	53	54	55	56	57	58	59	60
61	62	63	64	65	66	67	68	69	70
71	72	73	74	75	76	77	78	79	80
81	82	83	84	85	86	87	88	89	90
91	92	93	94	95	96	97	98	99	100
101	102	103	104	105	106	107	108	109	110
111	112	113	114	115	116	117	118	119	120

Share and Show

Look for a pattern to help you write the numbers.

Use a Counting Chart. Count forward.
Write the numbers.

1. 114, ___, ___, ___, ___, ___, ___

2. 51, ___, ___, ___, ___, ___, ___

3. 94, ___, ___, ___, ___, ___, ___

4. 78, ___, ___, ___, ___, ___, ___

✓5. 35, ___, ___, ___, ___, ___, ___

✓6. 104, ___, ___, ___, ___, ___, ___

Name ______________________________

On Your Own

MATHEMATICAL PRACTICE 7 **Look for a Pattern**

Use a Counting Chart. Count forward.
Write the numbers.

7. 19, ____, ____, ____, ____, ____, ____, ____, ____

8. 98, ____, ____, ____, ____, ____, ____, ____, ____

9. 60, ____, ____, ____, ____, ____, ____, ____, ____

10. 27, ____, ____, ____, ____, ____, ____, ____, ____

11. 107, ____, ____, ____, ____, ____, ____, ____, ____

12. 43, ____, ____, ____, ____, ____, ____, ____, ____

13. 68, ____, ____, ____, ____, ____, ____, ____, ____

14. THINK SMARTER Use a Counting Chart to write the numbers counting forward.

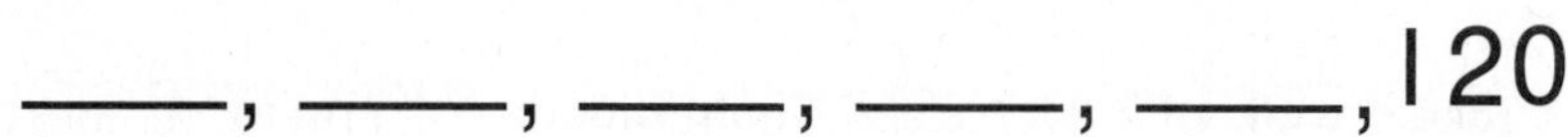

Problem Solving • Applications

Use a Counting Chart. Draw and write numbers to solve.

15. GO DEEPER The bag has 99 buttons. Draw more buttons so there are 105 buttons in all. Write the numbers as you count.

16. THINK SMARTER The bag has 56 buttons. How many more buttons do you need to add to the bag to have 64 buttons?

____ buttons

17. THINK SMARTER Tito counts 105 cubes. Then he counts forward some more cubes. Write the numbers.

105, ____, ____, ____, ____, ____, ____

TAKE HOME ACTIVITY • Take a walk with your child. Count aloud together as you take 120 steps.

FOR MORE PRACTICE: Standards Practice Book

Name ______________________________

Count by Tens to 120

Essential Question How do numbers change as you count by tens to 120?

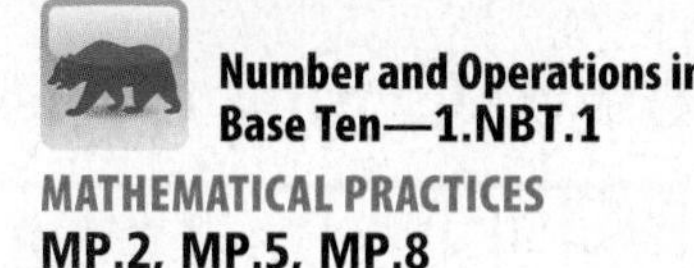

Number and Operations in Base Ten—1.NBT.1

MATHEMATICAL PRACTICES
MP.2, MP.5, MP.8

Listen and Draw

Start on 10. Count forward by tens.
Color each number as you say it.

1	2	3	4	5	6	7	8	9	10
11	12	13	14	15	16	17	18	19	20
21	22	23	24	25	26	27	28	29	30
31	32	33	34	35	36	37	38	39	40
41	42	43	44	45	46	47	48	49	50
51	52	53	54	55	56	57	58	59	60
61	62	63	64	65	66	67	68	69	70
71	72	73	74	75	76	77	78	79	80
81	82	83	84	85	86	87	88	89	90
91	92	93	94	95	96	97	98	99	100

FOR THE TEACHER • Ask children: How do you count by tens? Starting at 10 on the hundred chart, have children count forward by tens, coloring each additional ten as they count.

Math Talk Mathematical Practices

Which numbers in the hundred chart did you color? **Explain.**

Model and Draw

Start on 3. Count by tens.

1	2	3	4	5	6	7	8	9	10
11	12	13	14	15	16	17	18	19	20
21	22	23	24	25	26	27	28	29	30
31	32	33	34	35	36	37	38	39	40
41	42	43	44	45	46	47	48	49	50
51	52	53	54	55	56	57	58	59	60
61	62	63	64	65	66	67	68	69	70
71	72	73	74	75	76	77	78	79	80
81	82	83	84	85	86	87	88	89	90
91	92	93	94	95	96	97	98	99	100
101	102	103	104	105	106	107	108	109	110
111	112	113	114	115	116	117	118	119	120

THINK
When you count by tens, each number is ten more.

3, 13, 23, 33, ____, ____, ____, ____, ____, ____, ____, ____

Share and Show

Use a Counting Chart to count by tens.
Write the numbers.

1. Start on 17.

17, ____, ____, ____, ____, ____, ____, ____, ____

✓2. Start on 1.

1, ____, ____, ____, ____, ____, ____, ____, ____

✓3. Start on 39.

39, ____, ____, ____, ____, ____, ____, ____, ____

Name ______________________

On Your Own

MATHEMATICAL PRACTICE 5 **Use Patterns** Use a Counting Chart. Count by tens. Write the numbers.

4. 40, ___, ___, ___, ___, ___, ___, ___, ___

5. 15, ___, ___, ___, ___, ___, ___, ___, ___

6. 28, ___, ___, ___, ___, ___, ___, ___, ___

7. 6, ___, ___, ___, ___, ___, ___, ___, ___

8. 14, ___, ___, ___, ___, ___, ___, ___, ___

9. 32, ___, ___, ___, ___, ___, ___, ___, ___

10. THINK SMARTER If you start on 43 and count by tens, what number is after 73 and before 93? ___

11. You say me when you start on 21 and count by tens. I am after 91. I am before 111. What number am I? ___

Problem Solving • Applications  

GO DEEPER Use what you know about a Counting Chart to write the missing numbers.

12. 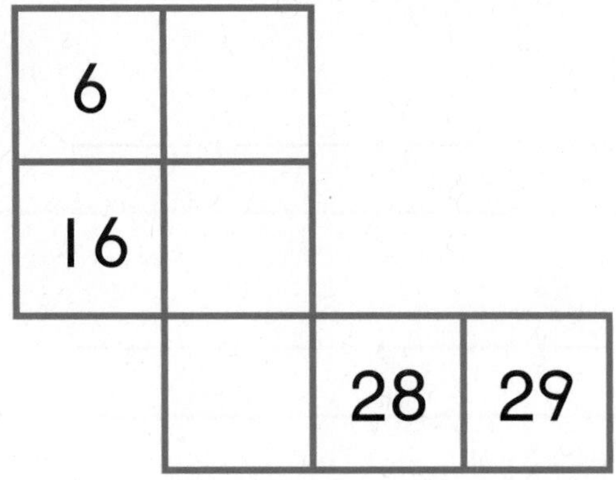

13.

54 55
64
72

14. 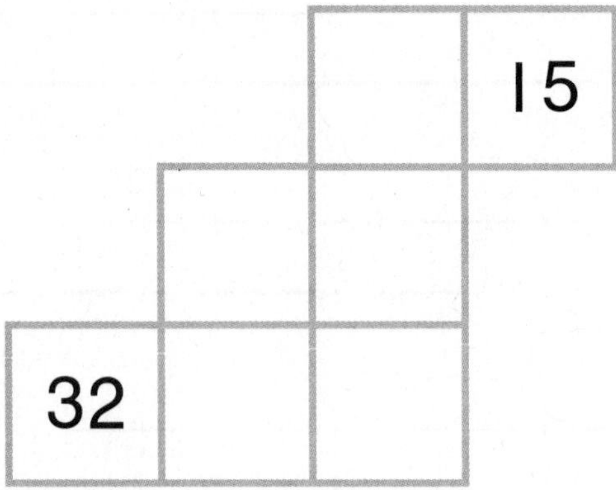

15.

97 98

16. THINK SMARTER Use a Counting Chart. Count by tens. Match each number on the left to a number that is 10 more.

57 •	• 103
73 •	• 67
77 •	• 87
93 •	• 83

TAKE HOME ACTIVITY • Write these numbers: 2, 12, 22, 32, 42. Ask your child to tell you the next 5 numbers.

FOR MORE PRACTICE: Standards Practice Book

Name ____________________

Understand Ten and Ones

Essential Question How can you use different ways to write a number as ten and ones?

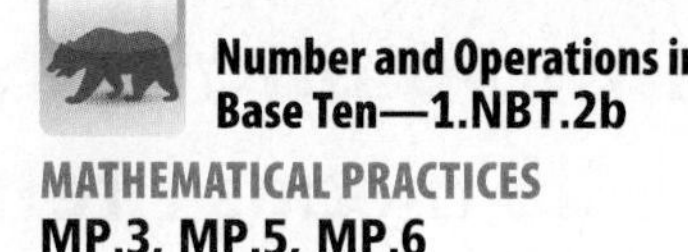

MATHEMATICAL PRACTICES
MP.3, MP.5, MP.6

Use [cube] to model the problem.
Draw the [cube] to show your work.

FOR THE TEACHER • Read the problem. Tim has 10 pennies. He gets 2 more pennies. How many pennies does Tim have now?

Math Talk Mathematical Practices

How does your picture show the pennies Tim has? **Explain.**

Model and Draw

13 is a two-**digit** number.
The 1 in 13 means 1 **ten**.
The 3 in 13 means 3 **ones**.

THINK
10 ones and 3 ones
is the same as
1 ten 3 ones.

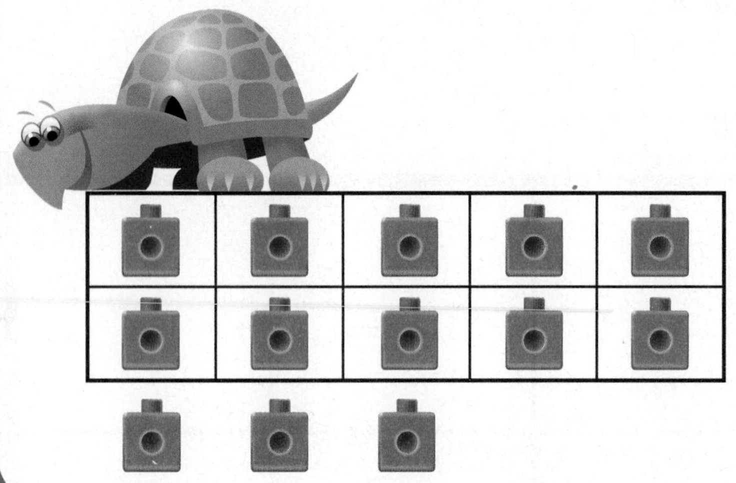

1 ten 3 ones

10 + 3

13

Share and Show

Use the model. Write the number three different ways.

1. 

____ ten ____ ones

____ + ____

____

2. 

____ ten ____ ones

____ + ____

____

Name ___________________________

On Your Own

MATHEMATICAL PRACTICE 6 **Make Connections**

Use the model. Write the number three different ways.

3.

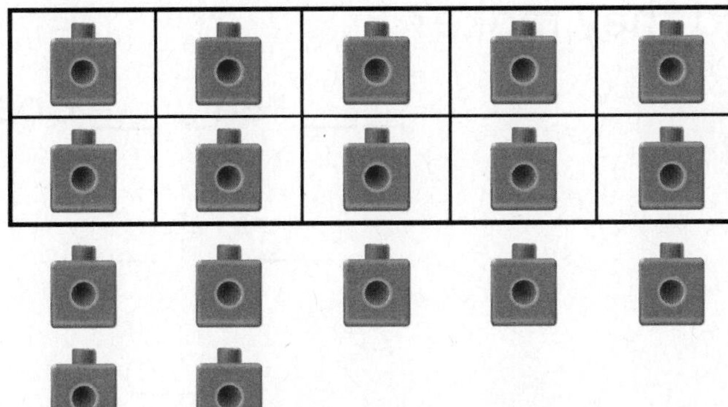

____ ten ____ ones

____ + ____

____

4.

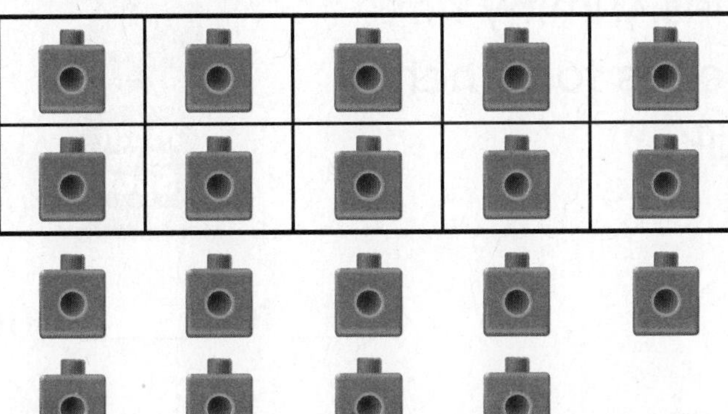

____ ten ____ ones

____ + ____

____

5. **GO DEEPER** Draw cubes to show the number. Write the missing numbers.

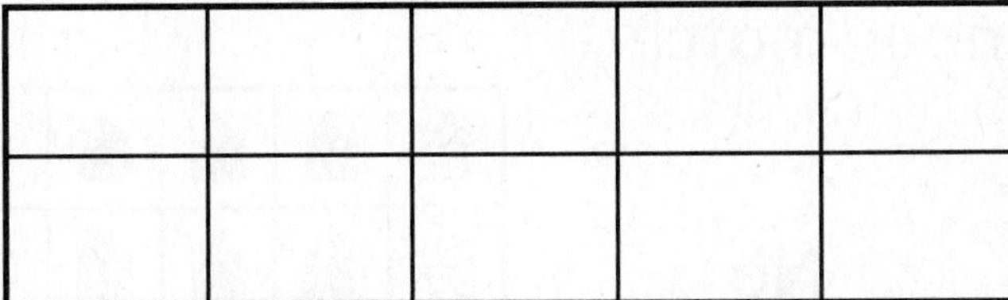

____ ten ____ ones

____ + ____

Problem Solving • Applications  

Draw cubes to show the number. Write the number three different ways.

6. David has 1 ten and 3 ones. Abby has 6 ones. They put all their tens and ones together. What number did they make?

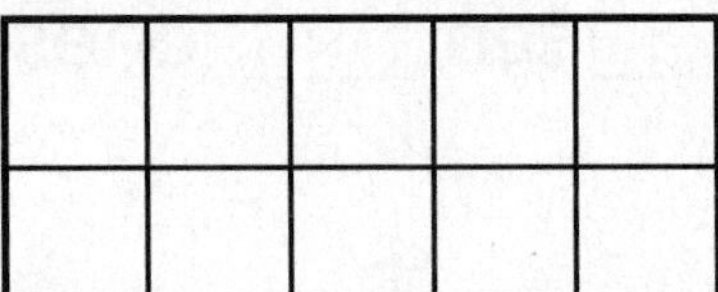

____ ten ____ ones

____ + ____

____

7. THINK SMARTER Karen has 7 ones. Jimmy has 9 ones. They put all their ones together. What number did they make?

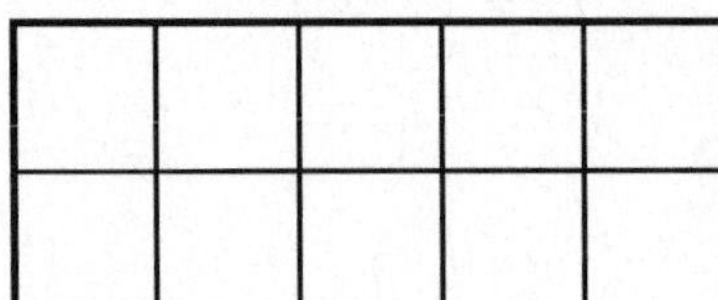

____ ten ____ ones

____ + ____

____

8. THINK SMARTER Does the number match the model?

10 + 5 ○ Yes ○ No

1 ten 15 ones ○ Yes ○ No

TAKE HOME ACTIVITY • Show your child one group of 10 pennies and one group of 8 pennies. Ask your child to tell how many tens and ones there are and say the number. Repeat with other numbers from 11 to 19.

FOR MORE PRACTICE: Standards Practice Book

Name ____________________

Make Ten and Ones

Essential Question How can you show a number as ten and ones?

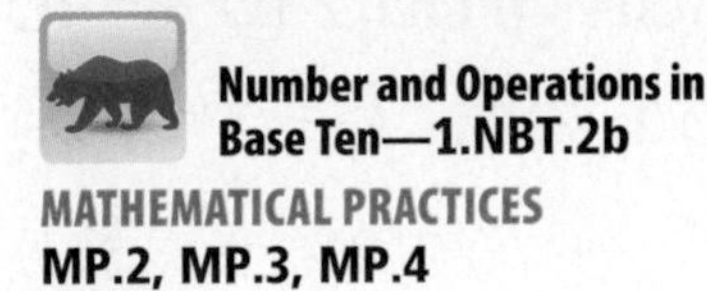

MATHEMATICAL PRACTICES
MP.2, MP.3, MP.4

Listen and Draw

Use ■ to model the problem.
Draw ■ to show your work.

Draw to show the group of ten another way.

Math Talk Mathematical Practices

How are the pictures the same? How are the pictures different? **Explain.**

FOR THE TEACHER • Read the problem. Destiny has 10 cubes. How can she show 1 ten?

Model and Draw

You can group 10 ◼ to make 1 ten.

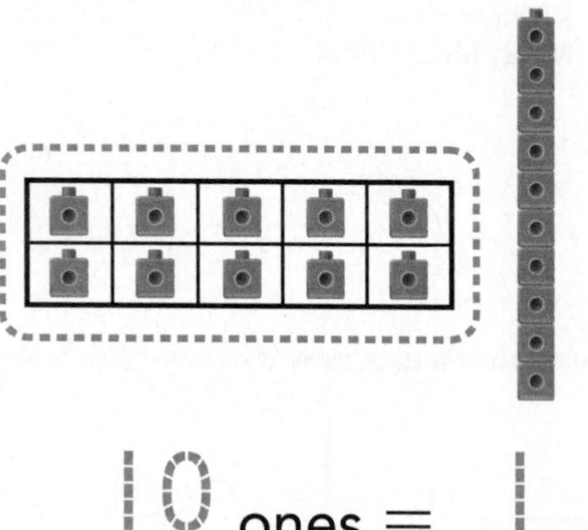

10 ones = 1 ten

Draw a quick picture to show 1 ten.

1 ten

Share and Show

Use ◼. Make groups of ten and ones. Draw your work. Write how many.

1.

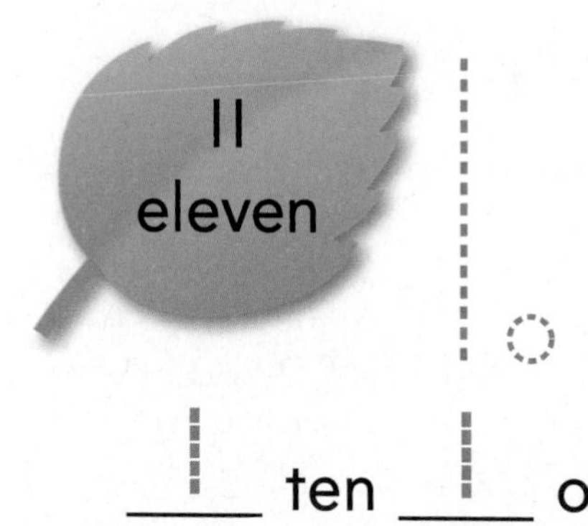

1 ten 1 one

2.

____ ten ____ ones

3.

____ ten ____ ones

4.

14
fourteen

____ ten ____ ones

Name ______________________

On Your Own

MATHEMATICAL PRACTICE 6 **Compare** Use ▪. Make groups of ten and ones. Draw your work. Write how many.

5. 

____ ten ____ ones

6. 16
sixteen

____ ten ____ ones

7. 17
seventeen

____ ten ____ ones

8. 18
eighteen

____ ten ____ ones

9. 

____ ten ____ ones

Problem Solving • Applications Real World

WRITE Math

Solve.

10. THINK SMARTER Emily wants to write ten and ones to show 20. What does Emily write?

20
twenty

____ ten ____ ones

11. GO DEEPER Gina thinks of a number that has 7 ones and 1 ten. What is the number? Draw to show your work.

____

12. Ben drew this picture to show a number. What is the number?

____

13. THINK SMARTER Circle the numbers that make the sentence true.

There are [1 / 4 / 10] tens and [1 / 4 / 10] ones in 14.

____ ten ____ ones

TAKE HOME ACTIVITY • Give your child numbers from 11 to 19. Have your child work with pennies to show a group of ten and a group of ones for each number.

FOR MORE PRACTICE: Standards Practice Book

Name ____________________

Tens

Essential Question How can you model and name groups of ten?

Number and Operations in Base Ten—1.NBT.2a, 1.NBT.2c
MATHEMATICAL PRACTICES
MP.7, MP.8

Listen and Draw

Real World

Hands On

Use ▪ to solve the riddle.
Draw and write to show your work.

Math Talk **Mathematical Practices**

Explain what you did to solve the first riddle.

FOR THE TEACHER • Read the following riddles. I am thinking of a number that is the same as 1 ten and 4 ones. What is my number? I am thinking of a number that is the same as 1 ten and 0 ones. What is my number?

Model and Draw

You can group ones to make tens.

Draw a quick picture to show the tens.

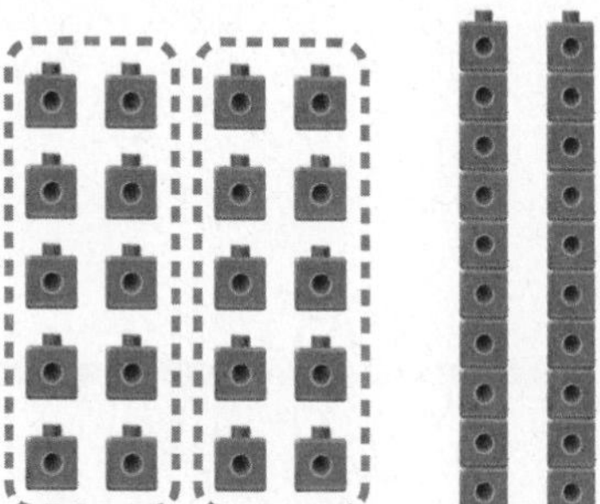

20 ones = 2 tens 0 ones

2 tens = 20
twenty

Share and Show

Use ▪. Make groups of ten.
Write the tens and ones.

Draw the tens.
Count by tens.

1.

30 ones = ____ tens ____ ones

____ tens = ____
thirty

2.

40 ones = ____ tens ____ ones

____ tens = ____
forty

Name ______________________________

On Your Own

MATHEMATICAL PRACTICE 8 **Use Repeated Reasoning**

Use [cube]. Make groups of ten. Write the tens and ones.

3. 50 ones

____ tens ____ ones ____ tens = ____ fifty

4. 60 ones

____ tens ____ ones ____ tens = ____ sixty

5. 70 ones

____ tens ____ ones ____ tens = ____ seventy

6. 80 ones

____ tens ____ ones ____ tens = ____ eighty

7. 90 ones

____ tens ____ ones ____ tens = ____ ninety

8. THINK SMARTER 100 ones

____ tens ____ ones ____ tens = ____ hundred

Name ______________________________

Mid-Chapter Checkpoint

Concepts and Skills

Use a Counting Chart. Count forward. Write the numbers. (1.NBT.1)

1. 63, 64, ____, ____, ____
2. 108, 109, ____, ____, ____

Use a Counting Chart. Count by tens. Write the numbers. (1.NBT.1)

3. 42, 52, ____, ____, ____
4. 79, 89, ____, ____, ____

5. Use the model. Write the number three different ways. (1.NBT.2b)

____ ten ____ ones

____ + ____

____

Use ■. Make groups of ten and ones. Draw your work. Write how many. (1.NBT.2b)

6.

____ ten ____ ones

7. THINK SMARTER Choose all the ways that name the model.

- ○ 60
- ○ 60 tens
- ○ 6 tens 0 ones

Name ______________________________

Tens and Ones to 50

Essential Question How can you group cubes to show a number as tens and ones?

Number and Operations in Base Ten—1.NBT.2

MATHEMATICAL PRACTICES
MP.4, MP.5, MP.6

Listen and Draw

Use ▪ to model the number.
Draw ▪ to show your work.

Tens	Ones

Math Talk — **Mathematical Practices**

How did you figure out how many tens and ones are in 23? **Explain.**

FOR THE TEACHER • Ask children to use 23 cubes and show them as tens and ones.

Model and Draw

The 2 in 24 means 2 tens.

Tens	Ones

2 tens 4 ones = 24

The 2 in 42 means 2 ones.

Tens	Ones

4 tens 2 ones = 42

Share and Show

Use your MathBoard and ▭ ▪ to show the tens and ones. Write the numbers.

1. 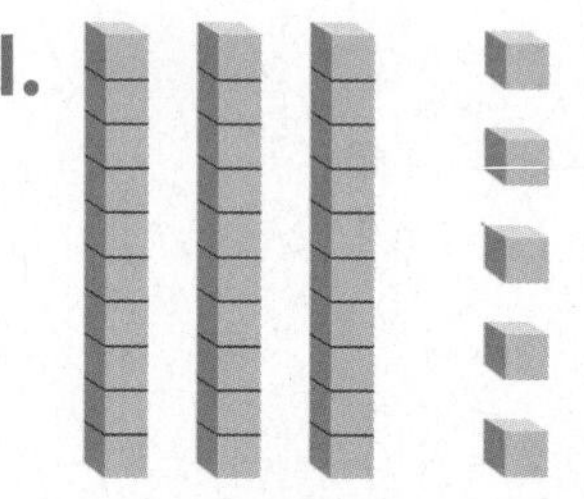

____ tens ____ ones = ____

2. 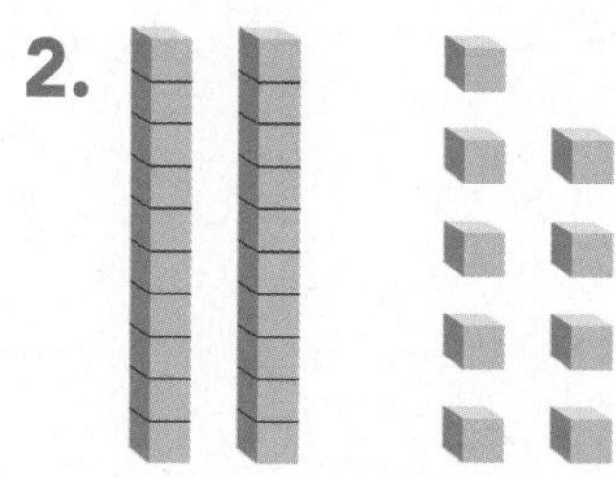

____ tens ____ ones = ____

✓ 3. 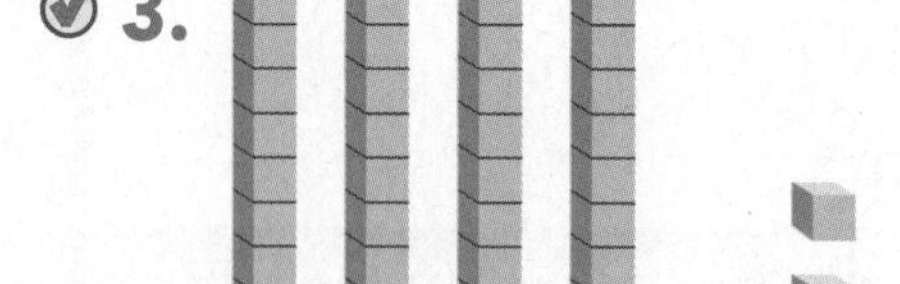

____ tens ____ ones = ____

✓ 4. 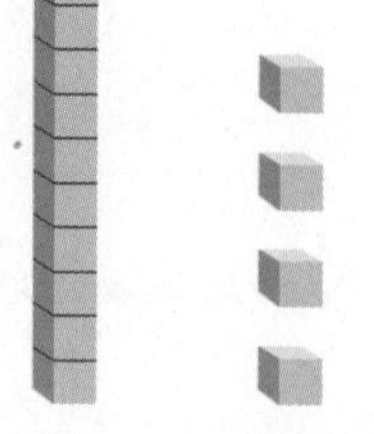

____ ten ____ ones = ____

Name ______________________________

On Your Own

MATHEMATICAL PRACTICE 6 **Make Connections**

Write the numbers.

5. 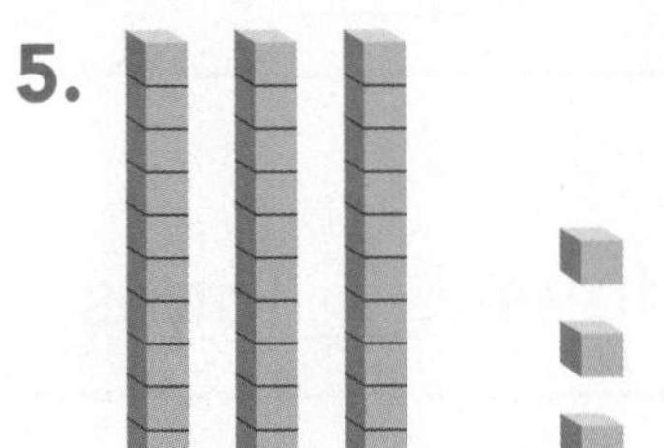

____ tens ____ ones = ____

6. 

____ tens ____ ones = ____

7. 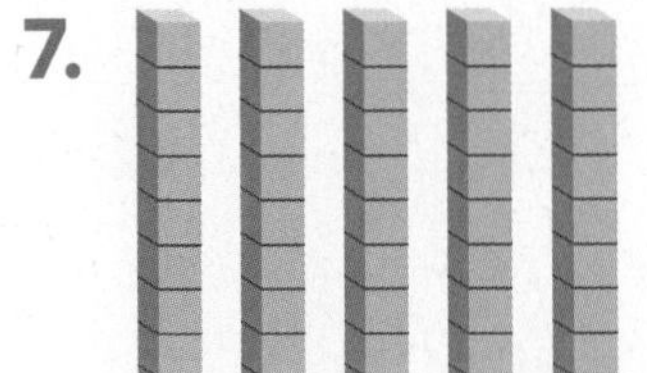

____ tens ____ ones = ____

8. 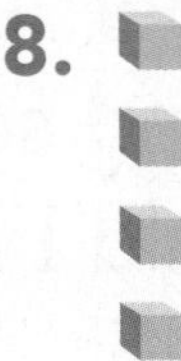

____ tens ____ ones = ____

9. GO DEEPER Mary drew tens and ones to show 32.
She made a mistake.
Draw a correct quick picture to show 32.
Write the numbers.

Tens	Ones
			o o o

Tens	Ones

____ tens ____ ones = ____

Problem Solving • Applications

Solve. Write the numbers.

10. I have 46 cubes. How many tens and ones can I make?

____ tens ____ ones

11. I have 32 cubes. How many tens and ones can I make?

____ tens ____ ones

12. I have 28 cubes. How many tens and ones can I make?

____ tens ____ ones

13. THINK SMARTER I am a number less than 50. I have 8 ones and some tens. What numbers could I be?

____

Personal Math Trainer

14. THINK SMARTER + There are 35 ▪. Jun says that there are 3 ones and 5 tens. Rob says that there are 3 tens and 5 ones. Who is correct? Circle the name.

Jun Rob

How can you draw to show 35?

TAKE HOME ACTIVITY • Write a two-digit number from 20 to 50, such as 26. Ask your child to tell which digit names the tens and which digit names the ones. Repeat with different numbers.

FOR MORE PRACTICE: Standards Practice Book

Name ______________________________

Tens and Ones to 100

Essential Question How can you show numbers to 100 as tens and ones?

Number and Operations in Base Ten—1.NBT.2

MATHEMATICAL PRACTICES
MP.2, MP.4, MP.6

Listen and Draw

Hands On

Use  to model the number.
Draw a quick picture to show your work.

25

50

52

Math Talk Mathematical Practices

How did you figure out how many tens and ones are in 52? **Explain.**

FOR THE TEACHER • Ask children to use base-ten blocks to show how many tens and ones there are in 25, 50, and 52.

Model and Draw

The number just after 99 is 100.
10 tens is the same as 1 **hundred**.

Draw quick pictures to show 99 and 100.

9 tens 9 ones = 99

10 tens 0 ones = 100

Share and Show

Use your MathBoard and [tens rod] [ones cube] to show the tens and ones. Write the numbers.

1. 

____ tens ____ ones = ____

2. 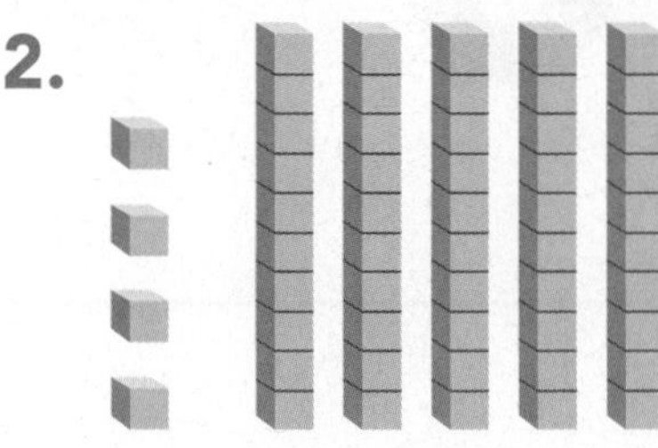

____ tens ____ ones = ____

 3. 

____ tens ____ ones = ____

 4. 

____ tens ____ ones = ____

Name ____________________

On Your Own

MATHEMATICAL PRACTICE 2 **Reason Quantitatively** Write the numbers.

5. 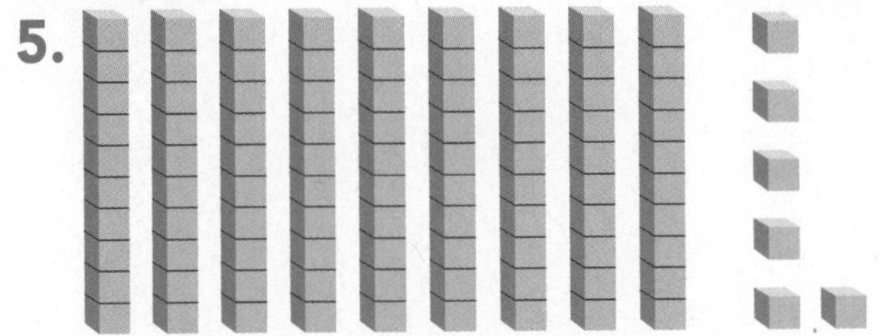

____ tens ____ ones = ____

6. 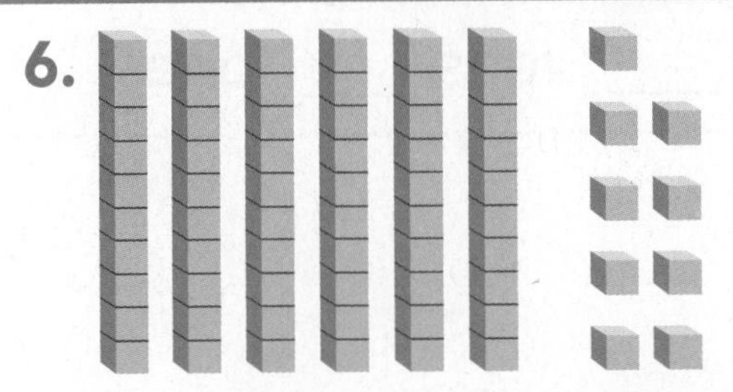

____ tens ____ ones = ____

7. 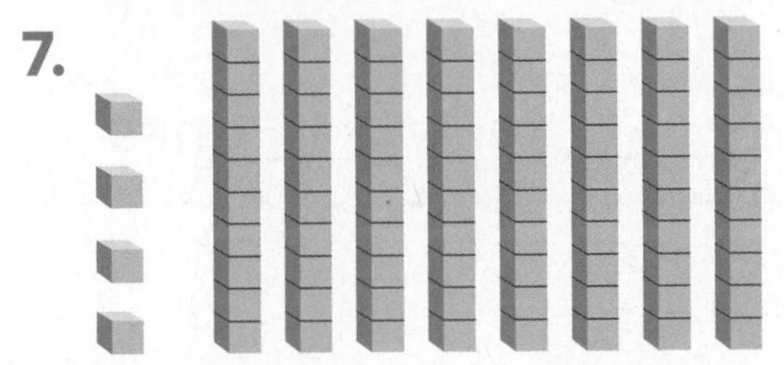

____ tens ____ ones = ____

8. 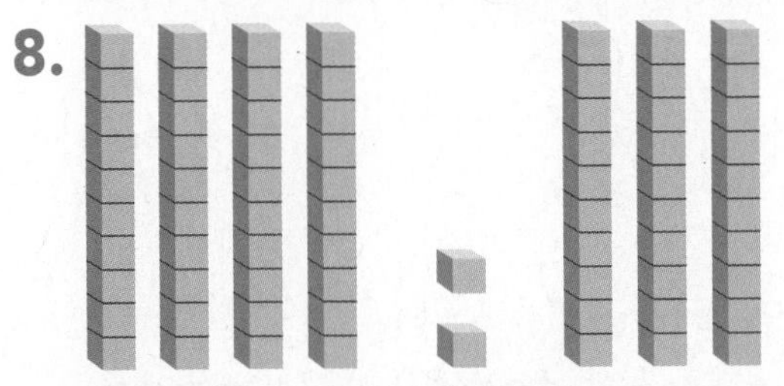

____ tens ____ ones = ____

9. 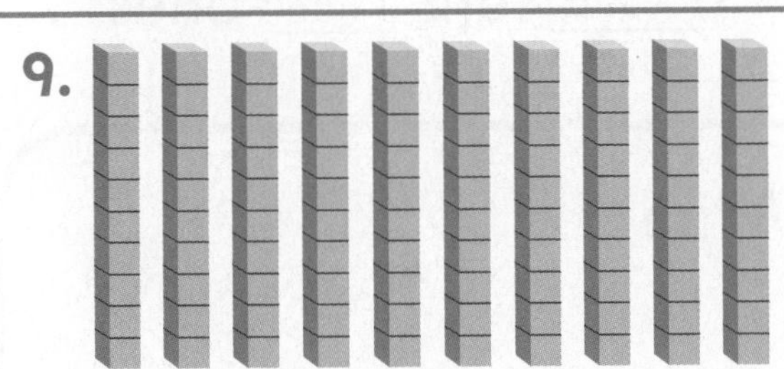

____ tens ____ ones = ____

10. GO DEEPER What number is the same as 7 tens and 20 ones?

____

11. GO DEEPER What number is the same as 5 tens and 13 ones?

____

Problem Solving • Applications

Draw a quick picture to show the number.
Write how many tens and ones there are.

12. Edna has 82 stamps.

____ tens ____ ones

13. Amy has 79 pennies.

____ tens ____ ones

14. THINK SMARTER Moe has a group of 70 red feathers and 30 brown feathers.

____ tens ____ ones

15. THINK SMARTER Read the problem. Write a number to solve.

I am greater than 14.
I am less than 20.
I have 6 ones.

____

TAKE HOME ACTIVITY • Give your child numbers from 50 to 100. Ask your child to draw a picture to show the tens and the ones in each number and then write the number.

FOR MORE PRACTICE: Standards Practice Book

Name ____________________

Problem Solving • Show Numbers in Different Ways

Essential Question How can making a model help you show a number in different ways?

Number and Operations in Base Ten—1.NBT.2a, 1.NBT.3
MATHEMATICAL PRACTICES
MP.1, MP.6, MP.7

Gary and Jill both want 23 stickers for a class project. There are 3 sheets of 10 stickers and 30 single stickers on the table. How could Gary and Jill each take 23 stickers?

Unlock the Problem

What do I need to find?

two different ways to make a number

What information do I need to use?

The number is 23.

Show how to solve the problem.

Gary

Tens	Ones

Jill

Tens	Ones

23 = 23

HOME CONNECTION • Showing the number with base-ten blocks helps your child explore different ways to combine tens and ones.

Try Another Problem

Use to show the number two different ways. Draw both ways.

- What do I need to find?
- What information do I need to use?

1. 46

Tens	Ones

Tens	Ones

___ ◯ ___

2. 71

Tens	Ones

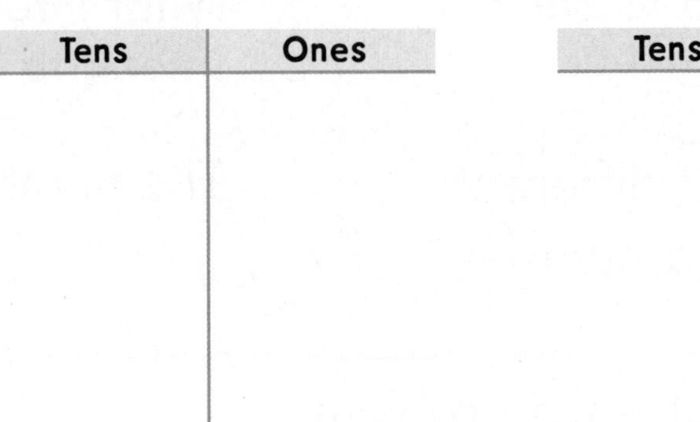

Tens	Ones

___ ◯ ___

3. 65

Tens	Ones

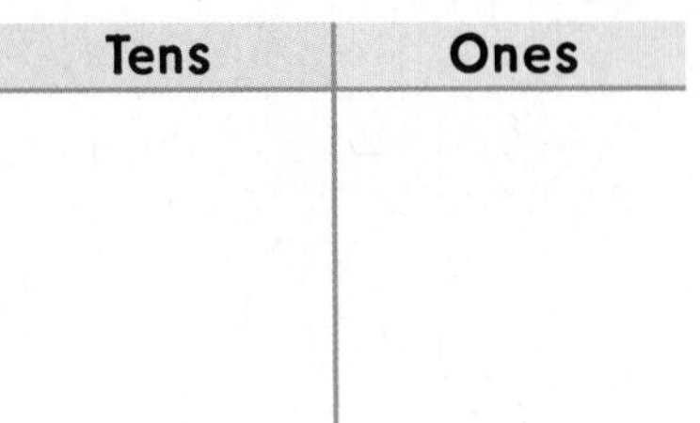

Tens	Ones

___ ◯ ___

Math Talk **Mathematical Practices**

Look at Exercise 3. **Explain** why both ways show 65.

Name ______________________________

Share and Show

Use [tens] [ones] to show the number two different ways. Draw both ways.

4. 59

Tens	Ones

Tens	Ones

_____ ◯ _____

5. 34

Tens	Ones

Tens	Ones

_____ ◯ _____

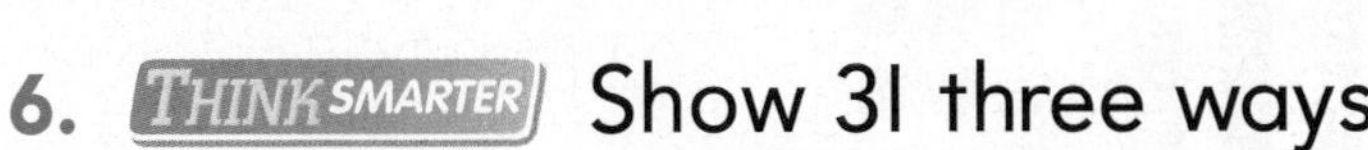

6. THINKSMARTER Show 31 three ways.

Tens	Ones

Tens	Ones

Tens	Ones

_____ ◯ _____ ◯ _____

On Your Own

WRITE Math

Write a number sentence to solve. Draw to explain.

7. MATHEMATICAL PRACTICE 4 **Write an Equation**
Felix invites 15 friends to his party. Some friends are girls. 8 friends are boys. How many friends are girls?

____ ◯ ____ ◯ ____ girls

GO DEEPER Solve. Write the numbers.

8. I am a number less than 35.
I have 3 tens and some ones.
What numbers can I be?

____

Personal Math Trainer

9. THINK SMARTER + Choose all the ways that show the same number.

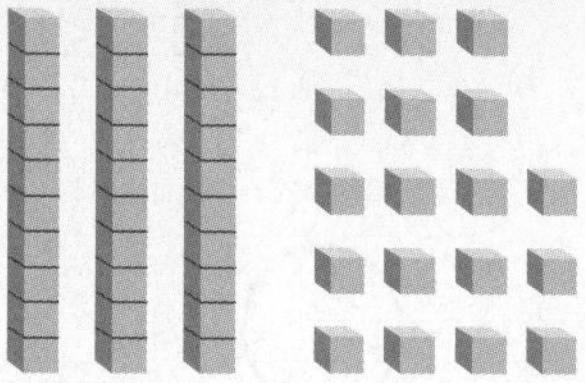

○ 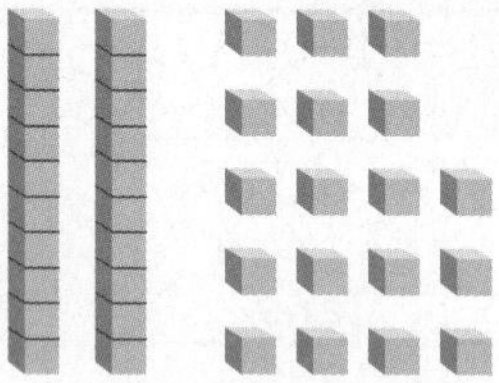

○ 

○ 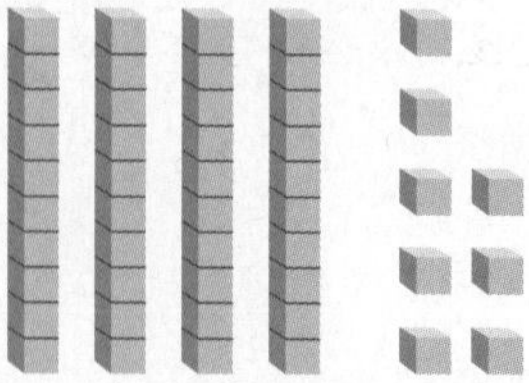

○ 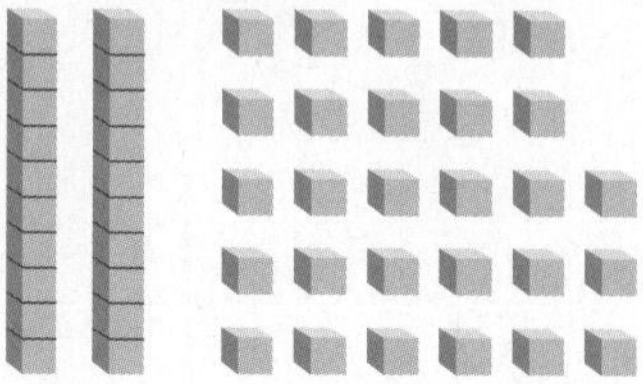

TAKE HOME ACTIVITY • Have your child draw quick pictures to show the number 56 two ways.

FOR MORE PRACTICE:
Standards Practice Book

Name ___________________________

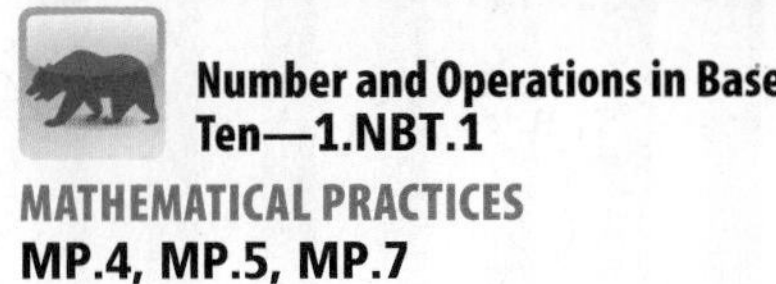

Model, Read, and Write Numbers from 100 to 110

Essential Question How can you model, read, and write numbers from 100 to 110?

Number and Operations in Base Ten—1.NBT.1

MATHEMATICAL PRACTICES
MP.4, MP.5, MP.7

Use crayons.
Circle a number to answer the question.

1	2	3	4	5	6	7	8	9	10
11	12	13	14	15	16	17	18	19	20
21	22	23	24	25	26	27	28	29	30
31	32	33	34	35	36	37	38	39	40
41	42	43	44	45	46	47	48	49	50
51	52	53	54	55	56	57	58	59	60
61	62	63	64	65	66	67	68	69	70
71	72	73	74	75	76	77	78	79	80
81	82	83	84	85	86	87	88	89	90
91	92	93	94	95	96	97	98	99	100

Math Talk Mathematical Practices

Explain why 100 is to the right of 99 on the hundred chart. **Explain** why 100 is below 90.

FOR THE TEACHER • Have children locate each number on the hundred chart. What number is the same as 30 ones? What number is the same as 10 tens? What number is the same as 8 tens 7 ones? What number has 1 more one than 52? What number has 1 more ten than 65?

Model and Draw

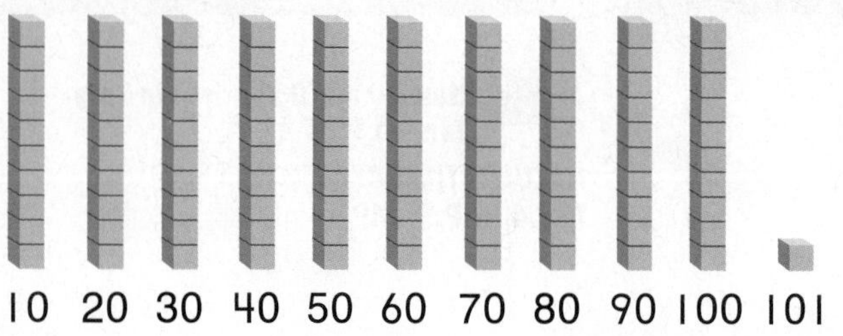

10 tens and 1 more = 101

10 20 30 40 50 60 70 80 90 100 110

10 tens and 10 more = 110

Share and Show

REMEMBER
10 tens = 100

Use to model the number.
Write the number.

1. 10 tens and 1 more ______

2. 10 tens and 2 more ______

3. 10 tens and 3 more ______

4. 10 tens and 4 more ______

✓5. 10 tens and 5 more ______

✓6. 10 tens and 6 more ______

Name ______________________________

On Your Own

MATHEMATICAL PRACTICE 4 **Model Mathematics**

Use [tens rod] [ones cube] to model the number. Write the number.

7. 10 tens and 7 more

_____

8. 10 tens and 8 more

_____

9. 10 tens and 9 more

_____

10. 10 tens and 10 more

_____

11. THINK SMARTER 11 tens

_____

Write the number.

12.

_____

13.

_____

14.

_____

15.

_____

Problem Solving • Applications

GO DEEPER Solve to find the number of apples.

THINK
● = 1 apple
crate = 10 apples

16.

There are _____ apples.

17.

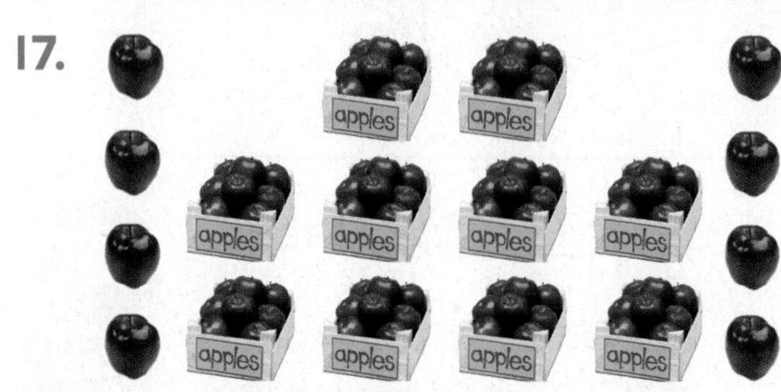

There are _____ apples.

18.

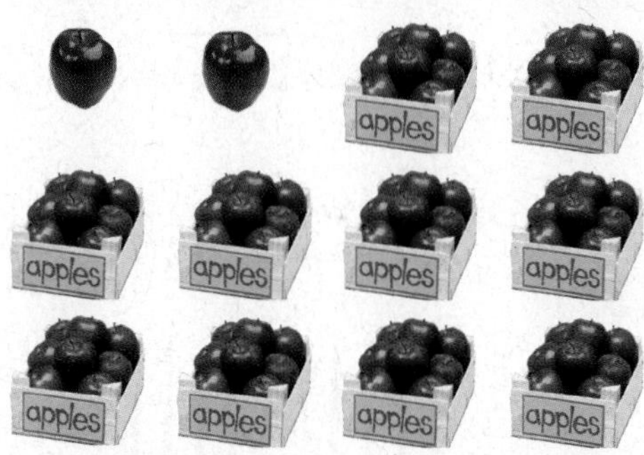

There are _____ apples.

19. THINK SMARTER What number does the model show?

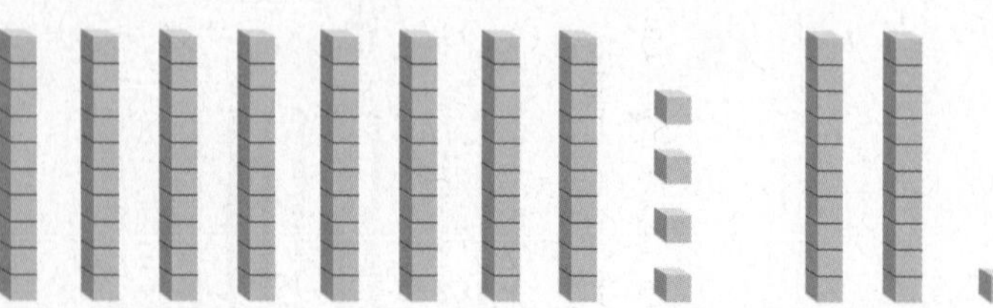

_____

TAKE HOME ACTIVITY • Give your child a group of 100 to 110 pennies. Ask him or her to make as many groups of ten as possible, then tell you the total number of pennies.

FOR MORE PRACTICE: Standards Practice Book

Name ______________________________

Model, Read, and Write Numbers from 110 to 120

HANDS ON
Lesson 6.10

Number and Operations in Base Ten—1.NBT.1

MATHEMATICAL PRACTICES
MP.2, MP.4, MP.6

Essential Question How can you model, read, and write numbers from 110 to 120?

Listen and Draw Real World

How many shells are there?

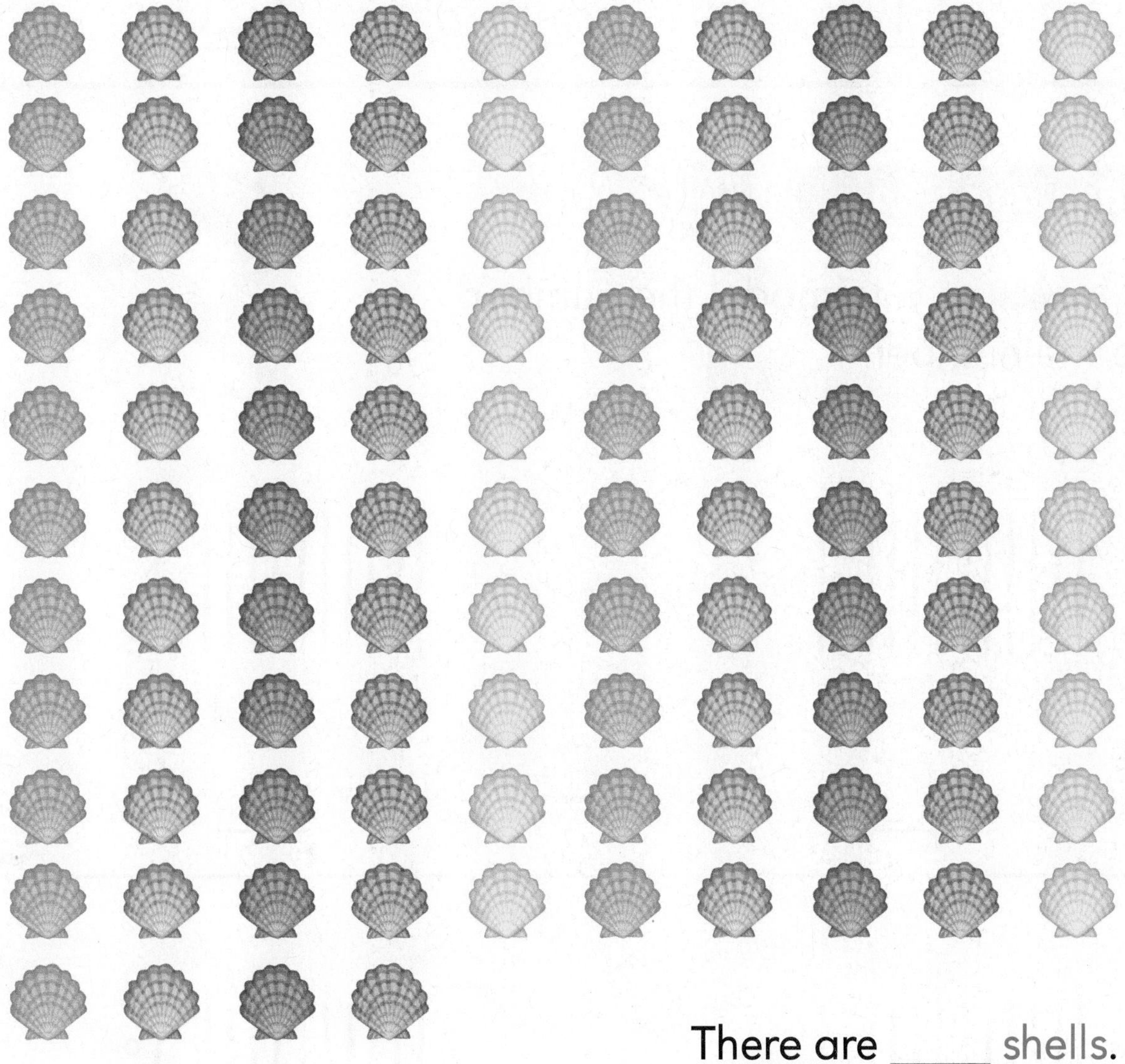

There are _____ shells.

Math Talk Mathematical Practices

How did you decide how many shells there are? **Explain.**

FOR THE TEACHER • The picture shows the shells that Heidi has collected. How many shells does Heidi have?

Model and Draw

11 tens is 110.

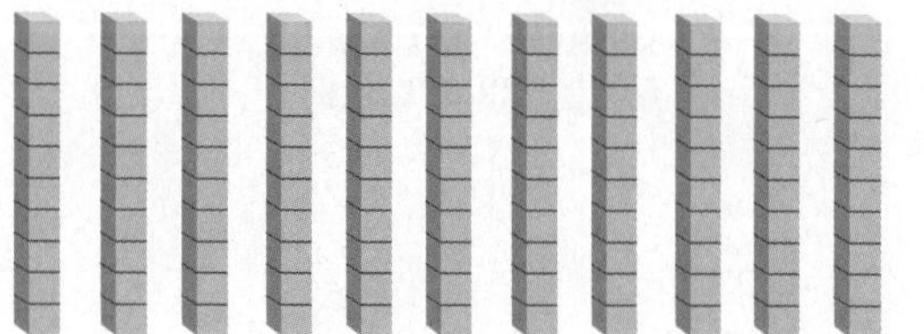

110

12 tens is 120.

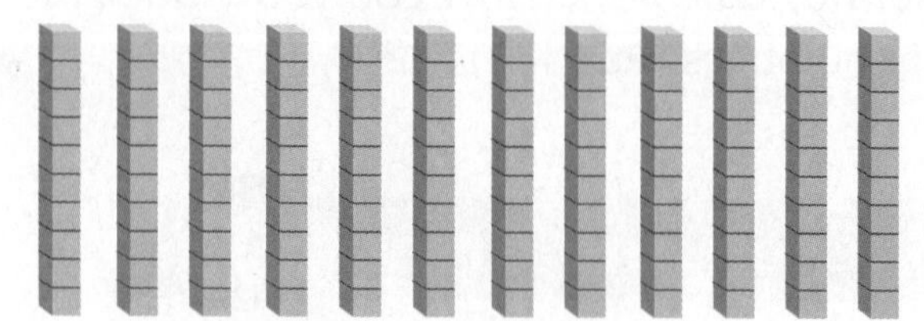

120

Share and Show

MATH BOARD

Use  to model the number. Write the number.

1.

111

2.

______

3.

______

4.

______

Name ______________________________

On Your Own

MATHEMATICAL PRACTICE 4 **Model Mathematics**

Use [tens rod] [ones cube] to model the number.
Write the number.

5.

______

6.

______

7.

______

8.

______

9.

______

10.

______

THINK SMARTER Write the number.

Math on the Spot

11.

______

12.

______

13.

______

Problem Solving • Applications  

GO DEEPER Choose a way to solve.
Draw or write to explain.

14. Joe collects pennies. He can make 11 groups of 10 pennies. How many pennies does Joe have?

_____ pennies

15. Cindy collects buttons. She can make 11 groups of 10 buttons and one more group of 7 buttons. How many buttons does Cindy have?

_____ buttons

16. Lee collects marbles. He can make 11 groups of 10 marbles and has 2 marbles left over. How many marbles does Lee have?

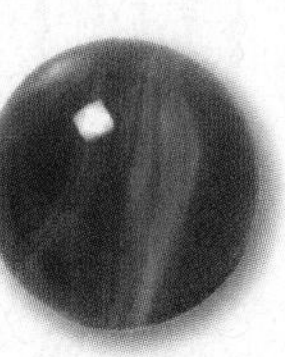

_____ marbles

17. THINK SMARTER Finish the drawing to show 119.

Write to explain.

_____

TAKE HOME ACTIVITY • Give your child a group of 100 to 120 pennies. Ask him or her to make as many groups of ten as possible, then tell you the total number of pennies.

FOR MORE PRACTICE: Standards Practice Book

Name ______________________

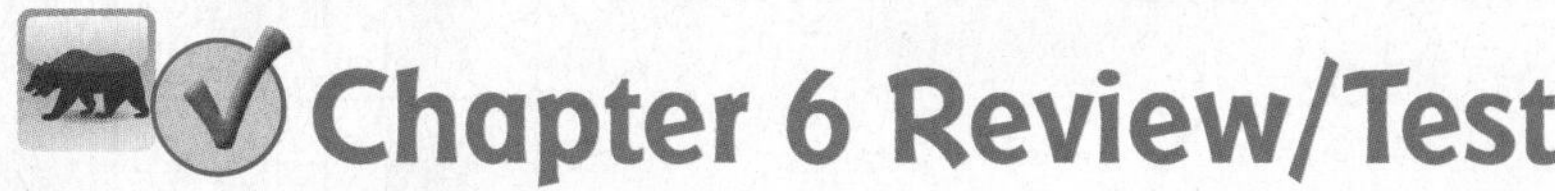

Chapter 6 Review/Test

1. Felix counts 46 cubes. Then he counts forward some more cubes. Write the numbers.

46, ____, ____, ____, ____, ____, ____

2. Count by tens. Match each number on the left to a number that is 10 more.

35 •	• 69
49 •	• 59
59 •	• 75
65 •	• 45
57 •	• 67

GO DIGITAL Assessment Options Chapter Test

3. Does the number match the model?
Choose Yes or No.

10 + 10	○ Yes	○ No
1 ten 4 ones	○ Yes	○ No
1 ten 5 ones	○ Yes	○ No
10 + 5	○ Yes	○ No

4. Circle the numbers that make the sentence true.

There are [1 / 2 / 10] tens and [1 / 2 / 10] ones in 12.

5. Choose all the ways that name the model.

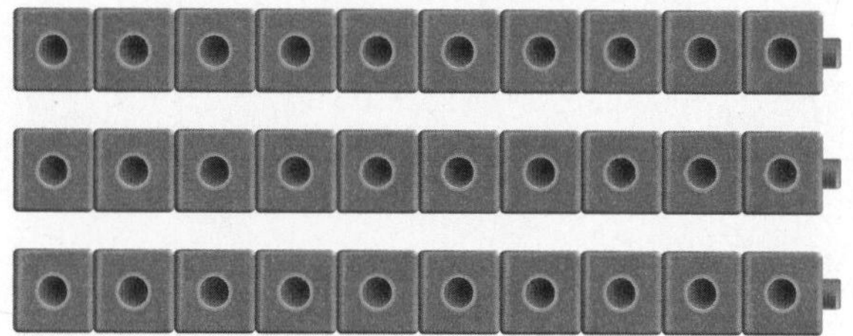

○ 3 ones

○ 3 tens

○ 3 tens 0 ones

○ 30

Name ____________________

6. There are 42 . Lisa says that there are 4 tens and 2 ones. Elena says there are 2 tens and 4 ones. Who is correct? Circle the name.

Lisa　　　　　　Elena

How can you draw to show 42?

---

7. Read the problem. Write a number to solve.

I am greater than 27.
I am less than 30.
I have 9 ones.

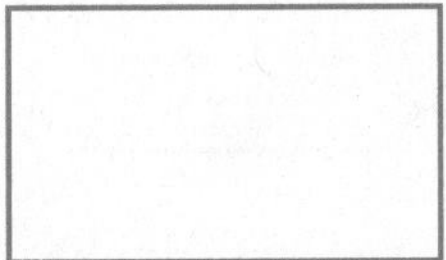

---

8. Choose all the ways that show the same number.

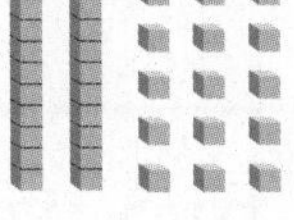

○ 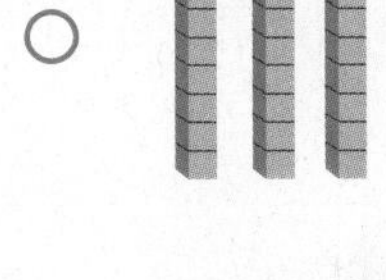

○ 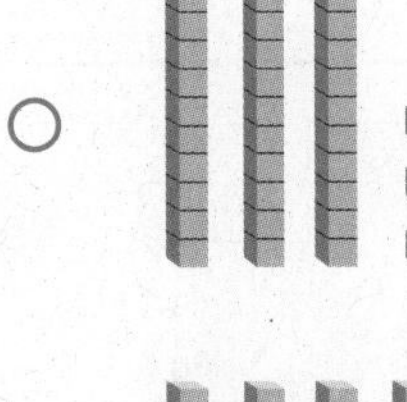

○ 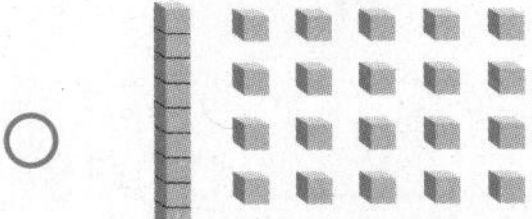

○ 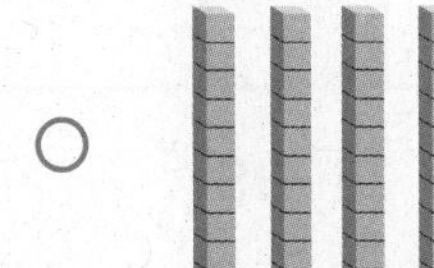

9. What number does the model show?

____

10. Finish the drawing to show 118.

Write to explain.

11. Count the acorns. Write the numbers.

How many tens? ________ tens

How many acorns? ________

________ acorns

12. Draw a quick picture to show 54 in two ways. Then write the number of tens and ones in each picture.

________ tens ________ ones ________ tens ________ ones

Chapter 7 Compare Numbers

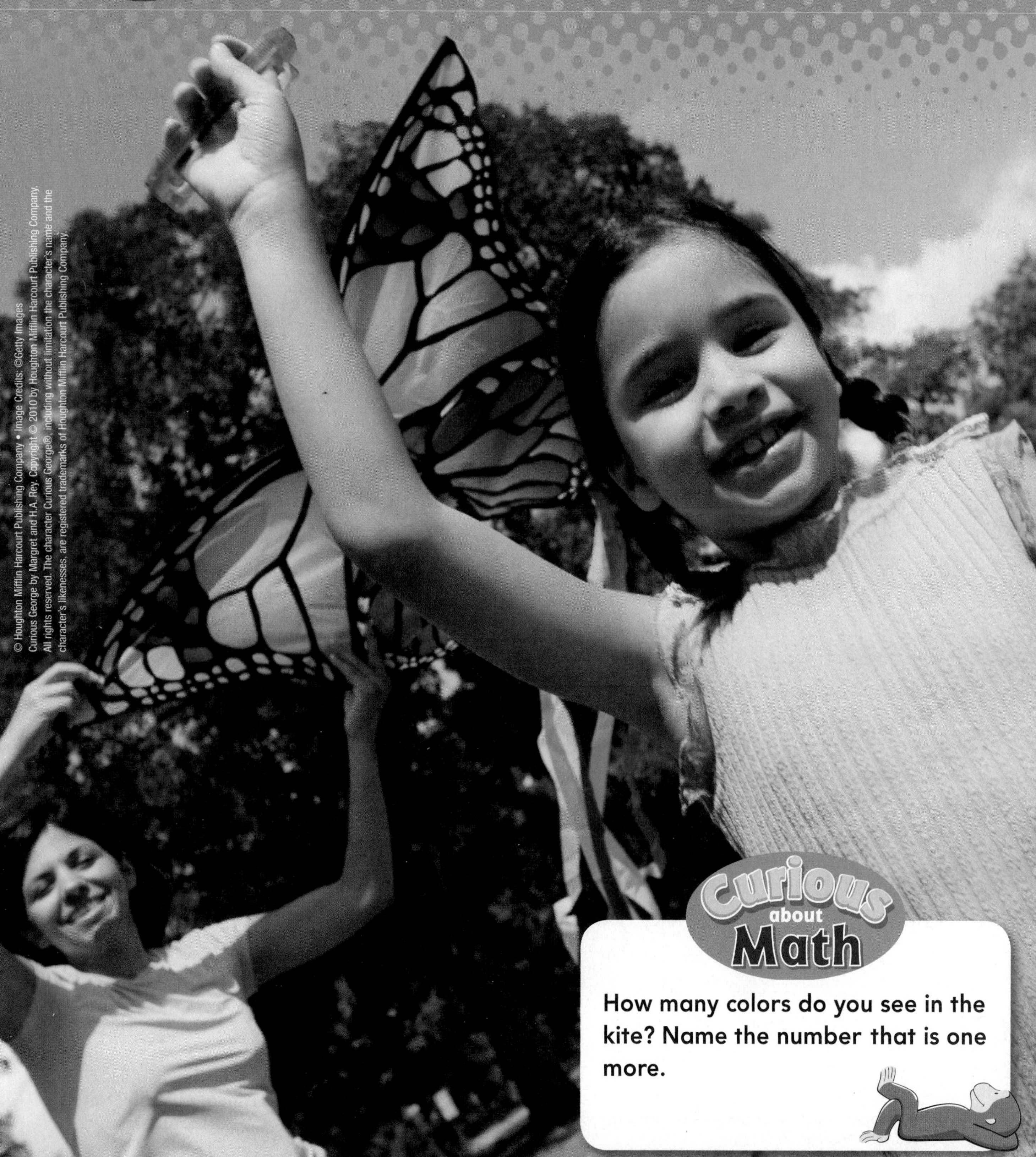

How many colors do you see in the kite? Name the number that is one more.

Name ____________________________________

Show What You Know

Model More

Draw lines to match.
Circle the set that has more.

1.

2.

More, Fewer

3. Circle the row that has more.

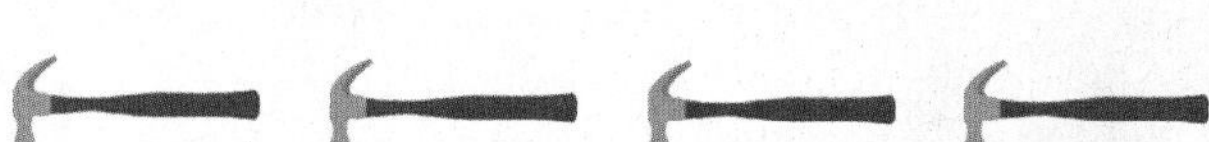

4. Circle the row that has fewer.

Draw Equal Groups

5. Draw a ball for each glove.

This page checks understanding of important skills needed for success in Chapter 7.

Name ______________________________

Vocabulary Builder

Review Words
fewer
more
same

Visualize It

Draw pictures in the box to show **more**, **fewer**, or the **same** number.

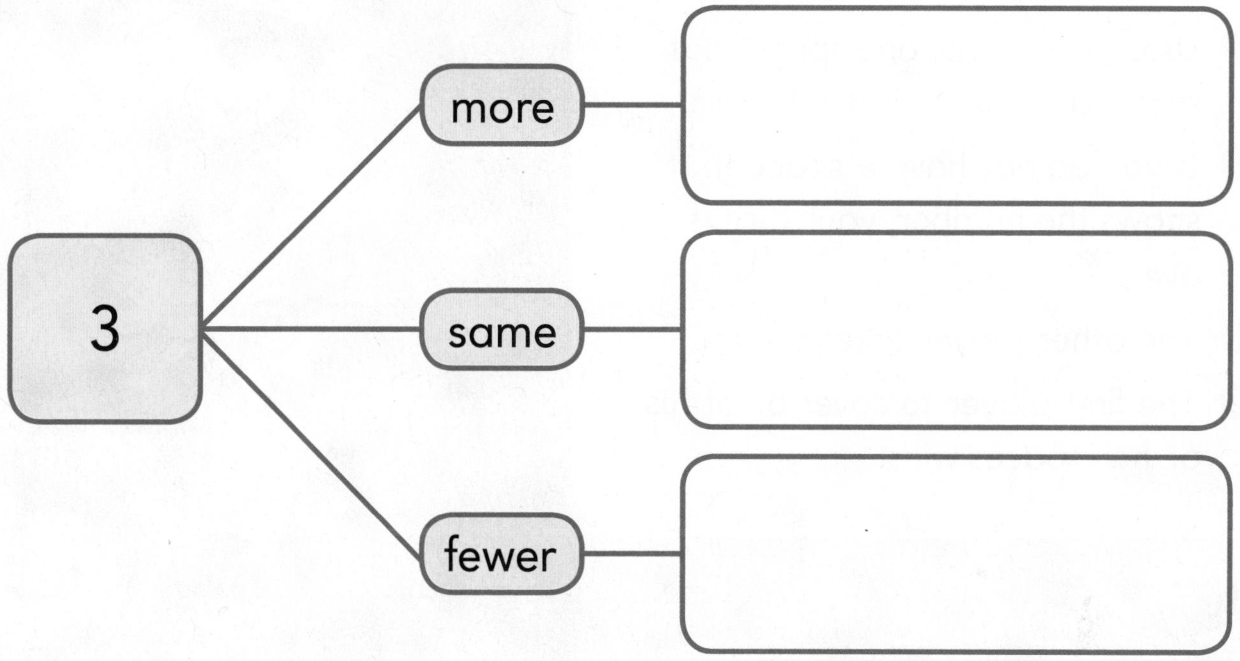

Understand Vocabulary

Complete the sentences with review words.

1. I see 2 white cats and 4 yellow cats. I see __________ yellow cats than white cats.

2. Dave has 9 grapes. Ann has 6 grapes. Ann has __________ grapes than Dave.

3. 5 ducks and 5 swans are at the pond. There are the __________ number of ducks and swans.

GO DIGITAL • Interactive Student Edition • Multimedia eGlossary

Chapter 7

Game Rainy Day Bingo

Materials •  • 9 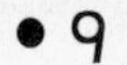 • 9

Play with a partner.

1. Toss the .
2. Use to cover one space that shows a number that is 1 more.
3. If you do not have a space that shows the number, your turn is over.
4. The other player takes a turn.
5. The first player to cover all of his or her spaces wins.

Player 1		
4	5	2
3	6	4
2	5	7

Player 2		
6	2	3
4	7	6
5	3	7

Name ______________________

Algebra • Greater Than

Essential Question How can you compare two numbers to find which is greater?

Number and Operations in Base Ten—1.NBT.3

MATHEMATICAL PRACTICES
MP.5, MP.7

Listen and Draw

Use [tens block] [ones block] to solve.
Draw quick pictures to show your work.

Tens	Ones

Math Talk **Mathematical Practices**

How did you decide which number is greater? **Explain.**

FOR THE TEACHER • Read the problem. Which number is greater, 65 or 56? Have children use base-ten blocks and draw quick pictures to solve.

Model and Draw

To compare 25 and 17, first compare the tens.

2 tens are more than 1 ten.

25 **is greater than** 17.

25 > 17

If the tens are the same, compare the ones.

7 ones are more than 5 ones.

17 is greater than 15.

17 > 15

Share and Show

MATH BOARD

Use your MathBoard and  to show each number.

	Circle the greater number.	Did tens or ones help you decide?	Write the numbers.
1.	62 (65)	tens (ones)	65 is greater than 62. 65 > 62
2.	84 48	tens ones	____ is greater than ____. ____ > ____
3.	72 70	tens ones	____ is greater than ____. ____ > ____

Name ______________________

On Your Own

MATHEMATICAL PRACTICE 5 **Use a Concrete Model**

Use [tens block] [ones block] if you need to.

	Circle the greater number.	Did tens or ones help you decide?	Write the numbers.
4.	57 75	tens ones	____ is greater than ____. ____ > ____
5.	94 98	tens ones	____ is greater than ____. ____ > ____

Write or draw to solve.

6. THINK SMARTER Pam and Jake play a game for points. Pam's points are 1 ten 6 ones. Jake's points are 1 one 6 tens. Who has the greatest number of points?

____

7. GO DEEPER John has 51 cards. Paul has 32 cards. George has a stack of cards greater than either Paul or John. How many cards might George have?

____

____

Problem Solving • Applications

8. THINKSMARTER Color the balloons that show numbers greater than 56.

46

59

1 ten 6 ones

100

80

50

65

1 one 6 tens

52

9. THINKSMARTER Compare. Is the math sentence true? Choose Yes or No.

37 is greater than 43.	○ Yes	○ No
41 is greater than 39.	○ Yes	○ No
48 > 52	○ Yes	○ No
86 > 68	○ Yes	○ No

TAKE HOME ACTIVITY • Write 38, 63, 68, and 83 on slips of paper. Show your child two numbers, and ask which number is greater. Repeat with different pairs of numbers.

FOR MORE PRACTICE: Standards Practice Book

Name ______________________

Algebra • Less Than

HANDS ON
Lesson 7.2

Essential Question How can you compare two numbers to find which is less?

Number and Operations in Base Ten—1.NBT.3

MATHEMATICAL PRACTICES
MP.5, MP.7

Listen and Draw

Hands On

Use [tens block] [ones block] to solve. Draw quick pictures to show your work.

Tens	Ones

Math Talk Mathematical Practices

How does your drawing show which number is less? **Explain.**

FOR THE TEACHER • Read the problem. Which number is less, 22 or 28? Have children use base-ten blocks to solve.

Model and Draw

Compare numbers to find which is less.

How do you know which number is less?

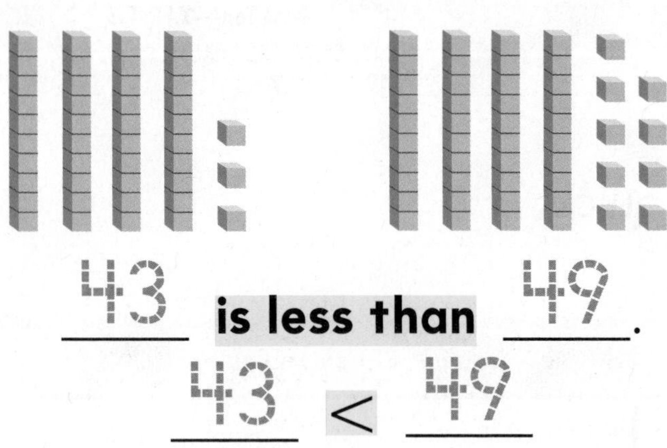

43 is less than 49.

43 < 49

Share and Show

Use your MathBoard and [tens and ones blocks] to show each number.

	Circle the number that is less.	Did tens or ones help you decide?	Write the numbers.
1.	39 (36)	tens (ones)	36 is less than 39. 36 < 39
✓2.	80 94	tens ones	____ is less than ____. ____ < ____
✓3.	57 54	tens ones	____ is less than ____. ____ < ____

Name ______________________________

On Your Own

MATHEMATICAL PRACTICE 5 Use a Concrete Model

GO DEEPER Use [ten rod] [unit cube] if you need to.

	Circle the number that is less.	Did tens or ones help you decide?	Write the numbers.
4.	47 48	tens ones	____ is less than ____. ____ < ____
5.	82 28	tens ones	____ is less than ____. ____ < ____
6.	96 90	tens ones	____ is less than ____. ____ < ____
7.	23 32	tens ones	____ is less than ____. ____ < ____
8.	65 55	tens ones	____ is less than ____. ____ < ____

Problem Solving • Applications

Write a number to solve.

9. THINK SMARTER Nan makes the number 46. Marty makes a number that is less than 46. What could be a number Marty makes?

_____

10. THINK SMARTER Jack makes the number 92. Kit makes a number that has fewer ones than 92. What could be a number Kit makes?

_____

11. THINK SMARTER Write a number that is less than 67.

How do you know your number is less than 67?

_____

TAKE HOME ACTIVITY • Write 47, 54, 57, and 74 on slips of paper. Show your child two numbers, and ask which number is less. Repeat with different pairs of numbers.

FOR MORE PRACTICE: Standards Practice Book

Name ____________________

Algebra • Use Symbols to Compare

HANDS ON
Lesson 7.3

Essential Question How can you use symbols to show how numbers compare?

Number and Operations in Base Ten—1.NBT.3 *Also 1.OA.7*
MATHEMATICAL PRACTICES
MP.1, MP.4, MP.8

Listen and Draw

Hands On

Use . Draw quick pictures to show your work. Write the numbers to compare.

___ < 36

___ = 36

___ > 36

Math Talk **Mathematical Practices**

Compare 47 and 32 in two ways. What two symbols do you use? **Explain.**

FOR THE TEACHER • Have children use base-ten blocks to show a number less than 36, a number equal to 36, and a number greater than 36.

Model and Draw

$21 < 24$

21 is less than 24.

$24 = 24$

24 is equal to 24.

$30 > 24$

30 is greater than 24.

Share and Show

MATH BOARD

Use . Draw to show each number.
Write $<$, $>$, or $=$. Complete the sentence.

1.

28 ◯ 35

28 ______________ 35.

2.

16 ◯ 16

16 ______________ 16.

✓3.

46 ◯ 31

46 ______________ 31.

✓4.

51 ◯ 52

51 ______________ 52.

Name ______________________________

On Your Own

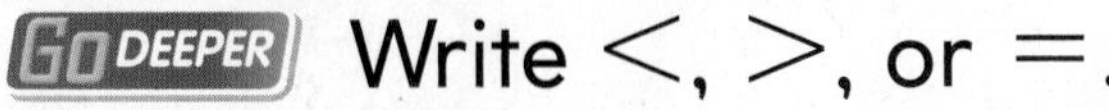

Draw a quick picture if you need to.

5. 45 (>) 42

6. 38 ◯ 50

7. 90 ◯ 93

8. 87 ◯ 87

9. 64 ◯ 59

10. THINK SMARTER Gill and Rob win tokens in a game. Gill has 86 tokens. Rob has 61 tokens. 70 tokens are needed for a prize. Who has enough tokens for a prize? Write the number. ____

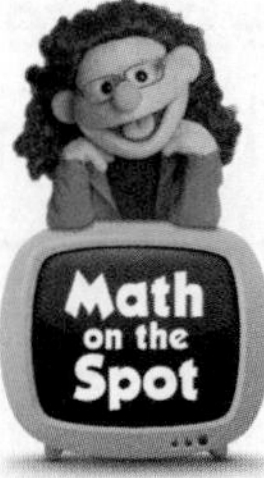

THINK SMARTER Write numbers to solve.

11. 96 = ____

12. 53 > ____

13. 83 < ____

14. 40 < ____

15. 71 > ____

16. 29 = ____

TAKE HOME ACTIVITY • Have your child show you how to write <, >, and = to compare two numbers. Ask him or her to use words to explain each comparison.

FOR MORE PRACTICE: Standards Practice Book

Name ____________________

Mid-Chapter Checkpoint

Concepts and Skills

Circle the greater number. Write the numbers. (1.NBT.3)

1. 38 83

___ is greater than ___.

___ > ___

Circle the number that is less. Write the numbers. (1.NBT.3)

2. 61 29

___ is less than ___.

___ < ___

3. Matt scores 34 points and wins the game. Lee scores points and does not win. The number of Lee's points is less than the number of Matt's points. Is Lee's score 49 or 29? (1.NBT.3) ___

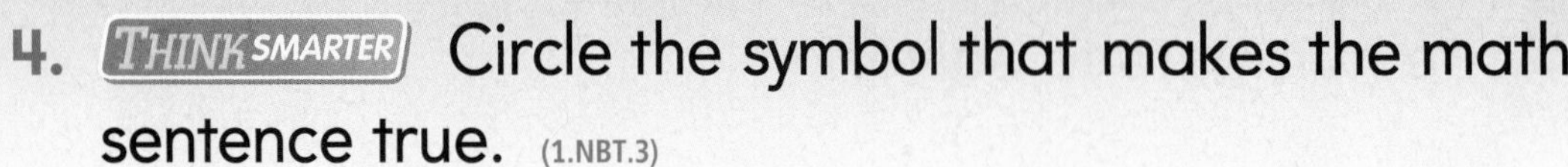

4. THINK SMARTER Circle the symbol that makes the math sentence true. (1.NBT.3)

44

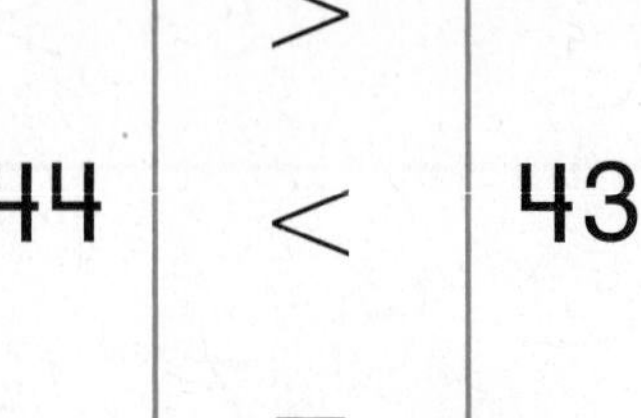

43

Name ___

Problem Solving • Compare Numbers

Essential Question How can making a model help you compare numbers?

Number and Operations in Base Ten—1.NBT.3

MATHEMATICAL PRACTICES
MP.2, MP.4, MP.6

Cassidy has the number cards shown below. She gives away the cards with numbers less than 49 and greater than 53. Which number cards does Cassidy have now?

Unlock the Problem

What do I need to find?

the number cards that Cassidy has now

What information do I need to use?

number cards < 49

and > 53

Show how to solve the problem.

Cassidy has number cards 51, 52.

HOME CONNECTION • Your child made a model of the problem. The numbers crossed out are less than 49 and also greater than 53. The remaining numbers solve the problem.

Try Another Problem

Make a model to solve.

- What do I need to find?
- What information do I need to use?

1. Tony has these number cards. He gives away the cards with numbers less than 16 and greater than 19. Which number cards does Tony have now?

15	17	18	20	22

Tony has number cards ______________.

---

2. Carol has these number cards. She keeps the cards with numbers greater than 98 and less than 95. Circle the number cards Carol keeps.

Carol keeps number cards ______________.

Math Talk **Mathematical Practices**

Explain how you can find the number cards Tony has now.

Name ______________________________

Share and Show

MATHEMATICAL PRACTICE 4 **Use Models** Make a model to solve.

3. Felipe has these number cards. He gives away cards with numbers less than 60 and greater than 65. Which number cards does Felipe have now?

Felipe has number cards ______________.

4. THINK SMARTER Molly underlines the number cards greater than 76 and circles the number cards less than 84. Which number cards are both greater than 76 and less than 84?

Number cards ______________ are both greater than 76 and less than 84.

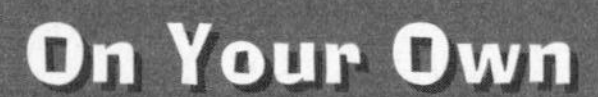

Choose a way to solve.
Draw or write to explain.

5. GO DEEPER Some cows were in the field. 6 more cows walked there. Then there were 13 cows. How many cows were in the field before?

____ cows

6. THINK SMARTER Ed has 6 marbles. How many marbles can he put in a red cup and how many can he put in a blue cup?

____ + ____ = 6

Personal Math Trainer

7. THINK SMARTER + Lani has these number cards. Write each number in the box to show **less than** 24 or **greater than** 24.

22 27 23 21 25

less than 24	greater than 24

TAKE HOME ACTIVITY • Ask your child to tell you a number that is greater than 59 and a number less than 59.

FOR MORE PRACTICE: Standards Practice Book

Name ____________________

10 More, 10 Less

HANDS ON
Lesson 7.5

Essential Question How can you identify numbers that are 10 more or 10 less than a number?

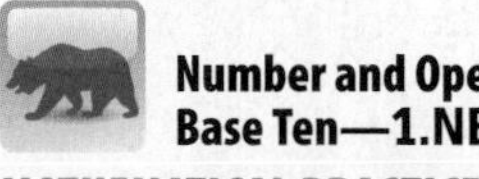

Number and Operations in Base Ten—1.NBT.5

MATHEMATICAL PRACTICES
MP.1, MP.3, MP.6

Use [tens rod] [ones cube] to solve. Draw quick pictures to show your work.

Pat

____

Tony

____

Jan

____

FOR THE TEACHER • Read the following problem. Tony has 2 boxes of markers and 2 more markers. Pat has 10 fewer markers than Tony. Jan has 10 more markers than Tony. How many markers does each child have?

Math Talk **Mathematical Practices**

What number has one less 10 than 12? **Explain.**

Model and Draw

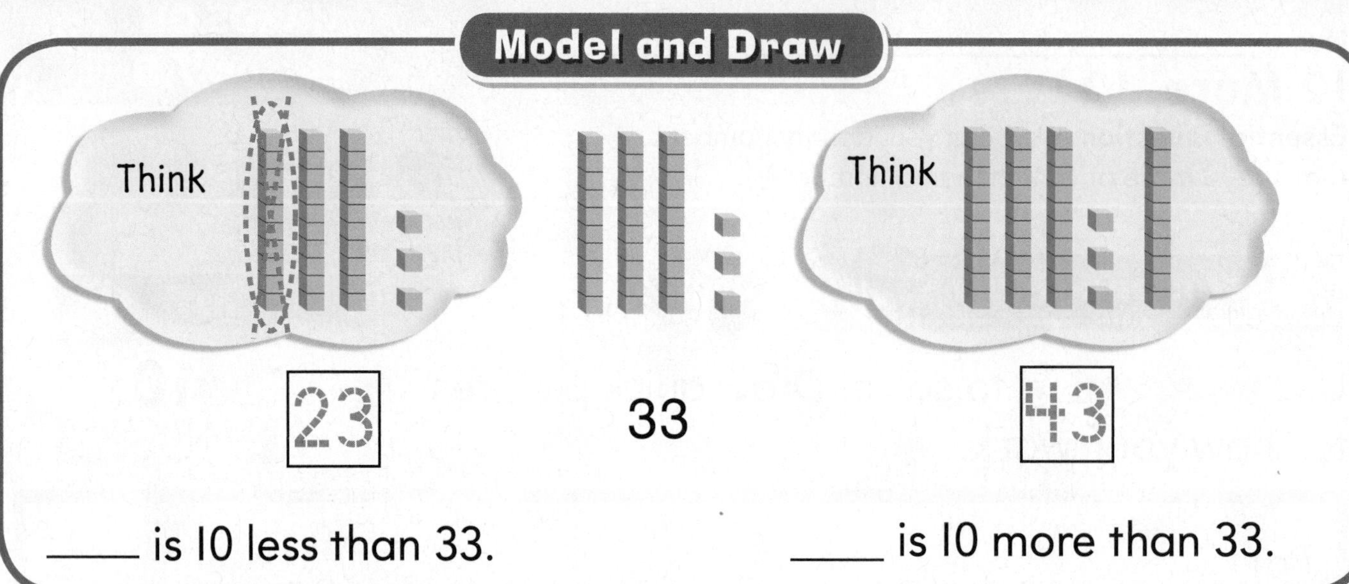

23 33 43

____ is 10 less than 33. ____ is 10 more than 33.

Share and Show

Use mental math. Write the numbers that are 10 less and 10 more.

1. 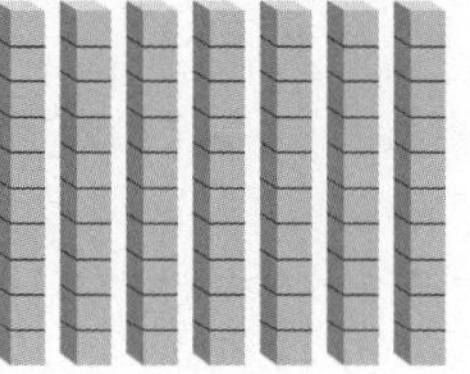

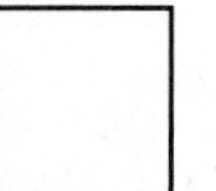 70

2. 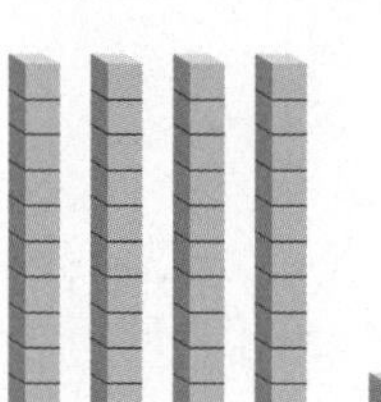

41 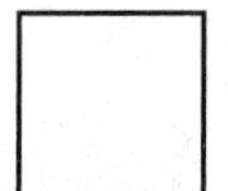

3.  58 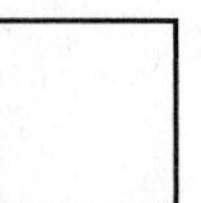

4.  66 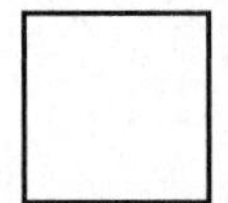

5. 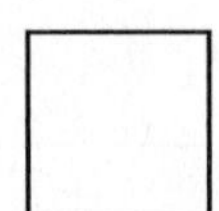 24 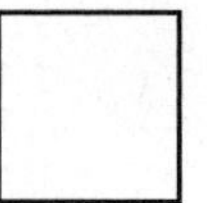

6. 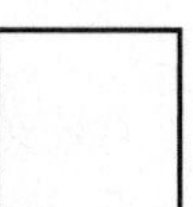 86 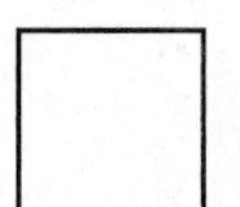

✓7.  37 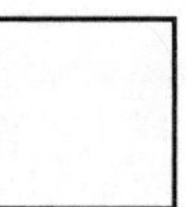

✓8. 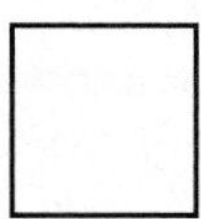 15 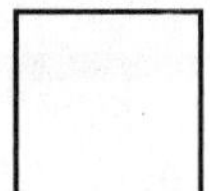

Name ______________________________

On Your Own

MATHEMATICAL PRACTICE 3 **Apply** Use mental math.
Complete the chart. Explain your method.

	10 Less		10 More
9.	____	39	____
10.	____	75	____
11.	____	64	____
12.	____	90	____
13.	____	83	____
14.	11	____	____
15.	____	____	26

16. THINK SMARTER Solve.
I have 89 rocks. I want to collect 10 more. How many rocks will I have then?

____ rocks

Problem Solving • Applications

Choose a way to solve. Draw or write to show your work.

17. The plant has 4 fewer ladybugs on it than the tree. The tree has 7 ladybugs on it. How many ladybugs are on the plant?

____ ladybugs

18. Amy has 7 ribbons. Charlotte has 9 ribbons. How many more ribbons does Charlotte have than Amy?

____ more ribbons

19. GO DEEPER Margo has 28 stamps. Chet has 10 more stamps than Margo. Luis has 10 more stamps than Chet. How many stamps does Luis have?

____ stamps

Personal Math Trainer

20. THINK SMARTER + Draw a quick picture to show a number that is 10 less than the model.

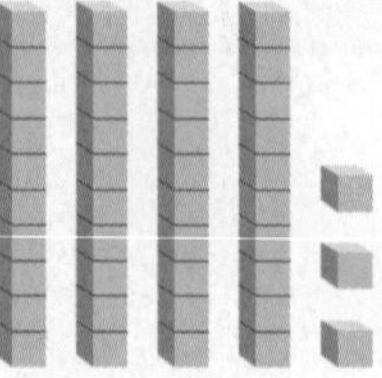

What is the new number? 

TAKE HOME ACTIVITY • Write a two-digit number, such as 25, 40, or 81. Ask your child to identify the numbers that are ten less than and ten more than that number. Repeat with other numbers.

FOR MORE PRACTICE: Standards Practice Book

Name ________________________________

Chapter 7 Review/Test

1. Compare. Is the math sentence true? Choose Yes or No.

54 is greater than 45.	○ Yes	○ No
37 is greater than 29.	○ Yes	○ No
$29 > 43$	○ Yes	○ No
$55 > 45$	○ Yes	○ No

2. Choose all the numbers that are less than 71.

○ 62 ○ 80 ○ 70 ○ 49

3. Circle the symbol that makes the math sentence true.

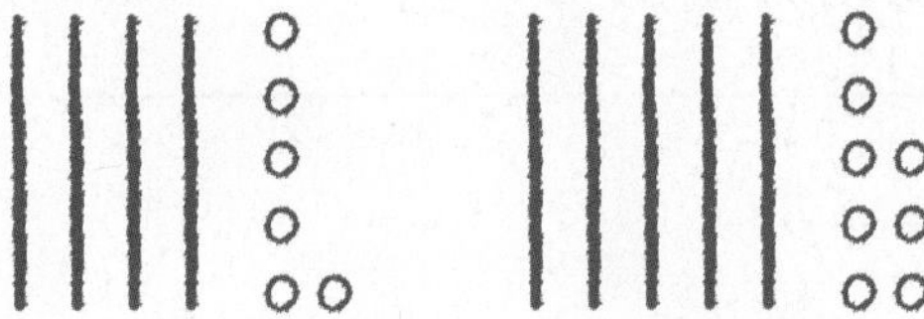

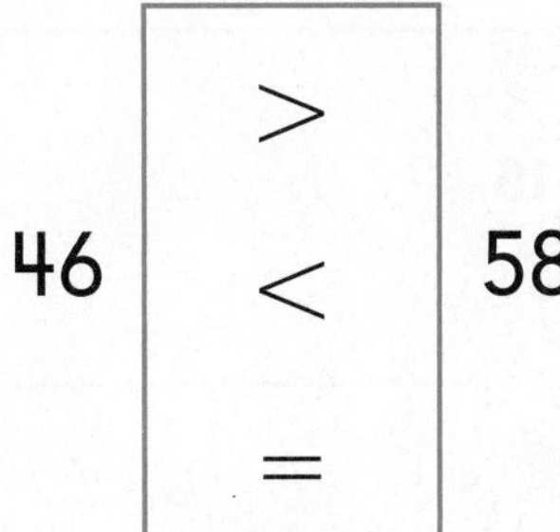

4. Megan has these number cards. Write each number in the box to show **less than** 33 or **greater than** 33.

37 34 31 35 32

less than 33	greater than 33

5. Use mental math. Complete the chart.

10 Less		10 More
____	33	____
____	57	____

6. Write a number that is less than 30.

How do you know your number is less than 30?

Name ______________________

7. Choose all the math sentences that are true.

- ○ $35 < 47$
- ○ $24 = 39$
- ○ $14 > 41$
- ○ $48 = 48$
- ○ $23 > 21$

---

8. James circles the numbers that are **less than** 87 or **greater than** 91. Which numbers does James circle?

86 88 89 90 92

James circles _____ and _____.

---

9. Draw a quick picture to show a number that is 10 more than the model.

10. Compare. Is the math sentence true?
Circle yes or no.

49 is greater than 57.	○ Yes	○ No
54 is greater than 53.	○ Yes	○ No
$60 > 50$	○ Yes	○ No
$72 > 68$	○ Yes	○ No

11. Write $<$, $>$, or $=$ to compare the numbers.

48 ____ 36

How do the drawings help you compare the numbers?

12. Circle the words that make the sentence true.

88 is [greater than / less than / equal to] 90.

Chapter 8

Two-Digit Addition and Subtraction

Curious About Math with Curious George

There are 4 boxes of oranges on a table. Each box holds 10 oranges. How many oranges are there?

Name ________________________

Show What You Know

Add and Subtract

Use ▪ and ▪ to add. Write the sum.
Break apart ▪ to subtract.
Write the difference.

1.

4 + 1 = ____

5 − 1 = ____

Count Groups to 20

Circle groups of 10. Write how many.

2.

____

3.

____

Use a Hundred Chart to Count

Touch and count. Shade the last number counted.

4. Start at 1 and count to 20.
5. Start at 30 and count to 56.
6. Start at 77 and count to 93.

1	2	3	4	5	6	7	8	9	10
11	12	13	14	15	16	17	18	19	20
21	22	23	24	25	26	27	28	29	30
31	32	33	34	35	36	37	38	39	40
41	42	43	44	45	46	47	48	49	50
51	52	53	54	55	56	57	58	59	60
61	62	63	64	65	66	67	68	69	70
71	72	73	74	75	76	77	78	79	80
81	82	83	84	85	86	87	88	89	90
91	92	93	94	95	96	97	98	99	100

This page checks understanding of important skills needed for success in Chapter 8.

Name ______________________________

Review Words
add
subtract
sum
difference

Vocabulary Builder

Visualize It

Sort the review words from the box.

Put Together

____

____

____

Take Apart

____

____

____

Understand Vocabulary

Use a review word to complete each sentence.

1. 8 is the ______________ for 17 − 9.

2. 17 is the ______________ for 8 + 9.

3. When you ______________ 4 to 8, you find the sum.

4. When you ______________ 4 from 8, you find the difference.

GO DIGITAL
• Interactive Student Edition
• Multimedia eGlossary

Chapter 8

Game Neighborhood Sums

Materials

- 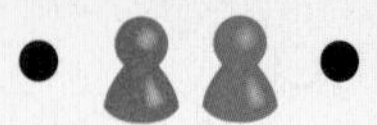
- 
- 9 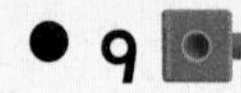
- 9 
- 9 

Play with a partner.

1. Put your on START.
2. Spin the . Move that number of spaces.
3. Make a ten to help you find the sum.
4. The other player uses to check.
5. If you are not correct, you lose a turn.
6. The first player to get to END wins.

2 4 +8	Move ahead one space.	4 9 +6	4 4 +6	9 1 +6	END
4 6 +3	5 3 +7	9 7 +1	Move back one space.	3 7 +7	5 8 +5
					6 6 +4
	START	2 4 +8	Move ahead one space.	6 1 +9	8 8 +2

Name ______________________________

Add and Subtract Within 20

Essential Question What strategies can you use to add and subtract?

Operations and Algebraic Thinking—1.OA.6

MATHEMATICAL PRACTICES
MP.1, MP.3, MP.6

What is 5 + 4?
Use a strategy to solve the addition fact. Draw to show your work.

5 + 4 = ____

Math Talk — Mathematical Practices

Explain What strategy did you use to find the answer?

FOR THE TEACHER • Have children choose and model a strategy to solve the addition fact. Then have them draw to show their work.

Model and Draw

Think of a strategy you can use to add or subtract.

What is $14 - 6$?

I can use a related fact.

$\underline{6} \oplus \underline{8} = 14$

So, $14 - 6 = \underline{8}$.

Share and Show

MATH BOARD

Add or subtract.

1. $5 + 3 =$ ____	2. $10 - 5 =$ ____	3. $3 + 6 =$ ____
4. $12 - 5 =$ ____	5. $15 - 9 =$ ____	6. $5 + 7 =$ ____
7. $8 + 7 =$ ____	8. $9 - 7 =$ ____	9. $5 + 5 =$ ____
10. $12 - 7 =$ ____	11. $18 - 9 =$ ____	12. $9 + 4 =$ ____
13. $2 + 7 =$ ____	14. $5 - 1 =$ ____	15. $9 + 1 =$ ____
16. $7 - 6 =$ ____	✓17. $13 - 4 =$ ____	✓18. $2 + 6 =$ ____

Name ______________________________

On Your Own

MATHEMATICAL PRACTICE 3 **Apply** Add or subtract.

19. $14 - 5$

20. $2 + 10$

21. $3 + 3$

22. $14 - 8$

23. $8 + 9$

24. $6 - 3$

25. $6 - 5$

26. $2 + 8$

27. $0 + 5$

28. $10 - 2$

29. $9 + 9$

30. $5 - 4$

31. $8 - 8$

32. $10 + 1$

33. $4 + 7$

34. $9 - 3$

35. $1 + 8$

36. $17 - 9$

37. $13 - 7$

38. $6 + 5$

39. $10 + 2$

40. $14 - 9$

41. $10 + 10$

42. $11 - 3$

43. THINK SMARTER Jamal thinks of an addition fact. The sum is 15. One addend is 8. What is a fact Jamal could be thinking of?

____ ◯ ____ ◯ ____

Problem Solving • Applications

Solve. Write or draw to explain.

44. THINK SMARTER There are 9 ants on a rock. Some more ants get on the rock. Now there are 18 ants on the rock. How many more ants got on the rock?

____ more ants

---

45. GO DEEPER Fill in the blanks. Write a number sentence to solve.

Lin sees ____ bees. Some bees flew away. Now there are ____ bees. How many bees flew away?

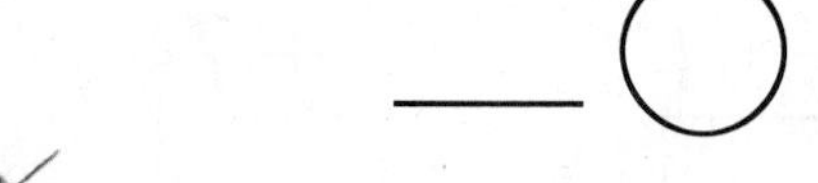

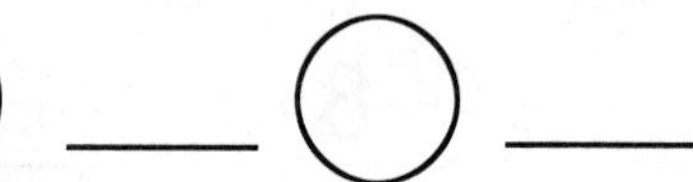

____ bees

46. THINK SMARTER Write each addition or subtraction in the box below the answer.

7 + 9   6 + 1   17 − 8   14 − 7   8 + 8

7	9	16

TAKE HOME ACTIVITY • Have your child tell a strategy he or she would use to solve 4 + 8.

FOR MORE PRACTICE: Standards Practice Book

Name ______________________________

Add Tens

Essential Question How can you add tens?

Number and Operations in Base Ten—1.NBT.4

MATHEMATICAL PRACTICES
MP.2, MP.7

Listen and Draw (Real World)

Choose a way to show the problem.
Draw a quick picture to show your work.

Math Talk **Mathematical Practices**

Explain why there will be no ones in your answer when you add 20 + 30.

FOR THE TEACHER • Read the following problems. Barb has 20 pennies. Ed has 30 pennies. How many pennies do they have? Kyle has 40 pennies. Kim has 50 pennies. How many pennies do they have?

Model and Draw

How can you find 30 + 40?

30 + 40 = 70

____ tens

Share and Show

MATH BOARD

Use . Draw to show tens.
Write the sum. Write how many tens.

1. 20 + 40 = ____

____ tens

2. 30 + 30 = ____

____ tens

3. 40 + 50 = ____

____ tens

4. 50 + 30 = ____

____ tens

Name ___________________________________

On Your Own

MATHEMATICAL PRACTICE 2 **Represent a Problem** Draw to show tens. Write the sum. Write how many tens.

5. 40 + 40 = ____

____ tens

6. 70 + 20 = ____

____ tens

7. 10 + 80 = ____

____ tens

8. 60 + 30 = ____

____ tens

9. GO DEEPER Draw two groups of tens you can add to get a sum of 50. Write the number sentence.

Problem Solving • Applications

WRITE Math

10. THINK SMARTER Complete the web. Write the missing addend to get a sum of 90.

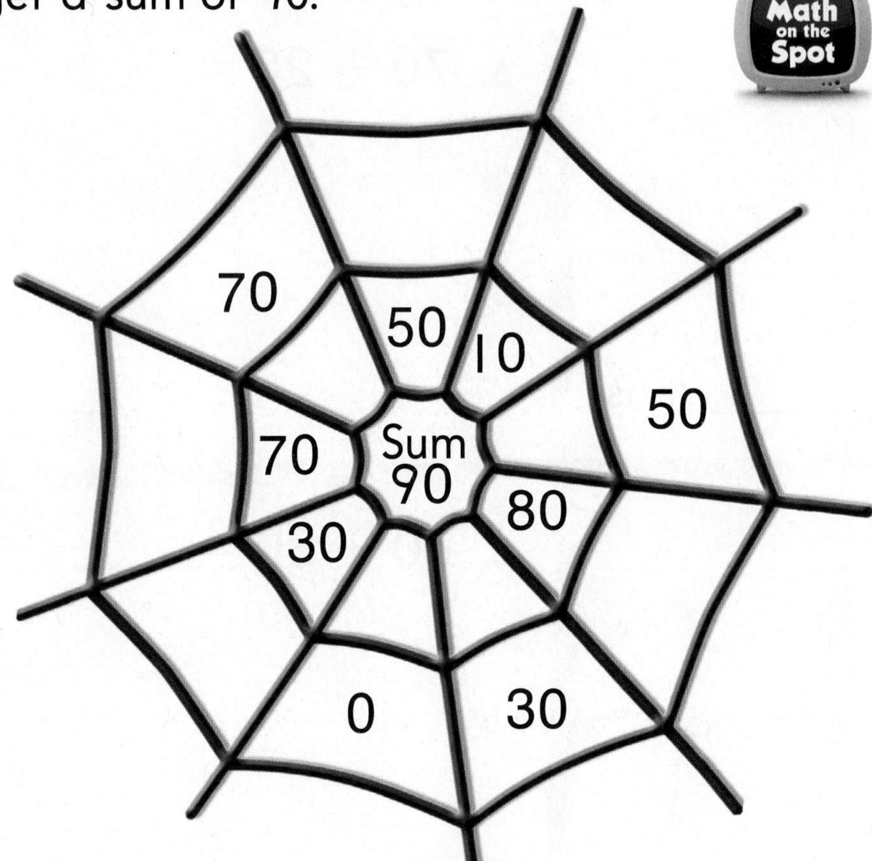

11. THINK SMARTER Choose all the ways that name the model.

- ○ 4 ones and 3 tens
- ○ 4 tens and 3 tens
- ○ 7 tens
- ○ 70

TAKE HOME ACTIVITY • Ask your child to explain how to use tens to find 20 + 70.

FOR MORE PRACTICE: Standards Practice Book

Name ________________________

Subtract Tens

Essential Question How can you subtract tens?

Number and Operations in Base Ten—1.NBT.6

MATHEMATICAL PRACTICES
MP.3, MP.8

Listen and Draw (Real World)

Choose a way to show the problem.
Draw a quick picture to show your work.

FOR THE TEACHER • Read the following problems. Tara has 30 seashells. 20 shells are big. The rest are small. How many small shells does she have? Sammy has 50 shells. He gives 30 shells to his friend. How many shells does Sammy have now?

Math Talk **Mathematical Practices**

Explain how your picture shows the first problem.

Model and Draw

How can you find 80 − 30?

80 − 30 = 50

____ tens

Share and Show

MATH BOARD

Use . Draw to show tens.
Write the difference. Write how many tens.

1. 60 − 20 = ____

____ tens

2. 70 − 30 = ____

____ tens

✓3. 80 − 20 = ____

____ tens

✓4. 90 − 40 = ____

____ tens

Name ______________________________

On Your Own

MATHEMATICAL PRACTICE 6 **Make Connections** Draw to show tens. Write the difference. Write how many tens.

5. 80 − 40 = ____

____ tens

6. 90 − 70 = ____

____ tens

7. 70 − 50 = ____

____ tens

8. 30 − 30 = ____

____ tens

THINK SMARTER Solve.

9. Jeff has 40 pennies. He gives some to Jill. He has 10 pennies left. How many pennies does Jeff give to Jill?

____ pennies

TAKE HOME ACTIVITY • Ask your child to explain how to use tens to find 90 − 70.

FOR MORE PRACTICE: Standards Practice Book

Name ____________________

Mid-Chapter Checkpoint

Concepts and Skills

Add or subtract. (1.OA.6)

1. $\begin{array}{r} 4 \\ +8 \\ \hline \end{array}$

2. $\begin{array}{r} 15 \\ -7 \\ \hline \end{array}$

3. $\begin{array}{r} 9 \\ -6 \\ \hline \end{array}$

4. $\begin{array}{r} 3 \\ +1 \\ \hline \end{array}$

5. $\begin{array}{r} 10 \\ +6 \\ \hline \end{array}$

6. $\begin{array}{r} 11 \\ -2 \\ \hline \end{array}$

Use [tens rod] [ones cube]. Draw to show tens.
Write the sum. Write how many tens. (1.NBT.4)

7. $30 + 50 =$ ____

____ tens

8. $40 + 20 =$ ____

____ tens

Use [tens rod] [ones cube]. Draw to show tens.
Write the difference. Write how many tens. (1.NBT.6)

9. $90 - 20 =$ ____

____ tens

10. $60 - 40 =$ ____

____ tens

11. THINK SMARTER Mike has 60 marbles. He gives 20 to Kathy. How many marbles does Mike have left? Show your work. (1.NBT.6)

________ marbles

Name ______________________

Use a Hundred Chart to Add

Essential Question How can you use a hundred chart to count on by ones or tens?

Number and Operations in Base Ten—1.NBT.4

MATHEMATICAL PRACTICES
MP.4, MP.6

Listen and Draw Real World

Use the hundred chart to solve the problems.

1	2	3	4	5	6	7	8	9	10
11	12	13	14	15	16	17	18	19	20
21	22	23	24	25	26	27	28	29	30
31	32	33	34	35	36	37	38	39	40
41	42	43	44	45	46	47	48	49	50
51	52	53	54	55	56	57	58	59	60
61	62	63	64	65	66	67	68	69	70
71	72	73	74	75	76	77	78	79	80
81	82	83	84	85	86	87	88	89	90
91	92	93	94	95	96	97	98	99	100

FOR THE TEACHER • Read the following problems. Alice picks 12 flowers. Then she picks 4 more flowers. How many flowers does Alice pick? Ella picks 10 strawberries. Then she picks 20 more strawberries. How many strawberries does Ella pick?

Math Talk Mathematical Practices

Describe how you can use a hundred chart to find each sum.

Model and Draw

Count on a hundred chart to find a sum.

Start at **24.**
Count on four ones.
25, 26, 27, 28

24 + 4 = 28

Start at **31.**
Count on four tens.
41, 51, 61, 71

31 + 40 = 71

1	2	3	4	5	6	7	8	9	10
11	12	13	14	15	16	17	18	19	20
21	22	23	24	25	26	27	28	29	30
31	32	33	34	35	36	37	38	39	40
41	42	43	44	45	46	47	48	49	50
51	52	53	54	55	56	57	58	59	60
61	62	63	64	65	66	67	68	69	70
71	72	73	74	75	76	77	78	79	80
81	82	83	84	85	86	87	88	89	90
91	92	93	94	95	96	97	98	99	100

Share and Show

Use the hundred chart to add.
Count on by ones or tens.

1. 42 + 7 = ____

2. 57 + 30 = ____

3. 91 + 5 = ____

4. 18 + 50 = ____

Name ______________________________

On Your Own

How can you use the hundred chart to find each sum?

32 + 5 = ___

48 + 30 = ___

1	2	3	4	5	6	7	8	9	10
11	12	13	14	15	16	17	18	19	20
21	22	23	24	25	26	27	28	29	30
31	32	33	34	35	36	37	38	39	40
41	42	43	44	45	46	47	48	49	50
51	52	53	54	55	56	57	58	59	60
61	62	63	64	65	66	67	68	69	70
71	72	73	74	75	76	77	78	79	80
81	82	83	84	85	86	87	88	89	90
91	92	93	94	95	96	97	98	99	100

MATHEMATICAL PRACTICE 5 **Use Appropriate Tools** 
Use the hundred chart to add.
Count on by ones or tens.

5. 13 + 70 = ___

6. 22 + 6 = ___

7. 71 + 3 = ___

8. 49 + 50 = ___

9. 53 + 4 = ___

10. 25 + 40 = ___

11. GO DEEPER Solve. Show your work.

31 + 20 + 40 = ___

Problem Solving • Applications

Choose a way to solve. Draw or write to show your work.

12. THINKSMARTER Rae put 20 books away. She put 20 more books away, then 11 more. How many books did Rae put away?

____ books

Personal Math Trainer

13. THINKSMARTER+ Use the hundred chart to add. Count on by ones or tens.

$62 + 9 =$ ____

1	2	3	4	5	6	7	8	9	10
11	12	13	14	15	16	17	18	19	20
21	22	23	24	25	26	27	28	29	30
31	32	33	34	35	36	37	38	39	40
41	42	43	44	45	46	47	48	49	50
51	52	53	54	55	56	57	58	59	60
61	62	63	64	65	66	67	68	69	70
71	72	73	74	75	76	77	78	79	80
81	82	83	84	85	86	87	88	89	90
91	92	93	94	95	96	97	98	99	100

Explain how you used the chart to find the sum.

TAKE HOME ACTIVITY • On a piece of paper, write 36 + 40. Ask your child to explain how to use the hundred chart to count on by tens to find the sum.

FOR MORE PRACTICE: Standards Practice Book

Name ______________________________

Use Models to Add

HANDS ON
Lesson 8.5

Essential Question How can models help you add ones or tens to a two-digit number?

Number and Operations in Base Ten—1.NBT.4
MATHEMATICAL PRACTICES
MP.4, MP.6

Draw to show how you can find the sum.

$14 + 5 =$ ____

Math Talk **Mathematical Practices**

Explain how you found the sum.

FOR THE TEACHER • Read the following problem. Amir counts 14 cars as they go by. Then he counts 5 more cars. How many cars does Amir count?

Model and Draw

Add ones to a two-digit number.

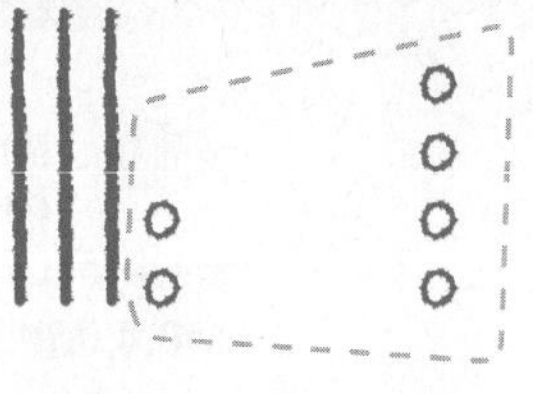

32 + 4 = 36

Add tens to a two-digit number.

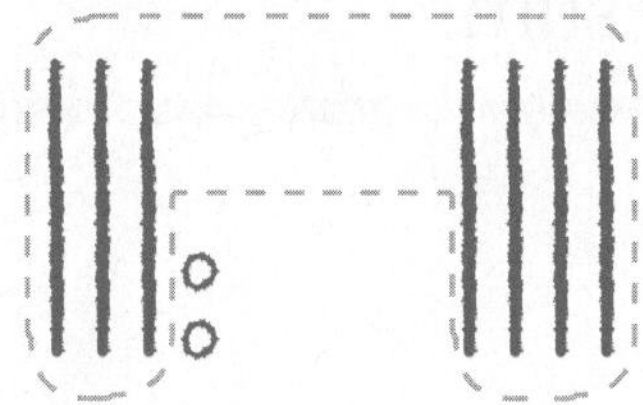

32 + 40 = 72

Share and Show

Use . Draw to show how to add the ones. Write the sum.

1. 27 + 2 = ____

2. 41 + 5 = ____

Use . Draw to show how to add the tens. Write the sum.

3. 13 + 50 = ____

4. 28 + 30 = ____

Name ______________________

On Your Own

MATHEMATICAL PRACTICE 4 **Use Models**

Use [tens] [ones] and your MathBoard.
Add the ones or tens. Write the sum.

5. 65 + 3 = ____

6. 81 + 8 = ____

7. 54 + 20 = ____

8. 32 + 10 = ____

9. 95 + 2 = ____

10. 25 + 60 = ____

11. 2 + 54 = ____

12. 70 + 29 = ____

GO DEEPER Make a sum of 45. Draw a quick picture. Write the number sentence.

13. Add ones to a two-digit number.

____ + ____ = 45

14. Add tens to a two-digit number.

____ + ____ = 45

Problem Solving • Applications Real World

WRITE Math

Choose a way to solve. Draw or write to show your work.

15. Rita picks 63 strawberries. Then she picks 30 more. How many strawberries does Rita pick?

____ strawberries

16. THINKSMARTER Kenny planted two rows of corn. He used 20 seeds in each row. He has 18 seeds left. How many seeds of corn did Kenny have?

____ seeds

17. There are 7 oak trees and 32 pine trees in the park. How many trees are in the park?

____ trees

18. THINKSMARTER Use the model. Draw to show how to add the tens.

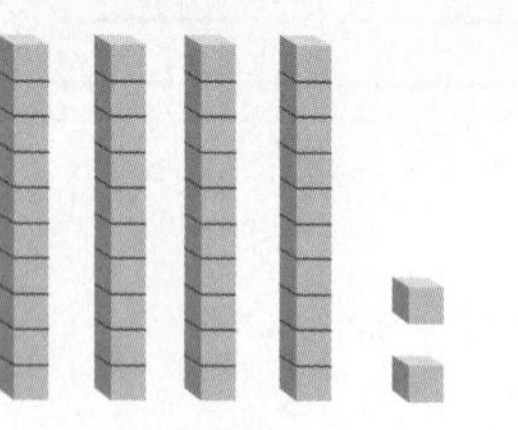
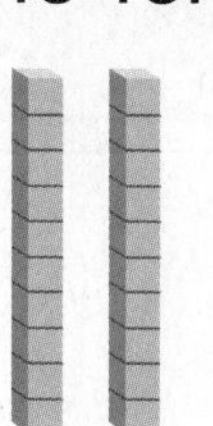

42 + 20 = ____

TAKE HOME ACTIVITY • Give your child the addition problems 25 + 3 and 25 + 30. Ask your child to explain how to solve each problem.

FOR MORE PRACTICE: Standards Practice Book

Name ______________________________

Make Ten to Add

Essential Question How can making a ten help you add a two-digit number and a one-digit number?

HANDS ON
Lesson 8.6

Number and Operations in Base Ten—1.NBT.4

MATHEMATICAL PRACTICES
MP.2, MP.5

Listen and Draw

Use . Draw to show how you can find the sum.

21 + 6 = ____.

Math Talk **Mathematical Practices**

Explain how your model shows the sum of 21 + 6.

FOR THE TEACHER • Read the following problem. Sally has 21 stickers in her sticker book. She gets 6 more stickers. How many stickers does Sally have now?

Model and Draw

Make a ten to find 37 + 8.

What can I add to 7 to make 10?

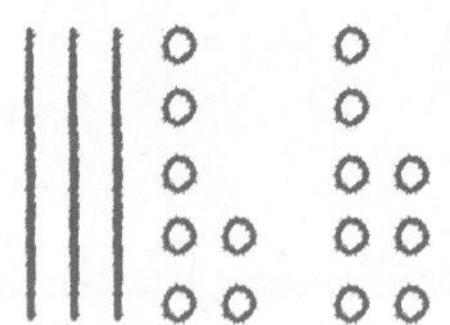

37 + 8

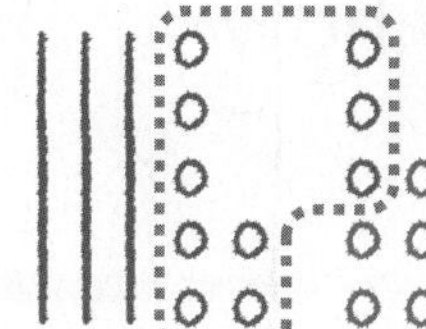

37 + 3 + 5

40 + 5

40 + 5 = 45

So, 37 + 8 = 45.

Share and Show

MATH BOARD

Use . Draw to show how you make a ten. Find the sum.

1. 49 + 3 = ?

____ + ____ = ____

So, 49 + 3 = ____.

Name ______________________________

On Your Own

MATHEMATICAL PRACTICE 5 **Use a Concrete Model**

Use [tens and ones blocks]. Draw to show how you make a ten. Find the sum.

2. $39 + 7 =$ ____

3. $72 + 9 =$ ____

4. $58 + 5 =$ ____

THINK SMARTER Solve. Write the numbers.

5. $46 + 7$

$46 + \square + 3$

$\square + 3$

So, $46 + 7 =$ ____.

6. $53 + 8$

$53 + \square + 1$

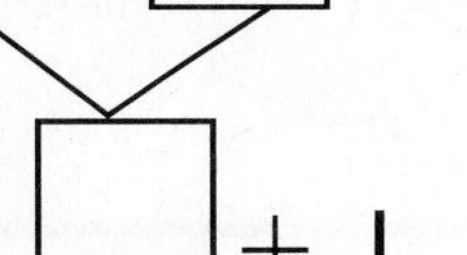

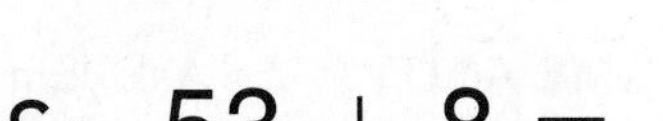

So, $53 + 8 =$ ____.

Math on the Spot

Problem Solving • Applications

Choose a way to solve. Draw or write to show your work.

7. THINK SMARTER Koby puts 24 daisies and 8 tulips in a vase. How many flowers are in the vase?

_____ flowers

8. GO DEEPER There are 27 ducklings in the water. 20 of them come out of the water. How many ducklings are still in the water?

_____ ducklings

9. Write the missing addend.

$46 + \square = 52$

10. THINK SMARTER Use the model. Draw to show how to make a ten.

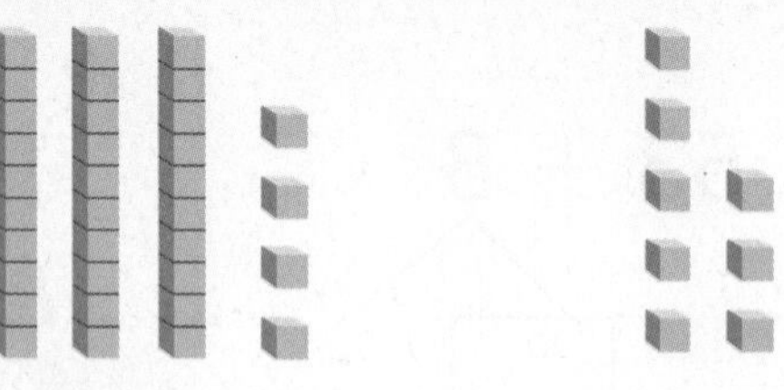

34 + 8 = _____

TAKE HOME ACTIVITY • Ask your child to explain how to find the sum for 25 + 9.

FOR MORE PRACTICE: Standards Practice Book

Name ________________________________

Use Place Value to Add

Essential Question How can you model tens and ones to help you add two-digit numbers?

Number and Operations in Base Ten—1.NBT.4

MATHEMATICAL PRACTICES
MP.1, MP.2, MP.7

Model the problem with ▭ ▫.
Draw a quick picture to show your work.

Tens	Ones

Math Talk Mathematical Practices

How many tens?
How many ones?
How many in all?
Explain.

FOR THE TEACHER • Read the following problem. Cameron has 30 shiny pennies and 25 dull pennies. How many pennies does Cameron have?

Model and Draw

How can you use tens and ones to add?

$$\begin{array}{r} 35 \\ +38 \\ \hline \end{array}$$

Tens	Ones

3 tens + 5 ones
3 tens + 8 ones

6 tens + 13 ones

60 + 13 = 73

$$\begin{array}{r} 35 \\ +38 \\ \hline 73 \end{array}$$

Share and Show

Draw a quick picture.
Use tens and ones to add.

1.

$$\begin{array}{r} 81 \\ +14 \\ \hline \end{array}$$

Tens	Ones

8 tens + 1 one
1 ten + 4 ones

____ tens + ____ ones

____ + ____ = ____

$$\begin{array}{r} 81 \\ +14 \\ \hline \end{array}$$

Name ____________________

On Your Own

MATHEMATICAL PRACTICE 6 **Make Connections**

Draw a quick picture. Use tens and ones to add.

2.

	43
+	37

Tens	Ones

4 tens + 3 ones
3 tens + 7 ones

____ tens + ____ ones

____ + ____ = ____

	43
+	37

3.

	62
+	23

Tens	Ones

6 tens + 2 ones
2 tens + 3 ones

____ tens + ____ ones

____ + ____ = ____

	62
+	23

THINK SMARTER Solve.

4. 28 + 17

28 + ____ + 15

____ + 15 = ____

So, 28 + 17 = ____.

5. 59 + 13

59 + ____ + 12

____ + 12 = ____

So, 59 + 13 = ____.

Problem Solving • Applications 

6. THINK SMARTER Draw a quick picture to solve. Kim has 24 marbles. Al has 47 marbles. How many marbles do they have?

____ marbles

Tens	Ones

7. GO DEEPER Choose two addends from 11 to 49. Draw them. Add in any order to solve.

Addend	Addend

____ + ____ = ____

____ + ____ = ____

8. THINK SMARTER Write the addition that the model shows. Solve.

Tens	Ones

____ + ____ = ____

TAKE HOME ACTIVITY • Write the numbers 42 and 17. Have your child tell how to find the sum by adding the tens and ones.

FOR MORE PRACTICE: Standards Practice Book

Name ____________________

Problem Solving • Addition Word Problems

Essential Question How can drawing a picture help you explain how to solve an addition problem?

Number and Operations in Base Ten—1.NBT.4

MATHEMATICAL PRACTICES
MP.1, MP.6, MP.8

Kelly gets 6 new toy cars.
He already has 18 toy cars.
How many does he have now?

Unlock the Problem

What do I need to find?

how many toy cars Kelly has now

What information do I need to use?

Kelly has 18 cars.

He gets 6 more cars.

Show how to solve the problem.

____

HOME CONNECTION • Being able to show and explain how to solve a problem helps your child build on their understanding of addition.

Try Another Problem

Draw and write to solve.
Explain your reasoning.

- What do I need to find?
- What information do I need to use?

1. Aisha picks 60 blueberries to make a pie. Then she picks 12 more to eat. How many blueberries does Aisha pick?

____ blueberries

2. Yuri collects 21 cans for the school food drive. Leo collects 36 cans. How many cans do Yuri and Leo collect?

____ cans

Math Talk Mathematical Practices

Explain the addition strategy you used to solve Exercise 1.

Name ______________________________

Share and Show

MATHEMATICAL PRACTICE 2 **Use Reasoning**

Draw and write to solve.

✓3. Tyra sees 48 geese in the field. Then she sees 17 more geese in the sky. How many geese does Tyra see?

____ geese

✓4. Jade paints 35 circles and 45 triangles in art class. How many shapes does Jade paint?

____ shapes

5. THINK SMARTER It takes 10 hops to get across the yard. How many hops does it take to get across the yard and back?

____ hops

On Your Own

Choose a way to solve. Draw or write to explain.

6. THINK SMARTER Julian sells 3 books of tickets for the school fair. Each book has 20 tickets. How many tickets does Julian sell?

____ tickets

7. GO DEEPER I have some red roses and pink roses. I have 14 red roses. I have 8 more pink roses than red roses. How many roses do I have?

____ roses

Personal Math Trainer

8. THINK SMARTER + Ella sees 27 caps. She sees 28 caps. How many caps does Ella see? Circle the number that makes this sentence true.

Ella sees 48 / 51 / 55   in all.

TAKE HOME ACTIVITY • Ask your child to solve 16 + 7, 30 + 68, and 53 + 24. Ask him or her to explain how they solved each problem.

FOR MORE PRACTICE: Standards Practice Book

Name ____________________

Related Addition and Subtraction

Essential Question How can you use a hundred chart to show the relationship between addition and subtraction?

Number and Operations in Base Ten—1.NBT.4
MATHEMATICAL PRACTICES
MP.2, MP.3, MP.7

Listen and Draw Real World

Use the hundred chart to solve the problems.

1	2	3	4	5	6	7	8	9	10
11	12	13	14	15	16	17	18	19	20
21	22	23	24	25	26	27	28	29	30
31	32	33	34	35	36	37	38	39	40
41	42	43	44	45	46	47	48	49	50
51	52	53	54	55	56	57	58	59	60
61	62	63	64	65	66	67	68	69	70
71	72	73	74	75	76	77	78	79	80
81	82	83	84	85	86	87	88	89	90
91	92	93	94	95	96	97	98	99	100

FOR THE TEACHER • Read the following problems. Trevor collects 38 acorns. He collects 10 more acorns. How many acorns does Trevor have now? Trevor has 48 acorns. He gives 10 acorns to his brother. How many acorns does Trevor have now?

Math Talk — Mathematical Practices

Describe how you can use a hundred chart to find the sum and the difference.

Model and Draw

You can use a hundred chart to find a sum and a difference.

1	2	3	4	5	6	7	8	9	10
11	12	13	14	15	16	17	18	19	20
21	22	23	24	25	26	27	28	29	30
31	32	33	34	35	36	37	38	39	40
41	42	43	44	45	46	47	48	49	50
51	52	53	54	55	56	57	58	59	60
61	62	63	64	65	66	67	68	69	70
71	72	73	74	75	76	77	78	79	80
81	82	83	84	85	86	87	88	89	90
91	92	93	94	95	96	97	98	99	100

Start at **29**. Count up four tens.
39, 49, 59, 69

$29 + 40 =$ 69

Start at **69**. Count back four tens.
59, 49, 39, 29

$69 - 40 =$ 29

Share and Show

Use the hundred chart to add and subtract.
Count up and back by tens.

1. $56 + 20 =$ ____

   $76 - 20 =$ ____

2. $48 + 50 =$ ____

   $98 - 50 =$ ____

Name ______________________________

On Your Own

How can you use the hundred chart to find the sum and the difference?

$28 + 60 =$ ___

$88 - 60 =$ ___

1	2	3	4	5	6	7	8	9	10
11	12	13	14	15	16	17	18	19	20
21	22	23	24	25	26	27	28	29	30
31	32	33	34	35	36	37	38	39	40
41	42	43	44	45	46	47	48	49	50
51	52	53	54	55	56	57	58	59	60
61	62	63	64	65	66	67	68	69	70
71	72	73	74	75	76	77	78	79	80
81	82	83	84	85	86	87	88	89	90
91	92	93	94	95	96	97	98	99	100

MATHEMATICAL PRACTICE 7 **Look for a Pattern** Use the hundred chart to add and subtract. Count up and back by tens.

3. $36 + 30 =$ ___

   $66 - 30 =$ ___

4. $73 + 10 =$ ___

   $83 - 10 =$ ___

5. $25 + 70 =$ ___

   $95 - 70 =$ ___

6. $18 + 40 =$ ___

   $58 - 40 =$ ___

7. THINK SMARTER Solve.

   There are 73 bees in a hive. 10 bees fly away. Then 10 more bees fly into the hive. How many bees are in the hive now?

___ bees

Problem Solving • Applications

WRITE Math

Solve. Draw or write to show your work.

8. THINK SMARTER There are 38 ants on a rock. 10 move to the grass. 10 walk up a tree. How many ants are on the rock now?

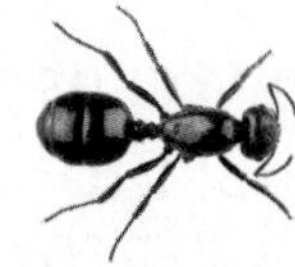

____ ants

9. GO DEEPER There are 27 birds at the park. 50 more birds come. Then 50 fly away. How many birds are at the park now?

____ birds

10. THINK SMARTER Match the math sentences that count up and back by tens.

$25 + 40 = ?$	$65 + 20 = ?$	$45 + 30 = ?$
$65 - 40 = ?$	$75 - 30 = ?$	$85 - 20 = ?$

TAKE HOME ACTIVITY • On slips of paper, write 36 + 40 and 76 − 40. Ask your child to explain how to use the hundred chart to count up and back by tens to find the sum and the difference.

FOR MORE PRACTICE: Standards Practice Book

Name ______________________

Practice Addition and Subtraction

Essential Question What different ways can you use to add and subtract?

Number and Operations in Base Ten—1.NBT.4, 1.NBT.6 *Also 1.OA.6*

MATHEMATICAL PRACTICES
MP.1, MP.3, MP.8

Listen and Draw Real World

Draw to show the problem.
Then solve.

___ ◯ ___ ◯ ___

Math Talk **Mathematical Practices**

How did you solve the problem? **Explain.**

FOR THE TEACHER • Read the following problem. The class collects paper bags for an art project. Ron brings 7 more bags than Ben. Ben brings 35 bags. How many bags does Ron bring?

Model and Draw

What ways have you learned to add and subtract?

$5 + 9 =$ ____

THINK
9 + 5 is the same as 10 + ? .

$50 - 30 =$ ____

THINK
5 tens − 3 tens.

$51 + 21 =$ ____

THINK
5 tens + 2 tens.
1 one + 1 one.

Share and Show

Add or subtract.

1. $30 + 60 =$ ____
2. $73 + 5 =$ ____
3. $10 - 4 =$ ____
4. $29 + 4 =$ ____
5. $9 + 9 =$ ____
6. $5 + 6 =$ ____
7. $25 + 54 =$ ____
8. $15 - 8 =$ ____
9. $40 + 10 =$ ____
10. $40 - 10 =$ ____
11. $14 - 7 =$ ____
12. $90 - 70 =$ ____
13. $86 + 12 =$ ____
14. $1 + 9 =$ ____
15. $6 + 7 =$ ____
16. $9 - 2 =$ ____
17. $8 + 31 =$ ____
18. $50 + 11 =$ ____

Name ______________________________

On Your Own

MATHEMATICAL PRACTICE 8 **Use Repeated Reasoning** Add or subtract.

19. $\begin{array}{r} 12 \\ -\ \ 3 \\ \hline \end{array}$	**20.** $\begin{array}{r} 10 \\ +10 \\ \hline \end{array}$	**21.** $\begin{array}{r} 7 \\ +42 \\ \hline \end{array}$	**22.** $\begin{array}{r} 41 \\ +36 \\ \hline \end{array}$
23. $\begin{array}{r} 8 \\ +10 \\ \hline \end{array}$	**24.** $\begin{array}{r} 16 \\ +\ \ 7 \\ \hline \end{array}$	**25.** $\begin{array}{r} 6 \\ -6 \\ \hline \end{array}$	**26.** $\begin{array}{r} 3 \\ +8 \\ \hline \end{array}$
27. $\begin{array}{r} 64 \\ +\ \ 3 \\ \hline \end{array}$	**28.** $\begin{array}{r} 60 \\ -30 \\ \hline \end{array}$	**29.** $\begin{array}{r} 2 \\ +7 \\ \hline \end{array}$	**30.** $\begin{array}{r} 5 \\ -1 \\ \hline \end{array}$
31. $\begin{array}{r} 13 \\ -\ \ 5 \\ \hline \end{array}$	**32.** $\begin{array}{r} 52 \\ +40 \\ \hline \end{array}$	**33.** $\begin{array}{r} 3 \\ +2 \\ \hline \end{array}$	**34.** $\begin{array}{r} 30 \\ +50 \\ \hline \end{array}$
35. $\begin{array}{r} 8 \\ +4 \\ \hline \end{array}$	**36.** $\begin{array}{r} 18 \\ -\ \ 8 \\ \hline \end{array}$	**37.** $\begin{array}{r} 20 \\ +13 \\ \hline \end{array}$	**38.** $\begin{array}{r} 70 \\ -50 \\ \hline \end{array}$
39. $\begin{array}{r} 29 \\ +\ \ 2 \\ \hline \end{array}$	**40.** $\begin{array}{r} 34 \\ +24 \\ \hline \end{array}$	**41.** $\begin{array}{r} 20 \\ +70 \\ \hline \end{array}$	**42.** $\begin{array}{r} 11 \\ -\ \ 7 \\ \hline \end{array}$

Problem Solving • Applications

Solve. Write or draw to explain.

43. THINK SMARTER Jane drew some stars. Then she drew 9 more stars. Now there are 19 stars. How many stars did Jane draw first?

____ stars

44. THINK SMARTER Adel drew 10 more stars than Charlie. Charlie drew 24 stars. How many stars did Adel draw?

____ stars

45. GO DEEPER Write three ways to get a sum of 49.

____ ◯ ____ = 49

____ ◯ ____ = 49

____ ◯ ____ = 49

46. THINK SMARTER Find the sum of 23 and 30. Use any way to add.

$23 + 30 =$ ____

Explain how you solved the problem.

TAKE HOME ACTIVITY • Have your child explain how he or she solved Exercise 43.

FOR MORE PRACTICE: Standards Practice Book

Name ______________________________

Chapter 8 Review/Test

1. Write each addition or subtraction problem in the box below the answer.

7 + 2	3 + 3	15 − 9	8 + 6	14 − 5

6	9	14

2. Choose all the ways that name the model.

○ 2 tens and 3 tens
○ 20 + 30
○ 5
○ 50

3. Sasha has 70 stickers. She uses 40 of them. How many stickers are left? Show your work.

_____ stickers

GO DIGITAL Assessment Options Chapter Test

4. Use the hundred chart to add.
Count on by ones or tens.

$37 + 5 =$ ____

Explain how you used the chart to find the sum.

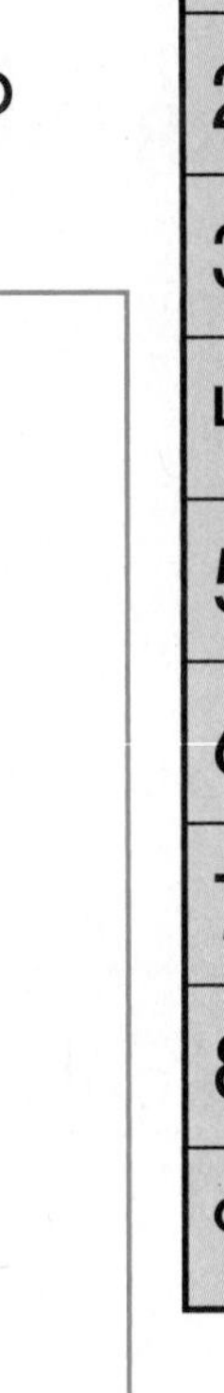

1	2	3	4	5	6	7	8	9	10
11	12	13	14	15	16	17	18	19	20
21	22	23	24	25	26	27	28	29	30
31	32	33	34	35	36	37	38	39	40
41	42	43	44	45	46	47	48	49	50
51	52	53	54	55	56	57	58	59	60
61	62	63	64	65	66	67	68	69	70
71	72	73	74	75	76	77	78	79	80
81	82	83	84	85	86	87	88	89	90
91	92	93	94	95	96	97	98	99	100

5. Use the model. Draw to show how to add the tens.

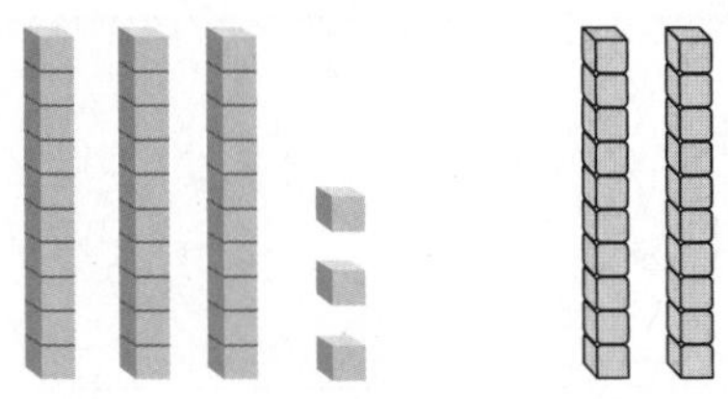

$33 + 20 =$ ____

Name ______________________________

6. Use the model. Draw to show how to make a ten.

$26 + 7 =$ ____

7. Write the addition sentence that the model shows. Solve.

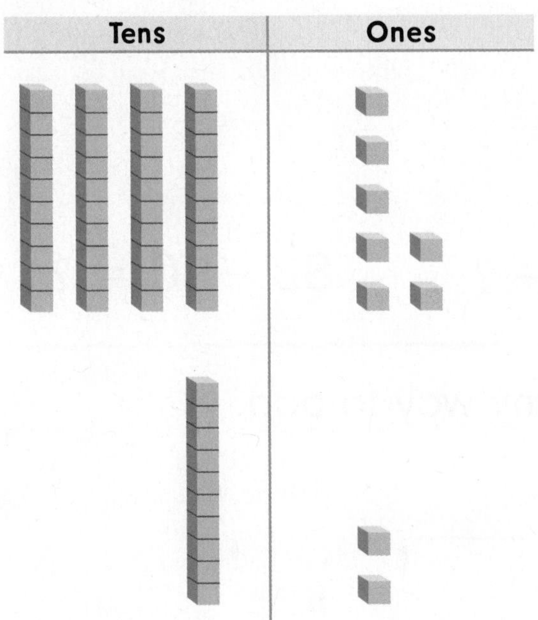

____ + ____ = ____

8. What is the difference?

$$\begin{array}{r} 15 \\ -\ 7 \\ \hline \end{array}$$

○ 7 ○ 8 ○ 10 ○ 12

9. What is the sum?

$$\begin{array}{r} 40 \\ +\ 50 \\ \hline \end{array}$$

○ 10 ○ 70 ○ 80 ○ 90

10. Luis has 16 leaves.

He has 38 leaves.

How many leaves does Luis have? Circle the number that makes the sentence true.

Luis has [48 / 54 / 59] leaves.

11. Match the math sentences that count up and back by tens.

38 + 30 = ?   48 + 40 = ?   38 + 20 = ?

58 − 20 = ?   68 − 30 = ?   88 − 40 = ?

12. Find the sum of 62 and 15. Use any way to add.

62 + 15 = ____

Explain how you solved the problem.

All Kinds of Weather

written by Margie Sigman

CRITICAL AREA Developing understanding of linear measurement and measuring lengths as iterating length units

In rainy weather,

We play together.

Things We Use for Rainy Weather

raincoats					
umbrellas					

Use ● to complete the graph.

How many raincoats do you see? _____

How many umbrellas do you see? _____

SCIENCE

Describe rainy weather.

In sunny weather,

We play together.

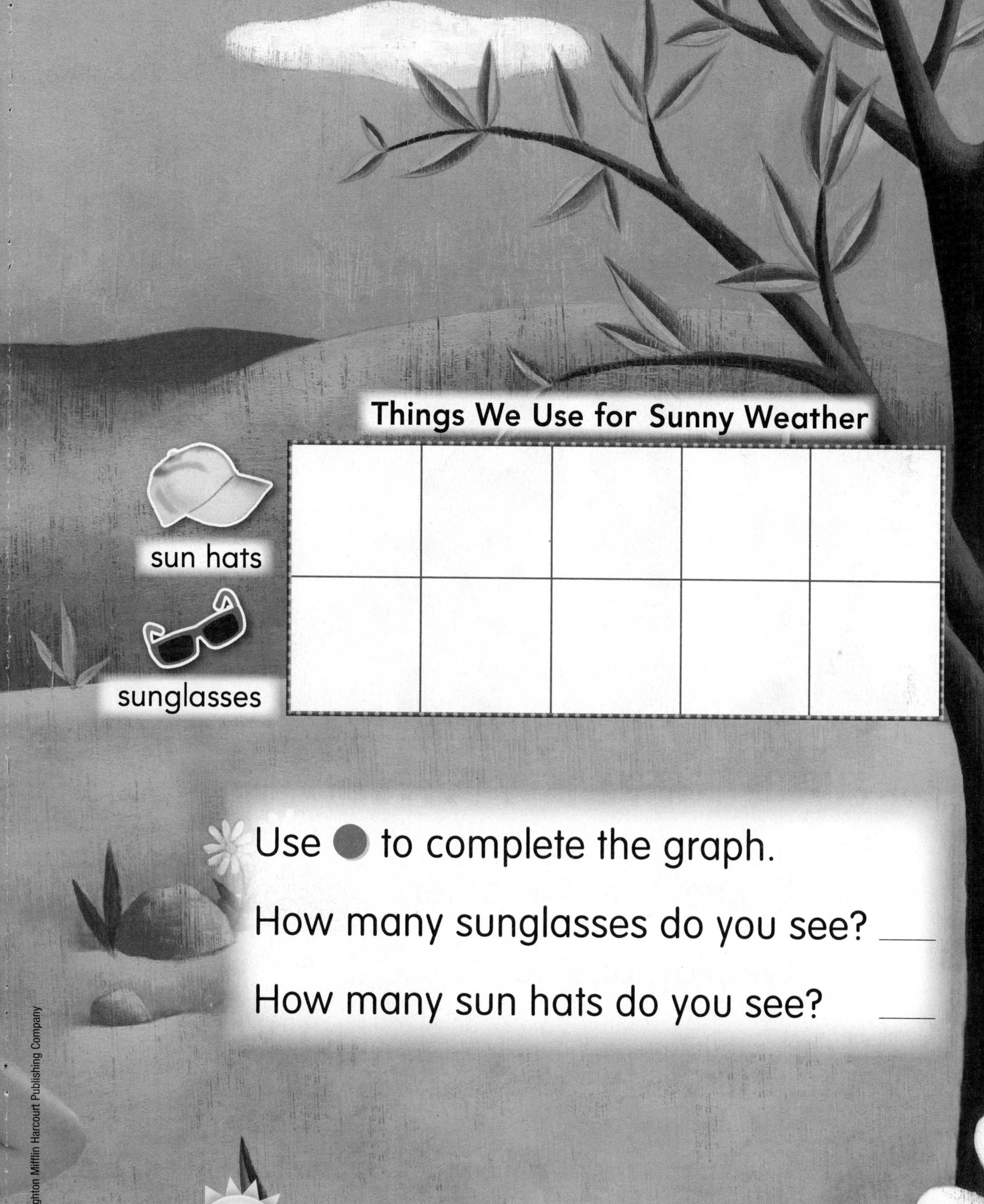

Things We Use for Sunny Weather

sun hats					
sunglasses					

Use ● to complete the graph.

How many sunglasses do you see? ____

How many sun hats do you see? ____

SCIENCE

Describe sunny weather.

Whatever the weather,

We play together.

SCIENCE

Describe the weather shown here.

Name ______________________________

Write About the Story

Use ●. Show some sun hats and sunglasses in each category on the graph.

Vocabulary Review
category
classify
graph

Things We Use for Sunny Weather

 sun hats					
 sunglasses					

WRITE Math Write a sentence telling how many sun hats there are. Write a sentence telling how many sunglasses there are.

____

____

____

____

More or Fewer?

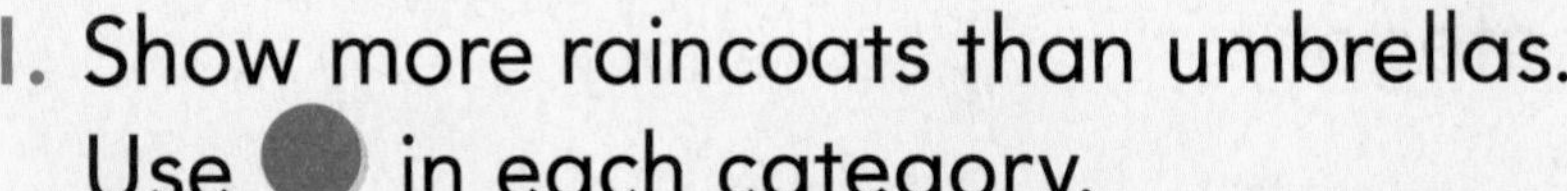

1. Show more raincoats than umbrellas.
   Use ● in each category.

Things We Use for Rainy Weather

raincoats					
umbrellas					

2. Show fewer raincoats than umbrellas.
   Use ● in each category.

Things We Use for Rainy Weather

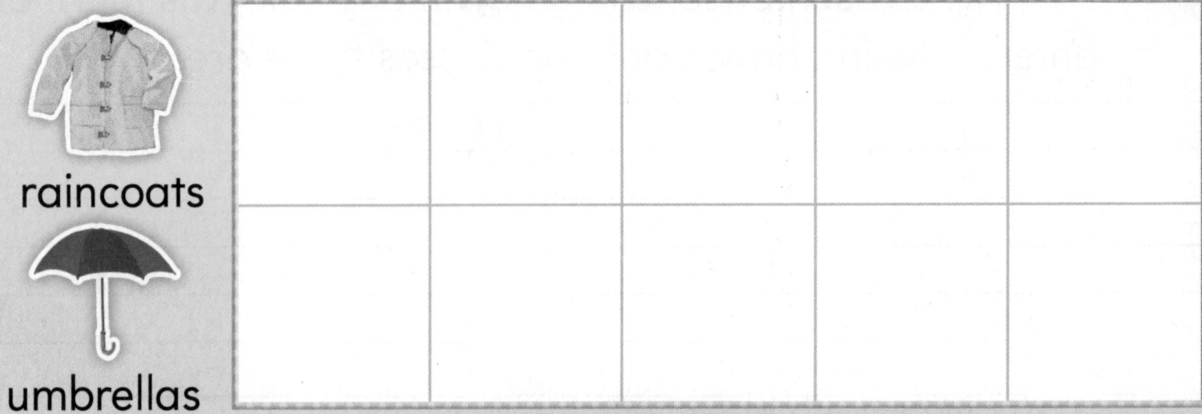

raincoats					
umbrellas					

Write a story problem about raincoats and umbrellas. Tell how to classify each item in the correct category.

Chapter 9
Measurement

Curious About Math with Curious George

What objects in the picture are shorter than the arch?

Name ___________________________

Show What You Know

Bigger and Smaller

Circle the bigger object.

1.

Circle the smaller object.

2.

Compare Length

Circle the longer object.
Draw a line under the shorter object.

3.

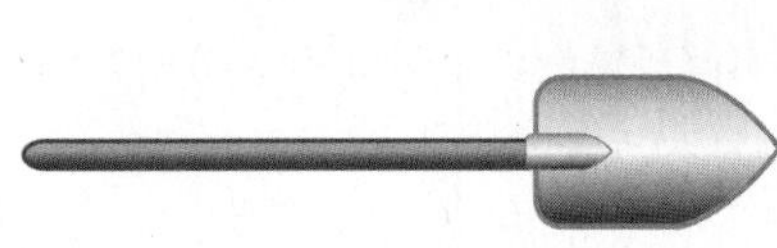

4.

Numbers 1 to 10

Write each number in order to 10.

5.

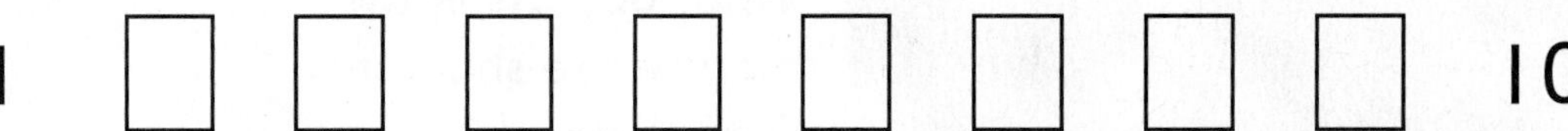

This page checks understanding of important skills needed for success in Chapter 9.

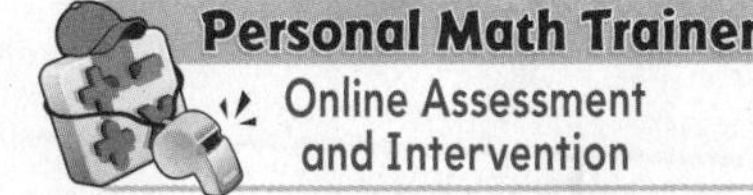

Name ____________________

Review Words	
nine	ten
eleven	twelve
long	longer
short	shorter

Vocabulary Builder

Visualize It

Sort the review words from the box.

length	numbers
long	nine
____	____
____	____
____	____

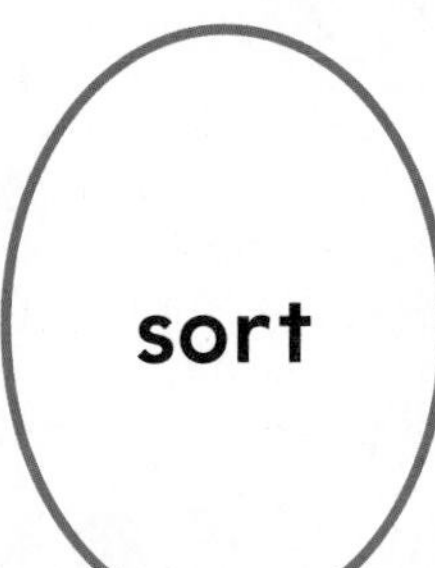

Understand Vocabulary

Complete the sentences with the correct word.

1. A crayon is ____________ than a marker.
2. A toothbrush is ____________ than a paper clip.

Write the name below the number.

3. 9 ________ 10 ________ 11 ________ 12 ________

GO DIGITAL • Interactive Student Edition • Multimedia eGlossary

Chapter 9

Game Measure UP!

Materials • 2 pawns • spinner

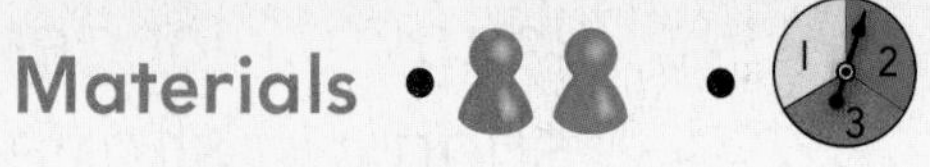

• 2 • 2 • 2 • 2

Play with a partner.

1. Put pawns on START.
2. Spin the spinner. Move your pawn that many spaces. Take that object.
3. Your partner spins, moves, and takes that object.
4. Compare the lengths of the two objects.
5. The player with the longer object places a counter on the space. If both objects are the same length, both players put a counter on the board.
6. Keep playing until one person gets to END. The player with the most counters wins.

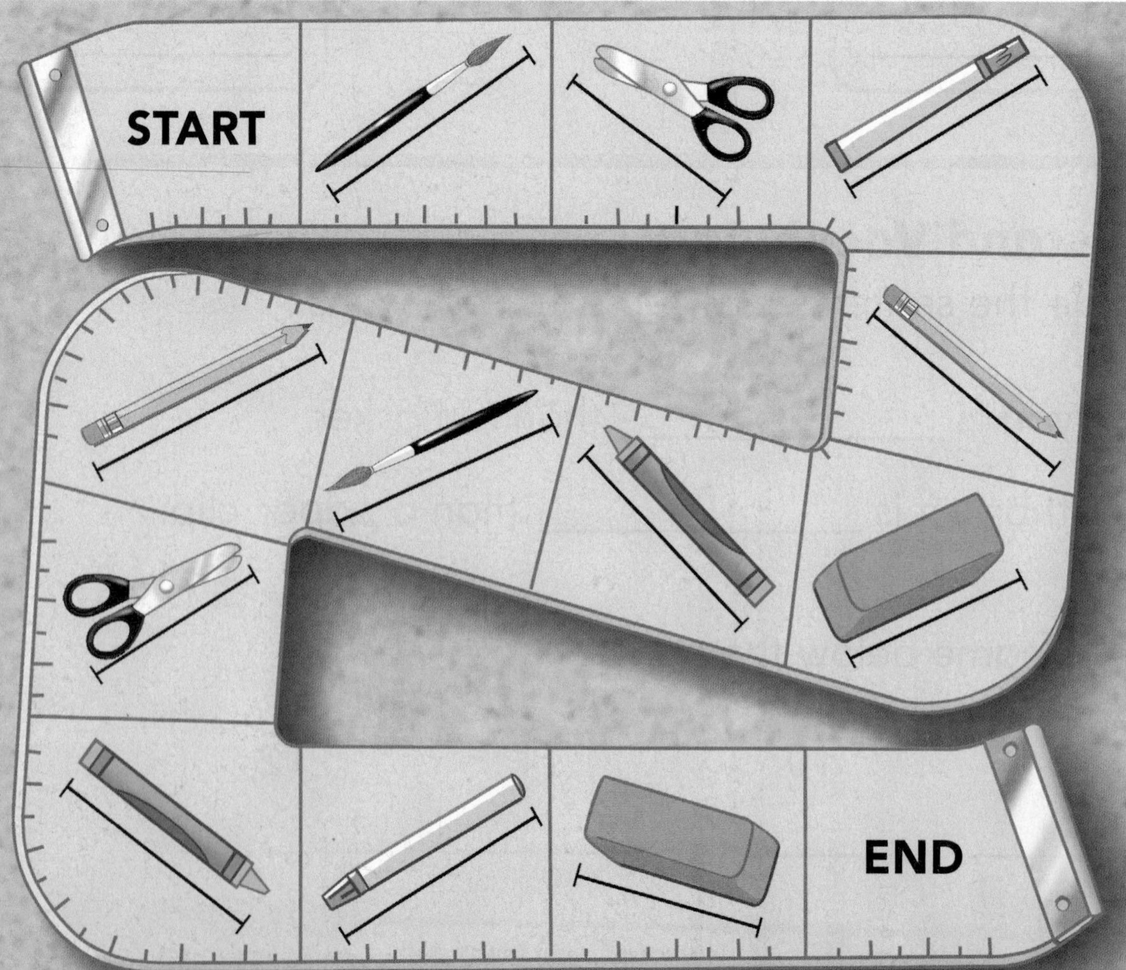

Name ____________________

Order Length

Essential Question How do you order objects by length?

Measurement and Data—1.MD.1

MATHEMATICAL PRACTICES
MP.1, MP.3, MP.6

Use objects to show the problem.
Draw to show your work.

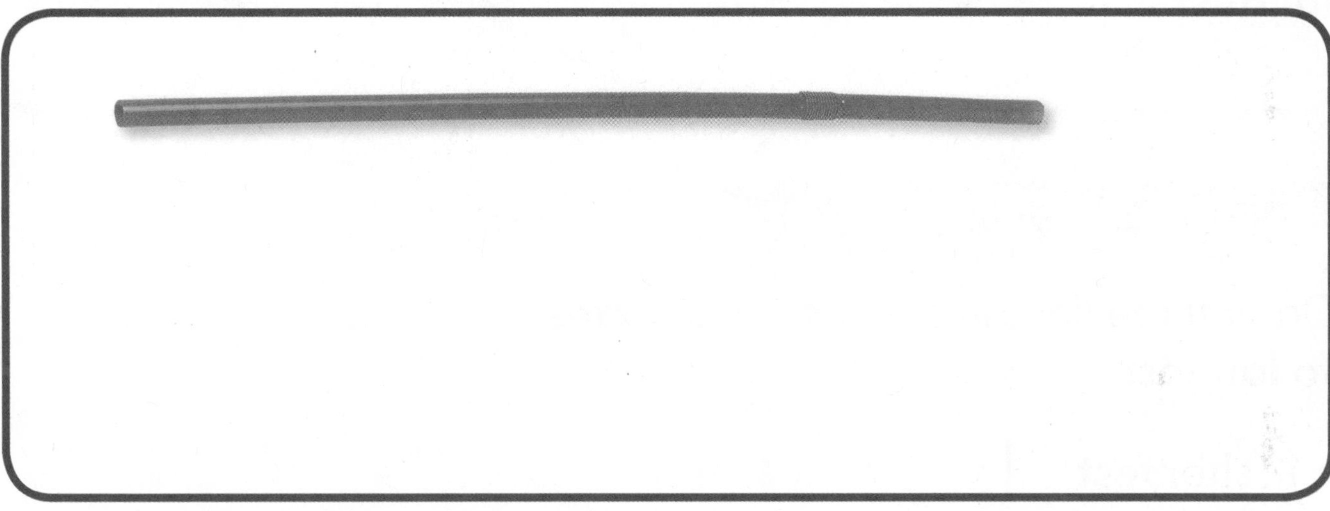

Math Talk **Mathematical Practices**

Explain Compare the straw and the key. Which is longer? Which is shorter?

FOR THE TEACHER • Read the problem. Have children use classroom objects to act it out. Rosa has something that is longer than the drinking straw. She has another object that is shorter than the key. What objects might she have?

Model and Draw

Order three pieces of yarn from **shortest** to **longest**. Draw the missing piece of yarn.

shortest

longest

Share and Show

MATH BOARD

Draw three lines in order from **shortest** to **longest**.

1. **shortest**
2.
3. **longest**

Draw three lines in order from **longest** to **shortest**.

4. **longest**
5.
6. **shortest**

Name ______________________

On Your Own

MATHEMATICAL PRACTICE 3 **Compare Representations**

Draw three crayons in order from **shortest** to **longest**.

7. **shortest**

8.

9. **longest**

Draw three crayons in order from **longest** to **shortest**.

10. **longest**

11.

12. **shortest**

13. THINK SMARTER Complete each sentence.

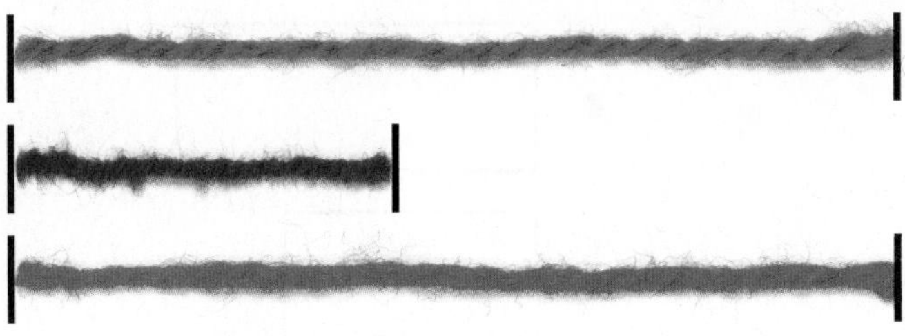

The ______ yarn is the shortest.

The ______ yarn and the ______ yarn are the same length.

Problem Solving • Applications

Solve.

14. GO DEEPER Draw four objects in order from shortest to longest.

Objects

15. THINK SMARTER The string is shorter than the ribbon. The chain is shorter than the ribbon. Circle the longest object.

string

ribbon

chain

16. THINK SMARTER Match each word on the left to a drawing on the right.

shortest •

longest •

TAKE HOME ACTIVITY • Show your child three different lengths of objects, such as three pencils or spoons. Ask him or her to order the objects from shortest to longest.

FOR MORE PRACTICE: Standards Practice Book

Name ______________________________

Indirect Measurement

Essential Question How can you compare lengths of three objects to put them in order?

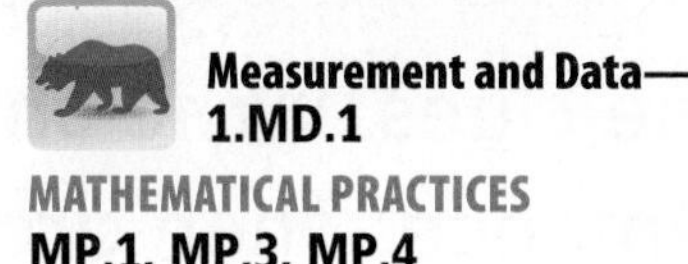

MATHEMATICAL PRACTICES
MP.1, MP.3, MP.4

Listen and Draw Real World

Clue 1: A yellow string is shorter than a blue string.

Clue 2: The blue string is shorter than a red string.

Clue 3: The yellow string is shorter than the red string.

yellow

blue

red

Math Talk Mathematical Practices

Explain how the clues helped you draw the strings in the correct order.

FOR THE TEACHER • Read the clues. Have children use the MathBoard to draw each clue. Then have children draw the strings in order from shortest to longest.

Model and Draw

Use the clues. Write **shorter** or **longer** to complete the sentence. Then draw to prove your answer.

Clue 1: A green pencil is longer than an orange pencil.

Clue 2: The orange pencil is longer than a brown pencil.

So, the green pencil is longer than the brown pencil.

brown	
orange	
green	

Share and Show

Use the clues. Write **shorter** or **longer** to complete the sentence. Then draw to prove your answer.

1. Clue 1: A red line is shorter than a blue line.
   Clue 2: The blue line is shorter than a purple line.

   So, the red line is __________ than the purple line.

red	
blue	
purple	

Name ______________________________

On Your Own

MATHEMATICAL PRACTICE 1 **Analyze Relationships** Use the clues. Write **shorter** or **longer** to complete the sentence. Then draw to prove your answer.

2. Clue 1: A green line is shorter than a pink line.
   Clue 2: The pink line is shorter than a blue line.

   So, the green line is ____________ than the blue line.

green	
pink	
blue	

3. Clue 1: An orange line is longer than a yellow line.
   Clue 2: The yellow line is longer than a red line.

   So, the orange line is ____________ than the red line.

red	
yellow	
orange	

Problem Solving • Applications

4. THINK SMARTER The ribbon is longer than the yarn. The yarn is longer than the string. The yarn and the pencil are the same length. Draw the lengths of the objects next to their labels.

ribbon	
yarn	
pencil	
string	

5. THINK SMARTER Is the first line longer than the second line? Choose Yes or No.

○ Yes ○ No

○ Yes ○ No

○ Yes ○ No

TAKE HOME ACTIVITY • Show your child the length of one object. Then show your child an object that is longer and an object that is shorter than the first object.

FOR MORE PRACTICE: Standards Practice Book

Name ______________________________

Use Nonstandard Units to Measure Length

HANDS ON
Lesson 9.3

Essential Question How do you measure length using nonstandard units?

Measurement and Data—1.MD.2

MATHEMATICAL PRACTICES
MP.2, MP.6, MP.8

Listen and Draw

Use ▇. Draw to show the problem.

Math Talk — **Mathematical Practices**

How do you draw the boat to be the right length? **Explain.**

FOR THE TEACHER • Read the problem. Jimmy sees that his boat is about 6 color tiles long. Draw Jimmy's boat. Draw the color tiles to show how you measured.

Model and Draw

You can use ■ to measure length.
Write how many.

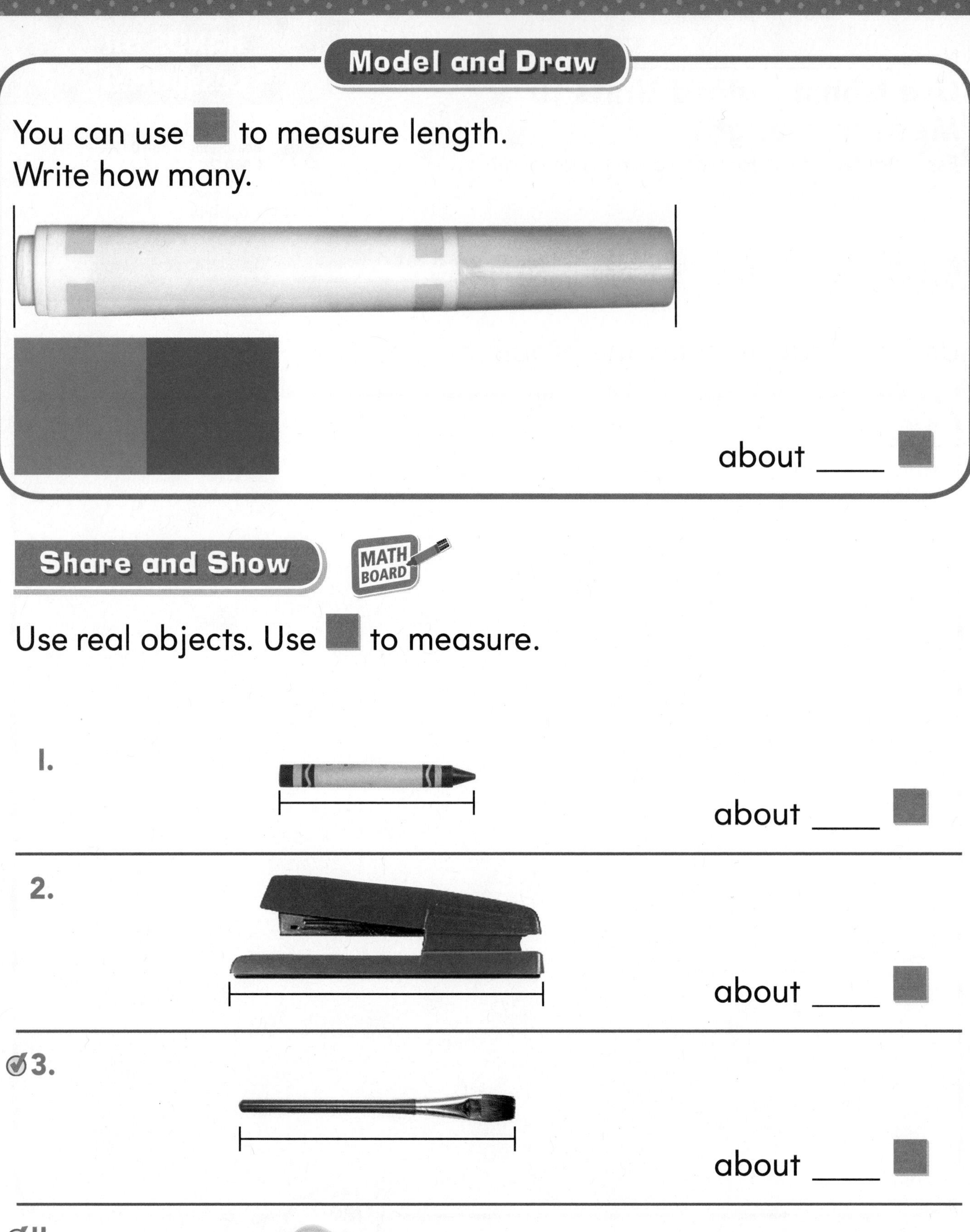

about ____ ■

Share and Show

MATH BOARD

Use real objects. Use ■ to measure.

1. about ____ ■

2. about ____ ■

3. about ____ ■

4. about ____ ■

Name ______________________________

On Your Own

Use real objects. Use ■ to measure.

5. 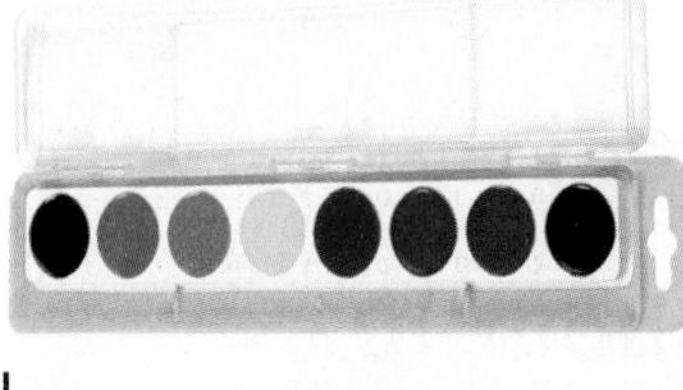

about ____ ■

6. 

about ____ ■

7. 

about ____ ■

8. 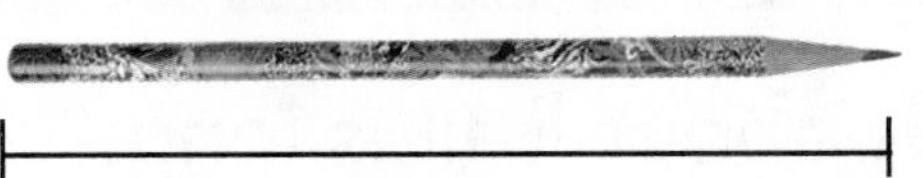

about ____ ■

9. THINK SMARTER The green yarn is about 2 ■ long. About how long is the blue yarn?

about ____ ■

Problem Solving • Applications

MATHEMATICAL PRACTICE 1 **Evaluate Reasonableness** Solve.

10. Mark measures a real glue stick with .
About how long is a glue stick?
Circle the answer that is most reasonable.

about 1 ■ **about 4** ■ **about 10** ■

11. GO DEEPER Bo has 4 ribbons. Circle the ribbon that is less than 3 ■ long but more than 1 ■ long.

12. THINKSMARTER+ The crayon is about 4 tiles long. Draw tiles below the crayon to show its length.

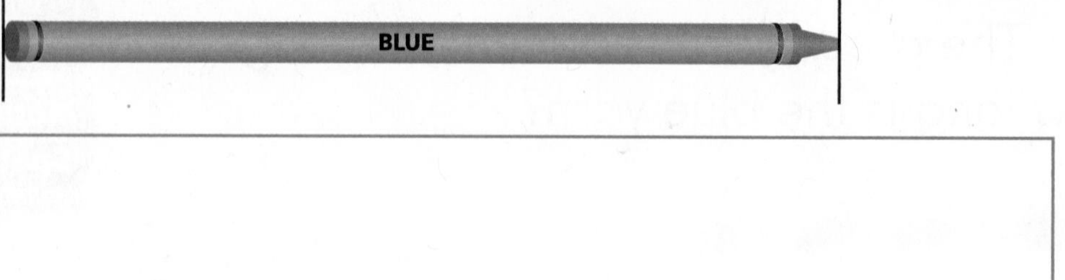

TAKE HOME ACTIVITY • Give your child paper clips or other small objects that are the same length. Have him or her estimate the lengths of objects around the house and then measure to check.

FOR MORE PRACTICE: Standards Practice Book

Name ___________________________

Make a Nonstandard Measuring Tool

Essential Question How do you use a nonstandard measuring tool to measure length?

Measurement and Data—1.MD.2

MATHEMATICAL PRACTICES
MP.2, MP.3, MP.5

Listen and Draw Real World

Circle the name of the child who measured correctly.

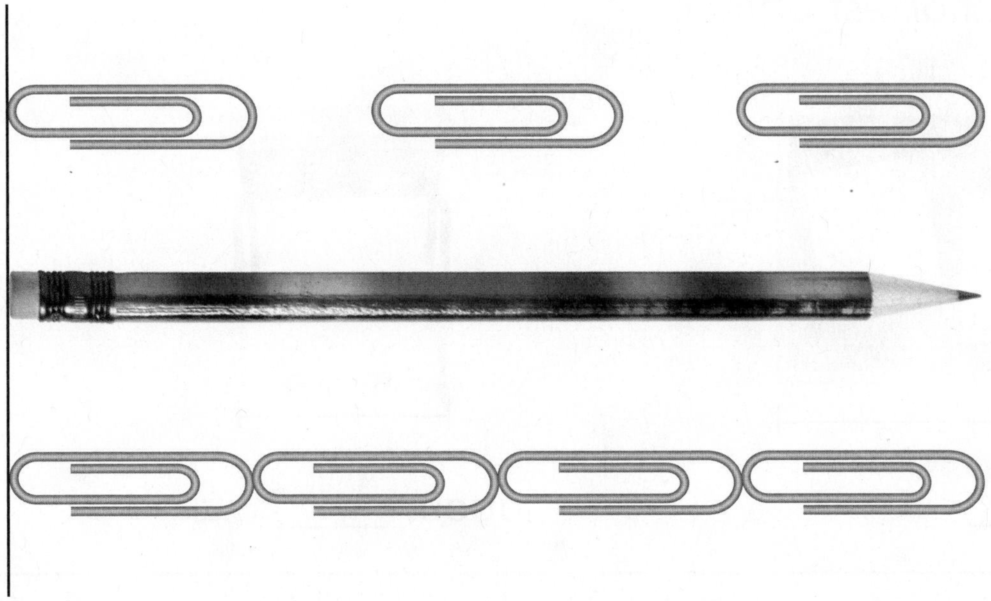

Alli

Mateo

FOR THE TEACHER • Read the problem. Mateo and Alli measure the same pencil. Mateo says it is about 4 paper clips long. Alli says it is about 3 paper clips long. Circle the name of the child who measured correctly.

Math Talk Mathematical Practices

Explain how you know who measured correctly.

Model and Draw

Make your own paper clip measuring tool like the one on the shelf. Measure the length of a door. About how long is the door?

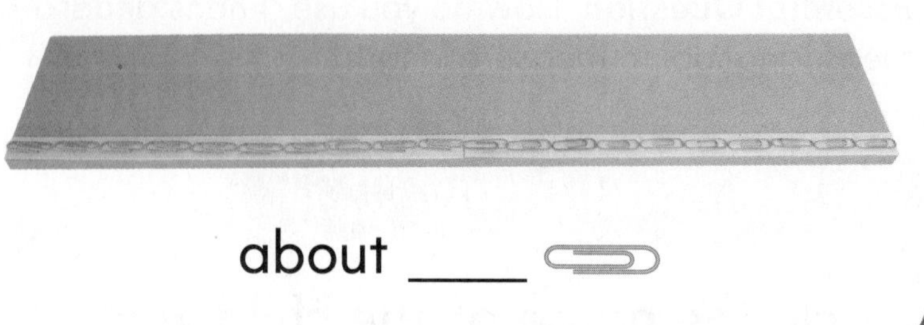

about ____

Share and Show

Use real objects and the measuring tool you made. Measure. Circle the longest object. Underline the shortest object.

1\.

about ____

2\.

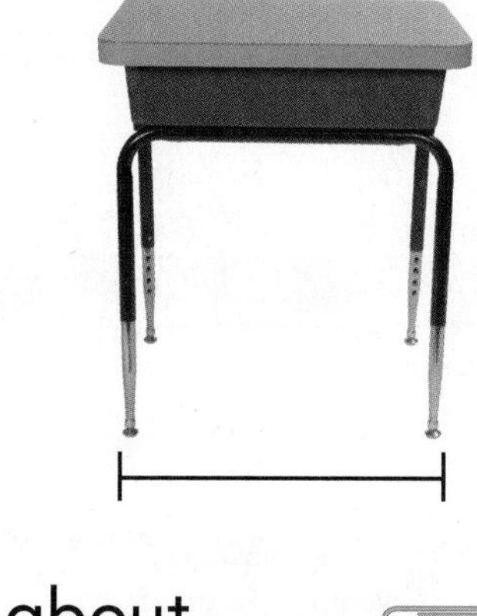

about ____

3\.

about ____

4\.

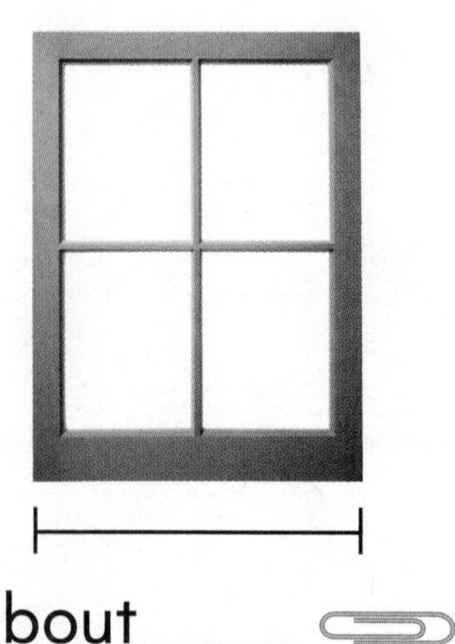

about ____

Name ___________________________

On Your Own

MATHEMATICAL PRACTICE 5 **Use Appropriate Tools**
Use the measuring tool you made.
Measure real objects.

5. 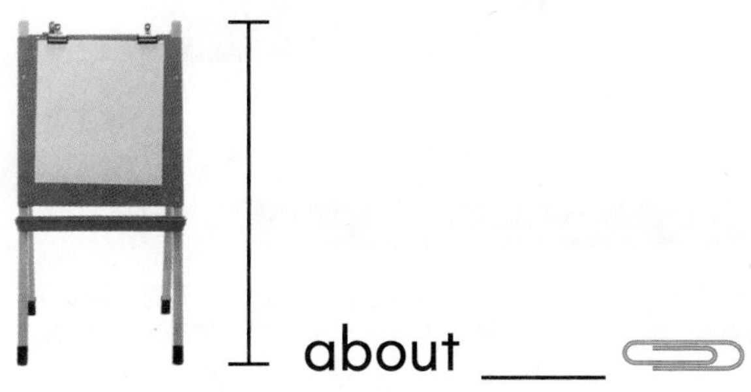
about ____ (paper clips)

6. 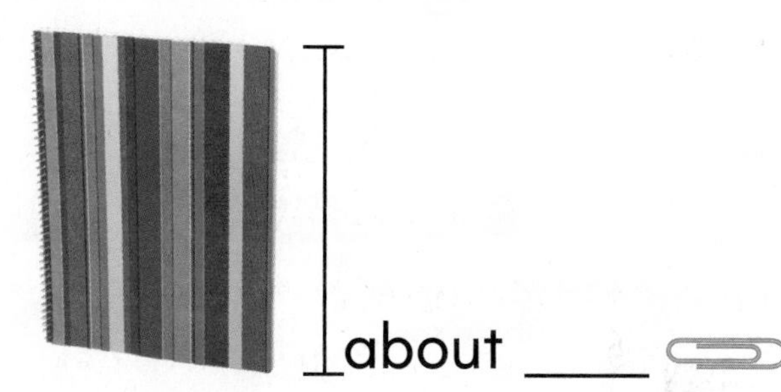
about ____ (paper clips)

7. 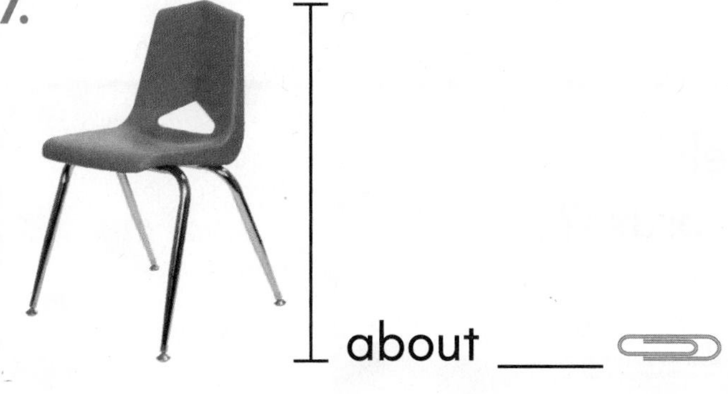
about ____ (paper clips)

8. 
about ____ (paper clips)

9. GO DEEPER Cody measured his real lunch box. It is about 10 (paper clips) long. About how long is Cody's real pencil?

about ____ (paper clips)

Cody's lunch box and pencil

Problem Solving • Applications Real World

Solve.

10. THINK SMARTER Lisa tried to measure the pencil. She thinks the pencil is 5 paper clips long. About how long is the pencil?

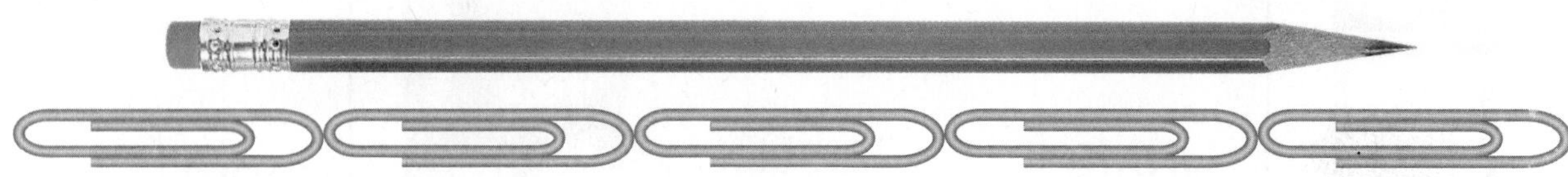

about ____

11. THINK SMARTER Use the below. About how long is the paintbrush?

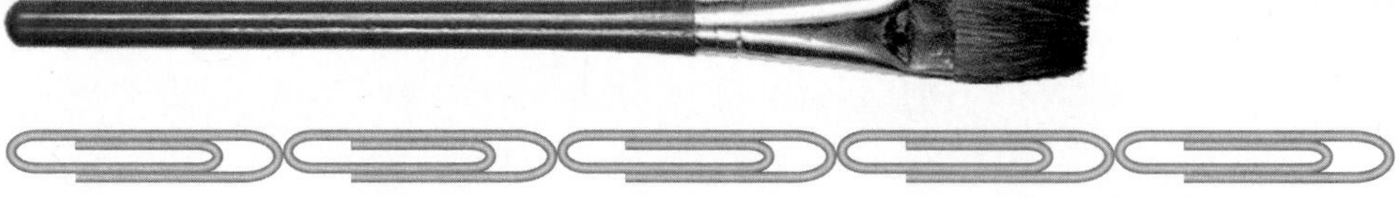

about ____

TAKE HOME ACTIVITY • Have your child measure different objects around the house using a paper clip measuring tool.

FOR MORE PRACTICE: Standards Practice Book

Name ______________________

Problem Solving • Measure and Compare

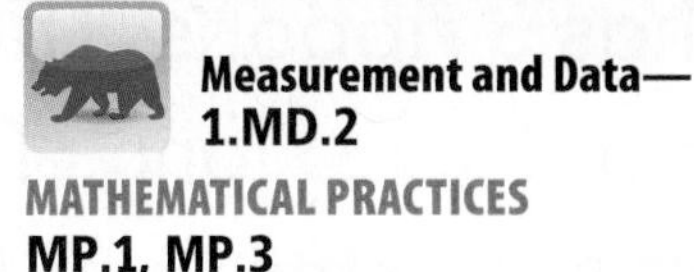

Essential Question How can acting it out help you solve measurement problems?

Measurement and Data—1.MD.2

MATHEMATICAL PRACTICES
MP.1, MP.3

The blue ribbon is about 4 paper clips long. The red ribbon is 1 paper clip long. The green ribbon is 2 paper clips longer than the red ribbon. Measure and draw the ribbons in order from **shortest** to **longest**.

What do I need to find?	What information do I need to use?
order the ribbons from shortest to longest	Measure the ribbons using paper clips.

Show how to solve the problem.

HOME CONNECTION • Have your child act out a measurement problem by finding the lengths of 3 objects and ordering them from shortest to longest.

Try Another Problem

Zack has 3 ribbons. The yellow ribbon is about 4 paper clips long. The orange ribbon is 3 paper clips shorter than the yellow ribbon. The blue ribbon is 2 paper clips longer than the yellow ribbon.

- What do I need to find?
- What information do I need to use?

Measure and draw the ribbons in order from **longest** to **shortest**.

1.

about ____ paper clips

2.

about ____ paper clips

3.

about ____ paper clips

Math Talk **Mathematical Practices**

How many paper clips shorter is the orange ribbon than the blue ribbon? **Explain.**

Name ______________________________

Share and Show

Solve. Draw or write to explain.

4. GO DEEPER Lisa measures her shoe to be about 5 paper clips long. Measure and draw an object that is 3 paper clips shorter than her shoe. Measure and draw an object that is 2 paper clips longer than her shoe.

Personal Math Trainer

5. THINKSMARTER+ Noah measures a marker to be about 4 paper clips long and a pencil to be about 6 paper clips long. Draw an object that is 1 paper clip longer than the marker and 1 paper clip shorter than the pencil.

TAKE HOME ACTIVITY • Have your child explain how he or she solved Exercise 4.

FOR MORE PRACTICE:
Standards Practice Book

Name ___________________________

Mid-Chapter Checkpoint

Concepts and Skills

Draw three crayons in order from **shortest** to **longest**. (1.MD.1)

I.

shortest	
longest	

Use ■ to measure. (1.MD.2)

2.

about ____ ■

3. THINK SMARTER Kiley measures a package with her paper clip measuring tool. About how long is the package? (1.MD.2)

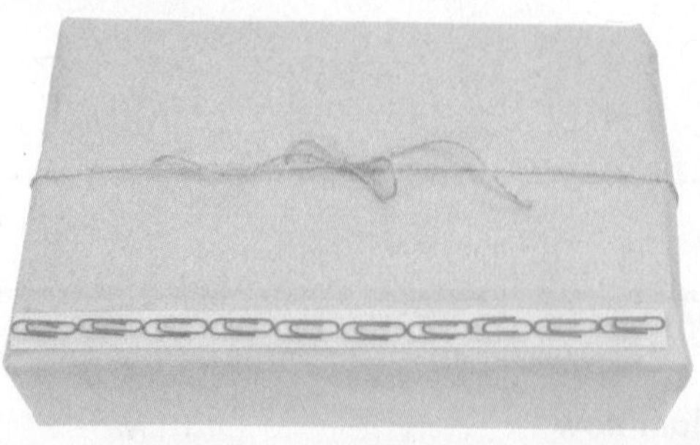

about

1
5
10
20

Name ______________________________

Time to the Hour

Essential Question How do you tell time to the hour on a clock that has only an hour hand?

Measurement and Data—1.MD.3
MATHEMATICAL PRACTICES
MP.5, MP.6, MP.7

Listen and Draw Real World

Start at 1.
Write the unknown numbers.

Start

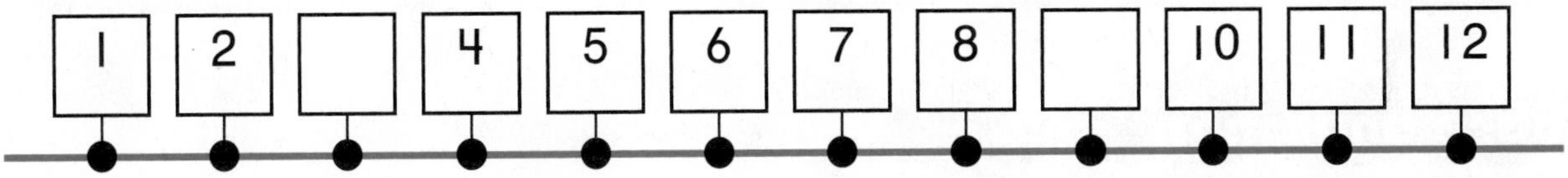
1
2
4
5
6
7
8
10
11
12

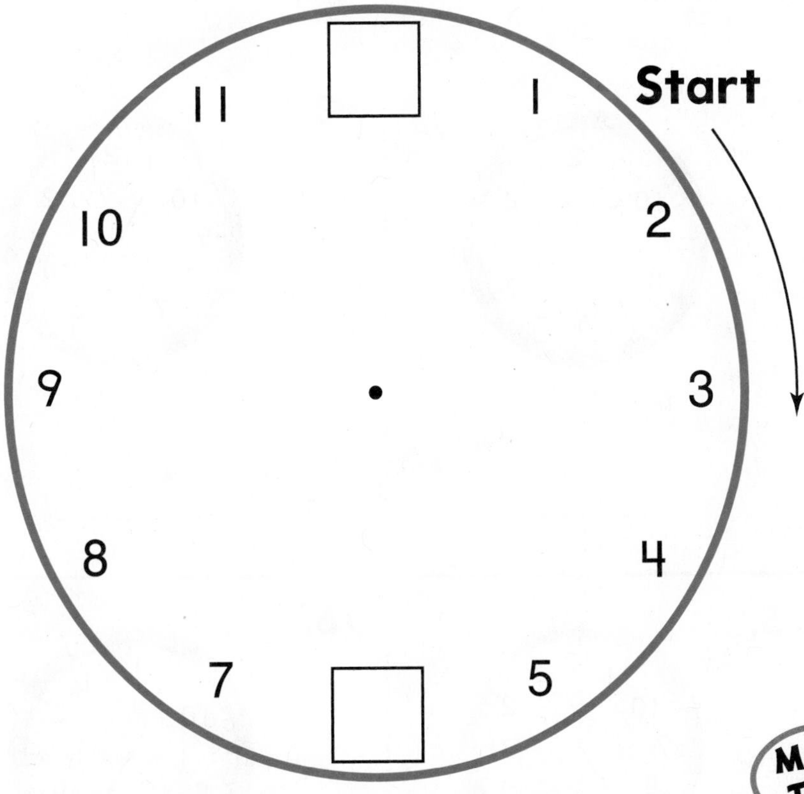
Start
11
1
10
2
9
3
8
4
7
5

Math Talk Mathematical Practices

Explain How are a clock face and ordering numbers alike?

FOR THE TEACHER • In the top workspace, have children write the unknown numbers in the squares on the green yarn. In the bottom workspace, have children write the unknown numbers on the clock face.

Model and Draw

What does this clock show?

The **hour hand** points to the 3.
It is 3 o'clock.

Say three o'clock.

Write 3:00.

Share and Show

Look at where the hour hand points.
Write the time.

1. 
_____

2. 
_____

3. 
_____

4. 
_____

5. 
_____

6. 
_____

Name ____________________

On Your Own

MATHEMATICAL PRACTICE 6 **Make Connections** Look at where the hour hand points. Write the time.

7. 

____

8. 

____

9. 

____

10. 

____

11. 

____

12. 

____

13. 

____

14. 

____

15. 

____

Problem Solving • Applications

16. THINK SMARTER Which time is **not** the same? Circle it.

1:00

1 o'clock

17. GO DEEPER Manny leaves for school at 8 o'clock. Write and draw to show 8 o'clock.

____

18. THINK SMARTER Look at the hour hand. What is the time?

- ○ 7:00
- ○ 8 o'clock
- ○ 9 o'clock
- ○ 12:00

TAKE HOME ACTIVITY • Have your child describe what he or she did in this lesson.

FOR MORE PRACTICE: Standards Practice Book

Name ______________________________

Time to the Half Hour

Essential Question How do you tell time to the half hour on a clock that has only an hour hand?

Measurement and Data—1.MD.3

MATHEMATICAL PRACTICES
MP.1, MP.2, MP.8

Listen and Draw

Circle **4:00**, **5:00**, or **between 4:00 and 5:00** to describe the time shown on the clock.

4:00

between 4:00 and 5:00

5:00

4:00

between 4:00 and 5:00

5:00

4:00

between 4:00 and 5:00

5:00

Math Talk **Mathematical Practices**

Use **before** and **after** to **describe** the time shown on the middle clock.

FOR THE TEACHER • Have children look at the hour hand on each clock to decide which choice best describes the time shown.

Model and Draw

As an **hour** passes, the hour hand moves from one number to the next number.

When a **half hour** has passed, the hour hand points halfway between two numbers.

half past 7:00

Share and Show

Look at where the hour hand points.
Write the time.

1. 

____

2. 

____

✓3. 

____

✓4. 

____

Name ______________________

On Your Own

MATHEMATICAL PRACTICE 2 **Use Reasoning** Look at where the hour hand points. Write the time.

5.

____

6.

____

7.

____

8.

____

9.

____

10.

____

Problem Solving • Applications

11. THINKSMARTER Tim plays soccer at half past 9:00. He eats lunch at half past 1:00. He sees a movie at half past 2:00.

Look at the clock.
Write what Tim does.

Tim ______________________________.

12. GO DEEPER Tyra has a piano lesson at 5:00. The lesson ends at half past 5:00. How much time is Tyra at her lesson? Circle your answer.

half hour

hour

13. THINKSMARTER What time is it? Circle the time that makes the sentence true.

The time is [5:30 / 6:00 / 6:30].

TAKE HOME ACTIVITY • Say a time, such as half past 10:00. Ask your child to describe where the hour hand points at this time.

FOR MORE PRACTICE: Standards Practice Book

Name ______________________________

Tell Time to the Hour and Half Hour

Essential Question How are the minute hand and hour hand different for time to the hour and time to the half hour?

Measurement and Data—1.MD.3

MATHEMATICAL PRACTICES
MP.2, MP.5, MP.6

Each clock has an hour hand and a minute hand. Use what you know about the hour hand to write the unknown numbers.

It is 1:00.

The hour hand points to the _____.

The minute hand points to the _____.

It is half past 1:00.

The hour hand points between the _____ and the _____.

The minute hand points to the _____.

Mathematical Practices

Look at the top clock. **Explain** how you know which is the minute hand.

FOR THE TEACHER • Read the time on the first clock and have children identify where the hour hand and minute hand point. Then repeat for the second clock.

Model and Draw

An hour has 60 **minutes**.

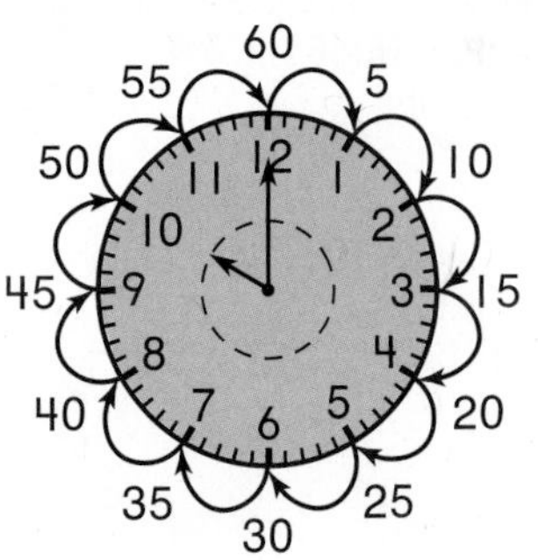

The clocks show 10:00.

A half hour has 30 minutes.

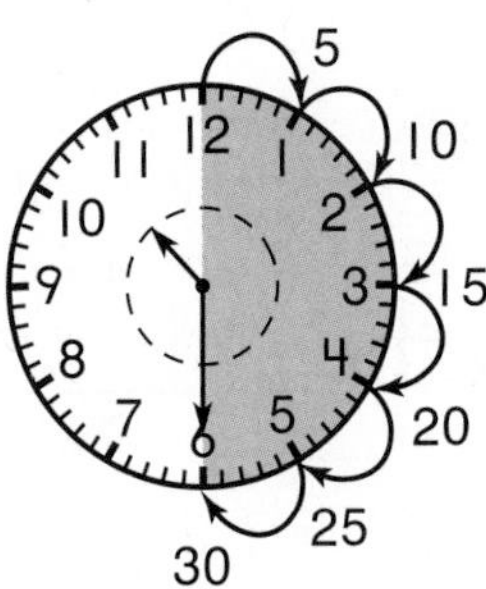

The clocks show half past 10:00. The **minute hand** has moved from the 12 to the 6.

30 minutes after 10:00

Share and Show

Write the time.

1.

2.

3.

Name ______________________________

On Your Own

MATHEMATICAL PRACTICE 6 **Attend to Precision** Write the time.

4.

5.

6.

7.

8.

9.

Circle your answer.

10. Sara goes to the park when both the hour hand and the minute hand point to the 12. What time does Sara go to the park?

1:00   12:00   12:30

11. THINK SMARTER Mel goes to the park when the hour hand points between the 3 and 4 and the minute hand points to the 6. What time does Mel go to the park?

3:00   3:30   6:00

Problem Solving • Applications

WRITE Math

Solve.

12. Linda wakes up at 6:30. Draw to show what time Linda wakes up.

13. David left school at 3:30. Circle the clock that shows 3:30.

14. GO DEEPER The hour hand points halfway between the 2 and 3. Draw the hour hand and the minute hand. Write the time.

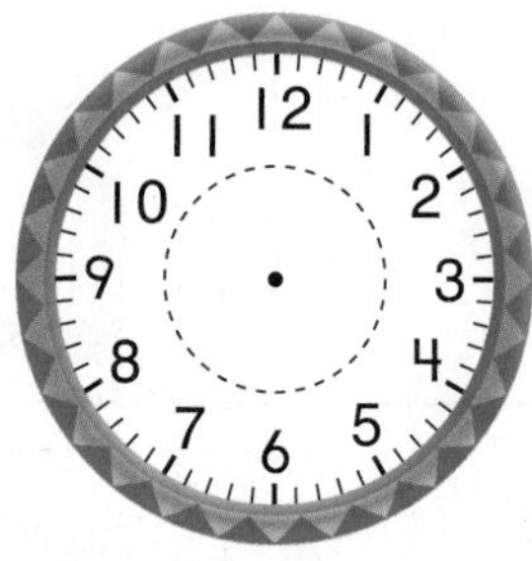

15. THINK SMARTER Choose all the ways that name the time on the clock.

- ○ half past 7:00
- ○ half past 6:00
- ○ 8:30
- ○ 7:30

TAKE HOME ACTIVITY • At times on the half hour, have your child show you the minute hand and the hour hand on a clock and tell what time it is.

FOR MORE PRACTICE: Standards Practice Book

Name ___________________________

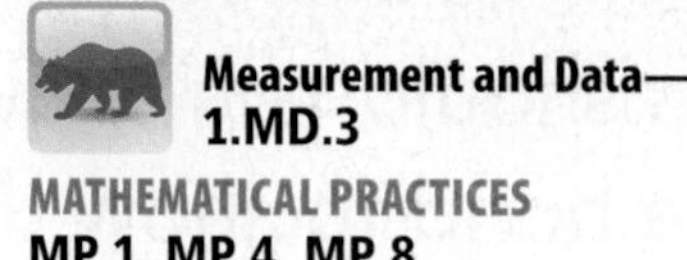

Practice Time to the Hour and Half Hour

Essential Question How do you know whether to draw and write time to the hour or half hour?

Measurement and Data—1.MD.3

MATHEMATICAL PRACTICES
MP.1, MP.4, MP.8

Circle the clock that matches the problem.

FOR THE TEACHER • Read the following problems. Barbara goes to the store at 8:00. Circle the clock that shows 8:00. Have children use the top workspace to solve. Then have children solve this problem: Barbara takes Ria for a walk at 1:30. Circle the clock that shows 1:30.

Math Talk Mathematical Practices

Describe how you know which clock shows 1:30.

Model and Draw

Where should you draw the minute hand to show the time?

Share and Show

Use the hour hand to write the time.
Draw the minute hand.

1.

2.

3.

4.

5.

6.

Name ____________________

On Your Own

MATHEMATICAL PRACTICE 4 **Use Diagrams** Use the hour hand to write the time. Draw the minute hand.

7.

8.

9.

10.

11.

12.

13. THINK SMARTER **What is the error?**
Zoey tried to show 6:00. Explain how to change the clock to show 6:00.

Problem Solving • Applications

Solve.

14. Vince goes to a baseball game at 4:30. Draw to show what time Vince goes to a baseball game.

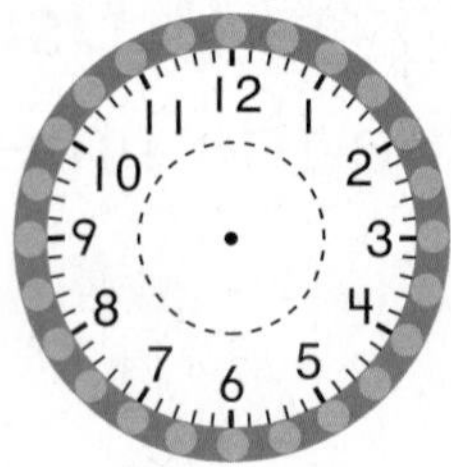

15. GO DEEPER Brandon has lunch at 1 o'clock. Write and draw to show what time Brandon has lunch.

16. THINK SMARTER Juan tried to show 8:30. He made a mistake.

What did Juan do wrong? Explain his mistake.

TAKE HOME ACTIVITY • Show your child the time on a clock. Ask him or her what time it will be in 30 minutes.

FOR MORE PRACTICE: Standards Practice Book

Name ______________________________

Chapter 9 Review/Test

1. Match each word on the left to a drawing on the right.

shortest •

longest •

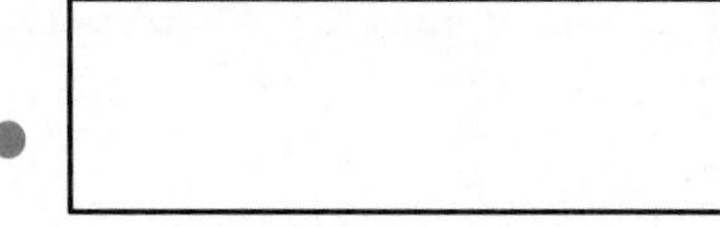

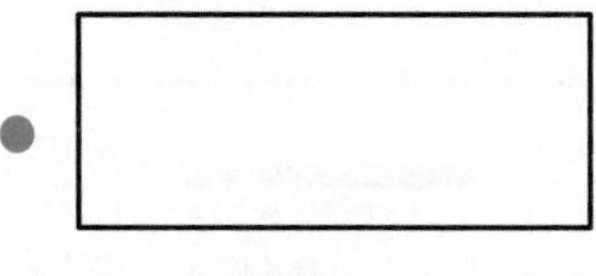

2. Is the first line shorter than the second line? Choose Yes or No.

○ Yes ○ No

○ Yes ○ No

○ Yes ○ No

3. The crayon is about 5 tiles long. Draw tiles below the crayon to show its length.

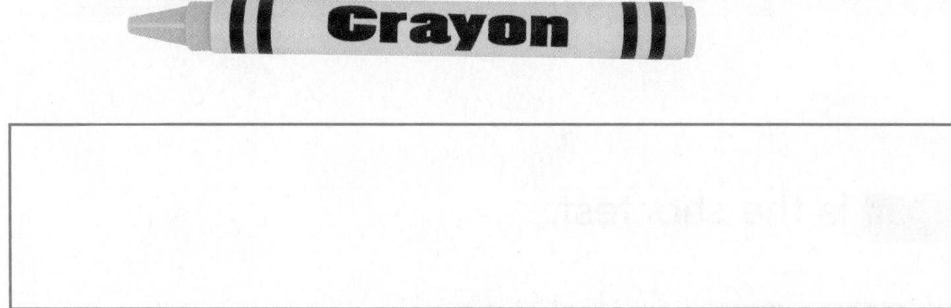

GO DIGITAL Assessment Options Chapter Test

4. Use the paper clips below. About how long is the worm?

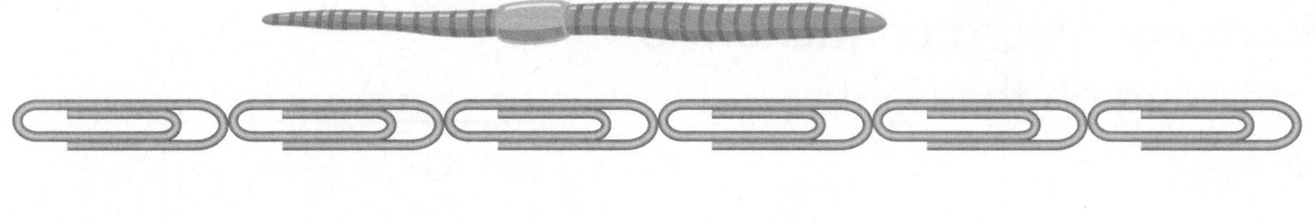

about ______ paper clips

5. Measure the ribbons. Use paper clips.

about ______ paper clips

about ______ paper clips

about ______ paper clips

The ______ ribbon is the shortest.

The ______ ribbon is the longest.

Name ______________________

6. Look at the hour hand. What is the time?

- ○ 9:00
- ○ 10 o'clock
- ○ 11 o'clock
- ○ 12:00

---

7. What time is it? Circle the time that makes the sentence true.

The time is [1:30 / 2:00 / 2:30].

---

8. Choose all the ways that name the time on the clock.

- ○ half past 6:00
- ○ half past 11:00
- ○ 6:00
- ○ 11:30

9. Draw the hand on the clock to show 9:30.

10. Lucy tried to show 5:00. She made a mistake.

Draw hands on the clock to show 5:00.

What did Lucy do wrong? Explain her mistake.

11. The is shorter than the  .
The  is longer than the  .
Draw the length of the .

Chapter 10

Represent Data

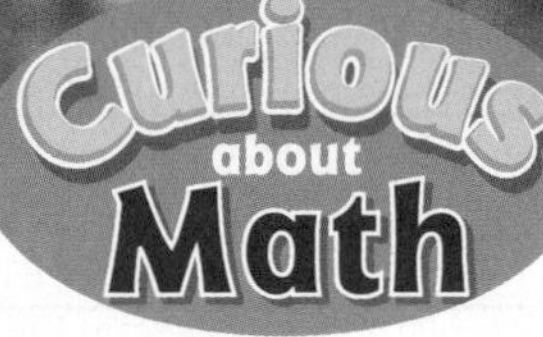

How many days will it snow or rain this week where you live? How can you find out?

Name ________________________________

Show What You Know

Make a Concrete Graph

Sort a handful of ■ and ■. Make a concrete graph.

Square Colors								
■								
■								

1. How many ■ are there? __________

More, Fewer

2. Shade to show a set of fewer.

Draw Equal Groups

3. Draw a ○ below each picture to show the same number of objects.

This page checks understanding of important skills needed for success in Chapter 10.

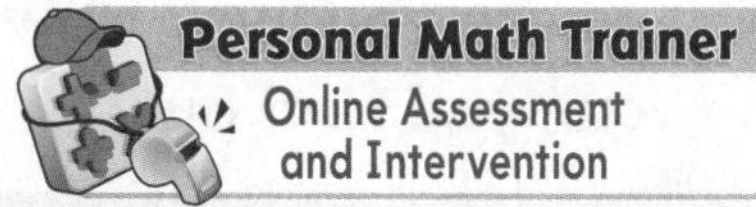

Name ______________________________

Vocabulary Builder

Review Words
graph
more
fewer
most
fewest

Visualize It

Complete the chart.
Mark each row with a ✔.

Word	I Know	Sounds Familiar	I Do Not Know
graph			
more			
fewer			
most			
fewest			

Understand Vocabulary

Use the review words. Label the groups.

1.  

______________ ______________

2.   

______________ ______________

GO DIGITAL
• Interactive Student Edi
• Multimedia eGlossary

Game

Materials 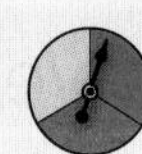 • 16 • 16 • 16

Play with a partner.

1. Spin the .
2. Put 1 cube of that color in the correct row of your graph.
3. Take turns. Play until each partner has 5 turns.
4. The player who went last spins again to get a color.
5. The player with more cubes of that color wins. Spin again if you both have the same number of cubes of that color.

Player 1

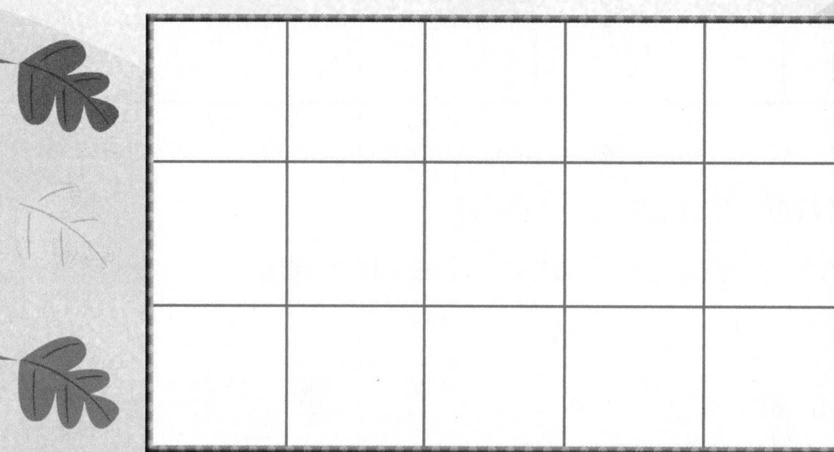

Player 2

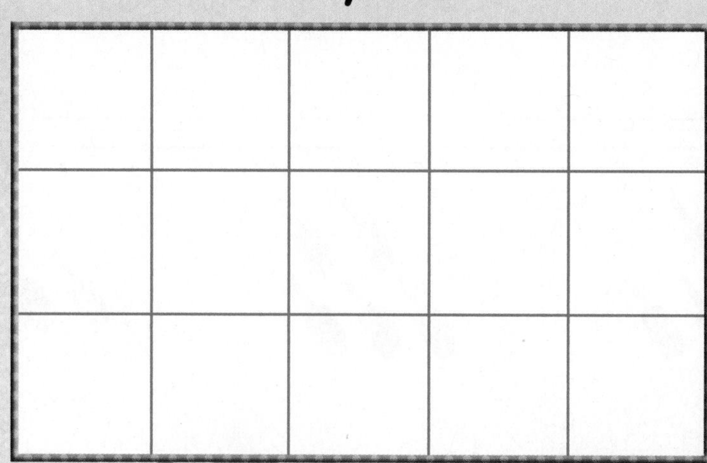

Name ______________________

Read Picture Graphs

Essential Question What do the pictures in a picture graph show?

Measurement and Data—1.MD.4

MATHEMATICAL PRACTICES
MP.3, MP.4

Listen and Draw

Use ▪ ▪. Draw to show the cubes.
Write how many more ▪.

_____ more ▪

Math Talk Mathematical Practices

Describe how you can use your picture to compare the cubes.

FOR THE TEACHER • Read the following problem. There are 2 green cubes and 4 blue cubes. How many more blue cubes are there than green cubes?

Model and Draw

Children at the Playground					
swings	웃	웃	웃	웃	
slide	웃	웃			

Each 웃 stands for 1 child.

A **picture graph** uses pictures to show information.

There are __4__ children on the swings.

There are ____ children on the slide.

There are more children on the ______________.

Share and Show

Our Favorite Activity at the Fair							
animals	웃	웃	웃	웃	웃		
rides	웃	웃	웃	웃	웃	웃	웃

Each 웃 stands for 1 child.

Use the picture graph to answer the question.

1. Which activity did more children choose? Circle.  

2. How many children chose ? ____ children

3. How many children chose ? ____ children

4. How many fewer children chose  than rides? ____ fewer children

Name ____________________

On Your Own

What We Drink for Lunch								
milk	웃	웃	웃	웃	웃	웃	웃	웃
juice	웃	웃	웃					
water	웃	웃	웃	웃	웃			

Each 웃 stands for 1 child.

Use the picture graph to answer the question.

5. How many children drink milk?

____ children

6. How many children in all drink juice and water?

____ children

7. How many fewer children drink water than milk?

____ fewer children

8. How many more children drink milk than juice?

____ more children

9. THINK SMARTER How many children in all drink milk, juice, and water?

____ children

10. GO DEEPER 4 new children join the class. They drink juice at lunch. Now, how many more children drink juice than water?

____ more children

Problem Solving • Applications  

Our Favorite Animal at the Zoo								
zebras	웃	웃	웃	웃	웃			
lions	웃	웃	웃	웃	웃	웃	웃	웃
seals	웃							

Each 웃 stands for 1 child.

 **Write an Equation** Write a number sentence to solve the problem.

11. How many children chose zebras and seals altogether?

    ___ ◯ ___ ◯ ___

    ___ children

12. How many more children chose lions than seals?

    ___ ◯ ___ ◯ ___

    ___ more children

13. 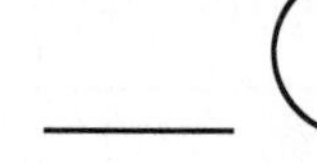 How many more children chose lions than zebras and seals altogether?

    ___ ◯ ___ ◯ ___

    ___ more children

14.  Use the graph at the top. How many children chose lions?

    ☐

TAKE HOME ACTIVITY • Keep track of the weather for one week by drawing a picture each day to show if it is sunny, cloudy, or rainy. At the end of the week, ask your child what the weather was like for most of the week.

FOR MORE PRACTICE: Standards Practice Book

Name ____________________

Make Picture Graphs

Essential Question How do you make a picture graph to answer a question?

Measurement and Data—1.MD.4

MATHEMATICAL PRACTICES
MP.3, MP.4

Listen and Draw

Use ● to solve the problem.
Draw to show your work.

Which has more?

FOR THE TEACHER • Read the following problem. Asaf has 6 baseballs. He has 4 bats. Does he have more baseballs or bats? Have children draw circles to show the baseballs and bats. Then have them circle the object with more.

Math Talk **Mathematical Practices**

Describe what the picture graph shows.

Model and Draw

Are there more black or white sheep in the picture? Make a picture graph to find out.

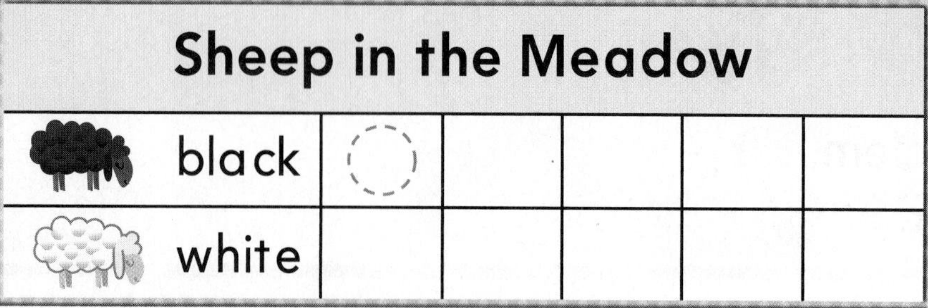

Sheep in the Meadow					
black					
white					

Each ◯ stands for 1 sheep.

There are more ________________ sheep.

Share and Show

Do more children like cats or dogs?
Ask 10 friends which pet they like better.
Draw 1 circle for each child's answer.

Our Favorite Pet										
cats										
dogs										

Each ◯ stands for 1 child.

Use the picture graph to answer each question.

1. How many children chose cats? _____ children

2. How many children chose dogs? _____ children

3. Which pet did more children choose? Circle.

Name ___________________________

On Your Own

Which activity do the most children like best?
Ask 10 friends. Draw 1 circle for each child's answer.

Our Favorite Activity										
reading										
computer										
sports										

Each ◯ stands for 1 child.

MATHEMATICAL PRACTICE 4 **Use Graphs** Use the picture graph to answer the question.

4. How many children chose (reading)?

____ children

5. How many children chose (computer) and (sports)?

____ children

6. Which activity did the most children choose? Circle.

7. Did all your classmates make picture graphs that look the same? Circle **yes** or **no**.

8. Write your own question about the graph.

____

9. GO DEEPER Look at the question you wrote. Answer your question.

____

Problem Solving • Applications

Matt made this picture graph to show the paint colors his friends like best.

Favorite Paint Color					
blue	○	○	○	○	○
red	○	○	○		
green	○	○			

Each ○ stands for 1 child.

10. How many children chose a paint color?

____ children

11. How many fewer children chose (green) than (blue)?

____ fewer children

Personal Math Trainer

12. THINK SMARTER+ Complete the picture graph to show the number of flowers.

Flowers in the Vase					
(red tulip)					
(yellow tulip)					

Each ○ stands for 1 Flower.

TAKE HOME ACTIVITY • Ask your child to make a picture graph showing how many glasses of water each family member drinks in a day. Discuss how to find who drinks the most water.

FOR MORE PRACTICE: Standards Practice Book

Name ______________________________

Read Bar Graphs

Essential Question How can you read a bar graph to find the number that a bar shows?

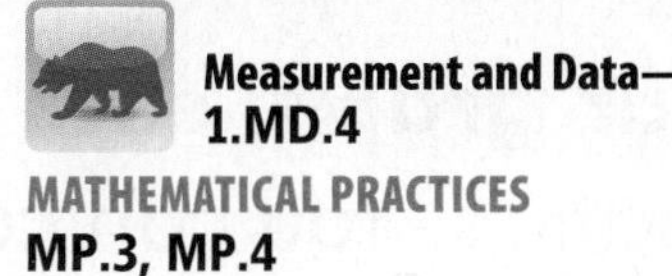

Measurement and Data—1.MD.4

MATHEMATICAL PRACTICES
MP.3, MP.4

Write a question about the graph.
Use ● to help solve the problem.

Type of Sneaker We Are Wearing

laces	○	○	○	○	○	○	○	○	○	○	
no laces	○	○	○	○	○	○					

Each ○ stands for 1 child.

____

____

____

FOR THE TEACHER • Read the following problem. Emma's class made this picture graph. What question could Emma's class answer using the graph? Write the question and the answer.

Math Talk — **Mathematical Practices**

Describe how the class made this picture graph.

Model and Draw

In a **bar graph,** each bar shows information. You can compare the lengths of the bars.

What title describes this graph?

Touch the end of a bar. Look down to see the number of children.

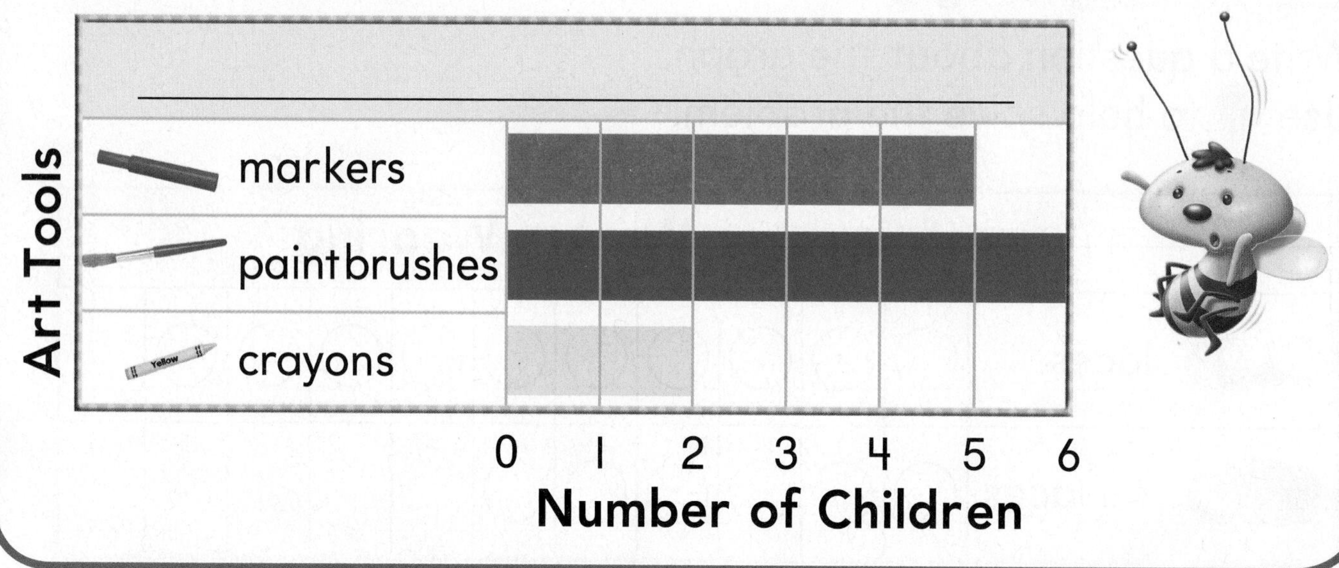

Share and Show

Use the bar graph to answer the question.

1. How many children chose ?

   ____ children

2. How many children chose ?

   ____ children

3. How many more children chose than ?

   ____ more children

4. Which art tool did the fewest children choose? Circle.

5. Which art tool did the most children choose? Circle.

Name ______________________________

On Your Own

MATHEMATICAL PRACTICE 4 **Use Graphs** Use the bar graph to answer the question.

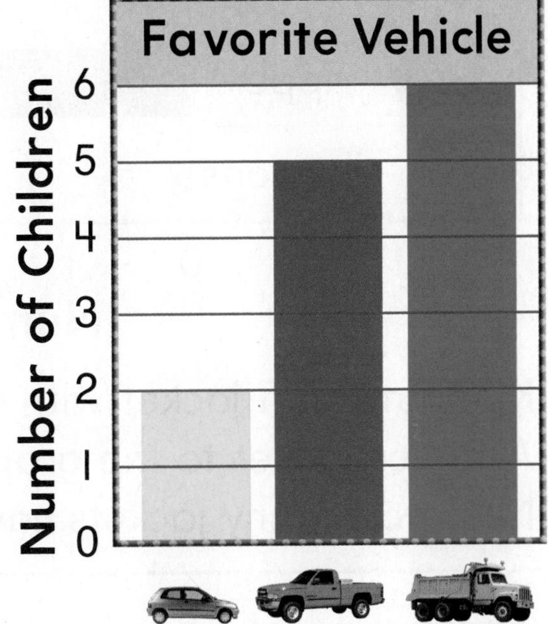

6. How many children chose car?

____ children

7. How many children chose dump truck?

____ children

8. How many children in all chose car and dump truck?

____ children

9. How many more children chose truck than car?

____ more children

10. Which vehicle did the most children choose? Circle.

11. THINK SMARTER Order the vehicles from least to most votes. Write 1 for the least votes and 3 for the most votes.

 ____

 ____

 ____

Problem Solving • Applications  

Use the bar graph to answer the question.

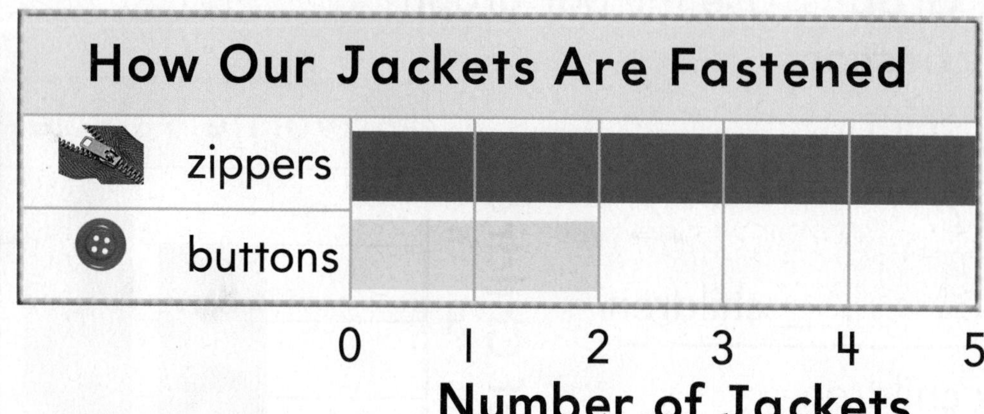

12. Kim puts on a jacket with (button). Add her jacket to the graph. Now how many jackets have (button)? _____ jackets

13. GO DEEPER Ed adds a row to the graph to show jackets with snaps. 2 fewer jackets have snaps than have zippers. How many jackets have snaps? _____ jackets

14. THINK SMARTER How many more jackets have (zipper) than (button)? Circle the number in the box.

7
5
3

more jackets have (zipper) than (button).

TAKE HOME ACTIVITY • Have your child look through newspapers and magazines for examples of bar graphs. Talk about what information is shown in each graph you find.

FOR MORE PRACTICE: Standards Practice Book

Name ______________________________

Make Bar Graphs

Essential Question How does a bar graph help you compare information?

Measurement and Data—1.MD.4

MATHEMATICAL PRACTICES
MP.3, MP.4, MP.8

Listen and Draw

Use ▪ to model the problem. Color 1 box for each food item to complete the graph.

Food Sold at the Soccer Game

Kinds of Food							
pizza							
hot dogs							
tacos							
	0	1	2	3	4	5	6 7

Number of Food Items Sold

Math Talk — **Mathematical Practices**

How do you know that you counted each food in the picture? **Explain.**

FOR THE TEACHER • Read the following problem. Dan keeps track of the food he sells at the soccer game. He sells all of the food on the table. Make a bar graph to show the food Dan sells.

Model and Draw

Are there more daisies or sunflowers in the garden?
Make a bar graph to find out.
Shade I box for each flower in the picture.

Flowers in the Garden

Kinds of Flowers							
daisies	■						
sunflowers							
	0–1	1–2	2–3	3–4	4–5	5–6	6–7

Number of Flowers

There are more ________________ in the garden.

Share and Show

Do more children write with their left hand or right hand?
Ask 10 friends which hand they use. Make a bar graph.

Hand We Use to Write

Writing Hand										
left										
right										
	0–1	1–2	2–3	3–4	4–5	5–6	6–7	7–8	8–9	9–10

Number of Children

✓ I. Which hand do more children use to write? ________________

Name ______________________

On Your Own

MATHEMATICAL PRACTICE 8 **Draw Conclusions**

Do children like bear, blocks, or marbles best?
Ask 10 friends which toy they like best.

2. Make a bar graph. Write a title and labels for your graph.

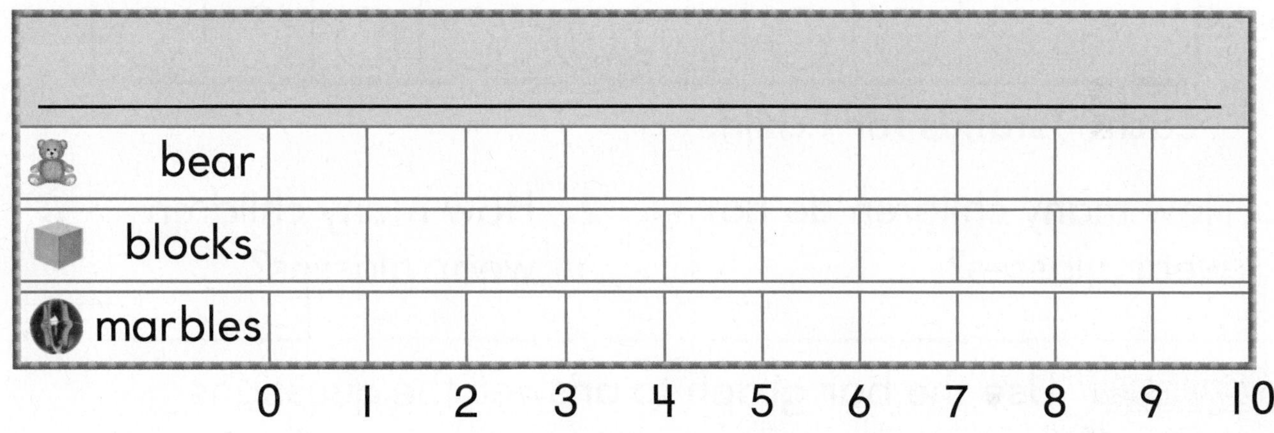

3. Which toy did the most children choose? Circle.

4. How many children chose blocks?

______ children

5. THINK SMARTER How are picture graphs and bar graphs alike?

____

____

____

TAKE HOME ACTIVITY • Your child has learned how to make picture graphs and bar graphs. Ask your child to explain how bar graphs are different from picture graphs.

FOR MORE PRACTICE: Standards Practice Book

Name ____________________

Mid-Chapter Checkpoint

Concepts and Skills

Use the picture graph to answer the questions. (1.MD.4)

Do you wear glasses?								
yes	○	○	○					
no	○	○	○	○	○	○	○	○

Each ○ stands for 1 child.

1. How many children do not wear glasses? ____

2. How many children wear glasses? ____

THINK SMARTER Use the bar graph to answer the questions. (1.MD.4)

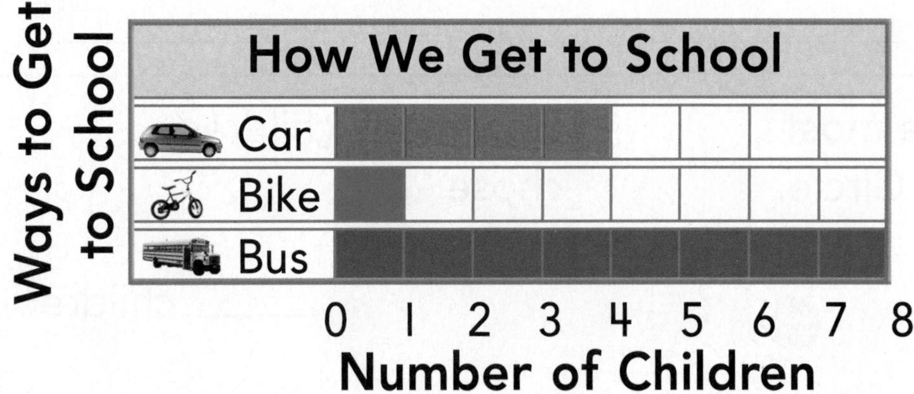

3. How many children take the bus to school? ____

4. THINK SMARTER Is the sentence true? Choose Yes or No.

5 children ride in a car or ride a bike.	○ Yes	○ No
More children go by car than by bus.	○ Yes	○ No
Fewer children go by bike than by car.	○ Yes	○ No

Name ______________________________

Read Tally Charts

Essential Question How do you count the tallies on a tally chart?

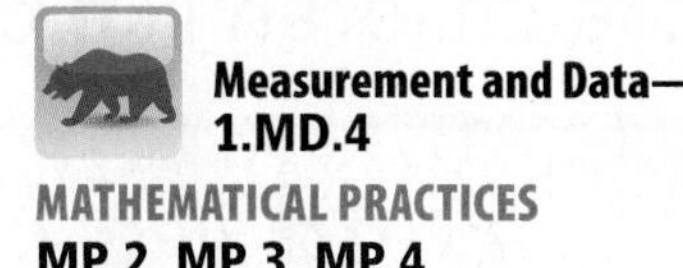

Listen and Draw Real World

Use ● to solve the problem.
Draw to show your work.
Write how many.

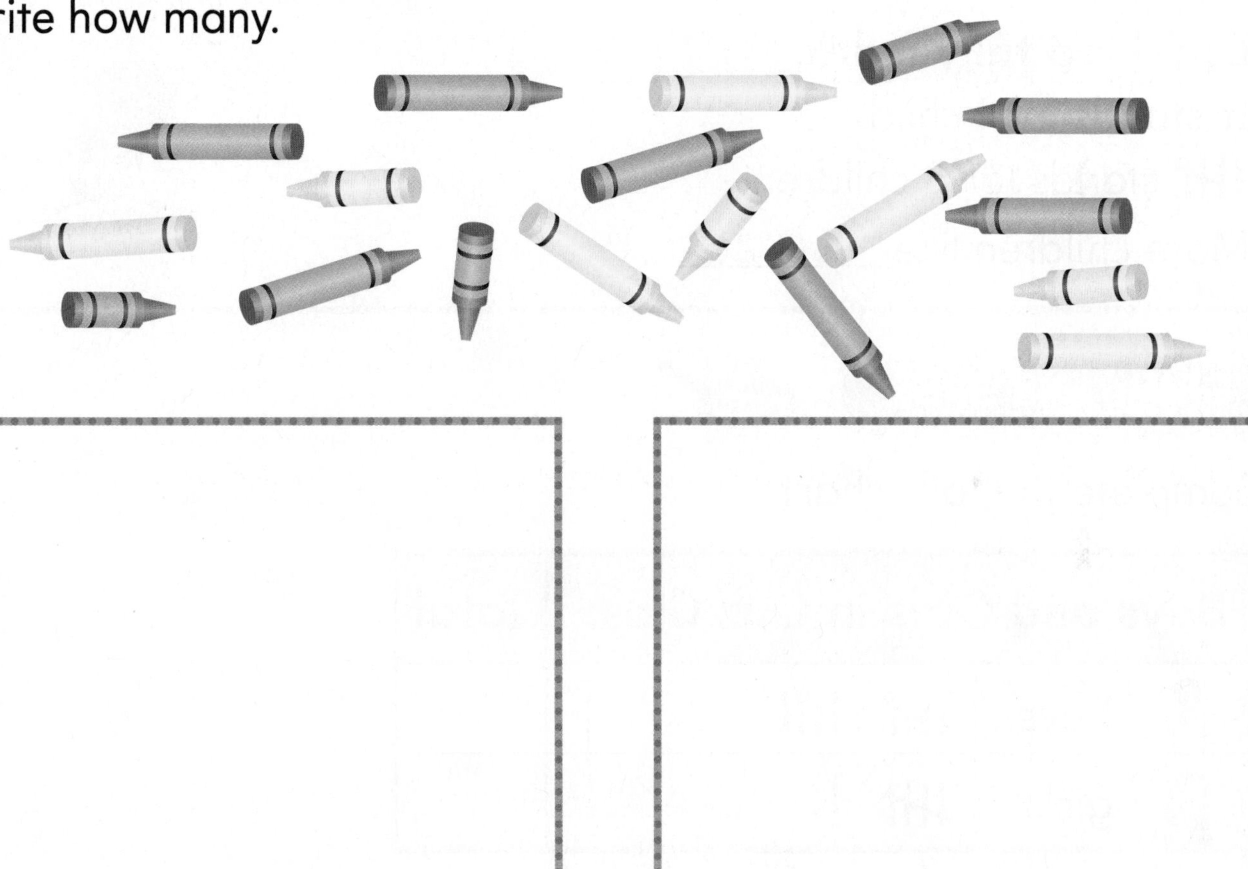

______ ______

Mathematical Practices

Describe how you sorted the counters.

FOR THE TEACHER • Read the following problem. Jane is sorting her crayons. Draw to show how she can sort the crayons into two groups.

Model and Draw

Do more children like chicken or pizza better?

Food We Like		Total
chicken	III	3
pizza	~~IIII~~ III	

You can use a **tally chart** to collect information.

Each | is a **tally mark.**
It stands for 1 child.
~~IIII~~ stands for 5 children.
More children like .

Share and Show

MATH BOARD

Complete the tally chart.

Boys and Girls in Our Class		Total
boys	~~IIII~~ IIII	
girls	~~IIII~~ I	

Use the tally chart to answer each question.

1. How many girls are in the class? _____ girls

2. How many boys are in the class? _____ boys

✓ 3. How many children are in the class in all? _____ children

✓ 4. Are there more boys or girls in the class? ____________

Name ___________________________

On Your Own

Complete the tally chart.

Our Favorite Sport		Total
t-ball	𝍸	
soccer	𝍸 II	
swimming	III	

Use the tally chart to answer the question.

5. How many children chose soccer? _____ children

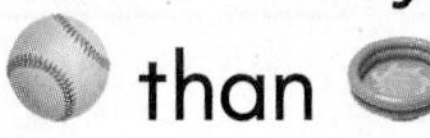

6. How many more children chose t-ball than swimming? _____ more children

7. Which sport did the most children choose? Circle.

8. THINK SMARTER Write your own question about the tally chart.

____

____

____

9. GO DEEPER Sam asked some other children which sport they like. They all chose swimming. Now the most children chose swimming.

How many children did Sam ask? _____ children

Problem Solving • Applications

Coins in the Bank		Total
dime	IIII	
penny	𝍸 𝍸	
nickel	IIII	

Remember to write the total.

MATHEMATICAL PRACTICE 2 **Connect Symbols and Words**

Complete each sentence about the tally chart.
Write **greater than, less than,** or **equal to.**

10. The number of tallies for (penny) is ______________ the number of tallies for (dime).

11. The number of tallies for (dime) is ______________ the number of tallies for (nickel).

12. The number of tallies for (nickel) is ______________ the number of tallies for (penny).

13. GO DEEPER The number of tallies for (penny) is ______________ the number of tallies for both (dime) and (nickel).

14. THINK SMARTER How many coins are in the bank?

○ 𝍸 III
○ 𝍸 𝍸 IIII
○ 𝍸 𝍸
○ 𝍸 𝍸 𝍸 III

TAKE HOME ACTIVITY • Together with your child, make a tally chart showing how many times you all say the word "eat" during a meal. Then have your child write the number.

FOR MORE PRACTICE: Standards Practice Book

Name ______________________________________

Make Tally Charts

Essential Question Why is a tally chart a good way to show information that you have collected?

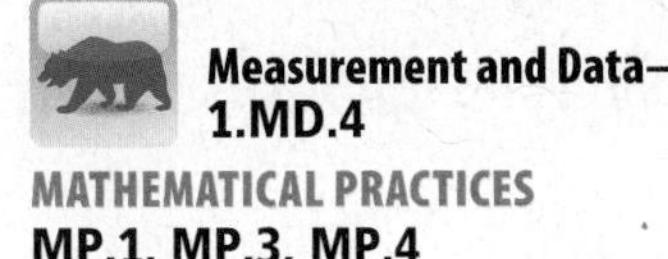

Measurement and Data—1.MD.4

MATHEMATICAL PRACTICES
MP.1, MP.3, MP.4

Complete the tally chart.

Our Favorite Game		Total
card game	卌	
puzzle	III	
board game	卌 卌	

Use the tally chart to answer the question.

Which game did the most children choose? Circle.

Which game did the fewest children choose? Circle.

FOR THE TEACHER • Read the following problem. Ava asks the children in her class which of three games they like the best. She makes a tally mark to show each child's answer. Which game did the most children choose? Which did the fewest children choose?

Math Talk **Mathematical Practices**

How do you know which game is the favorite? **Explain.**

Model and Draw

How can you make a tally chart to show the boats at the lake?

Decide if each boat has a sail.

Boats at the Lake		Total
boats with sails	||	
boats without sails		

Share and Show

Use the picture to complete the tally chart. Then answer each question.

Fish in the Tank		Total
zebra fish		
angel fish		

1. How many zebra fish are in the tank?

   ____ zebra fish

2. How many more zebra fish than angel fish are there?

   ____ more zebra fish

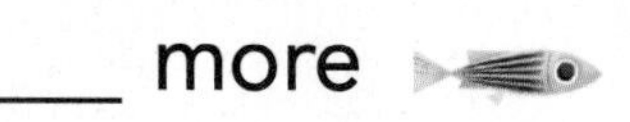

3. How many zebra fish and angel fish are in the tank?

   ____ fish

Name ____________________

On Your Own

Which of these snacks do most children like the best?
Ask 10 friends. Make 1 tally mark for each child's answer.

Our Favorite Snack		Total
pretzel		
apple		
yogurt		

Use the tally chart to answer each question.

4. How many children chose pretzel?

____ children

5. How many children chose yogurt?

____ children

6. Which snack do most children like best? Circle.

7. THINK SMARTER What if 6 children out of the 10 chose pretzel? Which snack would be the favorite? Circle it.

8. Explain Write your own question about the tally chart.

____

____

Problem Solving • Applications

MATHEMATICAL PRACTICE 1 **Analyze Relationships** Jenna asked 10 friends to choose their favorite subject. She will ask 10 more children.

Our Favorite School Subject		Total
math	卌 I	
reading	II	
science	II	

9. Predict. Which subject will children most likely choose?

10. Predict. Which subject will children least likely choose?

11. THINK SMARTER How can you prove if your prediction is good? Try it.

12. THINK SMARTER Complete the tally chart to show the number of votes.

Fruit We Like		Total
apple	IIII	4
banana		5
grapes		2

TAKE HOME ACTIVITY • With your child, survey friends and family to find out their favorite food. Draw tally marks to record the results and then prepare the food.

FOR MORE PRACTICE: Standards Practice Book

Name ___________________________

Problem Solving • Represent Data

Essential Question How can showing information in a graph help you solve problems?

Measurement and Data—1.MD.4

MATHEMATICAL PRACTICES
MP.3, MP.6

Brad sees many animals at the park. How can you find how many animals Brad sees?

Unlock the Problem

What do I need to find?

how many animals Brad sees

What information do I need to use?

the number of rabbits, birds, and deer in the picture

Show how to solve the problem.

Animals Brad Sees

Animals							
rabbit							
bird							
deer							
	0	1	2	3	4	5	6 7

Number of Animals

____ + ____ + ____ = ____ animals

HOME CONNECTION • Your child learned how to represent data from a picture in a bar graph. Have your child explain why it is easier to use data in a bar graph than in a picture.

Try Another Problem

Make a graph to solve.

- What do I need to find?
- What information do I need to use?

1. Jake has 4 more train cars than Ed. Ed has 3 train cars. Ben has 2 fewer train cars than Ed. How many train cars does Jake have?

____ train cars

Our Train Cars

Children								
Jake								
Ed								
Ben								
	0	1	2	3	4	5	6	7	8

Number of Train Cars

---

2. Marla has 8 dolls. Three dolls have blue eyes. The rest have brown. How many dolls have brown eyes?

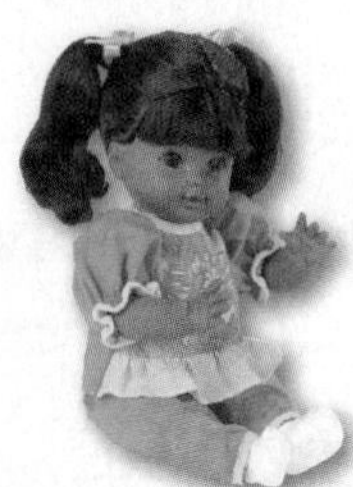

____ dolls

Dolls Marla Has

Eye Color								
blue eyes								
brown eyes								
	0	1	2	3	4	5	6	7	8

Number of Dolls

Math Talk — Mathematical Practices

Describe how the bar graph helps you solve Exercise 2.

Name ______________________

Share and Show

MATHEMATICAL PRACTICE 6 **Make Connections** Find out about the eye color of your classmates.

3. Write a question you can ask your friends.

____

4. Ask 10 friends your question. Make a tally chart.

______________________		Total

5. THINK SMARTER Use the tally chart to make a bar graph.

______________________								
	0	1	2	3	4	5	6	7	8

____

6. **Explain** What did you learn from the graph?

____

On Your Own

WRITE Math

What is your favorite fruit? Nina asked 20 children this question. Then she made a bar graph. But Nina spilled paint on the graph.

7. How many children chose grapes?

____ children

8. GO DEEPER How many children chose bananas?

____ children

Personal Math Trainer

9. THINK SMARTER + Write another question that can be answered by using the graph.

TAKE HOME ACTIVITY • Work with your child to make a tally chart and a bar graph showing the favorite color of 10 family members or friends. Talk about the results.

FOR MORE PRACTICE: Standards Practice Book

Name ______________________________

Chapter 10 Review/Test

Use the picture graph to answer the questions.

Color We Like							
RED red	웃	웃	웃	웃	웃		
BLUE blue	웃	웃	웃	웃	웃	웃	

Each 웃 stands for 1 child.

1. How many children chose RED?

☐

2. Is the sentence true? Choose Yes or No.

More children like blue than red. ○ Yes ○ No

5 children like red. ○ Yes ○ No

2 more children like blue than red. ○ Yes ○ No

3. 1 more child gets a BLUE. Draw what the blue row looks like now.

GO DIGITAL Assessment Options Chapter Test

Use the bar graph to answer the questions.

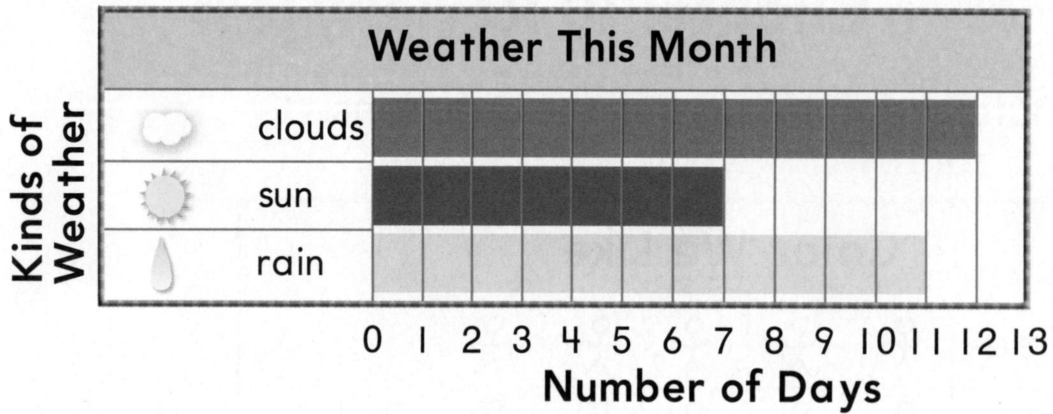

4. How many days had ☀ ?

☐

5. Compare 💧 and ☀ days. Circle the number that makes the sentence true.

There were [4 / 5 / 7] more 💧 days than ☀ days.

---

6. Ann says the graph shows 1 more rainy day than cloudy days. Is she correct?

Choose Yes or No.

○ Yes ○ No

Explain your answer.

☐

Name ______________________________

Use the tally chart to answer the questions.

Sam's Cars and Trucks		Total
cars		8
trucks	𝍸 |	6

7. How many  does Sam have?

☐

8. Draw tally marks for the number of cars that the chart shows.

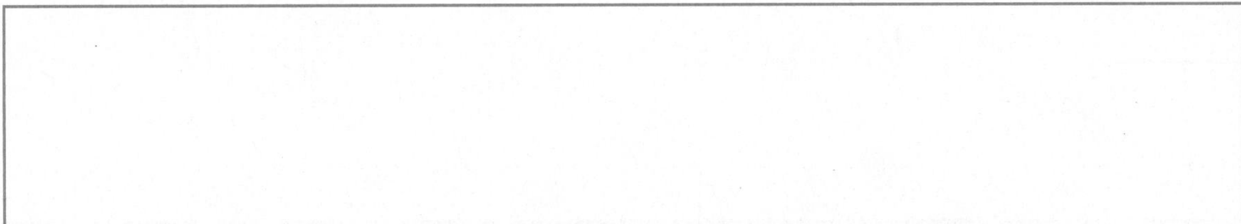

9. Circle the words that make the sentence true.

The number of tally marks for [truck] is

greater than less than equal to

the number of tally marks for .

10. Chung visits the zoo. He sees 3 . He sees 3 more than . He sees 2 fewer than . Graph the data.

What Chung Sees						
lion						
elephant						
monkey						
	0	1	2	3	4	5	6

Use Chung's graph to answer the questions.

11. How many does Chung see?

____

12. Write another question that can be answered by Chung's graph.

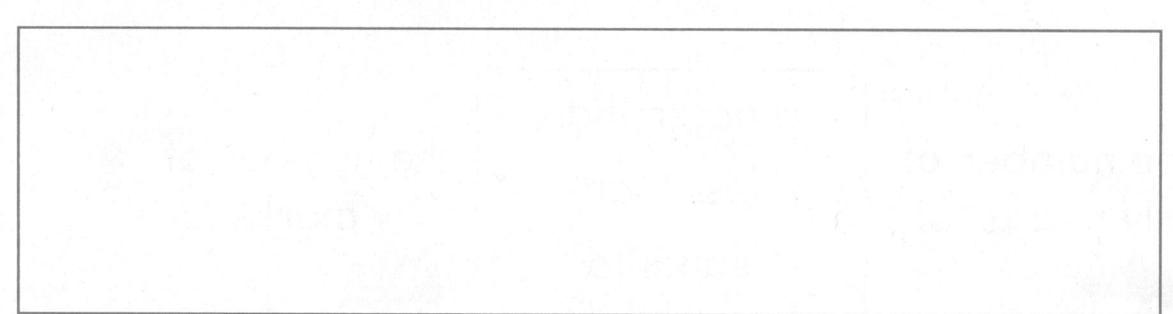

On the Move

written by Jennifer Earnshaw

CRITICAL AREA Reasoning about attributes of, and composing and decomposing geometric shapes

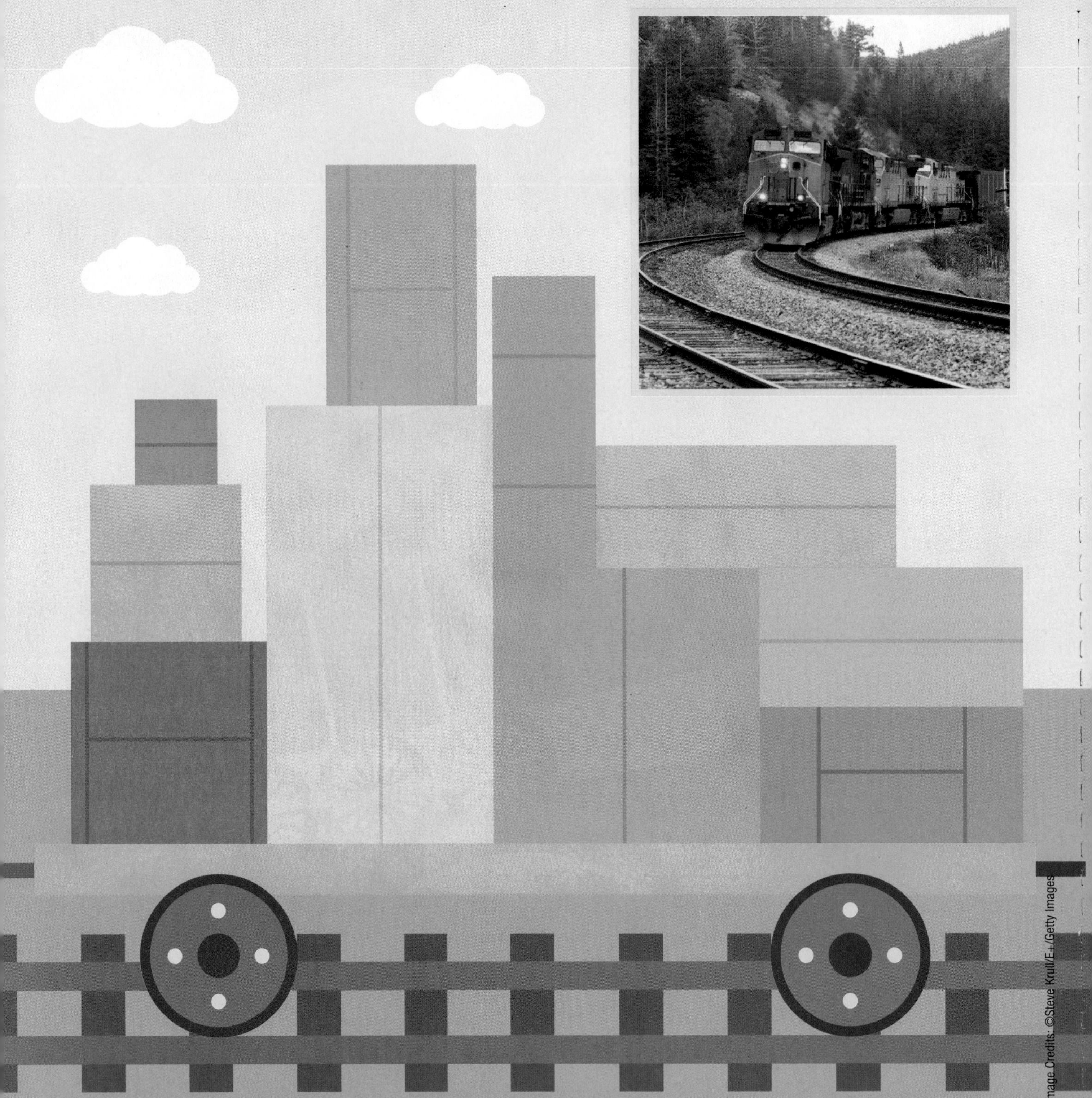

The train car waits for the engine.

Name some shapes you see.

What will this train bring?

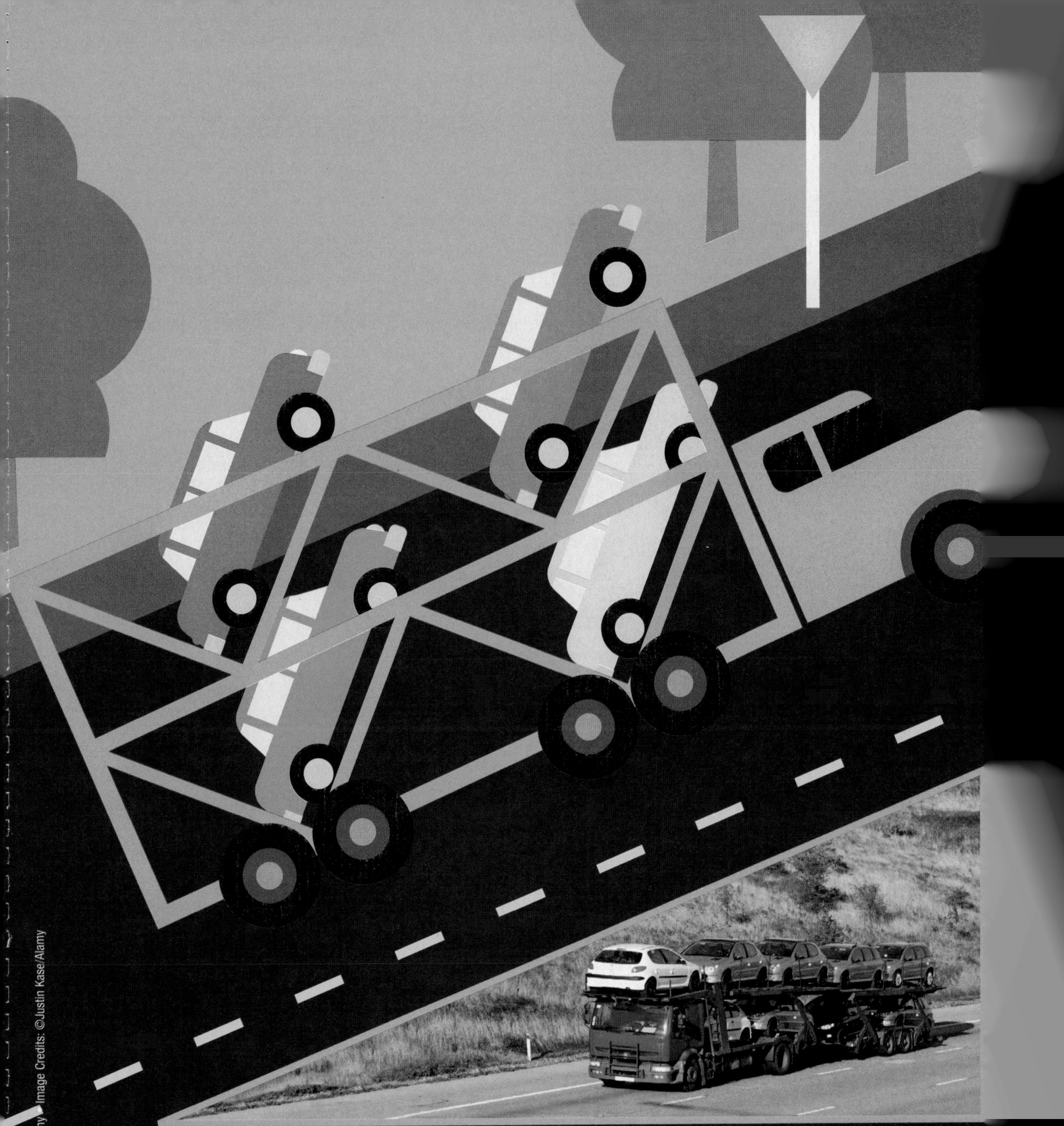

The big truck travels up the road.

Name some shapes you see.

What will this truck bring?

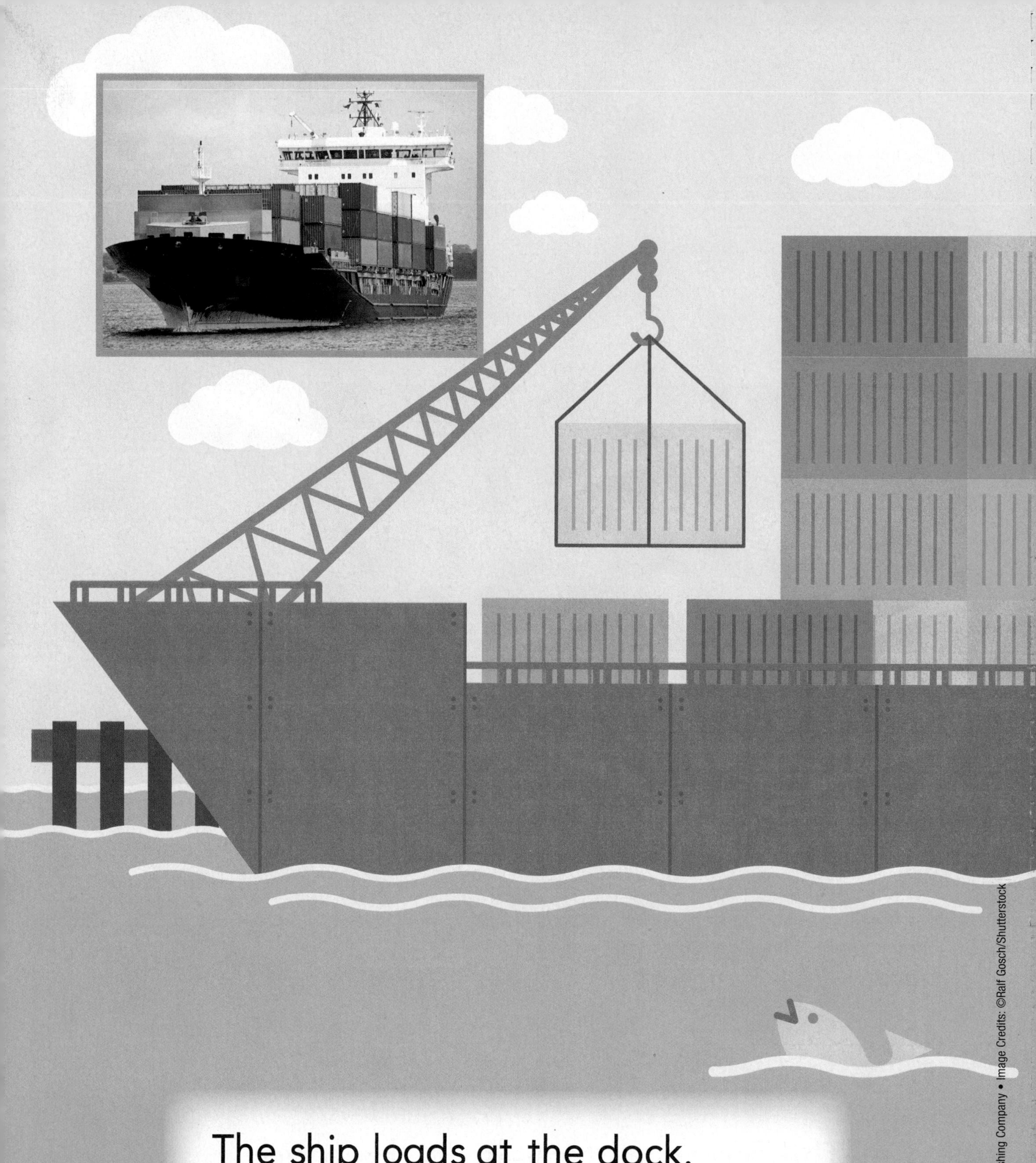

The ship loads at the dock.

Name some shapes you see.

What will this ship bring?

These trucks drive across town.

Name some shapes you see.

Social Studies

What will these trucks bring?

The airplane arrives at the airport.

Name some shapes you see.

Social Studies

What will this airplane bring?

Name ______________________________

Write About the Story

Think of another kind of truck that takes goods from one place to another. Draw a picture. Use circles, squares, triangles, or rectangles in your drawing.

Vocabulary Review

circle	triangle
square	rectangle

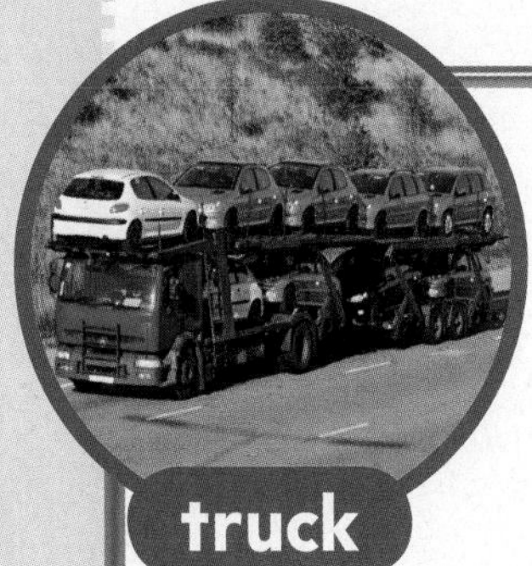

truck

WRITE Math Write about your drawing.

Figure It Out

1. Draw an airplane. Use some triangles and circles in your drawing.

2. Draw a train. Use some rectangles and circles in your drawing.

Choose two shapes to use to draw a ship. Draw the ship.

Chapter 11

Three-Dimensional Geometry

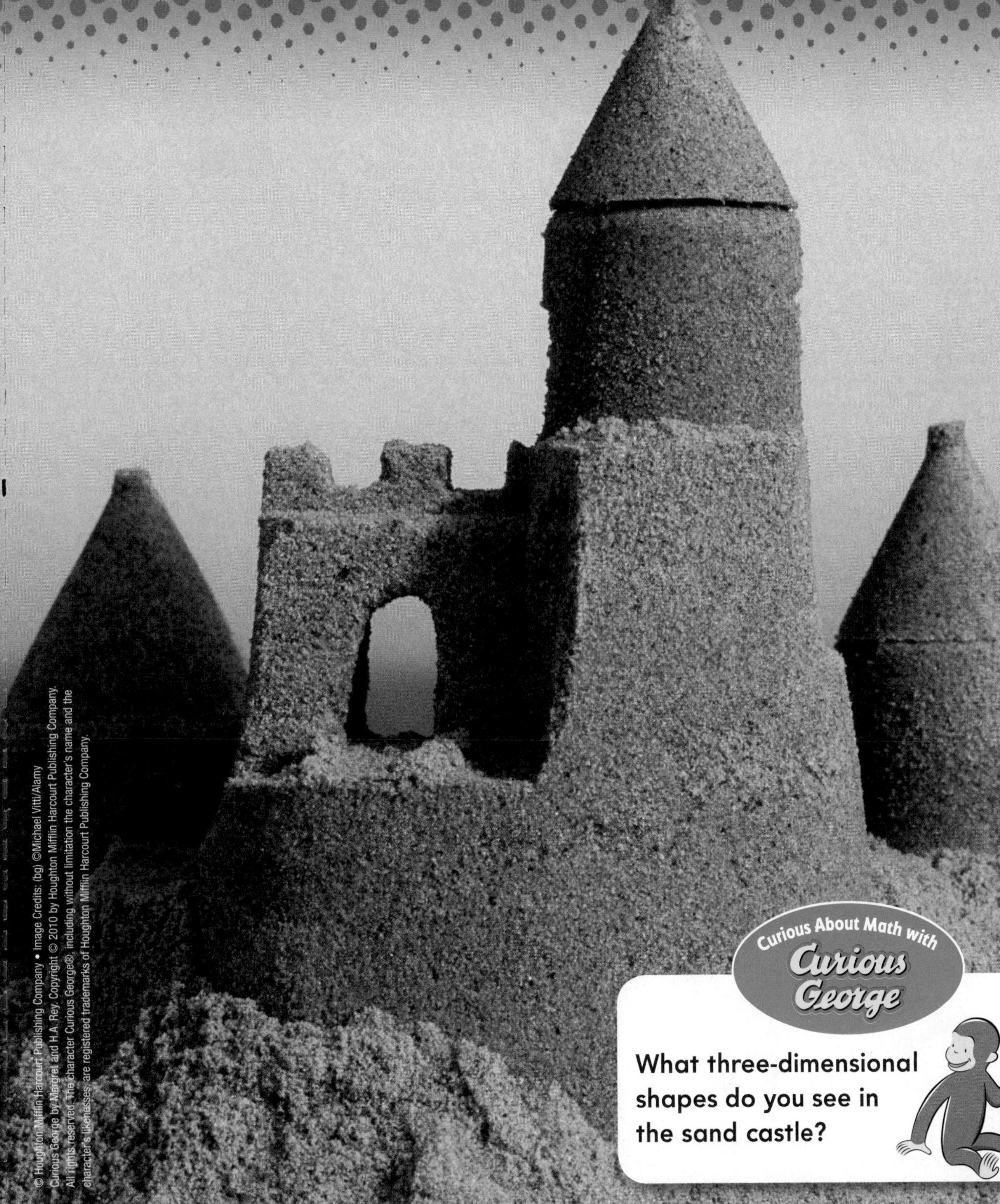

What three-dimensional shapes do you see in the sand castle?

Name ______________________________

Show What You Know 

Alike and Different

Circle the objects that are alike.

1.   

2.   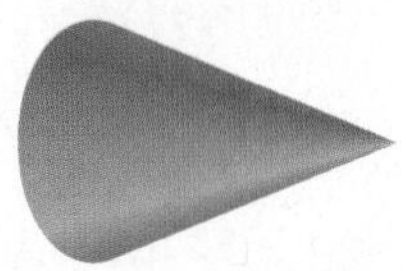

Identify Three-Dimensional Shapes

Color the sphere blue. Color the cylinder red.
Color the cube yellow.

3. 

4. 

5. 

Sort by Size

Mark an X on the object that does not belong.

6.  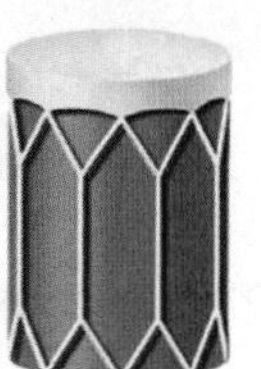  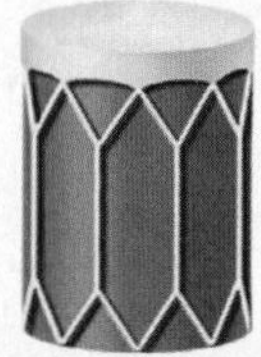

This page checks understanding of important skills needed for success in Chapter 11.

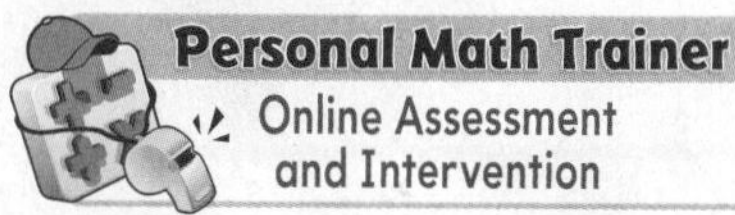

Name ____________________

Vocabulary Builder

Review Words
cone
cube
cylinder
sphere

Visualize It

Write review words to name the shapes.

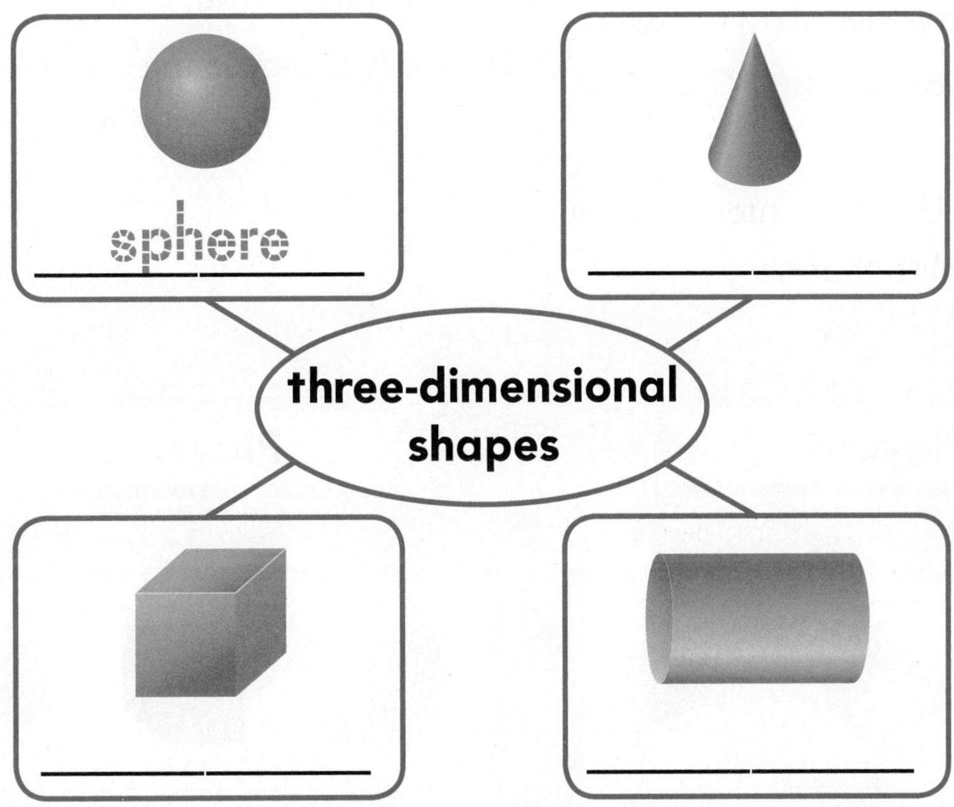

Understand Vocabulary

Look at the three-dimensional shapes.
Color the sphere. Color the cube.
Color the cylinder.

1.
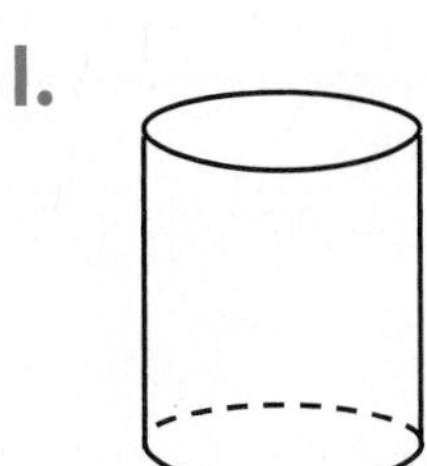

2.
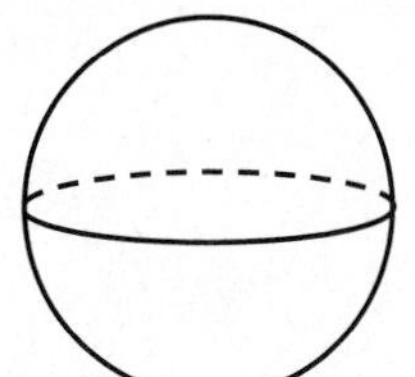

3.
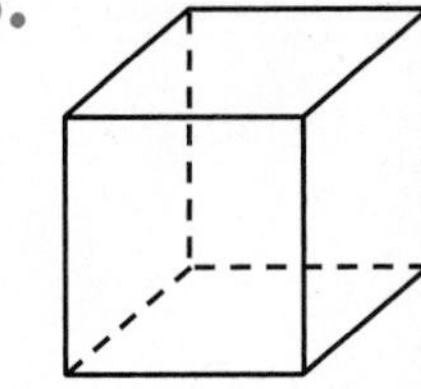

GO DIGITAL • Interactive Student Edition • Multimedia eGlossary

Chapter 11 Game

Shape Match Bingo

Materials • 9  • 9  •  

Play with a partner. Take turns.

1. One player uses ◯. The other player uses ●.
2. Spin the spinner. Use a counter to cover a space with that shape.
3. If you cannot cover a space, your turn is over.
4. The first player to cover all of his or her spaces wins.

Player 1

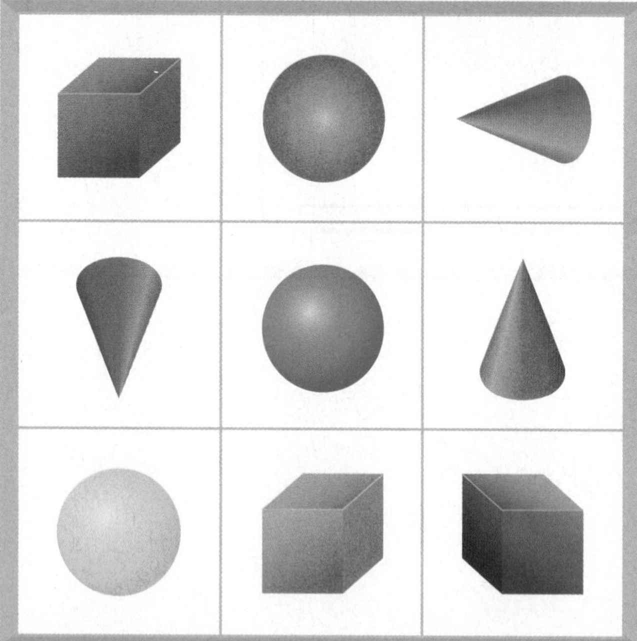

Player 2

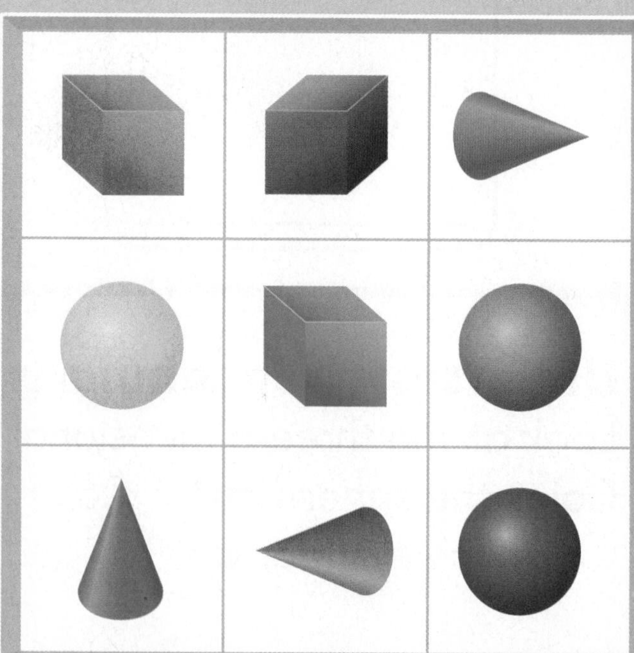

Name ______________________________

Three-Dimensional Shapes

Essential Question How can you identify and describe three-dimensional shapes?

HANDS ON Lesson 11.1

Geometry—1.G.1

MATHEMATICAL PRACTICES
MP.4, MP.8

Listen and Draw

Draw to sort the three-dimensional shapes.

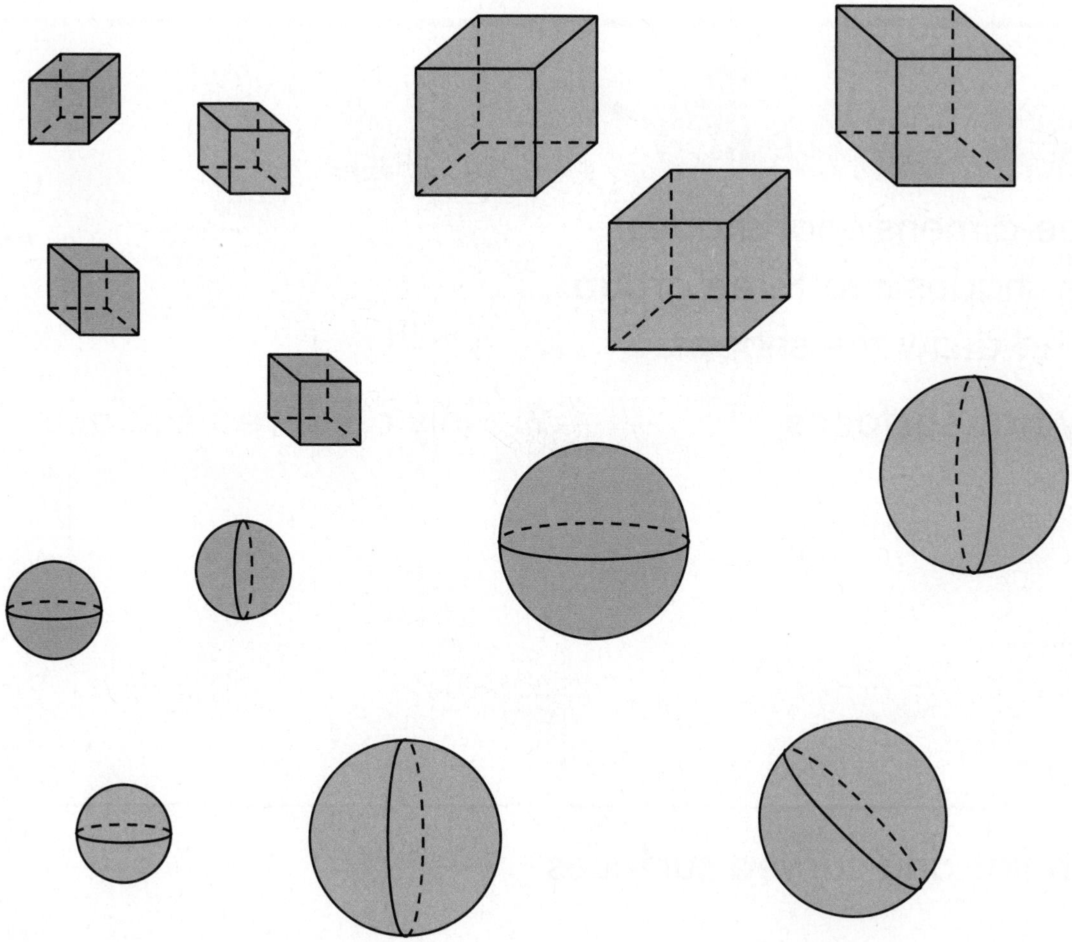

Math Talk Mathematical Practices

Explain how you sorted the shapes.

FOR THE TEACHER • Have children sort the three-dimensional shapes into two groups. Have them draw around each group to show how they sorted.

Model and Draw

These are three-dimensional shapes.

Why is a cube a special kind of rectangular prism?

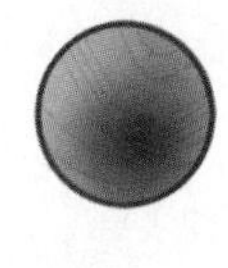
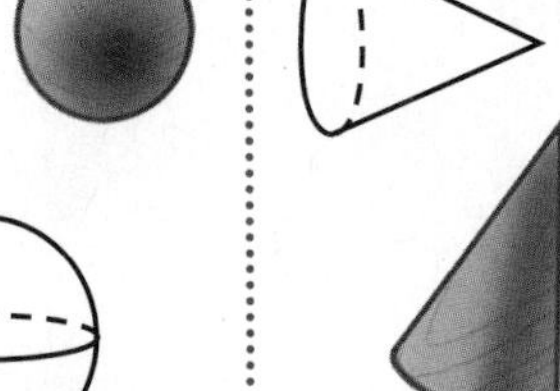
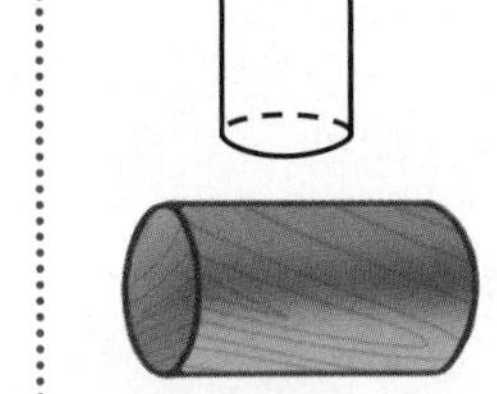
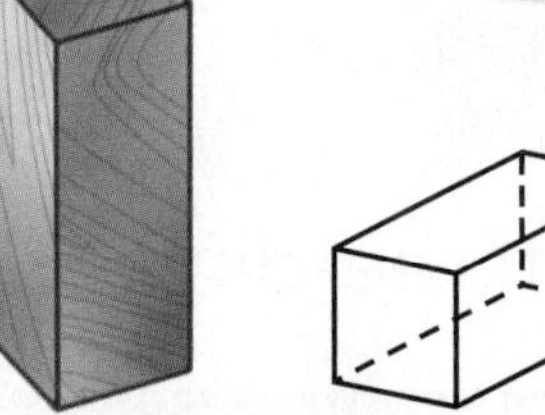
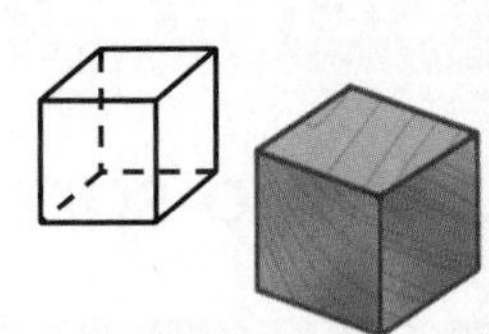

sphere	cone	cylinder	rectangular prism	cube

Share and Show

Use three-dimensional shapes.
Sort the shapes into three groups.
Name and draw the shapes.

1. only flat surfaces

2. only a curved surface

3. both flat and curved surfaces

Name ___________________________

On Your Own

MATHEMATICAL PRACTICE 4 **Use Models** Use three-dimensional shapes. Write the number of flat surfaces for each shape.

4. A rectangular prism has __6__ flat surfaces.

5. A cube has _____ flat surfaces.

6. A cylinder has _____ flat surfaces.

7. A cone has _____ flat surface.

GO DEEPER Write to name each shape.

Exercises 4–7 can help you write the shape names.

8.

sphere

9.

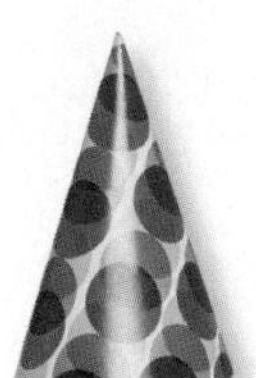

____

10.

____

11.

____

12.

____

Problem Solving • Applications

Circle the objects that match the clues.

13. Kelly drew objects that have both flat and curved surfaces.

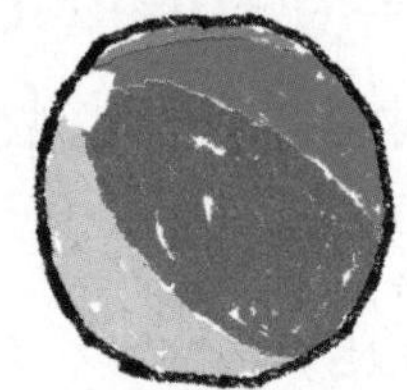

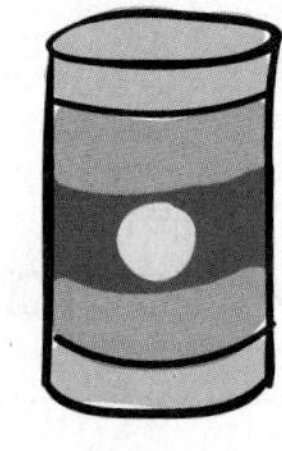

14. THINK SMARTER Sandy drew some rectangular prisms.

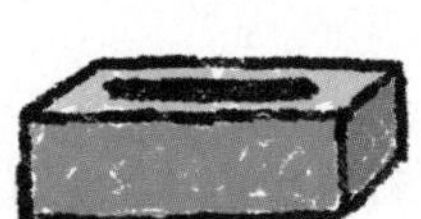

Personal Math Trainer

15. THINK SMARTER + Match each shape to the group where it belongs.

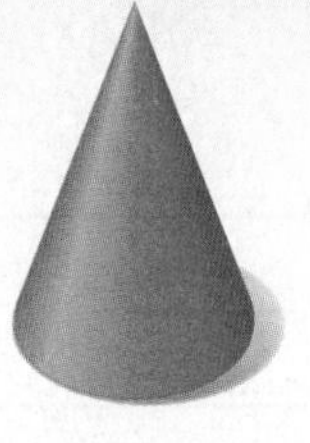

Both flat and curved surfaces	Only flat surfaces	Only a curved surface

TAKE HOME ACTIVITY • Ask your child to name real objects shaped like a sphere, a rectangular prism, and a cylinder.

FOR MORE PRACTICE: Standards Practice Book

Name ____________________

Combine Three-Dimensional Shapes

Essential Question How can you combine three-dimensional shapes to make new shapes?

Geometry—1.G.2

MATHEMATICAL PRACTICES
MP.1, MP.2, MP.3

Listen and Draw

Real World

Trace to draw the new shape.
Write to name the new shape.

Mandy	Carl
____________________	____________________

Math Talk Mathematical Practices

Describe the new shapes Mandy and Carl made.

FOR THE TEACHER • Have children trace the shapes to solve the problems. Mandy stacks one cylinder on top of another cylinder. Carl stacks one cube on top of another cube. What new shapes did Mandy and Carl make?

Model and Draw

You can put shapes together to make a new shape.

What other new shapes could you make?

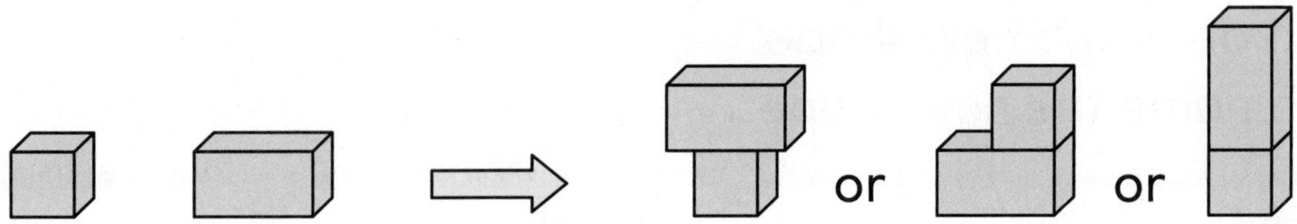

Share and Show

MATH BOARD

Use three-dimensional shapes.

Combine.	Which new shape can you make? Circle it.	
1. 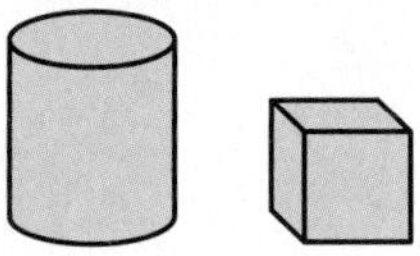	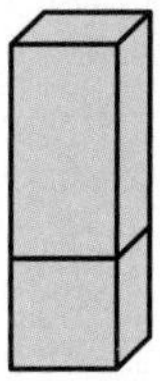	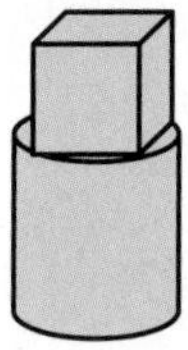
✓2. 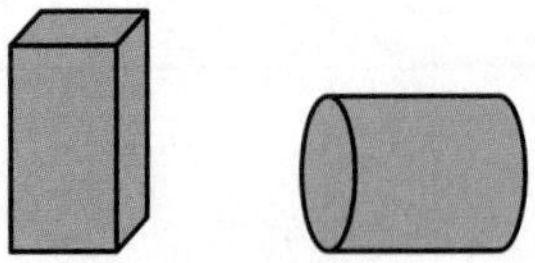		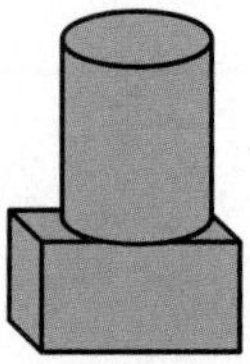
✓3. 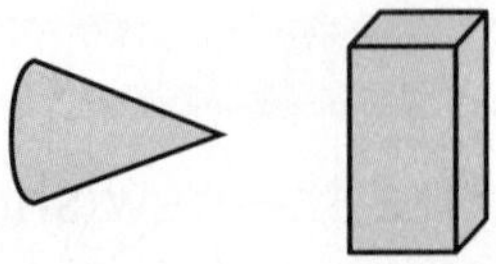	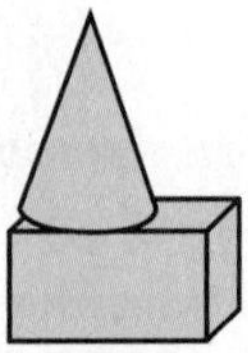	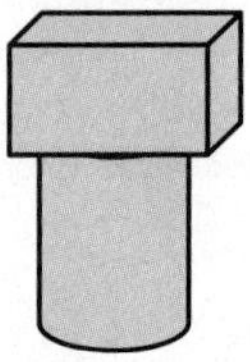

Name ____________________

MATHEMATICAL PRACTICE 6 **Attend to Precision**

Use three-dimensional shapes.

Combine.	Which new shape can you make? Circle it.
4.	
5.	
6.	
7.	
8. THINK SMARTER	

Problem Solving • Applications

GO DEEPER Circle the shapes you could use to model the ice cream cone.

9.

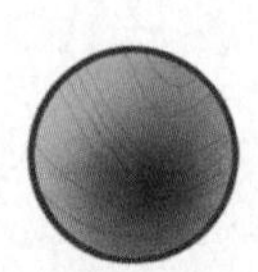

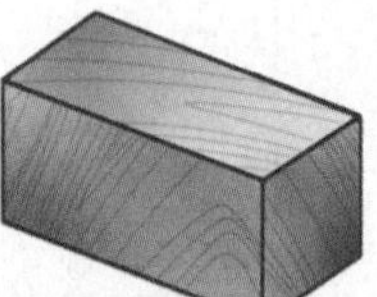

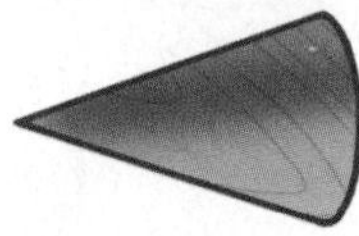

10. THINK SMARTER Circle the ways that make the same shape.

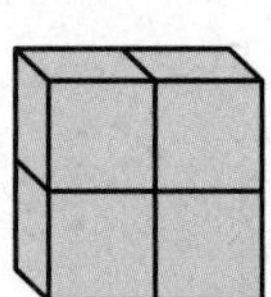

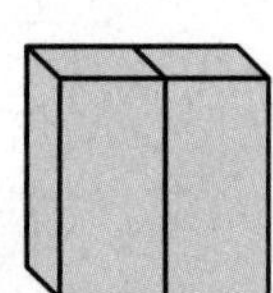

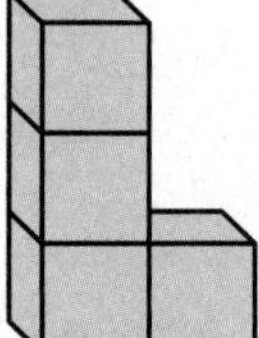

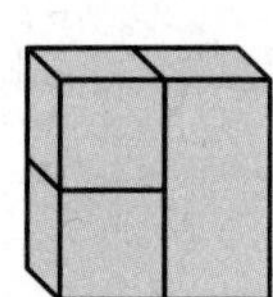

11. THINK SMARTER Combine [rectangular prism] and [cone]. Choose all the new shapes you can make.

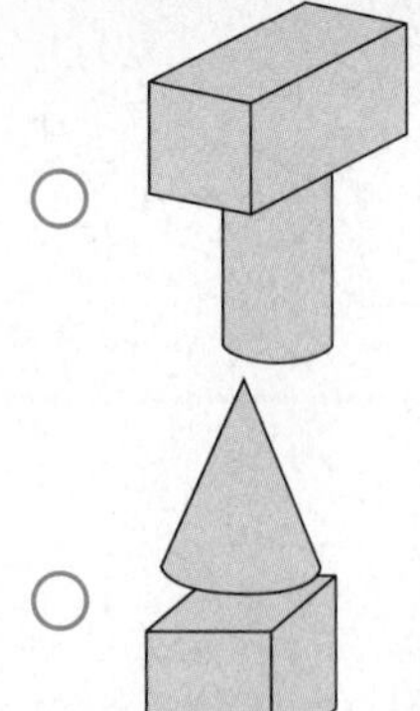

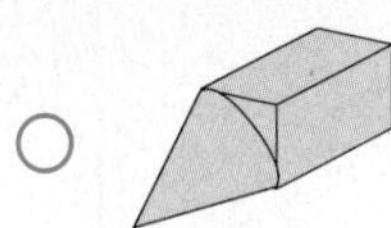

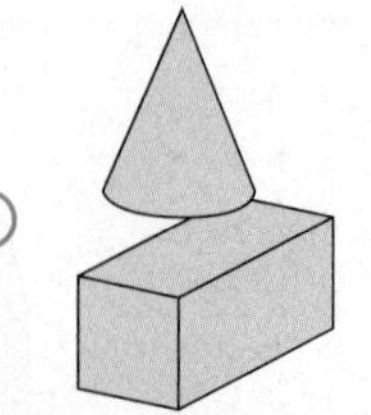

TAKE HOME ACTIVITY • Ask your child to show you two different new shapes he or she can make by combining a soup can and a cereal box.

FOR MORE PRACTICE: Standards Practice Book

Name ______________________________

Make New Three-Dimensional Shapes

Essential Question How can you use a combined shape to build new shapes?

Geometry—1.G.2

MATHEMATICAL PRACTICES
MP.1, MP.2, MP.3

Listen and Draw

Draw to copy the shape.

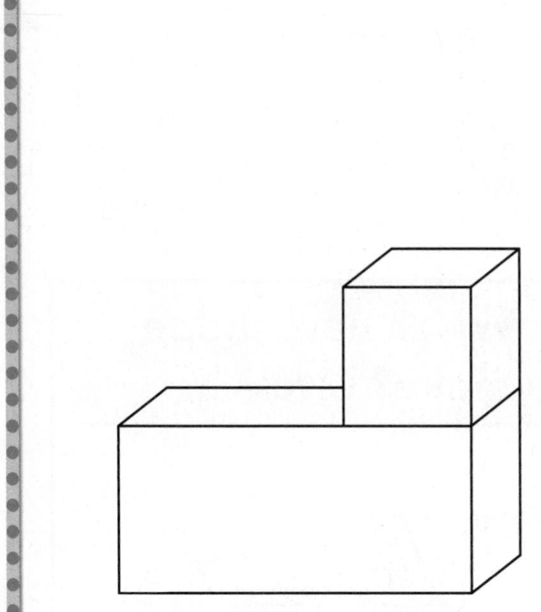

Math Talk **Mathematical Practices**

Describe how to draw to copy the new shape.

FOR THE TEACHER • Leila put a box on top of another box. Draw to copy the new shape Leila made.

Model and Draw

Circle a new shape you can make. **Explain** why you cannot make the other shape.

Step 1	Step 2	Step 3
Build.	Repeat.	Combine.

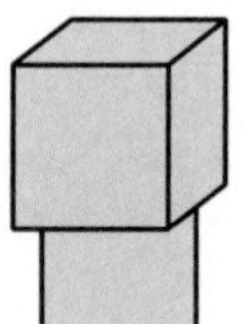

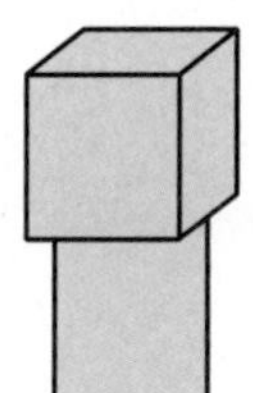

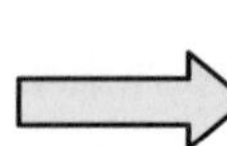

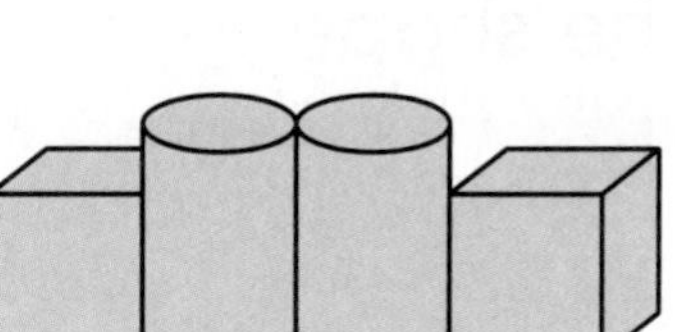

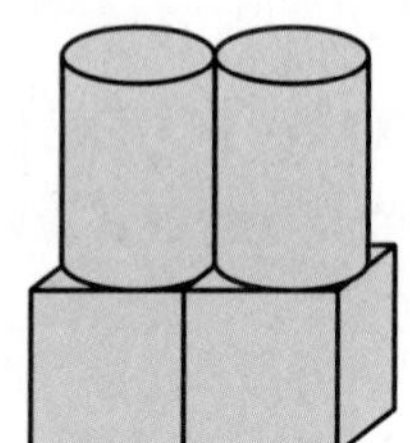

Share and Show

Use three-dimensional shapes.

Build and Repeat.	Combine. Which new shape can you make? Circle it.
1.	
✓2.	
✓3.	

Name ______________________________

On Your Own

MATHEMATICAL PRACTICE 5 **Use a Concrete Model**

Use three-dimensional shapes.

Build and Repeat.	Combine. Which new shape can you make? Circle it.
4.	
5.	
6.	

7. THINK SMARTER Look at the shape.

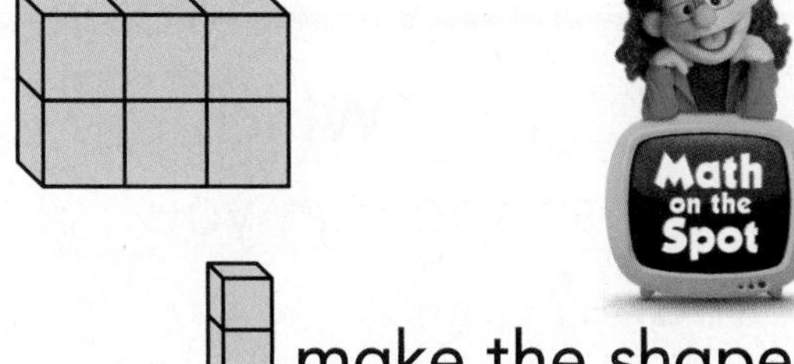

How many ▯ are used to make the shape?

_____ ▯ make the shape.

How many ▢ are used to make the shape?

_____ ▢ make the shape.

TAKE HOME ACTIVITY • Ask your child to explain how he or she solved Exercise 4.

FOR MORE PRACTICE: Standards Practice Book

Name ____________________

Mid-Chapter Checkpoint

Concepts and Skills

1. Circle the rectangular prisms. (1.G.1)
2. Draw a line under the shapes that have both flat and curved surfaces. (1.G.1)

Use three-dimensional shapes. (1.G.2)

Combine.	Which new shape can you make? Circle it.
3.	

4. THINK SMARTER Which new shape can you make? (1.G.2)

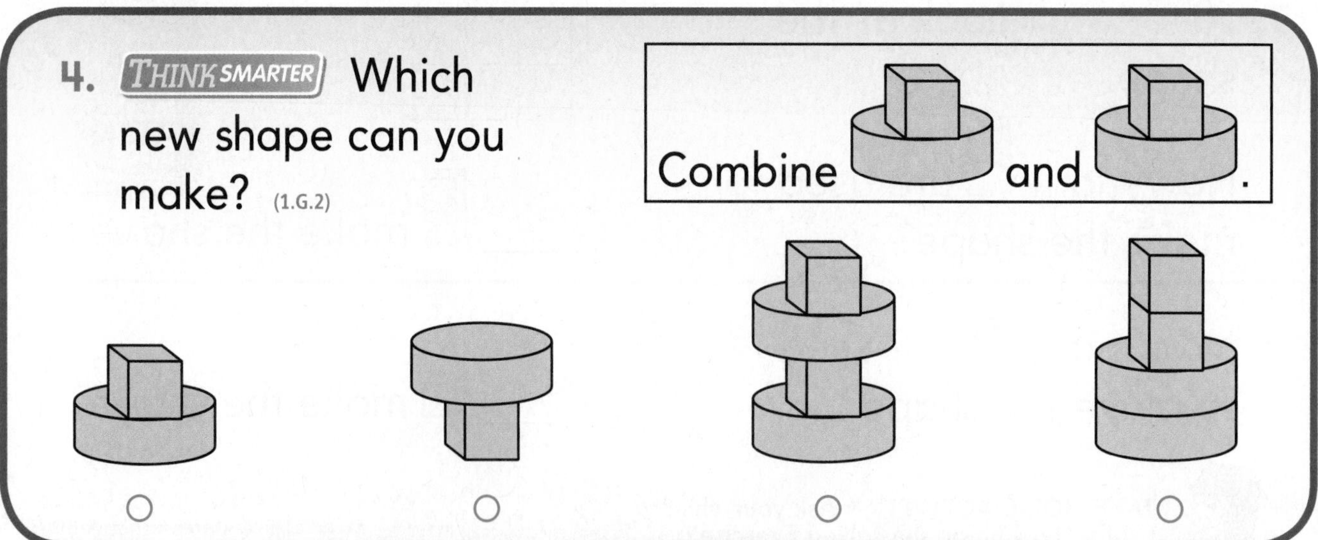

Name ______________________

Problem Solving • Take Apart Three-Dimensional Shapes

Essential Question How can acting it out help you take apart combined shapes?

Geometry—1.G.2

MATHEMATICAL PRACTICES
MP.6, MP.7, MP.8

Mike has  and . He chose some shapes to build a bridge. Which shapes did Mike use to build the bridge?

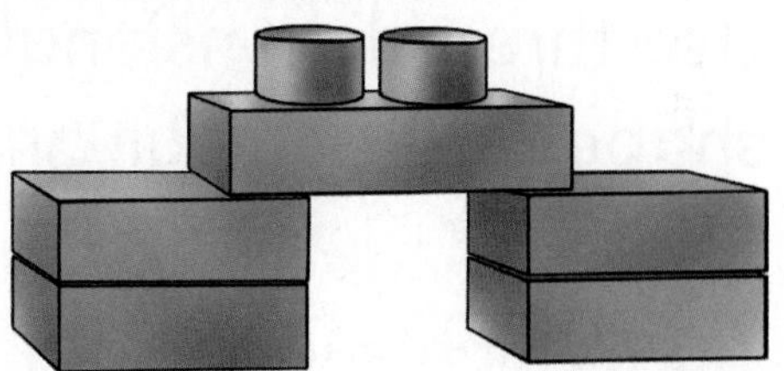

Unlock the Problem Real World

What do I need to find?

which shapes Mike chose to build the bridge

What information do I need to use?

Mike has these shapes.

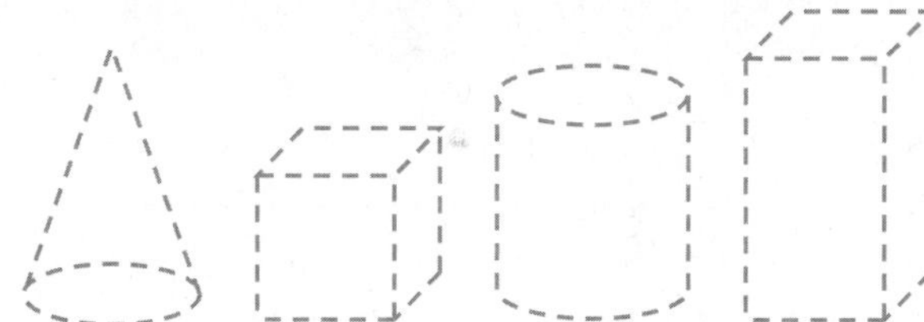

Show how to solve the problem.

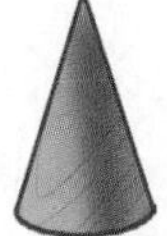

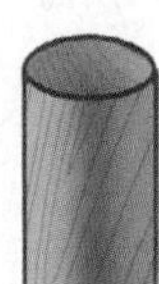

HOME CONNECTION • Your child is investigating how shapes can be taken apart. Being able to decompose shapes into smaller parts provides a foundation for future work with fractions.

Try Another Problem

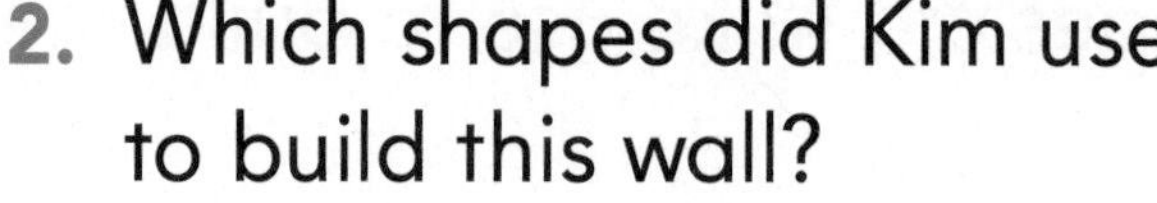

Kim used shapes to build this castle.

Use three-dimensional shapes. Circle your answer.

- What do I need to find?
- What information do I need to use?

1. Which shapes did Kim use to build the tower?

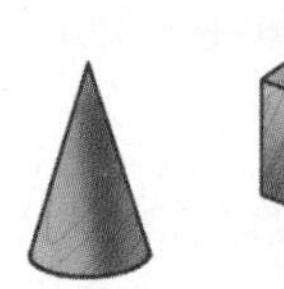

2. Which shapes did Kim use to build this wall?

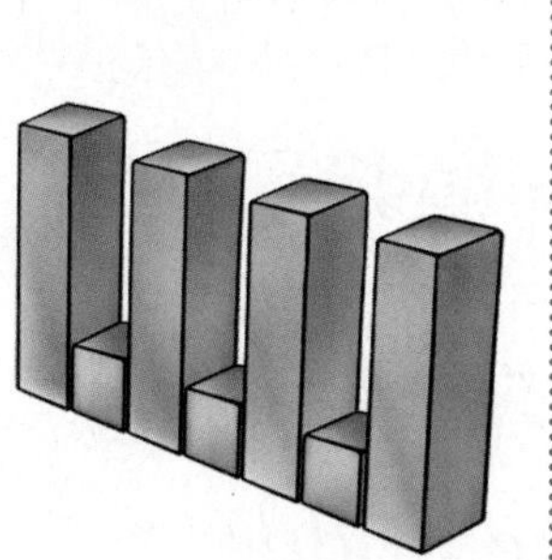

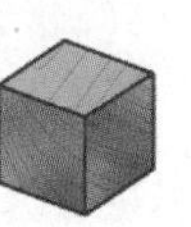

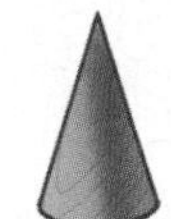

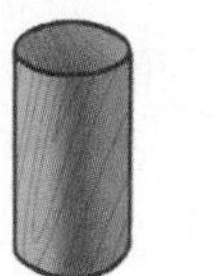

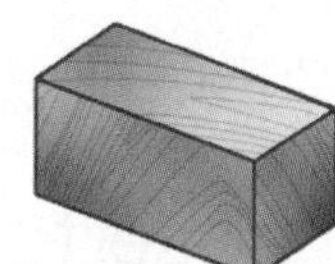

3. Which shapes did Kim use to build this wall?

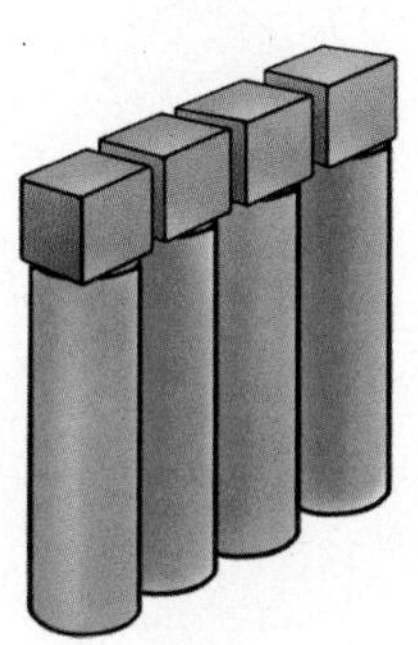

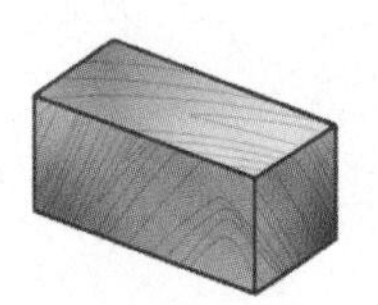

4. Which shapes did Kim use to build the gate?

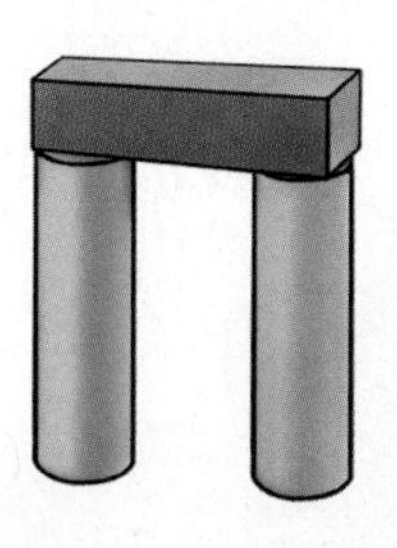

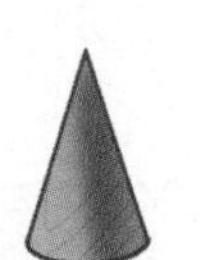

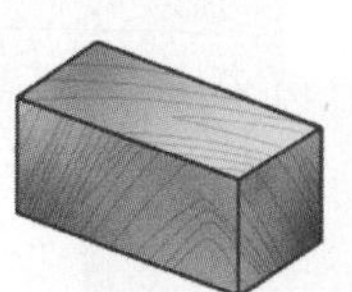

Math Talk **Mathematical Practices**

Describe how you know which shapes Kim used to build the tower.

Name ______________________________

Share and Show

MATHEMATICAL PRACTICE 1 **Analyze** Use three-dimensional shapes. Circle your answer.

5. Zack used shapes to build this gate. Which shapes did Zack use?

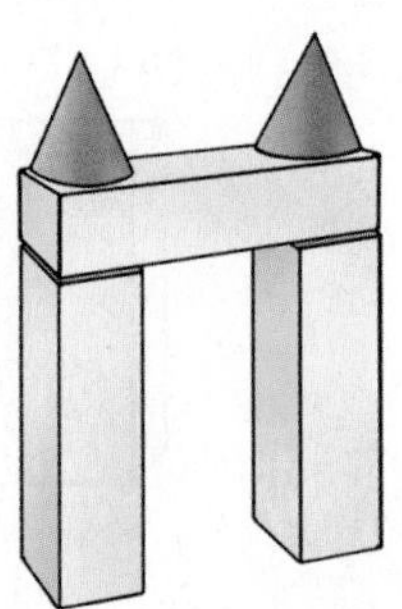

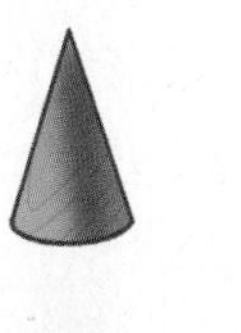
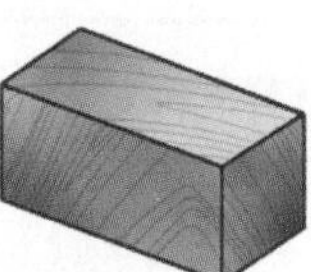

6. Chris used shapes to build this wall. Which shapes did Chris use?

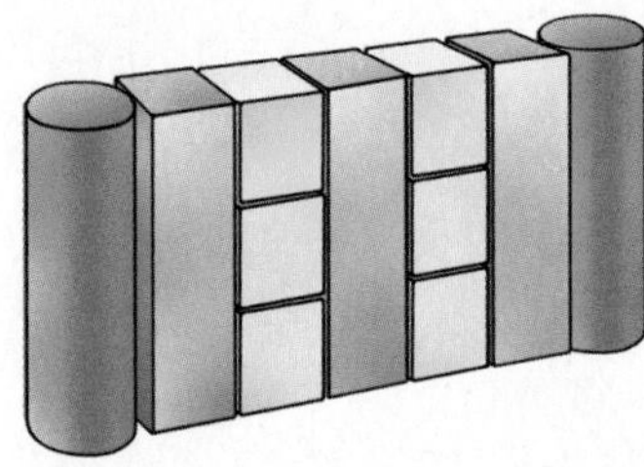

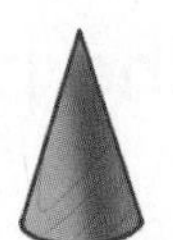

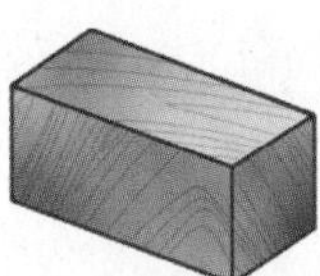

7. THINK SMARTER Rosa uses , , , and to build a tower. Draw to show a tower Rosa could build.

On Your Own

WRITE Math

GO DEEPER Circle the ways that show the same shape.

8.

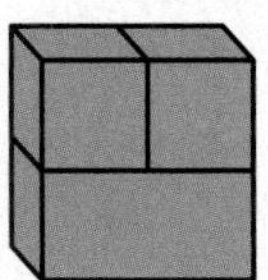
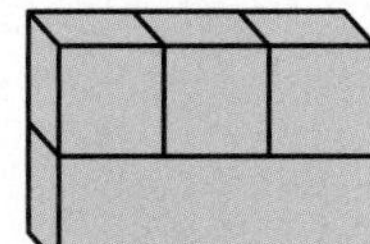
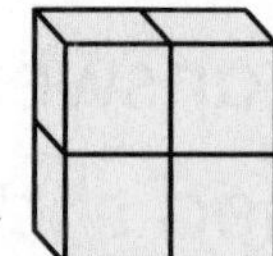

9. THINK SMARTER

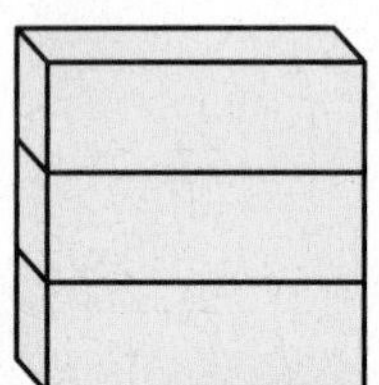
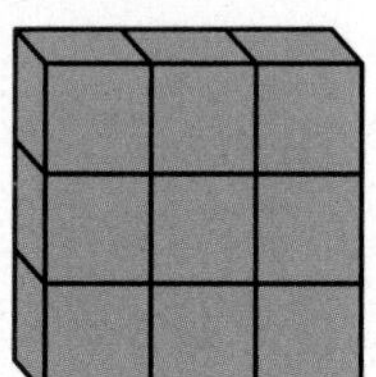
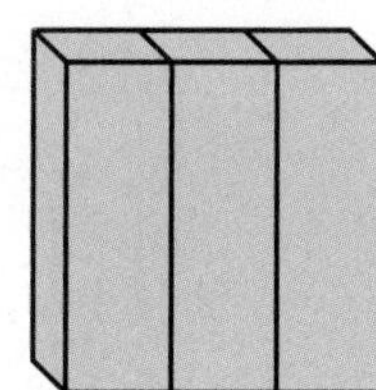

10. THINK SMARTER Sharon has many different blocks. She built this shape with her blocks.

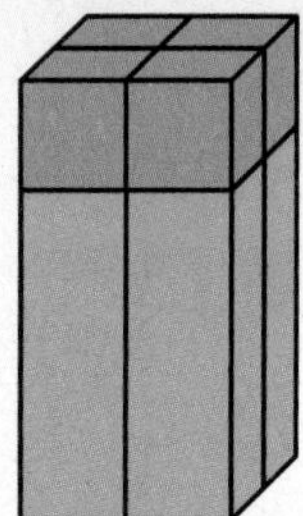

Choose all the shapes Sharon used.

○ 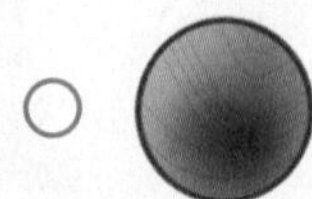

○ 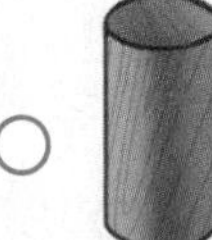

○ 

○ 

TAKE HOME ACTIVITY • Use real items such as a soup can (cylinder) and a cereal box (rectangular prism) to build a shape. Ask your child to name the shapes you used.

FOR MORE PRACTICE: Standards Practice Book

Name ______________________________

Two-Dimensional Shapes on Three-Dimensional Shapes

Essential Question What two-dimensional shapes do you see on the flat surfaces of three-dimensional shapes?

Geometry—1.G.1

MATHEMATICAL PRACTICES
MP.1, MP.4, MP.6

Listen and Draw

Real World

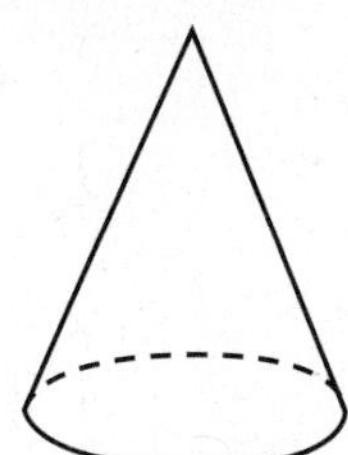

Use a cone.

Math Talk **Mathematical Practices**

What other shape could you use to draw the same kind of picture? **Explain.**

FOR THE TEACHER • Read the following problem and have children use the workspace to act it out. Lee places a cone on a piece of paper and draws around its flat surface. What did Lee draw?

Model and Draw

Trace around the flat surfaces of the three-dimensional shape to find the two-dimensional shapes.

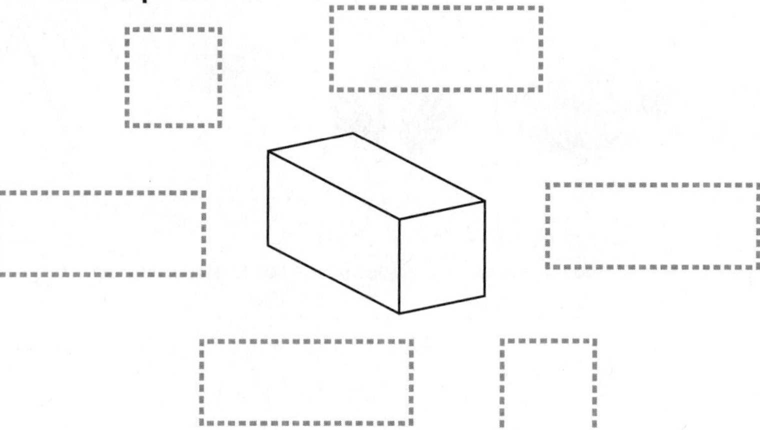

Share and Show

Use three-dimensional shapes. Trace around the flat surfaces. Circle the shapes you draw.

1.

✓2.

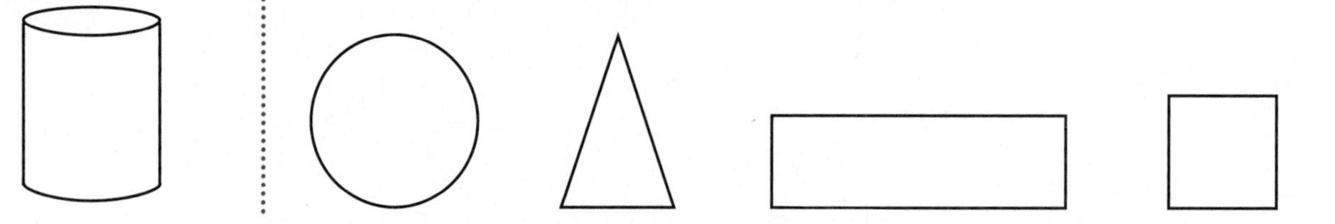

✓3.

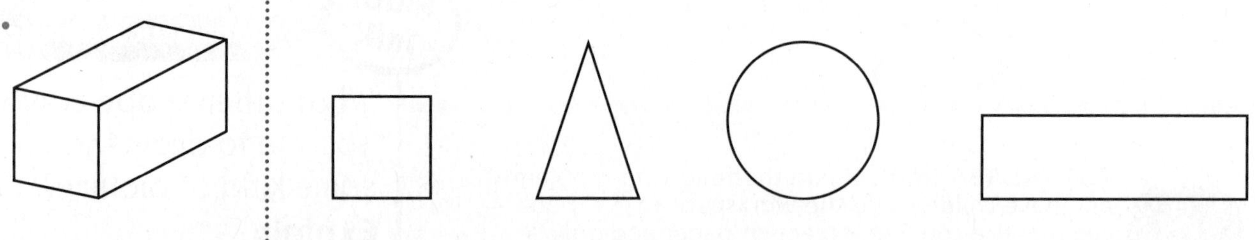

Name ______________________

On Your Own

MATHEMATICAL PRACTICE 6 **Make Connections** Circle the objects you could trace to draw the shape.

4. 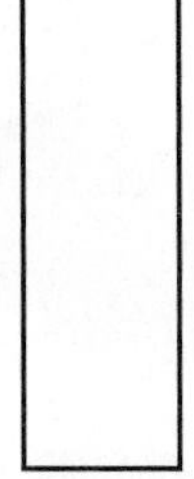

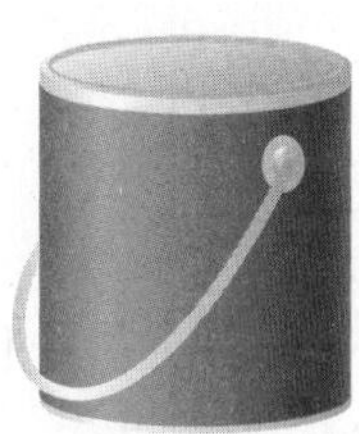

5. 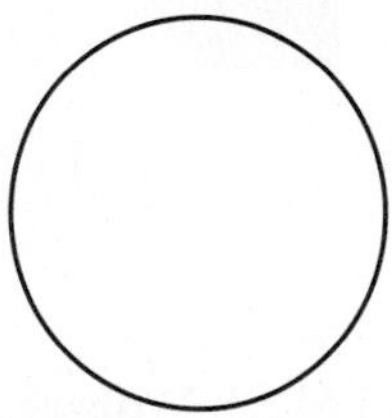

6. 

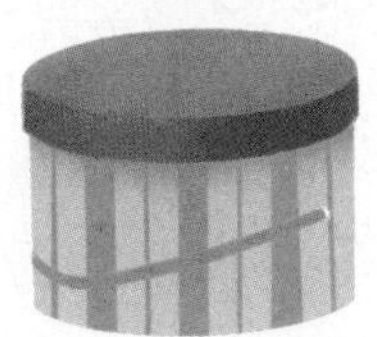

7. 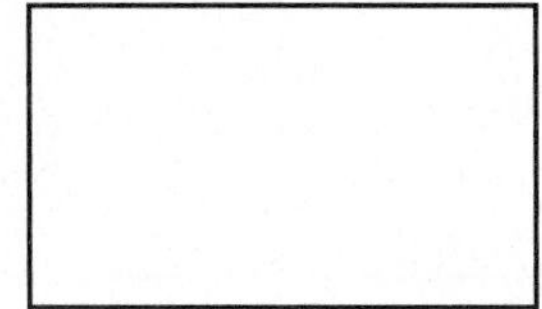

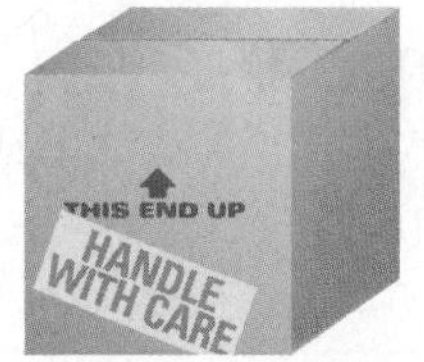

8. THINK SMARTER Draw a shape you would make if you traced this object.

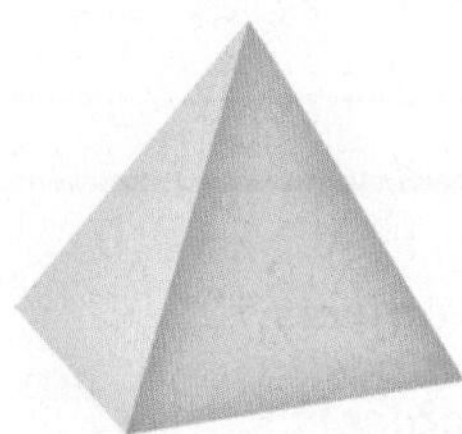

Problem Solving • Applications

Circle the shape that the pattern will make if you fold it and tape it together.

9. 10.

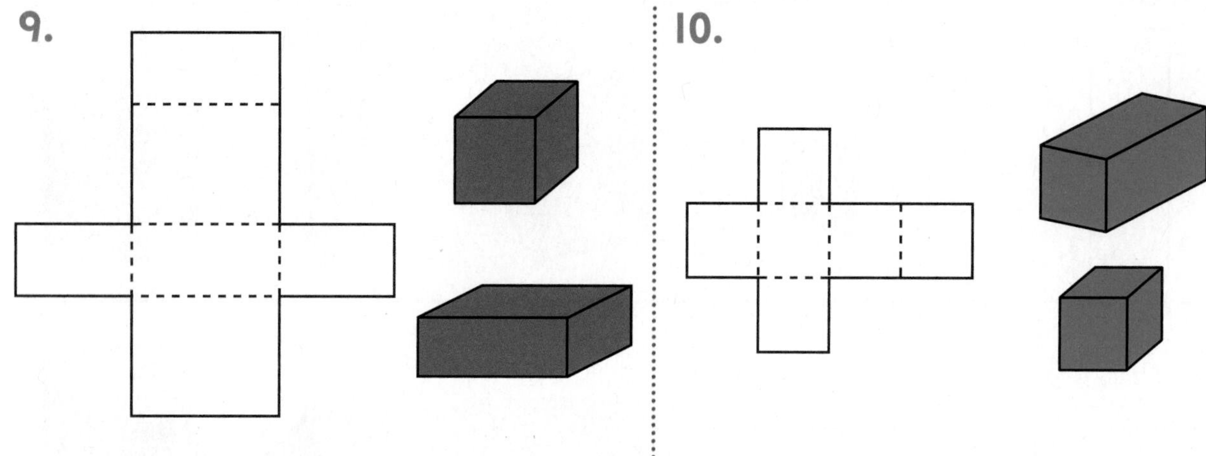

Personal Math Trainer

11. THINK SMARTER + Kei wants to trace a ▭.

She finds these objects.

Which object should she use?

______

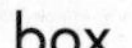

globe jar box

What would happen if Kei used the [jar] to trace a shape?

TAKE HOME ACTIVITY • Collect a few three-dimensional objects, such as boxes, that are shaped like rectangular prisms or cubes. Ask your child what two-dimensional shapes are on those objects.

FOR MORE PRACTICE: Standards Practice Book

Name ___________________________

Chapter 11 Review/Test

1. Match each shape to the group where it belongs.

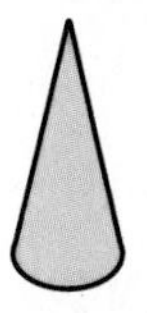
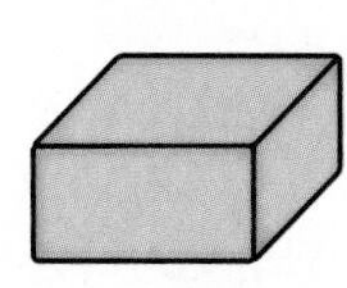
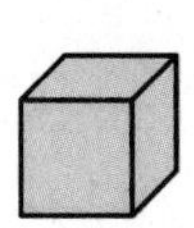
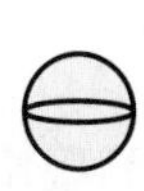
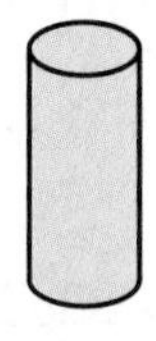

Only flat surfaces	Only a curved surface	Both flat and curved surfaces

2. Combine and . Choose all the new shapes you can make.

○ 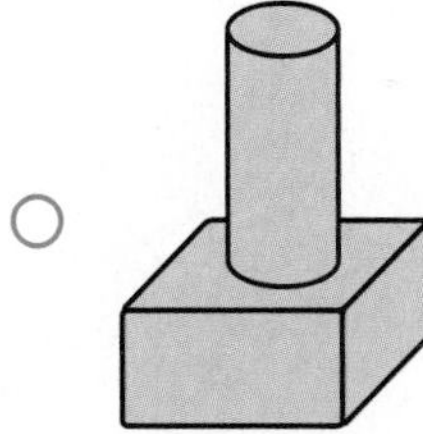

○ 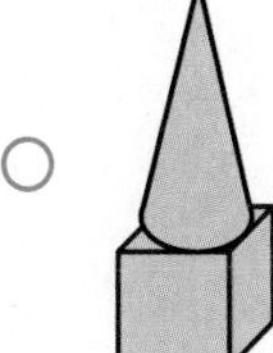

○ 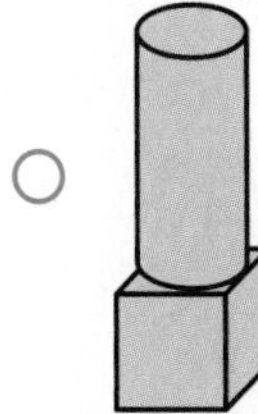

○ 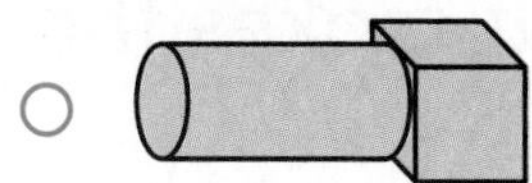

○ 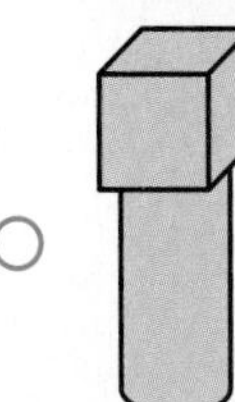

3. Build and repeat. Choose Yes or No.

Can two make ? ○ Yes ○ No

Can two make ? ○ Yes ○ No

Can two make ? ○ Yes ○ No

---

4. Damon built this shape.

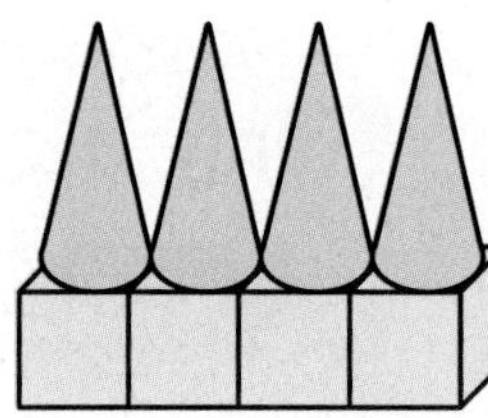

Choose all the shapes Damon used.

○ 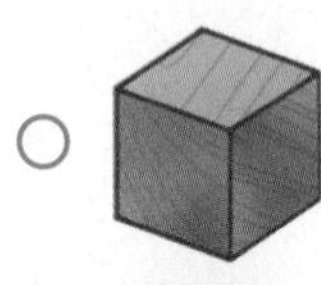

○ 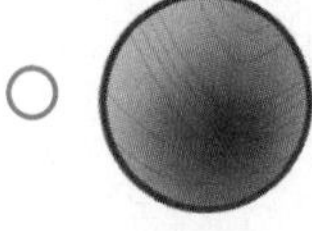

○ 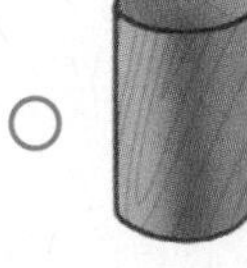

○ 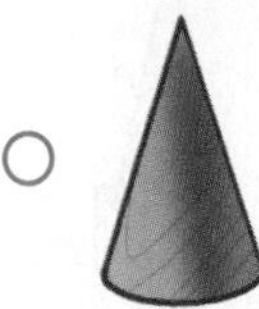

---

5. Circle the number that makes the sentence true.

There are

0
1
2

circles on a 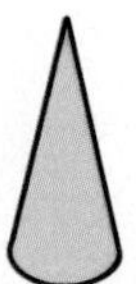.

Name ______________________________

6. Sara wants to trace a ○. She finds these objects.

Which object should she use?

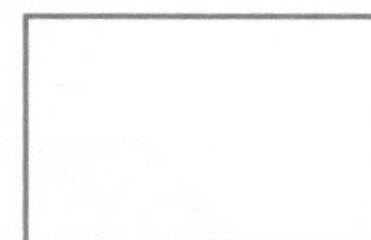

What would happen if she used the ▭ to trace a shape?

---

7. Which shape has only 2 flat surfaces?

○ 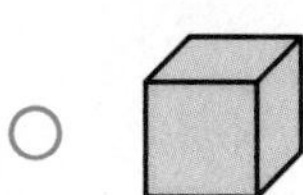

○ 

○ 

○ 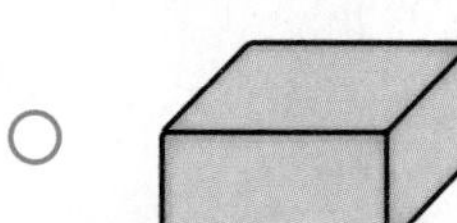

---

8. Look at the shape.

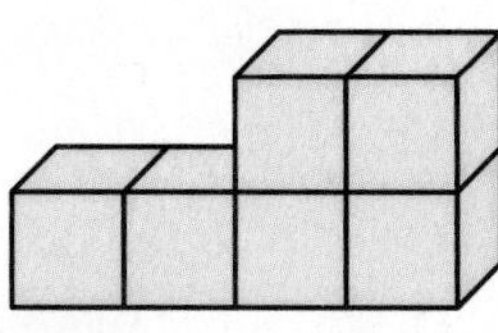

How many 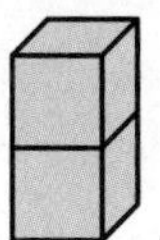 are used to make the shape?

☐

9. Ellen built this shape.

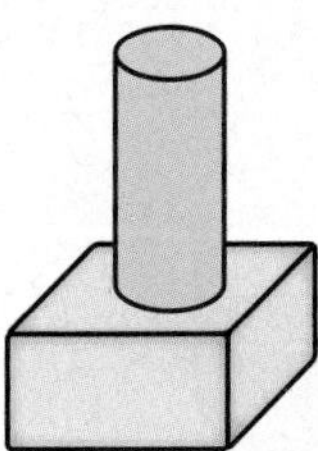

Which objects did Ellen use?
Circle them.

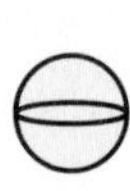 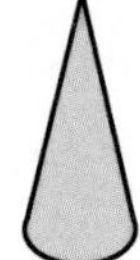 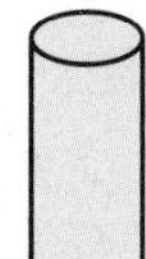 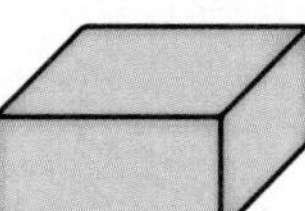 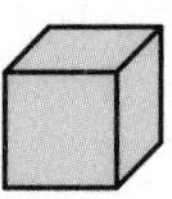

Draw another way to combine the objects.

---

10. Hector built this shape.

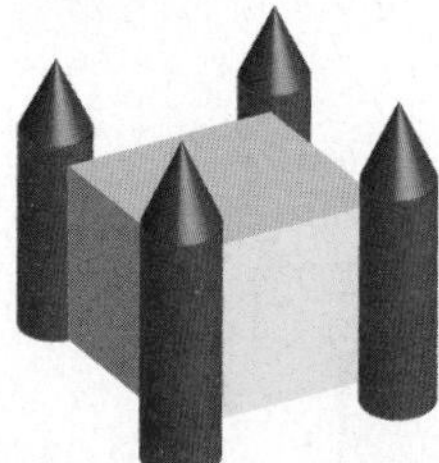

Choose all the shapes Hector used.

- ○ 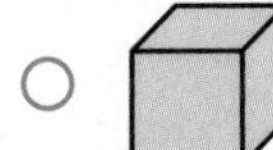
- ○ 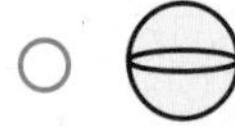
- ○ 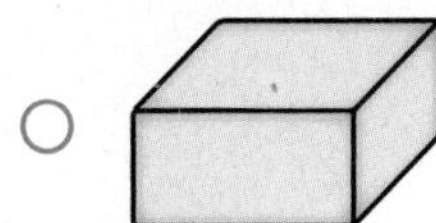
- ○ 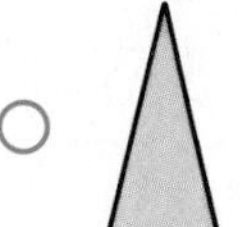
- ○ 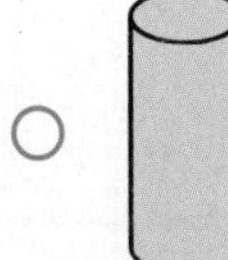

Chapter 12 Two-Dimensional Geometry

Curious About Math with Curious George

Shapes can be found in many places. What shapes might you see on a playground?

Name ___________________________

Show What You Know

Sort by Shape

Circle the shape that belongs in each group.

1. 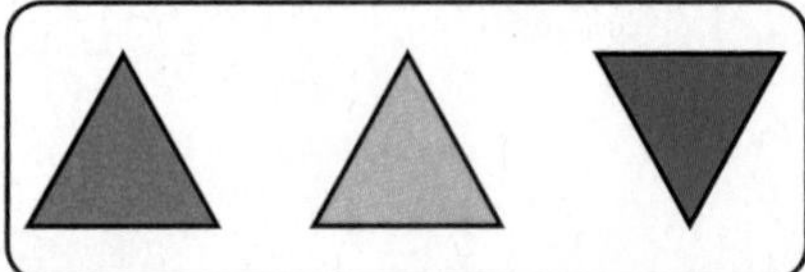  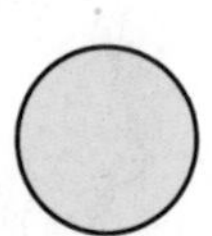 

2. 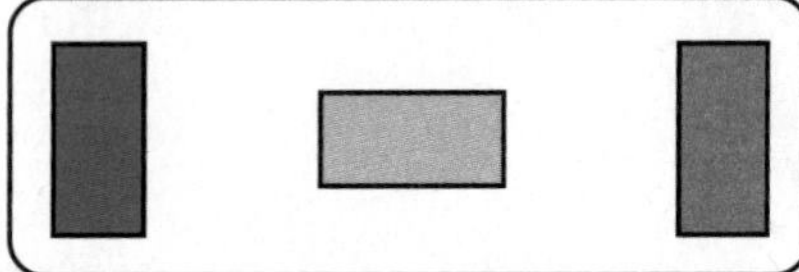  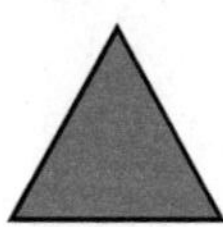 

Sort Shapes

Circle the shapes with 4 sides.

3.   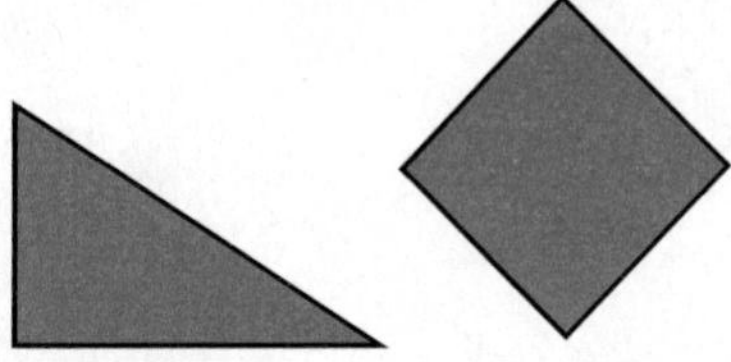

Identify Two-Dimensional Shapes

Color each square blue. Color each rectangle yellow.
Color each circle red.

4. 

This page checks understanding of important skills needed for success in Chapter 12.

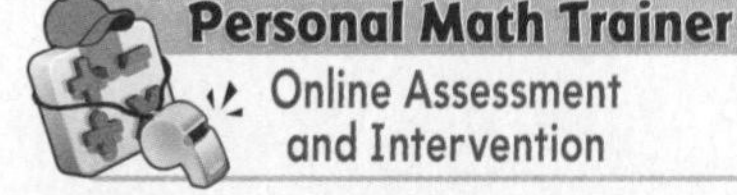

Name ____________________

Review Words
circle
hexagon
rectangle
square
triangle

Vocabulary Builder

Visualize It

Complete the chart.
Mark each row with a ✓.

Word	I Know	Sounds Familiar	I Do Not Know
circle			
hexagon			
rectangle			
square			
triangle			

Understand Vocabulary

Write the number of each shape.

1. ____ circles
2. ____ squares
3. ____ triangles

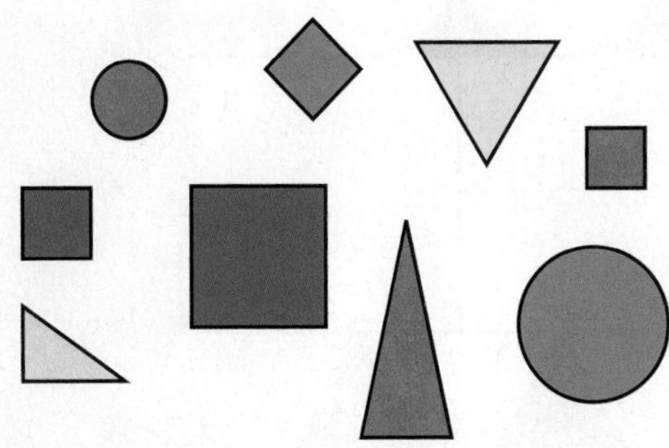

GO DIGITAL
• Interactive Student Edition
• Multimedia eGlossary

Chapter 12

Game Rocket Shapes

Materials

- 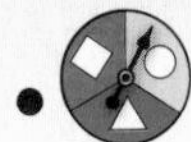
- 6 
- 8 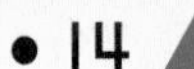
- 14 ▲

Play with a partner.
Take turns.

1. Spin the spinner.
2. Name the shape you spin.
3. Place that shape on the rocket if you can.
4. If you cannot place the shape, your turn is over.
5. The first player to cover a whole rocket wins.

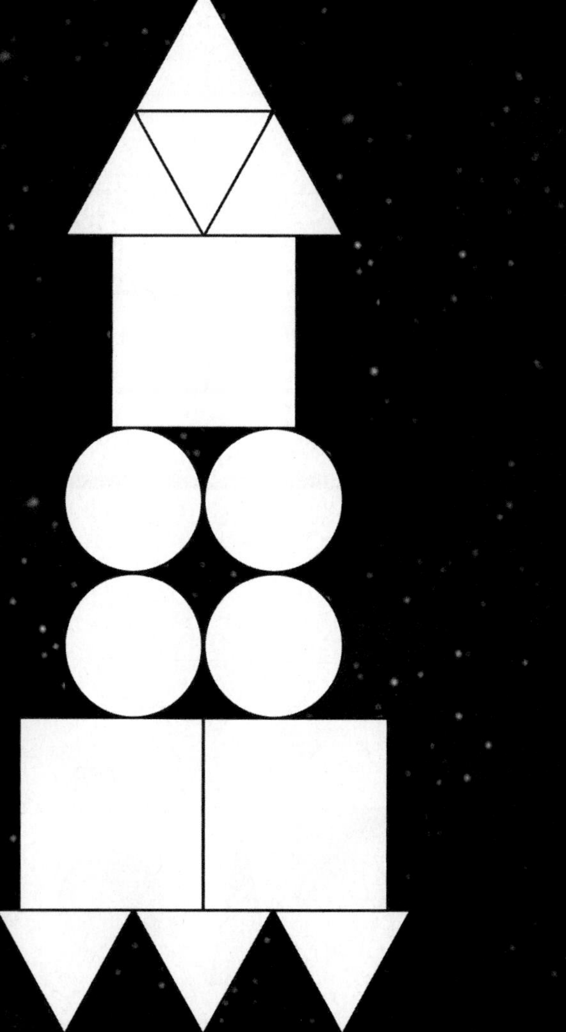

Player 1

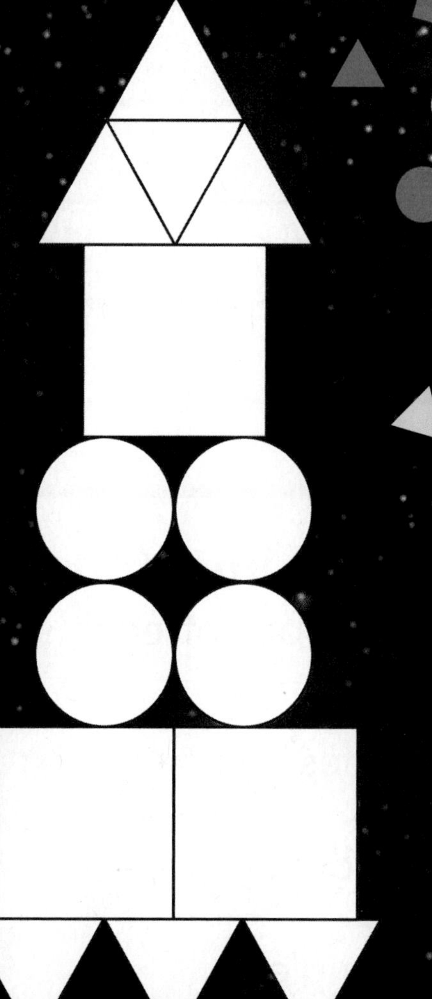

Player 2

Name ______________________

Sort Two-Dimensional Shapes

Essential Question How can you use attributes to classify and sort two-dimensional shapes?

Geometry—1.G.1

MATHEMATICAL PRACTICES
MP.6, MP.7, MP.8

Listen and Draw Real World

Draw to sort the shapes.
Write the sorting rule.

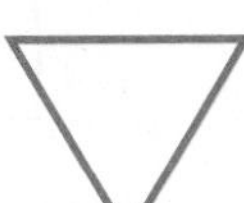

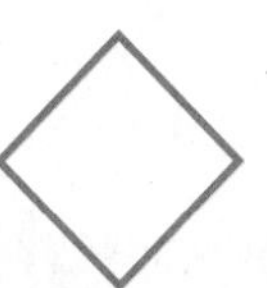

Math Talk **Mathematical Practices**

Explain Are there shapes that did not go in your groups?

FOR THE TEACHER • Read the following aloud. Devon wants to sort these shapes to show a group of triangles and a group of rectangles. Draw and write to show how Devon sorts the shapes.

Model and Draw

Here are some ways to sort two-dimensional shapes.

A **square** is a special kind of rectangle.

curved and closed shapes

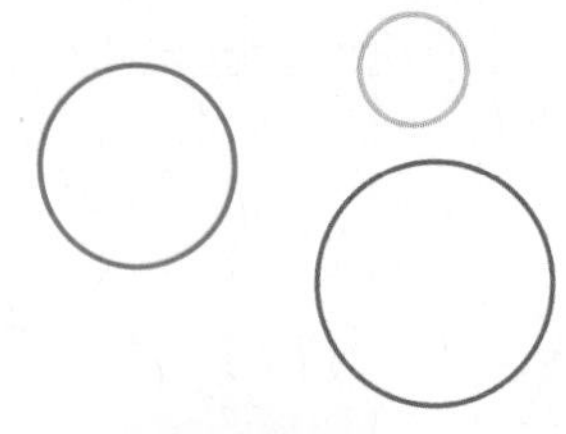

circles

closed shapes with ____ **sides**

triangles

closed shapes with ____ **vertices**

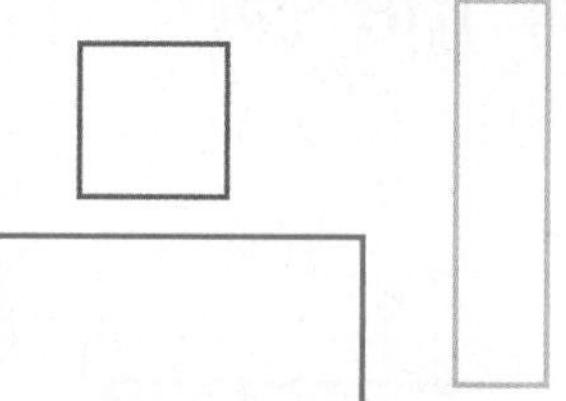

rectangles

Share and Show

THINK
Vertices (corners) are where the sides meet.

Read the sorting rule. Circle the shapes that follow the rule.

1. 4 vertices (corners)

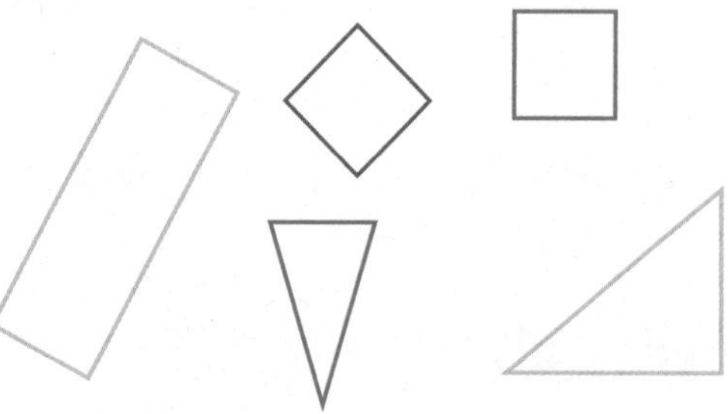

2. **not** curved

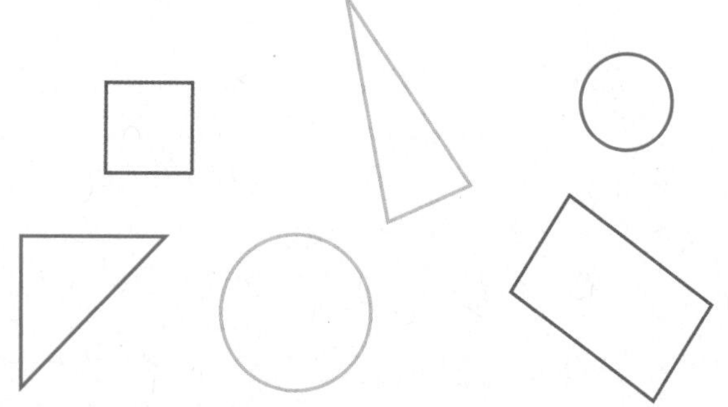

✓3. only 3 sides

✓4. more than 3 sides

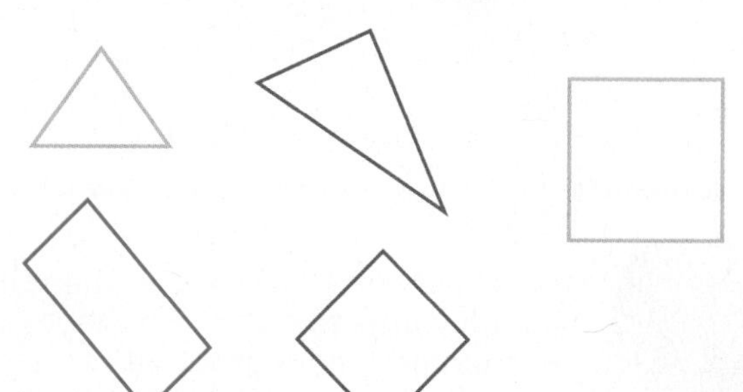

Name ____________________

On Your Own

REMEMBER
Read the sorting rule first.

MATHEMATICAL PRACTICE 6 **Use Math Vocabulary**

Circle the shapes that follow the rule.

5. curved

6. only 3 vertices (corners)

7. 4 sides

8. 4 sides are the same length

THINK SMARTER Draw 2 different two-dimensional shapes that follow both parts of the sorting rule.

9. 3 sides and
3 vertices (corners)

10. 2 sides are long and
2 sides are short

Problem Solving • Applications

Ted sorted these shapes three different ways. Write sorting rules to tell how Ted sorted.

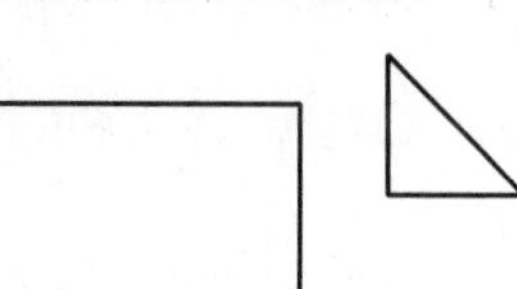
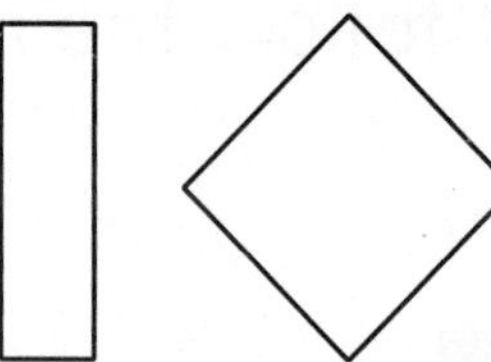
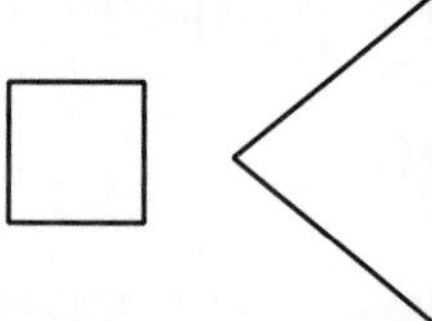

11. 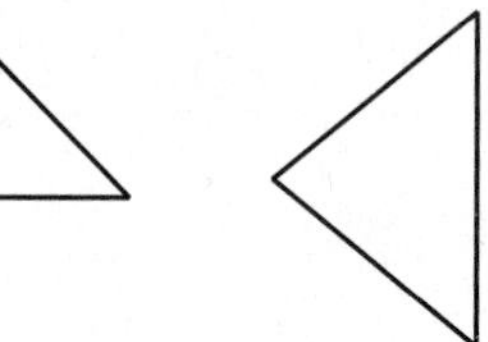

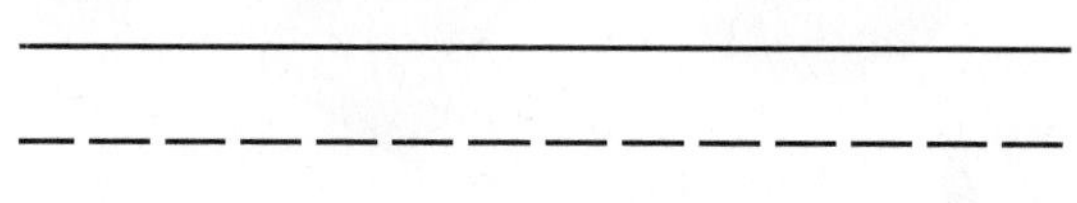

12. 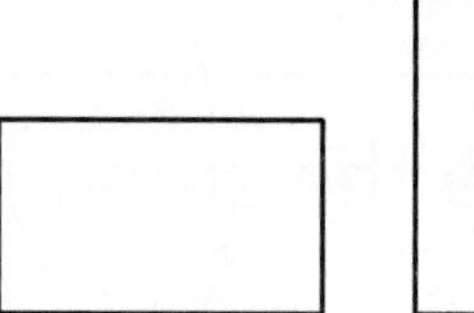
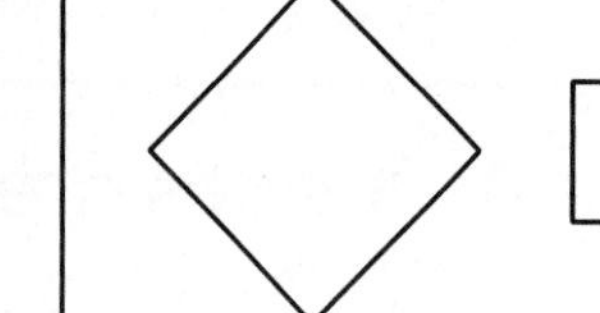

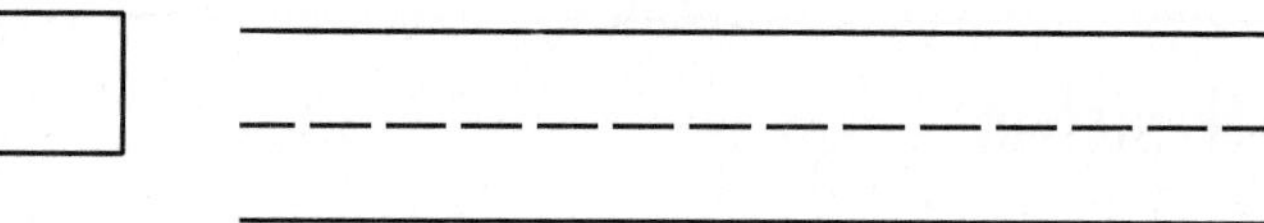

13. THINK SMARTER

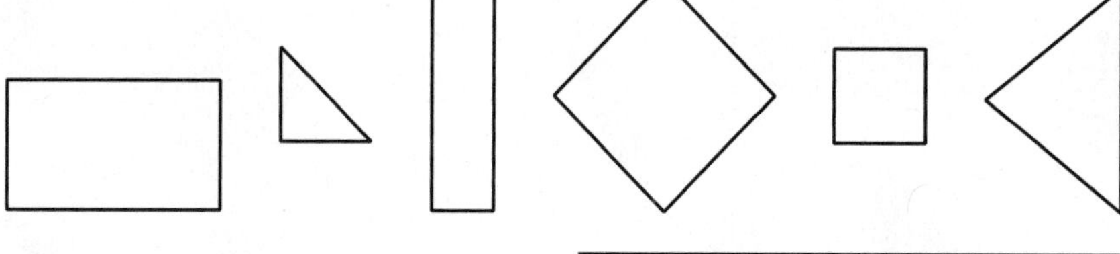

14. THINK SMARTER Which shapes have more than 3 sides? Choose all that apply.

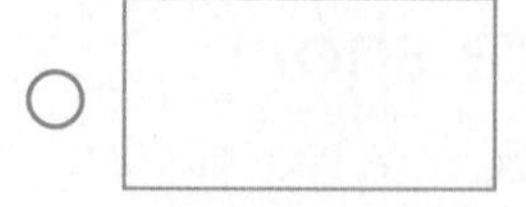
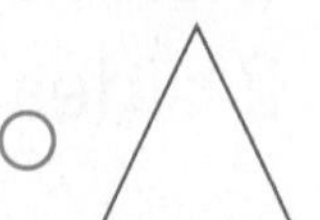

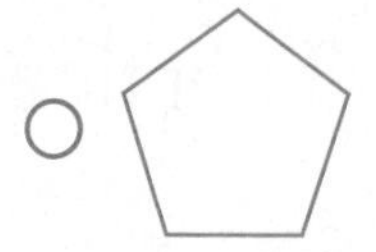

TAKE HOME ACTIVITY • Gather some household objects such as photos, coins, and napkins. Ask your child to sort them by shape.

FOR MORE PRACTICE: Standards Practice Book

Name ____________________

Describe Two-Dimensional Shapes

Essential Question What attributes can you use to describe two-dimensional shapes?

Geometry—1.G.1

MATHEMATICAL PRACTICES
MP.6, MP.7, MP.8

Listen and Draw

Use two-dimensional shapes. Sort them into two groups. Draw to show your work.

curved	straight

Math Talk Mathematical Practices

Explain how you sorted the shapes into two groups. Name the shapes in each group.

FOR THE TEACHER • Have children sort two-dimensional shapes into groups that are curved and straight. Have them draw the shapes to show how they sorted.

Model and Draw

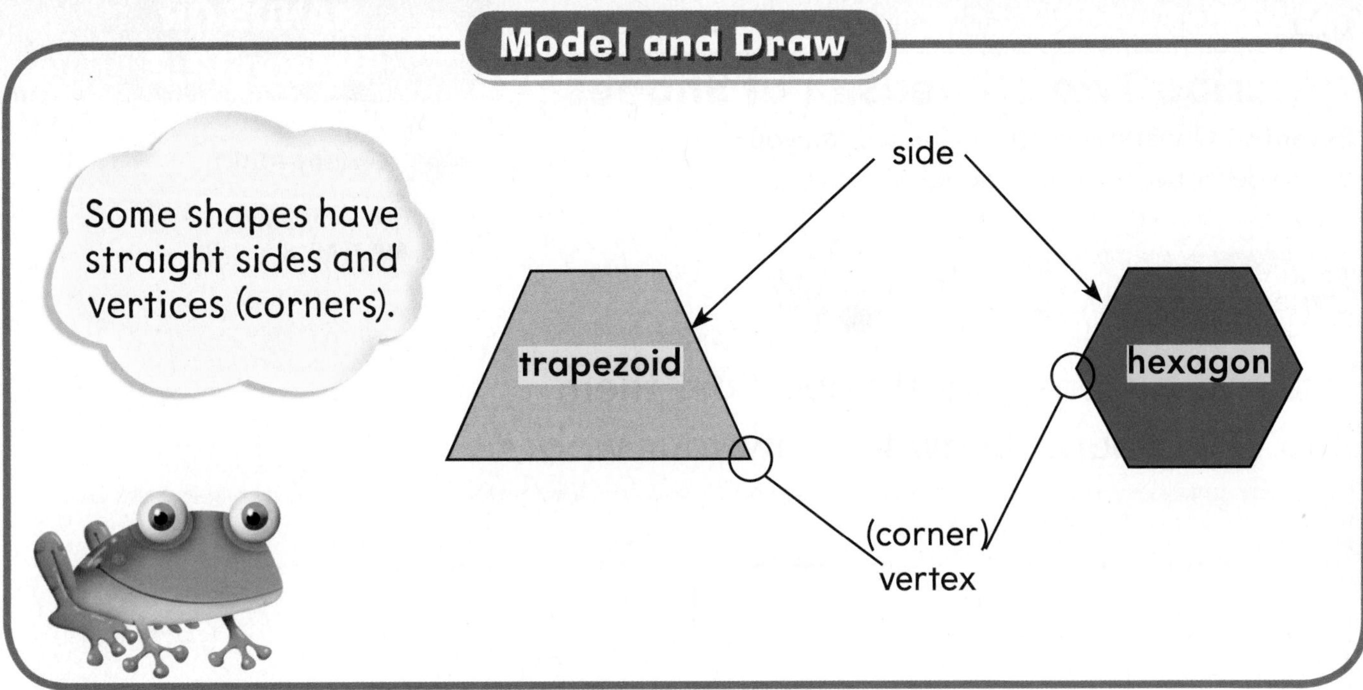

Share and Show

Use two-dimensional shapes. Draw and write to complete the chart.

	Shape	Draw the shape.	Number of Straight Sides	Number of Vertices (Corners)
1.	hexagon			
2.	rectangle			
3.	square			
✓4.	trapezoid			
✓5.	triangle			

Name ______________________________

On Your Own

Use [crayon] to trace each straight side.
Use [crayon] to circle each vertex (corner).
Write the number of sides and vertices (corners).

6. 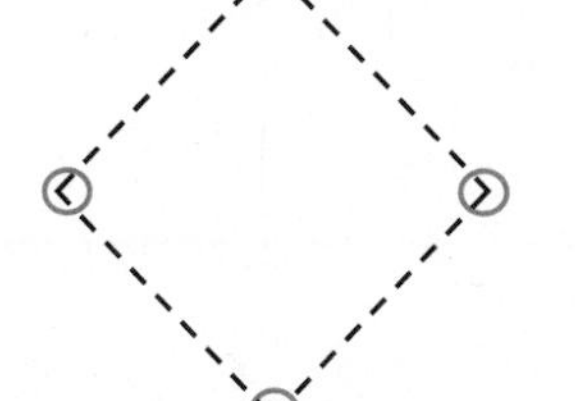

____ sides

____ vertices

7. 

____ sides

____ vertices

8. 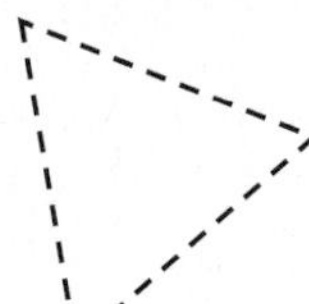

____ sides

____ vertices

9. 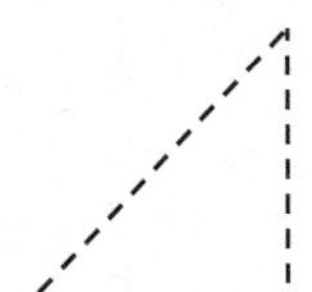

____ sides

____ vertices

10. 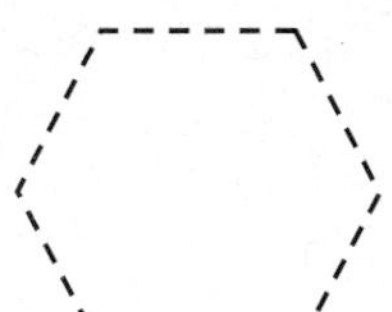

____ sides

____ vertices

11. 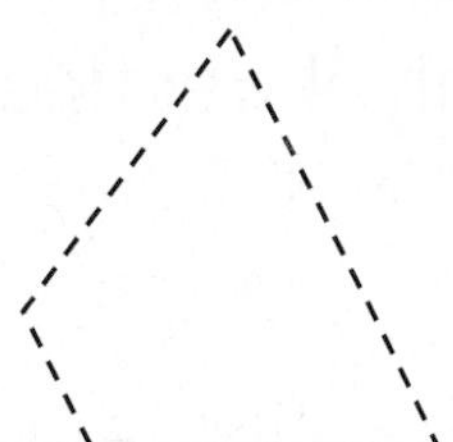

____ sides

____ vertices

THINK SMARTER Draw a picture to solve.

12. I am a shape with 3 straight sides and 3 vertices.

13. I am a shape with 4 straight sides that are the same length and 4 vertices.

Problem Solving • Applications

MATHEMATICAL PRACTICE 6 **Use Math Vocabulary**

Draw shapes to match the clues.

14. Jake draws a shape that has fewer than 5 sides. It has 3 vertices.

15. Meg draws a shape with 4 sides. She labels it as a trapezoid.

16. GO DEEPER Ben draws two different shapes. They each have only 4 vertices.

17. THINK SMARTER Circle the number that makes the sentence true.

A △ has [2 / 3 / 4] vertices (corners).

TAKE HOME ACTIVITY • Have your child draw a square, a trapezoid, and a triangle. For each shape, have him or her show you the sides and vertices and tell how many of each.

FOR MORE PRACTICE: Standards Practice Book

Name ______________________

Combine Two-Dimensional Shapes

Essential Question How can you put two-dimensional shapes together to make new two-dimensional shapes?

Geometry—1.G.2

MATHEMATICAL PRACTICES
MP.5, MP.6

Listen and Draw

Use pattern blocks. Draw to show your work.

Math Talk **Mathematical Practices**

Describe the new shape Karen made.

FOR THE TEACHER • Have children use pattern blocks to act out the following problem. Karen has some pattern blocks. She puts two triangles together. Draw a new shape Karen could make.

Model and Draw

How many do you need to make a ?

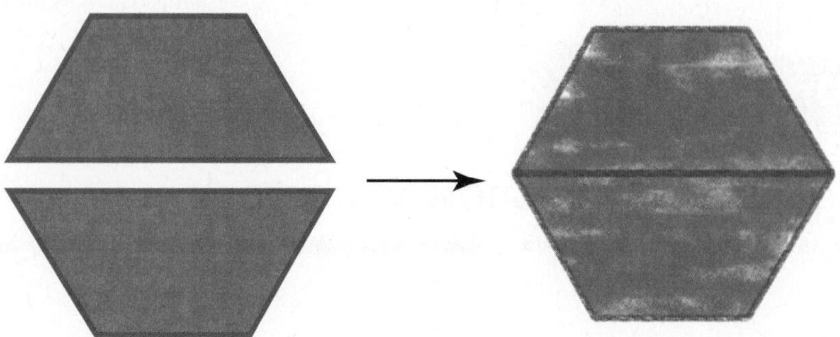

2 make a .

Share and Show

Use pattern blocks. Draw to show the blocks.
Write how many blocks you used.

1. How many make a ?

____ make a .

2. How many make a ?

____ make a .

Name ______________________________

On Your Own

MATHEMATICAL PRACTICE 5 **Use a Concrete Model** Use pattern blocks. Draw to show the blocks. Write how many blocks you used.

3. How many ▲ make a ⬡?

____ ▲ make a ⬡.

4. How many ▲ make a ◆?

____ ▲ make a ◆.

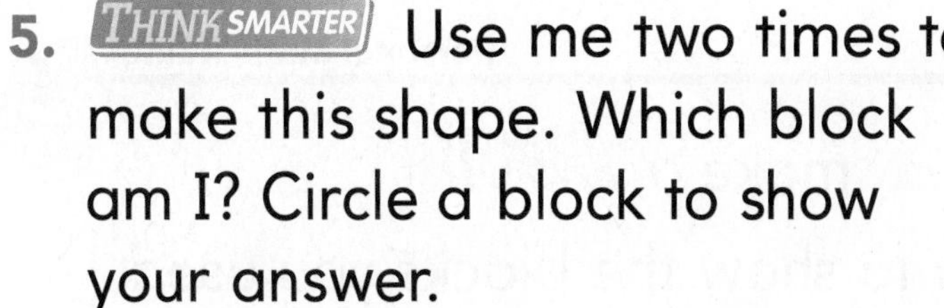

5. THINK SMARTER Use me two times to make this shape. Which block am I? Circle a block to show your answer.

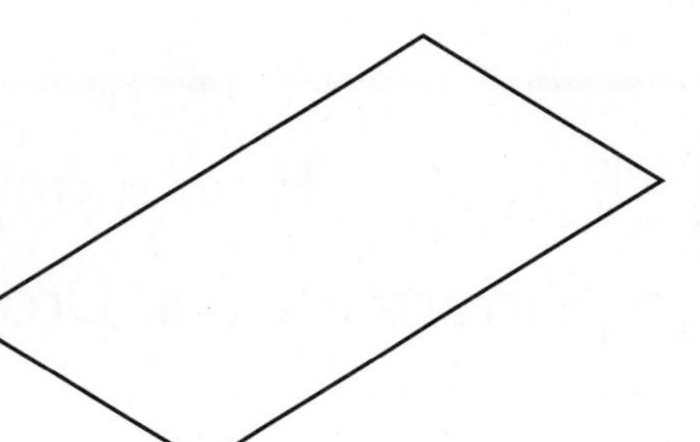

6. GO DEEPER Use these pattern blocks to make the shape. Write how many times you used each block.

____ ____ ____

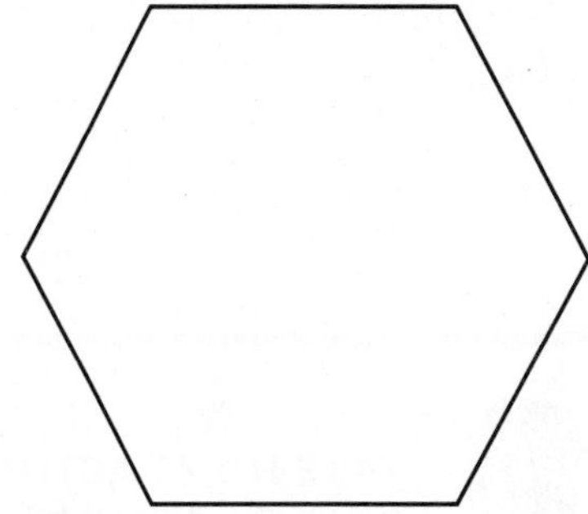

Problem Solving • Applications

GO DEEPER Use pattern blocks. Draw to show your answer.

7. 2 ▲ make a ◆.

How many ▲ make 3 ◆?

____ ▲ make 3 ◆.

Personal Math Trainer

8. THINKSMARTER+ How many ▲ make a ⏢?

Use pattern blocks. Draw to show the blocks you used.

TAKE HOME ACTIVITY • Have your child explain how he or she solved Exercise 7.

FOR MORE PRACTICE: Standards Practice Book

Name ___________________________

Combine More Shapes

Essential Question How can you combine two-dimensional shapes to make new shapes?

Geometry—1.G.2

MATHEMATICAL PRACTICES
MP.1, MP.4

Listen and Draw

Use shapes to fill each outline.
Draw to show your work.

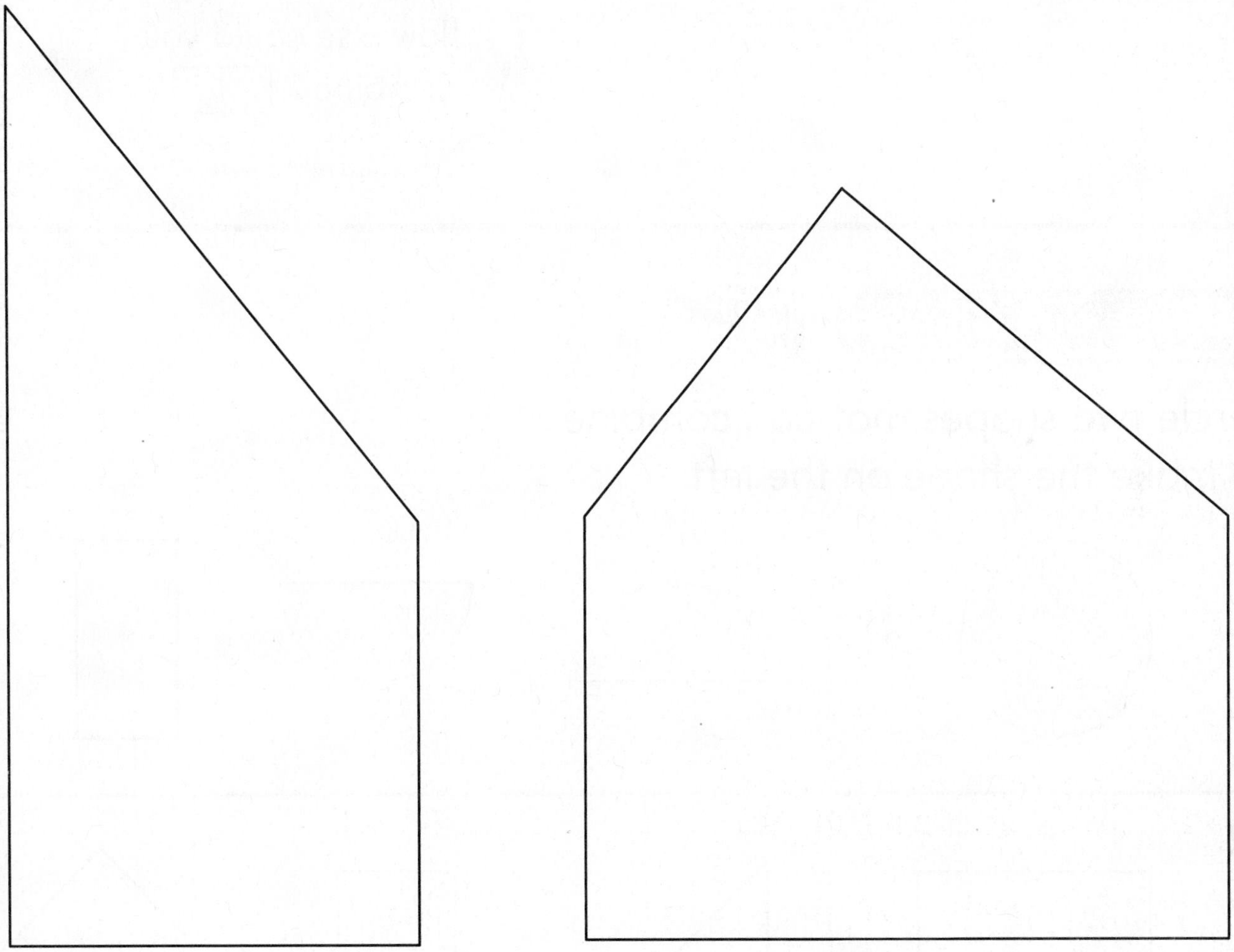

Math Talk

Mathematical Practices

Use the outline on the left to **describe** how two shapes can make another shape.

FOR THE TEACHER • Have children use two shapes to fill the outline on the left, and draw a line to show the two shapes. Then have children use three shapes to fill the outline on the right, again drawing lines to show the shapes.

Model and Draw

Combine shapes to make a new shape.

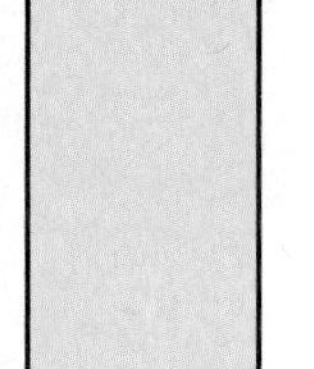

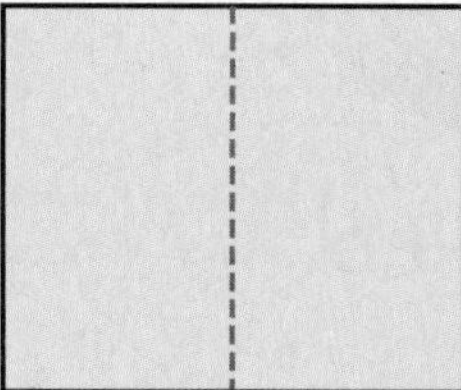
or
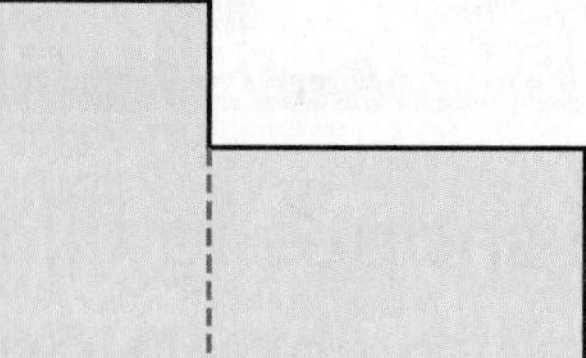

How else could you combine 2  ?

Share and Show

MATH BOARD

Circle two shapes that can combine to make the shape on the left.

1.

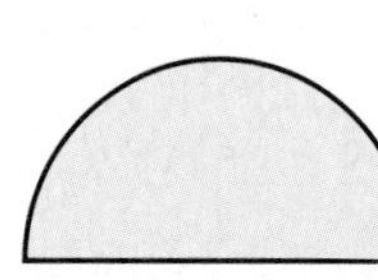
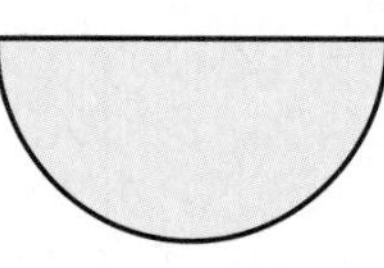

2.
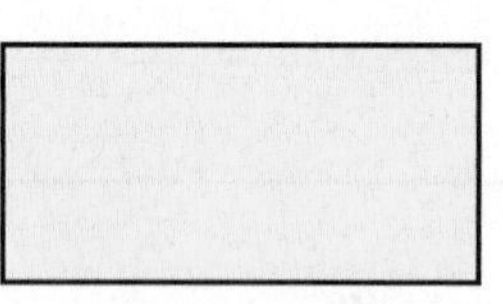
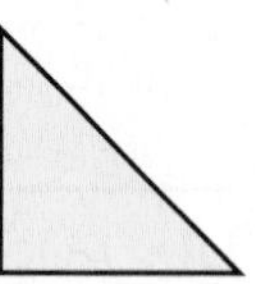
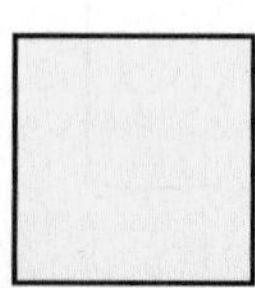
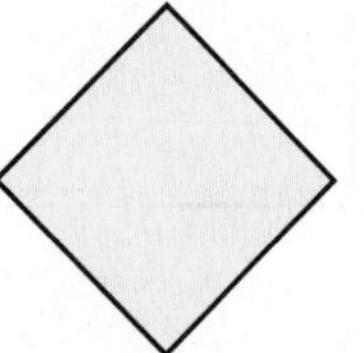

3.
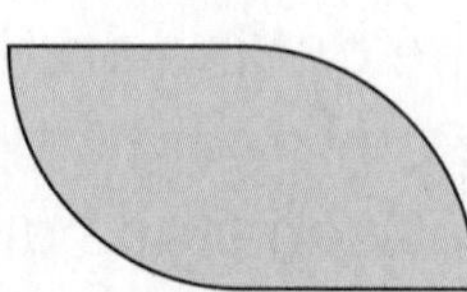
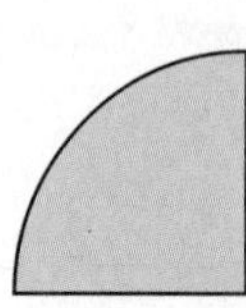
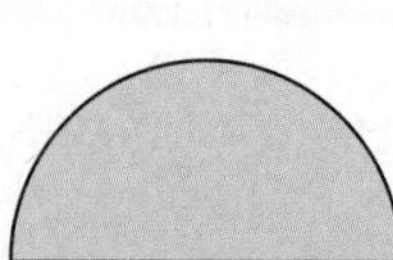
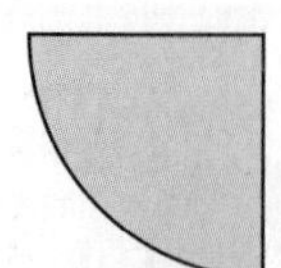

Name ______________________________

On Your Own

MATHEMATICAL PRACTICE 4 **Use Diagrams** Circle two shapes that can combine to make the shape on the left.

4. 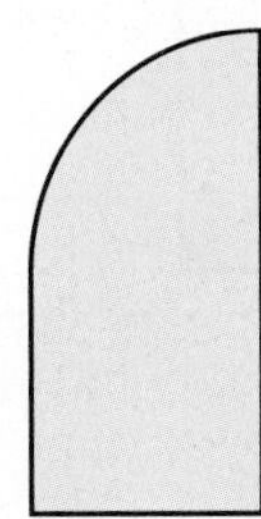 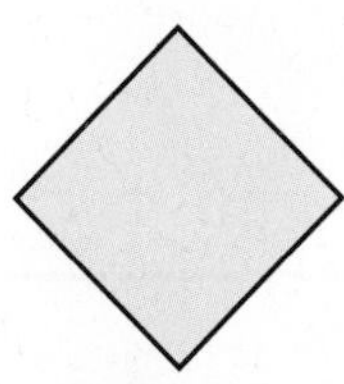 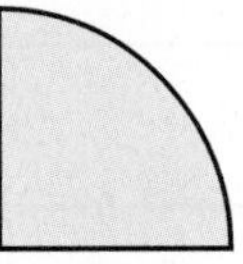 

5. 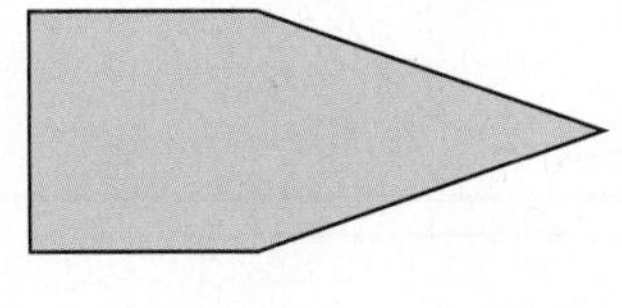 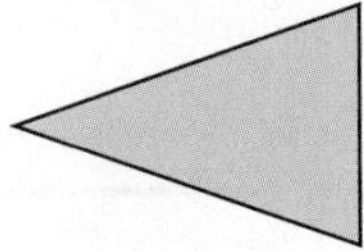 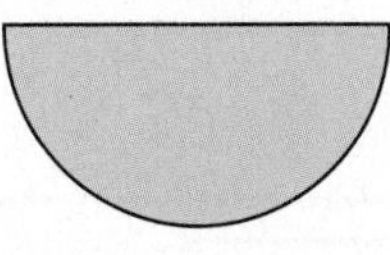 

THINK SMARTER Draw lines to show two different ways to combine the shapes on the left to make new shapes on the right.

6. 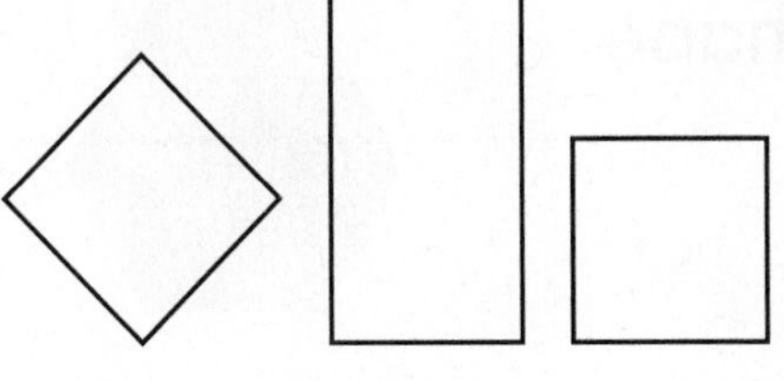 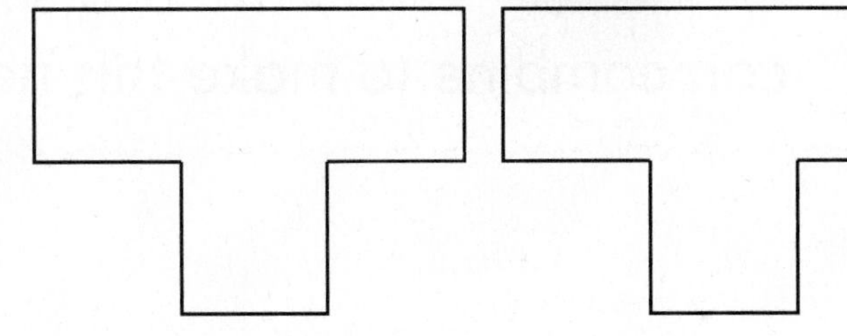

7. 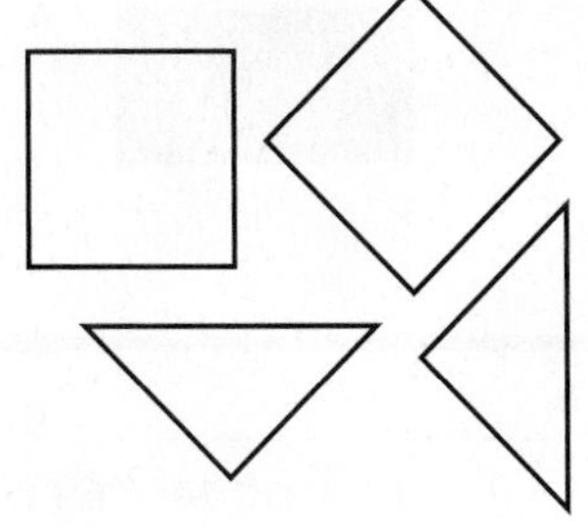 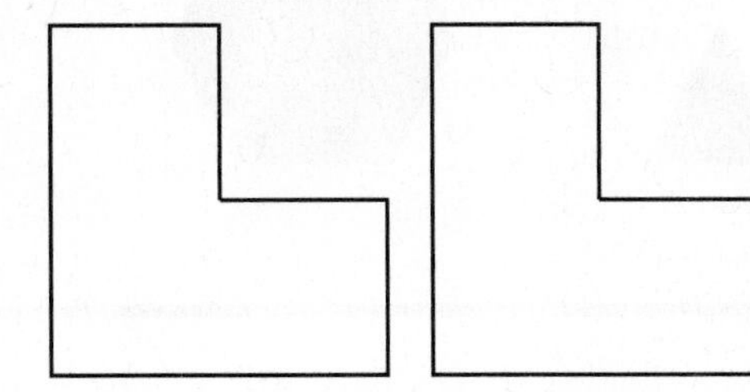

Problem Solving • Applications

THINK SMARTER Draw lines to show how the shapes on the left combine to make the new shape.

8.

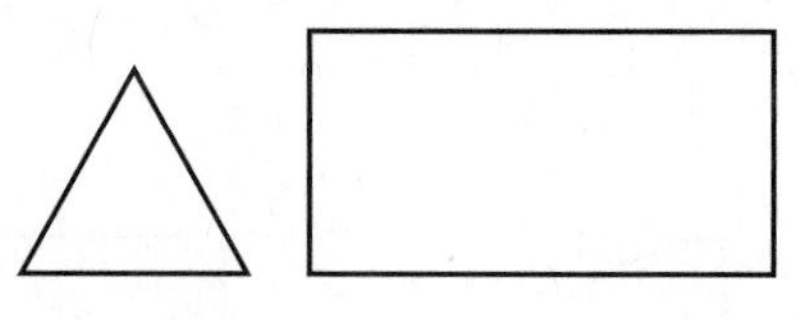

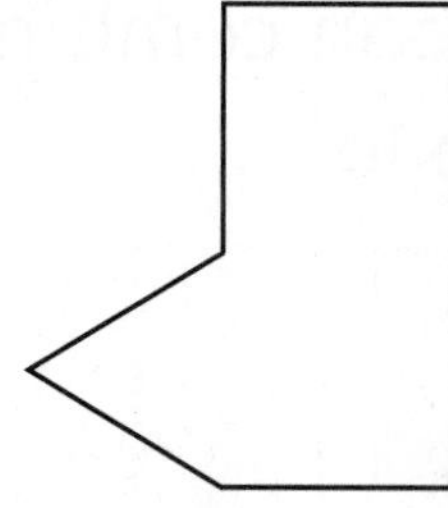

9.

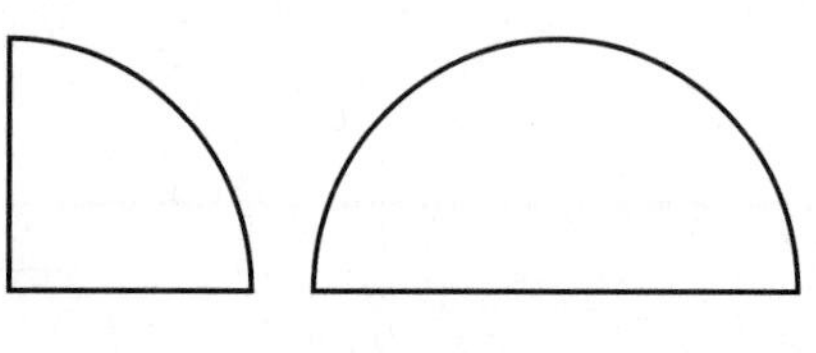

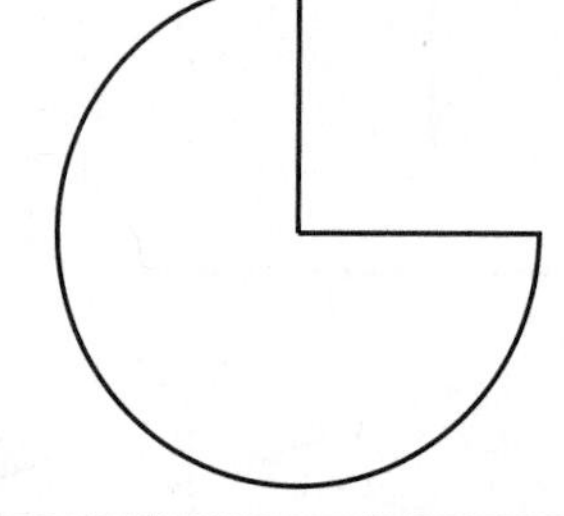

10.

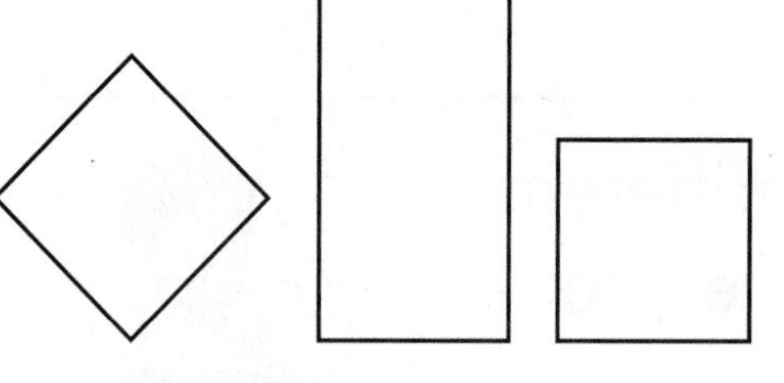

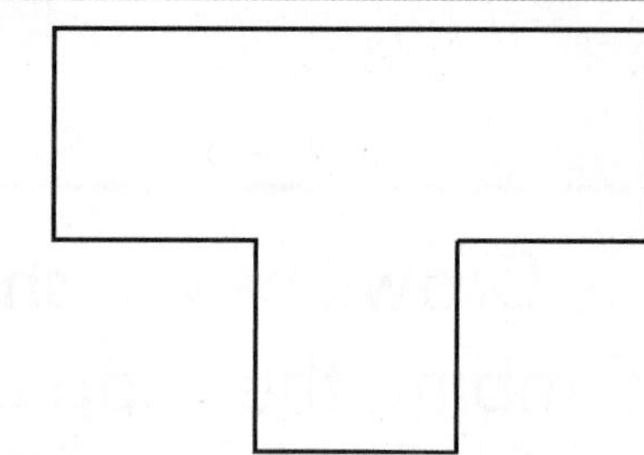

11. THINK SMARTER Circle the two shapes that can combine to make this new shape.

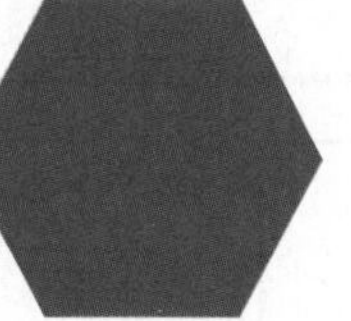

TAKE HOME ACTIVITY • Ask your child to draw a new shape he or she can make by combining two triangles.

FOR MORE PRACTICE: Standards Practice Book

Name ______________________________

Problem Solving • Make New Two-Dimensional Shapes

Essential Question How can acting it out help you make new shapes from combined shapes?

Geometry—1.G.2

MATHEMATICAL PRACTICES
MP.1, MP.4

Cora wants to combine shapes to make a circle. She has .
How can Cora make a circle?

Unlock the Problem

What do I need to find?

how Cora can make a

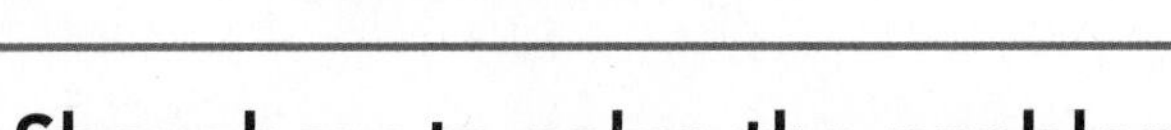

What information do I need to use?

Cora uses this shape.

Show how to solve the problem.

Step 1 Use shapes. Combine to make a new shape.

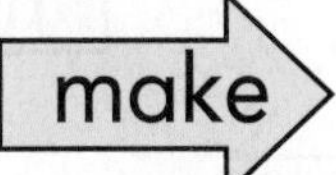

Step 2 Then use the new shape.

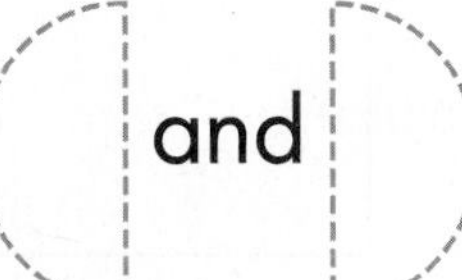

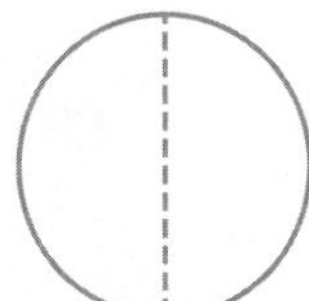

HOME CONNECTION • Recognizing how shapes can be put together and taken apart provides a foundation for future work with fractions.

Try Another Problem

- What do I need to find?
- What information do I need to use?

Use shapes to solve.
Draw to show your work.

1. Use □ to make a larger □.

Step 1 Combine shapes to make a new shape.

□ and □ make ▯

Step 2 Then use the new shape.

and make □

2. Use ◺ to make a ▭.

Step 1 Combine shapes to make a new shape.

◺ and ◺ make □

Step 2 Then use the new shape.

and  □

Math Talk **Mathematical Practices**

Describe how you made the rectangle in Exercise 2.

Name ______________________________

Share and Show

MATHEMATICAL PRACTICE 1 **Analyze Relationships** Use shapes to solve. Draw to show your work.

3. Use ◺ to make a ▭.

Step 1 Combine shapes to make a new shape.

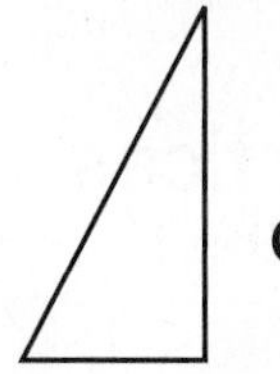 and 

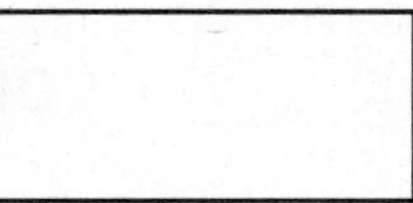

Step 2 Then use the new shape.

and

4. THINK SMARTER Use ⏢ and △ to make a ▱.

Step 1 Combine shapes to make a new shape.

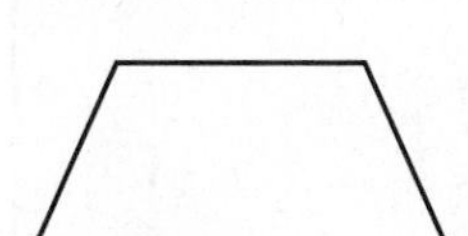 and 

make

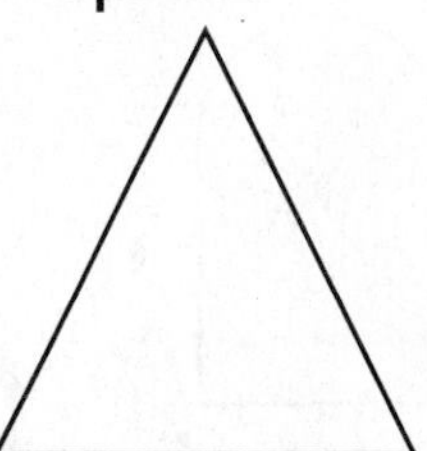

Step 2 Then use the new shape.

and

TAKE HOME ACTIVITY • Have your child explain how he or she solved Exercise 3.

FOR MORE PRACTICE: Standards Practice Book

Name ______________________________

Concepts and Skills

Write the number of sides and vertices (corners). (1.G.1)

1. 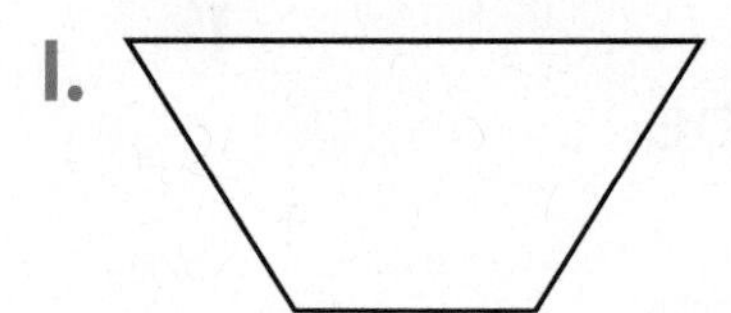 ____ sides

____ vertices

2.  ____ sides

____ vertices

Circle the shapes that can combine to make the new shape. (1.G.2)

3. 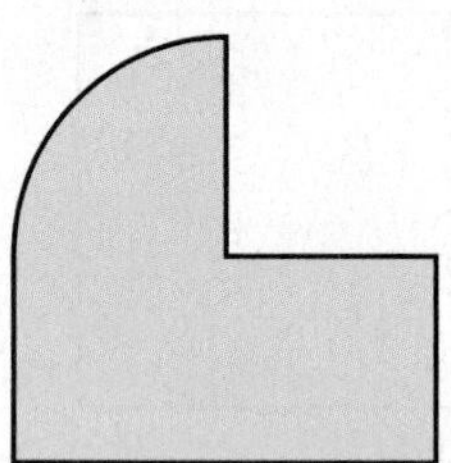 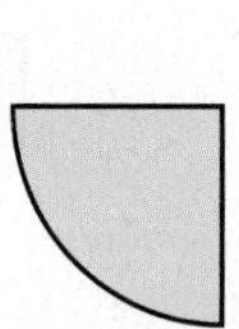 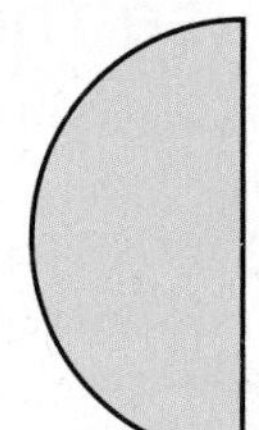 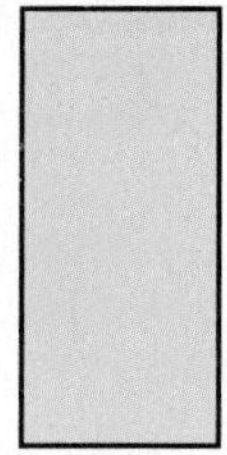

4. THINK SMARTER Which new shape can you make? (1.G.2)

 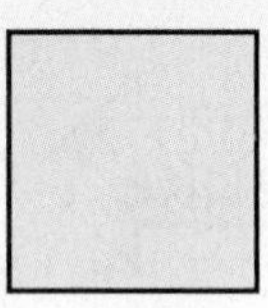 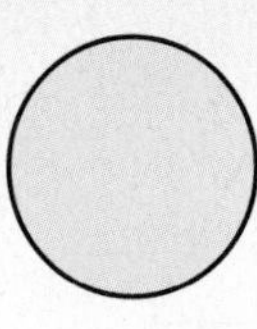 

○ ○ ○ ○

Step 1

Combine  and  to make .

Step 2

Then use and .

Name ______________________________

Find Shapes in Shapes

Essential Question How can you find shapes in other shapes?

Geometry—1.G.2

MATHEMATICAL PRACTICES
MP.4, MP.5

Listen and Draw

Use pattern blocks. What shape can you make with 1 hexagon and 2 triangles? Draw to show your shape.

Math Talk — Mathematical Practices

Explain Can you use the same pattern blocks to make a different shape?

FOR THE TEACHER • Have children explore making new shapes with the given pattern blocks. Discuss different shapes that can be made using the same pattern blocks.

Model and Draw

Which two pattern blocks make this shape?

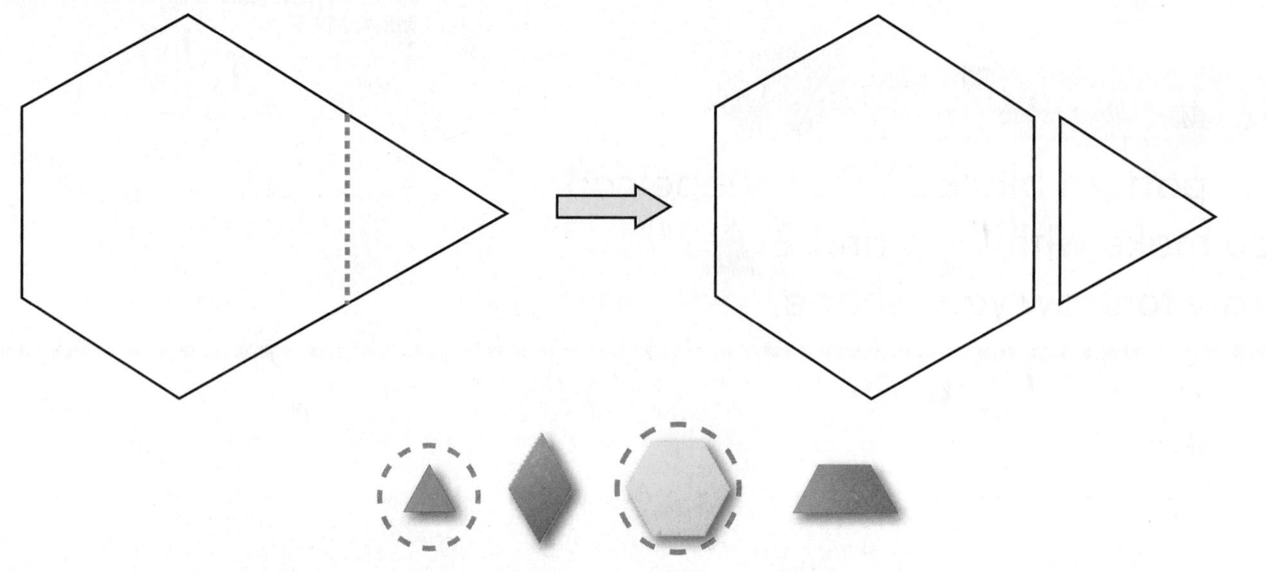

Share and Show

Use two pattern blocks to make the shape.
Draw a line to show your model.
Circle the blocks you use.

1.

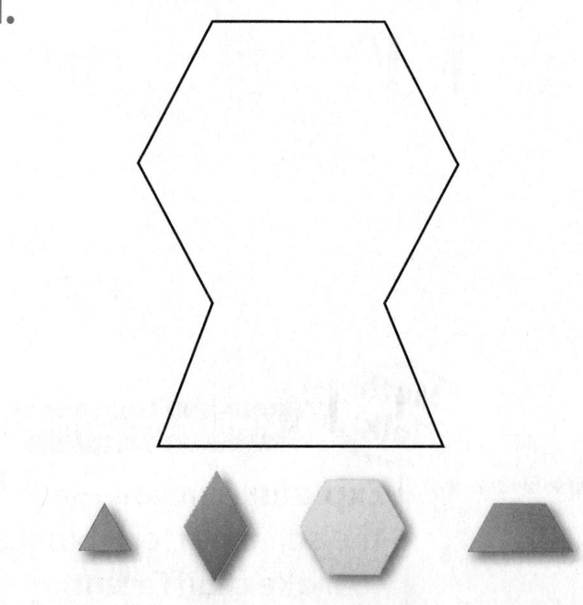

2.

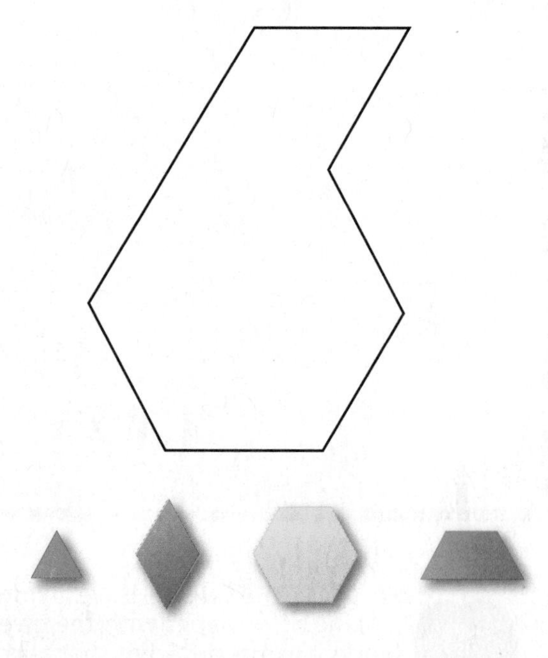

Name ______________________________

On Your Own

MATHEMATICAL PRACTICE 5 **Use a Concrete Model**

Use two pattern blocks to make the shape.
Draw a line to show your model.
Circle the blocks you use.

3.

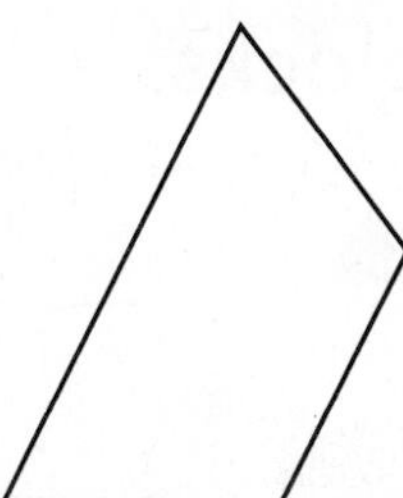

4.

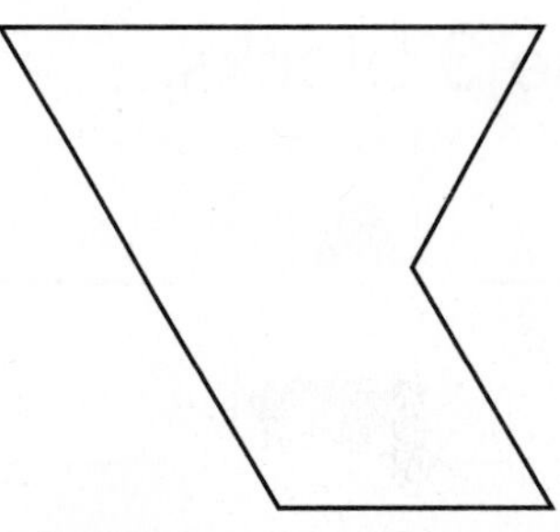

5.

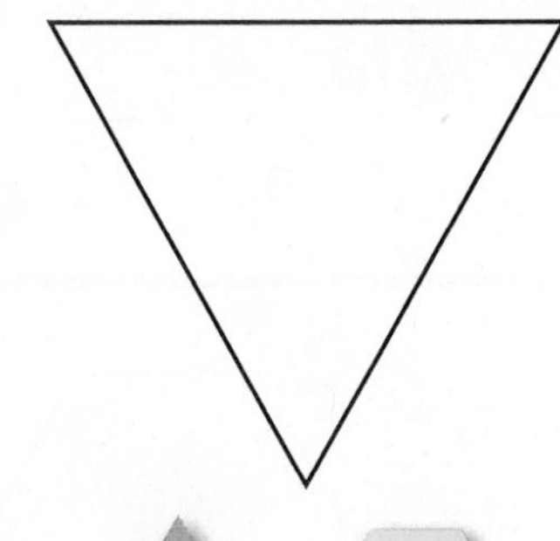

6.

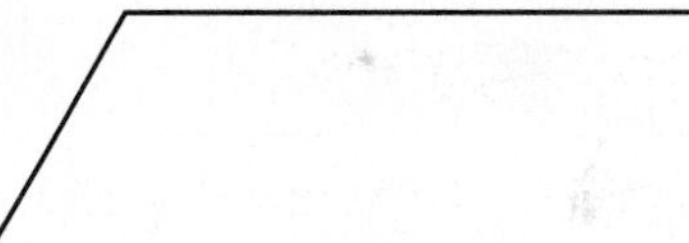

7. THINK SMARTER Use three pattern blocks to make the shape. Draw lines to show your model. Circle the blocks you use.

Math on the Spot

Problem Solving • Applications

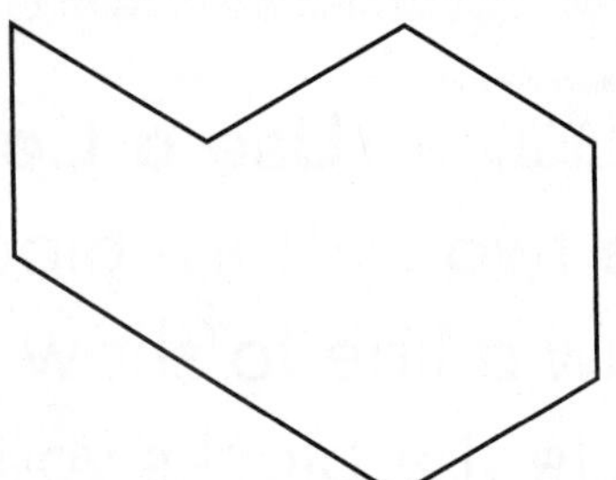

THINK SMARTER Make this shape. Use the number of pattern blocks listed in the exercise. Write how many of each block you use.

8. Use 3 blocks.

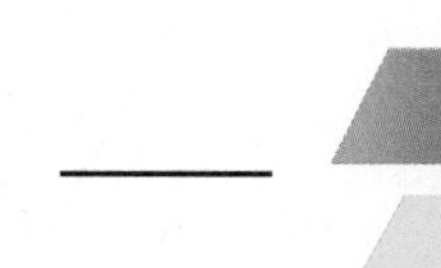

____ ____

____ ____

9. Use 5 blocks.

____ ____

____ ____

10. Use 7 blocks.

____ ____

____ ____

11. Use 8 blocks.

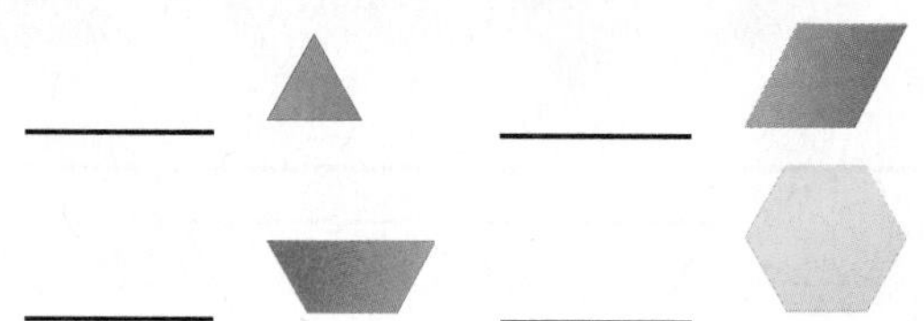

____ ____

____ ____

12. THINK SMARTER Use 4 pattern blocks to fill the shape. Draw to show the blocks you used.

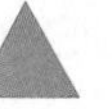

TAKE HOME ACTIVITY • Have your child use this page to explain how to find shapes within the given shape.

FOR MORE PRACTICE: Standards Practice Book

Name ______________________________

Take Apart Two-Dimensional Shapes

Geometry—1.G.2

MATHEMATICAL PRACTICES
MP.1, MP.7

Essential Question How can you take apart two dimensional shapes?

Listen and Draw

Color rectangles orange.
Color triangles purple.

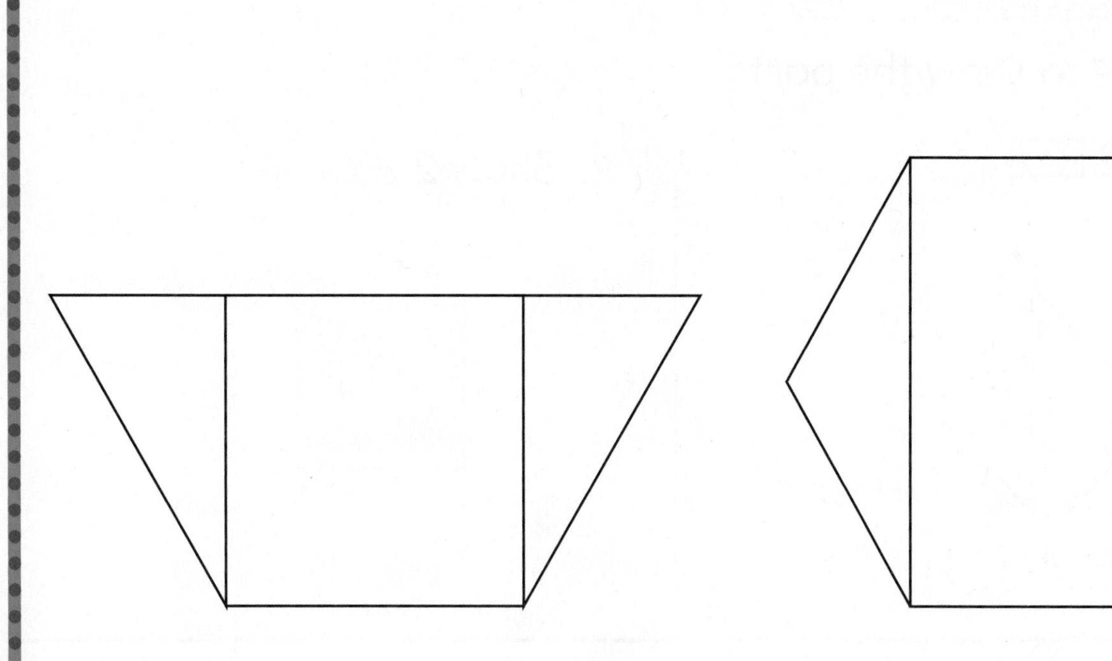

Mathematical Practices

Explain What shapes did Angelina make?

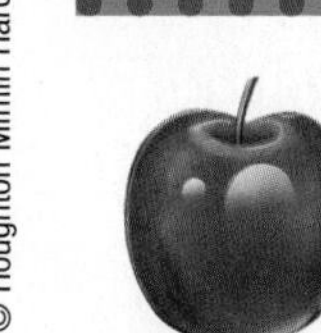

FOR THE TEACHER • Read the following aloud. Angelina put some triangles and rectangles together. She drew pictures to show what she made. Color to show how Angelina put the shapes together.

Model and Draw

You can draw to show parts of a shape.

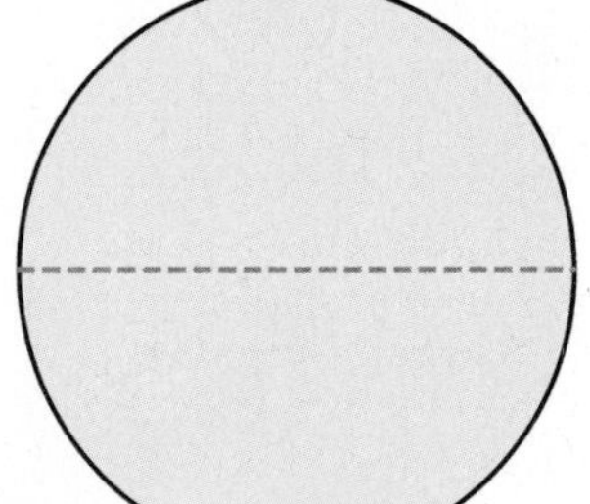 shows  and 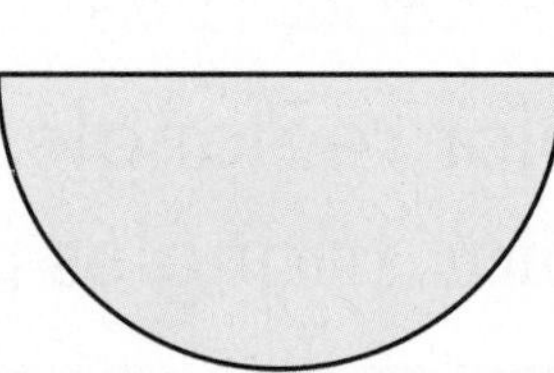

Share and Show

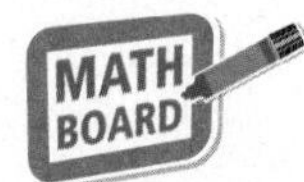

Draw a line to show the parts.

1. Show 2 ▭.

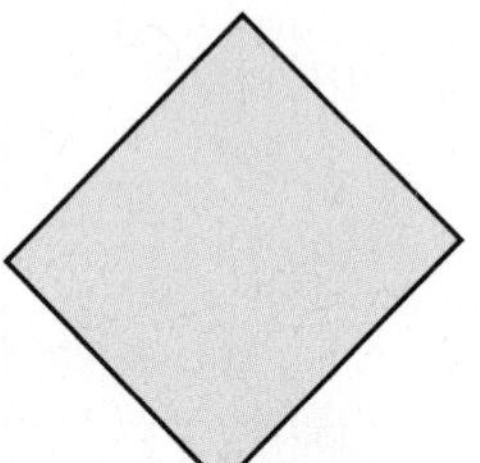

2. Show 2 △.

3. Show 2 □.

4. Show 2 △.

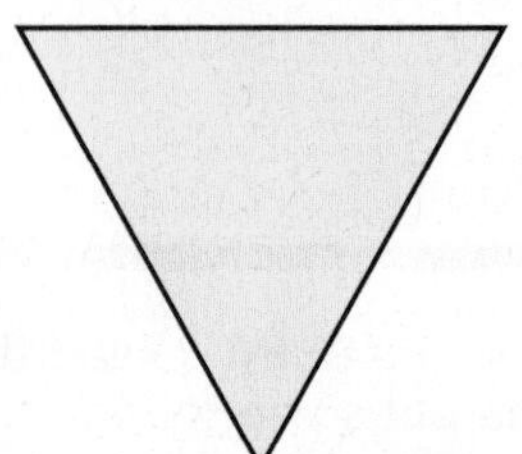

Name ______________________________

On Your Own

MATHEMATICAL PRACTICE 7 **Identify Relationships**

Draw a line to show the parts.

5. Show 2 △.

6. Show 2 ▭.

7. Show 1 ▭ and 1 □.

8. Show 1 △ and 1 ⏢.

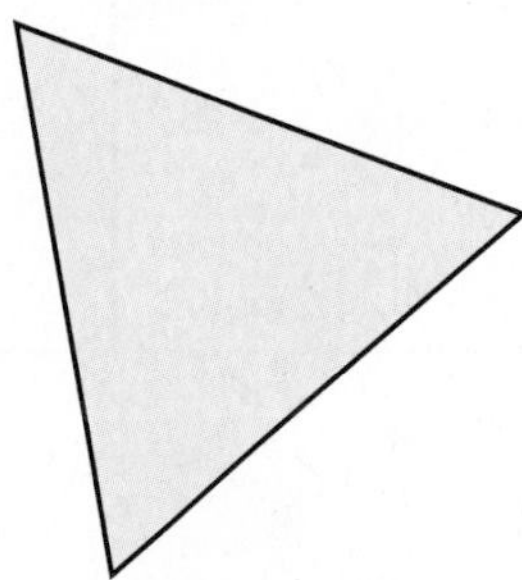

THINK SMARTER Draw two lines to show the parts.

9. Show 3 △.

10. Show 2 △ and 1 ⏢.

Problem Solving • Applications

11. THINK SMARTER How many squares are there?

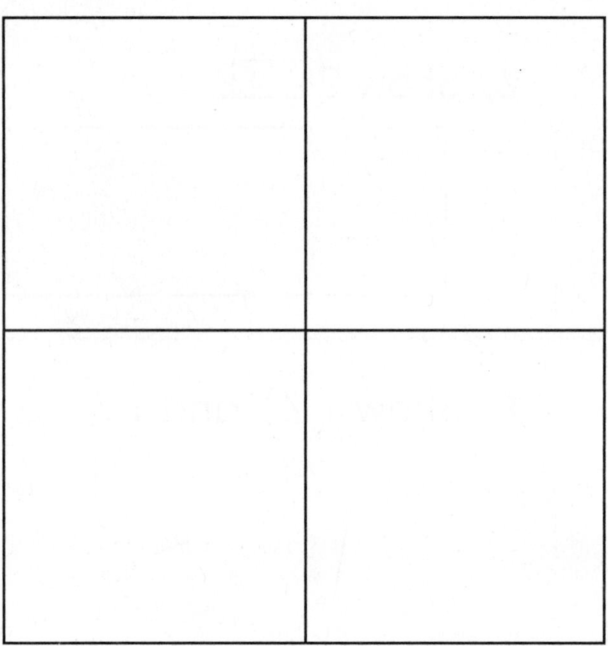

_____ squares

12. THINK SMARTER Draw a line to show the parts. Show 2 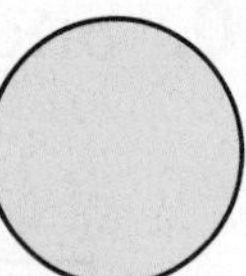.

TAKE HOME ACTIVITY • Ask your child to explain how he or she solved Exercise 11.

FOR MORE PRACTICE: Standards Practice Book

Name ______________________________

Equal or Unequal Parts

Essential Question How can you identify equal and unequal parts in two-dimensional shapes?

Geometry—1.G.3

MATHEMATICAL PRACTICES
MP.1, MP.3, MP.6

Listen and Draw

Draw to show the parts.

Show 2 △.

Show 3 △.

Math Talk **Mathematical Practices**

Describe how the triangles shown in each square compare.

FOR THE TEACHER • Have children draw lines to show two triangles in one square and three triangles in the other square.

Model and Draw

These show **equal parts**, or **equal shares**.

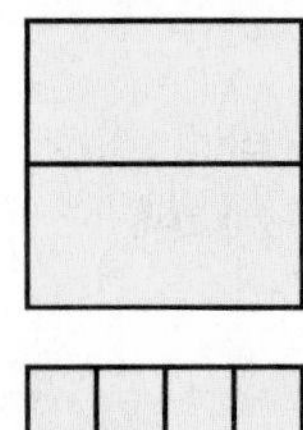

How can you describe equal shares?

These show **unequal parts**, or **unequal shares**.

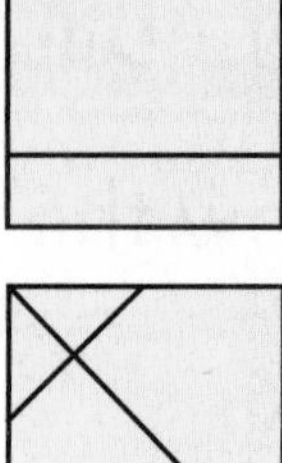

Share and Show

THINK
Are the parts the same size?

Circle the shape that shows equal parts.

1.

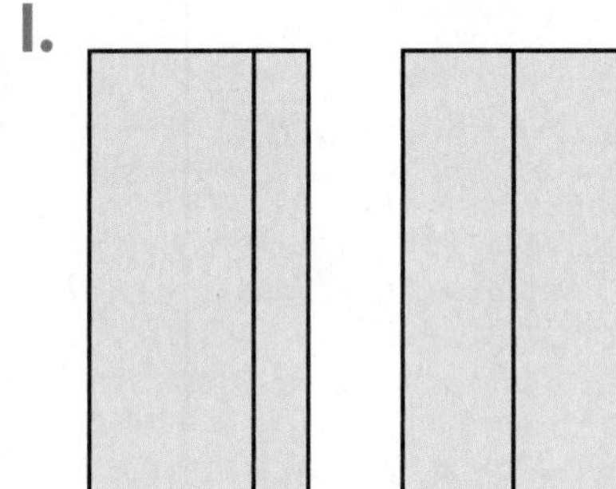

2.

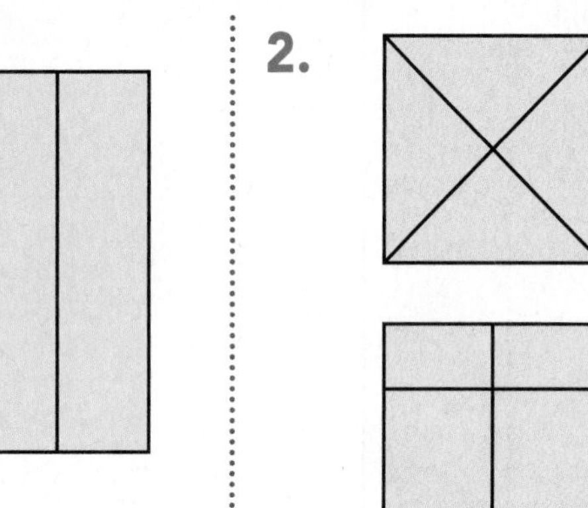

3.

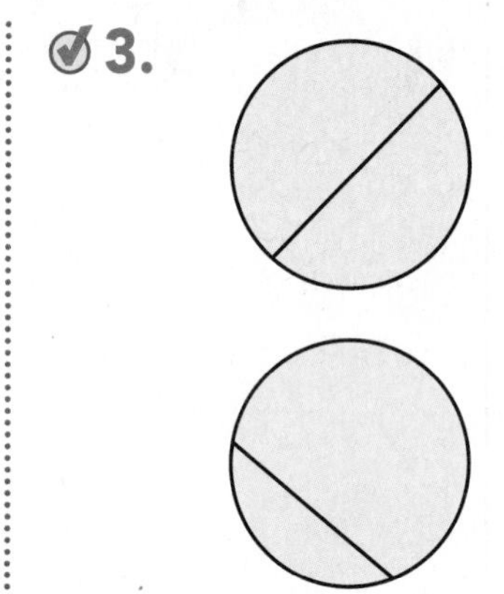

Circle the shape that shows unequal parts.

4.

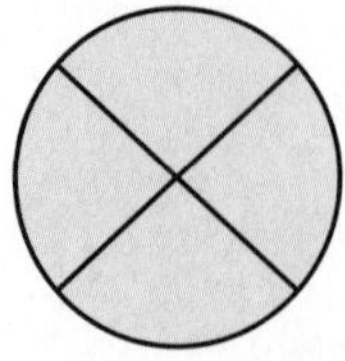

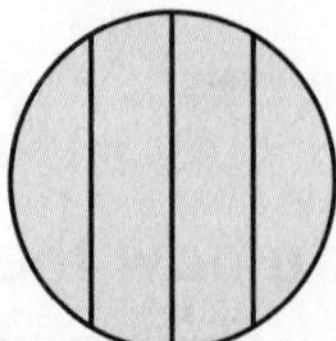

5.

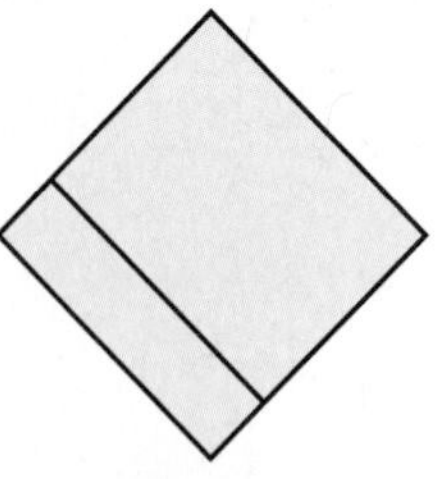

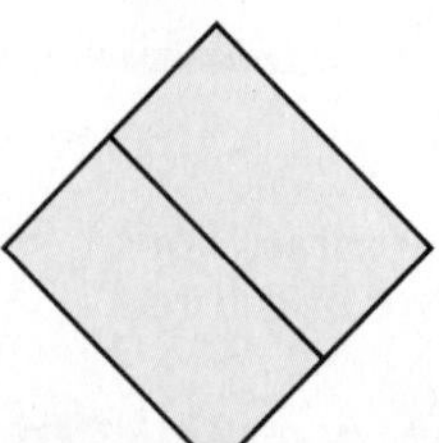

6.

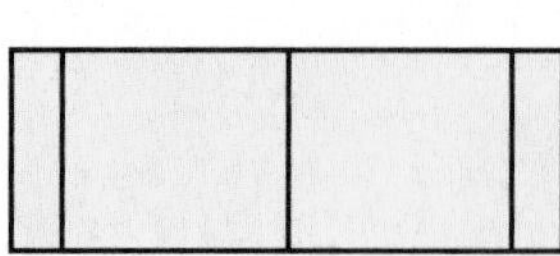

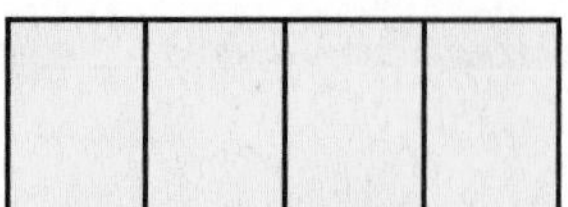

Name ______________________________

THINK
Equal shares means the same as equal parts.

On Your Own

MATHEMATICAL PRACTICE 6 **Use Math Vocabulary**

Color the shapes that show unequal shares.

7. 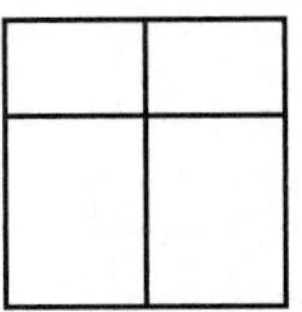 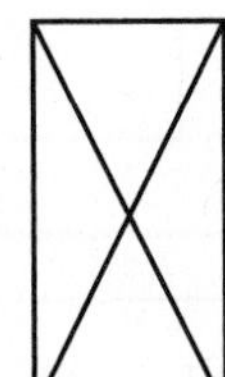 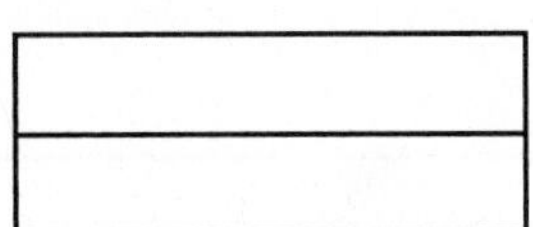 

8. 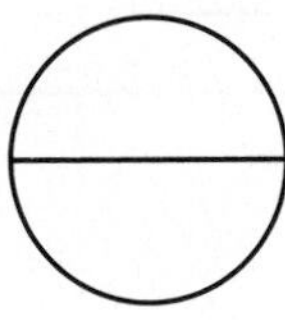 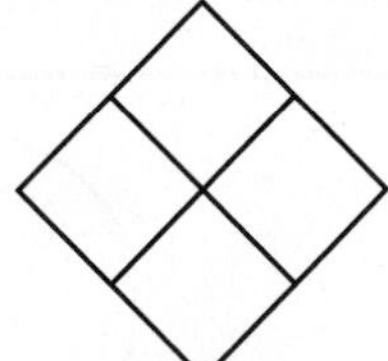 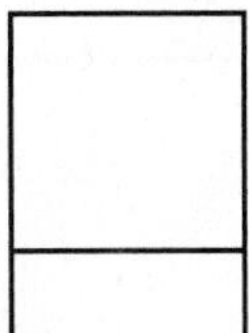 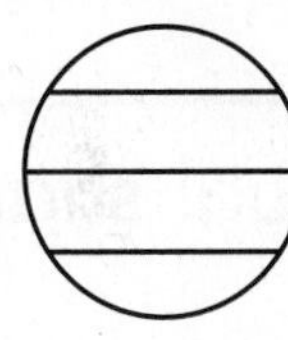

Color the shapes that show equal shares.

9. 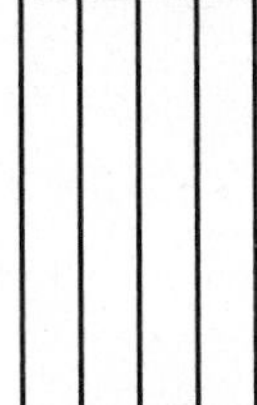 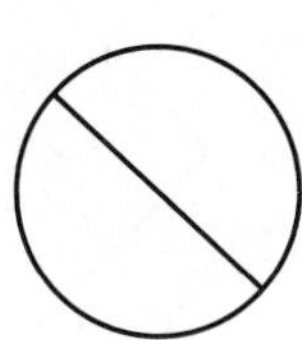 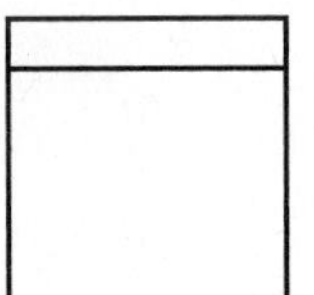 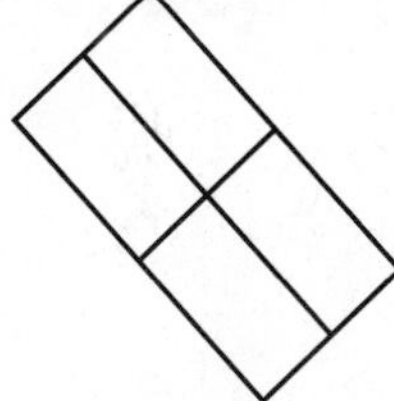

10. 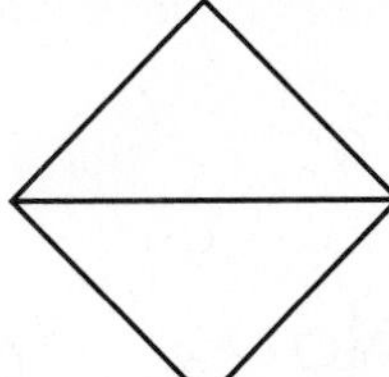 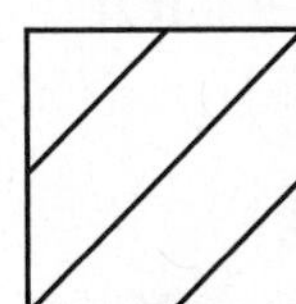 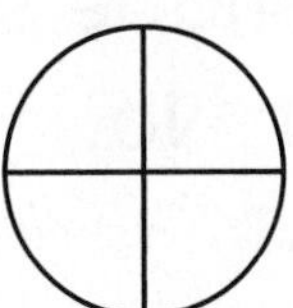 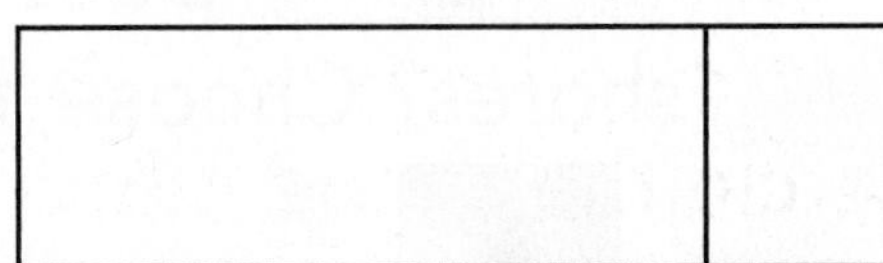

THINK SMARTER Write the number of equal shares.

11. 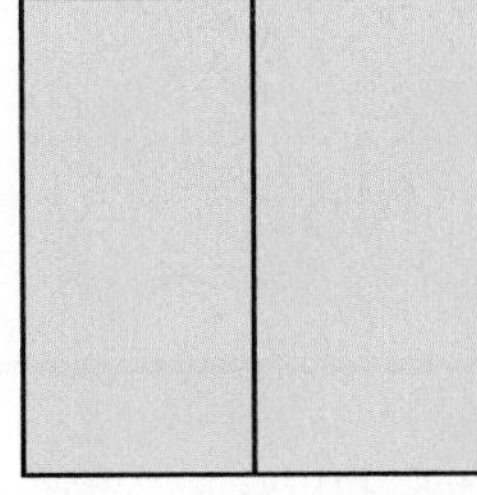

_____ equal shares

12. 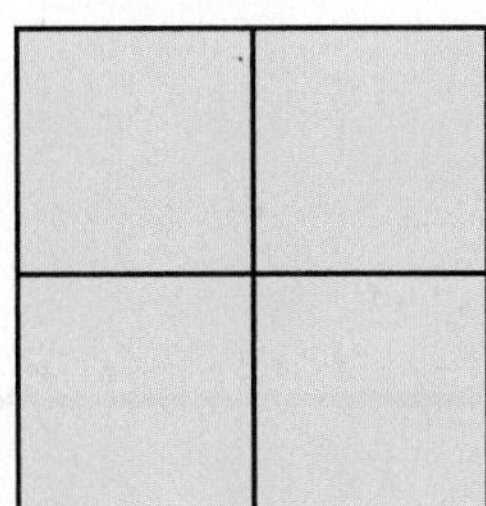

_____ equal shares

Problem Solving • Applications

WRITE Math

THINK SMARTER Draw lines to show the parts.

13. 2 equal parts

14. 2 unequal parts

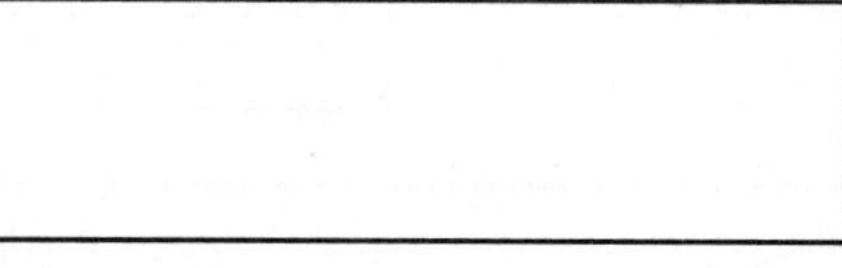

15. 4 equal shares

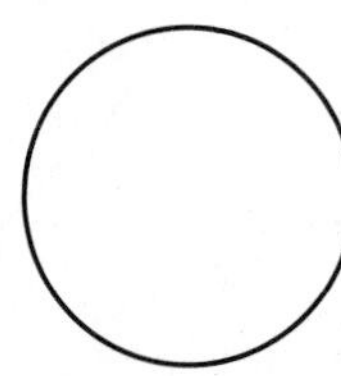

16. 4 unequal shares

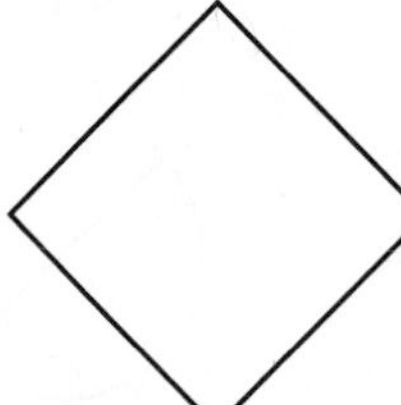

17. THINK SMARTER Does the shape show equal shares? Choose Yes or No.

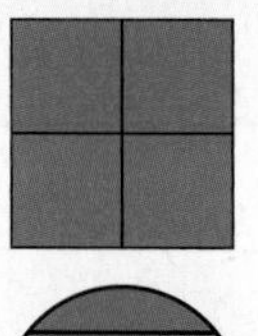

○ Yes ○ No

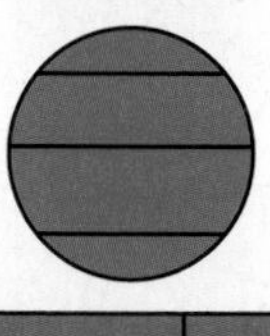

○ Yes ○ No

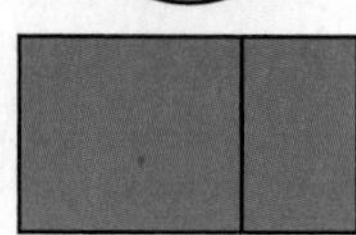

○ Yes ○ No

TAKE HOME ACTIVITY• Draw a circle on a piece of paper. Ask your child to draw a line so the circle shows 2 equal shares.

FOR MORE PRACTICE: Standards Practice Book

Name ______________________________

Halves

Essential Question How can a shape be separated into two equal shares?

Geometry—1.G.3

MATHEMATICAL PRACTICES
MP.1, MP.4, MP.6

Listen and Draw Real World

Draw to solve.

FOR THE TEACHER • Have children draw to solve this problem: Two friends share the sandwich on the left. How can they cut the sandwich so each gets an equal share? Then have children solve this problem: Two other friends share the sandwich on the right. How could this sandwich be cut a different way so each friend gets an equal share?

Math Talk **Mathematical Practices**

Describe Will all four friends get the same amount of sandwich?

Model and Draw

The 2 equal shares make 1 whole.

2 equal shares

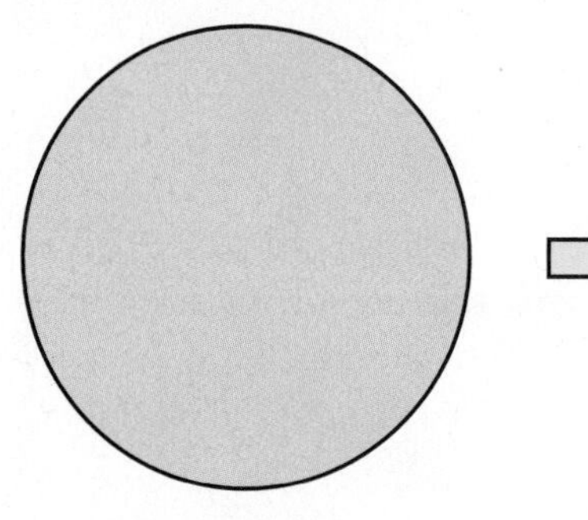

1 whole

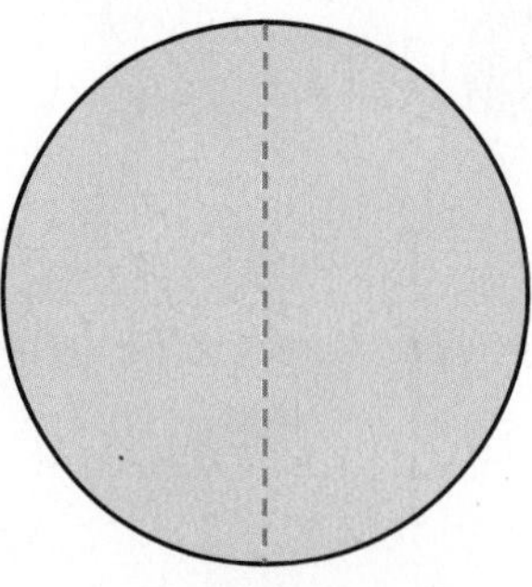

2 **halves**

Is **half of** the circle larger or smaller than the whole circle?

Share and Show

Draw a line to show halves.

1.

2.

3.

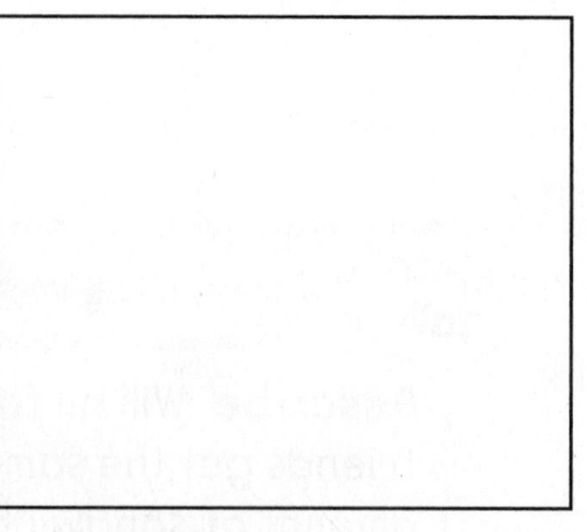

4.

Name ____________________________________

On Your Own

MATHEMATICAL PRACTICE 1 **Analyze Relationships**

Circle the shapes that show halves.

5. 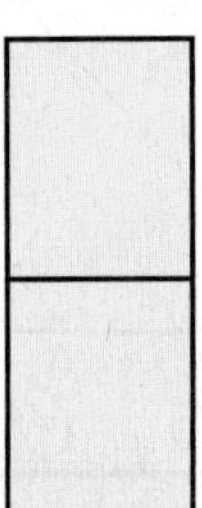

6. 

7. 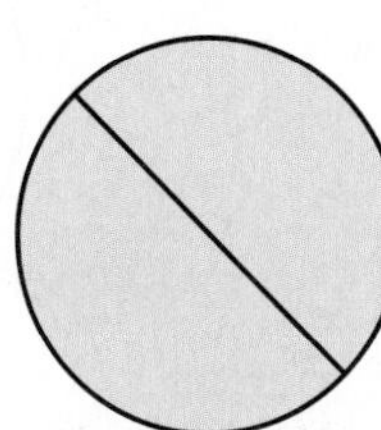

8. 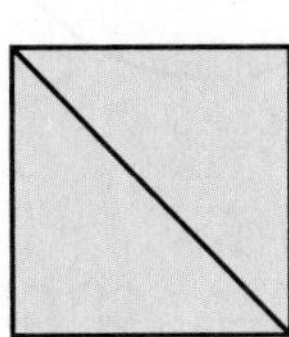

9. 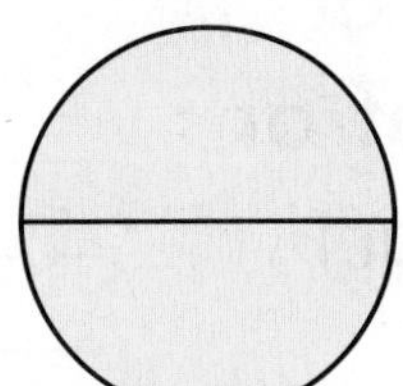

10. 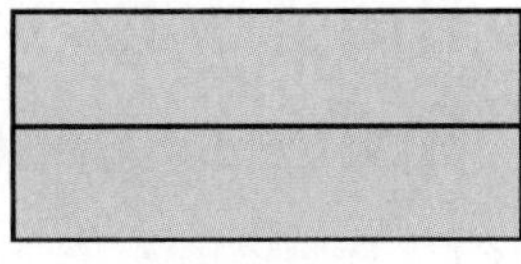

11. 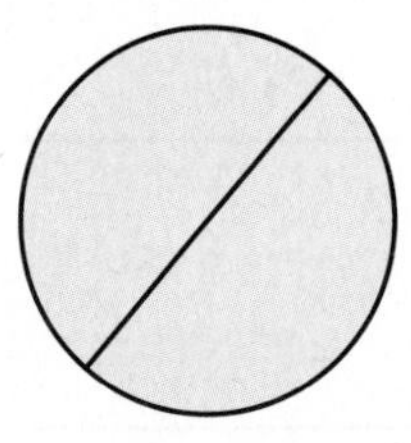

12. 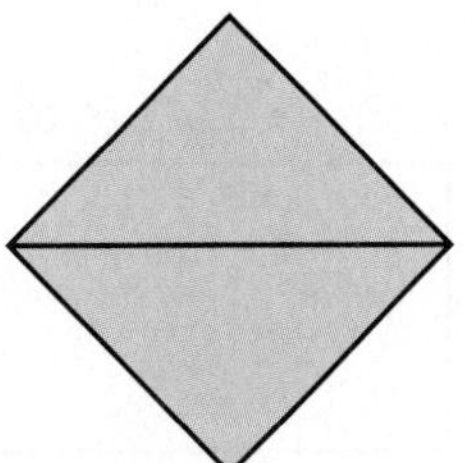

13. 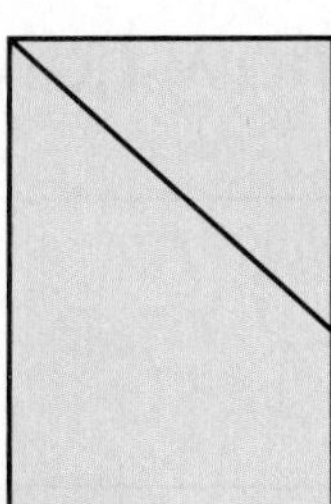

14. THINK SMARTER Use the picture.
Write numbers to solve.

Math on the Spot

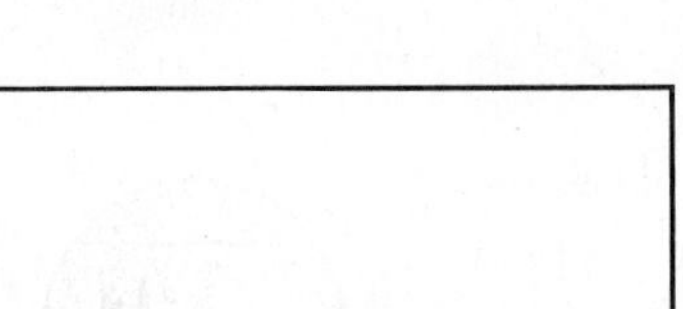

The picture shows _____ halves.

The _____ equal shares make _____ whole.

Problem Solving • Applications

Draw or write to solve.

15. Color half of each shape.

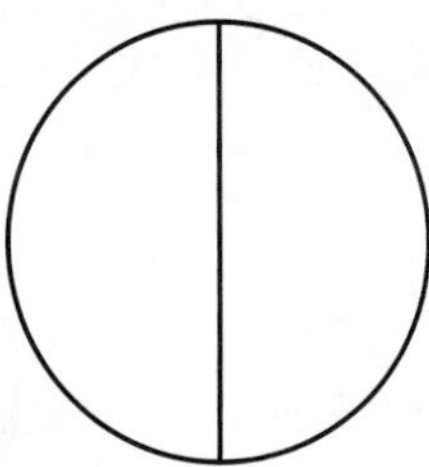

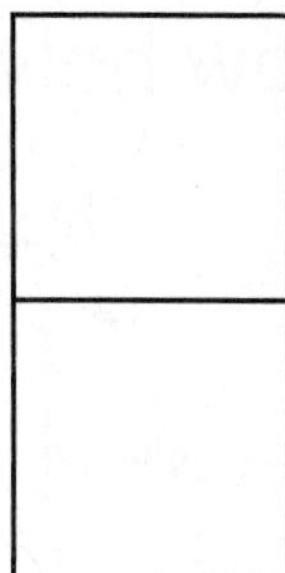

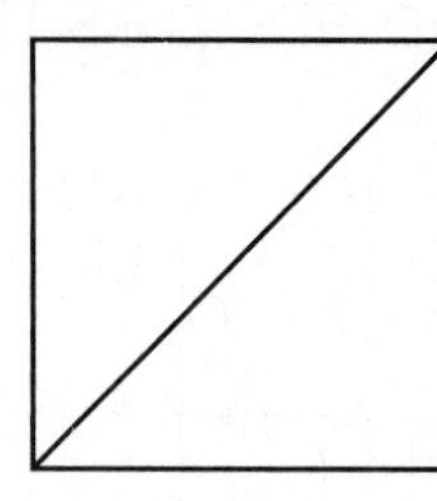

16. Linus cut a circle into equal shares. He traced one of the parts. Write **half of** or **halves** to name the part.

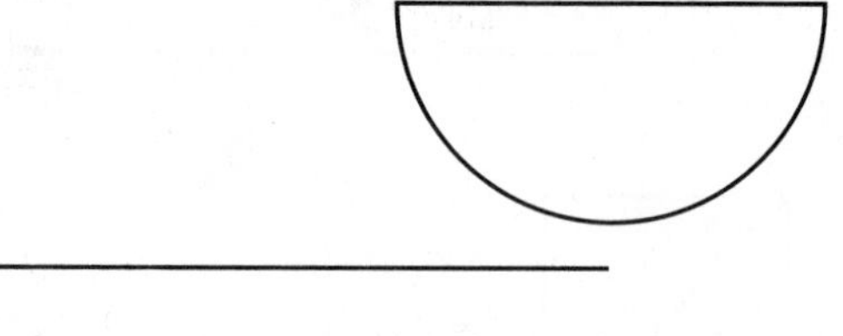

______________ a circle

17. GO DEEPER Draw three different ways to show halves.

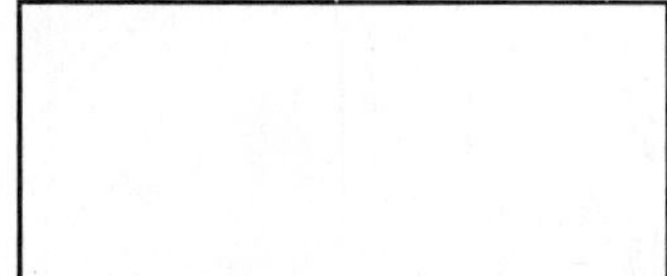

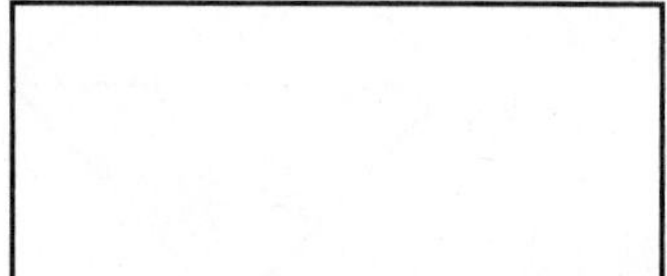

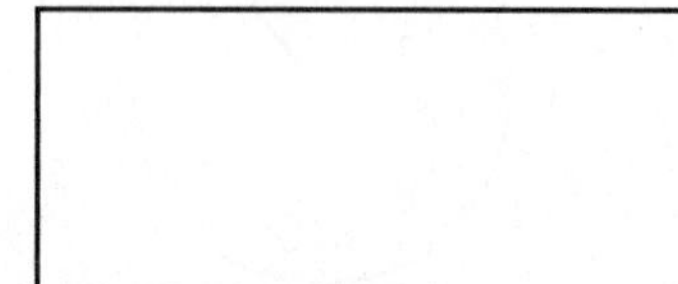

18. THINK SMARTER Circle the shapes that show halves.

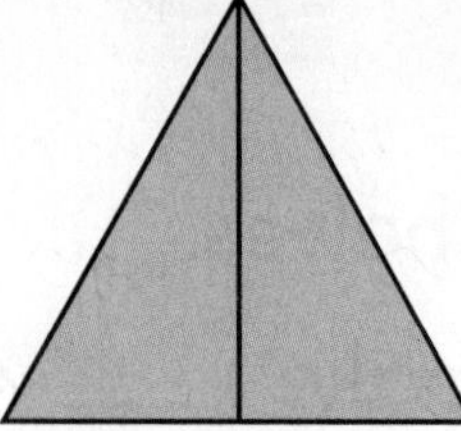

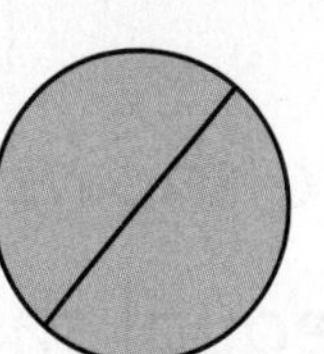

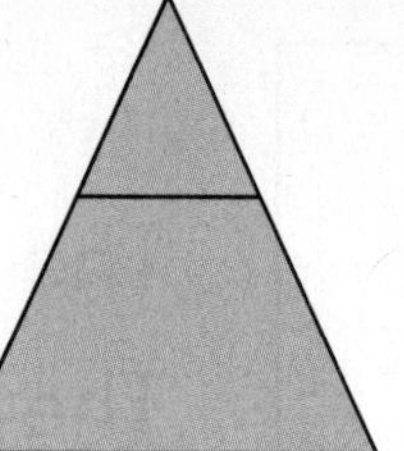

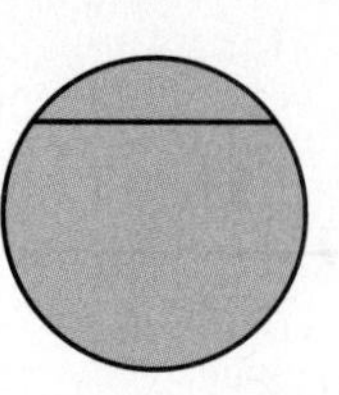

TAKE HOME ACTIVITY • Draw a rectangle on a piece of paper. Ask your child to draw a line to show halves.

FOR MORE PRACTICE: Standards Practice Book

Name ______________________________

Fourths

Essential Question How can a shape be separated into four equal shares?

Geometry—1.G.3

MATHEMATICAL PRACTICES
MP.1, MP.4, MP.6

Listen and Draw Real World

Use what you know about halves.
Draw to solve. Write how many.

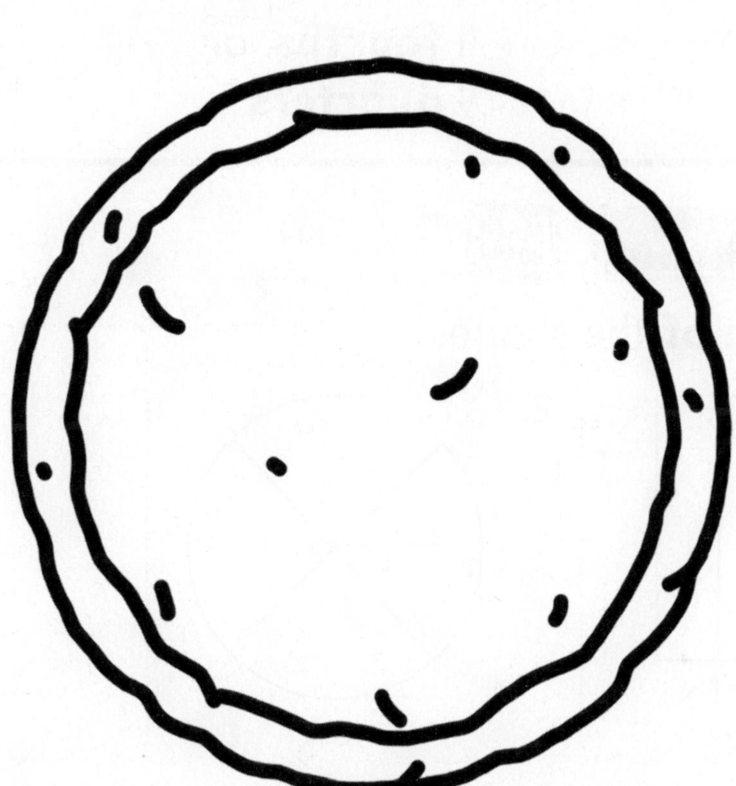

There are ____ equal shares.

FOR THE TEACHER • Read the following problem. Two friends will share a pizza. Then two more friends come. Now four friends will share the pizza. How can the pizza be cut so each friend gets an equal share? How many equal shares are there?

Math Talk Mathematical Practices

Explain How did you decide how to cut the pizza?

Model and Draw

The 4 equal shares make 1 whole.

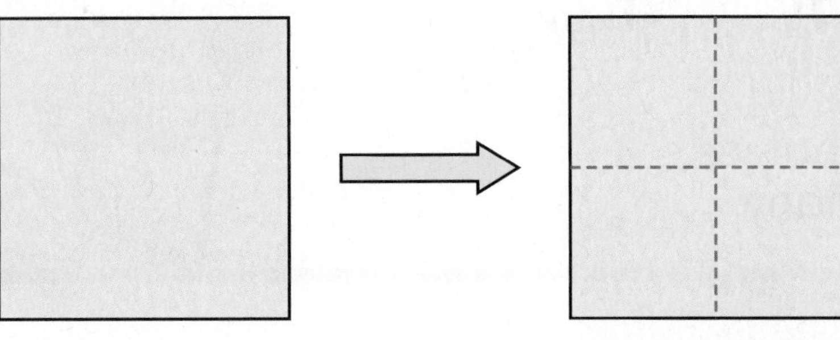

How can you describe one of the 4 equal shares?

1 whole

4 **fourths**, or
4 **quarters**

Share and Show

Color a **fourth of** the shape.

1. 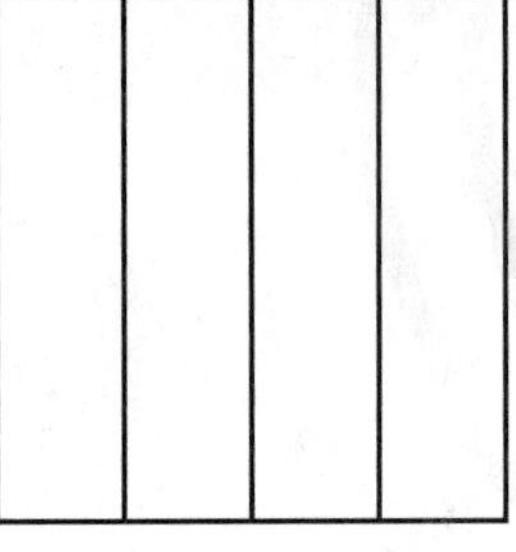

2. 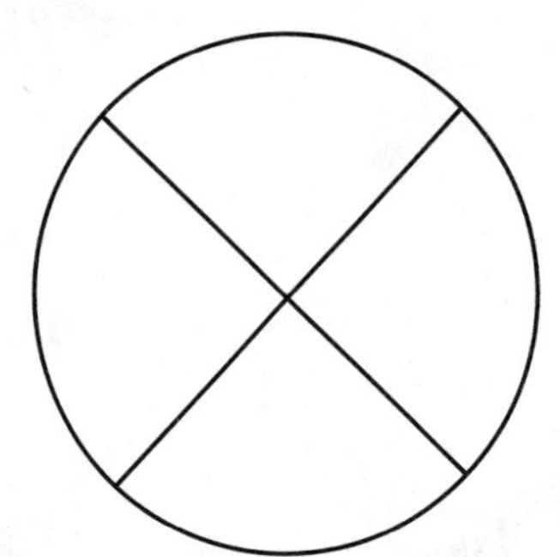

3. 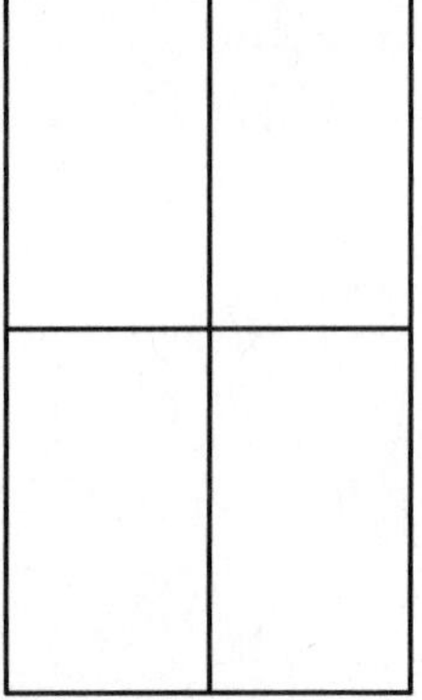

Color a **quarter of** the shape.

4. 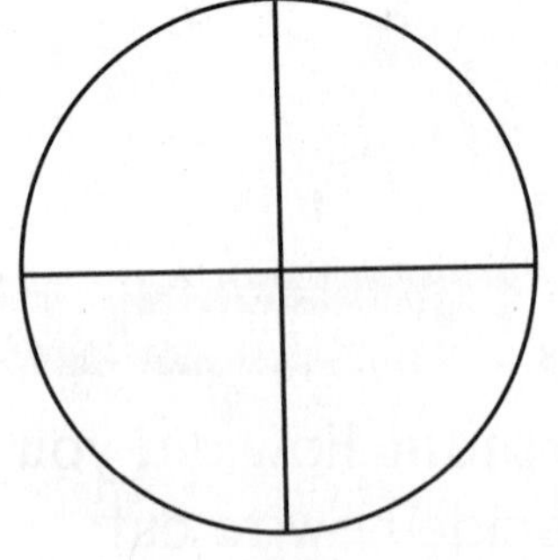

5. 

6. 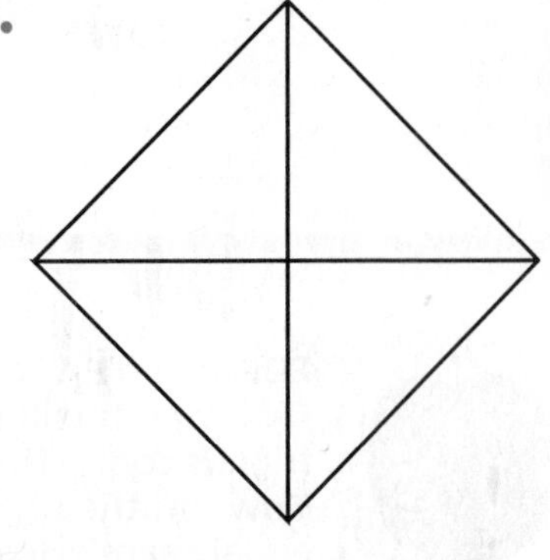

Name ______________________________

On Your Own

MATHEMATICAL PRACTICE 4 **Use Diagrams** Circle the shapes that show fourths.

7.

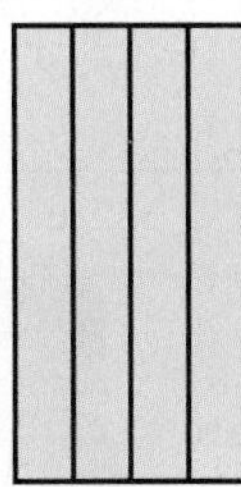

8.

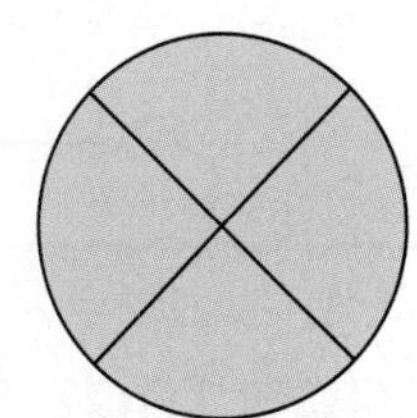

9.

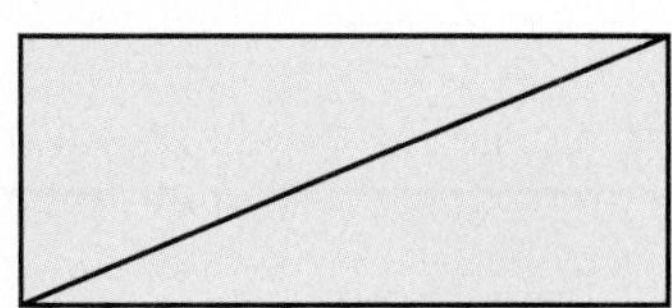

10.

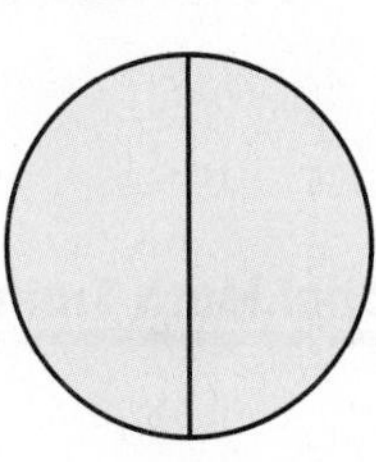

11.

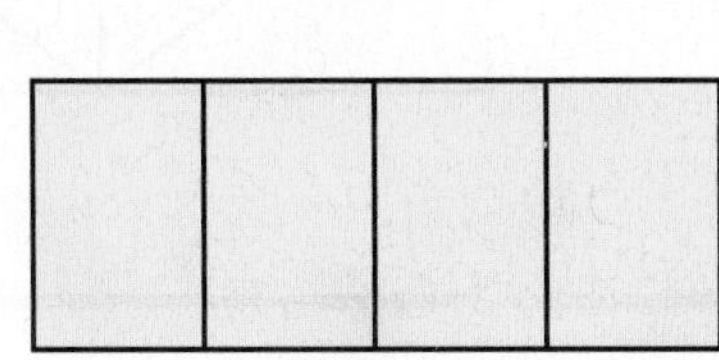

12.

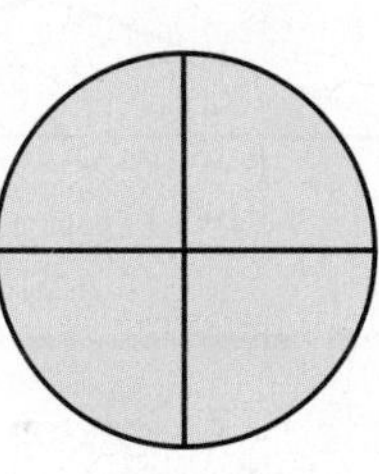

13.

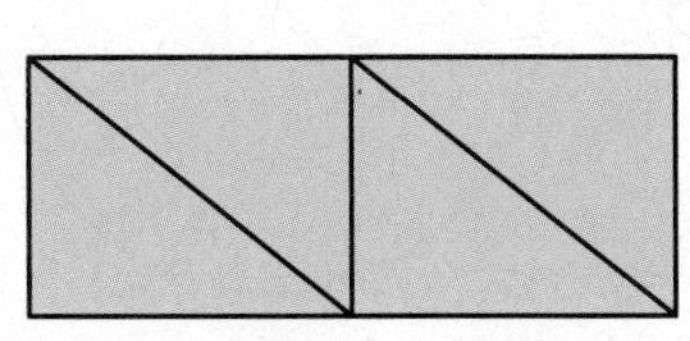

14.

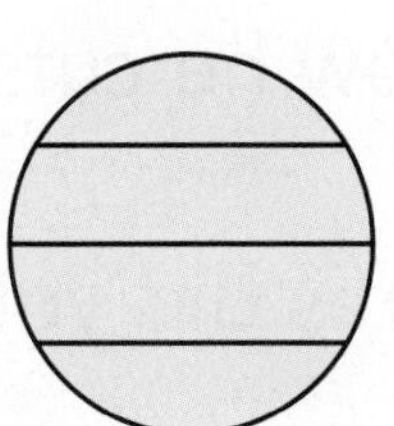

15.

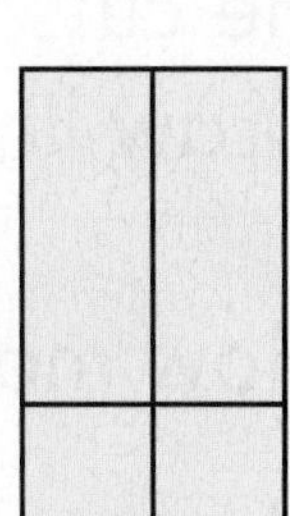

16. GO DEEPER Draw three different ways to show fourths.

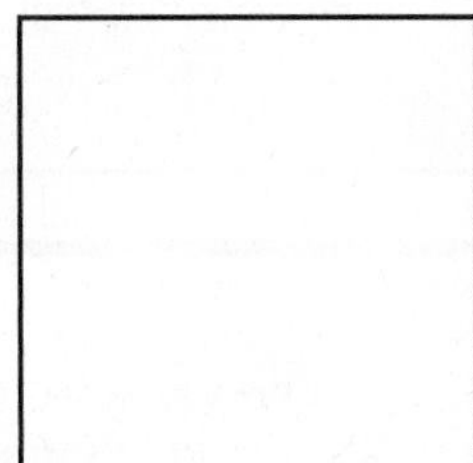

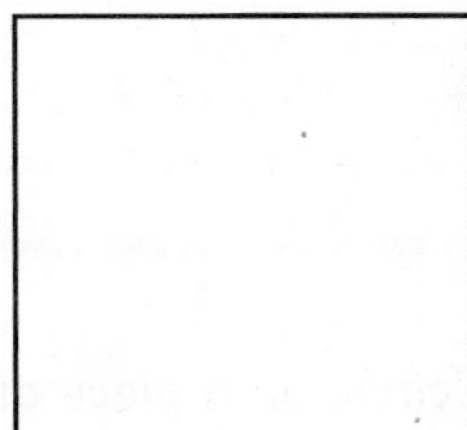

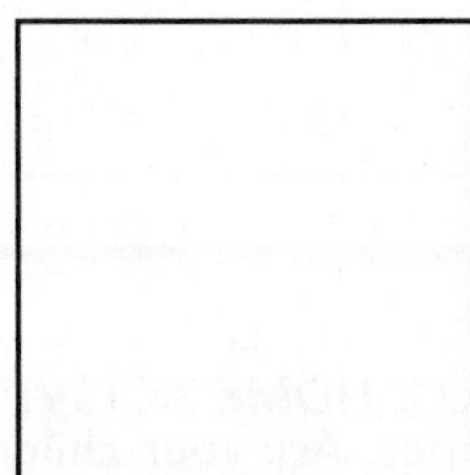

Problem Solving • Applications

Real World | WRITE Math

Solve.

17. Write **halves, fourths,** or **quarters** to name the equal shares.

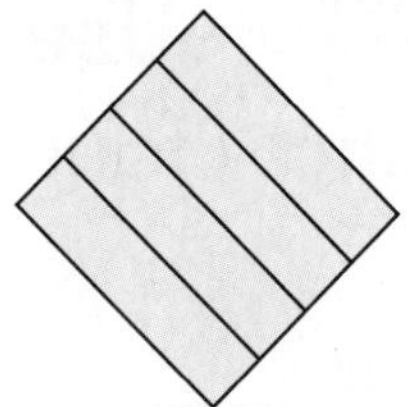

_______ _______

18. THINK SMARTER Circle the shape that shows quarters.

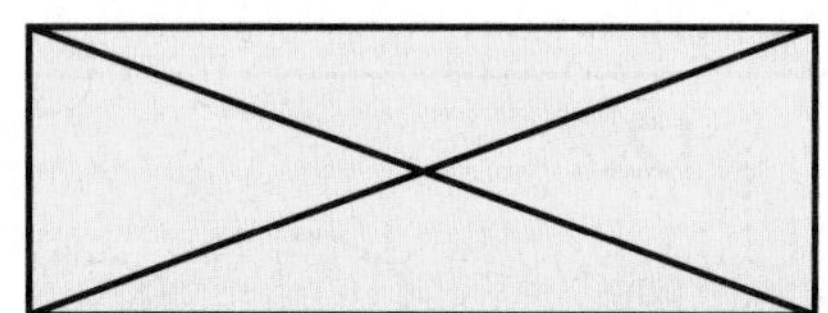

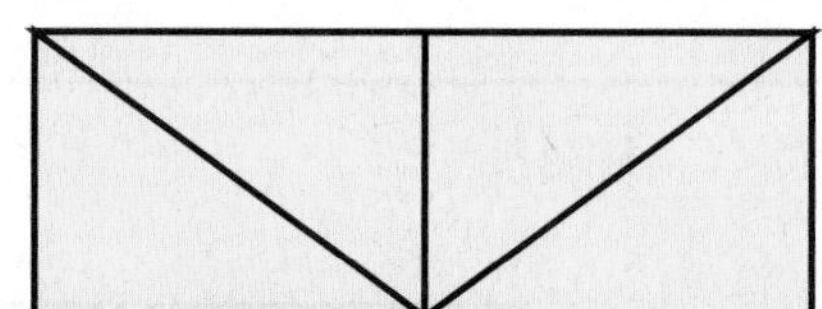

Personal Math Trainer

19. THINK SMARTER + Alano has a small pizza. He wants to share the pizza with friends. He cuts the pizza into fourths. Draw lines to show how he cuts the pizza.

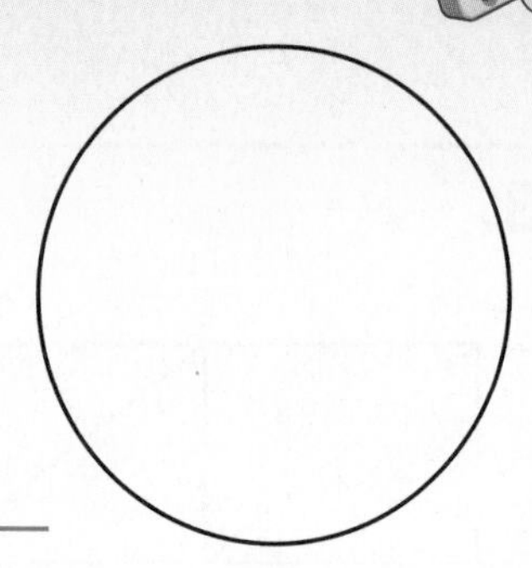

How many equal shares did you draw? _____

How many halves can you show in a circle? _____

Tell how you can solve this problem in a different way.

TAKE HOME ACTIVITY • Draw a circle on a piece of paper. Ask your child to draw lines to show fourths.

FOR MORE PRACTICE: Standards Practice Book

Name ___________________________

Chapter 12 Review/Test

I. Which shapes have only 3 sides? Choose all that apply.

○ 

○ 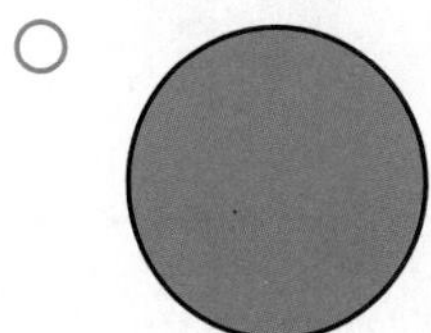

○ 

○ 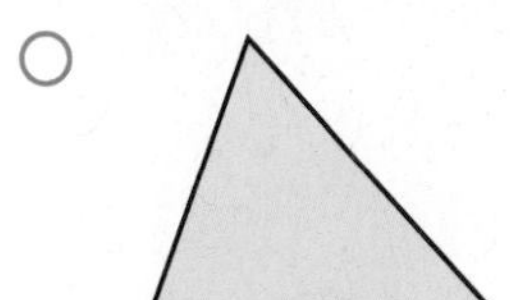

○ 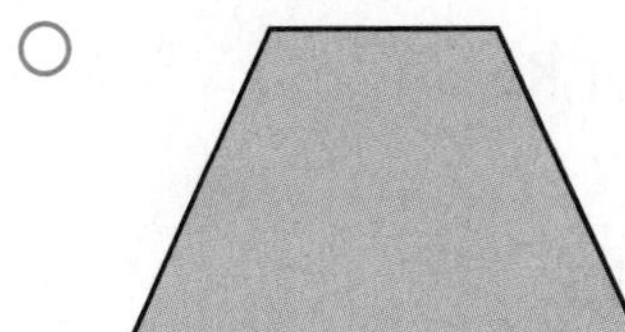

---

2. Circle the number that makes the sentence true.

A ▬ has [2 / 3 / 4] vertices (corners).

---

3. How many ⏢ make a ⬢?

Use pattern blocks. Draw to show the blocks you used.

4. Circle two shapes that can combine to make this new shape.

---

5. Use ◸ to make a ○. Use pattern blocks. Draw to show your work.

Step 1 Combine shapes.

◸ and ◸ make ◠

Step 2 Use the new shape.

◡ and ◡ make ○

How many ◸ do you need to make a ○?

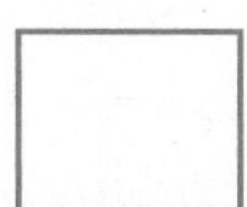

Can you make a △ with 3 ◸? Choose Yes or No.

○ Yes ○ No

Name ______________________________

6. Use 4 pattern blocks to fill the shape. Draw to show the blocks you used.

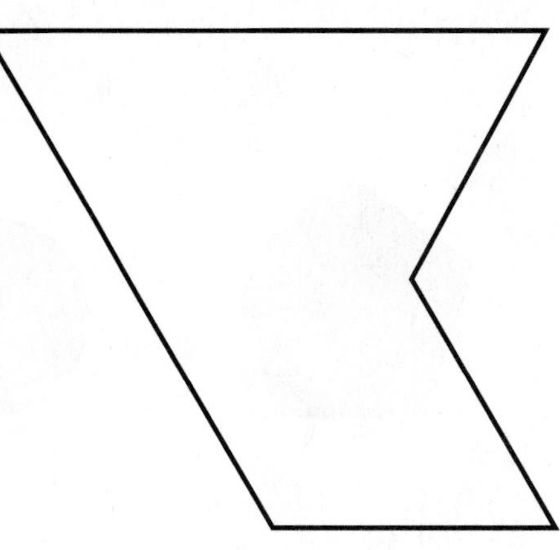

7. Draw a line to show the parts. Show 2 ▬.

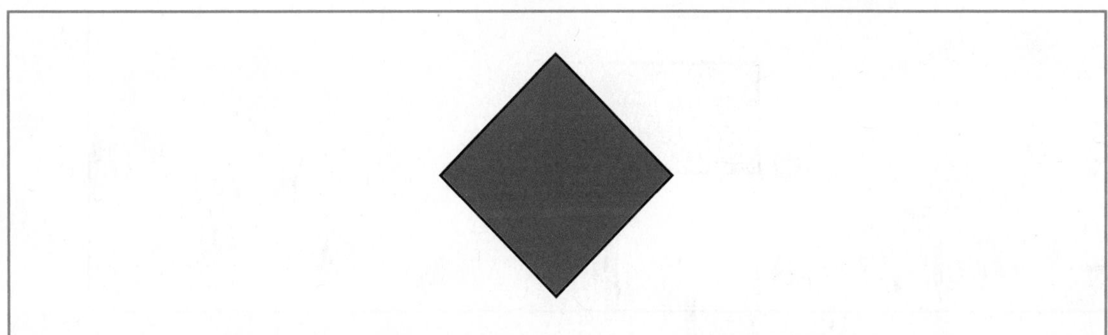

8. Does the shape show equal shares? Choose Yes or No.

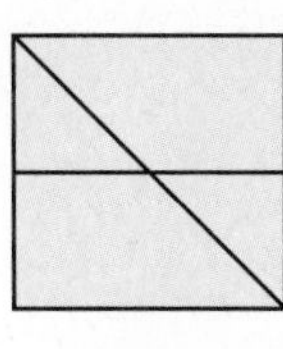

○ Yes ○ No

○ Yes ○ No

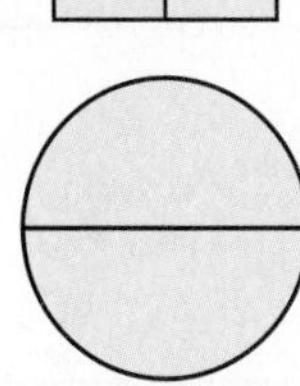

○ Yes ○ No

9. Circle the shapes that show halves.

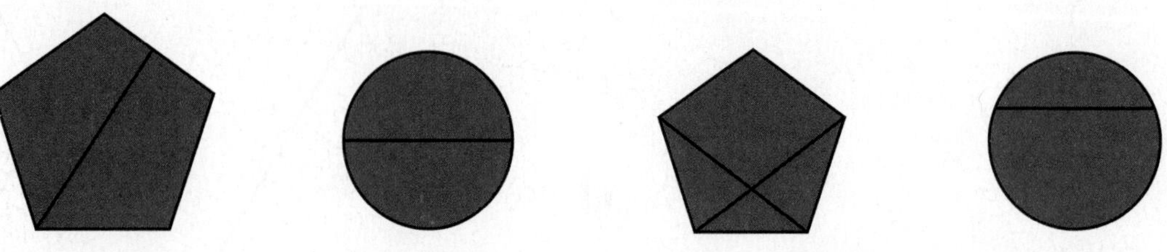

10. Draw lines to show fourths.

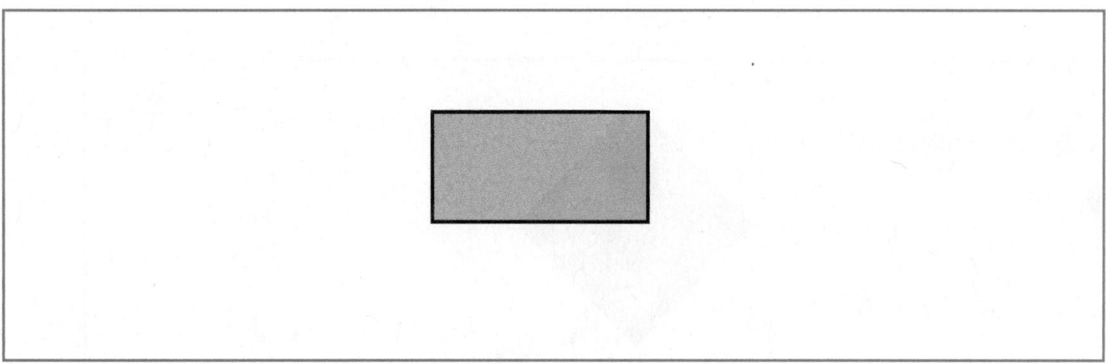

How many equal shares did you draw?

☐

How many halves can you show in a rectangle?

☐

Tell how you can solve this problem in a different way.

Picture Glossary

add sumar

3 + 2 = 5

addend sumando

1 + 3 = 4

addend

addition sentence enunciado de suma

2 + 1 = 3 is an **addition sentence.**

bar graph gráfica de barras

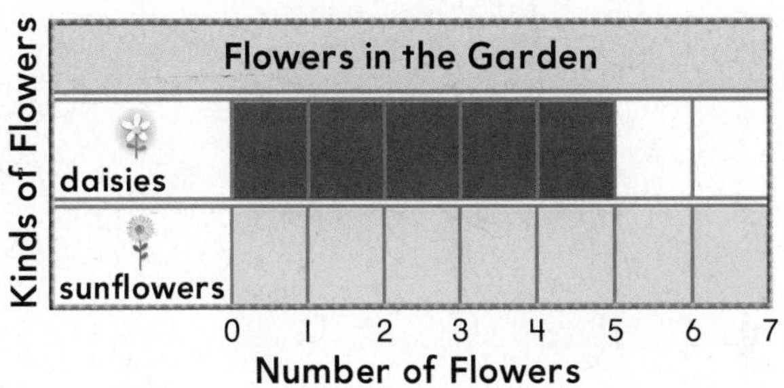

circle círculo

compare comparar

Subtract to **compare** groups.

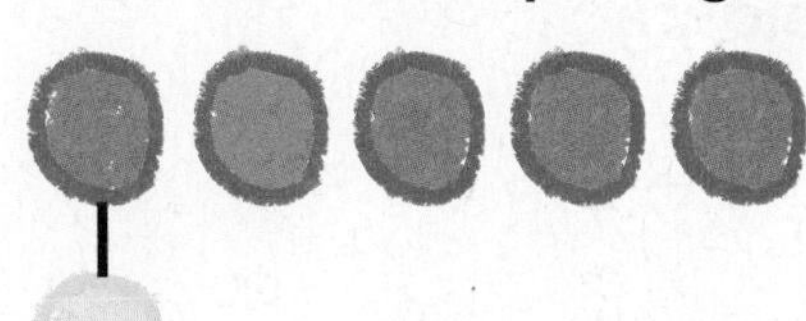

5 − 1 = 4

There are more ●.

cone cono

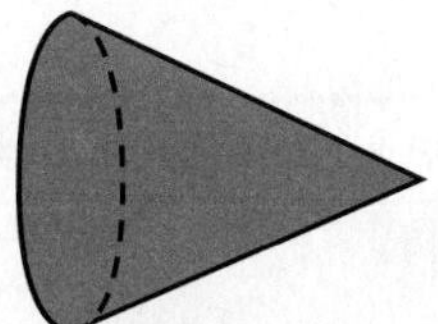

count back contar hacia atrás

8 − 1 = 7

Start at 8.

Count back 1.

You are on 7.

count on contar hacia adelante

4 + 2 = 6

Say 4.

Count on 2.

5, 6

cube cubo

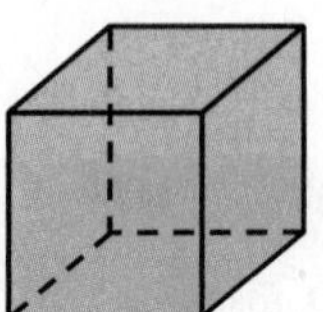

curved surface superficie curva

Some three-dimensional shapes have a **curved surface.**

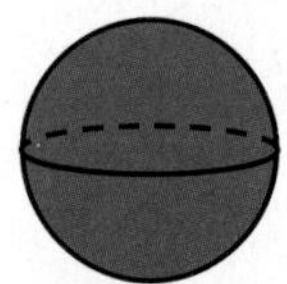

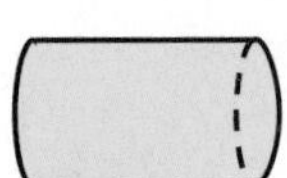

cylinder cilindro

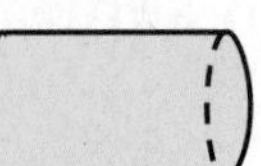

difference diferencia

$4 - 3 = 1$

The **difference** is 1.

digit dígito

13 is a two-digit number.

The 1 in 13 means 1 ten.
The 3 in 13 means 3 ones.

doubles dobles

$5 + 5 = 10$

doubles minus one dobles menos uno

$5 + 5 = 10$, so $5 + 4 = 9$

doubles plus one dobles más uno

$5 + 5 = 10$, so $5 + 6 = 11$

equal parts partes iguales

These show **equal parts**, or equal shares.

equal shares porciones iguales

These show equal parts, or **equal shares**.

fewer menos

3 **fewer** 🐦

flat surface superficie plana

Some three-dimensional shapes have only **flat surfaces**.

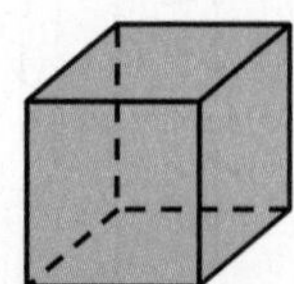

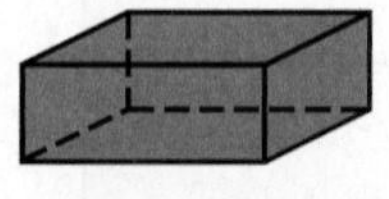

fourth of cuarto de

A **fourth of** this shape is shaded.

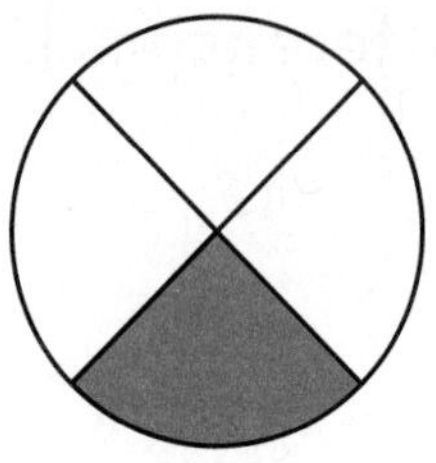

fourths cuartos

1 whole

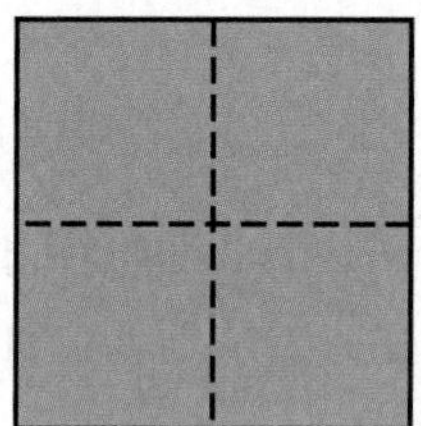

4 **fourths**, or 4 quarters

half hour media hora

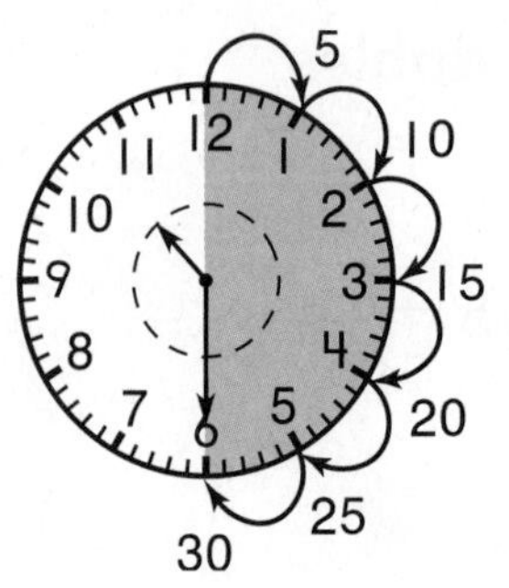

A **half hour** has 30 minutes.

half of mitad de

Half of this shape is shaded.

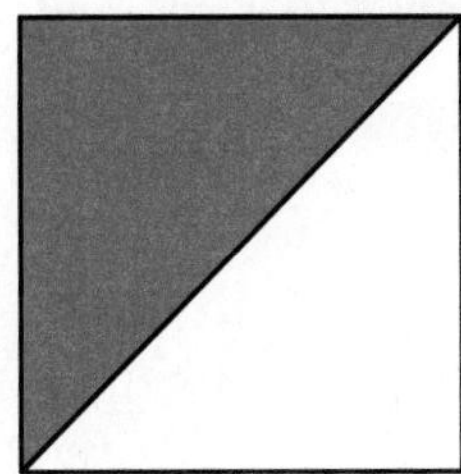

hour hora

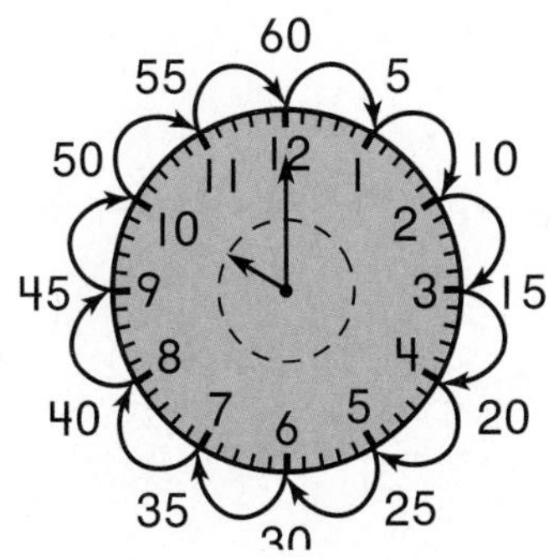

An **hour** has 60 minutes.

halves mitades

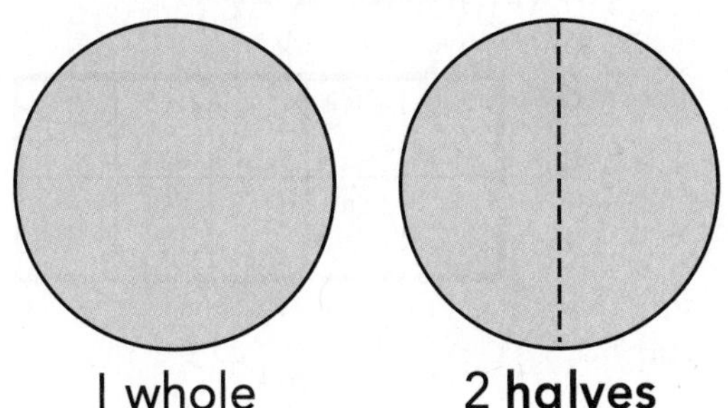

I whole

2 **halves**

hour hand horario

hexagon hexágono

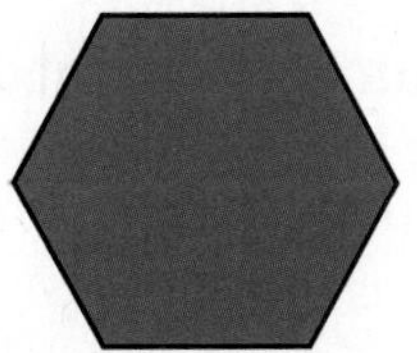

hundred centena

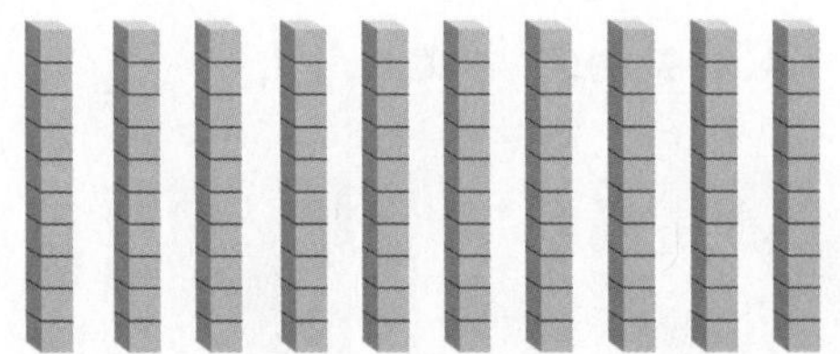

10 tens is the same as **I hundred**.

is equal to (=) es igual a

2 plus 1 **is equal to** 3.

$2 + 1 = 3$

is greater than es mayor que

35 **is greater than** 27.

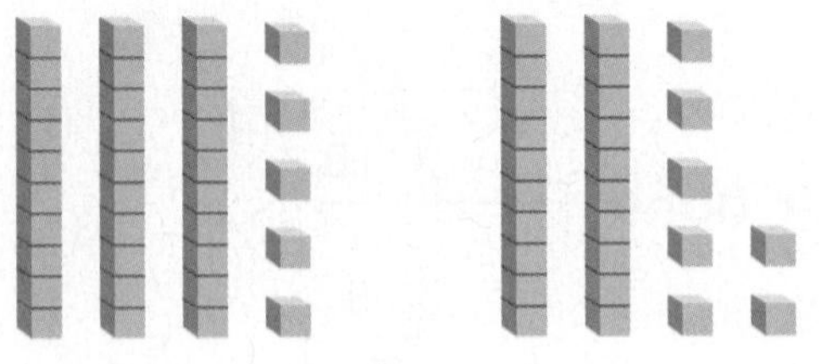

$35 > 27$

is less than es menor que

43 **is less than** 49.

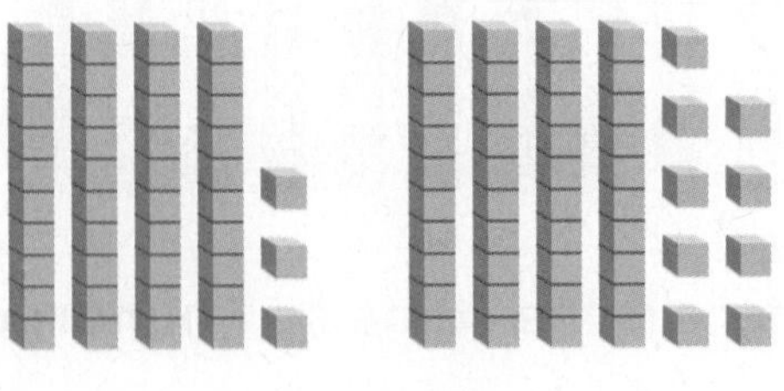

$43 < 49$

longest el más largo

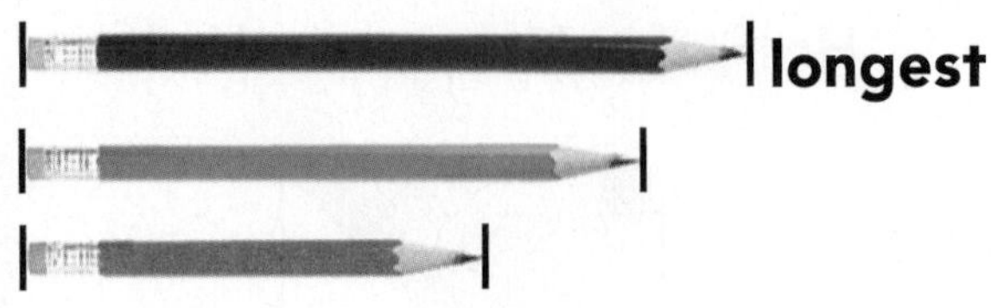

make a ten formar una decena

Move 2 counters into the ten frame. **Make a ten.**

$$\begin{array}{r} 8 \\ +\ 4 \\ \hline 12 \end{array}$$

minus (−) menos

4 **minus** 3 is equal to 1.

$4 - 3 = 1$

minute hand minutero

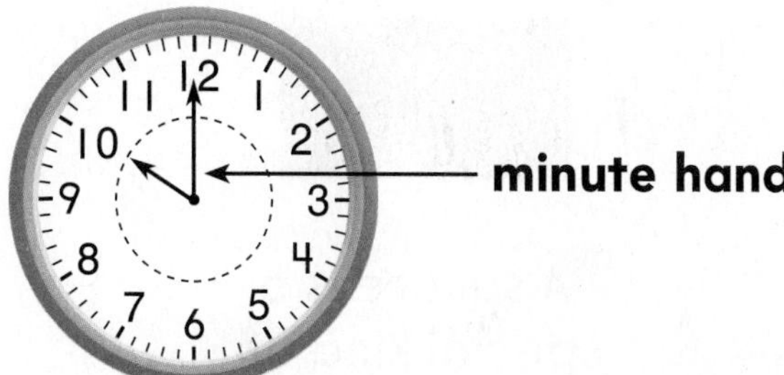

minutes minutos

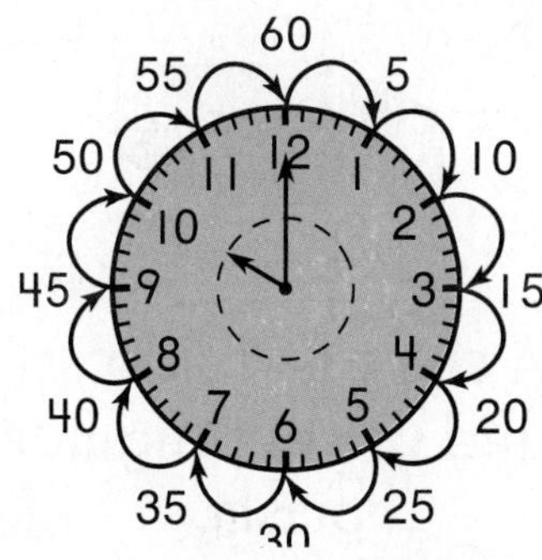

An hour has 60 **minutes.**

more más

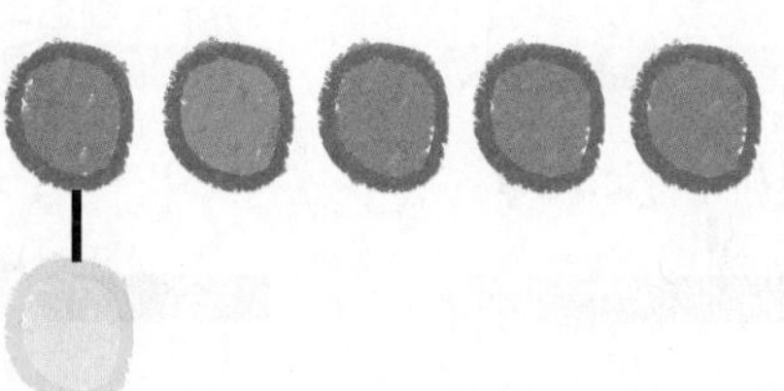

5 − 1 = 4

There are **more** ●.

ones unidades

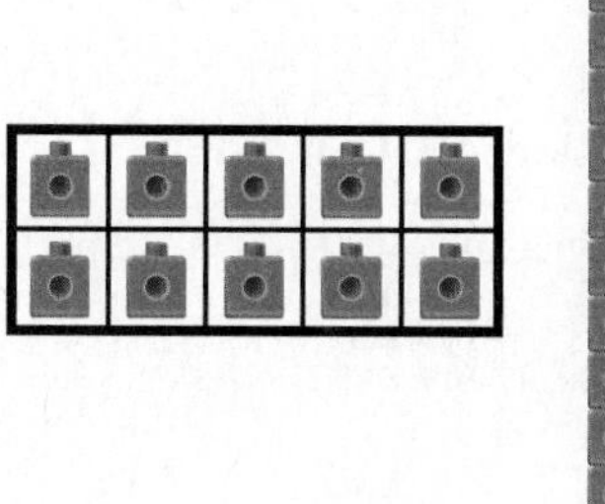

10 **ones** = 1 ten

order orden

You can change the **order** of the addends.

1 + 3 = 4

3 + 1 = 4

picture graph gráfica con dibujos

Our Favorite Activity at the Fair							
animals	웃	웃	웃	웃	웃		
rides	웃	웃	웃	웃	웃	웃	웃

Each 웃 stands for 1 child.

plus (+) más

2 **plus** 1 is equal to 3.

$2 + 1 = 3$

quarter of cuarta parte de

A **quarter of** this shape is shaded.

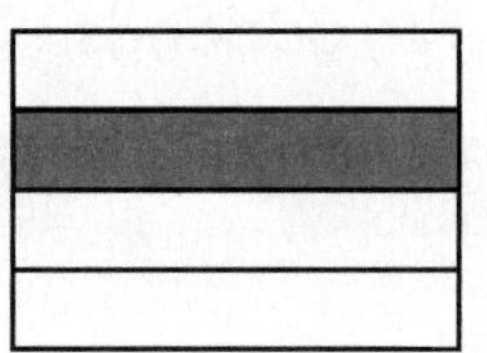

quarters cuartas partes

1 whole

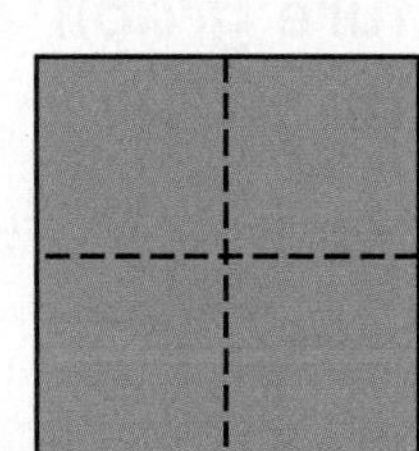

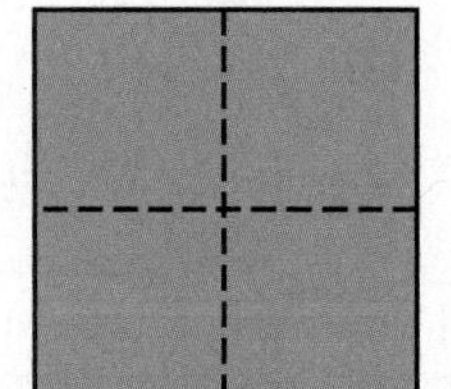

4 fourths, or 4 **quarters**

rectangle rectángulo

A square is a special kind of rectangle.

rectangular prism prisma rectangular

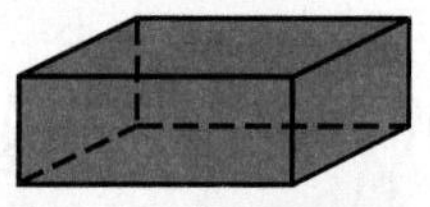

A cube is a special kind of rectangular prism.

related facts operaciones relacionadas

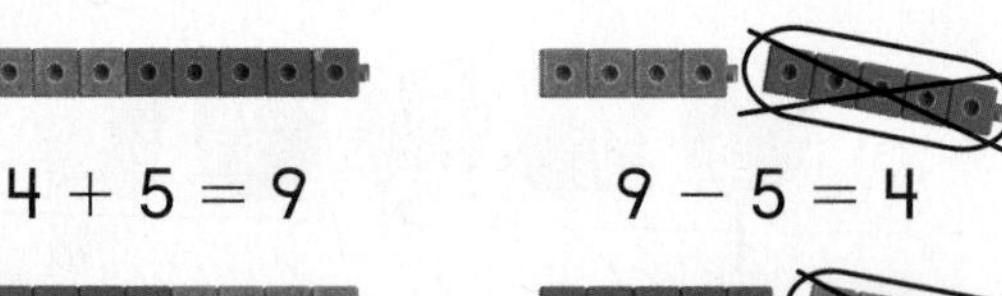

$4 + 5 = 9$

$9 - 5 = 4$

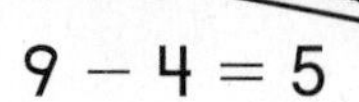

$5 + 4 = 9$

$9 - 4 = 5$

shortest el más corto

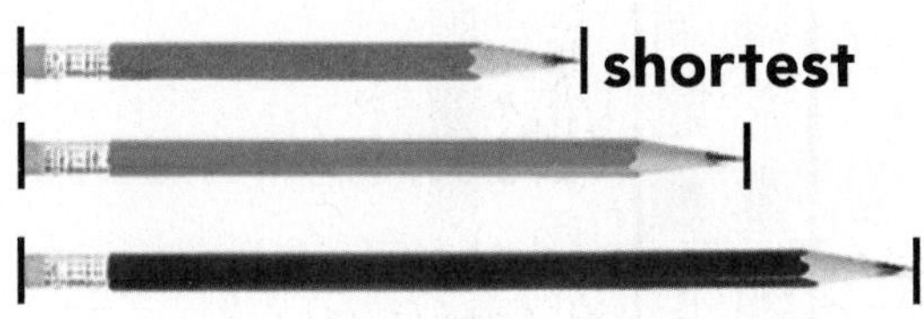

side lado

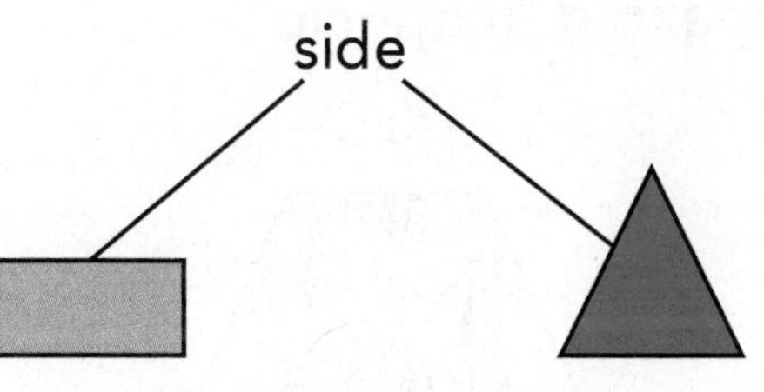

sphere esfera

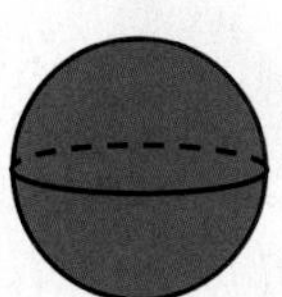

square cuadrado

subtract restar

Subtract to find out how many.

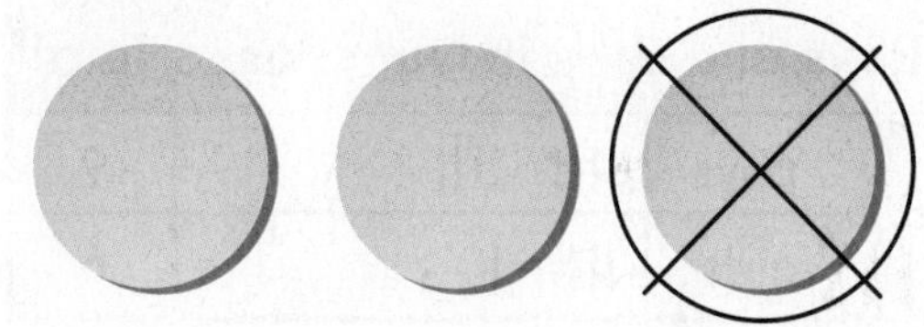

subtraction sentence
enunciado de resta

$4 - 3 = 1$ is a **subtraction sentence**.

sum suma o total

2 plus 1 is equal to 3.

The **sum** is 3.

ten decena

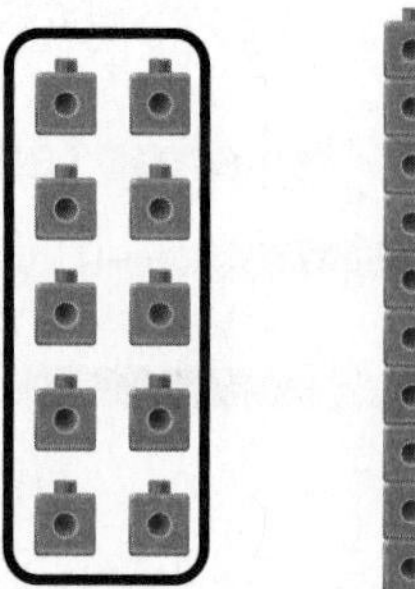

10 ones = 1 **ten**

tally chart tabla de conteo

Boys and Girls in Our Class		Total
boys	𝍸 ||||	9
girls	𝍸 |	6

trapezoid trapecio

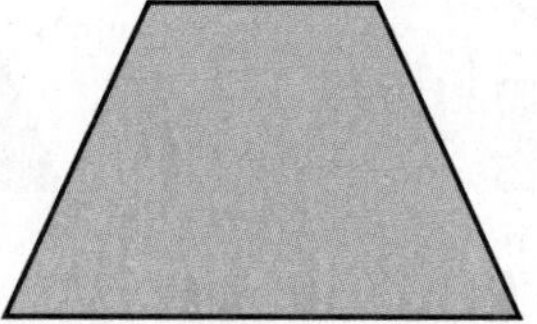

tally mark marca de conteo

𝍸

Each **tally mark** | stands for 1.
𝍸 stands for 5.

triangle triángulo

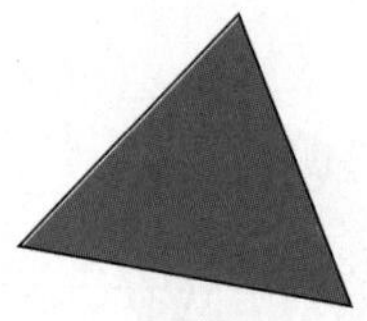

unequal parts partes desiguales

These show **unequal parts**, or unequal shares.

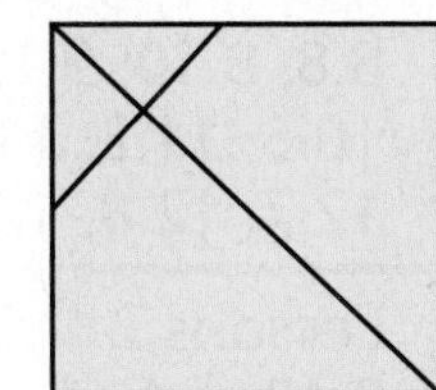

unequal shares porciones desiguales

These show unequal parts, or **unequal shares**.

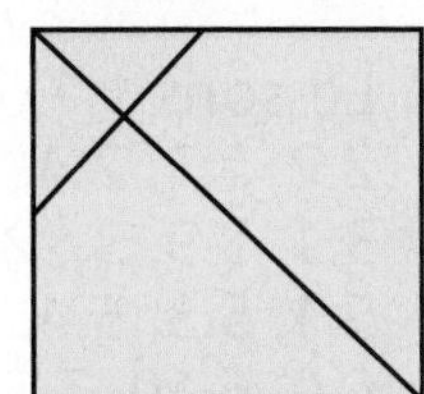

vertex vértice

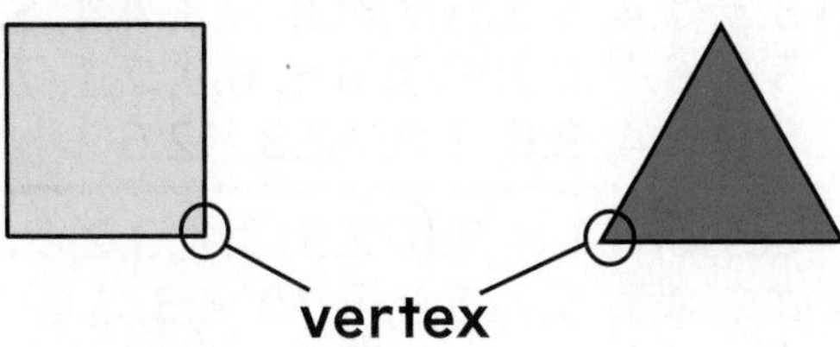

zero 0 cero

When you add **zero** to any number, the sum is that number.

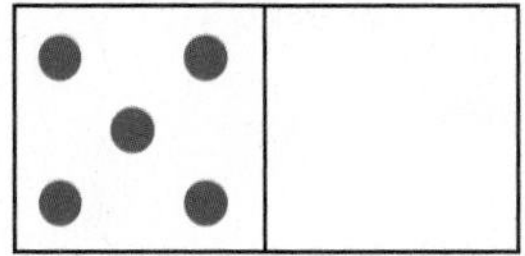

$5 + \mathbf{0} = 5$

Correlations

CALIFORNIA COMMON CORE STATE STANDARDS

Standards You Will Learn		Student Edition Lessons
Mathematical Practices		
MP.1	Make sense of problems and persevere in solving them.	Lessons 1.1, 1.2, 1.3, 1.4, 2.1, 2.2, 2.3, 2.4 2.5, 2.6, 3.2, 3.4, 3.12, 4.3, 4.6, 5.1, 5.5, 6.8, 7.3, 7.5, 8.1, 8.7, 8.8, 8.10, 9.1, 9.2, 9.5, 9.7, 9.9, 10.6, 11.2, 11.3, 11.5, 12.4, 12.5, 12.7, 12.8, 12.9, 12.10
MP.2	Reason abstractly and quantitatively.	Lessons 2.1, 2.2, 2.5, 3.7, 3.8, 3.9, 3.12, 4.1, 4.4, 4.5, 5.1, 5.6, 5.10, 6.2, 6.4, 6.7, 6.10, 7.4, 8.2, 8.6, 8.7, 8.9, 9.3, 9.4, 9.7, 9.8, 10.5, 11.2, 11.3
MP.3	Construct viable arguments and critique the reasoning of others.	Lessons 2.7, 2.8, 3.10, 3.11, 4.2, 4.6, 5.7, 6.3, 6.4, 7.5, 8.1, 8.3, 8.9, 8.10, 9.1, 9.2, 9.4, 9.5, 10.1, 10.2, 10.3, 10.4, 10.5, 10.6, 10.7, 11.2, 11.3, 12.8
MP.4	Model with mathematics.	Lessons 1.1, 1.2, 1.3, 1.4, 1.7, 2.1, 2.2, 2.3, 2.4, 2.5, 2.6, 2.7, 2.8, 2.9, 3.1, 3.9, 3.12, 4.1, 4.2, 4.5, 4.6, 5.1, 5.3, 5.4, 5.6, 5.7, 6.4, 6.6, 6.7, 6.9, 6.10, 7.3, 7.4, 8.4, 8.5, 9.2, 9.9, 10.1, 10.2, 10.3, 10.4, 10.5, 10.6, 11.1, 11.5, 12.4, 12.5, 12.6, 12.9, 12.10
MP.5	Use appropriate tools strategically.	Lessons 1.1, 1.2, 1.3, 1.4, 2.3, 2.4, 3.3, 3.4, 3.6, 3.7, 3.8, 4.3, 4.4, 5.2, 5.8, 6.1, 6.2, 6.3, 6.6, 6.9, 7.1, 7.2, 8.6, 9.4, 9.6, 9.8, 12.3, 12.6
MP.6	Attend to precision.	Lessons 1.8, 2.6, 2.9, 3.1, 3.2, 3.5, 4.1, 4.3, 5.7, 5.9, 5.10, 6.3, 6.6, 6.7, 6.8, 6.10, 7.4, 7.5, 8.1, 8.4, 8.5, 8.8, 9.1, 9.3, 9.6, 9.8, 10.7, 11.4, 11.5, 12.1, 12.2, 12.3, 12.8, 12.9, 12.10

Standards You Will Learn

		Student Edition Lessons
Mathematical Practices		
MP.7	Look for and make use of structure.	Lessons 1.5, 1.6, 1.7, 1.8, 2.8, 3.3, 3.4, 3.5, 3.6, 4.2, 5.2, 5.3, 5.4, 5.5, 5.8, 5.9, 6.1, 6.5, 6.8, 6.9, 7.1, 7.2, 8.2, 8.7, 8.9, 9.6, 11.4, 12.1, 12.2, 12.7
MP.8	Look for and express regularity in repeated reasoning.	Lessons 1.5, 1.6, 1.7, 2.7, 2.9, 3.2, 3.11, 4.4, 5.2, 5.3, 5.4, 5.5, 6.1, 6.2, 6.5, 7.3, 8.3, 8.8, 8.10, 9.3, 9.7, 9.9, 10.4, 11.1, 11.4, 12.1, 12.2
Domain: Operations and Algebraic Thinking		
Represent and solve problems involving addition and subtraction.		
1.OA.1	Use addition and subtraction within 20 to solve word problems involving situations of adding to, taking from, putting together, taking apart, and comparing, with unknowns in all positions, e.g., by using objects, drawings, and equations with a symbol for the unknown number to represent the problem.	Lessons 1.1, 1.2, 1.3, 1.4, 1.7, 2.1 2.2, 2.3, 2.4, 2.6, 2.8, 4.6, 5.1, 5.7
1.OA.2	Solve word problems that call for addition of three whole numbers whose sum is less than or equal to 20, e.g., by using objects, drawings, and equations with a symbol for the unknown number to represent the problem.	Lesson 3.12
Understand and apply properties of operations and the relationship between addition and subtraction.		
1.OA.3	Apply properties of operations as strategies to add and subtract. *Examples: If $8 + 3 = 11$ is known, then $3 + 8 = 11$ is also known. (Commutative property of addition.) To add $2 + 6 + 4$, the second two numbers can be added to make a ten, so $2 + 6 + 4 = 2 + 10 = 12$. (Associative property of addition.)*	Lessons 1.5, 1.6, 3.1, 3.10, 3.11

Standards You Will Learn

		Student Edition Lessons
Domain: Operations and Algebraic Thinking		
Understand and apply properties of operations and the relationship between addition and subtraction.		
1.OA.4	Understand subtraction as an unknown-addend problem. *For example, subtract 10 – 8 by finding the number that makes 10 when added to 8.*	Lessons 4.2, 4.3
Add and subtract within 20.		
1.OA.5	Relate counting to addition and subtraction (e.g., by counting on 2 to add 2).	Lessons 3.2, 4.1
1.OA.6	Add and subtract within 20, demonstrating fluency for addition and subtraction within 10. Use strategies such as counting on; making ten (e.g., 8 + 6 = 8 + 2 + 4 = 10 + 4 = 14); decomposing a number leading to a ten (e.g., 13 – 4 = 13 – 3 – 1 = 10 – 1 = 9); using the relationship between addition and subtraction (e.g., knowing that 8 + 4 = 12, one knows 12 – 8 = 4); and creating equivalent but easier or known sums (e.g., adding 6 + 7 by creating the known equivalent 6 + 6 + 1 = 12 + 1 = 13).	Lessons 1.8, 2.9, 3.3, 3.4, 3.5, 3.6, 3.7, 3.8, 3.9, 4.4, 4.5, 5.2, 5.3, 5.4, 5.8, 5.10, 8.1
Work with addition and subtraction equations.		
1.OA.7	Understand the meaning of the equal sign, and determine if equations involving addition and subtraction are true or false. *For example, which of the following equations are true and which are false? 6 = 6, 7 = 8 – 1, 5 + 2 = 2 + 5, 4 + 1 = 5 + 2.*	Lesson 5.9

Standards You Will Learn

		Student Edition Lessons
Domain: Operations and Algebraic Thinking		
Work with addition and subtraction equations.		
1.OA.8	Determine the unknown whole number in an addition or subtraction equation relating three whole numbers. *For example, determine the unknown number that makes the equation true in each of the equations 8 + ? = 11, 5 = [] – 3, 6 + 6 = [].*	Lessons 2.5, 2.7, 5.5, 5.6
Domain: Number and Operations in Base Ten		
Extend the counting sequence.		
1.NBT.1	Count to 120, starting at any number less than 120. In this range, read and write numerals and represent a number of objects with a written numeral.	Lessons 6.1, 6.2, 6.9, 6.10
Understand place value.		
1.NBT.2	Understand that the two digits of a two-digit number represent amounts of tens and ones. Understand the following as special cases:	Lessons 6.6, 6.7
	a. 10 can be thought of as a bundle of ten ones — called a "ten."	Lessons 6.5, 6.8
	b. The numbers from 11 to 19 are composed of a ten and one, two, three, four, five, six, seven, eight, or nine ones.	Lessons 6.3, 6.4
	c. The numbers 10, 20, 30, 40, 50, 60, 70, 80, 90 refer to one, two, three, four, five, six, seven, eight, or nine tens (and 0 ones).	Lesson 6.5
1.NBT.3	Compare two two-digit numbers based on meanings of the tens and ones digits, recording the results of comparisons with the symbols $>$, $=$, and $<$.	Lessons 6.8, 7.1, 7.2, 7.3, 7.4

Standards You Will Learn

		Student Edition Lessons
Domain: Number and Operations in Base Ten		
Use place value understanding and properties of operations to add and subtract.		
1.NBT.4	Add within 100, including adding a two-digit number and a one-digit number, and adding a two-digit number and a multiple of 10, using concrete models or drawings and strategies based on place value, properties of operations, and/or the relationship between addition and subtraction; relate the strategy to a written method and explain the reasoning used. Understand that in adding two-digit numbers, one adds tens and tens, ones and ones; and sometimes it is necessary to compose a ten.	Lessons 8.2, 8.4, 8.5, 8.6, 8.7, 8.8, 8.9, 8.10
1.NBT.5	Given a two-digit number, mentally find 10 more or 10 less than the number, without having to count; explain the reasoning used.	Lesson 7.5
1.NBT.6	Subtract multiples of 10 in the range 10–90 from multiples of 10 in the range 10–90 (positive or zero differences), using concrete models or drawings and strategies based on place value, properties of operations, and/or the relationship between addition and subtraction; relate the strategy to a written method and explain the reasoning used.	Lessons 8.3, 8.10
Domain: Measurement and Data		
Measure lengths indirectly and by iterating length units.		
1.MD.1	Order three objects by length; compare the lengths of two objects indirectly by using a third object.	Lessons 9.1, 9.2

Standards You Will Learn

		Student Edition Lessons
Domain: Measurement and Data		
Measure lengths indirectly and by iterating length units.		
1.MD.2	Express the length of an object as a whole number of length units, by laying multiple copies of a shorter object (the length unit) end to end; understand that the length measurement of an object is the number of same-size length units that span it with no gaps or overlaps. *Limit to contexts where the object being measured is spanned by a whole number of length units with no gaps or overlaps.*	Lessons 9.3, 9.4, 9.5
Tell and write time.		
1.MD.3	Tell and write time in hours and half-hours using analog and digital clocks.	Lessons 9.6, 9.7, 9.8, 9.9
Represent and interpret data.		
1.MD.4	Organize, represent, and interpret data with up to three categories; ask and answer questions about the total number of data points, how many in each category, and how many more or less are in one category than in another.	Lessons 10.1, 10.2, 10.3, 10.4, 10.5, 10.6, 10.7
Domain: Geometry		
Reason with shapes and their attributes.		
1.G.1	Distinguish between defining attributes (e.g., triangles are closed and three-sided) versus non-defining attributes (e.g., color, orientation, overall size); build and draw shapes to possess defining attributes.	Lessons 11.1, 11.5, 12.1, 12.2

Standards You Will Learn

		Student Edition Lessons
Domain: Geometry		
Reason with shapes and their attributes.		
1.G.2	Compose two-dimensional shapes (rectangles, squares, trapezoids, triangles, half-circles, and quarter-circles) or three-dimensional shapes (cubes, right rectangular prisms, right circular cones, and right circular cylinders) to create a composite shape, and compose new shapes from the composite shape.	Lessons 11.2, 11.3, 11.4, 12.3, 12.4, 12.5, 12.6, 12.7
1.G.3	Partition circles and rectangles into two and four equal shares, describe the shares using the words *halves, fourths*, and *quarters*, and use the phrases *half of*, *fourth of*, and *quarter of*. Describe the whole as two of, or four of the shares. Understand for these examples that decomposing into more equal shares creates smaller shares.	Lessons 12.8, 12.9, 12.10

Index

A

Q

R

S

T

U

Z